Guardians of the Horse: Past, Present and Future

Editors:
P. D. Rossdale, T. R. C. Greet, P. A. Harris, R. E. Green and S. Hall

British Equine Veterinary Association
and
Romney Publications

Published by

British Equine Veterinary Association
and
Romney Publications

British Equine Veterinary Association: 5 Finlay Street, London SW6 6HE, UK.
Romney Publications: 351 Exning Road, Newmarket, Suffolk CB8 0AU, UK.

First published 1999

ISBN 0-9528566-5-4 Hardback
ISBN 0-9528566-6-2 Paperback

Designed and Typeset by
Equine Veterinary Journal Ltd

Printed by
Geerings of Ashford Ltd., Ashford, Kent, UK.

Cover Designed by
Stephen Brendish, B Design, Suffolk, UK.

Contents

Preface

Foreword

Philosophy of the Horse

Past, Present and Future

Practice: the Frontier of Science and Application Across the Ages

Associations and Societies

Perspectives in:

Stud Medicine

Equine Feeding Practices

Equine Medicine

Equine Orthopaedics

Equine Surgery

Equine Anaesthesia

Recent Disciplinary Developments

Imaging Technology: Seeing is Believing

Preface

Within the covers of this book there is a wide spectrum of style, opinion, narrative and speculation contributed by 77 authors from nine countries. The diversity of the content matches that of life in all its variety. It represents a snapshot of the present, at a moment in the evolution of our profession and of its integration with the horse and the horse-owning and horse-loving public.

Veterinarians occupy an important place in society, as guardians of the horse's health and wellbeing, but they too are capable of the same emotions, sentiments, unease, triumphs and disasters as those in society itself. The contributors to be found herein reflect, therefore, both the professional and personal attitudes of the time, with all the frailties and strengths of mankind at the end of the 20th century.

The book contains descriptions of veterinary science, but also a number of views from the other side of the coin of equine welfare, such as that from Bonny Millar, who is a veterinary nurse, representing an essential ingredient of veterinary practice. Ian Robinson and Lindsey Abeyasekere contribute to the philosophy of caring man and willing horse and how the close relationship between man and horse has developed over time. Brigitte Heard writes of her debt to the horse and, in this, she speaks for the hundreds of thousands of those who, like her, have found it to be the focus and central theme of their working lives.

Rachel Green addresses the subject of herbal medicine and James Power describes the artist's approach, which has depicted the horse in all its glory throughout the ages. Peter Burrell, sadly not living to see the new century, recounts a life spanning 94 years of close association with the horse; and with the many equine and human greats of this period.

The guardians are composed of men and women, youth and age, bonded by common interest, expressed worldwide, in a respect for the horse and in the welfare of this most highly regarded species. The horse has rightly been described as a companion animal; the guardians are a team with interlinking responsibilities: vets dependent upon the handlers, nurses and farriers; owners, trainers and management relying on the vets for advice and action in prophylaxis and therapy; and the horse depending on each one of us for the dedication, humanity and respect worthy of the equine friend.

Readers may find themselves entertained, provoked, stimulated or enchanted; but never, we hope, bored or frustrated, as they turn the pages of this book. And in the years ahead, that objective of the book, which is to record the present, will become increasingly a source of reference to those who wish to reflect on change occurring during the 21st century; even, perhaps, enabling them to form a judgement as to the value of changes; and to answer the questions of what is improvement and what is deterioration, in the quest for a better way of life for man and horse.

By inviting contributors to cover the past, present and future of their subjects, our intention has been to provide the reader with the balance of progress and speculation about the future. The past forms the basis of experience and provides an opportunity to recognise those on whom progress has depended; the present is of immediate concern in the challenges of our own lifespan; and the future an intriguing vista, summed by Macbeth's admonition to the three witches, in Shakespeare's play,

> *"If you can look into the seeds of time and say which grain will grow and which will not, speak then to me, who neither beg nor fear your favour nor your hate."*

But, as Macbeth discovered, the response proved to be fatally equivocal:

> *"Then be these juggling fiends no more believed, that palter with us in a double sense, that keep the word of promise to our ear and break it to our face";*

and so, perhaps, we should treat all prognostications of the future with interest but also with some degree of scepticism.

Acknowledgements

We are most grateful to Merial for their substantial sponsorship of the book, through the kind auspices of Dr Frank Pipers; and to Schering Plough Animal Health, the Home of Rest for Horses and Organisation Mondiale des Equides for their financial contributions. The publishing team at EVJ, including Ann Monteith, secretarial support, Adam Boyle, sub-editing and proof-reading, and Selina Brendish and her support staff, typesetting, all provided invaluable support. Sue Dyson and Tim Mair gave substantial assistance in compiling the sections on imaging techniques and medicine, respectively.

PETER ROSSDALE AND RACHEL GREEN
351 Exning Road
Newmarket
Suffolk CB8 0AU
UK

TIM GREET
Beaufort Cottage
Equine Hospital
Cotton End Road
Exning, Newmarket
Suffolk CB8 7NN
UK

PAT HARRIS
Equine Studies Group
The WALTHAM Centre for
Pet Nutrition
Waltham on the Wolds
Melton Mowbray
Leicester LE14 4RT
UK

SHERWIN HALL
14 Huntingdon Road
Cambridge
Cambs CB3 0HH
UK

Giants and dwarfs, past and present

PETER ROSSDALE
Beaufort Cottage Stables
High Street
Newmarket
Suffolk CB8 8JS
UK

The Jesuit philosopher, Teilhard de Chardin, distinguished man from animals with the opinion that *"animals know, but man knows that he knows"*. And, in knowing that we know, we posses what is generally described as consciousness or awareness; both of ourselves and of the events of the world and, even, of the universe.

Memory and interpretation of experience provides the motivation and impetus to celebrate anniversaries in keeping with the rhythm of life imparted by periods in which the planets, sun and moon revolve around each other or on their own axis, thus giving us an awareness of day and night, weeks and months, years and eras. Man's mind and body have evolved against the background of the seasons of summer, autumn, winter, spring; and of a life span initiated by birth and ended by death.

Time, at least in the short term of millennia, is linear and not circular. Human existence is, therefore, measured as if a railway line extending back into the past with experience of events represented as stations on the way. The further the distance the more remote become both the experiences and those associated with them. However the past, with its memories and interpretations of significance, forms the basis of our identity, national group and/or family; the past is the platform to the present, as the present is a station on the journey to the future.

Celebrations of anniversaries, centuries and millennia are part of our heritage of consciousness and our awareness of the passing of time. Time, it is said, is the enemy of man; and, when time stretches out across the millennia, it is indeed an awesome and challenging concept for the human mind. In consciousness we can dwell upon the changing criteria of existence, from the environment in which the Battle of Hastings was fought, between Normans and Anglo Saxons, and the nuclear age and space travel of today. It is not surprising, therefore, that mankind wishes to celebrate two millennia, despite the illogicality of employing a specific Christian ethos as a marker of the period, rather than one based on biology common to all. We should, perhaps, be celebrating the landmark of when man first gained consciousness itself, which, according to Julian Jaynes in his book *The Origin of Consciousness in the Breakdown of the Bicameral Mind*, occurred some 4,000 years ago.

The end of this present millennium marks a temporal event the like of which we will never encounter again in our lifetime. The horse and those such as veterinary surgeons, who strive to better its welfare are, perhaps, very small cogs in the mighty sum of human enterprise but, to us, the horse is the alpha and omega of our professional and, in many cases, our personal life. To lay down a marker of equine status at this present milestone of the world will, hopefully, contribute to an understanding of future generations as to the hopes, fears, expectations, failures, triumphs and inadequacies of past and present veterinarians; a marker which may be used by historians and provide a better understanding of those who, in the future, look back like us upon the past. Let us therefore celebrate, within the pages of this book, our own existence and the understanding and progress we have made within our own lifetimes.

The idea for this book was developed within the office responsible for editing and publishing *Equine Veterinary Journal*, where a team led by my Deputy Editor, Rachel Green, put flesh around the bones of the concept. As Editor of *Equine Veterinary Journal* for the past 20 years, I have a strong instinct of the importance of recording history in the making and of providing a basis upon which future generations can understand (even appreciate!) the past. It was said by Isaac Newton that "*We stand upon the shoulders of giants*" and by Didactus Stella that *"A dwarf standing on the shoulders of a giant can see further than the giant himself"*!

The welfare of the horse is traced as a priority objective for the British Equine Veterinary Association since its inception in 1961. It is particularly appropriate, therefore, for the Association to have played a prominent role in furthering publication of a book dedicated to the multisighted aspect of human care for horses. This initiative, on the part of the Association, was led by the last and first Presidents of the old and new millennium, Pat Harris and Tim Greet, respectively.

Romney Publications was set up to publish Sharron Murgatroyd's book *Jump Jockeys Don't Cry*. Sharron had fractured her neck at the last fence at Bangor and, in consequence, became tetraplegic. She wrote the account of her life with the proceeds going to the Injured Jockeys Fund who supported her with great affection and completeness. Sharron typifies the lines of Kipling, "*If you can meet with triumph and disaster and treat those two impostors just the same*". It was a privilege to have been associated with such a venture. In a different dimension, it is a similar privilege for Romney Publications to be associated with the present project of identifying both giants and those like the present author, the dwarfs who stand upon their shoulders in the pursuit of progress in equine welfare.

"Si monumentum requiris, circumspice" (if you want a monument look around you) is the inscription over the North Door at St Paul's Cathedral, London, as a tribute to its architect Sir Christopher Wren. If readers of this present volume look around them, they will see that much loved animal, the horse, given the care and support it both needs and deserves; a care based on the contemporary

understanding of its natural processes, subject to the conditions and diseases inherent in the chances and purposes of its life. This book serves as a monument to those who have and are contributing to the progress of understanding and of equine welfare. There are, of course, many unsung heroes who have failed to receive mention; but they, like the unknown warrior, are part of the heritage on which we dwarfs now stand. And, as we face the new millennium, there are some of those recorded here who will be regarded as the giants, but they will still not see as far as those who stand upon their shoulders. We may conclude with Alfred Lord Tennyson, the poet, "*There, the great world spins forever, down the ringing grooves of change.*" This book is but a record of where we stand today.

The purpose and content of this book covers depth and breadth and height of the subject of the horse and its veterinary carers. The depth, in the spirit of endeavour, is represented by the milestones of events and personalities on whose shoulders we stand today. The breadth is the diverse disciplines, initiatives and technologies to which we have devoted and are now devoting to the ever-increasing dimension of medicine and surgery; in the older disciplines of feeding practices, medicine, surgery, orthopaedics and anaesthesia, in newer fields of imaging technology and exercise physiology. The height is brought by the few who have led the way in the past and will, in imagination, emerge to lead the way in the future.

"*Men my brothers men the workers ever seeking something new, that which they have done before them, but ernst of that which they will do.*"

Peter Rossdale

Philosophy of the Horse

Reminiscences of a nonagenarian

PETER BURRELL (1905–1999)
Long Hill, Moulton Road
Newmarket
Suffolk CB8 8QQ
UK

I am honoured to have been asked to contribute to this important book. *"Old men forget; yet all shall be forgot, but he'll remember with advantages what feats he did that day."* Thus Shakespeare puts, in the mouth of Henry V, the exhortation to his troops on Crispin's Day; and so we too remember the pleasures and excitements that our horses have given to us in days long gone.

All my life I have been interested in veterinary research. It dates back 80 years to when my father was Chairman of Governors of the Royal Veterinary College. At the same time he was Chairman of the Agricultural Research Council. So it was an education for me to listen to all the top men in the veterinary profession who would often be staying for the weekend at my home.

I now take the opportunity to thank all those who helped me in founding in Research Units for Haematology and Chemical Pathology at the Animal Health Trust. I formed these because for some time I believed that 'blood' was to be the important factor in training of racehorses in the future. And so it has proved.

A third research unit I also helped to establish at this time is what is now the Thoroughbred Breeders' Association Equine Fertility Unit. On the advice of Roger Short, who was at that time Reader in Animal Health at Cambridge University, I engaged a young man just finishing his PhD study at Cambridge Veterinary School. Now Professor 'Twink' Allen, he has been responsible for the Unit's great success and worldwide fame in subsequent years.

But above all, I now take the opportunity to give credit to my wife, Connie, who made all this possible. She financed all three Research Units mentioned above, the first two for 6 years and the Equine Fertility Unit for 10 years. The cost in both cases amounted to well over £1 million each. Without her help, progress in all three important equine veterinary subjects would have been delayed for years.

In the 34 years that I was Director of the National Stud we bred such classic winners as Big Game, Sun Chariot and Chamossaire, important names of their generation now past into the mists of pedigree history. After a lifetime connected closely with breeding Thoroughbred horses, pedigree is of great significance. My own ancestors can be traced back to Radulphus Burrell, born in 1270. Four generations later John Burrell de Woodland was knighted by Henry V in France, in 1414 Gerardus Burrell was made Archdeacon of Chichester and a further descendent, Merrik Burrell, bought West Grinstead Park Estate in Sussex in 1766. This was later sold after World War One to J.P. Hornung who built the studfarm now known as the Sussex Stud. After Hornung's death the estate was bought by Thomas Cook, the travel agent, and after his demise by the Governors of the Royal Veterinary College, intending to develop it as a field station.

However, they changed the minds believing it to be too far from their main college in Camden Town. The National Stud, at that time, required a studfarm as an overflow from their main unit at Gillingham in Dorset, at which to stand two or more extra stallions. The National Stud therefore took over West Grinstead Park. Thus the Burrell pedigree became linked with equine pedigree; and my father Sir Merrik Burrell, a renowned agriculturist, became President to the Royal Agricultural Society, Chairman of the Agricultural Research Council and Chairman of the Board of Governors of the Royal Veterinary College. My own interest in veterinary research stemmed from listening to eminent veterinary researchers who often visited at weekends. He was also a Council Member of the Hunter and Light Horse Improvement Society and bred many champion show horses himself. He was an excellent horseman and a keen hunting man, so that the stable yard was always full of homebred Hunters. My mother was the daughter of Walter Walter Winans, the noted American sportsman, who was renowned for the Trotting horses he himself drove in the showring. My father's mother was Ethelreda, the only sister to the five Loder brothers, all well-known sportsmen in their day. The fourth son founded the Eyrefield Lodge Stud in Kildare where Pretty Polly and Spion Kop, winner of the Derby, were bred.

In my book *Old Sportsmen Never Die* I recounted the story of Pretty Polly 's start in life. Nobel Johnson, stud manager and trainer in Ireland for Eustace Loder, was working some backward two-year-olds in April. He sent his head lad down to the start of the gallop to see that they jumped off properly. The lad was riding an even more backward filly and he was told that as he was there he might as well jump on off behind the others and go with them until she tired; surprise, surprise the filly finished about eight lengths in front of the rest. She was immediately despatched to Newmarket to Peter Gilpin who trained for Eustace Loder in England and it was at Eyrefield that I started my career in the Thoroughbred horse breeding industry when Pretty Polly was still there in happy retirement until she died age 28 the following year.

The first year I went to Goodwood, Mumtaz Mahal was a two-year-old running in the Molecomb Stakes. She looked magnificent and would have passed as a three-year-old. She was very much on her toes in the paddock, the layout of which was a single rail, which separated the horses from the spectators. As the filly turned a corner she lashed out at a man leaning on the rail and smashed his arm.

Noel Murless had just taken over Beckhampton following Fred Darling's retirement and he had a horse entered in the big Mile Handicap on the first day of the meeting. The horse was handicapped at a weight that Noel thought made it a certainty to win. Ante-post betting was 100 to 8 and Noel, who hardly ever bet, did so on this occasion and I too put on

Peter Burrell and H. M. Queen Elizabeth II unveiling his bronze at the National Stud.

more than I could afford. There was a good apprentice in the stable who claimed 5 lb and was given the ride to make it even more of a certainty. The boy was given instructions to jump off and settle in about fourth position, to remain there until they reached a black hut about 1.5 furlongs before the winning post. Then he was to pull out and go for home. In the race the field came into the straight with our horse pulling double and boy sitting quietly. He kept glancing to his right and passed the winning post in third place; it transpired that the hut had been painted white since the previous year. This probably saved me money in the end as I have rarely had a bet ever since.

In 1914 the mobility of the British Army depended almost entirely upon horses, with a few mules. When war was imminent and mobilisation ordered, the army was short of many thousands of the requisite number of horses. Colonel Hall-Walker, who founded the Tully Studfarm of 1,000 acres on the outskirts of Kildaire, offered to give his stud of horses to the nation to breed stallions suitable for getting horses of the army type. The gift depended on the land being purchased at the valuation of £47,000, to include a house and contents, stables, cottages and farm buildings. The stud consisted of six stallions, 43 brood mares, mostly Thoroughbred but with a number of half-bred mares, 10 two-year-olds, 19 yearlings and a large herd of cattle. However, towards the end of the war Major Albert Stern developed the armoured car and tank, so that by 1918 the horse was almost obsolete, although its usefulness was argued right up to the second World War. The future of the National Stud was thrown into question and, after much debate, it was decided to carry on the Thoroughbred side in order to maintain the world supremacy of the British Thoroughbred. Horses bred at Tully included Blandford, sire of four Derby winners; Stardust, sire of Starking, one of the greatest winners produced in Australia, Challenger, top sire in the USA in 1939; Royal Lancer, winner of the 1922 St Leger; Big Game, winner of the 2000 Guineas in 1942; and Chamossaire, winner of the St Leger in 1945. Among the female horses, there was Sun Chariot, winner of the Guineas, Oaks and St Leger in 1942, Myrobella and Carozza who won The Oaks.

At the age of 28, it was my responsibility to find a successor to lease the National Stud racehorses without showing favouritism to one person rather than another. At the time King George VI's racing fortunes were in the doldrums and, through the good auspices of his brother-in-law, Lord Athlone, the King became that man.

In 1944 it was pointed out that under the agreement between the governments when home rule for Ireland was established, all War Office property in Ireland was to be handed over. As the National Stud was supervised by the Ministry of Agriculture, the War Office connection had, until then, been overlooked. However, the Irish Government claimed the stud and lawyers advised that their claim was justified. Thus it came that all the bloodstock was moved to England, as these did not form part of the property. It was in this way that the National Stud was moved to Gillingham in Dorset and Big Game was the first stallion to stand there. His earnings were the salvation of the stud as he was a success from the beginning in his first season with two-year-old runners.

After the death of King George VI, Queen Elizabeth took over the lease of the horses. With her knowledge and enthusiasm it was a great pleasure to work for her. The West Grinstead Stud was bought in order to accommodate extra stallions but this, in turn, resulted in the economic problem of running two stud farms 100 miles apart. The decision was therefore taken to sell both the Gillingham and West Grinstead farms and build a new stud farm in the Newmarket area. And so it was that this was completed in 1963. The National Stud has been housed here for the remainder of the century.

It only remains for me to end by congratulating the veterinary profession as a whole for the high standard that has now been reached in the treatment of all our animals.

Caring man and willing horse: *all our history is his industry...*

LINDSEY ABEYASEKERE
Equine Veterinary Journal Ltd.
351 Exning Road
Newmarket
Suffolk CB8 0AU
UK

Look back at our struggle for freedom,
Trace our present day's strength to its source;
And you'll find that man's pathway to glory
Is strewn with the bones of a horse.

-Anon

From ancient to modern times, the horse has served as a beast of burden, a draught animal and a means of transportation; has helped wage wars and has provided recreation, companionship and even food; it is one of the most cherished subjects of art, revered by man in sculptures, carvings, drawings and paintings. It has been for centuries a symbol of power, freedom, superiority and triumph.

Undoubtedly the earliest relationship between man and horse was that of hunter and hunted, predator and prey. It is still the subject of great debate as to when the first taming and domestication of *Equus* occurred; it is probable that there existed a long association between the species, on the fringes of their respective habitats (horses being creatures of the open grasslands, the steppes of Central Asia and the Ukraine, while man preferred the game-rich area of the broken forest) which gradually developed into full domestication between 5000 and 3000 BC. Stone Age cave paintings throughout the Old World indicate that, by around 2000 BC, domestic horses were common from China to Mesopotamia and, by 1000 BC, archaeological records show that domestication of the horse had spread to almost every part of Asia, Europe and North Africa. Whenever the first incidence of taming and mounting the horse took place, it is certain that it would have been, as Stephen Budiansky says in *The Nature of Horses*,

> *"...surely more an act of daring, bravado, curiosity and yearning than of necessity...To have ridden upon the back of this powerful and dangerous animal at the dawn of its domestication must be ranked more as a sacrament than an invention."*

Invention of the wheel allowed the horse to come into its own as a draught animal: stronger, faster and more amenable than the asses and oxen used previously. Such a boon was the equine workforce to man that, even today, we evaluate the performance of tractors, trucks and cars in terms of 'horsepower'. Providing a means of travelling further and faster than ever before, use of the horse extended territorial boundaries, allowing the transformation of the pastoral nomads of the Central Asian steppes into mounted warriors and the first of the great 'horse cultures'. To these people, life without a horse became impossible; as well as transport for man and his belongings, the horse was food, drink, weapon, friend and god. Cultures such as these, including the Huns (led by Attila), the Mohammedans, the Mongols (under the infamous Genghis Khan) and the American Plains Indians, evolved where there was an abundance of horses and a mobile way of life; where horses were scarce, they were reserved for the wealthy and only for important business - generally warfare.

From this time, around 4000 years ago, until only a few decades ago, the primary role of the horse in man's history was as an instrument of war. Early Indo-Europeans spread West into the 'civilised' world, taking with them the domesticated horse and possibly the origins of today's European languages. Greek, Egyptian, Indian, Chinese and Roman paintings and sculptures of the time show many a

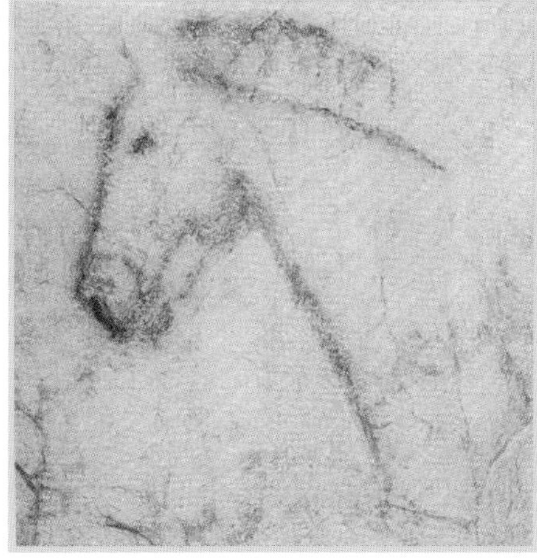

An Ice Age work of art - outline of a horse's head from the caves of Asturias in Spain, over 10,000 years old.

Coin of Roman Republic 67 BC, silver denarius showing Apollo on one face and a horseman on the other (Painting by Jim Power).

barbarian warrior being crushed beneath the wheels of a chariot, which had quickly become favoured over the ridden horse for use in battle. However, the chariot had its limitations (among them an inability to tackle obstacles such as water, walls and mountains), and proved no match for a well-trained cavalry. This, plus the considerable amounts of money required in order to obtain horses, to train them, feed and keep them, to pay grooms and stable staff and to build and maintain the chariots themselves, meant that the chariot came to be used mainly as an accoutrement and a symbol of wealth and power, owned by aristocrats and kings; throughout more peaceful times, it also became extremely important as the focus of the games where people came to relax and bet on the chariot races. The first known use of the horse as a means of sport and recreation, these games were particularly popular with the Greeks and the Romans - in *The Iliad*, Homer describes such races at the time of the Trojan War in the 13th century BC. Winners achieved respect and fame and were garlanded with laurels; if it were a 'funerary games', held in honour of the death of a king, the less fortunate may have ended up accompanying their late ruler to meet the gods. Ceremonial burial of horses was carried out in many countries and cultures, signalling the growing importance of the horse as a symbol of his owner's rank and wealth. In China, they tended to adopt the rather more peaceful method of honouring those they mourned by burying lifelike terracotta statues alongside the dead.

Although the image of the horse was inextricably linked with its role in warfare, history's greatest equestrian period began in Greece, where the horse was loved by men and gods more for its beauty than utility. Myths and legends were built around the animal, all based on the idea of the horse as a symbol of perfect motion, no mere earthbound creature but one of godly origin, capable of flight and speech. The Sun god Helios rose into the Eastern sky in a four-horsed chariot; Lampos and Phaeton draw the chariot of Eos, goddess of the dawn, and the moon goddess Selene, her sister, was also pulled by a horse-drawn chariot; the most famous of all, the winged horse Pegasus, dragged around the thunder and lightning of the all-powerful god, Zeus. Too expensive to be kept for everyday use, the horse achieved an air of exclusivity (which has to some extent been maintained to the present day); distinct from other domesticated animals, the horse was not submissive, each individual in a new generation having to be tamed and 'broken' anew. This feature appealed to man's image of himself as a fearless warrior, controlling the 'fiery steed'; again, this idea survives to the present, in a similar form - the rider whose mount goes quietly in a simple bit and on a loose rein around a course of jumps or in the hunting field never seems to command quite the same notice and admiration as the rider struggling, with the aid of bits and spurs, to control a snorting, leaping beast fighting for its head. However, 24 centuries ago Xenophon, a cavalry officer in the Greek army, wrote what have become the most influential books in the history of man's relationship with the horse, proposing that the basis of equestrianism was that horse and rider should work in harmony together. Until then, the riding horse had been a product of man's subjugation of the animal, and 'breaking in' taken literally, with brutal methods (such as bits with spiked cheekpieces to aid steering, or dropped nosebands so low as to interfere with breathing) often employed in order to effect mastery of the spirited horse. Xenophon also studied the horse's mind and believed in a system of reward and correction, for,

> *"...if you reward him with kindness when he has done what you wish and admonish him when he disobeys, he will be most likely to do what you want. This holds good in every branch of horsemanship."*

His writings dealt with the skills required in order to achieve the impression of the noble, powerful steed, teaching the horse movements such as the prancing curvet, for,

> *"...such are the horses that gods and heroes are depicted riding, and men who manage them will present a magnificent appearance".*

For the first time, this could be achieved through methods of persuasion and understanding, rather than force. The art of horsemanship was developed throughout the Greek cavalry, and spread as they did into Persia, led by the Macedonian prince Alexander the Great. Alexander's horse, Bucephalus, became as renowned as his rider and is probably the first horse in history to be recognised by name, indicating a closer relationship between the two than any before documented. First ridden by Alexander as a boy, Bucephalus was reputed to be extremely faithful to his master and, though a fierce and imposing warhorse, showed great jealousy if Alexander appeared to favour another mount. This loyalty and affection was reciprocated - when Bucephalus died in India (of old age) having helped his master to take 'civilisation' to Persia, Syria, Phoenicia, Egypt, Iran and parts of India, the city of Bucephala was founded on the spot where the great warhorse was buried.

With the death of Alexander, the Grecian civilisation began to crumble, allowing the Roman Empire to spread east. Having been forced rapidly to develop a cavalry with enough speed and manoeuvrability to conquer the Carthaginians (who had, with the use of elephants, previously defeated the infantry-based Roman army), the Romans proceeded to bribe the Parthians, horsemen and bowmen of the steppes, to be recruited as mercenaries. This enabled the Romans to retire to Rome to practice the art of decadence, to the extent of accepting a horse as a member of the senate. Having heard of the decline of the empire, the Huns (led by the notorious Attila) took full advantage, carrying out full-scale raids with huge numbers of horsemen, heralding the Dark Ages of western civilisation. Indeed, it would be no exaggeration to say that the horse brought about the collapse of the western Roman empire - cavalry having always been a neglected branch of their army, the Romans were unable to overcome the military superiority of the mounted enemy troops. To the Romans, the horse had always been considered more a symbol of affluence than of real power, signified also in the use of language; in ancient Athens, men who owned at least one horse were known as '*hippeis*' and legally recognised as a special upper class of society, while the English word '*cavalier*', the German '*Ritter*', French '*chevalier*' and Spanish '*caballero*' all indicated a socially superior citizen, usually of military nobility. The Latin equivalent, '*eques*', simply indicated that the holder of the title was wealthy enough to own a horse.

The mediaeval period in Britain was a time of myths and legends, of King Arthur and his Knights of the Round Table - who, in reality, would have been busy defending against Britons, Picts, Angles, Saxons and the Vikings. Alfred, rather than burning cakes, was more likely to have been found organising the first horse races run for reward. These races, originally a way of distributing a dead man's goods, resulted in the development of breeding horses purely for speed; the breeding of various types of horses for different purposes became widespread around this time. The Vikings, carrying out many of their lightning raids on horseback, bred a small, sturdy pony able to travel with them by ship. Having settled in northern France and become Normans, this ship-borne cavalry was used to great effect in 1066, when William also introduced to Britain a new type of horse, the Andalusian, large enough to allow the ruler to survey his troops, strong enough to carry the armoured soldier - and big enough to impress the opposition. To this end, these 'destriers' were all stallions and their natural aggression encouraged. Bred for size, these horses became slower and less mobile, so that other types of horses were needed for purposes other than fighting (or jousting, an activity developed in this Age of Chivalry to allow knights to impress the people and vye for ladies' favours when wars were scarce), including the messengers' horse the courser, bred for speed and tested against each other on the original 'racecourses'. When the 'infidels' took over the Holy Land and the Crusades began, the speed and agility of the lightly armed Arab horses was appreciated (compared to the heavy, armoured European horses), and the fact that the destriers were all stallions while the Saracens used only mares facilitated attempts to acquire Arab stock for breeding. At the same time, bands of perhaps the most famous horsemen were gathering on the steppes, this time under the command of Genghis Khan. The Mongolian warriors went around the Great Wall of China (taking with them the 'heavenly horses' that had been bred within the Forbidden City, using them to improve their own stock), round the Himalayas and, in the other direction, reached into Europe as far as Hungary. Here, however, the needs of their horses meant the Mongolian hordes could progress no further; 100,000 men with at least 20 horses each grazed out Eastern Europe.

The trend for the use of the horse in leisure began with Henry VIII. With the Crusades over, increasing amounts of free time were available (at least for the aristocracy). Hunting was one of his most popular pastimes, and riding purely for pleasure developed from this. A Royal Stud was established, crossing Italian stock from Padua with the now redundant courser, the descendants of which were to become known as the English Thoroughbred. Relative peace in Britain (prior to the Civil War) allowed 'native' pony breeds, actually ofViking and Saxon origin, to develop. Whereas the horse was generally perceived as a noble animal, identified with the warrior aristocracy, these ponies were to the peasants, farmers and ordinary citizens beasts of burden, a means of transport and travel and an indispensible aid in agriculture. As one of his methods for the improvement of horse breeding, Henry VIII decreed, in 1540, that all stock under 14 hh should be eliminated,

"Forasmuch as the breed of good and strong horses is a great help and defence to the realm",

- a dramatic and potentially catastrophic event in the history of pony breeds. However, this order could not have been implemented without the cooperation of all private owners, and so the consequences were limited and tended to be favourable; large numbers of the unfit, weedy and undersized were eliminated from breeding stock and there was no alternative for breeders but to introduce height into their ponies by introducing Thoroughbred and Arabian bloodlines, crosses which have led to the attractive, quality ponies seen today.

In the following century, the sport of horse racing received particular support from Charles I, under whom Newmarket became the centre of the racing scene. Although Cromwell, once in power, banned public horse races, they were soon reinstated and became more popular than ever under Charles II. A successful rider in his own right, he won the Newmarket Town Plate twice and his nickname of 'Old Rowley' (after a horse he owned of the same name) was passed on to the course on which he raced, the Rowley Mile. The onset of the Civil War encouraged the development of various breeding programmes, with the Royalists favouring a lighter, faster warhorse for the Cavaliers, while Cromwell and his Parliamentarians preferred the heavier, slower type. The Cavaliers were eventually defeated, but the lighter horse remained more popular in Europe where wars continued against the Cossacks and Turks. In Britain, the eventual defeat of the Scots at Culloden persuaded many (including Scots, various European refugees and others with less choice) to travel to the New World, taking only their most valued possessions - including the best of their stock. Some went to Australia or New Zealand, where the Aborigine and Maori people soon became excellent stockmen; others sailed across the Atlantic, and thus introduced the abilities of the horse to the natives of North America.

Equine ancestors disappeared from the American continent at the end of the last Ice Age, only reappearing on the mainland when Columbus landed in Hispaniola on 2 January 1494 (although this was his second voyage, having previously taken 30 Spanish horses ashore in Haiti on 6 December 1492). In the following years, the mounted Spanish Conquistadores introduced 'civilisation' to the Aztecs and, later, the Incas (who, having never seen this beast before, thought that man and horse were one, a kind of centaur). Not all of these Spanish horses returned to their native land; those left behind became the predecessors of the 'mustangs' on the great open grasslands of both North and South America. As with the people of the Central Asian steppes, the lives of the American Plains Indians were transformed by the horse, with many tribes soon prizing it above all else. Mounted, they could now kill buffalo by the thousand; and in war, the horse meant wealth and nobility, being status symbol, currency and bride-price. The death of a war leader led to the sacrifice of his favourite horses, in the belief that they would accompany him to the Happy Hunting Grounds. However, in general, Indians tended to be good riders rather than excellent horsemasters (with the exception of one tribe, the Nez Percés, who bred horses systematically and successfully, selecting in terms of speed, stamina, hardiness and character as well as good looks, and in so doing, developed the Appaloosa), with no attention paid if the animal were lame or had sores so long as it could still be ridden. If the pony were unable to work, it was abandoned or killed and eaten and another mustang caught.

Back in Europe, advancing civilisation was requiring faster and better communication. Roads were re-established and the redundant destrier was given a new role pulling the heavy vehicles needed to cope with the low standard of surfaces. Travel was therefore still very slow and so, since the aim of civilisation is always increased speed, the roads were improved, leading to the development of lighter coaches together with lighter, faster horse to pull them. While warhorses were still in demand in Europe, peace in England was maintained by her Navy, allowing the heavy horse to adapt to more mundane tasks such as ploughing and hauling. The rest of Europe was still producing only warhorses (leisure activities of the aristocracy in France having been 'cut short' by the Revolution), and the introduction of sufficient breeding stock of 'Barb' and 'Turk' stallions from Spain and Turkey enabled Britain to develop the types of horses suitable for various leisure activities. The introduction of bloodlines of the Godolphin Barb, the Darley Arabian and the Byerly Turk was so successful that the General Stud Book was begun in order to keep track of each horse's lineage - the Thoroughbred was born! Its exclusive pedigree added to the prestige of the owner and, more dramatically, to the value of the horse. When crossed with the older, heavier types, a suitable hunter and ladies' horse was also developed, providing a diversion for the gentry needing a pastime in the absence of war.

Improvement of facilities led to a general increase in travel by the common man. For those who could not afford carriages of their own (i.e. most of the population), scheduled coach services were established, travelling in stages of around 50 miles per day (thus 'stagecoaches') with overnight rests at inns. The invention of Tarmac allowed road surfaces to be improved again, raising the standard of travel. The best of these services carried the Royal Mail and were given priority over other road users, in addition to carrying passengers - 'third class' travelled outside the coach, while 'first class' were allowed inside in relative comfort. The presence of these obviously well-off passengers attracted the dashing figure of the highwayman, romanticised in legend as the 'gentleman of the road'. Another thriving nefarious industry was that of horse stealing, a highly organised activity throughout the country as coach horses were of high quality and much in demand. Taking account of these unforseen events meant that the coach was not a cheap method of travel even for those prepared to sit outside. Riding became, for many, a necessity, although the standard of equitation was often extremely low, encouraging the publishing of several books - Thompson's *Rules For Bad Horsemen*, for example - detailing the basic skills needed in order to be able to travel by horseback. Elsewhere in Europe the opposite was the case, with the classical Art of Horsemanship being revived, including the dramatic 'airs on and above the ground'.

At the end of the 18th century and beginning of the 19th, the constant threat of war provided the European horse-breeding industry with a great boost. Russian, British, Austrian and Prussian armies had well-established, well-stocked studs, while France had to rely on the taking of horses as booty during Napoleon's first campaigns, as the numerous Royal Studs providing cavalry horses had been abolished in the Revolution. When Napoleon became First Consul and, later, Emperor, he organised an intensive breeding programme and the reopening of many national studs to produce suitable horses. Although the rider of several well-known horses (including Marengo, whom the Emperor rode at Waterloo) he did not develop close relationships with them, as, for example, Alexander had with Bucephalus. His preference for grey Arab stallions as mounts was probably the result of his great need to be admired rather than from any particular love of horses. Napoleon fought against the British under Wellington at the last great cavalry battle on 18 June 1815 at Waterloo. At the end, around 75% of the horses involved lay wounded or dying on the battlefield.

With the return of peace, the role of the horse was once again altered. The best of the warhorses were selected by the 'Cadre Noir', the elite cavalry school dedicated to preserving the classical 'airs', while others went on to a more peaceful life, hunting or working on farms or on the road. The heavier horses, with bloodlines from the old packhorses, went on to develop into a range of draught breeds including the Shire, a popular choice in Britain as a plough horse or a barge horse, pulling cargoes equivalent to many wagonloads along the extensive canal networks of the time. This capacity inspired the development of faster and even more efficient means of transporting goods - although the first railways were still horse drawn, it was not long before civilisation had progressed beyond this and steam engines were the main method of bulk transport. In order to provide the railways with a purpose, the Industrial Revolution quickly followed, making the coachmen and carters redundant. However, the horse was still essential to the furtherment of civilisation, as both goods and people needed transporting and distributing once they had reached their destination, and cities such as London were crowded with horses pulling every sort of cart or carriage. The presence of up to 300,000 horses provided plenty of employment for the feed merchants, farriers stablehands and, even, the men who swept the street.

Increased earnings and improvements in the standard and availability of transport allowed the world of leisure to be enjoyed by the general population; racing in particular was popular, allowing as it did widespread gambling. The horse became a vital part of the social scene, with an ability to ride essential for those who aspired to greater social heights - although great skill was less important than style and appearance, as the limit of most people's equestrian forays was a trot along Rotten Row. True horsemanship was well respected and the secrets closely guarded; those few in the know were 'whisperers', often thought to communicate with horses via a secret language.

Recently, there has been a resurgence of interest in 'horse whisperers' and 'natural horsemanship', with many people claiming to have developed a unique method of bonding with horses. These techniques vary, but all are based on the horse's own methods of communication. In fact, these systems are no different in many ways to those that have been practised for centuries by all experienced and effective horse handlers - they may not have had a name for what they did, but the horse cultures of the past practised 'natural horsemanship' too, although the negative consequences would often have been aggressive rather than the body language used today. All of these 'unique' methods depend upon the basic understanding of why a horse acts as it does, why some problems may arise and how this may help to alleviate these problems, or even prevent them in the first place; the horsemen of old achieved this understanding through generations of experience.

The involvement of the horse in war continued into this century to a greater degree than may have been expected, since the cavalry was superior to infantry troops only up until the widespread use of guns rendered the horse too vulnerable. Over half a million horses were used in the Boer War in South Africa at the beginning of the 20th century; of these, 150,000 did not survive. By the onset of World War I, technological advances had resulted in mechanised transport and the automatic machine gun being available to the infantry, and traditional cavalry attacks were uncommon. The cavalry was deployed on the Eastern front where, in many cases, the cavalryman became a dragoon (i.e. a mounted infantryman whose horse was used to help him change position quickly rather than to attack), whereas on the Western front, horses were used mostly as pack animals, as the ground was too wet to allow the use of mechanised vehicles. However, in 1916, when these mechanical problems had been overcome and the tank made its first appearance, around a million saddle horses had been deployed on all fronts - more than in any previous war. The German army used a total of 14 million horses over the four years, and 256,000 died for Britain alone, a number which would have been much higher but for the work of the British veterinary organisation. Modern technology developed by the time of World War II rendered both horses and people even more helpless. Although use of the horse by Western troops was virtually obsolete, large numbers were deployed by Eastern Europeans, including the Polish army and the Russians (who always had mounted units to accompany their tanks - over 3.5 million horses were used by the Red Army). The German Wehrmacht was not entirely mechanised; 2.75 million horses were used in the war for the Fuhrer but, tragically, an average of 865 of these horses were killed each day for the length of the war - over 2000 days. For more about the role of the horse in war, see p 67.

The ultimate and most influential change in the history of man's relationship with the horse was preceded by a man carrying a red flag. The internal combustion engine was used in the tractor, which soon took over from the heavy horse in the fields. Civilisation's obsession with power and speed meant that the automobile or 'horseless carriage' was quickly accepted by most of the population and speed limits were lifted, allowing the vehicle to travel at a speed much higher than that of a coach and horses. In a few short years, the ubiquitous engine was used for everything of importance once done by the horse. However, this has not resulted in the demise of the horse, as may have seemed inevitable at the outset. The horse's relationship with man changed finally and dramatically from that of servant to that of friend.

The result of a true partnership...Pippa Funnell and Supreme Rock after winning the European Three-day Event Championship, Lümühlen, Germany, 1999 (Kit Houghton Photography).

Horses as work animals may continue to be used in some less developed countries, but oxen and asses tend to be more efficient in these areas and so it is possible that there will come a day when the last true workhorse is turned out to pasture. After a long and bloody history, it is inconceivable that the horse will have an influential role in any future war. Today and the future belong to the racehorse and the pleasure horse. Riding for pleasure is more popular and available to a wider section of the population than ever before, as increased free time and personal income have diminished the 'elite' image of the equestrian and leisure activities have become more affordable. The economic impact of the equine industry has been huge, particularly the racing industry, which is often said to be one of the biggest employers in the UK. There are many varied activities in which anyone with an equine interest may take part, each having evolved from a part of the intertwined history of horse and man. Show-jumping, racing, dressage, endurance, eventing (which combines all of these disciplines), polo, driving and hacking all have origins going back many centuries, while the working horse heading state occasions and controlling crowds continues his role as servant and partner.

Although it cannot be said that human culture has not been of benefit to the horse, it has both helped and hindered man's understanding of the animal. The horse is a free-ranging, trickle-feeding creature, evolved to live on the open plain with a flight response developed to combat its position as a prey animal. Man, however, expects it to live in a confined area, often shut in for as many as 23 out of 24 hours or more, in a relatively dark stable with dusty bedding and a limited number of feeds per day. We restrict horses' social relationships, expect them to allow us into areas that make them vulnerable to attack, and make them expend valuable energy travelling in circles and jumping over obstacles that could easily be avoided. However, in the last few years, academic studies and research regarding the horse have become more widespread than ever. Subjects such as evolutionary ecology allow us to begin to understand why horses behave as they do, and the increasing interest in nonaggressive communication via 'natural horsemanship' shows that many people are keen to develop a more sympathetic management system with this in mind. The next millennium is one in which the relationship of man and horse as companions will continue, with an understanding of equine behaviour developed through scientific studies. Our knowledge and therefore the standards of horse welfare can only be improved by an increase in understanding from the human side of this relationship.

"England's past has been borne on his back,
All our history is his industry;
We are his heirs,
He is our inheritance."

The Horse - Ronald Duncan.

My debt to the horse

BRIGITTE HEARD
Stoke-by-Clare
Sudbury, Suffolk
UK

My first experience of meeting a horse was age three years on my Uncle Edward's farm in Ashen on the Suffolk/Essex border. This was a 12.0 hh iron grey mare of uncertain age named Sally and I do not recollect how or why she was there.

My uncle did not have any children, so I guess I became more of a daughter than a niece and it was at this time that my love affair with the horse began. It was obviously then decided that I was old enough to sit on Sally, and my riding lessons began in earnest. Any spare moment was spent with her, not necessarily riding her but grooming her, plaiting her tail and, sometimes, it was just enough to be with her. Sally taught me a great deal, namely to be able to use my legs, because she required an awful lot of kicking, and also how to sit on a pony that could reverse far faster than it ever went forward. We tried to get her to join in a lesson at the local riding school, but she planted herself in the ring and wouldn't move, so that was the end of my lesson.

As children do, I soon tired of Sally and thought I needed something a bit faster. According to my uncle, when I was seven, he took me to Cambridge horse sales one day and whilst he was buying lunch I bid for, and bought, an unruly bay yearling colt. He said as he was returning to the ring he saw this red-faced child leaping up and down shouting at him, *"Uncle, we have bought a pony and they want your address!"* He said it cost him about four times as much as he paid for the pony to pay for its transport home. I cannot remember him taking me to the sales after that.

Once we got the colt home, we decided that he should be named Billy and he was turned out with another of my uncle's acquisitions called Silver and broken to tack about three years later. Billy and I learnt a lot together and it was from him I had my first fall when, I remember, I was winded quite badly. At that age (about ten), fear of the horse did not seem to exist; and I can remember my friend and I leap-frogging onto Billy and Silver from behind and crawling underneath them, until my mother caught us and lectured us on the dangers and responsibilities of being around horses.

My pony days seemed to pass all too quickly and, after various breeds, colours and sizes had passed through my hands, I found myself in 1976 without a horse for the first time in my life when we lived in Rippingale, South Lincolnshire. This was a new experience for me but, unfortunately, school and boyfriends took over for a short while. I still had contact with horses through friends, and it was through them that I sat on my first Thoroughbred racehorse, called Red Clip. In my mind, once you have ridden a Thoroughbred no other horse can quite match up. It is difficult to put into words, but perhaps the combination of speed, stamina and strength, so thrilling to experience, has something to do with it. To be on a galloping racehorse is comparable to a car enthusiast driving a Formula 1 car - nothing else could be so exhilarating.

When I left school, I obtained a job with Midland Bank in Bourne, Lincolnshire, and then, in 1983, applied for a transfer back home to Suffolk. I worked in Midland Bank, Cambridge, for several years and started to ride out racehorses for Robert Armstrong on Saturdays. I became friendly with his apprentice, who was about to spend the winter working for a trainer in Italy and asked me to go with him. I then made the decision to leave the Bank to work with horses. My mother was absolutely horrified and used all her powers of persuasion to stop me; but my mind was made up.

Italy was an absolute heaven for me. I was surrounded by my beloved horses in a beautiful warm country and being paid to be there! What more could one want! It is amazing how attached you can become to horses that are not yours. You get to know their moods, their likes and dislikes and almost to know what they are thinking. The hardest thing for me was to master the completely different style of riding from the 'heels down, grip with your knees, straight back' approach of Pony Club, to sitting with your knees almost at the top of the saddle and trying to imitate Lester Piggott. All in all, I thoroughly adored my time in Italy, and when I moved back to England I took up working in several different racing yards.

I found that one of the most difficult things about working with Thoroughbred horses was the fact that most are only in training for a couple of years or even less. It was a very sad moment when two fillies I looked after both went to stud in the same week. It was like losing friends and I still don't know how all the hundreds of stable lads and lasses cope with that. I guess that, if it is your chosen career, you just have to become hardened and accept it. The other thing I found hard was riding out during an English winter. I didn't realise that it was possible to feel so cold. I spent only a couple of years in this country working in racing, because I feel that there is not much chance, as a female in racing, to advance through the ranks. We actually had a head girl at the last yard I worked in, but this is by far the exception to the rule.

At that time I was lodging with a friend who was at the Royal Veterinary College at Potters Bar and she encouraged me to reply to an advert for a position at a local equine veterinary surgery. I have to say I didn't really rate my chances, but applied anyway and to my surprise got the job and started in January 1988; and am still working there today. I ride out for a local trainer as much as I can, so I still get my one-to-one contact with horses which is so important to me, and I own a seven-year-old pony called Geronimo, whom I have had since he was four months old.

I cannot imagine my life without horses in it, and my debt to the horse is that it has provided me with companionship, fun and inspiration. There is something about the horse that touches the soul of those who come into contact with them and I, for one, feel honoured that I am touched by that magic.

Horse and artist, artist and horse: a personal perspective

JIM POWER
Banstead Manor Stud
Cheveley, Newmarket
Suffolk CB8 9RD
UK

When I was invited to contribute to this book, with my views and observations of the horse from the perspective of an artist portraying them in a two dimensional plane, I was naturally pleased to accept.

I had never before analysed why I chose to make certain marks, strokes and daubs on canvas or paper in a particular way. Obviously, I have a methodical way of laying out a picture, of setting out its construction and composition, but analysing and committing this process into text I found quite challenging. So let me begin by returning to the origins of equine art; the first time the horse was painted.

Obviously, the observations and styles of neolithic man are very different to those observed by modern man. Neolithic and cavemen drawings of some 20,000 years ago are extremely interesting, considering the artists of that period had very limited materials with which to convey their drawings. These would have included burnt wood used as a charcoal, their own fingers employed as a primitive brush or, maybe, some chalk or whatever was lying around. Neolithic artists had very little colour or pigment, but perhaps had started crushing herbs, berries or fruit to create juices of different colours. Despite these great limitations, their observations were still very well studied because they depicted the horse, its gait and stride pattern with tremendous vigour and action, thereby capturing the image of movement.

They portrayed these drawings on the walls, not as a decorative feature but as teaching information for their families and the people who were to follow them in generations to come. This then was the proof of the first domestication of the horse. As the centuries rolled on, through Egyptian and Roman times, stone friezes as well as the pyramids portrayed the horse as a domesticated animal. By now horses had become a source of wealth, revolutionising contemporary lives with the use of their power in industry, transport, warfare and sport, not to mention the social side of human existence.

Two particularly good examples of recent finds are the horse's head of pentelic marble from the Parthenon friezes in Athens, which can now be seen as part of the Elgin Marbles collection in the British Museum in London, and the mosaics of a Roman Racer from a villa in Bath, dated around AD 300, one of the first pictures of a horse in sport.

As time went by, the horse became studied in more serious forms, as can be seen in individual pictures, particularly in the 16th, 17th and 18th centuries, and by looking at some of the early works of our European artists, who conveyed the horse in a totally different manner than did Neolithic man. Now they were painting for wealth, exaggerating the horse's body size and making it look more attractive than it actually was. Action and movement were changed to the 'rocking horse' type motion which was the fashion of the time and not very well observed; nevertheless that was the way the European world wanted their pictures painted.

George Stubbs was born in Liverpool in 1724 and was at the height of his fame in 1758 when he started his great work *The Anatomy of The Horse*, published in 1766 and illustrated with numerous engravings of the highest merit, etched by his own hand. One can imagine that he spent hundreds of hours dissecting the animal to see how it was constructed, logging all the information in a form that could be used as a reference. By this time, of course, pigments and raw materials were becoming more readily available and, consequently, large commissions were being offered to the artists of the day. Also the aristocracy and wealthy patrons of Europe were commissioning artists to portray them to the world in a favourable light in drawings and paintings. If George Stubbs' fame rested on nothing else, *The Anatomy of The Horse* alone entitles him to a niche in the halls of fame of both medical practitioners and artists. Horses from that moment changed and the inflated bladders on fixed frames and exaggerated cages of Velasquez and Van Dyke were no longer good enough. Even the horses of the great Michelangelo had to take a back seat; and between Stubbs and the advent of the camera there were very few artists who could portray a horse in a seriously true likeness.

There is one aspect that Stubbs struggled unsuccessfully to achieve, however, namely the action of the gallop. This was not for the want of trying. But for all his anatomical knowledge, he persisted with the conventional rocking horse action, often with all four of the animal's hooves off the ground (p 230).

Mention must be made of Ben Marshall, the English horse pictures of the 18th and 19th century, the Alken family, the Fernies and Herrings: these were all great masters of English sporting pictures. It was not, however, until 1887 that the photographer Muybridge concluded his studies at the University of Pennsylvania, where he published some 780 plates in a book entitled *Animal Locomotion*. Now that the truth of the matter was known, the problem was solved. What had always been too fast for the human eye was now set out in a clear sequence of 36 pictures from cameras with trip wires and clockwork shutter set-ups in a line through which the galloping horse passed.

Muybridge had also made many studies of the horse at a

Horse Head, Parthenon Frieze.

walk, from side, rear, front and diagonal views. He then proceeded with the trot, canter and, of course, the gallop, which enabled the artist to capture the horse in every conceivable movement he so wished.

The likes of Joseph Crawhall, one of the Glasgow school, was able to make some wonderful images armed with the knowledge of Muybridge's observations, as was Gilbert Holiday.

We then come to the wonderful 20th century artists, Alfred Munnings and Lionel Edwards, who drew so successfully on Muybridge's observations. Their own methods and interpretations were greatly studied and portrayed by other artists. The equine artist had moved into a completely new role.

It seemed strange that Gilbert Holiday had not been appreciated by the sporting masses. Only a small number of patrons, and in his latter years, Lionel Edwards and Alfred Munnings, admired his wonderful quality of his work.

In 1983 an exhibition was put on by William Marlan in London called *The Art of Gilbert Holiday*, and since that time he has been placed alongside the finest sporting artists.

Before I close this narrative, I would like to return to the beginning of the 19th century in order write about Edward Mayhew (1813–1868). Mayhew came from a very artistic family. His elder brother by a year, Henry, had great influence as the first editor of *Punch*; and his younger brother, Horace, was sub-editor: Mayhew's literary skills were therefore already instilled into him prior to his joining the veterinary profession. He wrote plays, loved to act, draw and to sketch. In 1845, Mayhew gained his diploma from the Royal Veterinary College in London and, while still a student, was invited to be a lecturer on anatomy, which he did with great verve and skill. His fellow students admired his professional outlook and the demonstration and illustration of this subject. He was elected to the RCVS Council in 1846 while still lecturing on anatomy. Unfortunately, this job did not last too long as he was asked to resign shortly afterwards. His character was quite strong and outspoken. He obviously upset colleagues within the London college and, slightly later in his life, he also upset those in Edinburgh. Nevertheless, it did not deter him from making his observations and statements; and his first papers and editorials were starting to appear. His accurate observations were absorbed very quickly and he managed to put them down in both literary and artistic terms. After losing his job as lecturer for anatomy, he opened a private

Roman Racer, Bath AD 300.

tuition course in London. This did not go down too well with the London School. But he persevered and then opened a veterinary practice, where he specialised in dogs and cats.

In 1847, he published a paper on the application of tubing a horse into the stomach, via a catheter through the nasal passages. This pioneered the work in respect of the nowadays common practice of getting medication into horses' stomachs quickly. This truly remarkable work and valuable method of treatment was disregarded totally for nearly half a century by the London and Edinburgh colleges; and was not rediscovered until around the 1900s. Nevertheless, Mayhew's determination and contributions to the *Veterinary Record* and the *Veterinarian* were never-ending. He wrote many, many different articles on diverse subjects, and was widely read in the subject matter he wished to examine.

In 1860, he published *The Illustrated Horse Doctor*, a specialist work intended for the amateur, and then, in 1864, reintroduced the work with a publication called *The Illustrated Horse Management*. He made 400 or so engravings, etchings and margin drawings which were really to help the layman and the groom observe the horse. The drawings depicted how to handle, restrain and diagnose simple problems the horse was showing, so that grooms could

Equine surgery through the ages.

A Champion.

convey the information back to the veterinary surgeon in attendance. This was a marvellous piece of work and the accuracy of the characters within each of the drawings and etchings, though the style might be slightly cartoonish, were well portrayed and executed.

Unfortunately, this was the last piece of work that Mayhew published. After a long illness he passed away in Plymouth, Devon, in 1868. Although he was far more skilled in the knowledge of dogs than horses, he pursued with great vigour his literary and artistic attributes; and the spirit of scientific enquiries he publicised was second to none. He touched on many fringe subjects that he felt important and the professional papers he wrote were publicised throughout the country, in many a different diary. If nothing else, we should really remember Mayhew for three major contributions. Firstly, the discovery and application of tubing a horse via the nasal passages; secondly, his last piece of work, *The Illustrated Horse Management*; and, finally, one of the finest pieces of work on the subject of the horse's mouth, in particular how to interpret age from the teeth. His draughtsmanship and skill in application of this piece of work was outstanding, using neutral colours to perfection. His drawings were guaranteed to be accurate right down to the smallest details; and he repeatedly confirmed this, time and time again, by his literary and artistic skills.

In conclusion, most of the trouble about art is caused by the fact that we are not agreed as to the proper definition of the term. Consequently, no one really knows what an artist is and the artist himself cannot therefore be clear about his own function. Take the simple case of the painter. He is obviously definable as a man who manipulates paint with skill. House painters are essentially skilled, but are they, therefore, painters or artists? We have the Society of Arts to remind us that practically everything for which 'skill' or 'science' is required is an art form. The usual interpretation of the word nevertheless makes a sharp distinction between the house 'painter' and the artist 'painter'; and describes even the incompetent picture painter as an artist and the most competent house painter an artisan.

The distinction is then not due to skill but the underlying idea. The artist, therefore, is a man who expresses ideas. The great artists are men who have great ideas and can express them. The minor artist, not less skilled but with lesser ideas, nonetheless knows how to express them.

This emphasis on 'canning' or 'knowing how' would appear to favour the definition of art, after all, as a question of skill; but that is only a very superficial conception since skill, though it be a means to an end, is not everything. The poem or picture depends entirely upon the emotions which underlie its making and that demand expression in one form or another; the actual making is only the carrying out of that which existed embryonically in the mind.

The idea is the important point; and the skill is requisite because man is a social and communicative animal. Imperfect expression may mar the idea but without it the most perfect power of expression spends itself in vain. No amount of skill can take the place of the idea or compensate for the lack of something to be expressed.

A picture that conveys nothing, however well executed, is not a work of art. Nor is it any justification if the artist claims that the picture expresses his or her feelings or conveys something quite superficially to oneself.

However, it is impossible to paint a picture that conveys nothing because, try as he may, no man can produce anything without some meaning or some significance, however obscure and unintelligible, even to himself. In this light I feel that I am in a stage in my own career where I feel my artistic skill and craftsmanship have moved on, so that I am more able to convey views, ideas, emotions of the wonderful animal that we love, work and live with and dream about. The more I paint and work, the more I am obsessed and frustrated by my lack of ability to convey the emotional effect that this animal has upon me and my life.

All the illustrations are the work of the author.

Final adjustment.

Chantilly paddock (exhibited at the 1999 SEA Palace House Exhibition).

A veterinary nurse's perspective: developments in caring as a team

BONNY MILLAR
Beaufort Cottage Equine Hospital
Cotton End Road
Exning, Newmarket
Suffolk CB8 7NN
UK

Introduction

It was now raining steadily but people were still not running for cover. Ladies in their best hats and gentlemen in morning suits walked around determined to savour the moment. The first clap of thunder sounded, then another. The hospitality tents started to fill rapidly. A flash of lightning in a group of trees behind the Royal tent, next to the ornamental lake, was followed by an ear splitting crash shaking the gardens.

Huddled together with my husband under an umbrella, I was loving every minute of this English summer weather. There I was, an American citizen, part of a team having worked for over a month on one of the Queen's stallions, enjoying the quintessential English experience: one of Her Majesty's summer garden parties at Buckingham Palace.

It all seemed a very long way from veterinary nursing in America, from the late nights, the smells and sights of surgery, the puzzling cases, the blood, the hard work, the work-ups and the letdowns.

Why do my colleagues and I work, day in, day out, on both sides of the Atlantic without thought or hope of such a reward? How did I get to be involved with horses? Where did veterinary nursing begin? Where would it lead?

I have watched the world of the veterinary nurse for almost 20 years, first as a student at Harcum College, then a veterinary technician at the University of Pennsylvania, New Bolton Center, USA, and finally a veterinary nurse at Rossdale & Partners in the UK. As the thoughts of many turn to the next millennium and the hopes it may bring, it seems an appropriate time to review veterinary nursing, or at least my perspective of it.

As we draw near to the end of the old century we are a part of a world undergoing political and economic upheaval. As I write, the Balkans are being ravaged by internal war, homes and lives in Oklahoma have been shattered by tornadoes - even our own community is full of people in desperate need. One is tempted to stop and consider whether or not the energy and skills invested in animals would have been better spent elsewhere.

For me, the answer lies, in part, in Scripture. Solomon noted in Proverbs, well over 2000 years ago, that:

> *"A righteous man cares for the needs of his animal, but the kindest acts of the wicked are cruel."*

In doing so he delivered with eloquent prose and timeless truth the heart of the veterinary profession: caring.

Experiences in the US

There are many different reasons for joining the ranks of veterinary professionals - intellectual challenge and academic research, financial reward or respect from society - a diversity matched perhaps by the variety of the animals in their care. When I look back, to September 1981, the date I started my Associates Degree course in Animal Health Technology, at Harcum College, Philadelphia, I cannot pinpoint why I chose a career in veterinary nursing.

There was no doubt, in my mind, that this was a career choice rather than a passing fad or fancy or something to occupy me until something more appealing came along.

A decision was probably made as a young teenager. I had quickly reached the conclusion that animals ('pets') are given to us to care for, to provide for, to develop and use, and most of all enjoy; that we do not own them, indeed we cannot, in anything more than a legal sense. Although their service can be enforced and compliance demanded, their devotion, willing obedience and eager companionship must be earned. Although I have never regarded myself as a passionate lover of all animals, I have had many of them as companions over the years. It is these characteristics which have always humbled and thrilled me.

Others will write in more detail and with greater insight about the relationship between man and the animal kingdom - and the evolution from worker to pet or companion. I can only describe my perspective on the common experience of my colleagues in the field of veterinary medicine, that of being a carer.

What does the future hold for veterinary nursing and veterinary nursing as a part of the veterinary profession? I hope that by recounting some of the stages in the development of the veterinary nurse/technician to date, a path will be traced that sets a direction for the future. It will remain up to us to maintain the momentum along it.

Developments

The mission statement developed by the North American Veterinary Technician Association (NAVTA), in the early 1990s, illustrates its future plans and strategies:

> *"The mission of NAVTA is to represent and promote the profession of veterinary technology. NAVTA provides direction, education, support, and coordination for its members and works with other allied professional organisations for the competent care and humane treatment of animals."*

Final days of training before starting work; New Bolton Center, USA, 1984.

The 1990s has also seen a three-fold increase in membership and, in 1993, NAVTA represented the USA at the meeting of the International Veterinary Nursing Congress, a worldwide forum. Held in London, this provided an opportunity for technicians and nurses from throughout the world to share their triumphs and concerns. Among the issues discussed were the criteria for recognising various speciality fields, for example, the American Society ofVeterinary Dental Technicians.

Clearly, the scope of nursing expertise is growing and its international recognition is certain, but the path to professional accreditation in veterinary care has been a long one and not without its battles and opposition. I will leave it to others to describe better than I can the development of the role, responsibilities and capabilities of the veterinary surgeon. What I offer here are some facts and thoughts about the developing role of the nurse within the veterinary profession.

It is recognised that the long-term development of any profession - or business or service for that matter - requires the development of an organisation or team to support the pioneers and exploit and consolidate the advances made. As expertise and sophistication increase, the sum of technical and organisational skill can no longer reside within the individual. Specialisation becomes inevitable and, in kind, must pass down through all levels of the organisation.

As the professional's enquiring mind travels down the path of knowing more and more about less and less, the weight of expectation in the public's mind increases; "*If the doctors mended Auntie Ruth's fractured leg, why can't you do the same for my horse's leg?*" Commercial pressure comes hard on the heels of public expectation and the professional must compete to provide a service to an increasingly knowledgeable and well-informed client.

Equipment has become more and more sophisticated and demands technical expertise. Funding and specialisation has led to more focused operations plus the demand for organisational and management skills. As caseloads increase so have the demands on the nurse, as extra eyes and ears for the veterinary surgeon.

I remember vividly my very first day as a nursing student, on a visit to New Bolton Center, the University of Pennsylvania's Large Animal Veterinary Hospital, for a tour. I was nervous about the big unknown ahead, but excited for the chance to see at first hand how the textbook was put into practice. As we walked around a corner heading towards the barns, we were met by a forklift with a freshly euthanased horse dangling high in the air on its forks. I was stunned - I had never considered how a horse is moved from one place to another when it can't use its own four legs. This was something I never expected; my textbooks had not elaborated on the grim technicalities of moving carcasses or the consequences when treatment fails.

Technicians in the US

In the US it was the veterinarians, not the academic institutions, who led the way in training assistants - on the job. It wasn't until 1961 that the first formal training programme for the veterinary nurse was established in the United States. The Associates Degree in 'Applied Science' was awarded after two years' full time study of a technically based curriculum and, in 1963, the first graduates joined the workforce as veterinary technicians. This course proved extremely popular, and soon colleges and universities throughout the United States were also offering similar courses.

As might have been expected, along with support for this development came fearful opposition from many professionals:

> *"Veterinary technicians would be competing with veterinarians - leading to confusion, an erosion of standards, a decentralised, discredited profession."*

Thus, in 1965, the American Veterinary Medical Association (AVMA) ruled against formal approval for the technician programmes that were being taught around the country.

Two years later, however, the attitude had softened and the AVMA's own Council on Education was made responsible for accreditation. At the same time, working guidelines were set up for the technician's use while modifications were instituted in the Model Practice Act to recognise this new profession. In 1968, the AVMA created the title of Animal Technician, granted to graduates of approved technician programmes.

The AVMA advisory committee was replaced by the Committee on Accreditation of Training for Animal Technicians (CATAT). In 1975, the committee was renamed the Committee on Animal Technician Activities and Training, to accommodate the expanding role of accrediting the technician programmes and coordinating with the AVMA on all aspects pertaining to the technicians themselves. The following year, 16 colleges were accredited and the CATAT committee was recognised by the United States Department of Education as the governing body for veterinary technician programmes. At this moment, there is a minimum of 71 AVMA accredited schools in the USA.

By 1977, a large number of graduates began employment in the veterinary field. An examination was soon developed by the Professional Examination Service (PES) that would enable new graduates the chance to become licenced, certified, or registered. The state-governed exam and the Veterinary Technician National Examination would also enable the results to be transferred to other states via the Interstate Reporting Service of the PES.

In the following years, many state organisations were formed to help the professional development of the technician. But, in 1981, a majority of the work force wanted a nationwide support group, with a mission to improve the public's awareness of the technician's role and to promote a professional image.

A group of technicians representing 20 states and

Canadian provinces met and formed the North American Veterinary Technician Association. This organisation formed a liaison with the AVMA and has been meeting together since 1990. Its purpose is to increase communication in all aspects of the field, with an emphasis on promoting professional recognition, and stimulating growth of the veterinary technology field through education and recruitment. It also came to light that the term 'animal technician' did not completely describe the role of the technician. A campaign to change the title to 'veterinary technician' ensued with great debate for many years. Finally, in 1989, the AVMA officially accepted the term 'veterinary technician' as the title given to graduates of accredited programmes.

Experiences in the UK

It is said that marriage, changing job and moving house are in the top five most stressful events to be experienced (or avoided). In the autumn of 1991, I found myself confronted by all of these, in short order. In addition, moving house was complicated by the process of emigrating to the UK within two weeks of being married, where my British husband and I had determined to spend our first years of married life together. The problems of jobs and somewhere to live seemed relatively small matters at the time.

After a couple of months, the dust started to settle on our move to Newmarket and life in the UK began to fall into a routine. The transition from professional environment and colleagues in a critical care situation to working in the distinctly nonveterinarian environment of supermarket checkouts was never going to be easy. It also proved to be a humbling and regularly eye-opening experience.

Never could one have hoped for a better position to see and hear people's thoughts, fears and passions than being 'imprisoned' behind one of those tills. In a country renowned for its love of animals, I saw how the fortune and failure of animals grabbed the headlines. I also realised what it was that I loved doing: working with animals and people. I quickly made a promise to get back into veterinary nursing as soon as possible, and to spend more time on the relationships with the people I worked alongside on a daily basis.

Two years later I experienced the famous British love for animals when I was involved in one of the biggest animal stories of the decade.

Desert Orchid, "*the nation's favourite racehorse*", an athletic grey, had captured the imagination of the public with his success over the jumps. He was given four consecutive awards as National Hunt Horse of the Year, won three King George's and the Irish Grand National - bookies hated him, the public loved him. But, in November 1992, they all held their breath when he was referred into Rossdale & Partners for evaluation of colic. Speculation was widespread and the pressure for photographs to accompany the front page headlines was intense - even the Windsor Castle fire had been relegated to the inside pages. Security guards had to be brought in to keep paparazzi off the property - they had to resort to hanging in trees and trying to climb a 12 foot wall to snatch a glimpse. Even Dr Peter Rossdale, the founding partner, was stopped at the gates as he came into the practice - he had been away on a lecture tour in Brazil and missed much of the excitement. Shaky long distance footage (out of range of our 500 ml dose syringes) of a grey horse's head peering out of its box appeared on the TV - but it wasn't Dessie's.

We enjoyed these pictures from our flat on the practice property - for two weeks I didn't leave the grounds on account of a horse I had never heard of; a horse that received over 1000 cards from well-wishers during the two week stay, many accompanied by flowers and small gifts, some via the post, addressed simply "*Desert Orchid, Newmarket*".

This care and passion for animals is not the prerogative of the professional. In many ways, I have learned as much from the various experienced lay people I have worked with as I did at college. A text book will never prepare you for the aggression you experience when you have taken a foal away from its mare. These people taught me about their 'sixth sense', an instinct for noticing the minute changes in the condition and demeanour of the patient.

Teddy Pitt was one such person. He started working at New Bolton Center on retiring from his own business. He was in his mid-seventies when I was just becoming confident as a nurse in my early twenties. As a team, the two of us spent hours each day in New Bolton Center's Isolation Unit dodging the projectile bursts of diarrhoea that unerringly hit that newly cleaned water bucket. I loved hearing about his life on the show-jumping circuit some 50 years earlier, and about the feelings he still had for a horse that he had cared for so long ago, feelings that were still strong and fresh half a century later.

Nursing Care in the UK

Working in the United Kingdom for seven years - almost as long as the time spent as a nurse in the US - has given me a tremendous respect for the veterinary nurse training scheme in the United Kingdom. I have had the opportunity to work alongside graduates, study and be examined (my US qualifications were not recognised at that time) - and most recently have been asked to contribute to the new certificate in equine veterinary nursing.

The story of the development of nursing care in the UK begins much earlier than in the US, but despite the head start, as is often the case, it has not reached the same level of respect within the profession.

Traditionally, the nursing care of domestic animals was

Desert Orchid goes home after colic surgery; November 1992.

left to the maid of the household. This posed a problem for the large number of households which could not afford a maid and so The Dogs' Protection League ran a home for sick dogs belonging to poorer people. Located in the heart of London, it provided free services for those who could not afford to pay for veterinary treatment. Records show that a certain Miss Groves was employed as a nurse there and was highly regarded for her quality of work. She and her fellow nurses even wore uniforms.

In 1908, The Canine Nurses Institute was established. It was run by the authoress and playwright, Mrs Lenty Collins, who had a tremendous affinity for dogs. Her school required nurses to wear uniforms also, and follow a code of practice not dissimilar to today's guidelines. The only requirement of the nursing candidates was that they were strong, healthy and tidy. Their training included instruction in veterinary care of sick animals, setting and bandaging fractured limbs, giving medications and general care.

An excerpt from the *Veterinary Student* magazine in 1908, commented on these canine nurses:

> *"Fully qualified canine nurses are provided by the Institute for ordinary cases at a charge of 1/5s a week. The nurse also receives her board and lodging while in attendance on her four footed patient, and her traveling expenses."*

Two months ago I lost my horse to pulmonary disease, while today my 8-month-old pup gave up fighting his battle against autoimmune haemolytic anemia and its complications. The whole trauma placed me on the other side of the nurse/client relationship. It has strengthened my belief of how vital a good nurse is when they are not just treating their patients. Compassion and understanding for your patient's owner is not a skill learned from a textbook. It is an area where the professional can really make a difference.

In the 1930s, the Royal College of Veterinary Surgeons was asked to recognise the status of nurses by instituting some form of supervised or accredited process of examination. It wasn't until the early 1960s, however, that practice-based training schemes were implemented for Royal Auxiliary Nursing Assistants (RANAs) by the Royal College of veterinary surgeons.

Little wonder that there was opposition to this: the Veterinary Surgeons Act was passed only in 1948, preventing members of the public from practising veterinary medicine; and the threat of undermining the Veterinary Surgeons' position from this new breed of trained nurses was real to many.

On the whole, however, the relationship and understanding between nurse and surgeon was good. Wilkinson's 1938 book *Canine Nursing* noted that:

> *"... the first principles in nursing are the comfort of the patient and the hygiene and sanitation of his surroundings...the good nurse observes and reports everything, even the apparently trivial or obvious, while the good surgeon appreciates the power of observation and the careful record of the progress of the case."*

In 1984, almost a quarter of a century after formal training schemes were implemented, the name was changed to veterinary nurse and, soon after, the British Veterinary Nursing Association was born.

By 1992, a two year intensive study course saw the first qualified Diplomates in Advanced Veterinary Nursing (surgical). At this time, there are 106 veterinary nurses who hold this diploma and deserve the highest of accolades. The syllabus for the Diploma in Advanced Veterinary Nursing (medical) has recently been approved, with the first candidates seeking qualification in 2002.

The last few years have seen rather swift progress in another aspect of veterinary nursing. The year 2000 will see the first holders of the new (RCVS-approved) certificate in equine veterinary nursing (VN Cert Eq). Now nurses can develop specialised skills in areas that were previously open only to veterinary surgeons. I still remember my surprise at learning, on my arrival in the UK in 1991, that there was no formal training for nurses with an interest in large animal species such as horses, cattle and sheep.

Personal Conclusions

In writing this chapter I have found myself drawn to two personal conclusions:

Firstly, the veterinary nursing profession is a noble and satisfying one as long as caring is at its heart. In this respect it stands shoulder to shoulder with its better known supporter, the veterinary surgeon. There has been a long and hard struggle on both sides of the Atlantic for recognition from veterinary surgeons; with hindsight a good thing, as excellence and nothing less has been demanded to earn their respect. Fears of usurping the veterinary surgeon have and will prove groundless, and contradict the true understanding of the present situation. The proper focus for considering the world of veterinary care in the forthcoming millennium is found by looking within, not outside the profession; looking to carers - not careers.

Secondly, veterinary care has developed tremendously, with the role of the nurse as an important part of that development. It must, therefore, be seen as a team effort if standards are to be maintained and advances in care built on. Progress is inevitable but this should not be regarded as purely technical. The need for and obtainment of organisational and management skills must also be recognised. These are critical factors affecting the quality of care delivered, although remote from the syringe and the blade. They are skills and qualities in themselves and, where deserved, given proper position in the team alongside the veterinary surgeon.

The various people I have spoken to about the future of veterinary nursing have offered many different comments. Many come from very different backgrounds and live in different cultures to my own. All have voiced a common desire, however; although technical skills are being recognised and encouraged, it is now time for recognition of decision-making skills, of management and people skills.

The partners in a multiskilled team providing excellent veterinary care are no longer solely veterinary surgeons. For this reason I am proud to be a veterinary nurse entering the next millennium.

Acknowledgement

I am grateful to Jean Turner VN for her work done in collecting and summarising much of this information and more in her article in Vol 9, No. 4, July 1994 of the *Veterinary Nursing Journal*.

The human-horse relationship

IAN ROBINSON
Waltham Centre for Pet Nutrition
Freeby Lane
Waltham-on-the-Wolds
Leics LE14 4RT
UK

Human interactions with horses have varied throughout history depending on our needs. Initially we used horses as a source of food, but later we valued their speed and strength in pulling or carrying a load. However, it was their ability to carry a man that has perhaps had the greatest impact on our relationship. In this century, although the use of horses for farm work and transport has declined in many countries, there has been an increasing involvement in riding as a sport or a hobby. In many developed countries the leisure horse population is possibly greater now than it has ever been.

The regular and very varied occurrence of the horse in a wide range of art gives a good indication of the importance of the horse in human society[1] (Fig 1). However, despite our long association with the horse and its current popularity, there have been few studies of the human-horse relationship. This is in contrast to the increasing number of studies conducted in the last 30 years exploring human relationships with companion animals, such as cats and dogs.

People can interact with horses in many different ways, from those who have occasional rides at weekends or while on holiday, to those who keep the same animal for many years and ride it regularly. Others may own a number of animals and change them as they strive for increased performance at a sport. In contrast to the many domesticated animals that we consider as companions, horse owners do not necessarily care for the animals they own. Some people own and ride their horses but are not responsible for their day-to-day care. Others care for horses day-to-day but never own these animals, while a further group both own, ride and tend to their animals. With such a wide range of type and intensity of interaction, the range of potential relationships with man is perhaps greater than for any other species.

There is little historical evidence of individual relationships with horses but indications of strong human-horse relationships have been noted in societies such as the North American Plains Indians (Fig 2) or the Mongols. These peoples established a strong feeling of identity with their horses and perceived their own fate as being intertwined with that of the horse. Mounted societies have been reported to be bold, aggressive, proud and defiant. It is unclear, however, whether these societal traits arose because of a close association with the horse or whether the societies were already proud and defiant; and the acquisition of horses simply provided a ready means by which these traits could be expressed. Studies of the Crow Indians of Montana, a North American Plains Indian Tribe[2], have shown that their entire society and culture changed after acquisition of the horse in the early 18th century. The horse gave Plains Indians the ability to travel further and faster than they could on foot. This caused an increase in warfare as traditional tribal boundaries, which previously had been based upon 'walking' distances, were contested. On the positive side, the horse stimulated greater trade by providing increased mobility and a means of transporting goods more efficiently.

Fig 1: The human-horse relationship is regularly portrayed in art.

Fig 2: North American Plains Indians established strong feelings of identity with their horses.

[1]Readers interested in an extensive review of the history of the horse in human society should see Juliet Clutton-Brock's book *Horse Power: A History of the Horse and Donkey in Human Societies*, published in 1992 by Harvard University Press.
[2]Readers interested in more details of Crow Indian or Mounted Police relationships with their horses should read Elizabeth Lawrence's book *Hoofbeats: Studies of Human-Horse Interactions*, published in 1986 by Indiana University Press.

Fig 3: Riding is often considered to be a 'female activity'.

Riding a horse has often been considered to give the rider increased power and an increased sense of power, as well as arousing a sense of inferiority and envy in pedestrians. The horse seems to provide a symbol and an image, which makes it desirable over and above its use as transport. Elizabeth Lawrence, in her review of horses in society[3], suggests that, if transportation had been the main issue, several African populations would have ridden quaggas (*Equus quagga*) rather than the horse. Until the mid-19th century the quagga was a common equid in central and southern Africa. It was docile, easily tamed and trained for riding, adapted for the local environment and readily available, in contrast to horses, which had to be imported. Quaggas, however, were hunted to extinction by English and Boer farmers who considered them to be vermin, while horses were imported for riding, at great expense. This was largely because of the belief that only a true horse represented status and was therefore the only animal suitable for a colonist.

In Europe too, horse riding was traditionally reserved for the ruling elite. It could be argued, therefore, that any perception of an elevated status by riders or pedestrians comes from these historical links between riding and the aristocracy or landed gentry. This argument is confounded, to a certain extent, by observations in North America, where riding is often associated with the tradition of the 'Old West' and a life of freedom, as represented by the cowboy. The cowboy, however, also held himself in high regard and considered himself to be superior to the nonmounted farm workers. The reasons for any real or perceived elevation of status of people who ride or associate with horses are probably influenced by many psychological and sociological factors. Its effect, however, has been turned to advantage with the development of therapeutic riding which has often been reported to help people with a variety of physical or psychological problems.

An elevation of status from riding a horse may also help mounted police in their work. A study conducted with the American mounted police[2] suggested that police horses were considered to be a great asset since they appeared to accentuate police presence, gave an officer increased visibility and appeared to reduce street crime. Police horses have also been reported to reduce public hostility towards the police and facilitate conversation with officers. Mounted police report a close relationship with their horses, spending a large amount of time with them each day. As the general rule is one rider to each animal, this allows officers to develop a sense of trust with their horse, because they can predict how it will react to most situations. Perhaps it is the strength of the relationship, which caused officers to report that they felt resentment if they had to share their horse with another officer.

Historically, the human-horse relationship was male dominated, reflecting the horses' role as a work tool and the traditional placing of power and power sources under the control of men. The traditional role of the equine veterinarian (another historically male-dominated area), was to ensure that the animals were fit to work. More recently this relationship has changed and many more women have become involved in riding as a sport or hobby (and involved in the veterinary profession). Recent surveys in the UK indicate that around three-quarters of riders are female, although men still dominate professional riding. Riding is also no longer restricted to those with higher socio-economic status. Popular surveys have indicated that the proportion of people in the lower socioeconomic classes who ride, is greater than their proportional representation in the population. Such information suggests that riding is an activity enjoyed by people from a wide variety of backgrounds. So, although availability of land and the relatively high cost of horse care may reduce the possibility of ownership for many people, the availability of riding establishments means that riding and interactions with horses are open to a large number of people.

There are many popular stereotypes associated with riding and horse ownership. For example, in the UK, riding is often considered to be a 'female activity', or only a developmental phase that children (especially girls) pass through (Fig 3). Such stereotypes could be simple reflections of rider demographics because we know that around three-quarters of all people who ride are female and around one third of all riders are aged between 5–15 years. Unfortunately there are so few data on human-horse interactions, that it is not possible to determine whether the demographic data are a cause or a consequence of the stereotypical image of horse riders. Do some men decide not to ride because they see the hobby as a 'female' activity or do men decide not to ride for some other reason, and so the hobby is perceived as a 'female' activity? People who ride may also sometimes be ridiculed by nonriders, because of a stereotypical perception of their reasons for choosing to ride (e.g. riding is undertaken by people who enjoy domination and control or as a bizarre form of sexual pleasure). However, there are no data to support these ideas and only a few small studies on the personalities of people who associate with horses.

One study conducted in the United States suggested that horse owners had high levels of assertiveness and self-concern, but low levels of cooperativeness, novelty seeking and nurturance. More specifically, male owners were found to be aggressive, dominant, and low in expressiveness. Such observations may correspond, to the traditional western cowboy stereotype. However, it is not possible to determine whether ownership of a horse causes an exaggeration of certain existing behavioural traits or perhaps encourages

[3]Lawrence, E.A. (1988) Horses in Society. In: *Animals and People Sharing the World*, Ed: A.N. Rowan, University Press of New England, Hanover, USA. pp 95-115.

Fig 4: Symbolising the loss of a companion animal with a gravestone is not a new phenomenon

individuals to adopt and 'act out' some perceived cowboy behaviour. Alternatively, it is possible that people with certain behavioural traits are more likely to become horse owners, perhaps because it is a route by which they can exhibit their traits. As the few studies conducted to date have involved small samples in few geographical areas, it is not possible to determine whether the participants are representative of the more general horse owning or riding population.

Although popular interest in human response to the death of a companion animal is a relatively recent phenomenon, symbolising the loss of an animal through a grave or the planting of a tree is a more ancient practice (Fig 4). There has been increasing veterinary interest in owner response to pet loss following a small number of studies of how owners want their veterinarians to handle euthanasia. Studies of horse owners suggest that the severity of response to the death of a horse is linked to the duration and intensity of the relationship (or 'bond') that the owner had with the animal. 'Bonded' owners were found in all age and social groups, but not all owners were 'bonded' to their animals. Some owners may also suffer a secondary loss associated with the loss of the social lifestyle that is associated with horse ownership, whereas other people have reported suffering distress at the financial loss associated with the death of their animal. The differences between owners noted in these observations again reflect the wide variety of potential human-horse relationships. That the response to loss is influenced by the strength of the human-horse relationship is perhaps to be expected but does not further our understanding of factors which affect that strength of relationship. In some areas, an increasing number of owners are choosing euthanasia of their animals via lethal injection, which in some cases may also be preferred by the veterinarian. Such a shift may be due to a general fear of firearms and perhaps a perception of shooting as being a 'violent' form of euthanasia. If this trend continues, owners need to be prepared for increased costs associated with euthanasia and disposal.

Given that we know so little about the human-horse relationship, how can we predict if our utilisation of horses or our relationship with them will change in the next century? We can gain some insight into trends in horse ownership by reviewing 'popular' surveys (e.g. from horse magazines). Demographic data, from these surveys, suggest that, in the UK at least, the types of people involved with horses may be changing. There appears to be an increasing proportion of male riders and an increasing number of older riders. Activities other than riding, such as showing and driving, also seem to be increasing in popularity. Some people keep horses just for the pleasure of ownership and the animals are rarely if ever ridden (a use that has been unkindly termed 'pasture ornaments' by some people!). Another reported change in horse keeping is the increasing number of people who keep their horses as companions long after their working life is over. Whatever the accuracy of these demographic data, they cannot tell us about the motivation of those people who associate with horses. Some popular surveys have attempted to do this and suggest that many people prefer their horse to their partners or getting a new horse to having a baby. However, similar results can be seen in popular surveys of dog and cat owners suggesting that this may be an effect of the questionnaire style rather than a true reflection of human-human or human-animal relationships.

Many owners appear to sacrifice a great deal to pay for the upkeep of their horses. Although the costs of keeping a horse varies considerably with the type of animal kept and the management practice, the experience of many people in the equestrian world is that many owners keep their horses in the best possible conditions that their disposable income allows. For some people, increasing the amount of their 'disposable income' so that they can afford to care for a horse, means taking no holidays, never having a new car and buying few new clothes. Other people may end up in debt, either by taking out an overdraft or loan or by failing to pay their suppliers (including their veterinarian!). The process by which an individual assesses personal costs of ownership vs. perceived benefits is fascinating and needs to be studied. Recent studies have suggested that dog and cat owners receive health benefits from their pet ownership, but although riding as an activity has long been considered to be therapeutic, there is no published information on the potential benefits of horse ownership. If such an effect exists it would need to be included in any 'cost/benefit' analysis.

I firmly believe that in the next century we need research focused on characterising the human-horse relationship, including its similarities to and differences from traditional companion animal species, and the degree of individual and cultural variation. Such information would provide benefits in many areas. A good understanding of human desire or motivation to ride or own horses could assist planners of land use or recreation and leisure services to identify when and where there may be increases in demand for land or services. An understanding of the psychology of horse ownership and particularly how owners perceive 'costs' vs. 'benefits' of ownership would be useful to equine veterinarians and the general equestrian trade, which support owners with products and services. For the veterinary profession in particular, a greater understanding of the human-horse relationships could also assist in identifying and supporting owners who may need support during times of stress (e.g. euthanasia). Whilst this would benefit owners, it could also have a benefit to a veterinary practice, by assisting in the acquisition and retention of clients. Finally, in the last few years, we have seen great advances in the field of equine veterinary medicine and equine nutrition, which have benefited the horse and its welfare. Although there is still much to learn in these fields, lets hope that in the first few years of the new millennium we can not only improve horse welfare but increase our pleasure from associations with horses, by increasing our understanding of the human side of the relationship.

The changing role of the horse in society

PETER WEBBON
Brelston Court
Marstow
Ross on Wye
Herefordshire HR9 6HF
UK

The evolution of the horse can be traced over the last 55 million years, with fossils of one-toed horses found in North and Central America from 15 million years ago. Records of domesticated horses exist for the last 5000 years, but the likelihood is that equids were used as riding or draught animals long before that.

In Britain, in the 19th century, much of transport, military strength and agriculture depended on the horse. One hundred years later, this is no longer the case. We no longer rely on the horse for its work, but as their use for work has diminished, their role in leisure and sport has increased. They now enrich the leisure time of 2.4 million of the British public who enjoy the profound relationship that develops between horse and rider and, in doing so, continue to provide employment within a thriving equestrian industry.

Much can be learnt about the changing role of the horse, and public attitudes to it, over the past 100 years by looking at the involvement of horses in the Boer War. This has been recorded in detail in *A Veterinary History of the War in South Africa 1899–1902* by Major General Frederick Smith, whose outstanding contribution to equine veterinary medicine is recognised by a biennial memorial lecture at the Annual General Meeting of the British Equine Veterinary Association. The foreword to Smith's detailed chronicle of neglect was provided by Field Marshall Sir Evelyn Wood and contained the following:

> *"The interesting work of Major General Frederick Smith is a severe though just indictment of a nation which prides itself on its love of horses. It is sad to reflect that, from 1856 to 1900, practically nothing was done to provide for the care and feeding of our animals with an Army in the field and it is a disgrace to Great Britain that, during the war in South Africa, we lost, mainly by insufficient feeding and overwork, 325,000 horses, 51,000 mules and 195,00 oxen, each of the latter averaging £20 in value."*

It is hard to imagine the outcry that would attend such losses today. The horses, drawn up side by side as if on parade, would have stretched 185 miles, from London to Manchester. Few of the deaths were the consequence of enemy action. Even if the horses were used to engage the enemy they were largely ineffective due to debility and disease. The problems were compounded when horses returning from the war zone for treatment and recuperation, debilitated and frequently showing the signs of glanders and mange, were mixed with remounts so that their replacements often went to the front line in a diseased state.

Some 20 years after the war in South Africa, the British forces again employed animals in large numbers in the Great War. The implications and consequences of this are recorded by Blenkinsop and Rainby in *Great War Veterinary Services*. Even they appear to be overwhelmed by the scale of animal involvement:

> *"The number of animals employed by the British forces in the Great War is difficult to imagine. At one period during 1917 the strength of animals on all fronts totalled over 1,000,000, of which 436,000 were in France. The average daily number constantly sick on all fronts rose during that year to over 110,000."*

At the end of the conflict, in November 1918, over half a million animals, mostly horses and mules, had been killed, half of them in France.

A century on from the war in South Africa, the only contact that the British public have with military horses is during ceremonial parades or in displays. The horses receive the best of care and attention, and if one of them should be injured during the Trooping of the Colour or the Kings Troop musical ride it would make front page news and probably lead to a late night television debate on the risks to which it is reasonable to expose horses during such events.

In much the same way as horses no longer play a significant role in the army, British agriculture has ceased to rely on the horse. The beginning of the second millennium saw the origins of the huge heavy horses that were at first used to carry over a quarter of a tonne of armour-clad rider into battle. Teams of oxen were used to perform all heavy agricultural work until the 15th century when draught horses started to replace oxen, although there was a resurgence in the use of oxen in the late 18th and early 19th centuries.

The number of horses in Britain has never been known precisely. In 1812 the number of horses in British farming was recorded as 800,000 by the returns of the excise duty. Horses were not included in the agricultural census until 1870, when 966,000 were recorded. This rose to 982,00 in 1886. In 1887, the numbers were boosted to 1,034,000 by the inclusion of mares kept for breeding and the peak was reached in 1910 when 1,137,000 horses were recorded as being employed in agriculture. However, these figures were misleading, since many horses were bred for sale as urban draught animals, but were included in the annual agricultural returns to gain exemption from excise duty. Indeed, from 1840 onwards the number of horses employed in agriculture probably, in reality, fell. This was in part due to the agricultural recession in the 40 years preceding the First World War and in part to the development of lighter, more efficient ploughs which, on many soils, allowed the use of two-horse teams ploughing abreast rather than three- or four-horse teams harnessed in line.

The period between the two World Wars saw increased mechanisation both in agriculture and in towns, with a corresponding decline in the working horse population. The farm horse population fell from 962,000 in 1921 to 649,000 in 1939 while the number of tractors increased from 22,000 in 1930 to 50,000 in 1939. However, during this period, horses and tractors worked side by side and the prevailing view was that there would always remain a place for the horse in agriculture. In the 1930s, farmers were encouraged to continue heavy-horse breeding since there was a fear that the falling horse population would be insufficient to meet the likely demand.

The Second World War compounded the pressure towards mechanisation so that, in 1946, there were 200,000 tractors and by 1951 Britain, alone in the world, had more tractors on farms than horses. The trend has continued, to the extent that the Rare Breeds Survival Trust has a number of indigenous draught horse and pony breeds on its priority list. The Cleveland Bay and Suffolk are both rated as critical (200 individuals or less), Dales and Fell ponies are vulnerable (600 individuals or less) and the Clydesdale is at risk (1000 individuals or less). Nevertheless, the outlook is good, albeit for the maintenance of small populations of working horses. Ploughing with horses is now a well established, traditional, competitive activity and horses are increasingly used in logging, both in Britain and abroad, since horses can work in areas inaccessible to mechanised equipment and with less damage to the environment. In all species, the value of genetic diversity is now more generally recognised, and the future for our native draught animals is hopeful, if not assured.

The total number of horses and ponies in Britain remains unknown but is estimated to be between 500,000 and 950,000. Some of these will be used for pleasure riding only and others for hunting, but there is also a well-organised programme of high quality competitions spread over several disciplines, predominantly racing, polo, show-jumping, horse trials (eventing), dressage, endurance riding, vaulting, mounted games and carriage driving. Each of these disciplines has its own governing body. With the change of use of horses in Britain over the last century has come a heightened concern for their welfare, coupled with confusion, exacerbated by the press and television, of animal welfare and rights. Although the two terms are often mistakenly used synonymously, they are in reality very different, and any consideration of the position of horses in modern society needs to recognise this.

Horse welfare is harder to define than it is to understand, but requires that a balance is maintained between what we expect of our horses and what we give back to them. The standards of nutrition, training, preventive medicine, housing and veterinary care for racehorses and top sports horses in Britain are extremely high and arguably better than those enjoyed by other species including farm and pet animals. The risks of sport and competition are also high, for both the horses and their riders, but risk, in itself, does not compromise welfare. After all, for most farm animals the risk of a premature death is very high, but their welfare is not related to their eventual fate, but to the quality of their lives leading up to their slaughter. It is, therefore, a social decision whether we eat meat, or ride horses, and we should aim for the highest standards of welfare within a structure of animal use which is socially acceptable.

Those who argue in favour of immutable rights for animals, on the other hand, deny us the opportunity to make social judgements about animal use, believing that any use of animals for pleasure, fibre or food is fundamentally wrong. The increasing popularity of horse sports in Britain suggests that this view finds little public support, but the public does need regular reassurance that riding horses are properly cared for, and this is particularly true for high profile sports which are regularly televised.

Of all uses of the horse during the last century, racing, at least superficially, has changed the least and no better record of the development of racing in Britain can be found than that in *Running Racing: The Jockey Club Years* by John Tyrrel. A comparison between the first Derby and the last Derby of the second millennium reveals the way in which racing appears to adhere to its traditional past. In 1780, the Derby was run for the first time over one and a half miles at Epsom. The 1999 Derby winner, Oath, competed over one and a half miles, at Epsom, over a course unchanged since 1872 and, still, little different from the course over which Diomed was the first winner of the race. Even the morning suits and silk hats worn by the winning connections are not significantly different from those of 100 years ago.

Racing started in Britain as an amusement for the occupying Roman garrisons and still continues on two courses, Chester and York, originally frequented by the Romans. Prior to 1605 Newmarket was nothing but a small market town. James I transformed it into a fashionable centre by transferring his court there so that he could hawk and hunt. Others saw its additional sporting potential and the first recorded match race took place in 1622. The origins of The Jockey Club itself are vague. It had no written constitution and, indeed, no early list of members. Its original London base was at Messrs Weatherbys while a coffee room was built in Newmarket in 1752. The restored coffee room can be found in the Jockey Club Rooms on the High Street in Newmarket. The Racing Calendar was first published in 1727, under a different title and carrying, in addition to the

A Kidney Dropper - When accompanying a Gig on horseback never ride close behind the vehicle. *From Edward Mayhew, reprinted with kind permission of the Royal College of Veterinary Surgeons Library.*

The Honest Manner of exhibiting the Horse's Teeth. *From Edward Mayhew, reprinted with kind permission of the Royal College of Veterinary Surgeons Library.*

racing fixtures, a record of all important cock fights. Racing increased in popularity and the daily papers, as today, started to carry racing reports. This was to the dislike of Parliament which, in 1740, passed an Act placing restrictions on racing and stipulating that the weights to be carried be related to age: for five-year-olds 10 stone, 11 stone for six-year-olds and 12 stone for seven-year-olds and older.

The regulation of racing is now in the hands of The Jockey Club. It is unclear how this originated, with the first reference to The Jockey Club appearing in the conditions of a race in 1752. Followers of modern racing may be surprised to learn that before 1727 the minimum age for horses to race was five, reduced to four in 1727 and three in 1756. In 1770, all races were followed by the examination of the participants to determine their ages and their certified ages were then posted in the Newmarket coffee house during the evening of the race meeting. Shortly afterwards two-year-olds (taking their age from 1 May) made their racing debut and, again, modern racegoers may be surprised to learn that they raced at distances of up to four miles against older horses, receiving as much as 58 pounds, with two-year-olds carrying four stone 8 pounds. The first race for yearlings took place in 1771 over a little more than two and a half furlongs. Never popular, it continued until 1859.

While racing continues in many respects much as it did 200 years ago, and the Chief Executive of The Jockey Club still enjoys the title of Keeper of the Match Book, much, in reality, has changed. The Jockey Club has as its mission statement: "*To set and maintain standards.*" These are standards of safety for horse and rider and standards of integrity so that punters can place their bets with confidence. To achieve these high standards, The Jockey Club employs a large team of officials, augmented by part time assistants in some areas. Few people not closely involved in racing realise the massive logistical exercise that is required to provide the technical and regulatory services on every one of about 1200 racing days at racecourses as distant as Perth and Newton Abbot, Yarmouth and Chepstow. In addition to the local stewards, doctors, veterinary surgeons and other staff, each race meeting generally requires two starters, a clerk of the scales, a judge, two stewards' secretaries, a veterinary officer, two veterinary technicians, a photo finish team, television and video recording of all races and a stalls team and starting stalls for Flat race meetings. At the end of each racing day, this entire entourage packs up its equipment and moves on to the next venue.

Central to the integrity of British racing is its policy on doping control. Racing in Europe and much of the rest of the world aims to be drug free and sets standards of doping control higher than any other sport. In Britain, 7000 horses (10% of all runners) are tested annually after racing and others are tested during their training. The small number of positive tests bears witness to the effectiveness of the testing programme, but all concerned in horse sports need to be constantly vigilant to ensure that the abuse of drugs, allegedly commonplace in human sport, is kept out of equestrianism.

Racing, and equestrian sport in general, although traditional in many respects, have embraced many of the changes seen in other activities. These are manifested as increasing concern for the safety of the participants, an unwillingness to acknowledge that accidents (unfortunately) can happen with nobody at fault and the inevitable influence of the computer and all that goes with it. So, at Epsom in 1999, the jockeys all wore approved patterns of hats and body protectors, the horses were closely monitored and the racecourse, in common with all others, had to employ a sports turf consultant to try to ensure the very best ground conditions. The judge had a sophisticated computerised system to help his adjudication and the bookmakers had been recently told that they would have to keep computer records of all their on-course bets. Wooden and concrete running rails had been replaced by plastic and the material from which the new rails are constructed is regularly tested for its strength and brittleness. Legislation requires that the public and horses are effectively separated. The jockeys could only carry whips of an approved pattern and their use was very closely scrutinised and controlled by video recording from four different camera angles.

What has the next century in store for horses and equestrianism? In 2100, will our only contact with horses be via a virtual reality riding simulator allowing us safely to negotiate Becher's Brook, a puissance wall and the Badminton water complex without moving from our in-house offices, and at no greater risk than of repetitive brain injury from manipulating our motorised mice by tiny brain-generated voltages? Or will the power and athleticism of one of the most graceful and exciting animals in creation prove too strong an appeal to be foregone? Will there ever be a substitute for the rain lashing in your face on a November morning or the priceless exhilaration of a steeplechase fence taken at speed? Even genetically modified pigs cannot fly, yet.

With horse in mind

ROGER SHORT
Department of Perinatal Medicine
Royal Women's Hospital
University of Melbourne
Victoria 3035
Australia

What promises does the new millennium hold for a better understanding of the horse? What is it that we still need to know about this magnificent animal? At the top of my list would be an understanding of the horse's mind. There seems to be general agreement in scientific circles that the coming century will be the 'Century of the Mind'.

The current euphoria over molecular biology will have run its course, and the challenge will be to assemble the hundreds of thousands of new pieces in life's jigsaw that it has generated, to give us a better understanding of the whole animal. For the first time, we will have at our disposal all the molecular, chemical, physiological and anatomical evidence that will eventually enable us to understand how the mind works. This may be biology's last frontier. I would like to think that the Thoroughbred racehorse may have an important, if unexpected, role to play in this new endeavour.

Walking through Newmarket one day and gazing with undiminished awe at the statue of Hyperion, it occurred to me that, while we know so much about his form and function, his pedigree and his progeny, we know nothing of the workings of his mind. History does not relate what his trainers made of his psychology, what his jockeys thought of his temperament. Was he born or made a champion?

The first person to provide a vital clue as to how to study the human mind objectively was Sir Francis Galton, Charles Darwin's cousin. In 1875, he showed how a study of human indentical twins made it possible to distinguish between the influences of nature and nurture (his wording), or genotype and environment, as we would say today. Galton's studies convinced him that, as far as behaviour was concerned, nature was far stronger than nurture.

This radical view initiated a furious debate that is still raging today, about where to give the credit for our brilliance, or lay the blame for our failure. Lawrence Wright has given a fascinating account of the history of human twins research since Galton's day, in his book *Twins*. First came the development of eugenics, the idea of selective breeding from the favoured few. This degenerated into the racist views of the Nazis, and led to the horrific experiments of Dr Josef Mengele on Jewish twins in Nazi concentration camps during the Second World War. Twin research fell into disrepute for a while, but it was revived as an academically respectable discipline by the likes of Dr Bouchard in Minnesota, who carried out detailed studies of a large number of pairs of human identical twins, some of whom had been raised in widely different social and cultural environments since birth, and were unaware of the existence of their co-twin. There were often chilling similarities in their behaviour, and the overall conclusion was that around 50% of our behaviour seems to be genetically predetermined. Educational psychologists like Jensen even went so far as to suggest that education might be a waste of time for those with a low IQ.

So how could the horse contribute to the debate about the control of behaviour? I can think of no domesticated animal to rival the Thoroughbred horse as far as the environmental control of behaviour is concerned. No animal is in such close daily contact with skilled and dedicated individuals whose sole objective over the centuries has been to produce an animal with the physical and mental ability to win races. Breeders, trainers, jockeys and owners have devoted their lives and, sometimes, enormous fortunes, to produce a winner. Isn't it about time that we were able to give them some scientific advice about how to apportion their efforts as between improvements in nature and nurture?

Suddenly, the answer to this age-old question is within reach, and it could transform the way in which we breed, train and race horses in the future. The scientific breakthrough has come by accident and has yet to be exploited. Thanks to all the basic research on equine reproduction carried out in Newmarket by Professor Twink Allen and his colleagues, we can now produce identical twins in horses by embryo splitting. The resultant clones, for that is what they are, are genetically identical to one another in every way, but can be raised in different environments from the moment of their formation by transfer to the uteri of different foster mothers, and by rearing and training them according to different regimes. Given the common genetic background, we should begin to get some invaluable clues about the influence of the intrauterine and postnatal environments on the wellbeing and performance of the Thoroughbred. We could instantly gain a wealth of new information about which behavioural characteristics are environmentally determined. For starters, how would a castrated stallion or mare compare with its intact co-twin? In what way do drugs modify performance? Which feeding, rearing and training regimes give one twin the edge over the other? If Sir Francis Galton, that eccentric genius, were alive how he would revel in the endless possibilities!

The ultimate test would come in the most fascinating two-horse race ever run. If it resulted in a dead heat, the breeders would be celebrating and the trainers would have to think again. If one twin were a clear winner, the hunt would be on for the environmental factors that has led it to its success. Soon, we would be able to rank trainers and jockeys by objective criteria.

My hope for the millennium would therefore be to see the establishment somewhere in the world (and preferably Newmarket) of an Institute for the Study of Equine Twins. And I hope that I might live long enough to see the running of the first Galton Stakes at Newmarket; but I am neither brave nor wise enough to place any bets.

Past, Present and Future

A veterinary surgeon looks back

JOHN HICKMAN
The White Lodge
57 High Street
Haslingfield
Cambs CB3 7JP
UK

The following is an abridged version of an account written by Colonel John Hickman, the first President of BEVA, which is to appear in full for BEVA Members in the year 2000. Here extracts are presented for the benefit of readers of this volume (Editors' note).

Veterinary School

When I entered the Royal Veterinary College, London in 1931 the buildings were in a very dilapidated state and the facilities left much to be desired. Sir Frederick Hobday was the principal and was actively engaged in raising money for a complete rebuild of the college.

In spite of this the staff continued to give lectures and demonstrations. The supply of cases for teaching purposes was obtained through the Outpatient's Clinic and the Subscribers Department. Professor J.G.Wright was in charge of the Outpatients' Clinic and Professors Hobday, Wooldridge and McCunn were responsible for the Subscribers Department.The subscribers' paid an annual fee, which gave them the privilege of having their animals seen by one or other of these three Professors.

After qualifying as a veterinary surgeon I was appointed house surgeon to the Subscribers' Department but in addition I had to do night and weekend duties at the free clinic. As Sir Frederick Hobday was almost permanently engaged in raising money, the majority of his cases were seen by Professor J. McCunn, the Professor of Anatomy and a medical doctor. At the end of World War I he had worked with his brother in a heavy horse practice in the East End of London. His brother let him off some of the daytime work provided he took all the night calls. This arrangement enabled him to attend the London Hospital during the day and qualify as a doctor. After qualifying as a doctor he stayed on at the London Hospital and worked in the bacteriological department.

It was only on rare occasions that Professor Hobday demonstrated to the students the operation named after him for the treatment of roaring in horses. He preferred to perform the operation at the premises of the veterinary surgeon referring the case and made him responsible for casting the horse with hobbles, administering the chloroform anaesthetic and positioning the horse for surgery. He never used a burr to evert the ventricles, always his finger and demonstrated to those present that they had been totally removed by pulling them over the tip of his finger. Before he left the premises he always explained to the groom that the horse might develop a choke and explained the symptoms to him. He then showed him a laryngeal tube and how to insert it and then made the groom insert it for practice. Finally he would point out to the groom that the stamped label attached to the tube was addressed to him and that should be posted if not required after ten days.

The Royal Army Veterinary Corps

During my year's appointment as assistant to the Subscribers' Department I had to decide what career I would pursue as a veterinary surgeon. I had made up my mind to join the Colonial Veterinary Service when an advert appeared in the *Veterinary Record* for applications to join the Royal Army Veterinary Corps (RAVC). As I had been in the Officers' Training Corps at school and also had obtained the Army Certificate A, I thought I would apply. In reply I was instructed to report to New Scotland Yard for a medical examination and then to the office of the Director General of the RAVC at the War Office in Whitehall for interview.

After a probationary period I was attached to the Station Veterinary Hospital, Woolwich, commanded by Major D.A. Gilmore. I lived in the RASC Mess and hunted with the Woolwich Drag which was organised by the Gunners. We all hacked to and from the meets, which meant a long day but was well worth it.

After we had been accepted as officers of the Royal Army Veterinary Corps we were presented by the Colonel Commandant of the Royal Army Veterinary Corps, Major General W.S. Anthony, CB, CMG to HRH King George VI at St. James's Palace.

I was next posted to India and returned to Aldershot to be kitted out. As it was out of the trooping season I had a normal passage booked for me and I sailed out of Liverpool on 26 June 1937 on the Anchor Line SS Britannia and arrived in Bombay on 20 July 1937.

India

I had a very enjoyable and informative voyage to Bombay via the Suez Canal. Many of the passengers were Indian civil servants, service personnel, planters, railway officials, etc., returning from leave and they gave me very helpful advice on life in India. On berthing in Bombay I reported to the Army Movement Control Unit and was informed that I had been posted to the Military Veterinary Hospital, Secunderabad, Decan, which is located in the state of the Nizam of Hyderabad.

Secunderabad

When waiting in the queue I was handed a letter by an

Indian servant, Major G.K. Shaw's batman, whom he had sent to meet me off the boat, to collect my luggage and accompany me on the train to Secunderbad. Major Shaw greeted me on arrival and took me to meet his wife and have breakfast. Afterwards we went to the veterinary hospital to meet the Indian staff and Lieutenant Miza of the Indian Army Veterinary Corps who had qualified as a veterinary surgeon at the Royal Dick School of Veterinary Studies, Edinburgh.

During my service in Secunderabad I gained experience of some tropical diseases. Rabies, being endemic, was the most important from a personal point of view.

Rabies

The first case of rabies that I encountered was a terrier belonging to an officer on the staff. He asked me if I would have a look at the family pet terrier as it did not seem to be its normal active self. On my way back to my quarters I called at his bungalow and as I entered the dog ran out from under a coat and hat stand and bit at my leg in passing. Fortunately I was wearing trousers and his bite did not break the skin of my leg.

This was obviously a suspect rabies case and I followed the normal procedure for such cases.

The dog was caught, two leads were fitted to his collar, each held by an individual to prevent the dog from biting anyone. It was then taken to the veterinary hospital and put in a special isolation kennel which was kept for suspected rabies cases. The dog died within 48 hours.

How to remove a portion of the brain, with no sophisticated laboratory facilities or rubber gloves, presented a problem. The following measures were adopted.

Wearing leather gloves (rubber gloves were yet to be standard issue), I placed the dog's head over a drain and had disinfectant poured over. Next the dog was then dropped into a sack and its head manoeuvred to one corner and fixed there with a strong string noose. With a farriers hammer the dog's head was hit through the sack until the skull was well and truly smashed. The carcass was then tipped out over a drain and again soaked with disinfectant. Then with forceps and scalpel, the overlying skin and fractured skull bones were removed to expose the brain. About half of it was removed and placed in a 2 lb jam jar (screw cap) with cotton wool at the bottom and top. It was then filled with formalin. I then secured the jam jar to my bicycle and took it to the pathologist at the local British Military Hospital. He found Negri bodies which are diagnostic of rabies and in consequence all in contact were subjected to a routine course of antirabies injections.

Later, while stationed in Lyallpur, I encountered two cases of rabies and had to deal with two outbreaks of glanders.

Rabies 1

Early one morning I received a message from Colonel Bruce to say that when rounding up some mares, one had slipped up and fallen against a manger in the paddock, hitting her head and getting concussion. When I arrived to examine her she was standing quietly by a tree. A little blood could be seen trickling from her mouth and as I approached she took a step towards the tree, seized a lower branch with her teeth, hung back and shook it like a dog shaking a rat. She was driven into a loosebox and was dead within three hours.

Rabies 2

On returning home from an inspection tour I asked to see the Senior Veterinary Assistant Surgeon only to be informed that he had gone to see a sick donkey stallion in stables about five miles distant. I decided to make a visit and when I arrived the donkey was standing in a pen, held by a syce, being examined by the Veterinary Assistant Surgeon. He immediately informed me not to worry as it was a case of colic. With that the stallion seized the arm of the syce and would not let go. It was necessary to force the donkey's mouth open with an iron bar before the man's arm could be freed. The stallion was then driven into a loosebox and as the wooden bar was put in place to keep him in, he seized it with his teeth.

Meanwhile the syce who had been bitten thought he had developed rabies and screamed for water, which the other syces would not give him. As they thought he had rabies they tied his hands behind his back with a length of rope and the end of the rope to a tree. I told them to let him have water which was held out to him in a bucket and into which he plunged his head and drank freely. He gradually settled down and I took him to the local hospital, restrained by two hefty syces in the back seat of my small Hillman Minx. After an injection of morphine, and the doctor explaining to him that he had not got rabies and that he would have an injection daily to prevent him developing rabies, peace reigned and all was well.

Glanders

The Army Veterinary Service in India was responsible for the control of glanders amongst the civilian-owned horse population.

I was instructed to examine a pony suspected of having glanders, belonging to a potter in a village some 50 miles from Lyallpur. Together with my senior veterinary assistant surgeon we set off and on arrival at the village were immediately shown a very emaciated pony. On examining the nasal septum for the classical ulcerations of glanders cases I discovered that ulceration was so extensive and had coalesced to such an extent that the septum was perforated by a large hole. Looking through the hole I could see the blue sky of the Punjab.

There was no doubt about the diagnosis of glanders and immediate action was taken to deal with the outbreak. A standstill order was issued for all horses and a clinical examination of all in contacts was carried out. No other clinical cases were discovered and so all in contacts had to be Mallein tested. The method employed was the intradermo-palpebral test (IDP) which results in positive cases developing a severe and painful swelling of the lower eyelid. Any doubtful reactor was immediately tested by the subcutaneous method which in positive cases resulted not only in a large and painful swelling but also a rise in body temperature up to 104°F.

The veterinary assistant surgeon informed me that doubtful reactors following the IDP test was probably due to the owners applying icepacks to the site of injection. I thought I could overcome this by immediately employing the subcutaneous test which, if positive, would see the swelling accompanied by a rise in temperature. On taking the temperature of the first doubtful reactor I discovered an ice cube in the rectum. To deal with this problem I let it be known that in future all doubtful reactors to the test would be considered positive, destroyed and the owner would receive immediate compensation. This was accepted with smiles all around and the outbreak was rapidly brought to a close by sending a telegram to the Commander In Chief in India to this effect.

In April 1944, I took command of No. 6 Veterinary and Remount Conducting Section, which was a unit of the 52nd Lowland Division located at Ballater which had two troops of pack ponies attached. Soon after I took over this unit I received instructions that all personnel in the unit had to be medical category A1, and if they were not, they were to be returned to the Doncaster Veterinary Hospital and replaced. On checking the identity cards of the unit personnel I found I required eight replacements, amongst which was one named Merk, nationality German. Apparently he was working with a circus in England, specialising in the training of circus horses, when war was declared.

It so happened that on my way to the office that morning I had seen a notice referring to a 'Salute the Soldier Event' for raising money. I asked if the unit was involved and was informed we were too small a unit to participate. I interviewed Merk and he told me he could train a pony to perform circus tricks within three weeks. We selected a grey pony which, with his expertise and much of the unit's sweet ration, was performing many circus tricks proficiently within three weeks. In consequence the veterinary unit was able to make a significant input and hold their own with much larger units in numerous 'Salute the Soldier' events.

The Division had trained for mountain warfare and it was presumed its role was a landing in Norway on D-day. This was not to be and almost overnight following D-day its role was changed to that of an airborne Division, signalling the end of any veterinary and remount input.

France and Germany

Within a few days I was posted as DADVS & RS of the Veterinary & Remount Branch of 21st Army Group. I joined the ADV & RS, Lt Colonel R.H. Stalker in a bivouac camp on the Wentworth Golf Course. The next day the V & R Branch of 21st Army Group comprising the ADV & RS, DADV & RS together with a staff car, driver and batman embarked with the Rear HQ at Portsmouth, crossed over to France in a tank landing craft and on landing bivouacked in a field near Bayeux. There were no Veterinary & Remount units in the order of battle or veterinary staff with Civil Affairs. In consequence we were called upon for technical advice concerning civilian-owned stock and also assumed veterinary responsibility for all dogs on the strength of units. These dogs had been inoculated against rabies and were employed by the Military Police and the Royal Engineers for mine detection.

It was expected that a large number of horses would be captured and in consequence a Veterinary & Remount Conducting Unit was requested which arrived early in September, its primary role being to collect and treat battle casualties. It was located at Le Bec Helouin as some 2000 horses had been captured south of the Seine. They were distributed to local farmers through the French authorities. Feeding captured horses presented no great difficulty as grazing was abundant at the time of the year.

To ease the strain on mechanical transport in the build up of the advance bases in Belgium, it was decided to form horse transport units for draught work on the lines of communication. During the Battle of Falaise a heavy mortar barrage fell on a large Thoroughbred stud, killing and wounding many mares and youngstock. I remained at the stud for four days treating a great variety of wounds and removing pieces of shrapnel. Fortunately an RAMC field unit was nearby and they kindly provided me with a supply of drainage tubing and sulphanilamine powder which greatly enhanced my surgical procedures.

The V & R Branch now moved its HQ from Bayeux to Brussels and was billeted in the Avenue Louise. During the winter months horse transport did invaluable work on the lines of communication but especially in the docks on short haulage from the quays to base supply depots. These units were manned with French and Belgium labour, supervised by RAVC personnel, the largest being located in the Antwerp docks. To meet the Antwerp docks requirement, some 200 horses were marched by road from Rouen, a distance of 220 miles, in 12 days by Captain Pearson, RAVC. Antwerp docks received more than its share of V1 and V2 rockets, one of which killed some 30 horses and two RAVC personnel. To meet this deficiency of horses, I was able with the assistance of the Belgium authorities to requisition 40 heavy draft horses, standing at the crossroads near the monument to the Battle of Waterloo.

One day a French farmer arrived at our headquarters in Brussels having travelled from Bayeux, saying the Germans had stolen his horse, that we had got it in our army and he wanted it returned. When asked how it could be identified he said it was grey. When told we had a number of grey horses he replied he could identify it and asked for a piece of paper and pencil. On it he drew a sign which he said was tattooed on the inside of its left ear. I told him to return home and if his horse was found he would be informed. A mare answering his description and with a similar tattoo was located in the dock stables in Antwerp. He was informed and in due course arrived complete with a webbing halter. I took him into the first stable block and he said she was not there. When we entered the second stable block, he looked down the line of horses, intimated that he had seen her and called out. The mare turned her head around and whinnied to him. I did not consider any paperwork was necessary. The last I saw of him was bareback on his mare, with a rope halter, trotting out of Antwerp docks on a 400 mile homeward journey. It made my day.

Contagious disease amongst captured horses at this time was to be expected. Sarcoptic mange was the most difficult to control owing to the shortage of clipping machines, but in no way was the working efficiency of the horse transport units seriously affected. In due course the War Dogs Training School was brought out from the UK and located near Brussels and V&R were made responsible for obtaining suitable dogs for training. These were obtained by requisitioning in Belgium, France and Germany.

After VE Day, the V&R staff moved into Germany and

were located in the German barracks at Herford. The immediate task was to dispose of the Wehrmacht horses and locate pedigree stallions and mares for return to their countries of origin.

Return to Civilian Life

On a visit by Brigadier Kelly, Director Army Veterinary Services, to the control commission for Germany I intimated to him that I was considering asking for permission to retire. He asked why I should want to do that, and I replied that my veterinary interest was in the horse and the total number of horses in the British Army was now less than I'd had to look after as a Lieutenant. He told me that if I could obtain a suitable appointment he would let me go. In due course I was appointed lecturer in surgery on the staff of the Royal Veterinary College, London, which was headed by Professor Formston and located at Goring-on-Thames where they had been evacuated during the war.

The accommodation for large animals was little more than three or four dilapidated wooden sheds. Dogs fared a little better. Farm animals for teaching purposes were provided by the surgical staff undertaking the routine veterinary work on a number of local farms. All instruments, drapes, swabs, etc., had to be sterilised by boiling in a fish kettle steriliser.

I soon came to the conclusion that there was not only an urgent need to raise the standards for the practice of routine surgery in the treatment and relief of disease and accidents but also that surgery had an important application to research. To this end I was fortunate in receiving a grant from the Animal Health Trust which enabled me to visit the Surgical Research Unit of the Mayo Foundation, University of Minnesota, USA for three months.

Not only did I see the application of surgical procedures to a great variety of disease investigations but also the information and results obtained. The standard of surgery practised was of the highest order and on being shown around the unit on my arrival I was more than impressed to see a technician canulating the thoracic duct of rats under ether anaesthetic.

Cambridge

At this time a school of veterinary medicine was being established by the University of Cambridge and I was invited to join the staff as Reader in Animal Surgery. Students were due to arrive but the buildings were not completed. However, excellent looseboxes for horses and farms animals, and dog kennels complete with outside runs, were ready for occupation. An excellent small animal surgical unit, staffed by a medically qualified theatre sister with two assistants were ready to receive patients and, from the outset, standards of excellence were established for operating theatre routines.

Requests for consultations gradually trickled in and it soon became obvious that the veterinary surgeons requesting the consultations did so because they did not have up-to-date radiological facilities or clinical pathology back-up for making or confirming a diagnosis. To this end it was decided that all members of the surgical staff must be general surgeons to meet the caseload but each member should be a specialist, not necessarily on an animal species but rather of a discipline.

As a result, Leslie Hall became responsible for all anaesthetics and pre- and postoperative care, Robert Walker abdominal and thoracic surgery, Mike Littlewort cardiology, Keith Barnett ophthalmology, and myself orthopaedics. In due time a radiology unit was established with a member of the professional staff in charge, alongside an assistant with a radiographer's qualifications.

An interesting variety of cases were always seen when Chipperfield's Circus came to Cambridge. These included the seal that had a bone in its flipper broken due to a flower pot tipping over onto it and I will always remember Mr Chipperfield walking down the corridor with a chimpanzee holding his hand on its way to have a tooth extracted. A sick lion was examined by Leslie Hall and Robert Walker in its cage at the circus site. They diagnosed an intestinal obstruction and decided a laparotomy was advisable. Hall anaesthetised the lion, which was then put in a small trailer and with him sitting beside it they were driven through the streets of Cambridge, to the surprise of passers-by. An obstruction was found and a section of the small intestine resected and anastomosed and the muscles and skin sutured. Just as he was putting in the last skin suture the lion stopped breathing. Routine resuscitation was applied but to no effect. With no further ado, Walker performed a thoracotomy, massaged the lion's heart and got it going. The lion made an uneventful recovery, was returned to the circus to perform again and eventually to the wild.

The official opening of the John Hickman Surgical Suite on 23 July 1998. Left to right: Professor Sir David Williams (Vice Chancellor Emeritus), Professor Leo Jeffcott (Dean of the Veterinary School) and Colonel John Hickman.

Colonel John Hickman greeting the Chancellor of the University, HRH The Duke of Edinburgh, on his visit to the Surgical Suite on 28 June 1999.

This millennium in retrospect

SHERWIN HALL
14 Huntingdon Road
Cambs CB3 0HH
UK

Introduction

The horse has always been of great utility to man and especially so in times of war. Throughout this millennium, from the first of the crusades through the period of the Hundred Years War and right up to the present century, the horse has been a military animal needing veterinary attention to stem the appalling losses from injury and disease. In the later mediaeval period the horse was also becoming more important for civilian purposes.

Notwithstanding the catastrophic losses due the Black Death, the long-term trend was an increase in the human population. Towns were getting bigger and a merchant class was emerging. The great explorations were opening up new lands and where the explorers went the horses followed. When Columbus arrived on the American continent, for instance, there were no indigenous horses and after his second voyage all consignments to the New World had to include breeding stock from Spain.

In Europe, mining, manufacturing and trading were expanding and requiring more power. Water wheels and windmills were in widespread use but they had the serious limitation that the power generated had to be used on the spot. For locomotion the horse was supreme. It was used as a fast conveyor of messages, as a pack animal and for draught power. The introduction of the rigid, padded horse collar, improved shafts and traces resulted in an increase in tractive effort, possibly by a factor of five. In the *Luttrell Psalter*, dated about 1338, there is an illustration of a three-horse team using a recognisably modern harness to draw a two-wheeled cart.

The rough road surfaces and the lack of bridges caused difficulties for the carters but under favourable conditions they could probably cover 36 miles in a day and compete with water transport. The poor condition of the roads persisted for centuries and it was not until the early years of the 19th century when Telford and McAdam achieved fame as road builders and brought big improvements in the efficiency of horse haulage. By 1832, the smooth, metalled roads, enabled stagecoaches to average 10 miles an hour with loads up to three times as heavy as was previously possible. It was a short, hard life for the horses. As might be expected, lameness, colic and injuries were an everyday problem and the postmasters and carriers regularly worked glandered horses, spreading the disease from town to town. The introduction of steam-powered locomotion on the railways made the stagecoach obsolete but the draught horse became even more important for short distance work and their numbers increased throughout the 19th century. Nowadays it is difficult to imagine roads jammed with horse-drawn traffic, buses, cabs, carts, vans, drays, private carriages, hearses and fire engines. Victorian Britain truly was the horse-drawn society. It was the development of the internal combustion engine in the 20th century that eventually caused the demise of the horse as an economic force.

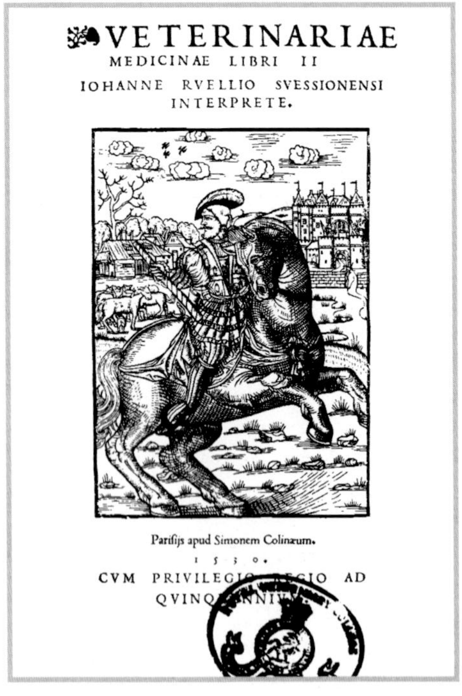

VETERINARIAE
MEDICINAE LIBRI II
IOHANNE RVELLIO SVESSIONENSI
INTERPRETE.

Parisijs apud Simonem Colinæum.
1530.
CVM PRIVILEGIO REGIO AD
QVINQ[illegible]ANNI[illegible]

Fig 1: The title page from the Hippiatrika, a compilation of the Byzantine veterinary texts by Ruellius, published in Paris in 1530. Reprinted with permission of the RVC.

Fig 2: The title page from The Proprytees and Medicynes of Hors, *the first printed book on horse medicine in English. Reprinted with permission of the RVC.*

Fig 3: The Muscle Man from Vesalius' De Humani Corporis Fabrica *published in Basle in 1543. Reprinted with permission of the Wellcome Trust Medical Photographic Library.*

Fig 5: The frontispiece to Snape's Anatomy of an Horse *1683. Reprinted with permission of the RVC.*

Fig 4: The Muscle Horse from Ruini's Anatomia del Cavallo Infermita et Suoi Rimedii *published in Venice in 1599. Reprinted with permission of the RVC.*

Development of the Veterinary Art

For centuries the diseases and treatment of horses had been essentially an oral tradition but the development of the printing press using movable type had stimulated the production of printed books and by 1500 there were nearly 40,000 recorded editions produced in Europe. The date of the first printed veterinary book is uncertain but there is evidence that *The Book of Marescalcia* was published in Rome in 1486. The author was Laurence Rusius, Marshal of the city, who had practised there in the first half of the 14th century. The mediaeval word 'Marshal' was derived from the Old French, '*mareschal*', denoting a person who tends horses, especially a person who practised marescalcia, marshalry or what came to be known as farriery. There was a similar use of the word in England: in 1356 the Company of Marshalls was founded in the City of London but, in the course of time, they became the Worshipful Company of Farriers and the term 'marshal' came to mean a high ranking officer. Although the word 'veterinarian' was first used in English in 1646 the word 'veterinary' did not appear until 1790 when the London Veterinary College was founded but thereafter it was widely used. The term 'veterinary surgeon' can be dated precisely to 1796 when it was stipulated by the Board of General Officers that every cavalry regiment should have one.

The first printed books were not original works but were compilations derived from manuscripts, many of which had been copied and recopied from classical times. One such book is nowadays known as the *Vegetius*, published in Basle in 1528 with the title *Artis Veterinariae, sive Mulomedicinae*. It represents the state of the veterinary art in the Western Roman Empire in the 4th or 5th century. Another work, known as the *Hippiatrika*, (Fig 1), translated from the original Greek by Ruellius and printed in Paris in 1530, was based on manuscripts derived from the Eastern Empire. The first printed book in English on horse diseases was the *Proprytees & Medicynes of Hors*. It came from the press of Wynkyn de Worde in about 1497. A copy of the first edition was sold at auction in London in July 1998 for £194,000; see Figure 2.

Knowledge of the classical manuscripts was largely due to the Arabs. The spread of Islam had led to a revival of interest in Greek science and for four centuries Arabic was the language of scholarship. To this day such words as 'alcohol', 'zenith', 'algebra' and 'almanac' display their Arab roots. 'Drug' is also derived from the Arabic and the enlargement of the materia medica was one of the Arabs more original syntheses. They had a strong, innate attachment to their horses which they did not separate from mankind in a religious or philosophical sense. The prominence of the horse and the state of the veterinary art in the Arab world is reflected in a 13th century treatise, *The Naceri*, by Abu Bekr, veterinarian to the Sultan of Egypt.

An engaging reference to horse diseases in the popular

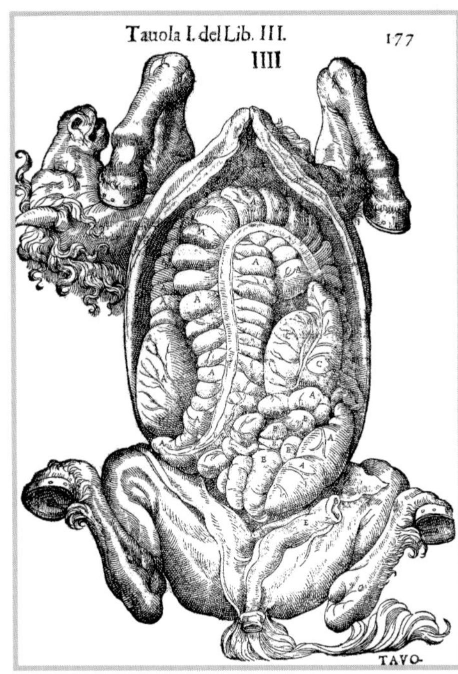

Fig 6: Another of the many fine plates from Ruini, 1598.

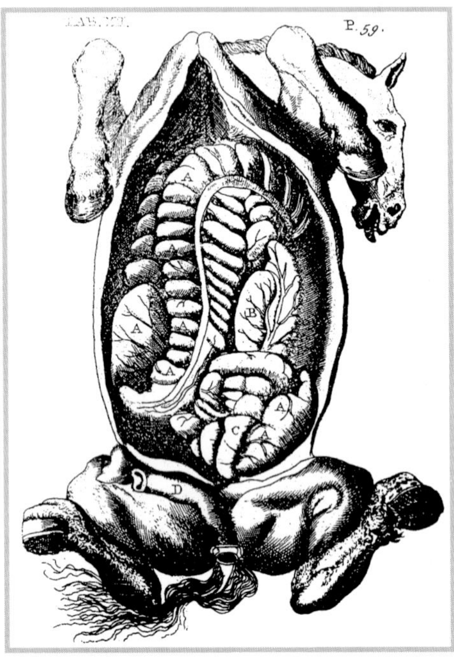

Fig 7: A plate from Gibson's New Treatise, *1751. See how closely it resembles Fig 6, printed 150 years earlier.*

literature of the midmillennium can be found in *The Taming of the Shrew*. There is a scene where Petruchio and Kate are about to get married. The guests are assembled but there are no signs of the bridegroom. Kate's father is beginning to get anxious when Biondello explains that Petruchio's delay is due to:

> *"... his horse hipped with an old mothy saddle, and stirrups of no kindred; besides possessed of the glanders and like to mose in the chine; troubled with the lampass, infected with the fashions, full of windgalls, sped with spavins, rayed with the yellows, past cure of the fives, stark spoiled with the staggers, begnawn with the bots, swayed in the back and shoulder shotten."*

Shakespeare's vernacular description of Petruchio's decrepit horse reveals what we may assume were the common equine ailments of that time.

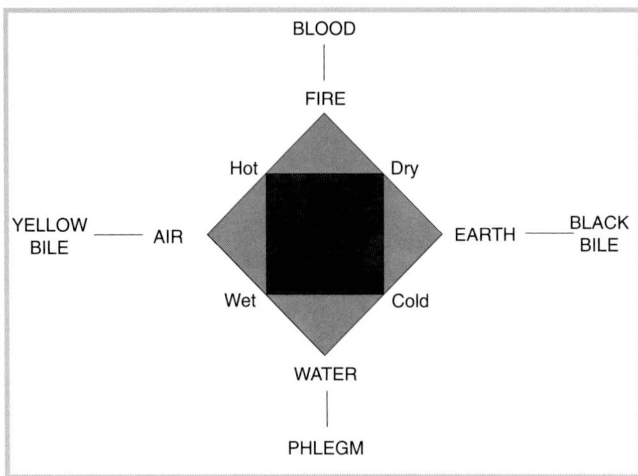

Fig 8: Diagram to illustrate the relationship between the four elements, Air, Earth, Fire and Water the four humours Yellow Bile, Black Bile, Blood and Phlegm the four qualities Hot, Dry, Wet and Cold.

The Renaissance

The year 1543 was remarkable for the publication of two momentous books that epitomised the Renaissance. One, by Copernicus, entitled *De Revolutionibus Orbium Coelestium*, proclaimed the belief that the earth was not the centre of the universe. The other, by Vesalius, entitled *De Humani Corporis Fabrica*, challenged the belief of centuries on the anatomy of the human body. It was based on the actual dissection of human cadavers rather than a abstract account of what it was said to be in the classical texts. Apart from its content, Vesalius's book is a masterpiece of creative art with some superb drawings by van Calkar, a pupil of Titian; see Figure 3. It set the standard of enquiry which later anatomists were to follow and it is tempting to suggest that it was Vesalius's 'anatomy' that inspired Carlo Ruini, a senator of Bologna, to produce an anatomy of the horse in 1598, entitled *Dell Anotomia, et Dell Infirmita Del Cavallo et Svoi Rimedii*. It was certainly in the Vesalian tradition of description from observation and although the production did not match the lavish standards of the *Fabrica* the similarity of the illustrations is striking; see Figures 3, 4. Nothing is known about Ruini other than he was the son of a wealthy lawyer and that the book was published posthumously. His anatomy was original but his section dealing with the diseases of the horse was based on earlier texts. It was well received and went into at least four more editions as well as translations into German and French. There was no English translation but almost 100 years later, in 1683, there appeared *The Anatomy of an Horse* by Andrew Snape, who borrowed heavily from Ruini. Many of the plates were copied directly from the Italian book but laterally transposed. Snape, who described himself as farrier to Charles II and his family as having served the Crown in the *"quality of farriers"* for 200 years, could command regal fees, for it was said that *"Snape the marshal farrier invariably presented a heavy bill for extras on account of the Royal Stud."* His son, another Andrew, was at Eton and became Provost of Kings College, Cambridge, in 1719, and Vice-Chancellor of the University in 1723.

After Vesalius, anatomical studies were focused on parts of the body. Thus Fallopia, Eustachia, Fabricius, Malpighi and de Graaf became eponyms which are instantly recognisable today by the structures they described. Fabricius' work on the valves of the veins influenced William Harvey who described the circulation of the blood in *De Motu Cordis*, published in 1628. It was a model for medical research, but the increasing application of science was not yet making much impression on clinical practice. By the middle of the 18th century there were good descriptive accounts of the gross lesions commonly affecting the organs but there was no proper understanding of the processes or the causes of disease. The emphasis was on the treatment. For the human population there were three classes of practitioner; the learned physicians who had been educated at one of the ancient universities, the surgeons and the apothecaries. The physicians treated their genteel patients according to their constitutions and advised them when to take the waters at one of the numerous spa towns like Bath and Tunbridge Wells that were then fashionable. The surgeons carried out the hands-on treatments such as setting fractures, trussing ruptures and dressing syphilitic chancres but they carried little prestige. The apothecaries prepared the medicines that the physicians prescribed but they also diagnosed and treated the servants' illnesses. Animals were referred to as *"the brute creation"* and it was socially demeaning to treat their diseases. That was a job for the lower orders, the farriers and, at the bottom of the social pile, the cow-leeches.

Thus the farriers were generally ill-educated persons and if they had any training it was an apprenticeship at the end of which they adopted their masters' secret remedies and continued the practice of generations as is described in a preface to a book, *The Gentleman's Pocket Farrier*, by Captain William Burdon in 1730:

"A farrier is as useful a Trade as any other in his Majesty's Dominions; we commonly call him Doctor, because he professes Physick and Surgery among Horses, and some are good sensible Men; but People who are able to give their sons Learning, seldom bind them to that Trade; so that Farriers are obliged to take such apprentices as they can get, without regard to their education. When an Apprentice has served out his Time, a few Recipes, the same (that for Time out of Mind have been secretly handed down from Master to Man, without any Variation or Amendment) set him up; and fully contented, he seeks to know no more: Thus many are illiterate, and some totally incapable of improvement. I have great Compassion for that noble and serviceable Creature a Horse, when I consider how precarious his Life is in the Hands of such Men."

The farriers 'exhibited' their drugs in various ways; as drinks, powders, balls, electuaries, clysters, blisters and charges. Bleeding and purging were everyday procedures, possibly because they were something the farrier could be seen to do that would have a predictable outcome. They could be confident that they would quieten a horse, distressed for whatever reason, when they bled 'to fainting' and they could predict precisely when a purging draught would take effect. Although the farriers were empirics there was a tenuous rationale to their practice. It stemmed from the classical belief that there were four elements - earth, air, fire and water - and four associated humours of the body: black bile, blood, yellow bile and phlegm. Health was a balance of the humours; when they were out of balance disease supervened and the rational treatment was to restore them by whatever means (Fig 8). By the end of the 18th century, when the London Veterinary College was founded, the humoral pathology was distinctly old-fashioned but customs die hard and there was nothing to put in its place. The remnants of it persist in our time with such words as 'phlegmatic', 'sanguine' and the black bile condition of 'melancholy'. The current fashion for holistic medicine with its emphasis on the body constitution is a revision of the humoral pathology.

Despite its reputation, farriery could provide a good living for some. There were complaints about the fees that were charged and there is published evidence that many of them were indeed high. Perhaps it was for this reason that several surgeons and even the odd physician swallowed their pride and demeaned themselves to treat horses and publish books on the subject. William Gibson was a prime example. He served as an army surgeon where he gained some experience with horses and on leaving the army he set up a horse practice in London. In quick succession, he published three books on farriery: *The Farrier's New Guide*, 1720, *The Farrier's Dispensatory*, 1721, and *The True Method of Dieting Horses*, also in 1721. Much of his text was copied from other sources but the books were well received and went into further editions. His anatomy has been described as *"consisting of 125 pages, wholly copied from Snape, errors included"*. In 1751, after 30 years experience in practice, he published *A New Treatise on the Diseases of Horses*, a handsome quarto that was largely an original contribution although it still used anatomical plates based on Ruini; see Figures 6 and 7. In its turn it was plagiarised, notably by Francis Clater, a farrier who produced a popular book entitled *Every Man His Own Farrier, or The Whole Art of Farriery Laid Open* which went into many editions over the next 60 years.

The second half of the 18th century was characterised by the agrarian and industrial revolutions. There were also notable advances in scientific knowledge and there was an air of optimism that farriery, too, could be improved if only it were subjected to scientific enquiry. In 1785 the Odiham Agricultural Society in Hampshire approved the motion

"...that farriery as it is commonly practised is conducted without principle or science and greatly to the injury to the noblest and most useful of our animals ... the society resolved: to open a voluntary subscription to forward such means as may be thought most likely to promote the study of scientific farriery."

This proposal led to the founding of the London Veterinary College in 1791 at which date the art of farriery had hardly changed in the 200 years since Shakespeare had described Petruchio's horse. The first professor was Charles Vial de Sainbel who had qualified at the Lyons veterinary school and attracted notice in London when he dissected the famous racehorse Eclipse. Unfortunately he died in 1793 from what is believed to have been glanders. His successor was Edward Coleman, a young surgeon who confessed to being *"little versed in veterinary matters and presumptuous to superintend the interests and growth of the infant school"*, but he held the post for 45 years. When the war with France started in 1793 the British army was badly organised and short of horses. An improved veterinary training was now a national necessity and Pitt's government was persuaded to make an annual grant-in-aid to the London College with the stipulation that veterinary surgeons should be trained for military service.

In 1839, foot and mouth disease broke out in London. It

rapidly spread throughout the country and was followed by an outbreak of bovine pleuropneumonia. These epidemics presented a challenge to the profession which it was ill prepared to meet. It had been known from biblical times that certain diseases could be 'caught' and there was empirical evidence that measures such as quarantine, *cordons sanitaires* and, in the case of animal diseases, stamping out by slaughter were sometimes effective methods of control. The farriers had experience of glanders and farcy and there had been serious outbreaks of what was probably equine influenza but it was not universally accepted that they were spread by contagion alone. The contemporary concepts of infectious disease were encapsulated in 1840 in a book by Jacob Henle entitled, in translation, *Concerning Miasmatic, Contagious and Miasmatic-contagious Diseases*. The miasmatic diseases were those that arose spontaneously from the environment, a miasma being a noxious emanation from organic matter and the names 'influenza' and 'malaria' stem from this belief. The miasmatic-contagious diseases were said to arise from a miasma which caused living parasites to be generated in the host which, in turn, carried the disease to other hosts by contagion. The third group, contagious diseases, did not arise spontaneously and were spread only by contagion. There were a few veterinary surgeons who believed that glanders was spread by contagion alone but the teachers at the London School believed that it was due to a miasma. William Dick, who had founded the Veterinary School in Edinburgh in 1823, expressed his opinion in a long article entitled, *On the Non-Contagious Nature of Epizootic Diseases*.

The New Laboratory Sciences

The 1840 publication by Henle was only one of many from Germany and France that were to show the way to a new, scientific understanding of disease. In Berlin, Rudolf Virchow published a set of lectures in 1858 in a book entitled *Cellularpathologie*. It set the pattern for a systematic, rational pathology and it gave a boost to the new science of morbid histology which was now made possible by using a microtome to cut thin sections that could be stained for microscopical examination.

One of Henle's students was Robert Koch, who, together with Pasteur, became world famous as a pioneer of bacteriology. Their work was revolutionary because it provided an entirely new framework, theoretical and practical, for understanding what previously had been so mystifying. Once the paradigm had been set, other workers were able to apply the techniques to great effect. The last 25 years of the century were the golden age of medical bacteriology and many of the discoveries related to animal disease; anthrax and fowl cholera were the first to be explained by the new germ theory. Pasteur lost no time in looking for ways to use the organisms to give protection against the diseases that they caused and at the International Medical Conference held in London in 1881 he described his method of protecting cattle and sheep against anthrax. He proposed, *"in honour of that great Englishman, Jenner"*, that the term 'vaccination' which hitherto had been used solely in connection with smallpox should from now on be used for the new process that he had pioneered. This was the beginning of another science, immunology.

The new sciences were a triumph for the French and Germans and the crowning achievement was the isolation of the tubercle bacillus by Koch in 1882. In that year, too, the organism of glanders was isolated by Loeffler and Schutz. Many of these early bacteriologists were veterinary scientists but there was no equivalent in Britain where veterinary training was still emphasising the art rather than the science.

The first bacteriological laboratory in Britain was established at Kings College, London, by Edgar Crookshank who had studied with the master, Koch, in Berlin in 1885. The students of the Royal Veterinary College had lectures from Crookshank and in 1890-91 steps were taken to radically improve their training. In 1892 John McFadyean was appointed Professor of Pathology and Bacteriology. A prodigious worker, he introduced postgraduate training and a degree course in Veterinary Science and he founded the *Journal of Comparative Pathology and Therapeutics*. This was the journal that published an amazing account of human glanders. The patient was Sidney Gaiger, who taught pathology at the Liverpool veterinary school. He had caught the disease in the army in India and from March 1911 until June 1913 he published detailed notes of how it progressed through his body to cause deep-seated abscesses. The treatment was excruciating and at one time he had 16 sinuses that had to be plugged daily while he was under morphia. At the height of the disease his arm was amputated. Finally, he wrote:

> *"not counting the smallest of the incisions, I have been operated on forty-five times and of these, twenty-seven operations were under general anaesthetic... I am writing this in July 1913. I have never been in better general health than at the present time."*

Such were the hazards of horse practice in the days before antibiotics.

Despite the great advances in bacteriology, there will still some diseases that had the characteristics of a contagion but for which no bacterium could be demonstrated. In 1892 the key to this problem was provided by a Russian worker, Dmitri Ivanowski, who showed that tobacco mosaic disease could be transmitted by the sap from a diseased plant even after the sap had been passed through a filter that was fine enough to remove bacteria. In 1898 Loeffler and Frosch, both pupils of Koch in Berlin, showed that foot and mouth disease could also be transmitted by an organism that passed through a bacteriological filter. Hence, these organisms came to be known as 'filtrable viruses' and the word 'virus' was thereafter used with the more specific meaning that we accord it today.

The concept of specific of disease that began with the discovery of infectious agents was thereafter applied with great effect to other kinds of disease, such as the metabolic and nutritional disorders. René Dubos has described it as:

> *" the most constructive force in medical research (over the last century) and the theoretical and practical achievements to which it has led constitute the bulk of modern medicine."*

What we recognise today, at the end of this millennium, when we discuss the pathology, microbiology, immunology and therapeutics of disease is almost entirely the product of the last one hundred years. Indeed, much progress has been within the living memory of the authors of this book as the following chapters will reveal.

Ancient and modern disease of the horse: a remembrance of things past

JIM ROONEY
204 Sportsman Neck Road
Queenstown
Maryland 21658
USA

In a sense one can say that pathology is one of the more ancient fields of endeavour and inquiry. The reading of entrails for signs and omens - haruspicy - is as old as the recording of human religious rituals. In that sense, the first haruspex - the religious practitioner responsible for such divination - was the first pathologist.

Such a view of pathology is in keeping, perhaps, with the human tendency to find, on every hand, omens associated with the millennium.

As far as we know, however, pathology in the sense of the study of disease processes began in the 18th century and developed rapidly in the 19th century in both human and veterinary medicine. The first textbook of veterinary pathology *per se* was probably that of Gurlt in Germany in 1831 though material about animal lesions had appeared earlier in human texts.

In this chapter, I shall try to develop but one broad idea: atavism and evolution as components of the pathogenesis of disease in modern horse medicine and pathology. Briefly said, this chapter addresses the interaction of genetics and environment in equine disease. As well, this is a plea for a broader and more historically oriented view of equine disease. While problems must be faced as they occur in the present - real time - understanding of the how and why of some problems, at least, can be obtained by considering what may be learnt from the past. The millennium not only suggests that we review the past hundred years but what, in the last hundred and the coming hundred, we owe and shall owe to even earlier centuries.

Such an approach is particularly relevant in equine pathology and medicine because of the gap in development of knowledge beginning with the widespread use of the internal combustion engine, a gap which has only begun to close in recent years. In my class at the New York State Veterinary College (1952) there were but two of us professing interest in the horse, and my lone soul mate died at the end of our first year. In 1960, when I interviewed for a position in the Animal Pathology Department at the University of Kentucky, Roger Doll - one of the great men of equine research - warned me that by working on the horse I was consigning myself to professional oblivion. He was right at the time, but no longer.

I should like to speculate about some conditions of the horse which may be called atavistic in the broad sense. Atavism is defined as: "*Recurrence in an organism or in any of its parts of a form typical of ancestors more remote than the parents, usually due to a recombination of ancestral genes.*" There is nothing in that definition to limit atavism to sporadic occurrence or, indeed, to regular recurrence.

Cement Hypoplasia

Hypoplasia of the cement on the occlusal surfaces of the maxillary molar teeth is an atavism which occurs in about 43% of modern horses. In fact, this is somewhat more than simple cement hypoplasia; rather it is dystrophic development involving absence of both cement and enamel folds. As a clinical problem, this manifests as an infection working into the tooth from the abnormal occlusal surface, leading to fracture, collapse, and eventual loss of one or more of the upper molars. Despite the prevalence of this condition, there has been little or no attention given to its pathogenesis, but we shall put that right here.

During the Miocene, some 20 million years ago, horses evolved from brachydont, low crowned browsing teeth, to hypsodont, high crowned grazing teeth. The low crowned tooth was quite adequate for browsing on tough forages but not gritty, abrasive foods. With the retreat of the forests and the evolution of savannahs and plains, grass became the primary food source and grazing involved heavy exposure to abrasive, gritty siliceous food materials.

Several strategies evolved, including long, hypsodont teeth which could slowly wear away over the animal's lifetime. Coincident with the evolution of the long teeth were, of course, changes in the proportions of the cranial skeleton to accommodate those longer teeth. Of interest to us, at this juncture, was the appearance of cementum on the occlusal surfaces of the teeth. Cementum is a coarse fibre bone with good resistance to abrasion. The hypothesis, then, is that the cement hypoplasia which has been with the horse for so many years (and is still with it today) had its origins

Fig 1: Maxillary molars of an Equus. *The first and second molars, above the left-hand label, are lacking enamel folds and cementum.*

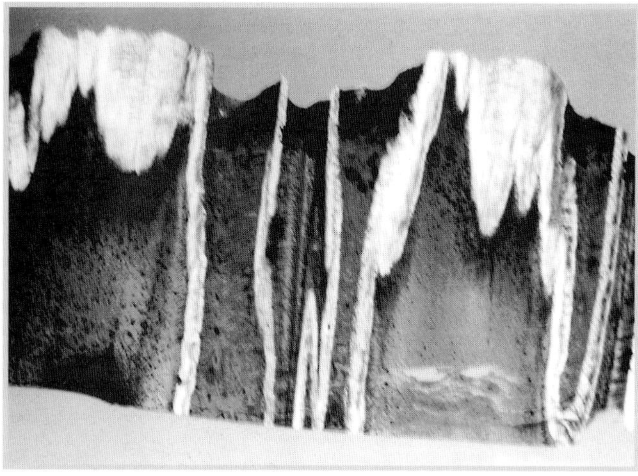

Fig 2: Low magnification of a ground sagittal section of a normal maxillary molar with well-developed enamel folds, dentine, and cementum.

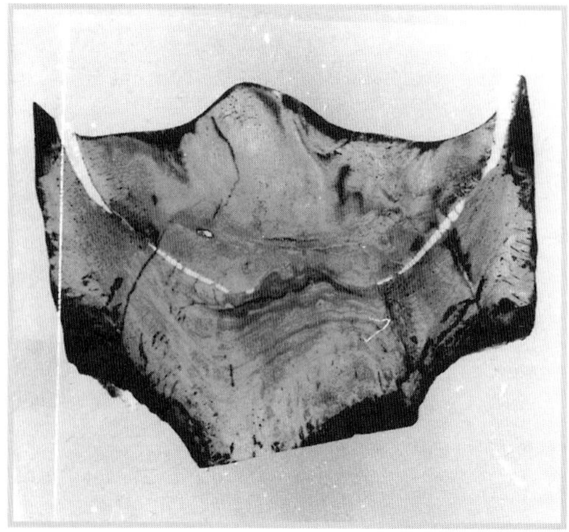

Fig 3: Low magnification of a ground sagittal section of an abnormal maxillary molar. Only a single enamel fold is present. There is no cementum and the dentine is disorganised.

some 20 million years ago when the teeth were evolving from brachydont to hypsodont. That is, controlling factors (presumably genes) remain in the modern horse population which specify molar teeth without adequate cementum on the occlusal surfaces.

The hypothesis was tested by examination of large numbers of teeth of fossil equids (Figs 1, 2 and 3). Evidence of cement hypoplasia was found as early as Miocene *Pseudohipparion* 10–15 million years ago and with some frequency in Pleistocene *Equus* as early as 5 million years ago (million years will be abbreviated henceforth as MA.)

The restriction of hypoplasia to the maxillary cheek teeth, particularly the first molar, is striking and so far unexplained.

I should like to pursue this matter of atavistic teeth anomalies a step farther. We know the situation with sickle cell anaemia in man, for example: homozygous normals - susceptible to malaria; homozygous recessive - lethal sickle cell anaemia; and heterozygotes - resistant to malaria. Can we look for something similar in the teeth of the horse, recognising that this is speculation based on limited data? According to Cohrs, Becker, Baker and others, the teeth are normal in about 18% of the population; 58% have enamel

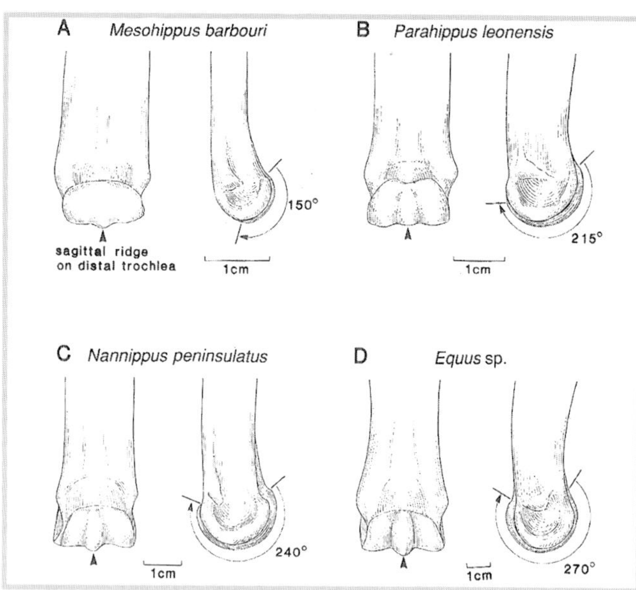

Fig 4: Evolution of the distal end of Mc3 after MacFadden. See text for further details.

and/or cement hypoplasia; and 24% have more severe anomalies such as malfitting teeth, extra teeth and so on. One discerns, however tentatively, a 1-2-1 ratio: 18% normal, 24% severely abnormal, and 58%, the heterozygotes, with a reasonable, if imperfect, adaptation to siliceous forage.

Contracture of the Neonate

This is the most common congenital defect of Thoroughbred and Standardbred foals, with an incidence of about 15%. It occurs in other breeds as well, but incidence data are not available. Please note that this section deals only with contracture of the newborn and not contracture which appears later during the first year of life. That is another problem altogether.

I reported, in 1969, that a characteristic lesion of newborn contracture was hypoplasia of vertebral articular facets and, of specific interest here, the distal articulation of metacarpal three (Mc3). Cohrs had already reported this in a foal in 1929. The pathogenesis of the contracture, as it relates to such hypoplasia, is arguable but appears to be related to loss of equilibrium of moments[1] about the metacarpophalangeal joint. This loss of equilibrium, in turn, is caused by the hypoplasia which entails a smaller than normal moment arm for the extensor as compared to the flexor tensile elements.

The pathogenesis of the hypoplasia itself is unknown. We know that it appears early in fetal development, at least as early as the cartilaginous model of Mc3. Figure 4 shows the evolution of the distal end of Mc3 from *Mesohippus*, about 30 million years ago, to modern *Equus*. The distal end of Mc3 of *Mesohippus* and *Parahippus* is what I call hypoplasia in a modern foal (Fig 5). I hypothesise that neonatal contracture is an atavism, an ancestral trait, reappearing at a rather constant rate for many years, millions of years. Eighty-five percent normal and 15% abnormal suggest, at least, a recessive character never deleted from the population.

[1]A moment in mechanics is a turning force. A moment is exerted when one twists off a bottle cap or turns a nut with a wrench (spanner). In this case "*equilibrium of moments*" means the joint does not move because the turning force exerted by the extensor tendons is equalled by the turning force exerted by the flexor tendons and suspensory.

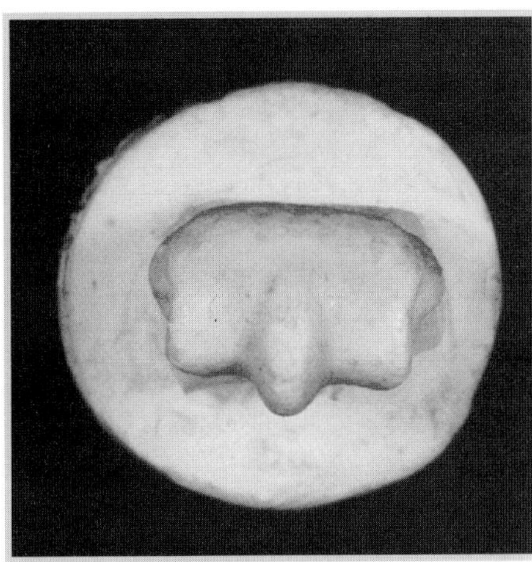

Fig 5: Cast of the distal end of Mc3 of Mesohippus *(about 30 MA), distoproximal view showing complete absence of the dorsal part of the sagittal ridge. The palmar part of the ridge is lower than that of the comparable* Equus *Mc3.*

Size

Over the about 55 million years of evolution of the members of the Superfamily *Equoidea* there have been a number of examples of larger (for their time) animals and quite small animals, that is, dwarfs. While estimates of body weight from fossil material is fraught with caveats, *Hypohippus* (20–15 MA), for example, may have weighed about 400 kg, large for the spectrum of equids of its time. *Archaeohippus,* which occurred about the same time was a dwarf race, and the fossil bones show this was proportionate dwarfism. One can speculate that chondroplastic dwarfs, if they occurred, would have died young, their bones not preserved by fossilisation. It is generally true that bones of young animals are uncommon in the fossil record, either because they did not fossilise or were destroyed by predators.

In more recent times, dwarfism has been seen in inbred Friesian horses and in Shetland ponies. The Friesians were proportionate dwarfs while the Shetlands were dysplastic. It is of considerable interest that the Shetlands had complete ulnas and fibulas rather than the incomplete, reduced bones characteristic of modern *Equus*. That in itself is atavistic since very early equids (e.g. *Mesohippus*, 30 MA; *Hyracotherium*, 55 MA) had complete ulnas and fibulas.

This brings us to the modern miniature horse, so-called. While objective data are sparse, it appears that there are three results of breeding these animals: 1) usual size animals; 2) proportionate small animals; and 3) frank dwarfs. This suggests that there could be a 1:2:1 segregation of homozygous normals (dominants), heterozygous miniatures, and homozygous dwarfs (recessives). Breeding experiments, although unlikely, would obviously be of considerable pathological and paleontological interest. Dwarf lines of fossil horses, proportionate or dysplastic, died out, and the variety of apparently congenital problems in the modern 'mini' suggest why. Without human intervention, the miniature horse probably would die out as well.

Guttural Pouch

These enigmatic structures peculiar to the *Perissodactyla* (horse, rhinoceros and tapir) are not, of course, hereditary diseases, but they do become diseased, and we might ask, first, why are they there at all?

The guttural pouches are outpouchings of the Eustachian tube, said to be necessary adjuncts to the pharyngeal apparatus of *Equidae* in order to allow normal swallowing. Incidentally, a French veterinarian invented an instrument to examine the guttural pouches in 1790.

The pharynx of the *Perissodactyla* differs from that of other animals. The rostral third of the dorsal wall is directly applied to the skull; the remainder of the dorsal wall and the lateral walls are enveloped by the guttural pouches. In the horse, during swallowing, there is considerable movement of the caudal pharyngeal wall rostrally, this movement permitted by the flexible attachment of the pharyngeal wall to the guttural pouches.

Skoda argued, in 1911, that this movement is necessitated by the long, narrow pharynx, so that a bolus of food could pass from mouth through oropharynx to oesophagus without entering the larynx. Abnormal swallowing does occur with disease of the guttural pouches, such as tympany, empyema or inflammation, supporting, but not proving, Skoda's hypothesis.

It can be suggested that the long, narrow pharynx and the long, narrow, and deep head of horses developed as the short (brachydont) teeth of the early browsing equids evolved to the long, grazing (hypsodont) teeth of later equids and *Equus* as already discussed.

Disease of the guttural pouch, then, is predisposed by the necessary evolutionary adaptation of the dentition of equids to the change from browsing to grazing. That the guttural pouches may have other functions as well as that described is certainly possible, but there is no information at this time suggesting such functions.

Lameness

One of the major endeavours of pathology is the elucidation of pathogenesis. Many years of study of the lesions of lameness have led to some of the following considerations.

First, some data on lameness may be of interest. Bartke (1900) provided a wealth of information on the frequency of disease in Prussian army horses. There were about 100,000 cavalry and artillery horses in any given year between 1886 and 1895. There were 278,323 sick horses during the ten year period, or about 27,832 horses per year. Of that number, 94.6% recovered, 1.3% were turned out or disposed of, 3.3% died, and 0.9% were killed. About 27% of the horses were on sick call in any given year. The locomotor system, including the foot, accounted for 65% of horses on sick call.

Jeffcott provided similar data for 314 Thoroughbred horses in six racing stables in Newmarket, England, for one year. A one-to-one comparison cannot be made, but it was apparent that locomotor problems retained pride of place in the English horses. The one significant difference was a high rate of respiratory disease in the young English as compared to the older Prussian horses.

Some years ago, based on the study of the nature and distribution of lameness lesions in horses, I suggested that conformation could be thought of in two related ways in the pathogenesis of many types of lameness. The first is obvious and hallowed: the phenotype, the conformation, of the horse, as determined by the genotype, mechanically predisposes particular anatomical structures or areas to damage. One thinks immediately of the relationship between sickle hock, the smaller than average dorsal angle of the hock joint, and spavin arthrosis. Also, consider the type of American Quarter Horse with a large body, small feet, and navicular disease.

Somewhat less obvious, perhaps, is what I call functional conformation. That is the horse which because of the work being done places the legs in the same positions as the predisposed phenotype. Space does not permit a full explanation, but the sickle hock horse is predisposed to spavin arthrosis and the horse which works in a sickle hock manner also is predisposed to spavin arthrosis. Examples include the jumping horse, crouching in order to generate sufficient force to leap into the air, and the animal under draft, crouching in order to generate sufficient force to move the load. Clearly, the anatomically - phenotypically - predisposed horse is even more likely to develop spavin arthrosis when working in the sickle hock manner.

The horse with a heavy body and small feet is predisposed to navicular disease because of rocking or oscillation of the hoof on the surface: too much energy is delivered for the small foot to store and dissipate quickly and safely. The functional equivalent is the jumper, predisposed by work to navicular disease, because a large amount of energy is delivered - at the drop from the jump - to a foot which impacts toe first.

While the two examples may not seem comparable, they are. The hoof normally impacts flat-footed, at the slow walk, or heel-quarter-toe at faster gaits. With toe first hoof impact, there is out-of-phase rotation of the distal interphalangeal and metacarpophalangeal joints. This increases the force exerted by the deep flexor tendon on the palmar articular surface of the navicular bone and, so, increases the friction on the surface. The same out-of-phase rotations occur when the small foot impacts with the surface, the excess energy causing oscillation of the foot: heel-quarter-toe.

The police or carriage horse working long hours on hard surfaces, such as city streets, is also at risk. The energy which would have been absorbed and dissipated by a more 'usual' surface is not absorbed and dissipated by hard surfaces.

The interaction of genes and environment in the pathogenesis of lameness is not a simple one to one: gene A causing lameness B. Multiple genes and environmental factors can and do interact to produce the unhappy end result.

I realise that what comes next may cause immediate brain shutdown. I can only hope that reader will persevere and ponder. The interaction of genetics and environment may be mathematically summarised:

$$E = \surd A\text{-}G \; dt$$

E, here, is the normal animal with E equal to zero. A is environment and G is genetic constitution. The integral sign, $\surd$, and the notation dt indicate that the interaction of environment and genetics is evaluated continuously over time... a day, a week, a lifetime. Obviously this is an equation that cannot be solved, but it does provide a succinct statement of what is to be discussed next.

If a mare kicks a normal foal and fractures the radius, there is a uniquely large environmental factor with no necessary genetic inadequacy, and the value of E is not zero.

On the other hand, in a foal with combined immunodeficiency, G, the genetic component, is large while the environmental component can be normal. E is not zero, and the foal sickens and dies.

So, we have: 1) genetic disease, pure or nearly so; 2) environmentally induced disease, pure or nearly so; and 3) variably interacting genetic/environment, multifactorial disease.

There is no need to discuss at length purely genetic disease, but with purely environmental disease, there is a dilemma. With the exception of frankly traumatic events, is there such a thing as a purely environmentally induced disease? While many fractures can be so considered, the role of genetically controlled conformation as a factor in the fracture cannot be overlooked, even if it is difficult or impossible clearly to define. Do we include ingestion of senecio and Crotalaria, yellow star thistle, Russian knapweed? Do all horses eating the same amount of such poisonous materials invariably develop cirrhosis of the liver or encephalomalacic lesions? Do they all develop it at the same time and to the same degree? You know the answer. There is variability in all populations and that variability is in large measure genetic. In the majority of disease states, both genetic and environmental factors are interacting.

Lesions Not Seen

To conclude, it is of interest to mention some lesions *not* seen in fossil horse material. It is well known that human use is directly and indirectly responsible for many of the disease and lameness problems of the modern horse, whether environmental *per se* or predisposed to by human genetic selection. While that seems obvious, the point is fully made for skeletal structures and lesions, at least, by consideration of the lesions seen and not seen in fossil horses prior to domestication.

In a large series of fossil material, from about 20 million

Fig 6: Sagittal sections of the central and third tarsal bones of Archaeohippus *(about 20 MA) with fusion and new bone formation on the dorsal aspect indicative of spavin arthrosis.*

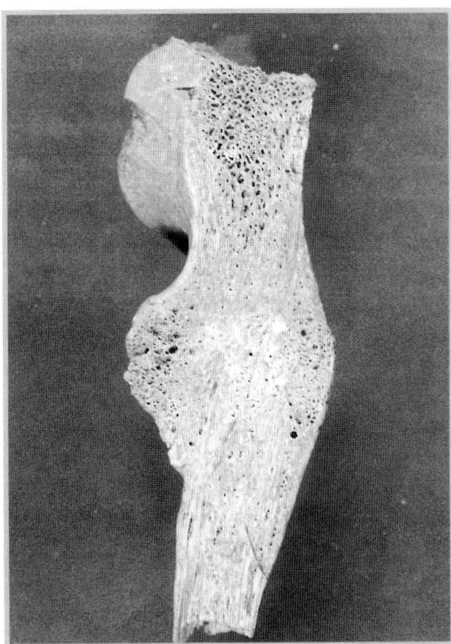

Fig 7: Fractured rib of an equid with callus formation. Radiographs showed incomplete healing of the fracture line.

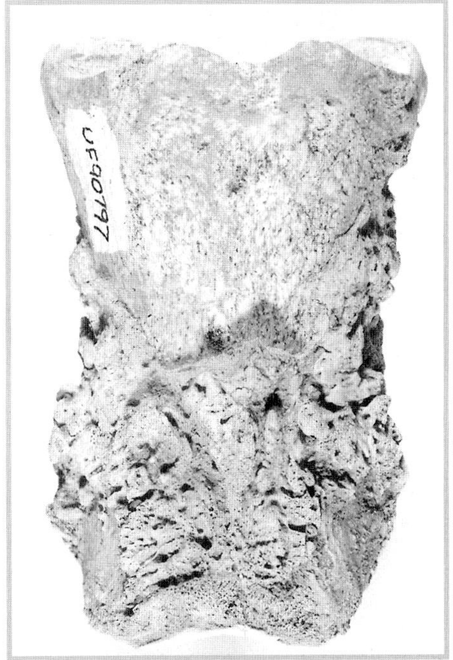

Fig 8: Dorsal view of the proximal phalanx of Equus *with abundant new bone formation (periostosis) on the dorsal surface and both borders.*

years ago up to the time of domestication, perhaps about 6000 years ago, the following lesions were not seen:

- Osteochondrosis at any site, including the cervical vertebrae (wobblers).
- Navicular disease.
- Sesamoiditis.
- Splints. A single example was seen in an *Equus* from Bolivia.
- Spavin. Fusion of central and third tarsal bones was seen in a few specimens. In only one was there new bone formation to suggest spavin arthrosis (Fig 6). The others appeared to be congenital.
- There was no evidence of chronic laminitis as far as could be determined from examination of distal phalanges (hooves are not preserved).
- Arthrosis was found in only one appendicular joint, the stifle of an *Hipparion* (about 10 MA). Arthrosis was seen in the articular facets of a lumbar vertebra and the osteophytes characteristic of spondylosis in a thoracic vertebra of *Hipparion*.

While fractures undoubtedly occurred in these ancient horses, their presence could be recognised only if healing with callus formation was present. One such healing fracture of a rib was found (Fig 7).

It is of anatomical interest that there was no evidence of synovial fossae, including the fossa of the glenoid of the scapula, in equids earlier than 1-5 MA *Equus*, and then in only about half of the specimens. Such fossae are present in virtually all modern *Equus* scapulae.

Most of the lesions found were nonarticular periostoses which occur as a result of ligamentous avulsion or partial avulsion from bone (Fig 8). While speculative, it appeared that these lesions might be associated with the transition from the three-toed to the one-toed (tridactyl to monodactyl) condition. It is true, however, that such nonarticular periostoses are more frequent, in the modern era, in slower moving animals while articular damage with reparative periostosis is seen in animals which work at speed. This makes it clear (I trust) that early equids did not indulge in much racing, jumping or other equine athletic events.

In summary, we have looked at several disease conditions of modern horses which can reasonably be defined as atavistic, genetic, in nature. Also, we have examined genetic and functional conformation in the pathogenesis of equine lameness. The concept of functional conformation enforced by human use of horses is complemented by consideration of lesions found and, more importantly, not found in the bones and joints of fossil horses which lived long before horses fell into the hands of man.

Further Reading

For an history of veterinary pathology see:

Saunders, L.Z. (1996) *Biographical History of Veterinary Pathology*, Allen Press. Lawrence, Kansas.

MacFadden, B.J. (1992) *Fossil Horses*, Cambridge University Press. New York. Rooney, J.R. (1997) *Equid Paleopathology. J. equine vet. Sci.* **17**, 430-446.

References for all authors cited may be found in: Rooney, J.R. and Robertson, J.L. (1996) *Equine Pathology*, Iowa State University Press, Ames, Iowa.

Factors which may influence the future of equine medicine

BRIAN SINGLETON
Vine Cottage
60 Morston Rad
Blakeney, Holt
Norfolk NR25 7BE
UK

Introduction

The operative word in the title is 'may' for there are so many factors which may influence the future of equine medicine. It seems a reasonable start to consider available statistics relating to equine matters. It has been known for some time that accurate statistical data concerning the equine population in the UK, its distribution and uses, have been difficult to obtain.

The situation is now improving and in 1996 the British Equestrian Trading Association produced a comprehensive report on the equine industry and its trading potential. A follow-up report is expected in 1999 from which, by comparison, it may be possible to identify trends.

Sadly, accurate figures on the overall equine populations reflecting the situation in the past are not available except in the Thoroughbred and from certain associations representing pony breeds. Currently, the British Horse Society is conducting a detailed parish census in Devon, Essex, Denbighshire and a district census in Lancashire. This study is to be extended and is clearly a large undertaking; when complete it should provide accurate figures and a good starting point for establishing future trends.

The equine population and its uses is only one factor to consider in attempting to forecast equine veterinary activities. Although perhaps less directly relevant, there are others which will have an influence, such as human population growth and distribution, the gradual spread of urbanisation, sociological changes, public perceptions regarding veterinary services and attitudes and expectations, as well as national and international politics and economics. In addition, ecological and environmental issues will all play a part. Predicting the future is, therefore, even more difficult than it has always been in the past.

While several of the factors mentioned may have marginal effects upon our concern others, such as economic trends, could profoundly influence the call for veterinary services in one way or another. At the present time, when the European single currency debate is still in full flow, it is impossible to know which way the UK economy will swing. Owning and/or using horses is almost entirely a leisure pursuit, popular in the affluent western societies, but it is a luxury and, in many cases, an expensive one. It is therefore vulnerable to adverse economic changes, as are equine veterinary services.

Currently there is no reason for pessimism; even though equine population figures have been somewhat vague, two independent surveys undertaken in the mid-1990s arrived at similar figures for the total number of horses in the UK. At the time of writing, equine veterinary practice is buoyant and there is expansion in the number of veterinarians engaged. Specialist centres and hospitals are being established and research is arguably much better supported than in other areas of 'companion animal medicine'. These are all upbeat factors which, although difficult to quantify, nevertheless suggest a positive trend.

Surveys

In the mid-1990s Peat Marwick & McLintock (PMM) were commissioned by the British Horse Society to study the economic contribution of the horse and pony industry. PMM estimated the equine population at the time to be 550,000 and calculated that 3.3 million people, namely 5.6% of the population, rode regularly, of whom 600,000 rode three or more times a week.

In 1996 the BETA Equestrian Survey estimated the equine population as 565,000, of which 216,000 were Thoroughbred/Thoroughbred-cross. The number of people over age five years who were classified as riders was 2 million or 3.8% of the total population. While the two surveys are remarkably close regarding the equine population, the number of people quoted as riders differ. So far as veterinary

TABLE 1: Figures (in thousands) from the Office of National Statistics in the 1997 edition of Social Trends 27.

	1961	1971	1981	1991	1995	2011	2031
England	43,561	46,412	46,821	48,208	48,903	50,757	51,150
Wales	2635	2740	2813	2891	2917	2955	2886
Scotland	5184	5236	5180	5107	5137	5083	4934
Northern Ireland	1427	1540	1538	1601	1649	1699	1750
United Kingdom	52,807	55,928	56,352	57,808	58,606	60,493	60,720

TABLE 2: Actual (1995) and predicted (2011 and 2021) population percentages in three age groups.			
	1995	2011	2021
Under 16 years	21	18	18
16–34 years	27	24	23
35–54 years	26	29	26

services are concerned, the equine population figures are the most relevant. Whether the percentage of the population that rides is 2% or 3.8%, it is unlikely that these figures will change appreciably in relation to the forecasts of the total populations of the UK.

Trends during the last 40 years, extrapolated to the year 2031, are shown in Table 1. A peak to 61.2 million is forecast for 2023. In Table 2 the actual and predicted populations of riders according to age are given. This indicates that the group under 34 years will decline by approximately 3%. The majority of people who ride regularly probably fall within that age span, but the decline will be compensated for by the overall rise in the UK population. Although it is interesting to consider these figures it seems probable that a *status quo* in terms of numbers of horse riders will exist for many years to come.

Influence of Urbanisation

The Department of Environment, Transport and the Regions, in the document 'Planning for the Communities of the Future' (1997), predict that for the period 1997–2106 about 175,000 new homes *per annum* will be required in the UK. This figure compares favourably with the following house-building rates *per annum*:

1950s	230,000
1960s	300,000
1970s	260,000
1980s	180,000
1991/97	176,000

It is an interesting point that, since 1950, the population of the UK has grown by 8 million but over 10 million dwellings have been created. Reasons for this discrepancy include the facts that more elderly people are living alone, younger people are delaying marriage, there is an increased rate of divorce and, consequently, more single parents. Little wonder then that over the last 50 years there has been a steady erosion of the countryside due to spreading urbanisation. While the process must have had adverse local and regional effects upon horse and pony ownership and access to good riding opportunities, it would seem that nationally those effects have not had a profound effect upon ownership.

It is heartening to find that the policy of the last and present governments regarding the siting of new houses is the expectation that 50% (rising to 60% by 2010) will be built on reused sites i.e. on previously developed land. However, this means that some 70,000 dwellings will be built *per annum* on green field sites - still a considerable encroachment upon the countryside year by year. Let it be hoped that some of the sociological factors referred to earlier as contributing to the ever-increasing demand for new houses can be reversed, but that is unlikely to happen.

Clearly, the effect of urbanisation will vary greatly from district to district. In some areas it may have minimal effect upon horse ownership and pursuits whereas in others it may be profound. Factors such as these will need to be taken into account by young graduates intent on setting up new equine practices.

Economics and Public Expectations

According to the BETA National Equestrian Survey 1996, based upon a population of 565,000 horses, the total expenditure in one year was £915 million of which £55 million or 6% was spent on veterinary fees. This averages out at approximately £100 per horse based upon the total population - not a high figure but, nevertheless, the public expectations of the quality of facilities and service provided by practices, specialist centres and hospitals continues to rise.

In recent years, there has been a remarkable increase in media attention to the veterinary profession. Many of the feature programmes have been shallow, slanted towards entertainment instead of reality and unrepresentative of the high standards which many people in practice and in the veterinary schools adhere to. Clearly, such programmes have done the profession no favours. To a large extent, the equine branch of our profession has escaped such degrading exposure. Nevertheless the whole profession must be vigilant for, although we continue to ride high in public esteem, those in practice must give real value for money. They must not fall into the trap of using technological progress irresponsibly by providing and charging for more than is truly necessary for the welfare of the patient simply to enhance the bank balances. There is a risk that veterinary services could become so expensive as to be counterproductive. Whenever it is genuinely necessary to pull out all the stops in order to provide an accurate diagnosis and the best possible treatment then every stage should be carefully explained to the client so that they understand why a high bill is being levied.

Many people owning horses and ponies are from urban backgrounds, many have been highly successful in business and they expect, and even demand, very high standards. It is imperative that practice attitudes in every aspect of the service provided can respond accordingly.

The trend towards multiperson practices, the equine veterinary centres of excellence, often including certificate and diploma holders on the staff, as well as the provision of state-of-the-art hospital facilities all enhance the standing of the equine veterinarian. Such developments, subject to a healthy economy, are certain to continue so that eventually a sound referral service will be available to the horse-owning public throughout most of the country.

TABLE 3: RCVS certificate holders according to category.

	1991		1997	
	No. Enrolled	Holders*	No. Enrolled	Holders*
Equine practice†	35	25	74	51
Equine orthopaedics	18	13	14	17
Equine stud medicine*	12	12	18	22
Totals	65	50	106	90

†Only taken to Certificate level; *Now superceded by Equine Medicine (Stud Medicine).

TABLE 4: RCVS diploma holders according to category.

	1991		1997	
	No. Enrolled	Holders*	No. Enrolled	Holders*
Equine orthopaedics	3	7	4	9
Equine stud medicine	6	8	7	6
Equine soft tissue surgery	N/A	N/A	32	3
			13	18

*Including Foundation Diplomats.

The Development of Specialisation

The introduction by the Royal College of Veterinary Surgeons of Certificates and Diplomas in specialised fields has, in recent years, done more than anything else to enhance the standing of the veterinary profession. It has given individuals a goal to aim for and every justification to pursue special lines of interest. The job satisfaction provided by these opportunities has been immense. The recognition by the RCVS of a Diploma (Table 4) or other approved qualifications as a means of gaining specialist status has been a major step forward. There is every reason to believe that the trend, albeit gradual, will continue.

The rewards for veterinarians who participate in referral work are great, especially in terms of academic dialogue, job satisfaction and the possibility of involvement in collaborative research with colleagues in the universities. This point is important because more and more research is being undertaken at the molecular level far removed from the clinical case. It is therefore essential that, in appropriate circumstances, a meaningful link between the field and research team be established.

The Importance of Research

A statement in the Pew National Veterinary Education Programme Report 1989 contains a passage which is as true today as when it was written and which will be equally true in the future. Under the heading *The New Vision of the Veterinary Profession - Greatly Expanded Collective Competency*, it reads "*The future welfare of the veterinary profession will depend more upon the quality of the national veterinary research programme than any other single factor.*" That statement is as true for equine medicine and surgery as it is for every other aspect of veterinary science.

Sadly the immediate future for veterinary clinical research in the UK is arguably the least encouraging component of all the factors which may influence the future of equine medicine. In giving the plenary Wooldridge Memorial Lecture at the 1998 BVA Congress, Dame Bridget Ogilvie presented a most compelling case for ascertaining that the quality of veterinary research is declining in this country. She spoke from her experience, as the recently retired director of the Wellcome Trust, which over the previous decade had invested some £30 million into veterinary research and training awards. This sum is less than 10% of the budgeted allocation of the Wellcome Trust for research grants spanning biomedical, medical and veterinary research. The Trust had been *"prepared to invest more money into veterinary research but the weakness of veterinary clinical research had prevented the Trust from giving as many grants as it was prepared to do."* This is surely a depressing omen for the future. What are the root causes and what can be done to safeguard the future?

It is a strange anomaly that the veterinary schools can select students from the cream of university entrants. Among these bright graduates there must be research potential. Yet at the time of graduation few elect for veterinary academia. The majority enter practice for which the courses, almost without exception, have trained them. Once in practice, where graduates command relatively high salaries (because of the continuing shortage of veterinarians), it is difficult to attract recent graduates back to the schools or other research institutes because the salaries offered are relatively low and security of tenure is fragile. Even those graduates who do elect to enter research and obtain a PhD, few stay on to establish a research career. This situation is in turn putting an increasing burden upon the core of people who have made teaching and research their chosen calling. Increasingly, they are having to spread their time and energy to cover matters of administration and fundraising at the same time as their teaching responsibilities increase. The result is that they have less time for research and some become disillusioned and unhappy in their work. That scenario may be another reason why our brighter young graduates are not attracted to research.

Another major factor in the equation is that research has become so technologically sophisticated and expensive that it is seldom easy for an individual to undertake worthwhile research unless part of a multidisciplinary team which can share equipment and interact academically. Critical mass in relation to research is vital and was one of the pivotal points made by the Riley Committee Report (1989) which led to the recommendation to merge some of the veterinary schools - partly to resolve the 'one man deep phenomenon'.

A recurring problem for the veterinary schools is the overall lack of resource from Government. A result, no doubt, of the policy to grant individuals the right to a university education, subject to educational attainment. Although commendable, this policy has nevertheless led to available resources being spread too thinly. There is no doubt at all that currently our schools are grossly under-resourced. Some authoritative voices maintain that the quality of veterinary education is gradually falling. That is difficult to quantify but it does seem, with a small number of notable exceptions, that things are becoming more and more difficult and this must eventually be reflected in the quality of teaching and amount of research undertaken.

The problems highlighted by Dame Bridget Ogilvie and shared by many other people are not at all easy to resolve for the future. Clearly, increased resources for veterinary education and research, linked with a more attractive salary structure for those in academia, will be essential if the present trends are to be reversed. It has been suggested that the animal-owning public should help. However, although there is substantial support for animal welfare charities, especially those concerned with horses, the very people who subscribe are often the same people who have benefited from research, but if asked to support research or education directly they demur (fortunately the Home of Rest for Horses and the International League for the Protection of Horses are both generous in their support of research and facilities at veterinary schools.)

Should the money be raised from levies on the clients of veterinary practices? This is not a very popular suggestion for many reasons. Veterinary practices, centres and hospitals are the result of private enterprise; no grants from local authorities are available as they are in Sweden, for instance. Capital outlay is enormous and running costs very high. The whole enterprise is labour intensive. Fees are already of necessity substantial and any idea of, say, a 5% levy to be directed towards education and/or research would pose real problems. In any event, as the amount spent on equine veterinary services is £55 million *per annum* a 5% levy would only raise £2.75 million - useful but not really significant in terms of overall funding.

The problems that have been outlined can only be resolved by substantial increases in funding from the Department of Education and Employment into veterinary education. This almost inevitably means higher taxation, because the whole of higher education in the UK is under-resourced. This takes us into the political arena which is dangerous ground. Realistically, it seems unlikely that in the foreseeable future adequate funding will be forthcoming. The veterinary schools will continue to struggle and education and research will need increasing support from trusts, charities and businesses with direct interests such as insurance and nutrition.

In the specific area of equine clinical research the contributions provided annually by the Horserace Betting Levy Board, Thoroughbred breeders and owners and the Animal Health Trust will hopefully continue to play a vital role in sustaining research programmes.

Amid the doom and gloom which currently exists, there are several shining examples of equine-orientated research being undertaken to a standard of excellence in veterinary schools and departments of research institutes in the UK. Their success results from the establishment of the factors already referred to, namely the quality and experience of the researchers and supporting staff, good leadership and coordination, and state-of-the-art equipment. Above all, it is vital to have the right size of team to meet the criteria of critical mass, with each member eager to collaborate with their close colleagues and colleagues in other institutes as appropriate. Such teams will compete successfully for funding but the rest will struggle. It will be the quality of the science which will dictate success or failure. Unless equine-orientated research can be organised and sustained along these lines it is unlikely to survive effectively into the 21st century,

Undergraduate Education

One of the most important issues relating to the future wellbeing of equine practice concerns the persistent policy in this country, still insisted upon by the RCVS, that every graduate should leave university capable of dealing with any contingency relating to any animal species. The Royal College is undoubtedly giving considerable thought to this unrealistic situation. The Pew Report had this to say on the subject, that *"the universal veterinarian is outmoded and should be abandoned...it is an anachronism and should be buried with honour."* It goes on to say that *"the concept is inhibiting the progress of our profession and is at the very root of serious problems facing veterinary educational institutes today."*

The section ends with the following sentence: *"To be prepared for the 21st century, a veterinarian must be knowledgeable about health and disease in animals in general and have experience in depth in the application of this knowledge clinically to a single class of animal or species."* Such changes in approach to undergraduate education will have to be adopted in this country eventually. Equine practice, relating as it does to a single species, can only benefit from such changes. Electives within the curriculae are a step in the right direction but what is required is a form of 'streaming' along species lines during all the clinical years. There would have to be the opportunity to switch during the first year of 'streaming' if a student felt that a wrong decision had been taken.

Veterinary Nurses (Equine)

However well qualified and experienced veterinarians in practice may be and however good the facilities in which they work, the ultimate success of the practice depends greatly on the quality and dedication of lay staff.

There is no doubt that the scheme to train and register veterinary nurses (previously known as RANAs) instigated and administered by the RCVS since the mid-1960s has been an enormous success. There are now 2867 veterinary nurses registered and 5700 have qualified since 1963. The effect upon the efficiency and quality of service in small animal practice has been phenomenal. It is therefore very pleasing that, since 1995, the RCVS, BVNA and BEVA have been working towards the introduction of Veterinary Nurses (Equine). Such a move is long overdue and one cannot but wonder why it has taken so long. Currently the RCVS is considering possible changes to Schedule 3 Amendment Order 1991 to the Veterinary Surgeon Act 1966. The range of activities which are currently so restrictive may be eased for all VNs. At the same time, plans for trainees to select modules relating to their specific species interests are being considered. If the outcome of both these potentially important changes are positive then equine practice and equine undergraduate and postgraduate training will be enhanced in the long term.

Conclusion

No doubt additional points could have been made in relation to the future of equine medicine but, hopefully, enough has been covered to suggest what is likely to happen. In summary, little effect is likely from a national standpoint from changes in human and equine populations into the foreseeable future. Urbanisation may have local and/or regional consequences but on a limited scale. If the UK economy falters as a result of joining the European Single Currency or for other reasons, then the extent of horse ownership may change and equine veterinary practice could be the most vulnerable section of the overall veterinary activity. On the other hand, equine practice and even the research which is currently well supported by sections of the equine industry and equine-related charities are all in a satisfactory state with steady expansion occurring. In this regard it seems safe to be optimistic.

The main cloud on the horizon reaches far wider than equine matters and involves veterinary training and research in the long term; and whether or not there may be a decline in the quality of both due to underfunding. The outlook is not encouraging but the teaching staff and particular groups of research workers are doing a superb job in spite of increasingly difficult circumstances. Let us hope the help they need is forthcoming.

Horses and herbs: the ancient and modern

RACHEL GREEN
351 Exning Road
Newmarket
Suffolk CB8 0AU
UK

"...and what I have been preparing to say, that in wildness is the preservation of the World. Every tree sends its fibres forth in search of the Wild. The cities import it at any price. Men plow and sail for it. From the forest and wilderness come the tonics and barks which brace mankind..." -Henry David Thoreau in *Walden, or Life in the Woods,* 1854

The use of herbal medicine to treat horses has become very popular in recent times with a large increase in the variety of herbal supplements now available for many different conditions. Some horse owners may already use herbal therapy on themselves and may choose this form of treatment for their horses either together with, or instead of, more conventional veterinary medicine.

Most of the literature currently available to promote the use of herbal medicine in horses is based on hearsay, folklore and tradition. However, herbal medicine itself is one of the oldest forms of medicine, having been practised by mankind for many centuries. Around 5000 BC it is known that there were Chaldean herbalists and by 3000 BC the ancient Egyptians undoubtedly had a sophisticated knowledge of herbs. Together with their use in the treatment of disease, herbs also formed an important part of their diet and their effects on the body were well known.

One of the earliest recorded herbals, or *materia medica*, came from China. It was written by a Chinese herbalist, Shen Nong, who lived around 2700 BC and studied herbs in great detail. This listed the medical use of over 350 herbal substances which were grouped into three categories: nontoxic, mildly toxic and toxic. Included in this book were the *Ephedra* species, used for bronchial difficulties, the purgative *Ricinus communis* and the opium poppy, *Papaver somniferum*. These plants form the basis for the modern medicines ephedrine, castor oil and morphine, respectively.

The *Ebers Papyrus*, thought to have been written about 1500 BC, is perhaps one of the most famous and earliest herbal pharmacopoeias. It lists over 800 remedies containing plants and many other substances such as minerals and details long usage of herbs, such as elder and wormwood.

In the 1st century AD, Pedanius Dioscorides, who journied with the surgeons of the well-travelled Roman armies, wrote the authoritative reference *De Materia Medica*. This has been called *"the most influential Western herbal of all time"* and was a standard reference for 1500 years. *De Materia Medica* describes some 600 herbs, many of which remain today in modern pharmacopoeias, and Dioscorides was particularly famous for the section which detailed many previously unknown plants.

Around 460–380 BC, the Greek physician Hippocrates whose discoveries were so influential that the modern world called him 'The Father of Medicine', studied the effects that various foods had on the body, advocating the use of diet and plant medicines to prevent and cure disease. He recognised both the beneficial and harmful effects of plants and prescribed amongst others the bark and leaves of the willow tree which contained salicin to help relieve pain and fever. He also understood that a close relationship existed between nutrition and medicine, nutrition being vital for the maintenance of good health. In addition, he put forward the fundamental theory that illness was caused by an imbalance of body fluid, i.e. the 'four humours', blood, phlegm, yellow and black bile. The 'Hippocratic Oath' enshrined in the medical profession today bears his name and medical practices were based on the philosophy of Hippocrates up until the time of Paracelsus in the 16th century. However, although Hippocrates was considered the most important medical intellect of early times, it was Galen (AD 131–200), surgeon to the gladiators, who achieved greater fame. Personal physician to Emperor Marcus Aurelius, he adopted the Hippocratic teaching of the four humours and made it the cornerstone of an elaborate system of medicine whereby he brought order and a complete classification of the herbal materia medica, evaluating all medicinal plants in terms of their reaction with a patient's 'humours'.

From 1493–1541, a Swiss-German doctor Philippus Theophrastus Bombastus von Hohenheim, or Paracelsus as he was later known, became famous for his unconventional views on medicine and for his professional skills. He was of the opinion that a thorough familiarity with the causes and symptoms of disease, and the ability to prescribe successfully for them, was imperative. He wrote: *"All substances are poisons; there is none which is not a poison. The right dose differentiates a poison and a remedy."* The alliance of medicine with commerce at the patient's expense always aggrieved Paracelsus and he repeatedly denounced it. Much emphasis has been placed on Paracelsus's advocacy of chemical medicine and of drugs prepared from minerals and his thinking was certainly influenced by the traditions of Swiss-German folk medicine, which three centuries later became famous as homeopathy.

The herbs used today in modern medicine have been in use for centuries as historically recorded by Dioscorides and Hippocrates. However, today, in China alone, there are around 7000 species of plants which are used in herbal medicine but only 230 of the most commonly used ones have been subjected to in-depth pharmacological, analytical and clinical studies. It is still a mistaken belief that the species of plants being used today are the same species used historically, but the actual chemical characteristics of the plant may have changed for many reasons, for example due to changes in the environment. It has also been discovered that certain herbs thought previously to have been safe have now been found to contain carcinogens, for example, comfrey.

Herbal medicine has evolved over many centuries and different cultures have different approaches to the subject. However, a significant percentage of the modern medicines currently used today originated from wild plants, including salicylic acid (aspirin), obtained from the bark of the white willow (*Salix alba*) and digitalis which was originally derived from dried leaves of the foxglove plant (*Digitalis purpurea*). Herbal medicine is mainly concerned with the study of those plants which may be used for therapeutic purposes. However, a difference exists between the modern medicines of today and the more traditional therapies which use only natural materials; modern drugs are used to attack the symptom whereas traditional therapies actually treat the body itself.

The chemistry of most herbs is also very complex. Their active constituents include alkaloids, which are the most common ingredient in plants and may have varying toxic or medicinal effects on the body. Some herbs - *Cantharathus roseus*, for example - have been found to contain over 75 different alkaloids. These exist in small quantities in many plant species and form the basis of many of today's modern drugs such as morphine, quinine, atropine and codeine. Herbs may also contain flavonoids, bioflavonoids, glycosides, mucilage, saponins and tannins. The foxglove plant contains over 30 different glycosides which have cardiotonic properties, each differing in potency, time of onset and duration of activity.

In their natural state, herbs have a unique make-up as individual as a fingerprint and the proportions of the constituents contained within herbs may fluctuate as they are dependent on many variables, e.g. the time of day in which they are harvested, weather and soil conditions. It should also be remembered that, contrary to popular wisdom, because herbal medicines are natural does not necessarily mean they are harmless. The natural toxins contained within herbs have the same mechanisms of toxicity as those produced synthetically.

Knowledge is still extremely limited of the constituents of herbs and their pharmacological and possible toxic effects and one should always be cautious before administering herbal medicine.

Before coming to a decision about when, and for what reason, to use a herbal product to treat a condition in a horse, it is important to try and establish which part of the plant was used, its active ingredients, the conditions in which it was harvested and processed, its safety and potential side effects and whether it has been shown to be the same or superior than pharmaceutical products available for the same purpose. Some herbal products may actually have been formulated from books on the use of herbs in human medicine, which could be dangerous, mainly because of what is known as species difference. This obviously also has implications in the complex area of toxicology.

Nowadays, the horses that live and work for us do so in an environment which is very different from that of their predecessors. For example, their place in our society and the demands man has placed upon them have changed dramatically over time. They do not live a natural life because of man's expectations of their ability to adapt to new and improved diets, their living conditions and physical capabilities. Generally, they appear to thrive well on it, but the physical, mental and environmental pressures involved have almost certainly led to an increase in the number of horses affected by chronic and recurrent health problems rarely observed in their ancestors. Imbalances or deficiencies in a horse's diet will obviously predispose it to disease and over the past few years, the number of products containing herbs available on the market for horses has considerably increased to try and help prevent and alleviate a wide variety of medical conditions.

Herbal supplements for horses are now available in several different forms, i.e. dried, powders and tinctures, and may be recommended for many different purposes including the treatment of digestive, respiratory and joint problems and disorders. They are also being increasingly used in the field of behaviour with a range of herbal products claiming to have calming effects, e.g. valerian, scullcap and chamomile.

Unfortunately, legal standards do not currently exist for the processing, harvesting or packaging of herbs as they do with manufactured drugs. Even if herbs suitable for use by man are used, there can be risks regarding products which have been imported. Some may even contain unidentifiable toxic substances. Environmental pollution and the use of chemicals in the husbandry of herbs are also clearly undesirable influences.

Generally, the labels of herbal remedies do not list any information about the side effects, dangers and contraindications of their use as well as not providing the required dosage. The lack of regulations regarding good manufacturing practices for these products and the lack of requirements for disclosure of all ingredients makes it very difficult to know what one is actually giving a horse when you provide a herbal supplement. Even if it is possible to obtain accurate information and determine the correct dosage and route of administration of a herbal remedy, few herbal medicines have both the scientific name of the herb and expiry date on the bottle. Common names may also be shared by several herbs, only one or two of which are medicinal.

For centuries, in their natural environment, horses have instinctively selected specific foods to obtain and maintain optimum nutrition. However, as already mentioned, the diet of the modern horse is far removed from its natural requirements and one of the most important aspects of this is the lack of specific herbage in modern pasture and consequently in most hay. One reason for this decline is the advancement of monoculture involving the use of quick-release fertilisers. Whilst this undoubtedly causes rapid growth in a few species of grasses, the herbage which takes longer to grow is suffocated. Also, vital minerals may be depleted from the soil and disappear into drainage water. The traditional pastures where horses once grazed may have contained many species of grasses and herbage; however, the modern pastures of today contain much fewer. It is for this

Modern management of pasture is increasingly shifting the balance in herbage away from the horse's natural fodder (illustration by John Fuller).

reason that herbs are now included in some compound feeds for horses and many can be purchased as separate supplements sold for different purposes.

It is thought that horses, together with other grazing animals, commonly suffer from the effect of mild toxicity, possibly because they are forced to feed on certain plants in the absence of more suitable species, although it is very unlikely that feral horses poison themselves with plants because they usually have access to an abundance of natural food.

However, many species of poisonous plants e.g. bracken and ragwort still grow today in our forests and fields, and their poison may build up slowly over time in the system and cause a gradual decline in health with the accumulation of toxins. These are capable of irritating, damaging or impairing tissue activity which can be the direct result of a single substance or a combination of substances producing a poisonous effect. Other poisonous plants, such as yew, can kill a horse immediately. However, the most common causes of fatal or serious poisoning in horses are as a result of the ingestion of ragwort, yew, laburnum or bracken.

Equine veterinarians should be familiar with the wide variety of toxicities related to the treatment of horses with herbal medicine and be aware of the contraindications and side effects of the administration of herbs before giving advice to horse owners. Conversely, horse owners should also advise their vet if they are using herbal medicines, particularly if herbs known to have a calming or sedatory effect have been used in an emergency situation.

Because some herbs contain active pharmacological ingredients the veterinarian, together with unsuspecting horse owner and trainer, may encounter difficulties with regard to the reporting of positive drugs tests resulting from the administration of commercially available herbal products to horses, particularly those used in competition or racing.

Unfortunately, the demand for those with expertise in veterinary herbal medicine and nutrition is not balanced with the availability of appropriately qualified people. For the safety of the horse and to comply with the law, the animal should be examined by a veterinary surgeon before any advice is given.

Herbal remedies have also been shown to reduce the effectiveness of some concurrently administered conventional medications and this is one of the reasons why many equine veterinarians remain sceptical about their use. There is also a lack of substantial clinical evidence and published results in peer-reviewed journals on the efficacy of herbal medicine; and veterinarians do not widely recommend its use to horse owners instead of conventional treatment with veterinary medicine. More studies on the interactions between traditional and modern medicines will certainly be required before veterinarians feel comfortable prescribing herbal remedies alongside conventional medicine.

As we enter the third millennium, there can be few, if any, forms of medicament that so unites the distant past with the present, as that of herbal remedies.

Looking out from the ivory towers: some personal reflections of the role of the equine academic clinician

ROGER SMITH
The Royal Veterinary College
Hawkeshead Lane, North Mymms
Herts AL9 7TA
UK

"To study the phenomenon of disease without books is to sail an uncharted sea, while to study books without patients is not to go to sea at all" Sir William Osler

Introduction

What is the role of university academic clinicians? My personal viewpoint, from within the British system, is that their role is, has been, and hopefully will continue to be, to make a central contribution to the welfare of the horse by promoting the development of equine clinical practice and clinically relevant research, and by education of equine veterinarians to high standards.

Veterinary schools emphasise three areas in which academic clinicians should perform – education, research, and clinical work. All areas complement each other and cannot be prioritised. The veterinary schools occupy a unique place within the university system. They are the only departments engaged in clinical service, situated entirely within the university system – the medical profession relies heavily on the National Health hospitals to contribute to clinical teaching. Objective assessment of research quality is used increasingly as a standard by which to determine government funding within the universities. This leads to additional pressure on university clinicians to compete for research funding with other university departments that are entirely devoted to research and have no clinical responsibilities.

Is there, therefore, any place for the academic clinician? Might the universities' needs not be better served by full-time researchers? The academic clinician has a critical role in ensuring quality, relevance and clinical applicability in both veterinary research and clinical education. With respect to research, academic clinicians can be regarded as a communicator, both in bringing questions from the clinic floor to a basic science research facility and in translating advances in fundamental knowledge into practical solutions to clinical problems. These roles cannot be fulfilled by either full-time research scientists or clinicians working without the support of scientific resources. Effective research into clinical problems cannot be provided without quality clinical material and input from experienced and highly trained clinicians.

On the other hand, Teaching Quality Assessment is here to stay. It is no longer acceptable for institutes maintained by the public purse to be unaccountable. All university departments document clear learning objectives, and demonstrate that they provide the environment necessary for students to attain them. Therefore, should the universities employ individuals whose sole responsibility is to teach? It is critical that those responsible for determining and executing the content of the veterinary undergraduate curriculum are experienced clinicians active in the practice of veterinary medicine and surgery.

But, can one person be involved actively in all three areas effectively? This is the constant dilemma that faces every academic clinician. In recent years, universities have recognised this problem and are addressing it by ensuring that individual areas of clinical service are not 'one-deep' allowing staff to divide blocks of time more effectively to concentrate on these activities.

Education

Education of Veterinary Undergraduates

"The professional is more than a bundle of competencies"

There is much debate on the selection of our future generations of veterinarians, our methods of education within the university system, and the quality of the final product. This debate arises frequently from the observation that new graduates are not well suited to the practice environment in which they are placed immediately after qualifying. The universities have a clear responsibility to provide the new graduate with a theoretical knowledge that is broad, detailed and current. This must be coupled with competence in basic technical tasks, communication skills and with experience in clinical decision making. However, employers of new graduates also have a responsibility to allow these individuals to continue to develop, expand and refine their technical skills and to continue their education.

Are we selecting the wrong people to enter the veterinary course? Demand for places in veterinary school far outstrips supply. While this may be considered a disadvantage by some, I consider that it is the one of the major methods for maintaining a well-respected profession. Universities are often criticised for taking 'boffins'. Ten years of experience of working with veterinary students has convinced me that a talent for science and common sense are by no means mutually exclusive characteristics. The profession requires more than technicians, and we are presented with the most gifted of our youth, an opportunity of which every other profession is aware and jealous.

The universities now demand not only high A-level grades but also evidence that applicants have experienced the nature of the profession and spent time within the agricultural and veterinary industry before applying to veterinary school. This ensures that veterinary undergraduates are cognisant of the profession they are entering and are not surprised (or disappointed) when they graduate. Another important facet of the selection at the Royal Veterinary College (RVC) is the interview when a panel of both university academics and clinical practitioners assess whether the character of the applicant is appropriate. It is hard to appreciate an improvement in this rigorous selection procedure which causes those near to it to marvel at the quality of the applicants who gain entry to the veterinary schools.

In recent years, educationalists have recognised the need to move away from the simple transmission of factual knowledge to more emphasis on attaining higher learning skills, such as analysis, synthesis and evaluation. It is no longer reasonable or desirable to expect veterinary undergraduates to amass and regurgitate a colossal number of unrelated and random facts, with no understanding of their clinical relevance. The modern veterinary curriculum

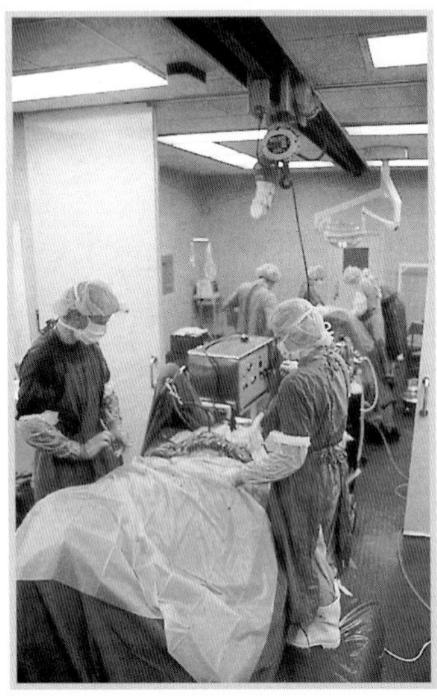

The author (left) at work.

incorporates fewer lectures and problem-based seminars occupy a central role in teaching methods. Rather than the traditional four or five years spent yawning in a lecture theatre, students are presented with clinical problems, from the earliest years of the course. Pre- and paraclinical sciences are integrated with clinical teaching throughout the course and the final year at the RVC and other veterinary schools is now free of all lectures. It follows then, that the academic clinician has an expanding role in veterinary education, as we are called upon to provide contributions to components of the course that were, in the past, executed by the pure scientists. Students are made responsible for their own learning by researching a series of practical, real-life clinical problems. These principles enable professionals to progress more rapidly in the development of their knowledge and skills in what is always a rapidly expanding field.

Is it essential that universities maintain teaching hospitals to provide clinical experience for veterinary undergraduates? Could we revert to a system of apprenticeships as practised in previous centuries? In my opinion, such a move would be disastrous both for veterinary education and for the profession as a whole. The alternative of transferring full responsibility for clinical education to private practice is unworkable – not least because there would be great difficulty in defraying the costs associated with the considerable time that would have to be spent by practitioners on education. Furthermore, the maintenance of standards and consistency of education would be impossible and increased variability would ensue. However, I recognise that it is essential that students spend time in practice and this is achieved in extra-mural studies and in the universities' first-opinion practices. Throughout the five year course, students spend a minimum of 26 weeks in practice and it is a credit to our profession that practitioners welcome, educate and supervise them.

It is essential that the universities maintain high quality clinics for the education of veterinary undergraduates. The universities possess some of the best facilities for clinical work, funded largely by charitable organisations. At veterinary school, undergraduates spend blocks of time within the clinics, subdivided into different disciplines, such as surgery, medicine, anaesthesia, and reproduction. During this time, students have intimate contact with the cases where they have responsibilities for monitoring and treating in-patients under supervision. They are expected to become accomplished record keepers, a vital skill for their subsequent career, and participate in case discussions concerning management options and financial implications of treatment. This would not be possible without the presence of an active, competitive and quality clinic staffed by experienced clinicians.

In addition, there is increasing specialisation within our profession after qualification and it may not be long before veterinary students qualify as either 'large animal' or 'small animal' veterinarians. Many students have already decided which branch of the profession they wish to enter before they qualify and the final phase of their education seeks to advance their knowledge and practical skills in the field they have chosen. At the RVC, as at other veterinary schools, considerable pride and importance has been placed on the Electives system – a three month period at the end of the course when undergraduates chose one of many subjects which are either species or discipline based. The students receive more detailed tuition, often similar to Royal College ofVeterinary Surgeons (RCVS) certificate level, and spend one month engaged on a small research project. The latter provides them with some basic research training, an essential generic skill, whether in practice or pure research. The accompanying preparation of reports and presentations in front of their peers ensures that they develop communication skills, so important to a veterinarian in practice, education, or research.

Education of Postgraduates

Clinical education within the universities is not restricted to veterinary undergraduates. There is now an established programme in every university for clinical training scholarships (internships and residencies). In the equine field, we are particularly fortunate that these programmes are generously funded by the Horserace Betting Levy Board and The Home of Rest for Horses, with additional scholarships being funded by clinical income. Scholarships provide an opportunity for young veterinarians to obtain further qualifications such as certificates and diplomas from the RCVS and European-based qualifications within a specialised equine clinic. Although, currently, such qualifications are not regarded as essential for equine practice, there is an increasing move within society to expect that professional individuals cannot only claim, but also document their competence.

Universities are increasingly involved in providing opportunities for continuing professional development (CPD). This is now perceived by most graduates as a necessity, rather than a luxury. Courses of CPD are often provided in collaboration with veterinary associations, such as the BEVA, and university clinicians play a prominent role. This is an important aspect of equine veterinary education and, for the academic clinician, often presenting an enjoyable and constructive opportunity to discuss clinical problems with colleagues from practice.

Education in Other Areas

As paraclinical professions evolve and are, hopefully, licensed and regulated in future to ensure minimum standards, teaching of these allied disciplines will be necessary. I believe universities, and in particular university clinicians, to be integral in this process. Nursing and physiotherapy courses are already becoming established within the university system.

Neither should education finish here. The welfare of the horse relies on the knowledge of horse owners; and it is an important role of equine clinicians within and outside academia, to provide formal and informal education to the public.

Research

If the veterinary profession neglects research we can expect to stagnate in our clinical practice. However, it is imperative that the profession and the horse's needs are carefully targeted. Advances made on a wide research front are slow and costly. Our research should be appropriate for the problems in our patients and for this reason clinical input is essential and it is in this area that the equine academic clinician can excel. But research should not be directed only at the applied level, we also need basic science investigations into mechanisms to provide future advances.

The research community can be justifiably criticised for failing to transmit the results of its research to the horse-owning public in a format which they can understand. This failure to explain research objectives and findings frequently causes research to be considered expensive but ineffective. It is essential that academic clinicians are active in this area.

Clinical Work

The university clinic is an essential asset for the education of veterinary under- and postgraduates; and as an important vehicle for applied research and audit. The modern university clinic has facilities that are second to none but is still required to be run economically; not only because it is not supported by government funding but also so that undergraduates appreciate the financial constraints under which equine veterinarians frequently have to work. Because the universities are involved in teaching and research, they are often considered in a different light to the private clinics; however, they function in a very similar fashion and have the added benefit of a wide breadth of expertise. The Royal Veterinary College clinic has six RCVS specialists in equine clinical sciences, not to mention comparative specialities, such as ophthalmology and dermatology, also led by RCVS Specialists. Such powerful university bases maximise clinical progress and many of the clinical advances in recent years have been initiated or developed within the university clinics by academic clinicians. Furthermore, many of the stars of equine veterinary practice work in, or began their careers within, the academic sector. The university and private clinics are synergistic in these advances – it has been impressive how new techniques have been transferred rapidly to the private sector. It is the close cooperation between practice and university that continues to offer the answer to rapid progress in caring for the horse.

The most up-to-date facilities, large staff base and the presence of large numbers of enthusiastic and capable students within the university clinic enable the provision of intensive care, a multidisciplinary approach to cases and the ability to collaborate with experts from comparative disciplines, e.g. in pathology and the small animal clinic. Academic clinicians can also coordinate multicentre trials of new treatments and methods with other universities and private clinics.

Does the clinic provide an enjoyable and functional environment for the academic clinician? The answer to this question is yes, without a doubt. I thrive on the discussions of cases with colleagues and with students and, in my experience at least, this provides the most balanced, and therefore best, decision-making in clinical cases, not to mention maintaining the standard of the individual clinicians! The extra time involved with the teaching of students while in the clinic is a small price to pay in the goal of effective care and welfare of the horse.

The Future

What is the future for the equine academic clinician? We have a wealth of academic talent in this country both within the universities and in practice. It is essential that this talent is harnessed effectively and in a fashion that enables us to advance our care of the horse. We must encourage a proportion of our graduates to pursue a career in the academic sector – it can be an immensely satisfying job. While this may have been difficult in the past for financial reasons, universities are now augmenting salaries for academic clinicians.

The universities continue to expand their clinical services, spearheading both applied and basic research with the academic clinician central to its structure. They should maintain a breadth of experience in the clinic and foster collaborative links with other universities and especially their colleagues in practice. The continued flourishing of the academic clinician can, I believe, reap dividends in the new millennium for the individuals concerned, the universities, and the profession as a whole.

Acknowledgements

I would like to thank Professors Stephen May and Sandy Love, and Drs Celia Marr and Eddy Cauvin for valuable discussions during the writing of this article.

Historical perspectives of the Cambridge Veterinary School

LAWSON SOULSBY
The Old Barn House
Swaffham Prior
Cambs
UK

The subtitle of this article was proposed as 'The Ups and Downs of the Cambridge Veterinary School' but, in fact, I prefer 'The Downs and Ups' because every 'down' did, in fact, galvanise a positive response to the betterment of the School. One of the advantages of a 'down' is the realisation of mistakes made, the opportunity to correct them and turn them into an 'up'.

Not quite 50 years ago in 1956, the School ofVeterinary Medicine facilities at Madingley Road were opened by H. M. Queen Elizabeth II accompanied by H. R. H. Prince Philip, this being a fine beginning to a venture which had been long in debate and planning.

The need for teaching and research in comparative medicine and veterinary science in Cambridge was recognised at the turn of the century when Sir Clifford Allbutt, Regius Professor of Physik (Fig 1), urged the establishment in Cambridge of an institute for comparative pathology:

> *"To establish in Cambridge a central institute of comparative pathology, which must include professorial units for the diseases of plants and animals and the means of blending these departments with the neighbouring departments for the diseases of man, will no doubt cost much money, but a sum which when compared only with the waste and destruction of stock and crops would prove to be small indeed. Such is the utilitarian promise, but far beyond this we cannot tell how bright will be the cross-lights which, in a system of comparative medicine, will be thrown reciprocally upon the fields of the several pathologies of all kinds of life."*

Fig 1: Sir Clifford Allbutt.

Developments apposite to this included the establishment, in 1923, of the Institute of Animal Pathology, Milton Road and the appointment of a Professor of Animal Pathology endowed by the Agricultural Research Council. Prof. J. B. Buxton was the first holder of the chair and later became Principal of the Royal Veterinary College, London.

Who was this man Allbutt? Undoubtedly, a man of prodigious intellect and energy, MA MD FRS 1880, when he was 44; KCB (1907); Privy Councillor (1920); Regius Professor of Physik when he was 56; first in Natural Sciences at the age of 24; Fellow of Caius College; Honorary Colonel RAMC; several honorary degrees; Honorary Fellow, Royal Society of Medicine and, perhaps of significance, the first President of the Comparative Medicine Section of the RSM in 1923. His inaugural address *The Integration of Medicine* makes most interesting reading: *"As physic is divorced from surgery and mind from body, so the diseases of animals and plants are separated from those of mankind."* Allbutt died on 22 February 1925, aged 89.

The Institute of Animal Pathology (1923) fared well and quickly became a major research and training centre in the UK and many of its staff and graduate students went on to senior positions at home and overseas. It provided annual reports of animal research and its visitors' book contained the names of the international scientific elite.

But this was a time also when both medical and veterinary education were under detailed scrutiny - probably as a result of Flexner's Report to the Carnigie Foundation in the USA in 1910:

> *"Two kinds of medical schools were private money-making ventures; bickering and feuding was standard means of faculty communication. Standards were low, apart from anatomy, teaching was wholly didactic, many schools had no clinical facilities...".*

This report revolutionised thinking on medical education in North America, sweeping away the apprenticeship system and established the concept that teaching and research go hand in hand.

Veterinary education had yet to tread that road. Perhaps it started in the late 1920s with a Ministry of Agriculture and Fisheries Report on *Reconstruction of the Royal Veterinary College* in 1929. The report stated that the condition of the Royal Veterinary College was a "*national disgrace*" and noted

TABLE 1: Value for money - Cambridge viewpoint.	
Budget from University Grants Committee (1987-1988) Current research funding Hospital income Research income (new grants)	£ 1,131,481 £ 429,639 £ 200,000 £ 624,500
	£ 2,385,620

For this, Cambridge • Produces 45 veterinary graduates per year • Conducts research comparable to AFRC institutes undertaking full-time research (2.05 publications per staff member vs. 1.8 for AFRC Institutes of Animal Health) • Trains postgraduates (25) • Runs referred hospital services (5000 patients) • Runs consultative services • Provides training for overseas veterinarians (12) • Undertakes joint research and research training with Sri Lanka.

that a way out of this situation had been offered by the Ministry of Agriculture and Fisheries - namely the transfer of the Royal Veterinary College to the University of Cambridge, where there was a thriving Institute of Animal Pathology. This was not accepted by the governors of the RVC! Some 60 years later, the working party, chaired by Sir Ralph Riley, made similar recommendations but the other way around. These were not accepted either!

Now, however, veterinary education began to feel the blast of enquiries, reports and investigations. In 1933, a syndicate on Agriculture Research Organisation recommended, to the University of Cambridge, that a Veterinary Diploma be established and a Committee of the General Board was set up to confer with the Council of the Royal College of Veterinary Surgeons on the courses and examinations for such a Diploma. That committee reported in 1934 and, in 1938, following the Report of the Committee on Veterinary Education in Great Britain (the first Loveday Report). Agreement was reached with the Royal College of Veterinary Surgeons on a scheme whereby not more than ten students per year would undertake their preclinical work in Cambridge and complete their clinical work elsewhere. In 1944, the Second Loveday Report recommended the establishment of veterinary clinical training facilities in Cambridge with an annual output of about 30 graduates. The first Loveday Report was scathing about veterinary education.

> *"The basic sciences are in general not adequately taught. The prescribed courses of study concentrate on animal sickness and treat the maintenance of health altogether too lightly. Attention is focused too completely on the curative aspect to the neglect of the preventive; animal husbandry in its wider sense...is not stressed. The farm animal receives too little consideration relative to that given to the horse, the dog and the cat."*

The Second Loveday Report (1944), which recommended that veterinary colleges (as the Schools were then) should become part of universities stated:

> *"Nothing short of this will give veterinary education the standing and the opportunities for development which the increased and still increasing importance of the progression to the national economy deserves and requires."*

In 1949, the School of Veterinary Medicine was established, made up of two new departments, the Department of Animal Pathology (incorporating the former Institute of Animal Pathology), Faculty Board of Biology 'B', and the Department of Veterinary Clinical Studies, Faculty Board of Clinical Medicine, and the Madingley Road site for the School was identified. The first graduates of the School were admitted to membership of the Royal College of Veterinary Surgeons in 1955. The main building was delayed by some two years due to a problem with piles and foundations. One-third of the planned building was not constructed due to increased cost. The proposed join of the existing building, originally to house the library, is still clearly visible.

From the start the School was unusual. The course was six years, not five, as elsewhere. It took time and patience to explain to outsiders the Tripos System and the uniqueness of a system that utilised the strengths of the basic biological sciences departments, and permitted a major element of elective choice in the third year of the course through the Part II system. This was and is a deliberate effort to integrate veterinary education with the rest of biological science in the university. Entry to the veterinary course was, via the colleges, not a single portal entry system as with all the other five schools in the UK. Essentially the School has no say in the students who are admitted. This has led to marked variations in the number of students admitted per year with attendant difficulties in planning clinical teaching.

Over the years, there have been many discussions with admissions tutors on numbers of students to be admitted each year. The colleges shied away from any mention of a 'quota' similar to that for medical students, though in due course colleges grouped together and accepted the concept of a 'quota' in quotes. It was a happy day when the quotes came off the quota!

But a major problem in the early years was the number of students, sometimes not even reaching the teens per year, a far cry from the initially proposed 30 per year. This was nearly its downfall and certainly the cause of the first threat of closure. The Swann Report of 1972 had recommended an entry of 300 students nationally. The University Grants Committee decided it could not justify the School because of low numbers and threatened to withdraw funding. A major effort was made to increase student recruitment at schools and in the colleges. This, with rationalisation of staffing, saved the School.

Following this 'down', the resulting 'up' was the amalgamation of the two Departments of Animal Pathology and Veterinary Clinical Studies into the Department of Clinical Veterinary Medicine, and the appointment of a Head of Department, equivalent to a Dean, with a syndicate to look after its affairs.

Much later, the Department was to acquire faculty status, with its own Faculty Board. A further small step for veterinary students but a giant leap for the profession was the renaming of the Medical Sciences Tripos to the Medical and Veterinary Sciences Tripos. Recognition and respectability for basic teaching in the veterinary course at last!

But the years between the first threat of closure and its solution and the second major threat in 1989 were not easy. Universities in general were underfunded; the high hopes that the Swann Report and its recommendations would solve a number of problems with respect to staffing and facilities were not supported by the government of the day. Nevertheless useful progress was made in staffing; a dairy unit was built; the School took over the Huntingdon Road site after the AFRC vacated it; we established the first chair of Animal Welfare; created the Veterinary School Trust

(CAMVET); set up the first major Cancer Radiation Therapy Unit in a Veterinary School; and built a new teaching block with pathology diagnostic laboratories.

As with many veterinary schools in the world, the needs which dictated the original location of the Cambridge School may change or even cease to exist. Some of the older schools were located in the centre of large cities where horses provided the draught power for transport, public and personal, and milk and meat was produced in a myriad of small dairies and piggeries. Much of this has been swept away by changes in livestock production, now characterised by intensive units of hundreds, sometimes thousands, of animals.

Major changes in agriculture in Cambridge and its environs left, therefore, only a few intensive animal production units in the area and to the casual observer the landscape was bereft of animals, giving rise to the erroneous comment that the Cambridge School had no access to farm animals (Table 2). The School did have a sufficiency of horses because of the high density in the area, but also because of the great surgical skills of our clinicians, particularly Colonel John Hickman and the late Robert Walker. We also had excellent relations with the two major equine practices in Newmarket. This was most welcome since there is much to be gained by a close collaboration between private practices and academic institutions.

Then disaster threatened: the Riley Report recommended the closure of the Clinical Veterinary School at Cambridge and also the Glasgow School, the latter to be united with Edinburgh as a new school at the Edinburgh site.

It is useful to dwell on the effect of the recommendation because it united the University behind the Veterinary School as never before and having vociferously defended the survival of the School it then proceeded, perhaps with a little pushing here and there, to provide additional support and continues to do so!

The news the School was to be closed down in five years' time was received on Monday 23 January 1989 at 8.30 am in the Secretary General's Office. All staff and students were informed immediately. I remember well a student asking, "*We're going to fight this aren't we, sir?*" and the answer was, "*Yes*". The following Saturday the students organised a demonstration in Cambridge protesting at the proposed closure. It was a cold and very wet day but this was ignored as town and gown rose to the defence of the School. Support for survival came from many sources, including those unrelated to veterinary medicine such as the Music School and Oriental Languages. In building a case against closure we needed to look critically at our operations and many interesting points emerged. Thus, while teaching was an important component in the education of veterinary students, we also undertook research and, in fact, published more papers per head of academic staff than a comparable AFRC institutes of animal health where only research was done.

The battle to save the School owes much to a wide range of people: the Vice Chancellor of the day, Michael McCrum; James Wright, Secretary General; Peter Vaugon (deceased) and Gerald Burke of the Old School; Sir Arnold Burgen; David Williams of Wolfson College; the students and staff of the School; the surrounding veterinary divisions of the British Veterinary Association, particularly Lord Kimball; Robert Rhodes-James, MP for Cambridge at the time; the Prime Minister; and Her Majesty The Queen!

The Page Report of 1990 on the number of veterinary graduates required in the UK recommended no closures and with one bound we were free! A subsequent internal review of the School made wide-ranging recommendations on organisation teaching and research, many of which have come or are coming to fruition.

TABLE 2: Animal Populations in the Cambridge Area*

15 mile radius from Cambridge**	
Cattle	31,000
Pigs	134,000
Sheep	31,500
Seven counties around Cambridge	
Cattle	484,469
Pigs	1,683,028
Sheep	816,455
Poultry	19,836,000
Human population	
East Anglia	2 million
East Midlands	4 million

*Figures provided by MAAF regional office Cambridge. Horses are not included in the animal census as they are not classified as agricultural animals.
**We had been criticised for having few farm animals for teaching. In fact, the supply was adequate for 450 visits per year at that time.

And so to the modern stage, of new facilities and innovations growing all the time. But physical facilities important as they are, are not the only requirement for an outstanding School. An important component is the student body. Although, in the early days of the School, student members were low, dangerously low, we have been blessed with an outstanding student body. It has been a bit of a mystery how this came about, especially when the School was not responsible for the selection process. We must put it down to the wisdom of admission tutors. In our analysis of student academic records and performance during the Riley crisis it became apparent that the A levels of veterinary students were significantly higher than the average in the university and that veterinary students gained more 'firsts' than the average.

It would be an easy and pleasant task to detail the graduates who have distinguished themselves in one way or another, but I will not inflict such a list on the reader. Suffice it to say, they are well represented in the important forums of the profession and elsewhere.

At one time it was thought the School would give more emphasis to the production of research workers than general veterinary practitioners. As it turns out, it has emphasised both, with postgraduate training particularly strong in Cambridge, a legacy of the days of the Institute of Animal Pathology and now the reality of a recently constituted postgraduate school in veterinary and biomedical science. Over the 50 years of its existence there has been a steady and increasing flow of postgraduates with PhD degrees, some of whom have gone on to the highest echelons of science.

Some of the more recent developments in postgraduate training include a very strong programme in clinical speciality certificates and diplomas and a particularly important development of a Vet MD degree, allowing the equivalent of the MD degree to be undertaken by clinicians, including those in practice. Perhaps it is somewhat fortuitous that our 50 years of existence comes at the dawn of a new millennium, when the School is stronger and more secure than it has ever been and can advance with pride in its achievements and in step with the other departments of the University of Cambridge.

The story of a skeleton: Eclipse

SHERWIN HALL
14 Huntingdon Road,
Cambridge
CB3 0HH
UK

On 27 February 1789, the celebrated racehorse Eclipse died and there began a fascinating association between his skeleton and the developing veterinary profession in Britain. But before describing the history of the skeleton something should be said of the horse and his owner.

Eclipse

Eclipse was born on 1 April 1764, the day of an eclipse of the sun. He was bred by the Duke of Cumberland and was by Marske out of Spiletta. Marske was a third-generation descendent of the Darley Arabian and Spiletta was a granddaughter of the Godolphin Arabian, on her sire's side. Thus Eclipse combined the blood of two of the famous three foundation sires of the English Thoroughbred.

On the death of the Duke of Cumberland, his stud was sold and Eclipse was purchased by a Leadenhall merchant and grazier called Wildman, who paid 75 guineas for him as a yearling. Wildman did not race Eclipse until he was five years old, when he was entered for a 50 guinea plate at Epsom, in May 1769. That was the beginning of a short racing career. In 18 races, Eclipse was either unbeaten or walked over and, in 1770, he was put to stud. By this time he was owned by Colonel Dennis O'Kelly who had bought a half share in the horse after his second race at Ascot, in 1769. That had cost 650 guineas but, before the year was out, O'Kelly purchased the other half share for 1100 guineas and it has been said that "*no better bargain in horseflesh was ever made*".

Dennis O'Kelly

The new owner of Eclipse was a remarkable man. There is some doubt about his early life because the contemporary references were few or have since been declared scurrilous, but they make a good story and the details are to be found in T.A. Cook's book, *Eclipse and O'Kelly,* published in 1907. In brief, O'Kelly was born to a poor squireen of an old house in County Carlow. He and his brothers had to make their own way in the world and they came to England at an early age to do it. It seems that Dennis had that innate affinity of the Irishman for horses and racing, which served him well in the gambling circles in Georgian London.

He also had a persuasive way with the ladies. It set him on the first rung of the social ladder when he was the 'front legs' of a sedan chair and came to the rescue of a lady whose carriage was blocked in St James's. Another step in his career was a spell in the Fleet Prison, but debt has never been a bar to social progress. While in the Fleet, O'Kelly's fellow inmates called him the 'Count', a name which stuck with him for the rest of his life although he also acquired the title of 'Colonel' in the Westminster Militia. To rank he added fame and fortune; when he died in 1787 he owned a stud in Epsom, a town house in Piccadilly and an estate called Cannons at Stanmore in Middlesex.

The Death of Eclipse

It was at Cannons where Eclipse died on 27 February 1789, 14 months after his colourful owner. At that time there happened to be in London a young French veterinarian, Charles Vial. *"To a good heart and a very generous way of thinking, he united a wonderful share of vanity"* (Bracy Clark, 1861) and, perhaps, it was this that prompted Vial to adopt the cognomen 'Sainbel' for that is how he was known in London where he was living in some style in a house that had been the residence of Sir Isaac Newton. His ambition was to establish a veterinary school in England but his first proposals in 1788 met with no success.

The attention that Sainbel was seeking was rewarded with an invitation to make a *postmortem* examination of Eclipse. Sainbel was said to have performed this in a masterly fashion, proceeding to dissect out the entire skeleton, cleaning it of every covering but the ligaments. The study he made of the skeleton was published in 1791 as *An Essay of the Proportions of Eclipse.* It was printed in French and English and included plates and tables to demonstrate the relative proportions of the various parts of the body and the motions of the limbs. He explained his purpose as threefold:

> *"1. As a sure guide to the brush or chisel of the artist who commonly only employs them in opposition to nature.*
>
> *2. It would teach a better choice of the animals, and to exact from it no greater exertions than Nature had rendered it capable of yielding.*
>
> *3. By means of this table we should be enabled to establish the true conformation of the racehorse and at any given time to discover whether the breed had improved or degenerated."*

According to Blaine in *The Outlines of the Veterinary Art,* 1802, the immediate inspiration for Sainbel was to be found in the first volume of Bourgelat's *Elements d'Hippiatrique,* published in Lyons in 1750, where *"the subject matter itself may be seen with little alteration".* Bourgelat had been Sainbel's professor at the Paris veterinary school and had taken his inspiration from Leonardo da Vinci's concept of perfect proportions established 300 years previously. Leonardo's diaries describe how he divided the horse's head into 12 units as a reference for modelling the proportions of the body.

Sainbel used the same system of units. At that time his dissection was acclaimed and it helped in achieving his ambition. Two years later the first veterinary school in the English-speaking world was established in London and Sainbel was the first professor, although not for long; he died in 1793, it is said, of glanders.

The Skeleton

It is not certain what happened to the skeleton in the first few years of its existence. Cook traced its history to the beginning of this century and cites a reference by Bracy Clark in which it is said the skeleton was given to Edmund Bond of Lower Brook Street, Grosvenor Square by Dennis O'Kelly. There is some confusion here: as noted above, Dennis O'Kelly predeceased Eclipse. He willed the bulk of his estate to his nephew Andrew Dennis O'Kelly whose father, Philip O'Kelly, appears to have been in charge of the stud. To compound the confusion, Andrew Dennis was also known as Colonel O'Kelly. So it was either Philip or Andrew Dennis who gave the skeleton to Edmund Bond who was the veterinary surgeon for the horses in Philip's charge. Bracy Clark said that when Bond died he assisted the widow in some business matters in consequence of which he acquired the skeleton. It is not known when Bond died but, many years later, Bracy Clark's daughter, at the age of 91, recalled seeing the bones in her father's study in 1825. At that time the skeleton was not mounted.

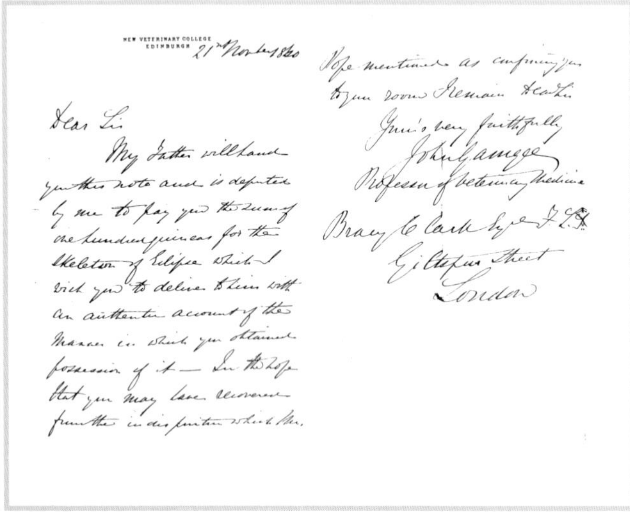

NEW VETERINARY COLLEGE
EDINBURGH 21st Nov 1860

Dear Sir

My Father will hand you this note and is deputed by me to pay you the sum of one hundred guineas for the skeleton of Eclipse which I wish you to deliver to him with an authentic account of the manner in which you obtained possession of it — In the hope that you may have recovered from the indisposition which Mr. Hope mentioned as confining you to your room I remain Dear Sir

Yours very faithfully
John Gamgee
Professor of Veterinary Medicine

Bracy Clark Esq F.L.S.
Giltspur Street
London

The letter from John Gamgee to Bracy Clark, confirming purchase of the skeleton.

In November 1860, the skeleton was purchased by John Gamgee for 100 guineas and his receipt, signed by Bracy Clark, can be seen today, mounted with the skeleton. It was John's father, Joseph Gamgee, who collected the bones from Bracy Clark and removed them from London to the Edinburgh New Veterinary College which John had established in 1857. The Gamgees mounted the bones for display as a complete skeleton and reexamined the measurements for the first time since Sainbel's dissection. In 1861 there is an account in the *Edinburgh Veterinary Review* pointing out *"some very important errors which found their way into M. Sainbel's essay"* and it is known that John Gamgee's brother-in-law, Clark Stanton, the artist, made a drawing of the skeleton which was used as a frontispiece for volume one of Gamgee and Law's two volume work entitled *A General and Descriptive Anatomy of the Domesticated Animals*. The removal of the bones to Edinburgh had aroused some doubts in the press on their authenticity but, in a letter to *The Scotsman* dated 30 November 1860, Joseph Gamgee cited the verbal authority of Bracy Clark given to him when he collected the bones, as evidence that they were those of Eclipse.

In 1865 John Gamgee moved his veterinary school from Edinburgh to London where it was known as the Albert Veterinary College. Soon after this move the school failed; John went on a visit to the USA and Joseph, his bitterly disappointed father, remained in Edinburgh. Having no further use for the skeleton, the Gamgees presented it to the Royal College of Veterinary Surgeons, in January 1871.

For many years thereafter the skeleton mouldered in the museum of the Royal College. There was a passing reference to it in 1891 and, in 1902, it became an item of council business. The secretary reported that the director of the British Museum (Natural History) had *"ventured to ask whether the RCVS would consider the question of presenting the skeleton of Eclipse... to the trustees of the British Museum"*. The secretary had been instructed to say that, *"he could hold out no hope that the skeleton would be handed over to the museum; it was the gift of an eminent veterinary surgeon and much prized by the profession"*. The council approved that decision although one cannot believe that the skeleton was much prized by the profession. Mr Wragg had examined it that morning and wished *"to call attention to the very dirty and dusty state it was in ... if it is not kept in a clean state there will soon be no skeleton of Eclipse at all"*. Professor Mettam asked:

> *"Is the museum committee ornamental or is it useful? Does it ever meet or has it anything to do with the museum? I was in the museum this morning and I think it more a place to set potatoes in than anything else."*

Nothing was done and two years later it was again a topic of council business when Colonel Duck complained that:

> *"Such a memento, I might almost venture to call it a national one, should not be relegated to a garret in this house."*

Professor Mettam proposed that it should be referred to the museum committee and added:

> *"I have been on the museum committee for 12 months and we have never met yet, and I think it is about time we should."*

Eventually the so-called museum of the Royal College was needed to provide space for the library and, in 1920, 18 years after the request, the council resolved that the skeleton of Eclipse should be offered on loan to the Natural History Museum at South Kensington. It seems that it was no longer *"much prized by the profession"* and was now in the way. The trustees of the museum were glad to accept the offer made by the Royal College and for the next 62 years the skeleton was in their care.

In April 1983, the National Horseracing Museum in Newmarket was opened by Her Majesty, the Queen. One of the prominent exhibits is the skeleton of Eclipse, brought from the Natural History Museum. Before leaving London, the bones were measured once more, this time by a method used by archaeologists for recording details of animal bones. This examination revealed that the pedal bones had been transposed; not only were the 'fore' ones obviously from the hind limbs but the 'hind' ones were showing extensive changes due to laminitis. It was well known that Eclipse was 'foundered'. In the book by Cook there is a series of photographs of the skeleton which were taken in 1906. Close examination of these reveals that one of the affected pedal bones was on a hindlimb while the other was on a forelimb. At that time the skeleton was at the Royal College of Veterinary Surgeons.

The same photographs reveal that, apart from the wooden base, the skeleton had not been remounted, presumably since the Gamgees did it in 1861. If this conclusion is correct one wonders why the neck is not in a more natural position. Surely the Gamgees would not have had it sticking out straight and low as it is now and in the 1906 photograph? The Clark Stanton drawing, done in Edinburgh, does portray it in a more natural position but even that appears to be somewhat straight.

The story now comes full circle back to the Royal Veterinary College. To mark the bicentenary of the College in 1991 and its association with Eclipse and Sainbel, Mr Paul Mellon, the American collector of sporting art, donated a picture of Eclipse painted in 1770 by George Stubbs and a bronze statue of the horse by James Osborne.

There remains yet another twist. A few years ago Mr Norman Comben MRCVS, bibliographer and keen collector of veterinary printed books and artifacts, saw a copy of Cook's book *Eclipse and O'Kelly* listed in a catalogue of a London sale. The description stated that the lot included a letter about the Eclipse skeleton from a Mr Gamage. He immediately realised its provenance and bought it. Not only did he have the 1860 letter from John Gamgee to Bracy Clark, but there was also a receipt signed by D. O'Kelly for a stud fee to Eclipse paid to Colonel O'Kelly. A second receipt, signed by Edmund Bond, was for a stud fee to

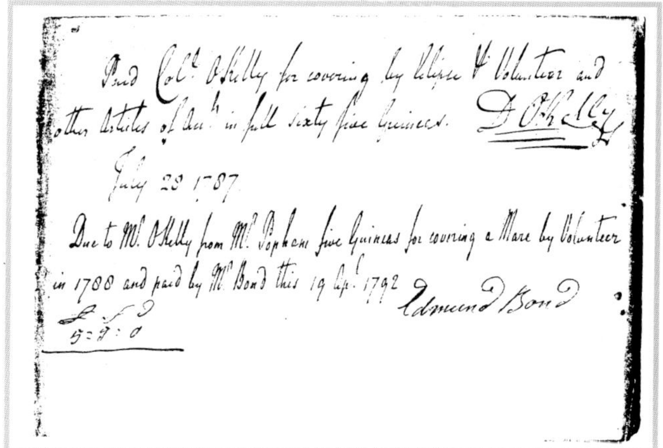
Paid Colˡ O'Kelly for covering by Eclipse & Volunteer and other Articles of Accᵗ in full sixty five Guineas. D O'Kelly

July 28 1787

Due to Mʳ O'Kelly from Mʳ Popham five Guineas for covering a Mare by Volunteer in 1788 and paid by Mʳ Bond this 19 Sep. 1792 Edmund Bond

£ s d
5 : 5 : 0

Reeipt for a stud fee to Eclipse, July 1787.

Volunteer, another of Colonel O'Kelly's stallions and also painted by Stubbs. As mentioned above, Edmund Bond was veterinary surgeon to the O'Kellys. He was the first student to qualify from the London school; and it was his widow who gave the skeleton to Bracy Clark.

Acknowledgement

I am indebted to Miss Katherine Whitwell FRCVS for details of the transfer of the skeleton from London to Newmarket.

Further Reading

Blaine, D. (1802) *The Outlines of the Veterinary Art,* Longman and Rees,. London.

Cook, T.A. (1907) *Eclipse and O'Kelly*, William Heinemann, London.

Thompson, Ruth D'Arcy (1974) *The Remarkable Gamgees*, Ramsey Head Press, Edinburgh.

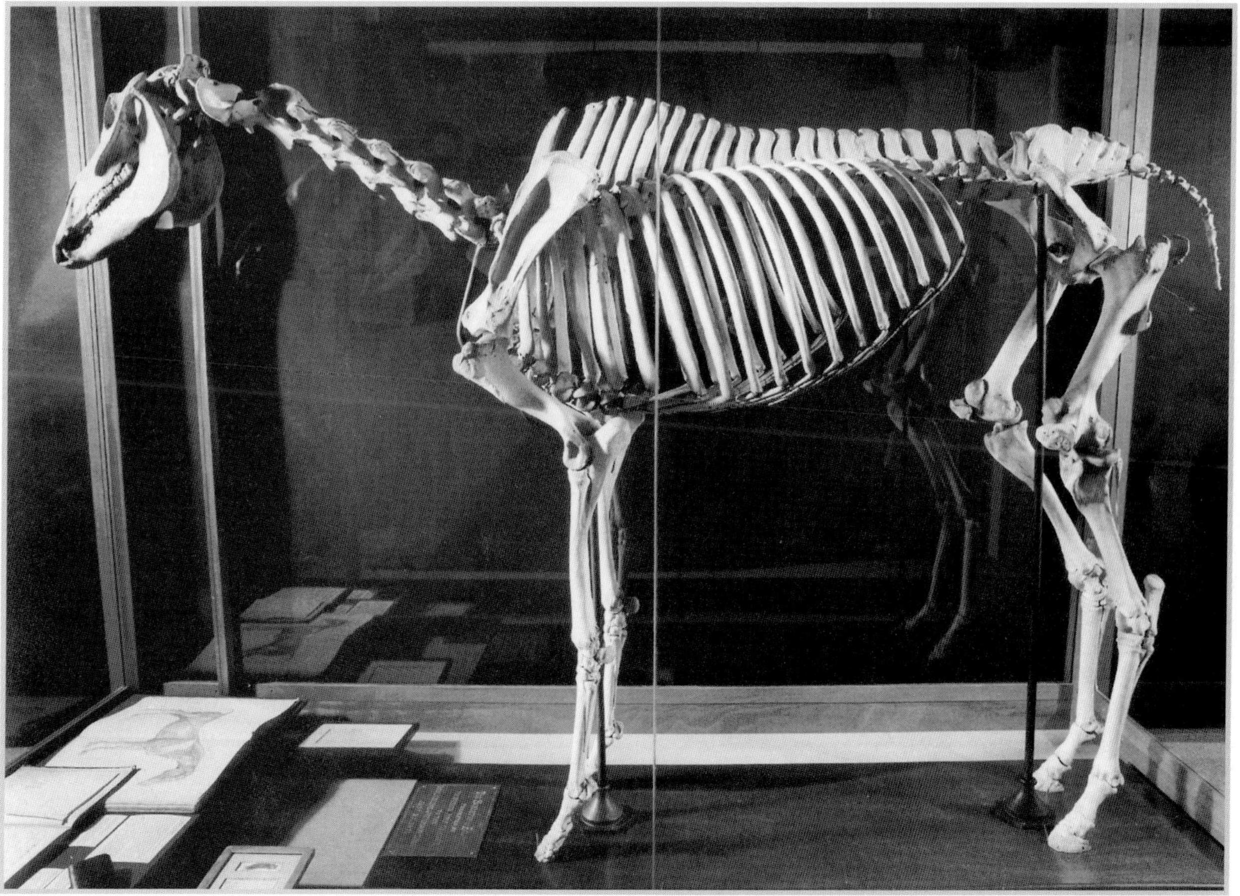
The skeleton of Eclipse today in Newmarket (Courtesy of the National Horseracing Museum).

The Mooi river, then and now: 1899–1999

SANDY LITTLEJOHN
202 High Street
Newmarket
Suffolk CB8 9AP
UK

One hundred years ago, the village of Mooi River in the Colony of Natal was a remount depot for the cavalry of General Sir Redvers Buller's forces of the British Army, despatched to subdue the Boers. Commandos of the Transvaal Republic had invaded the Colony after the British rejection of Paul Kruger's ultimatum in October 1899.

When I arrived in the village in 1952 to take over the veterinary practice, one of the oldest practices in the territory, there were veterans of both armies still farming in the province. However, it was my good fortune to meet a veteran of a different sort - Charles Cordy, a veterinary surgeon who had been recruited in the 1890s by the Colonial Office to serve as Veterinary Officer in the Crown Colony of Natal (later incorporated as a Province of the Union of South Africa). His proud boast was that he had drawn a Colonial Service Pension for longer than he had served as a vet. In spite of his 80-plus years and his long superannuation, he had a quick enquiring mind, sharp as a scalpel.

Charles H. Cordy graduated from the Royal Veterinary College in December 1890. After a number of appointments in London he joined the Veterinary Department of Natal. There he worked tirelessly until his retirement around 25 years later, a working life broken only by service during the 1914–1918 War in the Army Veterinary Corps, a period about which he was very reticent.

"*My first job,*" he recalled, "*was Assistant Vet at the transport yards of the Great Western Railway. They had over 2000 horses therein. Sometimes there would be more than a hundred horses for examination every morning in the sick lines. There were two of us to do the rounds. At the end of two years I knew a few things about lameness.*"

His job as Veterinary Officer in Natal was very different. When calls for help arrived at his Pietermaritzburg office (often in the form of a note in a cleft stick borne by a sweating Zulu runner), he would saddle up two horses, one of which carried his equipment, rifle and bedding, and set off on a journey which could take up to two weeks if rivers were in spate. In the 20,000 square miles of bush and forest of Northern Natal there were no veterinarians, no railways, few roads and fewer bridges. Once, chatting to the Governor of Natal at a garden party in the capital, Pietermaritzburg, he recounted how he had to wait on the bank of the Tugela river until it subsided sufficiently to allow his horses to ford it.

"*Cordy,*" boomed the Governor. "*The only way we'll get a bridge over the Tugela is for you to be drowned crossing it!*" The bridge was eventually built without such dire necessity.

Mooi River is now the Thoroughbred breeding centre of Natal and, although lacking a lime soil, has produced countless winners of good races in Southern Africa and elsewhere. In the mid-20th century there were no equine hospitals in the province, the nearest being 300 miles away at the Onderstepoort Veterinary Faculty near Pretoria. Equine veterinarians had perforce to make do with equipment and facilities which today would be considered primitive, if not downright dangerous. For example, before the pioneering work of L. W. Hall, anaesthesia for protracted operations was a chancy business involving chloroform, chloral hydrate and/or barbiturates. Chloroform administered by mask was particularly hazardous owing to the high concentrations resulting from the stifling heat of the subtropics.

One of my colleagues confessed to me that he didn't enjoy ops above the knee or the hock. "*I can do nearly all my ops under local,*" he said. "*Then I have no worries about general anaesthesia, all my firings stand nice and quiet under pethidine and nerve blocks.*" The same colleague claimed that he wasn't happy with a pin-firing unless he saw joint fluid oozing out of the pinholes. "*And then biniodide of mercury rubbed in well does the trick!*" When I tentatively suggested that the stress of the operation possibly released a flood of steroids into the joint over a period of weeks, he looked at me quizzically. "*And so? That'll help too, won't it?*"

When Charles Cordy visited the Royal Veterinary College, while on leave from Natal in 1908, one of the patients was Persimmon, HRH The Prince of Wales' Derby winner of 1896 and champion sire. He had slipped in his box and fractured his pelvis and was unable to take weight on either hindlimb. "*He was threatening to go down and would never have got up again,*" Cordy recalled. "*They tried slinging him but he wouldn't take to the sling, quite uncontrollable he was. They had to put him down, a terrible loss.*"

In those days a horse which won at the highest level over six furlongs (Coventry Stakes) and went on to win over one and a half to two and a half miles (Derby, St Leger and Ascot Gold Cup) was not just a great racehorse and champion sire, he was a national institution.

Cordy must have been one of the last persons to see Persimmon alive, albeit in pain and distress. In the final years of the reign of his owner HM King Edward VII there was no alternative to euthanasia.

We asked Tim Greet, widely respected equine surgeon of Newmarket, if Persimmon would have had a better chance of surviving the accident if the technology and medicines of today had been available.

"Horses with pelvic fractures that cannot bear weight on at least one hindlimb, with or without the benefit of sling support, are doomed, even at the end of the 20th century, to euthanasia on humane grounds," he wrote.

"Major advances in fracture repair over the last 25 years have revolutionised the success of fracture management in middle and distal appendicular skeleton. However, fractures of the long bones of the proximal appendicular skeleton and of the pelvic girdle which produce significant disturbance to skeletal integrity and weight bearing are beyond the scope of even the most up-to-date restorative surgery in adult horses. Thus, I fear Persimmon, whose statue stands proudly at the Royal Stud at Sandringham, would have suffered a similar fate had he sustained the same injury nowadays.

"One can only hope that improvements in equine surgery in the next millennium will allow salvage of patients suffering such injuries. However, we can take comfort in the fact that gamma scintigraphy practised in a number of centres in the UK has reduced dramatically the incidence of long bone and pelvic fractures by allowing readily the identification of precursory stress fractures. This has been the single greatest orthopaedic advance in equine welfare in the latter part of the millennium."

Is there any discipline of equine science which has not made quantum leaps in knowledge and application during the 20th century? In addition to the basic veterinary skills of medicine and surgery, specialist disciplines such as ethology, exercise physiology and biochemistry, and genesiology have contributed immeasurably to the sum of knowledge about the minutiae of performance on racecourse and at stud. Charles Cordy would have been tickled pink to time-travel for a while, visit a modern equine hospital and see how formerly lethal conditions such as fractures, twisted gut and septicaemia can be tackled today.

Although he served his country faithfully for close on half a century, Cordy received no obituary in relevant veterinary publications. Perhaps these few recollections of a fine veterinarian and gentleman may serve, not remotely as an appropriate obituary, more as a reminder of the problems awaiting solution in the first century of the third millennium.

Acknowledgement

The author wishes to express his sincere thanks to Tom Roper, Librarian of the Wellcome Library of the RCVS, and to Tim Greet of the Beaufort Cottage Equine Hospital, Newmarket.

Springbok photographed at Etosha National Park - Namibia, August 1998 (Photograph by Sidney Ricketts).

Sent flying into the future: air transport then, now and thereafter

DES LEADON
Irish Equine Centre
Johnstown
Naas
Co. Kildare
Ireland

DAVE BARTLE
Curragh Bloodstock Agency
Newbridge
Co. Kildare
Ireland

The air transport of horses may have begun in the UK in the 1920s. Perhaps the most significant early flight, however, took place in 1949, when Vincent O'Brien sent Cottage Rake and Hatton's Grace from Ireland to the Cheltenham National Hunt Festival in England. Both won. In 1946, eight horses were flown across the Atlantic Ocean from Shannon in Ireland to what is now JFK airport in the USA. The journey took 22 hours and necessitated many technical stops. Faster Douglas DC6/DC7 pressurised aircraft were used to transport horses on this route from 1952.

The international horse breeding industry began to be enhanced by access to air transport services when regular horse-carrying flights between Ireland, England and France were initiated in the early 1950s. Bristol Freighter aircraft were used for this service. Their front-loading facility made it easier to load than other contemporary aircraft, but they were felt to be noisy and slow by the personnel that travelled with the horses. The volume of traffic was sufficient to justify staff dedicated to providing horse care from departure to destination, familiar with the environments and requirements at airports and at altitude. They became known as 'flying grooms'. Their numbers have grown from a handful, to the stage at which there are international efforts to recognise their chosen profession by accreditation and certification. The 'jet age' arrived with the first carriage of horses in a Boeing 707 in the early 1960s. Stalls were built around the horses after they had walked up a ramp into the aircraft. These were so-called 'open stall systems' which, although they surrounded the horses, did not fully enclose them. In 1968, the first widely noted tragedy occurred, when an Elizabethan aircraft with three crew, five grooms and eight horses on board crashed on landing at London's Heathrow airport. All of the crew, all of the horses and three of the grooms died. The accident was attributed to metal fatigue.

Fast and efficient, regular air services from Europe to the USA, Japan and Australia became commonplace in the 1970s, using the then state-of-the-art Boeing 707 and DC8 aircraft. Palletised freight systems in which three horse stalls, with a grooms' compartment, were loaded with horses on the ground and then lifted onto the aircraft, led to faster loading and unloading. Thirty horses could now be loaded onto an aircraft in an hour. As many as 112 horses could be carried in a Boeing 747 when these and other so-called 'wide-bodied' jets became available for horse charter flights in the 1980s. Improved access to scheduled services also took place and three horses and a groom could, from then onwards, travel almost anywhere in the world in fully or partially enclosed 'air stables' or 'jet stalls'. Specialised horse air transport services are so extensive today that they can rightly be described as forming a global industry. The horse air transport industry is an integral part of the racing, breeding, sport and pleasure horse industries worldwide. There is a need for investment in research into the challenges that ever-increasing globalisation will impose on our willing equine accomplices. Let's hope that we can transport them, supersonic business class, from home in the EU or USA to Melbourne for the Cup, in 90 minutes, in the not too far distant future!

Preparing to load horses into a Boeing 747.

The 'open stall system' in the aircraft.

Sortie to ceremony

The horse's battle in the 20th century: a personal view

JOHN REILLY
Normandy Barracks
Sennelager
BFPO 16
Germany

The use of the horse in war is probably best exemplified by turn of the millennium images of mediaeval knights in armour mounted on heavy horses of agricultural lineage. The combined power of man and horse is illustrated in Shakespeare's *Henry V*:

"Steed threatens steed, in high and boastful neighs
Piercing the night's dull ear, and from the tents
The armourers, accomplishing the Knights
With busy hammers, closing rivets up,
Give dreadful note of preparation."

The age of the knight was ended by developments in the range and power of artillery in the middle of the 16th century. However, the reputation of the knight in shining armour for chivalrous behaviour and noble horsemanship has never been extinguished. It is still remembered today in fairs and pageants across the country and is possibly still reinforced by the spectacle of the Household Cavalry parading as the Sovereign's Escort in central London. Many would say this is now anachronistic and there is an increasing economic and political pressure to end such display. However, as we near the end of the 20th century it is important not to forget the very real contribution that the horse has made to the defence of our lands.

It was Oliver Cromwell who pioneered the use of cavalry, deployed to charge at the critical moment of combat, as a timely battle-winning asset. The victory won by such tactical use of mounted troops has immortalised many now famous charges, such as those of the Light (and the more successful Heavy) Brigades at Balaclava. However, there was a price to pay. The number of men that fell at Balaclava is in dispute, but they were few when compared with the colossal and catastrophic loss of horse flesh. Five hundred and seventeen horses were killed or wounded in that single valiant but misguided charge towards the Russian guns during this particular part of the Crimean War. As Lord Tennyson's famous poem testifies:

"When can their glory fade?
O the wild charge they made!
All the world wondered.
Honour the charge they made!
Honour the Light Brigade,
Noble six hundred!"

The courage of horses at the Battle of Waterloo is depicted in Scotland Forever, *1881 (oil on canvas) by Lady Butler (Elizabeth Southerden Thompson) (1844–1933) (Leeds Museums and Galleries (City Art Gallery) UK; ©Courtesy of the artist's estate/Bridgeman Art Library).*

The horse continued to battle into the first half of the 20th century; the Boer War, for example, resulted in the appalling loss of 326,073 horses. This privation is movingly commemorated in a memorial statue in Port Elizabeth with the ironic words:

"The greatness of a nation
Consists not so much in the numbers of its people
Or the size of its territory
As in the extent and justice of its compassion."

In condolence and in order to seek an explanation for such carnage, an investigation by Parliamentary Committee was commissioned in 1902. It concluded that few of these losses were caused by bullet wounds or shelling. It had been a lack of veterinary knowledge and provision for basic health care and animal husbandry that had led to such a great loss of animals through disease. The result was a Warrant signed by King Edward VII in 1903 creating the Army Veterinary Corps. Its leader was Major General Frederick Smith who retired in 1910 but was recalled when the Great War broke out in 1914.

The British Expeditionary Force (BEF) began the war with 53,000 animals and six veterinary hospitals. By 1918, there were 450,000 animals in the lines of the British Cavalry and Yeomanry and 18 veterinary hospitals. Nearly all artillery was also horse drawn: six horses to each field gun and eight or twelve for the medium and heavy types. Clabby[1] however, estimates that including all fronts, and not only Europe, the British Army had more than 1 million animals by 1917, with an average daily sick parade of 110,000!† Between 1914 and 1918, over 2.5 million patients were admitted to veterinary hospitals and of these, over 2 million, or 78%, were returned to duty[2]. Tennyson could well have written then:

"Thank god for the success of the Veterinary Corps!
For it was MAN who sent the beast to war!"

Following the Great War Major General Frederick Smith was knighted and King George V conferred the title 'Royal' on the Army Veterinary Corps in 1918[3]. The postwar figures recount, in contrast with those from the Boer War, that the loss of horse flesh was accounted for by direct rather than indirect circumstance. The draft horses of the artillery that hauled ammunition by night through the cratered and torn warscape sustained the heaviest losses††. In the last two years of the First World War, gunshot wounds killed 77,410 animals and the later introduction of mustard gas left 211 dead and 2,220 injured[2]. In addition, bombs began to take their toll in the summer of 1918 and particularly affected the heavy horses that had been used in logistic support roles. Various guises of shire horse had been used in this capacity, a shift from their much earlier role of carrying heavily clad knights in armour to the battlefield. The need for speed and incision had relegated these heavy horses to the thankless support roles while the lighter types of horse supplied the heroic cavalry with their intrepid steeds.

In the years between the two World Wars there were huge advances of mechanisation, and it was obvious that the armoured fighting vehicle would supercede the horse as the cavalryman's mount. In 1928, the first regular cavalry in Britain, the 11th Hussars and the 12th Lancers were converted to armoured car units and, by 1938, the process was practically complete. The failure of weaker allies to embrace the necessary changes in technology, which represented advances in armour, fire power and mechanisation, were made apparent in 1939, when the brave Polish Lancers charged invading German tanks - to no avail.

Thus, in 1940, the BEF deployed to France without a single horse. In the same year the Shire Horse Society was bombed out of its prestigious premises in Hannover Square[4] as if to stress the end of this magnificent horse's military role. With increasing sophistication in the conduct of armed conflict, the turn of the millennium's original warhorse no longer had a role to play on the battlefield. Nevertheless it continued, unabashed, to make a significant contribution to fuelling the war effort. Despite the government making tractors available to farmers, the Shire horse was still essential in fulfilling the requirement to produce as much home-grown food as possible[4].

Mounted troops and equine transport did however find their niches in the Second World War. The British used pack animals in jungle warfare against the Japanese and surgically stifled mules were moved in silent gliders to provide a muted tactical transport for the troops. (A certain Major Frederick Hobday had been consulting Veterinary Surgeon to the Field Army during World War One and Colonel C. M. Stewart published the method for total excision of the vocal cords in 1946.)

Specialised use of the horse is still currently employed in operations other than war. Horses have been used in border patrols in the Balkans and pack training is still carried out and has proved useful where the vagaries of weather has made the prima donna helicopter fallible.

With massive leaps in technological and defence engineering, weaponry and science, that the days of massed mounted cavalrymen and supporting horse-drawn artillery are gone is not in doubt.

The horse is unlikely to struggle in the 21st century as it did in the past. As a direct result of its valiant efforts, man is now liberated to enjoy the freedom of greater leisure time. Fittingly, the increased use of the horse as a pleasure animal features significantly in this more comfortable future. Horses are highly unlikely to have to undertake the tasks, or their consequences, that have been asked of them in the past. However, the future is unpredictable, and it may be that the use of the horse in military sense, in certain situations, will endure. Perhaps at some stage in the future, in response to the damage caused to the environment by the use of nonrenewable fuels, the horse will return as a major form of transport and power. With the increasingly

†For tales describing the workloads of military veterinarians at this time read, for example, the chronicles of W. Hamilton-Kirk (1968) *The Veterinarian* **5**, 281-285. Pergamon Press, GB.
††For poignant descriptions of the Royal Horse Artillery in action during World War One and other facts, figures and stimulating thoughts about the time read Holmes, R. (1995) *Riding the Retreat: Mons to the Marne 1914 Revisited.* Jonathan Cape, London.

sophisticated technological arming of the modern battlespace, and yet a simultaneously increasing threat from wholly unsophisticated armies in different parts of the world, perhaps the horse will even return to battle again on man's behalf.

For the moment, though, the horse can enter the new century with head held high. The contribution that this loyal creature has made to the defence of our lands should never be forgotten. With the Royal Tournament, during which the sheer professionalism and awesome capabilities of the horsed soldier were honoured, now no more, isn't the role of the horse in state ceremony, as escort and coffin bearer, a fit and proper honour that should remain for a noble animal with a noble history?

The horse has won its battle with the 20th century and should now enjoy a healthy future in the next century and indeed, the next millennium. It has been well earned.

Acknowledgements

I am indebted to Dr Paul Skelton-Stroud FRCVS for late night faxes containing useful sources and for steering me towards Brigadier Professor Richard Holmes who generously gave of his thoughts.

References

[1]Clabby, Brigadier J. (1963) *The History of the Royal Army Veterinary Corps* 1919-1961. J.A. Allen and Co., London.

[2]Dunlop, R.H. and Williams, D.J. (1996) *Veterinary Medicine: an Illustrated History.* Mosby-Year Book Inc., St Louis, Missouri.

[3]Smith, Major General Sir Frederick (1927) *A History of the Royal Army Veterinary Corps* 1796-1919. Bailliere, Tindall and Cox, London.

[4]Chivers, K. (1996) *RAVC Bicentenary Symposium.* Royal College of Veterinary Surgeons, London.

Vignettes of a veterinary life with horses

PETER ROSSDALE
Beaufort Cottage Stables
High Street, Newmarket
Suffolk CB8 8JS
UK

The Millennium: from Start to Finish

If we look back across the years of the millennium and, in particular, to those of the recent century, it is possible to discern the evolution of parallel strands of veterinary art and science, as with its medical and physiological counterparts.

It is a fascinating story, bound up with the development of man, because both art and science are but extensions of human intellect and experience. Knowledge and its use form the basis of the veterinary ethos, as of civilisation itself.

Members of the veterinary profession are dedicated to the concept of animal care and what, at the end of this century, is now termed welfare. However, the relationship of man with animals is one clouded by extremes of logical and illogical subjectivity, arising from tribal, national and religious circumstances. As the century draws to a close, we can still discern ancient attitudes and habits mixed with more recent developments, tinged with ecological, sociological, cultural and anthropomorphic influences.

For a history of the influence of animals on civilisation and culture we may turn to the account by Morus, *Animals, Men and Myths*. In the first place, man gained control of animals by extermination or domestication; hunting or the taking and keeping in captivity animals either useful or pleasurable to man. From these early beginnings, grazing animals for slaughter as a source of food has, somewhat paradoxically, saved many species otherwise doomed to extinction. Stone Age weapons and cave paintings show that hunting was mankind's oldest vocation. Cave paintings also indicate that smart animals, like the horse, were regarded seriously in comparison with caricatures of mammoths and rhinoceroses. The horse, therefore, became man's 'friend' as a beast of burden, source of food and means of transport. The riding of horses is first mentioned in historical records about 2000 BC and the Babylonians were possibly the first to use the horse for military purposes.

However, the great equestrian period originated in Greece, where the horse became the favourite of both gods and men. In Greek mythology, horses symbolised foaming waves of the sea and belonged in imaginary space. They drew Poseidon's cart over the ocean; and Pegasus bore poets up into the realms of fantasy. Horses had wings and were able to talk, Achilles inherited the steeds Balios and Xanthos, gifts from Poseidon; and Alexander's horse Bucephalus received the highest mortal honours, including the founding of the city of Bucephala to mark the spot where this warhorse died, having carried his master to India.

This century has seen a marked decline in the horse population worldwide due to its loss of utility to man in the form of transport, military usefulness and, to a large extent, preference for other sources of meat. However, the horse has not lost its glamour and is increasingly used for pleasure in forms of riding, show-jumping, three-day eventing and racing.

The veterinary art has always been closely identified with the care, medicine and surgery of horses; and with a resurgence of this relationship during the latter decades of the 20th century.

Horses appear to have been pre-eminent among animals in the practice of medicine up until the early 18th century, whereas cattle, swine and sheep received little attention. Rinderpest, the highly infectious and fatal disease of cattle was introduced into Europe and southern Russia in the early 18th century. This coincided with a dynamic expansion of effort to promote medical sciences; and the consequent establishment in Berlin of a college of medicine and surgery. In addition, anthrax, foot and mouth disease and pleuropneumonia threatened the economic existence of nations and caused pressure on medical establishments worldwide; and produced an awareness in physicians and those in medical schools to the importance of animal diseases and veterinary medicine.

In the time of the 4th century, Apsyrtos, the chief veterinarian of Emperor Constantine the Great, differentiated glanders from other illnesses of horses and recognised that the disease was transmitted from horse to horse. In 1664, Jacques de Solleysel transmitted glanders experimentally from horse to horse. This, and the renewed epidemics of rinderpest in the 1750s led to the setting up of the first school of veterinary medicine in Lyon (1762) and Alfort (1765). In France a National Academy of Science was established and, in 1802, the transmissibility of strangles demonstrated by veterinarian Erik Viborg. In 1859, Anginiard showed that equine infectious anaemia was a disease also transmitted from horse to horse.

The impetus that brought schools separate from medical establishments for the education of veterinarians was based on the recognition by European governments of the need to train persons to study and manage increasingly crippling problems of epizootic diseases and because of military requirements, large numbers of competent horse practitioners to maintain cavalries and horse- and mule-drawn artilleries in the pursuit of increasingly global war.

It was the physicians of the 19th century who provided the key to modern veterinary medicine and surgery. Edward Jenner, his tutor John Hunter and Claude Bernard (1813-1876) were dedicated to the concept of comparative medicine, as was Louis Pasteur (1822-1895). Their teaching and progress was, at first, opposed by many physicians who considered veterinary art to be beneath their intellectual status. This opposition lasted well into the 20th century but is now largely abandoned. Sir William Osler (1849-1919) became one of the most active members of the Montreal Veterinary Medical Association founded in 1875, presenting a paper on *The Relation of Animals to Man*. He represented Canada at the British Veterinary Association's meeting in 1881.

The practice of medicine began in ancient societies as comparative medicine, specialist healers found in Mesopotamia practising on draft and transport animals. The progress to modern comparative medicine is well described in Calvin Schwabe's book *Cattle, Priests and Progress in Medicine*.

Schwabe argues that comparative medicine provided the key to medical progress, first by an accumulation of an initial critical mass of biological and medical information by ancient Egyptian priests, followed by systematic observation of the biology and behaviour of other animals, better to understand man. The third step was the development of comparative medical research that was followed and influenced by the establishment of the first schools of veterinary medicine. On this basis, Schwabe suggests, should be created circumstances for completely uninhibited interaction of animal and human medicine.

However, the prime responsibility for veterinarians is to contribute to the health and welfare of animals. This has always been the case; and there is no reason to expect it to change in the 21st century. The collaboration between the veterinary and medical ethos is, however, a much broader subject and of greater importance than research *per se*. The end objectives are the same for medical and surgical practice, whether that practice be on animals or man. Those who practise have the same reasons and aspirations for both their art and science; the only major difference being related to the species differences of anatomy and function, allied to what may be termed intellectual levels. The human species occupies a special place because of an awareness that sets man apart from animals and introduces the concept expressed by Hamlet that "*conscience doth make cowards of us all*".

Veterinary practice, therefore, carries with it the logic of euthanasia, and is limited by economics to the lengths that it will go in the practice of medicine and surgery: For man these lengths are virtually what can be achieved, and what can be achieved lies largely in what can be imagined as future progress and opportunity.

Comparative medicine does, however, share a large measure of the objectives of both professions, as indeed do the objectives of many other branches of science, of physicists, chemists, molecular biologists and engineers to mention but a few. There is logic, therefore, in a common educational programme for medical and veterinary graduates in preclinical years. In clinical training and subsequent practice, the two branches need not diverge entirely, since medical and veterinary skills can be learnt in parallel and their practice shared for mutual benefit. The current law in the UK, which prohibits medical and veterinary interchange at the level of the patient, is one that will surely have to be amended as the new century progresses.

Equine Practice - The 20th Century

Perhaps the best way of placing present practice in the perspective of the past is to contemplate what it is in our armoury of diagnosis and therapy that we could forgo and still count ourselves to be among the progressive element of medicine and surgery aimed at helping, if not curing, the horses under our care and contributing to their welfare.

We would all, perhaps, place differing items in our list of priorities. But what of today's attributes in practice would have been available to us in 1899, let alone in 1799 or 1699? Each year as we progress through this century, the choice of priority would increasingly be personal to each reader. This writer would find imaging techniques to be high on the list of essential diagnostic tools of today, particularly ultrasonography, and nuclear scintigraphy, for diagnosis is everything in practice, before therapy can proceed in a logical and effective manner. However, diagnosis is nothing if the means of cure or alleviation are not available. In equine practice, anaesthesia, providing the opportunity for surgery of colic and caesarean section, is perhaps the most important contribution to the welfare of horses with colic and mares suffering dystocia; and, of course, to the clinician's peace of mind. Those of us who were in practice even as recently as the 1960s can remember the frustration of facing horses suffering from conditions such as volvulus or an intractable malpositioning of the fetus at delivery, without the means of alleviating pain except by euthanasia. Pain-relieving drugs and antibiotics are, perhaps, next on the list of musts for practice which were not available, certainly at the start of the century or well into its course.

Veterinary practice has now the technology, drugs and background knowledge to provide a service of high quality for horses and their owners, unimagined at the beginning of the century and, in the future, limited only by the high cost of technology as it develops in the future. The young graduate of today takes all these advantages as the prerogative of their training; much as previous generations may have viewed the world at the outset of their career, but with expectations based more on hope than substance. How many of today's graduates look back with gratitude to those, such as Koch and Jenner, Semmelweis and Hunter or even Crick and Watson for their discoveries which has lead to improvement in diagnosis, therapy and understanding of conditions caused by microbes or those involving immunological and genetic pathways. One has only to imagine attending a case of any sort today and contemplate the absence of diagnostic or therapeutic procedures based upon the observations of our predecessors to comprehend the debt we owe to them. The dichotomy of the 20th century is centred around the 1960s. Prior to this decade, advances in veterinary medicine and surgery were limited; subsequently they have advanced with increasing rapidity, each decade offering greater knowledge and application to the armoury of clinicians.

In the first half of the century, clinical skills were confined largely to a relatively small number of individuals whose sense of horse mastership and of equine form and function made them as much horseman as veterinary surgeon. These clinicians were pre-eminent in their field, establishing their reputation upon commonsense, experience and an ability to form diagnostic conclusions.

Equine practice consisted of medicine, largely of the application of blisters and cautery, black skin dressing (*Picis carb*), astringent lotions and purgatives and, of surgery, castrations, ventriculectomies and application of orthopaedic splints; skills were more personal than a consequence of professional aids to diagnosis and therapy, as today.

The '50s and '60s ushered in medical developments, especially the advent of antibiotics, which initiated the progress of the second half of the century. We can trace this progress in terms of professional development, the broadening of the basis of clinical expertise and the evidence which indicates that veterinary science now plays an equal, if not greater, part in practice as the art of bygone ages.

All branches of the profession have benefited and new endeavours introduced. Many of these developments are described in other chapters. Here, let us contrast the veterinary art and science of the '50s with that of the '90s.

Improvements in drug therapy have undoubtedly provided clinicians with enormously improved means of treating infection, of a systemic or local nature, caused by bacteria, mycoses or, to a lesser extent, virus. Besides antibiotics, two classes of drugs have, perhaps, made the greatest impact, namely, those involved in anaesthesia and sedation and those with anti-inflammatory properties.

At the sharp end of practice, where the clinician has to perform diagnostic or therapeutic procedures in the stable or field on a fractious individual, the alpha-2 agonist tranquillisers have revolutionised the approach. No longer is it necessary to apply a twitch nor to expose oneself, one's patient or handlers to injury, as was formerly the case. Tranquillisers have not only provided clinicians with the means to approach their patients unhindered but, consequently, enabled them greatly to increase their skills in minor surgical and medical procedures. Further, tranquillising drugs have contributed to markedly better anaesthesia. This has resulted in an enormous increase in the scope of surgery, involving complicated and lengthy procedures which, prior to about 1970, would have been possible only with great difficulty and risk to the patient's life.

During the first half of the century, veterinarians in practice were unable to relieve the suffering of individuals with acute abdominal problems of volvulus, intussusception or other forms of fatal colic; they had to resort to administering morphia, chloral hydrate and, in the last event, euthanasia. Colic surgery is now a routine procedure (p 233).

Orthopaedic surgery was similarly limited, initially, by corresponding limitations in anaesthetic techniques to allow lengthy and intricate procedures to be undertaken with appropriate depths of anaesthesia. A diagnosis of systemic and orthopaedic problems have been substantially enhanced through technologies of radiology then ultrasound and, more latterly, scintigraphy (p 292), together with improved understanding of an increasingly widening spectrum of clinical pathological tests. The clinical acumen of the first half of the 20th century, in which palpation, vision and hearing were the main attributes of the 'horse doctor' have now been supplemented by means of verification; subjectivity has given way to objectivity.

A number of adjuncts have been developed, largely from human medical experience, such as disposable plastic syringes and hypodermic needles, plastic drapes and improved antiseptics, flexible fibreoptic endoscopes and laparoscopes, improved biopsy punches and uterine forceps, video recording and computerised databases.

Again, it has been during the later decades of the century that the impact of new technology and new knowledge has changed the face of practice. In the early and midcentury decades, the veterinary schools and Equine Research Station, at Newmarket, were the centres of excellence of equine practice. Groups of veterinarians at Lambourn, Newmarket and Malton and individuals in Thirsk, Aylesbury and Cambridge ran practices with some specialist support of radiological facilities backed by practical expertise of colleagues who, as discussed earlier, possessed reputations for clinical acumen. The effect of these technologies was to impose both a need for, and a recognition of, specialism within the profession.

Up to about the 1970s, specialism was strenuously opposed by the Royal College of Veterinary Surgeons. The reasons for this opposition are difficult to comprehend today, as the new century begins. The path of specialisation has enormously enhanced both the skills and status of individual clinicians; and has led to the setting up of group practices that are currently gathering reputations as centres of excellence. Competition for clinical cases between privately run group practices and the university veterinary schools is an unfortunate situation which the next century will surely resolve in favour of private practices becoming increasingly involved in the role of clinical teaching.

The last decade has seen increasing emphasis being placed on continuing education and audit of standards in all professions. In the case of veterinarians, this process is gathering pace, but against a background of increasing financial pressures on the veterinary schools and upon students themselves. With the schools being placed under increasing pressure by universities and government to concentrate on research rather than upon teaching, there is a corresponding requirement for the definition of the role of the veterinary profession to be more apparent. It is a truism that to conduct research, one does not have to have a veterinary qualification, whereas to be a veterinary surgeon in practice it is essential; and for that degree to be meaningful in terms of the standards of clinical medicine and surgery.

As we peer into the new century we may discern that eventually the logic of the situation will prevail and the profession will harness the excellence of private practice in order to teach clinical skills to undergraduates in a system replacing 'seeing practice' and function as a pre- and, to some extent, postgraduation means of imparting knowledge and understanding of equine clinical matters in a way which mirrors the age old concept of apprenticeship.

In this speculative view of the future, the Royal College of Veterinary Surgeons and colleges of specialisation would then have the responsibility of maintaining standards and of approving and of monitoring those who teach and the methods of their tuition. This would enable the clinical arm of veterinary schools to be closed down and replaced by research endeavours which would include collaborative research with clinicians in practice, especially with reference to epidemiology and the collection and collating of data from cases in the field. Veterinary schools may be centres for teaching of basic science with courses common to medical, veterinary and allied scientific students who would subsequent to, say, three years training, diverge into the branches of science that they favoured for their careers. Veterinary schools would also act as postgraduate schools of continuing education and research.

Research into the physiology and pathology of horses has been attempted on too many subjects to achieve specific progress in any one area. Much has been accomplished by the support of funding bodies, such as the Horserace Betting Levy Board and Home of Rest for Horses, but the majority of advances applied to clinical practice, as the century closes, have been the result of application of developments outside both veterinary and equine disciplines. For example, echography, anaesthesiology, gait analysis and surgical procedures have been adapted, largely from human applications, by veterinarians; and it is support for the veterinarians in veterinary schools and in practice, together with the encouragement of young scholars and residents, which has been the most successful feature of funding during the last quarter of the 20th century.

In summary, the 20th century has seen an enormous increase both in the development of technologies and capabilities of clinicians to apply these in their diagnostic, therapeutic and prognostic acumen to the benefit of the horse and horse's owners and managers. This trend seems certain to continue into the 21st century. The cost, in terms of capital expenditure for facilities and for supporting an increasing number of physicians in their particular specialisms, will have to be borne by the client and, to paraphrase Shakespeare, "*Aye, there's the rub, for in the ideals of practice what costs may come, that shuttle off the Utopian dream, must give us pause.*" Group practice involving an increasing number of vets corresponding to increasing need for specialism, will continue to an end point where equine centres of excellence will service clinicians, in general or nonequine specialist practices, who have little or no depth of equine expertise but who, nonetheless, are responsible for the health and welfare of individual horses in their locality.

Referral to centres of equine excellence should provide the extra throughput needed to support expensive technology and specialist approaches in these centres, which are and will be particularly necessary against a background of litigation, for less than excellent attention and outcome in equine cases. Equine practitioners now refer small animal cases; and there is therefore ample scope within the profession for collaboration along specialist species lines.

The generalist must be supported by referral facilities in all species, particularly the horse, where expertise is much more limited by numbers, species difficulties, and other criteria. This necessitates careful economic control which, in itself, requires sufficient throughput of cases to justify expensive facilities. This is the main reason why clinical departments of veterinary schools find financial control so difficult to justify within the university system; and their transfer to the private sector will be, in this writer's opinion, a feature of the 21st century (for a different view see p 55). Equine research must continue, but its definition will require alteration in order to fit both veterinary and equine research into the context of a pursuit of knowledge and understanding of comparative medicine, pathology and surgery. Much can be learnt from comparative studies and the horse probably fits more readily into this field of vision than as a subject of investigation on its own. Epidemiology would seem to be the most advantageous discipline to pursue with respect to the horse itself and this subject is considered elsewhere (p 196).

Dipping Into the Future

At the end of the last century, the poet Alfred Lord Tennyson wrote in the poem *Locksley Hall*:

> *"For I dipped into the future far as human eye could see,*
> *Saw the vision of the world and all the wonder that would be."*

In a book to celebrate the beginning of the third millennium, it is appropriate that we authors peer into the future but, of course, the human eye has its horizons as does the mind; and these horizons may be extended only by a few gifted in the art of extrapolating from present and past into the future. For most of us, the horizons are very limited. Tennyson envisaged much, some of which has, indeed, come to pass:

> *"Saw the heavens fill with commerce and there rained a ghastly dew From the nations' airy navies grappling in the central blue."*

These words were written in the 1840s, before the invention of the aeroplane, and its sad sequelae in such as the Blitz and the dropping of the atomic bomb on Hiroshima. But his vision has not yet reached its conclusion:

> *"Far along the worldwide whisper of the south wind rushing warm, With the standards of the people plungeing through the thunderstorm, When the war drums throb no longer and the battle flags are furled, In the parliament of man, the federation of the world.*
>
> *"There the common sense of most shall hold a threatful realm in awe And a peaceful earth shall slumber wrapped in universal law."*

We can all attempt to prophesise and hope that when we are gone, someone will note the accuracy of our forecast. But where science and the development of our professional skills are concerned, forecasting can itself become an objective for the future; and in this respect may serve a useful purpose.

On science, Tennyson noted that *"Science moves but slowly slowly, creeping on from point to point"*, and when we peer into the future, within each of our disciplines, we must recognise also that progress is based as much on the negative side of failure as on the positive side of success. Hypotheses are there to be tested; and in the testing, the negative outcome of one person's study may point the way to a positive outcome in another's. Progress is not linear, but starts often as a mountain stream which pursues its tortuous path before entering the mainstream of the river leading to its conclusion in the ocean itself.

So what can we discern of probable equine veterinary progress during the next century? The prior objectives of the profession are to maintain and improve the welfare of horses and, through this objective, to assist owners, handlers and all those associated with the many pursuits for which horses are bred. Within these objectives there may be conflicts of interest as, for example, usage of the horse versus the deleterious effects of injury or disease that follows use. Our profession is there to bridge the gap and achieve a balance which is both humane and effective.

It is against this background that our profession must harness the developments of science within the practicalities of application in any given instance. There can surely be little doubt that science will offer increasingly sophisticated means, as it has done, particularly, in the past quarter of a century. We are on the threshold of genetic and molecular manipulations that will bring new horizons to prophylaxis, therapy, diagnosis and understanding of pathogenesis. In applying these wonders to the horse, we shall be constrained inevitably by cost: the availability of funding and human resources for research and the willingness of the fee-paying animal owner to support the application of inevitably expensive technology in practice. In addition there is likely to be a continuing trend for legislation on a national or European basis to restrict experimental procedures on animals, as well as the ethical considerations regarding the pursuance of new medical and surgical developments applied to horses. As is the case in human patients, all these influences will operate at one or other level as advances in veterinary science during the next century.

We in the world of Thoroughbreds are already constrained by embargoes placed on the use of artificial insemination while the rest of the world moves on to *in vitro* fertilisation, embryo transfer and the manipulation of genetic material which assists in eliminating certain genetic diseases and conditions debilitating to the individual.

With regard to performance horses, there is, of course, a minefield of untoward and unknown side effects which could lead to a serious long-term decrease in athletic performance and soundness (structural stability) of the breed. No approach has yet determined how sensible culling of defective individuals and breeding, from those possessing intrinsic unsoundness of structure and function, can be replaced by artificial biological means; Darwin's theory still rules OK insofar as natural selection is concerned, but for horses, as with some other species, survival of the fittest is replaced by the survival of traits admired by man.

The responsibility of veterinarians must be to ensure that, whatever improvements 'science offers' for practical application to the equine problems encountered in practice, those that carry the risk of side effects that, in the long term, may diminish the health and welfare of the breed, are vigorously rejected. Of course, the $64,000 question will always be how to interpret the cause and potential effects of any new development before its effects appear, perhaps many years after the introduction of the programme. Ultrasonography has given us the capacity to eliminate twins in Thoroughbreds and other breeds, a technicological advance of the last decade now developed to a high level of efficiency. However, the question must be addressed as to whether or not this will lead to a high incidence of twin conceptions in future generations as the natural safety valve afforded by the failure of twins to survive is replaced by continuance in the breed of individuals carrying the genes for twins. In some species we appear to be on the brink of enabling scientists to inseminate females with spermatozoa selected by technology for ensuring a higher bias (perhaps 80 or 90%) towards male or female offspring according to choice. As these manipulative measures become available, it will be the responsibility of veterinary surgeons to attempt to achieve the balance between short-term commercial ventures on the one hand and health of the equine population, on the other hand.

The vulvoplasty introduced by Caslick in the 1930s was, perhaps, the most striking and significant single procedure that has been introduced in order to assist subfertile mares to conceive and carry a foal to full term. However, Reg Pascoe, Queensland veterinarian, demonstrated in a paper to the International Equine Reproduction Symposium, that mares with inferior perineal conformation, predisposing to pneumovagina, have a heritable tendency to produce mares which have similar or more deleterious conformation. We breed from these mares because we select for athletic and not breeding performance. The incidence of the condition therefore rises and, probably, worsens over decades. This has not, as yet, introduced a serious liability, largely because of the simplicity of the Caslick operation and the willingness of veterinarians and owners to employ the technique.

Nevertheless, there are many conditions, such as osteochondritis (OCD), degenerative joint disease, tendon sprains, susceptibility to infections, left-sided laryngeal paralysis and other conditions of the respiratory system which may have a heritable basis. We should at least define the genetic basis of individual conditions based on laboratory studies and epidemiological investigations in the field. This approach will surely develop in the first quarter of the next century; and the use which veterinarians, owners and breed societies make of this information will be the test of their sincerity when they speak of progress in furthering the welfare of the horse and the sanctity of the breed.

As the century draws to a close, another exciting approach is the sequencing of the equine genome which seems sure to lead to a better understanding of heritable conditions in horses, Thoroughbreds and other breeds. These developments are described in detail on pages 275-285. Here, let us speculate briefly on the potential of this tool in breeding to avoid the deleterious influences on which injury and disease are based. Horse owners and breed societies will have to come to terms with the benefits that this information could bring and themselves adjust to the new era of genetic counselling based on scientific principles. May we not see, even those responsible for the Thoroughbred, allowing some hybrid vigour to be introduced into the breed in order to promote improved soundness and a reduction of wastage in the chain between the birth of a foal and a consistent appearance and performance on the racecourse? We breed horses for a purpose and surely in the next millennium the 'penny will drop' and breeders will be enabled, yes, to select for speed and endurance, but at the same time to avoid the propagation of defects in their equine progeny which defeat their objective.

If we cast our minds back to the beginning of the present century, could our minds have envisaged computerisation or the unravelling of the structure of DNA? But now, a hundred years later, we glimpse the real prospects of possessing knowledge of the individual's genetic composition that could open the way to hitherto undreamed of capabilities of preventing and curing diseases, from cystic fibrosis to cancer in the human species; but what of the horse? The subject of the human genome is discussed elsewhere, but the application of this particular science will depend upon first determining what conditions and diseases have a genetically related component; and the number of genes involved. Before this information is established, speculation as to the future can be confined only to generalities of potential therapy.

Scientific advances are a challenge and the more sophisticated and in-depth they become, the greater the challenge to those who employ their methods. What can be envisaged? The development of much more effective vaccines based on genetically engineered microbes, viruses or bacteria, which induce a more solid immunity in the host. These will undoubtedly become available to equine veterinarians and their clients. It must be always remembered that it is better to prevent invasion of the enemy rather than to overcome an intrenched opponent by therapy. However, the environment plays a large part in infection; and science should complement the basic tenets of good husbandry (e.g. dust-free environments and avoidance of overcrowding).

Improvements in vaccine technology such as DNA vaccines may help control diseases where parasites are involved. By injecting fragments of DNA derived from the organism causing Equine Protozoal Myeloencephalitis (EPM), an immune response may be stimulated to prevent this debilitating infection.

The scientific assessment of novel techniques for treating joint, tendon and bone injuries will surely follow new technologies, such as nuclear scintigraphy, which already aid diagnosis. The clinician of the future may have the means to employ drugs which have a selective action. For example, targeting pain relief to a joint, cytotoxic drugs to neoplasia and immunomodulators to sites of inflammation and infection will enable clinicians to treat more effectively and with fewer or no side effects compared with current conventional therapies. These means will fuel and affect the arguments concerning the use of drugs in performance horses, as in human athletes. Such issues will have to be faced with greater precision and logic than they, perhaps, are at present, in order to rationalise the rules under which performances are held.

Surgical techniques have improved substantially in the last quarter of the 20th century and this trend will continue, with the increasing effectiveness and use of tissue transplantation and the introduction not only of biological but also of plastic and other material prostheses.

Biological mediators can now be manufactured in large quantities in a highly pure form by recombinant DNA technology. These could be used to enhance wound healing (platelet derived growth factor), prevent adhesions (tissue plasminogen activator) and glue bone (a protein secreted by mussels to stick to rocks). Articular resurfacing using autologous chondrocytes has already been reported in man and with the development of stem cell transformation a ready supply of chondrocytes could become available. Perhaps arthroscopic joint resurfacing could be performed between races!

Advances in drug therapy and, particularly, in abolishing drugs which act perhaps centrally but are targeted to desensitisation to a confined local area, may enable surgeons to perform major surgical procedures in the standing as opposed to the recumbent individual. One can envisage hindlimb fractures being repaired under these conditions in the standing horse, thereby avoiding the risk of refracture as the horse recovers from general anaesthesia. The extent to which these techniques can be applied to the horse and the ethics of doing so is sure to be a further source of debate and progress in the 21st century.

Research workers seeking new knowledge are the flagbearers of every profession; contributing to the process of progress to which mankind is dedicated in that unexplained motivation described by Tennyson as:

"Men my brothers, men the workers, ever seeking something new,
That which they have done before them but earn'st of the things that they shalt do."

However, as argued elsewhere, research workers need not be veterinarians, but clinicians must be so qualified. One of the primary aims of those responsible for the educational and career structures of the veterinary profession, in the next century must be surely be to communicate the thrill of research to veterinary undergraduates and graduates and adjust the discrepancies between lack of financial reward in science and the pull of the pound in practice.

Elsewhere in his text, Tennyson wrote:

"Knowledge comes but wisdom lingers and I linger on the shore,
While the individual withers and the world is more and more;
Knowledge comes but wisdom lingers and he bears a laden breast,
Full of sad experience moving towards the stillness of his rest."

It is the individuals who are responsible for the education of undergraduates and influence the various avenues of their career endeavours throughout life, which will determine the way that knowledge evolves into wisdom; and wisdom itself is achieved within the objectives of the profession.

What is the purpose of the equine veterinary profession is a question rightly to be asked. The objectives are essentially those of clinical acumen applied for the benefit of the horse, with a subsidiary aim of involvement in scientific progress by means of research which improves our ability to perform our primary objective.

One can envisage that university veterinary schools will become centres of excellence for research into diseases of animals, with comparative links to man and researchers on human disease. The schools will continue to teach basic science to undergraduates and prepare them not only for practice but also for their role as teachers in the field; and to train the undergraduate for collaborative epidemiological studies involving clinicians in the field. The staff of veterinary schools will also be employed to monitor standards and supervise continuing education at all professional levels. If we dip into the educational future, do we not see a fundamental shift developing towards the emphasis on practical training within the practice environment; and that this training should continue throughout the professional life of the individual?

The profession will inevitably come to be composed of generalists willing and able to provide primary veterinary care to many species supported by clinicians with specialisms by species and/or discipline providing secondary care; the species specialism will probably start as soon as the basic science course has been completed, but there will be opportunities for graduates to change their professional direction at any stage via the gateways of further training and examination for levels of competence.

As the century develops there will be an increasing number of centres of excellence for equine practice, providing tertiary care, to which nonspecialist equine clinicians will refer their cases; and where teaching of a high standard will be possible, directed both at undergraduates and postgraduates. These centres will have the most advanced facilities and be funded privately, perhaps with some state funding to support teaching while, at the same time, ensuring a contractual arrangement whereby control of standards may be imposed by continuing audit of results.

Finally, can you the reader any more than I the author envisage the creation of a technology of the future comparable to Tennyson's vision of the 1840s and its likely consequences? Whatever this might be, let us hope that it is not associated with the "*ghastly dew*" but one which enhances the quality of life of both horse and man.

Acknowledgements

I would like to thank Drs Julia Kydd and St John Collier for their assistance with the 'Dipping Into the Future' section of this article.

A French view of equine veterinary science entering another millennium

EDOUARD POURET
Le Manoir
Aunou Le Faucon
61200 Argetan
France

The Horse

For many centuries, horses have been the means of transport for man and his equipment throughout the world. As far back as 2000 BC, the horse was essential to the lives of both individual tribes and whole populations, enabling, for instance, the Arabic countries of the Middle East to invade North Africa and western Europe.

The horse later helped develop the power of Romans, thanks in part to the veterinary wisdom of their predecessors, the Greeks. Indeed, in ancient times it was by means of the horse that merchants, warriors, scientists and missionaries of all religions were able to establish supremacy of their respective cultural, religious, political and social systems, some of which lasted practically until the end of the first millennium. The horse was associated with man and all his migrations at different stages of history in Europe, Asia and America, whether North, Central or South.

The importance of the horse has been so great that it could be said that no civilisation could develop without its help, at least until the relatively recent discovery of motorised power at the end of this present millennium.

Equine Veterinary Science

Attention to the health of this unique form of transport of populations on earth has been of vital importance to the development of modern civilisation. The oldest texts show the concern of man for his companion. A long time before the 18th century, we know that man was often more careful about his horse than himself or his friends. For centuries, veterinary treatment of horses was primarily empirical, as was medical treatment of man. However, equine veterinary science - and its human medical counterpart - evolved gradually in Europe during the 17th and 18th centuries.

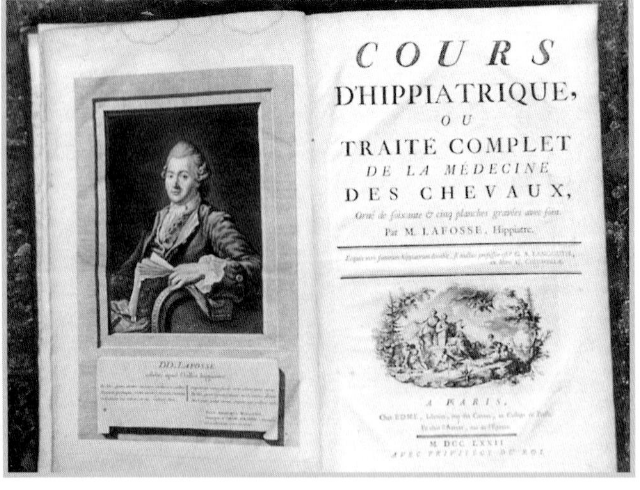

Fig 1: Cours D'Hippiatrique, ou Traité Complet de la Médecine des Chevaux.

The Literature

Many texts were published around this time, starting of course with the basis of all medical studies, anatomy, followed by further publications of medical importance. Certain bold surgical techniques, however, had been used for centuries (e.g. trephining the skull, repairs of fractures, extraction of foreign bodies, etc.).

Perhaps the best known book in Europe at this time was *Cours d'Hippiatrique ou Traité Complet de la Médecine des Chevaux (Hippiatrique's Lectures or A Complete Textbook of Equine Medicine)* by Lafosse, Hippiatre (Fig 1). Printed in France in 1772, this was the best complete book on anatomy and medicine for many years.

Equally important was *The Anatomy of the Horse* by George Stubbs (published in England in 1766). This amazing book, which contains the most beautiful drawings and paintings, can justifiably be called one of the greatest masterpieces ever printed.

Many other books and texts about the care and use of the horse were published in many countries during the 18th century. One of the most fascinating endeavours was produced in 1775, again by Lafosse, and consisted of four books under the title *Dictionnaire Raisonné d'Hippiatrique, Cavalerie, Manége et Maréchallerie (Explanatory Dictionary of 'Hippiatrique', Cavalry, Management, Hoof Care and Shoeing)* (Fig 2).

Veterinary Science

During the 18th century, veterinary education became scientifically based. The great French contribution was the foundation of the first veterinary school in Lyon in 1762 by Bourgelat, an equerry to the king. He also started the Alfort school in Paris-Alfort in 1765, some 27 years before the London school was first opened in 1792. Strangely enough, however, the French veterinary profession was not established by law until as late as 1938, when it became necessary to hold a diploma before being granted the right to look after the health and welfare of animals.

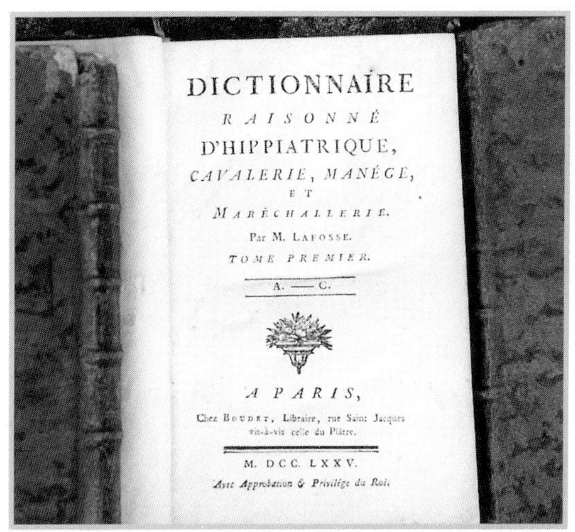

DICTIONNAIRE
RAISONNÉ
D'HIPPIATRIQUE,
CAVALERIE, MANÉGE,
ET
MARÉCHALLERIE.
Par M. LAFOSSE.
TOME PREMIER.
A. — C.

A PARIS,
Chez BOUDET, Libraire, rue Saint Jacques vis-à-vis celle du Plâtre.
M. DCC. LXXV.
Avec Approbation & Privilége du Roi.

Fig 2: Dictionnnaire Raisonné D'Hippiatrique, Cavalerie, Manége, et Maréchallerie.

The World Over

Since the foundation of the Lyon school in 1765, the teaching of veterinary medicine has spread to all parts of the world. Schools, colleges and universities were built in every country to allow the best professors and practitioners to teach theoretical and practical knowledge.

The quality and quantity of subjects that modern veterinary students are expected to learn increases every year. As well as anatomy, medicine and surgery, many other subjects and related sciences are now taught, studied, published and codified as much as possible. The result is that a lifetime is too short to store and memorise all this information, hence computers have became necessary. This international diversity of knowledge has been spread everywhere by the associations of veterinary equine practitioners and other scientific groups, as well as by a plethora of publications and a number of individual teachers.

Personal Experience

For myself, it all started after my French doctorate in Lyon 50 years ago, when I won a scholarship from the British Council to study physiology of reproduction in Cambridge under Sir John Hammond. At the same time, I was allowed to gain practical experience under a number of knowledgeable and generous horse practitioners in Newmarket, notably Fred Day and Bob Crowhurst.

After Cambridge, Sir John Hammond sent me to Kentucky to study under Professor W. W. Dimmock and a team of horse practitioners in Lexington. From Kentucky, I went to work on a large studfarm in Argentina for four years.

I came back to France in 1951 to work among racehorses and every year since I have endeavoured to increase the field of my veterinary activities and to keep up with the constant evolution of medical science.

The Horse at the End of the 20th Century

Since 1951, I have delved deeper and deeper into study of the problems of the horse, its breeding, racing and the practice of equine sports. I have travelled the world over to attend conferences, look after sick or injured animals or try to solve breeding problems. I have worked with, or been in contact with, many veterinary surgeons in other countries, as well as the most important breeders, owners, trainers and riders.

This contact with horses and horsemen around the world showed me that we all spoke the same language, had the same problems, the same ideas about success or defeat and the same sense of humour. We passed on our information about what we found useful and everyone learned and gave a lot, fair and square.

The Horse and the New Millennium

The latest communication technologies, the Internet, live television coverage of all sorts of equine competitions - all these ignore the traditional frontiers. Now, together with the horse, we are 'citizens of the world'. We can interact from our homes as easily with other horsemen in Hong Kong or crowds of fans in Sydney as with our next-door neighbours. Supersonic flight has increased our field of action, with transport times getting ever quicker. What's more, this whole irreversible headlong rush towards the new millennium has taken place before my very eyes over the last 50 years. It has been a marvellous life.

Martin Purcell: a voice from the past

BRODDY CORCORAN
Tallaghan
Mullingar
Co. Westmeath
Ireland

In the early days of the 1940s, I, at age 16 years, went to the Veterinary College, Dublin, and simultaneously was lucky to be apprenticed to a famed and fearful veterinary surgeon in my hometown, Mullingar, Co. Westmeath. This was Mr Martin Purcell, then quite elderly and nearing the end of a notable career.

Now, try to visualise in your mind's eye how, in the early part of the century, a mainly equine practitioner would look. He would be a big powerful man with great arms, never youngish looking. The job aged him instantly. All vets, then, were appraised on their physique as much as anything else as the stern, almost Herculean work demanded. By the way, I was very conscious of this too, being then the eight stone weakling that gets the sand kicked in his face in the famous Charles Atlas ads (remember them?).

To continue: he would be wearing riding boots of surpassing quality made by someone like Fitzpatricks, breeches from O'Callaghans, woollen shirts and cravats from Tysons, all of Dublin; a hunting-style jacket from Wickhams, Mullingar; a good quality cap, or a reinforced bowler at shows, point-to-points and race meetings. Well, this is how our Mr Purcell looked to me. He once owned a young National Hunt horse who won Ireland's premier Maiden Chase at Fairyhouse and gave the great Prince Regent a run for his money in a Red Cross Chase at Naas Racecourse. I was there. I rode a bike to it, it was wartime. Like so many of his colleagues (there were about 250 vets in Ireland at the time), he was a master of his craft, with a faultless, not to be questioned, professional opinion.

Also, like all his colleagues, his irascibility was legendary and that could lamentably be translated into physical action. I was terrified by many instances, though I managed, by luck and cunning, never to have it directed my way. Once, a big lump of a country fellow was restraining a bonham pig, almost a store, and he was squatting on a stool and the pig was in his lap while he held on to the struggling back legs. It was for castration. A quick incision was made by The Boss, the pig's screaming became a roar, and it wrenched one leg free from your man and gave Purcell a very smart kick on the wrist. He shouted, *"Ye humper ye!"*, his favourite admonition, and let a huge kick go that almost sent the stool, the assistant and the pig into orbit. I headed for the hills, honestly!

We were tubing and dosing an elderly hunting horse in a rather grand establishment. The stable door was shut and bolted on the inside for practical reasons too difficult to explain here, but a large window without glass or frame, high up, gave plenty of light. Old horses can be difficult to intubate - the swallow reflex seems weaker, and time after time the tube slips into the trachea. This was happening here, and because he was used to having his own way, he flung his massive and heavy head all over the place. He also had a neat trick of bringing a forefoot sharply forward, with horrendous possibilities for Martin Purcell. Things were going badly and he grew silent - an ominous sign. He was tired and frustrated. At last the tube went down the gullet and was confirmed to be right, in the usual ways. Just in case, a little water was funnelled down. The dose, a mixture of linseed oil, liquid paraffin and oil of Chenopodium (where are they all now?) was slowly administered.

Meanwhile, the lady of the house, who rode the horse, arrived, At the critical time, she pushed, then rapped the door, calling,: *"Hello in there, hello - whatever's the matter?"*; then she moved to the window and shouted out: *"Hey are you not finished? Hello? Hello?"*

The dose had gone, water was passed down the tube, the funnel was detached and the tube was slowly withdrawn. It was dripping greasy water and covered in liquid paraffin, mucus, nasal discharges and some blood from all the efforts to place it.

Martin gathered it into coils and calmly lobbed it out the window! There was a scream of fright, a howl of rage and an obscene oath no lady should know, never mind use. He apologised profusely and insincerely, saying he couldn't allow the infected tube to contaminate the horse's bedding. Beat that!

On a horse fair day, our 20 veterinary boxes would be full of horses of every description, even a Clydesdale stallion on show. Horses were tried for wind in a nearby field. One fair day Martin came back from it after trying a few - he had a legendary reputation - and walked through the horses standing about, into our small dark office-cum-surgery, passing two men who were arguing loudly as to who would pay for the veterinary examination of a horse they were dealing in. He gave the trio (the men and the horse) a cursory look in passing, like all the others waiting for him.

Presently, they came in or got into the office. *"Mr Purcell,"* one said, *"We has a horse for examinin'." "Which of you are paying me for same examination,"* he boomed. He was inclined to boom when it counted. *"I am,"* one said, reluctantly. *"My fee is five guineas"* - a princely sum at the time. The client slowly produced a fiver and proffered it. *"The fee is five* guineas," Purcell said, and pocketed the extra five bob. Then he slowly boomed again, *"The horse in question is the half-bred bay with the stripe; you,"* pointing to the other chap, *"were holding it?" "Yes,"* he answered. *"Well,"* Purcell pronounced, *"that horse has a spavin. Now take yourselves and it out of here."* The crestfallen pair did.

The trouble with this episode is that I cannot remember it clearly; I was marginally involved and I didn't understand it. It happened just before I was taken on by Mr Purcell, and the very first thing I did with him was to copy a letter he had written to a famous London Insurance Brokers who specialised in insurance of Thoroughbred horses. At 16, the contents meant very little; anyway, I was concentrating on my very best penmanship.

Now, there were always world famous studs in Westmeath and Meath, carrying bloodstock of the highest class. In one of these, a foal at foot became incoordinated but continued to suck an indulgent mare. It was insured with the London Brokers. Mr Purcell attended, as did others, but the condition remained static. Then a very eminent 'Opinion' declared that the foal should be put down in the interest of humanity, and this was done and a claim instituted (if that's the word).

The insurance company wrote to Mr Purcell, enquiring why he did not order same. In his reply, which I copied, it was indicated to him from the symptoms that a paralysis of some nature existed. He continued - this is my remembrance - that he could not recommend destruction on humane grounds as there is no pain in paralysis. The company famously and successfully quoted, *"No pain in paralysis"*. They naturally did not quote Mr Purcell's rider, that the foal was most probably, at best, useless for any purpose. Mr Purcell, naturally, lost a valuable client but benefited in many commissions from insurance companies.

I've often wondered how near to the actuality this remembrance is. His tightfistedness was historical, too. There were many who averred that he squeezed an Irish half-crown so tight that he put the harp on it out of tune! He didn't count generosity or dispense it: *"Neither a borrower nor a lender be."* He hated being owed money as much as being indebted to anyone.

He had a particular client, Billy Robinson, from whom he got a lot of difficult work in appalling conditions and with useless help, and he paid nobody except under extreme duress. Purcell was writing out accounts one day, growling to himself as he went along. Suddenly, the fountain pen made a savage attack on the innocent headed notepaper. Then he quickly thrust it right into my face; I was about 18 at the time. *"Here, Corcoran, read this, it'll be of use to you sometime."* It read:

To Wm Robinson

Robinson,
To account furnished many times
If I don't have payment within 14 days
I won't be surprised, but you will.

Signed Purcell

He loved to go to the Grand National every year, it was his only indulgence, and he devised a neat little trick to subsidise same.

Another client who was a slow payer would be sent an itemised account in mid-January; no reply of course. Further demands would be made through late January and February. Then, in early March, he would send a final notice threatening legal proceedings for double the amount, with 14 days to pay! The client would come storming in, demanding apologies and showing a previous account. Purcell would apologise, the client would pay the correct amount and off Purcell sailed for Liverpool with

The Test for Rick of the Back. *From Edward Mayhew, reprinted with kind permission of the Royal College of Veterinary Surgeons Library*

the proceedings.

He hated boozing, betting and fags. If you came in to him puffing a fag, smelling of liquor or gabbing about the horses, you were a goal down immediately.

One night he had to calve a cow for one of the countless 'triple treats' in our area. This is probably the one job above all we expect to get paid for, and usually do. Purcell successfully delivered a live calf, to the fulsome thanks and blessings of the client, who was, of course, half drunk as well.

Purcell demanded his fee, £3. Said 'Curly' (his nickname), *"Well sir, I don't have the money for you now, but I'll be in your office the evening of Mullingar November Races. I'll be hearin' about a yoke that is a certainty to win."* Purcell bellowed his usual imprecations, with additional material, at him, warned him never to darken his door again and stamped out to the car and home.

November Races came, ending in almost darkness. Purcell was in his office, having attended in an official capacity - no bets, of course. The door burst open and a dark figure missed the step down, hurtled in and fell flat on the small floor space - as drunk as old boots. It was, of course, Curly. He staggered to his feet and had a dead half of a cigarette in his idiotically grinning face; the other half glowed on the floor. He swayed and grinned at the glowering Boss and said, *"Howaye Purcell."* He swept a blue Irish tenner out of his pocket. *"Here! - take it outa dat."*

Martin and I got on very well. We never quarrelled, I always obeyed him and he never abused his authority. That I survived over 50 years in large animal practice was almost entirely due to his vast experience, his practicality and his wonderful intellect. I'm afraid my college tuition, though essential, was, in the event, only marginally helpful. And I can thank Martin too for my having no smoking and no drink problems.

But his brusque methods with his clients and the public generally were bad for an impressionable young person. It may have worked in his time - not in mine. So too were his money-grabbing propensities. His ascetic life is not the balm for the hardships of living that ordinary people know levity to be.

His funeral was a quiet one as he did not originate from these parts. He never courted friendships or expected any. His was largely a solitary existence, being a long-time widower. We all wore bowler hats - well, mainly. He might have been impressed - but, then again, maybe not.

Practice: the Frontier of Science and Application Across the Ages

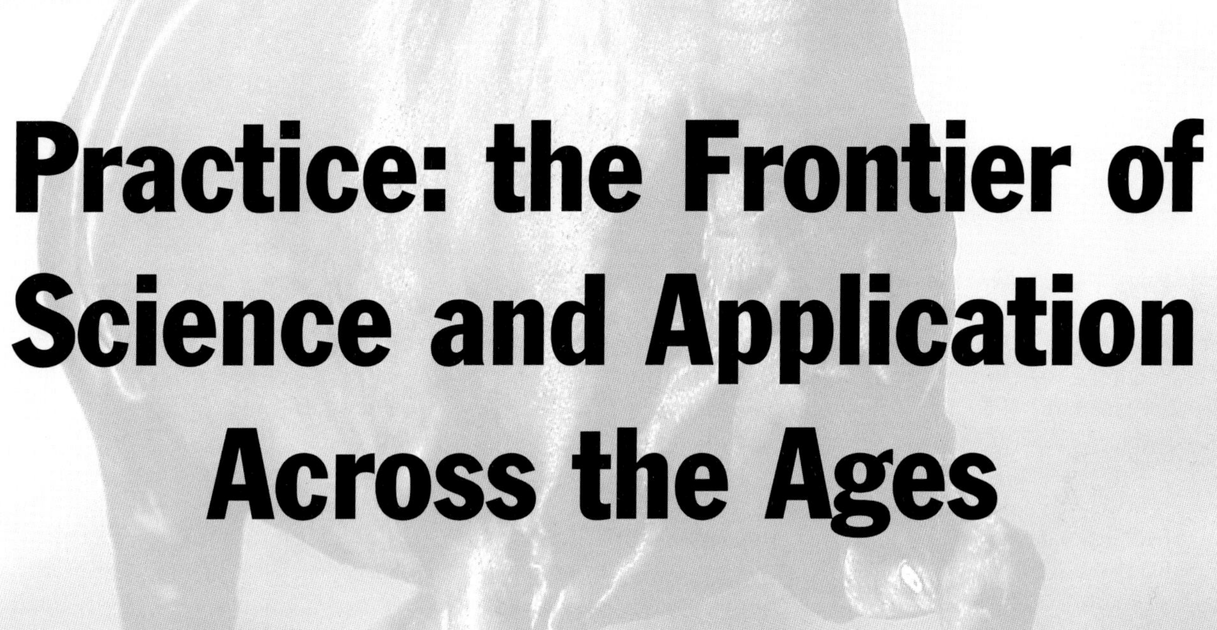

From father to son

JOHN BROOK
Spring Paddocks
Bishops Itchington
Leamington Spa
Warwicks CV33 0QX
UK

I was born in 1945 and one of my earliest memories is of my mother urging me not to follow in my father's footsteps and become a veterinary surgeon. This was fairly rapidly followed by my being stood on the tallest stool so that I could watch, fascinated, as Dad performed some operation or other. There were interludes of aspirations to be a fighter pilot, but slowly I realised that no other career had the overall appeal that the veterinary profession could offer. My mother has never forgiven me!

My father started out as an academic and did not come into general practice until after World War II, which was a good 20 years into his veterinary career, so rather later than most. In the mid-1920s, whilst at the 'Dick' Vet School, studying for his PhD on '*Radio-opaque Techniques on the Spine of the Dog*', he was sent over to the 'Meadows' to work in the medical school where his work established the basis of spinal anaesthesia. The Brook spinal needle is still in occasional use today and he was for many years the youngest student to have been awarded the DSc. Continuing his research he was awarded a Fellowship of the Royal College of Veterinary Surgeons and a Fellowship of the Royal Society of Edinburgh. He won virtually every academic award, unlike his son, who at the same stage was resitting, repeating years, "*wasting his time*" eventing, riding under rules, ski racing and sailing. Even my tutors agreed that for me academic studies were really an aggravating distraction. My father, meanwhile, was also a Blue and captained the University of Edinburgh cross-country team in 1924. He travelled Europe and North America between the wars on research projects, which included TB eradication. He learnt the language of the countries he visited, including Swedish when he studied with Professor Forsell, and brought details of equine surgical techniques back for Professor Hobday at London where he was house surgeon.

It was with great pride that I accompanied him up to London in 1983 when he received The Livesay Medal for his "*contribution to alleviating pain and suffering in animals*".

Following the departure of Professor Hobday from the Royal College, Dad decided he was not cut out for the political infighting of university life. At the outbreak of war he joined up with the RAF as he was already a competent pilot, only to be told that with his qualifications he would be of more use "*behind the scenes*". This involved stretching his mind with the MAFF, TB testing cattle in South Wales and advising on poultry diseases in Derbyshire. It was while lecturing at Derby that he met and married my mother. He finally settled down to general practice in Leamington Spa in 1946.

It was therefore with an enquiring mind that he approached everything. I well remember one poor lady fleeing the surgery clutching her dog in both arms when he had informed her that he didn't know what was wrong with her pet but it would make an interesting *postmortem*!

The family did not see a great deal of him – he'd leave early in the morning and was home late, sometimes operating into the night because something had diverted him during the day. Taking me to school one morning he heard on the news that the square-rigger *Pamir* had docked in London. (He had sailed on a sister ship as a midshipman just after qualifying.) He telephoned the surgery, postponed all appointments and instead of going to school we drove down to London for the day on a very important educational jaunt. (Similarly, I suppose, it has been known for me to phone in from the car, when hounds are nearby, and tell my assistant that she's on her own and I'm off hunting! A chip off the old block, perhaps…)

When I could, I would join him on his rounds. An early morning call at a dairy farm usually meant a pint of milk drunk straight from the churn, followed by a slap-up breakfast of fat bacon and eggs in the kitchen. This was still so in the late 1960s when I first came back to practice but, as time went on, the fat bacon disappeared and the breakfasts became fewer. We have one client who still recalls how, when the weather was clement, Dad would arrive on his horse having ridden miles down the 'green lane' with everything he required in his saddlebags, attend to the client's animals, and sometimes camp the night before returning home again. There seemed to be none of the pressures of veterinary life today. At that time, there were only three practices in the Leamington/Warwick area; now there are eight, employing dozens of veterinary surgeons all chasing the same slice of the cake. Hopefully the cake will continue to expand.

Further occasions that remain very vivid in my memory include days out in the Forest of Dean with my father and Alf Walker, a member of a well-known, long-established family of veterinary practitioners, whose nephew Alan has brought the family practice into the 20th century. My father felt it was an important part of a veterinary student's career to learn "*the old ways*". Alf was a veterinary practitioner who had spent the war in the Warwickshire Yeomanry working with RAVC staff and had come back to South Warwickshire to practice. A large part of his time was spent cutting colts. These were often unhandled and had hardly seen any human beings, resulting in a degree of sport not seen today. After lassoing the less friendly individuals, they would manage to get on a rope halter, twitch and blind, and a rope onto the tail. With two strong men on the latter, Alf would dive in with knife and pegs and the colt had been castrated and released certainly faster than I could get local anaesthetic into both testes today, and with arguably less stress to the animal. These sessions were always the precursor to monumental liquid lunches; how we arrived home safely I shall never comprehend. Even when I qualified it was commonplace to have a pub lunch and finish up there after a day's work, something that has become a rare occurrence in modern practice. After I had qualified in 1969 I would still occasionally spend a day or two with Alf; as he grew older and less agile I would go down to help him and sedate the colts for him. He would be amazed at the ease with which most colts can be cut these days using the modern sedatives which have made life so much easier and safer for us.

In Dad's time clinical life was relatively simple: you examined an animal, made a diagnosis with little or no laboratory back-up, and administered the drug(s) of your choice. There were no requirements on packaging and labelling, and 'cascade' merely related to some form of waterfall. Some years ago, Dad and I were having a quiet 'jar' with one of his surgeon pals from the local hospital. They were discussing the case of a horse for which a recently released human medicine had been administered and which is now used routinely with great success. It seemed perfectly normal and rational in those days to try out new medicines and so increase our knowledge and ability to heal; I can hear the outcry from eight furlongs today.

From a very early age I was fascinated by horses and ponies and, after learning to ride, had my first pony in 1951 at the age of six years. They were my means of freedom and, living in the country, my only means of transport. I would happily hack 20 miles to see a friend, whereas my own children balk at having to ride their ponies and latterly horses for five miles on exercise. Hunting or competition is their main interest and they definitely fall into that modern category of horse owner who is only interested in a 'turnkey' horse. I always wanted to be a 'horse vet', in those days a rare species outside the major racing centres; most practices were very general with an element of equine work.

When I was still a schoolboy, the wonderful art of casting a horse, hobbling (the more ropes around the place the better) and anaesthetising with a chloroform mask was the order of the day. Castrations, rigs, etc., were all carried out in 'the field', sometimes under an umbrella. Holding the latter was of course a highly skilful job, one, according to the old man, that I couldn't get right, either. The smell of burning flesh was commonplace – tendons, suspensories, etc., were line-fired and spavins were pin-fired ready for another round of hunting and racing. It was many years before I even considered the humanitarian aspects involved. I can't honestly say that I witnessed much in the way of suffering but I have to say that we have not 'fired' a horse in the last 25 years.

There were little or no 'case records' kept, bills 'for veterinary attention' went out once or twice a year, and a week never went by without a heated discussion with the bank manager. 'Business' was definitely a dirty word and would be likely to trigger off a visit to the local hostelry for suitable tranquillisation (some things never change).

Seeing practice at the Animal Health Trust under Colonel Langley and Dr Roberts in 1967-69, while still a student at the 'Dick' Vet, confirmed my wish to specialise in horses. After a short spell in Gloucester and Yorkshire I had the opportunity to return to Newmarket, but a call from my mother asking me to come home as my father was ill, put a stop to all my plans. In 1970 I took over a practice deeply in debt. We had no horses, virtually no small animals and a widespread farming clientbase well used to a very haphazard and eccentric veterinary service. A challenge. The small animal side was rapidly developed with an unheard of 'cash only' rule, while a regular accounting system on the large animal side rapidly improved the situation. I worked singlehandedly for three years and then took on an assistant, whereupon the growth stopped, the overheads increased, the debts grew! However, we survived and grew again. By now I had started to increase the equine side of the practice and with a third vet this rapidly increased into taking up most of my time; then, nine years ago, I decided to split away to specialise.

This entailed another three year spell of singlehanded practice (not something I would recommend) until there was sufficient work to justify an assistant; history repeated itself. Over a period of years we have converted an empty barn into an equine clinic with radiography facilities, lab, good examination areas with stocks, drop box/recovery box and surgical facilities that enable us to carry out elective surgery, and stables to 'hospitalise' both surgical and medical cases and admit mares for AI. We still seem to have fairly hefty bank loans, which happily at last seem to be under control, but we have a frightening amount of paperwork compared to the 'good old days'. How on earth I remembered all the cases then I just can't imagine; in fact I can't actually remember being able to remember the days when I could remember what happened yesterday without referral to the VDU!

Both my two elder children say that they had never really considered veterinary practice, as for one thing I had given them no encouragement, and for another it was synonymous with home. As I have always run the equine side of the practice from home, they were frequently called upon if an extra pair of hands was required. They readily helped out when we were operating, or with lab work, or simply brushing the yard or holding a horse, and my son is expert at sorting out problems with the computer. My youngest daughter, now eight years old, has been totally brought up in the practice and is very useful fetching and carrying; she is passionate about horses, has no fear and is the most likely one to follow the family tradition.

I occasionally glance through some of my father's research papers and books. The quality of radiographs taking in the 1920s put our own efforts to shame, as does the wonderful prose and use of English, which will always elude me. However, our radiographic safety procedure and standards have improved out of all recognition. Our ability to examine and carry out various procedures helped by minimal staff, with good stocks, modern sedatives, tranquillisers and anaesthetics, have transformed the equine veterinary scene, but not entirely, I hasten to add, as I nurse some significant bruises inflicted by a heavily sedated colt. In fact, most of my injuries, fortunately superficial, over the last 10 years have occurred while carrying out various procedures on sedated horses. Maybe I'm a little more careful and less trusting when they are unsedated.

As time progresses and specialisation increases, the 'general' bit of general practice, even within species specialisation, becomes less so. A realisation of limitation of skills, equipment, facilities and the increase of litigation

W.R. (Bill) Jermyn MRCVS who practised in Bristol in the North Somerset area at the turn of the century, with a pony and trap. He was much respected by his clients (Courtesy of Sidney Ricketts).

makes every professional person narrow his or her field of work in a way which only 30 years ago was definitely in some other generation's future. The 'I don't care how much it will cost' quickly followed by the 'if only you had told me how much it was going to cost' brigade has an increasing fertility rate. I am amazed that with the incredible increase in CPD courses and specialist media information rarely do I increase my 'hands-on' practical skills. Talking in the bar afterwards I always feel totally inadequate when certain techniques are discussed yet when such cases turn up at our clinic these experts disappear and the few long established centres of excellence remain the only ones with the necessary experience and/or facilities. These centres have vastly increased their own skills and equipment, keeping apace with the increase in the 'baseline' of expertise and therefore point of referral of general practitioners.

Veterinary life has become more stressful with the arrival of pagers, mobile phones, etc. (I desperately try, unsuccessfully I might add, to escape from the clinic without a student or work experience pupil in tow.) There was a time when one could drive along listening to *The Archers* with no interruption, but there is now always someone trying to get hold of us and clients know we are more accessible and are therefore more demanding. Gone are the days when you would call in the next few days; now everyone demands a call today and a time.

Our chosen profession has been good to most of us. It has proved stimulating, has provided us with an income (arguably something that is becoming much more unreliable), and has allowed us to meet an incredible cross section of society among whom we have made many good friends. These are the important things in life, and have not changed between this and my father's generation.

Major Oxspring: times remembered

STEWART HASTIE
Overton, Maids Moreton
Buckingham MK18 1RE
UK

Major G. E. Oxspring OBE FRCVS was born in 1893 and died in April 1949. He served with the Veterinary Corps in France from 1915 until the end of hostilities, during which he was mentioned in despatches. Postwar service was on secondment to cavalry units in the Sudan and then Egypt. Thereafter, his tours of duty abroad took him to China and India after which he was gazetted with a Military OBE.

Back in Britain, he eventually worked with and then succeeded Major Pryer OBE in command of the veterinary school at Aldershot. Uncertainty regarding further promotion in a diminishing army and particularly his Corps, caused his decision to resign in 1935. Following a refresher course in small animal practice at the Royal Veterinary College, he took over a mixed (mainly equine) practice in Ashford, Kent.

At his funeral service the then Director of the Army Veterinary and Remount Services, Brigadier Plunkett CBE, remembered Oxspring's distinguished service to his profession and to his Corps. In particular, he praised his zeal and devotion in all his appointments and particularly that in his research and development of radiography, with emphasis on the navicular bone in disease. The thesis written from this work led to his Fellowship of the RCVS. The Brigadier said that his retirement from this work had been a great loss to the Corps and inevitably to the horse world.

A great friend, Dr J. T. Edwards FRCVS, paid written tribute to Oxspring in the *Veterinary Record*. He, too, remarked on the reasons for men of Oxspring's calibre leaving the service but emphasised that Oxspring did so because of his wife's poor health and her desire for him to take up more lucrative work in general practice so as to enable their one and only child, a son, to receive a better education. Dr Edwards regretted that Oxspring had not opted for academic life as a clinical research worker and teacher but he was sure that all had understood the reasons for this decision.

The First Experience

I first heard of Major Oxspring when the names of the July 1944 final year examiners were announced. As students we were sure that the army rank implied a more than passing interest in matters equine. This was serious in implication as the equine species was the least important in the Glasgow Veterinary School curriculum and, for many of us, the opportunity to amend this when 'seeing practice' in the West of Scotland was extremely limited. We could but hope that these circumstantial deficits would be taken into account by the examiners. I can't remember the written paper contents but 'horse' problems either didn't loom large or were selectable.

It was only on the day of the 'oral' that word spread of Oxspring being equated not only with horses but with radiography and navicular disease. How insular and parochial we were in Glasgow! As it turned out I do not believe he asked any student about either of these subjects; perhaps he knew that it would be a waste of time.

Before university status was mandatory for the profession, the existing schools were set papers and orally examined by the same group of examiners in any one subject. Their itinerary varied year by year; this year Glasgow was last. As it happened, I was the last student. It was too late to worry about my ignorance of Oxspring's specialities; as one optimist among us said, "*Mules don't get navicular disease so I doubt if a requirement for call up into the Corps would focus on this disease*."

At Glasgow, agricultural work was held to be of greater importance for the war effort than the clinical knowledge of the horse. I doubt if navicular disease was dealt with in great detail; the College didn't possess an x-ray unit!

I walked into Oxspring's room; a stocky man with close-cropped hair and a military moustache, he was not quite what I expected for a dashing Cavalry Veterinary Officer. He was immediately affable and began his questioning on bovine teat surgery, after which he talked about military service and veterinary surgeons. He emphasised that this war didn't seem to need horses and, even in Burma, the use of mules was apparently restricted. A career with the RAVC, as distinct from war service, was not in his opinion to be contemplated.

Of course I didn't know then of his personal disappointment at having to leave the Corps when he did; had he stayed in beyond 1935, he probably would have made wartime Director rank. His only comment about Glasgow College and its teaching facilities was indirect, in suggesting to me, and no doubt others of us, that we would have gained considerably having seen so much practice with the freedom from lectures in comparison with other colleges.

Our Joint Clinical Cases

All he had on his desk were my earlier notes on the examination of two milkfloat cobs, a coal lorry halfbred Clydesdale and a fat pony. These had earlier in the day been 'walked away and trotted back' by their surly drivers in Buccleugh Street where streeetwise urchins gave us dubious advice and opinions, the latter being more of a personal nature. Oxspring referred to my notes almost *en passant*. Had I listened as well as looked, felt the leg contralateral to the one I suspected as being the lame one? Naturally, I concurred; he did not give me the impression of being a tricky examiner.

Did I think that lameness was possibly associated with the work done? Could I give examples? The carthorse was curbed in my selected lameness. I had often seen such horses being made to start off with a heavy load up a steep hill; I had, in fact, done my stable management in a city yard of around 100 such horses, few of which were given veterinary help as the drivers or carters had much more experience than many of the available veterinary surgeons. Oxspring stopped me before I floundered into 'founder'.

Practical surgery had been extremely limited in all species both at College and especially with horses; it wasn't much better while 'seeing practice'. In the former, dead subjects earmarked for anatomy specimens were first used to demonstrate denerving, resection of the sole and, where relevant, docking; chronic tendinitis subjects were dissected or fired, if only to delineate the sites.

Only front row forward-sized students were able to see these instructive interferences. Lesser mortals viewed the end results later and then referred to Dollar's *Surgery* textbook.

Bill Weipers (later Sir William and Principal of a much different Glasgow University Veterinary School) took rotas of students to his upmarket small animal practice to watch radiography in dogs. His fingers, disfigured from radiation trauma, left more lasting impressions on us than the eventual diagnostic viewing. The more ambitious, and no doubt foolhardy, offered to restrain the patients; general anaesthesia if given was for radiographic quality rather than assistant safety. Despite the obvious dangers, it was many years before greater care was taken when performing an x-ray examination.

Most equine limb fractures seen in practice were subjected to euthanasia, although occasionally heroic efforts were made with external splinting, usually in vain; no clinical cases in my time were ever brought to the College. Carpal and tarsal chip fractures were never in our case lists in either situation as young racehorses were not among our patients; nor did older Thoroughbreds and galloping horses figure in Donald Campbell's practice in North Lanarkshire.

Thanks to excellent pathology teaching by Professor Emslie, we had a very sound knowledge of traumatic inflammation and wound repair as it was then understood. Emslie taught that:

- One should always apply first principles - common things are common but uncommon ones still have the basic morbidity.
- Inflammation is a post-traumatic, natural, essential tissue reaction; it is not a disease but a temporary diseased state for survival; assist it whatever the cause, infection or wound.
- Laudable pus is not acceptable if it continues and/or worsens; it will do so in the presence of foreign material, such as dead tissue and/or bacteria. Debridement is essential, as is lavage (saline) and subsequent antisepsis. The wheel has turned again!
- In general 'seek and ye shall find'. This was particularly relevant to microbiology in these days, but it became a very important aphorism to me in many aspect of professional work, not least with radiographic plates.

These all came to mind with Oxspring's next question: "*Describe site, cause, treatment and convalescence duration in quittor.*"

Despite many final year inadequacies, trauma in draught horses' lower limbs was well taught by Professor Willie Robb in his lectures. Quittor, he emphasised, is a specific syndrome associated with necrotising trauma of a lateral (accessory) cartilage. It is not ascending 'pus in the foot'. This, with Emslie's dicta in mind, I offered in reply. "*Debridement, drainage, sterile saline lavage, antiseptic 'dyes' and perhaps glycerine or magnesium sulphate topical applications, should see the horse back in work within six weeks.*"

A slight nod of Oxspring's head was followed by: "*Would you be interested in joining me as my assistant?*"

I accepted, pending call-up (which never came). It was some time before the significance of being the last student at the last College on the examiner's itinerary dawned on me; the present incumbent had given him notice. It was even later that I experienced the power of the old boy's network, when a Colonel friend of Oxspring's visited and was introduced as the Corps Officer responsible for call-up.

August 1944

It was then that I came to the Garden of England, by now variably pockmarked by exploding flying bombs, dropped on the regular flights from the Continent that passed over Ashford. Here I became an agricultural and small animal practitioner and permitted to look, sometimes with awe and often with admiration, at English equine practice, but usually only from a distance; it was safer for the horse!

Oxspring was then a widower, the death of his wife following soon after the loss of their merchant navy cadet son by enemy action early in the war, and the strains of wartime Kent had left him a tired, slightly sad, somewhat disillusioned man.

Oxspring The Practitioner

After 20 or so years of regular Corps service, the work of a mixed practice in which horse work had declined in wartime reduced his interest but never his diligence.

Tuberculin testing, milk and dairy inspections, even the added work from the NVMA bovine health scheme inaugurated by his friends and colleagues George Gould, Sam Hignet and Henry William Steel Bodger, did not inspire him in the same way that his research and development work at Aldershot had done. For many years to come, the loss of dairy cows, in particular, to tuberculosis was dishearteningly high, as was the incidence of Brucella abortion.

His involvement with the South-East division of NVMA and eventually his appointment as an RCVS examiner did much to help his ego. His earlier Corps reputation and his horse work since, such as war allowed, had made him a much-respected equine practitioner. In East Kent he was "*the horse doctor*" and travelled far and near to carry out prepurchase examinations, work which increased from 1945 onwards. His 'vetting' opinions were of the old school, and consisted of three categories:

- Buy it.
- Buy it but beware of 'x'. The risk is worth taking and I shall advise you how to minimise this risk.
- Don't buy it.

Many of us have heard the oft-quoted maxim from older practitioners that a competent vet can 'pass' a doubtful horse, whereas an inexperienced one is more likely to fail it. Oxspring always qualified this by explaining that the good vet should be able to pick up defects and be able to analyse and assess their importance in the declared future use of the horse. A poor vet, unsure if a defect even existed, played safe. In particular, Oxspring could differentiate atypical, individual horse action, its natural way of going, from a low grade, potentially serious lameness. It was a matter of looking and seeing and then thinking. I can't remember him having recourse to radiography as an ancillary aid to his decision.

The medical treatment of dogs and cats and the usual range of spays and castrations did not enthuse him. He often threatened to put up a notice saying "*no dogs, no cats, no time*", but, of course, cash flow was important in those days.

The Man at Work

His appearance was always that of a country squire: Donegal tweed suits, raglan-sleeved overcoat, long scarf as required, snap brim trilby hat and, always, highly polished shoes. Wellington boots were never worn off a farm and cleaning them between farms was obviously important.

At work, the hat rarely came off. Even when calving cleansing a cow or stomach tubing a horse, it stayed on unless difficulties arose. As he was usually accompanied by his yardman, Strover, a muttered command to him was sufficient to have his hat removed; and for all who knew the situation to become more attentive to possible problems thus signalled.

To his discredit, most difficulties were in the first instance due to someone else: the embryotome wouldn't thread, the stomach tube pump connection was loose and so on. All concerned knew about this idiosyncracy and ignored it; helpers were always ultimately and courteously thanked whatever the outcome.

On one occasion when calving a heifer on the Romney Marsh, the group were strafed by a German fighter. Whilst helpers ran for a ditch, Strover removed Oxspring's hat and stayed with him and the recumbent animal; fortunately the gunner's aim was poor.

Army Work Abroad

Oxo, as he was fondly known, but never addressed as such by mere assistants, was never very talkative about his work or life. He was only ever reluctantly forthcoming about his spell at Aldershot, but occasionally, when driving me to a mutual case, he did open up a little and would reminisce about his times abroad.

In his opinion, the prevention of sand colic in Egyptian cavalry horses required regular administration of oil by stomach tube. On the first occasion when this order was to be expedited, the Egyptian veterinarians complained that it was too difficult and too dangerous. Oxspring himself proceeded to stomach tube a squadron of horses between lunch and tea, "*and without a single bleeder*" he proudly added.

In China, he captained the British Army Polo Team, but had little to say about veterinary work there except that, on one occasion, he was ordered north by train to be met at a station, well up country, where he was put blindfolded into a car and driven eventually to reach some mandarin's palatial estate and stables where he examined a Thoroughbred entire. The secrecy was apparently for internal political reasons. The return journey was similarly made, but before boarding the train a Chinese Officer handed him a parcel, a gift from the mandarin. It was a gold half-hunter in which bejewelled figures struck the hours and half hours and in which the numbers and the hands were of rare metal. Oxspring showed it to me once but he never carried it. I had the impression that it was to have been left to his son.

I would suggest that his Fellowship thesis, as published in the *Veterinary Record* (1935) **15**, 1433-1447, be read and studied. In conjunction with this I recommend the *Equine Veterinary Journal* (1984) **16**, 403-410, being the Sir Frederick Smith Memorial Lecture given by Colonel John Hickman, in which much reference is made to Smith's work on equine foot physiology and into his research into navicular disease at the end of the last century.

Oxspring's work, as set out in his thesis some 30–40 years later, complements Smith's pioneering research and clinical findings. The Aldershot radiography underlines and often confirms the earlier clinicohistopathological investigations. Further relevant reading is referred to in both Oxspring's and Hickman's papers. The former published another article, *Veterinary Radiology*, in the *Veterinary Record* **48**, 1145-1154.

He did eventually give me the original publications to help me to try to understand the disciplines involved, but I had the impression that he had lost some of his interest in teaching; perhaps he felt it was too late for a Glasgow graduate.

He was keener to describe the excitement he and Pryer experienced when they developed suitable radiographic techniques and settings which caused with each exposure flashes of blue light and sparks racing across the concrete floors. The horses he said were less concerned with these than were the troopers involved.

In Ashford, he used a portable Newton Victor machine which he considered adequate for horse limbs and small animals. He emphasised that success was due to using the correct settings which had to be determined for each tube no matter how it was described in the specifications. Focal distance and accurate alignment of the main beam, so that it eventually met the centre of the bone concerned at a right angle, were essential for success. The ability to go on to meet the plate at a similar angle was more difficult because of the positioning of the limb. This difficulty, he said, was much reduced once a human machine was so adapted that it could 'go to the horse' as with a portable model. It was impracticable to have the horse 'go to the machine'.

He was adamant that all sulci and other depressions which left edges must be thoroughly filled in. In those days, before Play-doh, hoof parings were ground down to a granular consistency and thoroughly mixed with lard. A refinement was to dry the horn slowly to produce a powdered form which, of course, would give better results. He pointed out that the two positions of the limb, as used in the 1930s and 1940s, required the rays to pass through the short pastern bone to reach the navicular and, as a result, variations in the all-important bone density were masked. The use of a grid was essential to minimise scatter and, of course, the shoe should always be removed. Finally, he emphasised that accurate 'reading' of the plates was essential, but that this required practice and a knowledge of the morbid changes which had taken place and which could be seen on a plate; many early stages of bone changes were not presented, even in ideal x-rays; hence later repeat plates were often necessary. This last finding he had determined from the large number of autopsies that he had carried out including the contralateral limb. He described the autopsy technique involved in getting at the podotrochlea without destruction of the vital areas of the associated tendon and the proximal and distal ligaments.

Like Smith, Oxspring found the earliest lesions of navicular to be in the bone's fibrocartilagenous posterior surface in apposition to the flexor perforans tendon (DDFT).

To me, the more important aspects of his knowledge were his clinical findings. I gathered these, some piecemeal and over long intervals. Epidemiologically, navicular disease was rarely seen in animals younger than age four years. It was associated with work on hard ground, especially with excessive trotting in the early stages of conditioning and also with excessive road work when fit. Compression rather than concussion was the underlying overstress; and he felt that this could possibly explain the cases which developed in a limb which was bearing excessive weight during box rest for the treatment of a contralateral limb. The onset is insidious and was invariably asymmetrically bilateral which was an important differential feature. Although of little clinical significance, he believed the primary lesion to be a hyperaemia and not an ischaemia.

He never seemed very concerned with hoof imbalance and, certainly, I don't remember comments about the mediolateral unlevelness but he did emphasise that an acquired overlong toe was often a contributory factor. In retrospect, I presume he did not see this as producing a broken back hoof axis. He did, however, think that a 'boxy' foot was more a consequence than a cause, but in his large sample of navicular disease cases he does not mention evidence of hoof deformation. Perhaps they had not been lame long enough to produce the presumably protective elongated heel that is discussed nowadays.

In this respect I remembered Professor Jimmy McCunn quoting the Arab horse breeders' maxim "*Keep the toes short but just level the heels, do not lower them*" and Rooney's later observation that, at least in American pleasure horses, significant conformation was small, high, hard (sic) hooves. The latter's theory of third order acceleration associated with a hard surface and a hard hoof and consequent inelegant step theory was not, of course, known to Oxspring but it does relate to some extent to the constant working on hard ground mentioned earlier.

Despite the requirements of stallion licensing in those days, Oxspring did not see navicular disease as a straight inherited disorder, only a susceptibility to it. This seemed most likely in crossbred animals - the Thoroughbred and something else - in which a heavy trunk, neck and head were supported by relatively small hooves, a genetically induced morphological deficiency which more readily fitted a concussion aetiology than the more generally accepted compression; it did not, however, rule this possibility out.

From 1945 onwards, we noted a surprisingly high incidence of navicular disease in recently 'late broken' horses, particularly those which came forward for prepurchase examination. No records were kept, but from memory some were Thoroughbred and others crosses with Irish Draught or Cleveland Bays. Most had been bred in the early war years and turned away on the relatively softer pastures of weald and marsh. Significantly, owners were keen not only to get them on the market as hunters but also to catch the increasing point-to-point trade and no doubt short cuts were taken in conditioning and training with considerable road work or work on summer dried fields. They were all in good to very good condition.

Clinically, Oxspring looked for early evidence of a shortened foreleg anterior phase stride, sufficiently more so in the primary limb to produce a patent one-leg lameness. This 'wore off' with warming up to return at the next day's start of work.

He would also look out for a 'pointing' foot posture to ease the heel, in fact to ease the pressure of the deep flexor tendon on the navicular bone which, as the disease progressed, involved alternate limb pointing.

In such there was usually a difficulty in turning in-hand to the worse limb side, a dislike of going on the hard and eventually a bilateral shortening of foreleg action to give a shuffling, stumbling gait as the horse tried to keep most of the weight towards the toes. There was a later evasion and refusals when jumping, especially on the hard. From memory, no mention was made of any characteristic hollow band over the wall of the hoof as described in other literature.

Oxspring felt that any advantage by fitting rolled toes and raised heels made little difference, except that the greater care required in preparing the foot must coincidentally have improved the length of the toes; this gave temporary improvement in many cases but, of course, the end result was always the same. I can't remember the use of bar shoes of any type.

In those days there were no efficient analgesics. In confirmed cases, neurectomy was widespread but Oxspring himself was against this procedure for the safety of the rider and the welfare of the horse. Present day discussed syndromes such as 'navicular-like disease' or 'posterior third of the hoof lameness' were not in Oxspring's vocabulary. A suspected case was considered on the basis of:

- Age.
- Work done or doing.
- Speed of onset (relative to the observational skill of the horsemaster) and duration.
- Posture in the box.
- Action, in-hand, in straight line, on the turn and in a circle on a hard, level surface, seen and heard at both walk and trot.
- Observation of the hoof conformation.
- Palpation of the limb.
- Comparative heat, presence of venous engorgement and local pulse increase.
- Careful search of the horn, wall, sole and frog before and after shoe removal; shoe wear is also assessed.
- Inducible pain as judged by a hoof tester on a searched, cleansed hoof.
- Possible low (volar) nerve block repeated in the contralateral limb if that went secondarily lame.
- Possible radiography if lameness was of several weeks duration but, if not, this ancillary aid was delayed to allow for improvement with good hoof trimming and shoeing following any treatment for incidental sole bruising, corns, etc. - the posterior third condition of today?

Oxspring did not pretend to know all the answers but he was usually spot on in suspecting navicular disease as later confirmed radiographically. I don't remember inferior border enlarged foraminae being discussed, although in his thesis he does consider them, but more as a result rather than a cause.

If navicular disease was present he was convinced that the classic distal central bone morbidity would progress to produce positive radiographic lesions in 4–6 weeks and that the early bone changes would have started, but were still negative, some time before that shortly after the fibrocartilage had become ulcerated.

His award of a Fellowship for his thesis obviously gave

him much quiet satisfaction but I never heard him 'throw rank' about it.

Other Equine Practice

He always cast a horse for castration using chloroform or chloral hydrate intravenously as the eventual anaesthetic. The inhalation method was often applied to the standing horse, especially if it was mature; the horsemaster then walked it round, with occasional toppings up into the canvas mask, until it went down and was then roped. I can remember one occasion when the surgical area was in an orchard. Perhaps the horseman had inhaled too much chloroform unintentionally; the now circling horse eventually fixed him to an apple tree as the rope, too long to begin with, encircled both. Oxspring was not amused!

Chloral was too risky to give intravenously to a standing horse, as there were no intravenous giving sets in those days and dislodgement of a needle had somewhat horrible consequences.

Actual cautery was effected under local anaesthesia but if the horse was difficult it had to go down under a general. The subsequent blistering, then deemed obligatory, was patently the real cause of the pain of 'firing'. Double racking and neck collars were essential in such cases. Towards the end of his practising days, Oxspring stopped blistering and I was glad to follow. I have a feeling that his new wife, a competent and caring horsewomen, had more than a little say in this decision.

Colic cases were invariably stomach tubed with linseed oil, occasionally aloes or turpentine and, in later days, with 'Altan', an anthraquinone, the dose of which had to be carefully assessed to avoid superpurgation. He avoided using injectable purgatives, even when obstructive colic was diagnosed but, come to think of it, rectal examinations were noted by their absence!

The difficulties and disadvantages, not only of the preantibiotic era, but the dubious effects of the simpler sulphonamides in horses were problems in all horse practices and certainly not common to Oxspring's. He, too, depended on the management of wounds by debridement and lavage but we never were heroic enough to counteropen infected tendon sheaths. Setons were very much in vogue for the treatment of bursal enlargements and indolent abscesses.

Employer/Employee Relationship

His attitude towards assistants was of the old school. Time off was a privilege, not a right. Mine was a Sunday afternoon, provided his prelunch sherry, only taken on a Sunday, did not cause a headache. It often did!

His sense of humour was not great, but he often recalled an occasion during his refresher course at the RVC under the great Hobday when, at a free clinic in Camden Town, he asked a small Cockney boy what ailed his cat. "*Me muvver says to take its back teef out, guvnor.*" Hobday turned to the students: "*Never underestimate the standard of learning of the poor and their quality care for their animals; here we have a case where dental problems have been perceived.*" As he opened the cat's jaw the lad quickly retorted: "*Not them teef. Me muvver means the ones between its hindlegs.*" This recollection had Oxo chortling for some time.

His willingness to help an assistant with a difficult horse case, when such an occasion arose, was always ethical, never patronising and invariably instructive. The request for his second opinion invariably came from his assistant.

In agricultural work the request usually came from the farmer, especially if the 'young vetinry' had had the temerity to diagnose a condition not seen by the owner before. On one such occasion, I diagnosed a bovine pyelonephritis to differentiate it from the suspected *postpartum* metritis. "*Better get the boss,*" I was told. Oxspring arrived, parking his car as close to the byre door as he could. Following a quiet discussion he said: "*Go back to the cow, Hastie.*" It was some 15 feet down the shed. "*Now press down with your finger on to the side of the backbone over the kidney in question.*" This I did and the cow responded to this spinal stimulation with the usual dipping of the back. "*Just as I thought,*" said he to the farmer, "*a painful kidney disease.*" The farmer was awestruck with admiration and showed no reluctance in having to cycle back to the surgery for a bottle of Mist. Chelidon Co. When I handed it to him he commented on my good fortune in working for such a clever man. I fear cattle medicine was not Oxspring's forte.

His Later Days

Oxspring married again in 1946 and soon after moved with his wife, Marjorie, to a country cottage and left me in charge, which I took to be a compliment; it certainly meant a dramatic increase in salary to £1000 per year. I could now afford my own car so the bicycle, my previous means of conveyance on time off, could be relegated.

The Oxsprings took to hunting in a serious way. He became a much happier, more relaxed man, but didn't have much time left to enjoy his new bliss. New horses were bought in Ireland and his wife, although an experienced rider, found she couldn't hold the proverbial one side of her mare in the hunting field. There was no argument from him about warranties; he could hold it, so the problem was his wife's. The financial loss in selling through a local dealer was not great. As a vendor he explained why and thus felt that he had behaved correctly in the whole deal, as indeed he had; if only present day purchasers behaved in such a sensible manner.

Conclusion

I must pay tribute to the fact that he encouraged me to become involved in veterinary politics, which led to my appointment to the Council of the National Medical Association via the South-East Division Committee.

These were the days of Presidents W. M. Mitchell, L. G. Anderson, R. F. Montgomerie and J. W. Brouford. I remember, too, the charismatic A. J. Wright. Most of these were actively involved in the work preliminary to the new Veterinary Surgeons Act and the licensing of Veterinary Practitioners.

In 1952, under A. M. Graham, a Regional Veterinary Officer, the NVMA was reconstituted (somewhat reminiscent of wartime dried egg) as the British Veterinary Association.

Major Oxspring was always willing to encourage one to engage in field research along with, for example, the Wellcome Research Station at Frant, Sussex, under Sam Hignet, with particular regard to bovine infertility and nutrition.

I shall always be grateful for Oxspring's support if and when things went wrong. His attitude to my driving was another matter!

Like many others, I regretted his premature death following a heart attack.

The Swedish contribution to equine veterinary science and practice in general; and to BEVA in particular

HARRY PETTERSSON
The Regional Animal Hospital
Box 22097
Helsingborg S-250 23
Sweden

History of Veterinary Medicine in Sweden

The first veterinary school in modern times was founded in Lyon, France 1762. At the same time Carl von Linné, one of Sweden's best known scientists of the 18th century, realised the lack of knowledge in veterinary medicine in our country. He advised the government of the day to send Peter Hernquist, one of his most intelligent pupils, to Lyon to study 'Art Veterinaire'.

On his return, Hernquist became the founder of veterinary education in Sweden, by setting up the first Swedish veterinary school in Skara in 1775. Veterinary education was moved to Stockholm in 1821, where a new school was built. This school was succeded by two other schools in Stockholm, the most recent being built in 1909–1911, and incorporated design features which at that time were quite unique.

In particular the facilities were built so that horses could be examined on an indoor track, a feature which proved to be important for advances made there in the field of lameness examination. Forssell introduced diagnostic nerve blocks and intrasynovial anaesthesia as tools for use in the examination of lame horses. This institute was honoured, in 1915, by being granted the status of Royal Veterinary College. In 1935, veterinary scientists were given the right by the government to present and defend their scientific work in theses at the Royal Veterinary College. Up to 1998, 360 theses have been presented and accepted, 49 of them on subjects of equine research.

Veterinary education remained in Stockholm until 1976, when the college became a faculty and was integrated with the Swedish University of Agricultural Sciences, in Uppsala.

The Swedish Contribution to Equine Veterinary Science and Practice

At the start of veterinary education in Sweden, teaching and practice were focused on the horse. This situation remained so until the early part of the 20th century. From the 1930s to the 1970s the horse population in Sweden diminished from 720,000 to 65,000 and so did, to a certain extent, teaching, research and practice in the equine field.

During the last three decades, the horse population has increased to around 230,000 horses. Furthermore, most of the horses are today used for sport and pleasure. The horse has become more valuable both economically and, especially, emotionally. The sport of professional trotting has an annual turnover of 10 billion SEK. The total turnover for the horse industry is 15 billion SEK. Riding has become the second biggest sport in Sweden with around half a million participants.

Altogether one million people have some connection to the horse, which is again in focus. With this development there is a growing demand from the horse-owning public for increased knowledge both in equine science and practice.

Equine Science in Sweden

Earlier this century unique scientific research on laminitis was published by Åkerblom in 1934 and Obel in 1948. In the 1960s Sune Persson presented an excellent thesis on blood volume and working capacity in the horse. This was the start of the study of exercise physiology in the horse and was followed by many other important scientific contributions in this field.

Ingvar Fredricson built a unit for equine joints kinematics and coordination. Several theses in this area have followed. Other areas of equine research, where Sweden has made significant contributions include anaesthesia, biomechanics, breeding, conformation, 'doping', immunology, infectious diseases, intestinal diseases, laminitis, muscular function and dysfunction, orthopaedics, osteochondrosis, respiratory diseases, reproduction, racetracks and stables design and training and competition.

The main portion of equine research is done at the veterinary faculty. But clinical research is common and necessary at the larger equine clinic, with the substantial clinical material at their disposal. During the last decades, a growing cooperation in equine clinical research has developed between the faculty and the larger equine clinics. This collaboration will become stronger in future. A major problem today is funding for all the proposed projects. Only around six million SEK are available every year. Half of that sum comes from 'external' sources such as sport or sponsorship from insurance companies.

Equine Practice in Sweden

Up to the beginning of the 1950s, almost all equine practice was ambulatory. Only the Royal Veterinary College in Stockholm and the state-managed animal hospital in Skara could treat horses in ward units.

The Region Animal Hospital in Helsingborg was founded in 1954 by Fritz Sevelius to coincide with the start of hospitalisation of animals in Sweden. Today there are eight animal hospitals of high standard available for treatment of injured and diseased horses at 24 hours per day. The National Trotting and Racing Association has, during the last 20 years, built 19 well-equipped horse clinics at racetracks all over Sweden. These see patients during day time and at race times. They have no ward units for hospitalisation of patients. Problematic cases and cases presented out of hours are referred to the animal hospitals. State district veterinarians and private practitioners take care of the ambulatory practice. It is fair to say that equine practice is of high standard and available throughout the whole country.

The Swedish Contribution of Equine Science and Practice to BEVA

Fritz Sevelius was also a leader of continuing education in Sweden. He was one of the founders of the Association of Swedish Veterinary Special Practitioners in 1949. Provision of continuing education in small animal and equine practice was one of its aims. Several British veterinary surgeons were invited to speak at the annual conferences. When BEVA was founded in 1963, an important step was taken to stimulate equine science, practice and continuing education both on national and an international basis. In 1964 Fritz Sevelius was invited to speak at the annual BEVA congress. He became an ambassador for BEVA in Sweden. Very soon Swedish equine veterinary surgeons were the most numerous foreign participants at the annual BEVA meetings. And it remained so for many years. Later Sevelius was made an Honorary Member of BEVA.

Sevelius also stimulated young Swedish veterinarians to produce papers in the equine field. I was very happy to be invited and to present the first paper on Bone Cysts in the Horse in 1968 and, later, on fracture treatment, among several other papers. Swedish equine basic and clinical research was recognised by BEVA, when many Swedish equine scientists and practitioners were invited to present papers at the annual conferences over the years. Notable contributions to BEVA have been made in areas of exercise physiology (Sune Persson), equine joints kinematics and coordination (Ingvar Fredricson) osteochondrosis (Rejnö, Strömberg, Dalin and Sandgren) orthopedics (Nilsson, Knudsen, Ahlengärd and Dalin) muscular function and exercise physiology (Lindholm and others). Many Swedish colleagues have contributed to the *Equine Veterinary Journal.* But it is also important to mention that many British veterinarians have given guest lectures and refresher courses in Sweden during many years. These have included Rossdale, Cook, Barnett, Jeffcott, Edwards, Dyson and McEvoy, to mention a few.

The communication and cooperation between British and Swedish equine scientists and practitioners has been very fruitful and BEVA has played a central role here. It is also important to mention the outstanding value of the *Equine Veterinary Journal* and *Equine Veterinary Education.* These publications, spread all over the equine world, have had an enormous influence on equine science and continuing education.

BEVA is to be congratulated for its admirable work during the 20th century. It is my true belief that BEVA will play an even greater role for the equine veterinary profession in the next millennium.

Theses in Equine Science in Sweden 1931–1998

Carlström, Birger (1931) *Über die Ätiologie und Pathogenese der Kreuzlähme des Pferdes Haemoglobinaemia paralytica*, Berlin & Leipzig.

Åkerblom, Eric (1934) Über die Ätiologie und Pathogenese der Futterrehe beim Pferde. *Skandinavisches Archiv für Physiologie* **68**, *Suppl.*

Lehnert, Edvin (1939) *Ein Beitrag zur Kenntnisder Bluttypen des Pferdes mit Hilfe arteigener, hochwertiger, gruppenspezifischer Isoimmunsera*, Uppsala.

Obel, Nils (1948) *Studies on the Histopathology of Acute Laminitis*, Uppsala.

Tufvesson, Gunnar (1952) *Studier över Hästens Ospecifika Bakbenslymfangit*, Stockholm.

Månsson, Ingmar (1957) The intestinal flora in horse with certain skin changes, with special reference to the coliform microbes. *Acta. pathol. et microbiol. Scand., Suppl.* **119**.

Hansson, Claes-Henry (1958) *Studies on Succinylcholine as a Muscle-relaxing Agent in Veterinary Medicine*, Lund.

Björck, Gustaf (1958) Studies on the draught force of horses. Development of a method using strain gauges for measuring forces between hoof and ground. *Acta. Agric. Scand., Suppl.* **4**.

Persson, Sune (1967) On blood volume and working capacity in horses. Studies of methodology and physiological and pathological variations. *Acta. vet. Scand., Suppl.* **119**.

Schubert, Bertil (1967) Identification and metabolism of some doping substances in horses. *Acta. vet. Scand., Suppl.* **21**.

Strömberg, Berndt (1971) The normal and diseased superficial flexor tendon in racehorses. A morphologic and pathologic investigation. *Acta. radiol., Suppl.* **305**

Persson, Lars (1971) On the synovia in horses. A clinical and experimental study. *Acta. vet. scand., Suppl.* **35**.

Fredricson, Ingvar (1972) *Equine Joint Kinematics and Coordination: Photogrammetric Methods Involving High Speed Cinemathography*, Stockholm.

Hyllseth, Björn (1973) *A Study of Equine Arteritis Virus with Special Reference to Serology and Structure*, Stockholm.

Nilsson, Gunnar (1973) De Distala Lederna och Falangerna hos den Varmblodiga Travaren. En Morfologisk, Klinisk Kemisk och Ergonomisk Undersökning. *Acta. vet. Scand., Suppl.* **44**.

Lindholm, Arne (1974) *Muscle Morphology and Metabolism in Standardbred Horses at Rest and During Exercise*, Stockholm.

Bergsten, Gunnar (1974) Blood pressure, cardiac output, and blood-gas tension in the horse at rest and during exercise. *Acta. vet. Scand., Suppl.* **48**.

Rydén, Lars (1975) *On Equine Infectious Anemia (EIA): A Serological and Field Study*, Stockholm.

Klingeborn, Berndt (1976) *Studies on Differentiation between Attenuated and Wild-type Strains of Equid Herpes Virus 1*, Uppsala.

Rejnö, Sven (1976) *Osteochondros, Synovit och Synoviaförändringar hos Unga Sporthästar*, Stockholm.

Wierup, Martin (1977) *Equine Intestinal Clostridiosis. An Acute Disease in Horses associated with Intestinal Counts of Clostridium Perfringens Type A*, Uppsala.

Drevemo, Stig (1980) *Racing Trot: Computerised Analysis of Linear and Temporal Gait Characteristics based on High Speed Cinematography*, Uppsala.

Hoppe, Fredrik (1984) *Osteochondrosis in Swedish Horses: A Radiological and Epidemiological Study with Special Reference .to Frequency and Heredity*, Uppsala.

Dalin, Göran (1984) *On the Back of the Horse: A Morphological, Clinico-pathological and Experimental Study with Special Reference to Sacroiliac Joint*, Uppsala.

Ronéus, Bengt (1985) *Betydelsen av Tillskott av Selen och E-vitamin Till Häst. En Kliniskbiokemisk och Morfologisk Studie på Friska Hästar och Hästar med Muskelsjukdom,* Uppsala.

Magnusson, Lars-Erik (1985) *Studies on the Conformation and Related Traits of Standardbred Trotters in Sweden*, Skara.

Lindberg, Ronny (1985) *On Granulomatous Enteritis and Eosinophilic Granulomatosis in the Horse*, Uppsala.

Carlsten, Johan (1986) *Imaging of the Equine Heart: An Angiocardiographic and Echocardiographic Investigation*, Uppsala.

Valberg, Stephanie (1986) *Skeletal Muscle Metabolic Responses to Exercise in the Horse, Effects of Muscle Fibre Properties, Recruitment and Fibre Composition*, Uppsala.

Nyman, Görel (1987) *Pulmonary Function in the Anesthetised Horse Analysis of Gas Exchange and Effects of Selective Ventilation of Dependent Lung Regions,* Uppsala.

Gottlieb-Vedi, Marianne (1988) *Circulatory and Muscle Responses to Draught Work of Varying Intensity and Duration in Standardbred Horses*. Uppsala.

Abusugra, Izzeldin (1989) *Epizootology of Influenza in Sweden in Horses, Pigs and Mink*, Uppsala.

Junkergård, Jörgen (1989) *Studies on Cerebral Mediation of ACTH-cortisol Secretion and other Responses to Systemic Angiotensin ll,* Uppsala.

Björkman, C. (1989) *Methodological and Biochemical Aspects of Acetylcholinesterase and Acetate in Blood from Cattle and Acetyl-CoA Synthesising Enzymes in Spinal Cord from Ruminants and Monogastrics Animals*, Uppsala.

Berg, Mikael (1991) *Studies of Genetic Relationships and Variation of Negative-strand RNA Viruses Causing Infection in Animals Equine Influenza (H3N8, Mink Influenza (H10N4) and Porcine Paramyxovirus (LPMV)*, Uppsala.

Ekfalck, Anders (1991) *Studies on the Morphology and Biochemistry of the Epidermal Tissue of the Equine and the Bovine Hoof with Special Reference to Laminitis,* Uppsala.

Ingvast Larsson, Carina (1991) *Pharmacodynamic Effects and Pharmacokinetics of Theophylline and Clenbuterol* in vitro *and* in vivo *studies in the Horse and Rat,* Uppsala.

Ronéus, Merike (1992) *Muscle Characteristics in Horses in Relation to Age, Sex and Training*, Uppsala.

Darenius, Kerstin (1992) *Early Pregnancy Loss in the Mare,* Uppsala.

Sandgren, Björn (1993) *Osteochondrosis in the Tarsocrural Joint and Osteochondral Fragments in the Metacarpo/metatarsophalangeal Joints in Young Standardbreds*, Uppsala.

Holmström, Mikael (1994) *Quantitative Studies on Conformation and Trotting Gaits in the Swedish Warmblood Riding Horse*, Uppsala.

Karlström, Kristina (1995) *Capillary Supply, Fibre Type Composition and Enzymatic Profile of Equine, Bovine and Porcine Locomotor and Nonlocomotor Muscles*, Uppsala.

Broström, Hans (1995) *Equine Sarcoids, a Clinical, Epidemiological and Immunological Study*, Uppsala.

Roethlisberger-Holm, Karin (1995) *Transtracheal Pressure Recordings in the Exercising Horse*, Uppsala.

Ronéus, Nils (1997) Muscle metabolic response to track exercise in Standardbred trotters. *Acta. Universitat. Agric. Sueciae Vet.* **6**.

Johnston, Christopher (1997) On the kinematics and kinetics of the distal limb in the Standardbred trotter. *Acta Universit. Agric. Sueciae Vet.* **22**.

Roepstorff, Lars (1997) A force measuring horse shoe applied in kinetic and kinematic analysis of the Trotting horse. *Acta. Universitat. Agric. Sueciae Vet.* **14**.

Otte, Kerstin (1997) The equine IGF genes, structural and transcriptional features. *Acta. Universitat. Agric. Sueciae Vet.* **24**.

Kallings, Peter (1998) Effects of bronchodilating and non-steroidal anti-inflammatory drugs on performance potential in the horse. *Acta. Agric. Sueciae Vet.* **30**.

Radiological and other memories of Victor Berwyn Jones

VICTOR BERWYN JONES (1898–1968)

The following extracts are taken from the family memoirs of Victor Berwyn Jones, who worked in general practice at Wonersh Yard Stables, near Guildford in Surrey. They have been edited by his son, Michael.

Radiology

We became a family on Boxing Day, 1925, when Michael was born. He was a lusty lad with hazel eyes and his mother Nora's very dark brown hair. His arrival provided us with an added incentive to make the practice thrive, and may have unconsciously been responsible for my decision to expand my facilities and services.

My interest in radiology was started by a medical friend who had installed a set of Roentgen tubes in a room adjoining his surgery in Guildford. Radiology was just beginning to be more generally used in human medicine, and sometimes I had taken a canine casualty into him when I thought a picture was essential for an accurate diagnosis.

This room of his was full of a fearsome collection of coils of wire, insulating cups and transformers which emitted explosive cracks and sparks when it was switched on, and sounded highly dangerous. Of course, it was not appreciated at that time just how dangerous it could be, because the damaging effects of continued exposure to the rays were slow to make themselves known; but many of those early operators became maimed, or even died, as a result of pioneering work that had yet to reveal the precautions needed to avoid the ill effects of irradiating themselves.

The procedure took so long, and was so frightening to an animal, that I always had to give it a narcotic before taking it in. The pictures were usually surprisingly good, and provided invaluable information for me on many occasions. I became so impressed and got so involved in the technicalities, reading all the available books and catalogues on the subject, that I resolved to get a set for myself. Only a few firms sold the sets, but I found out that an American firm would shortly be the first to sell a set small enough to pack into a suitcase - at a price. The temptation proved too much for me, and I sent in my order.

The next essential stage in my plan was to advertise my specialist ability in the veterinary press in order to generate enough work to recover the vast expenditure, but I could not do this until I had learned how to operate the machine properly; so I spent a long time calibrating it by trial and error to find the electrical output needed for the sort of radiographs I would be likely to take.

An old student friend, Gerald Langford of Ardenrun, Lingfield, replied to my advertisement by telephone, asking me if I would travel down to x-ray one of his cases, a dog belonging to a wealthy client of his. We set off bravely that day, Nora being more frightened than I was of the newfangled apparatus.

On arrival at the dog owner's home, a footman ushered us into an upstairs room where we unpacked and assembled the set. Then, to our dismay, we discovered that the house was powered by a private plant and, although I had brought a transformer with me, I had not calibrated for low-power direct current in my experiments. It had never occurred to me.

When I thought I had probably got things right to cater for this unexpected difficulty, I switched on. There was a blinding flash of blue light across the exposed wires of the set, and all the house lights failed. Servants started dashing about, doors banged and orders were being echoed around the depths of the mansion in the general confusion that resulted. We groped our way to the door to find that the staff had reached the stage of distributing candles.

We were handed a couple of these in an uncivil, rather aloof silence, and then had to poke about the passages until we found the fuse boxes. Nobody knew where they were because the estate electrician had gone home. I removed the porcelains one by one, replacing the burnt-out wires with Nora's hairpins for lack of any proper fuse wire. We exposed four films, and sent up a silent prayer that they would be adequate.

The hairpins stood the test of all my x-ray work on the dog and, for all I know, may still be in place. After processing the films late that night back at home, it was a great relief to find that Lady Luck had been a friend to us; the pictures were good enough to make quite clear the extent of the damage, and would be useful to my friend in repairing it.

We had now (1926) been working every day of the week, and often late at night, for nearly two years. We had needed a holiday for some months. Thanks to my fees from work I'd done for the Ministry of Agriculture and, more recently, the extra money earned from my radiography, which proved to be in great demand, we decided to find a locum tenens to look after things for us while we left Michael with my parents in the neighbouring village of Shamley Green. An Irish friend kindly agreed to undertake the task, and we left him with the kennels full of dogs to treat, and a parrot and monkey as well.

I had persuaded Nora that the happiest holiday for us could be spent on the Norfolk Broads, and had arranged to hire a sailing cutter with a comfortable cabin from Wroxham. Although Nora was initially a little anxious about the prospect, as she had not been sailing before, her fears were soon allayed by lovely weather and the serenity of sailing in the charming Fens. It was not quite as serene as I had expected from my youthful experiences there, however; the fenlands had been discovered by many more holidaymakers, and some of them had introduced noise, litter and oil pollution to the area with their motor-boats. All the same, we managed to find a deserted sea-beach adjoining one of the meres where we sunbathed and swam for a couple of days.

We returned home feeling refreshed and relaxed to find

our locum had done us proud. All the cases had progressed well, except the parrot which had died. When we left, it had been suffering from nudity due to persistent feather-picking which I thought might be caused by skin mites, so I had left instructions for it to be sprayed daily with an appropriate parasiticide. I had forgotten to be more specific, and should have said once daily. It turned out that poor Polly had been sprayed many times each day, in fact every time it was seen plucking itself, and expired from too much of such attention.

Our other unusual patient, the monkey, was just fine, and greeted us in the red flannel jacket that had helped him recover from pneumonia by waving his banana in front of a broad, toothy grin!

The Practice Thrives

New clients arrived in rapid succession soon after I had recovered from my hunting accident. Work that came along to expand the practice naturally tended towards my own special interest in horses, as word of this was spreading. A wealthy commercial magnate, Michael (Inky) Stephens, owned an estate at Ewhurst not far from us called Coverwood, and a large string of racehorses, both chasers and hurdlers.

His trainer was Morgan D. Blair, whose hobby was breeding miniature Bull Terriers with Yorkshire Terriers to produce a very attractive small dog. This crossbreeding created difficulties during whelping, and Blair discussed this with a breeder of Dachshunds, who had had similar trouble. She told him I had overcome the problem by Caesarean operations, usually successful provided the cases were presented in good time. So Blair noted my name and telephone number on the back of an envelope, which he later put on his desk with instructions to his Head Lad to call me if such a difficulty arose during one of his frequent absences on business, or for any other matter requiring veterinary attention.

One summer's day, when Blair was away playing polo, one of the horses in his home paddock was seriously savaged by a dog. His Head Lad rang me (at a time when I was lucky enough to be free) so I rushed over to dress the mare who had been badly mauled about the throat. During my visit to see how the mare was progressing the next day, Blair was there and asked me to have a look at another horse that had a small tumour on its fetlock. He was worried because he thought it was affecting its performance at the gallop. I advised a careful bit of surgery under a local anaesthetic.

I dissected out the small growth the next day, encountering the usual difficulties associated with a very fit and highly nervous Thoroughbred; after I had sutured and dressed the wound, they told me that it was entered for the Champion Hurdle race at Cheltenham, and that was less than three weeks away! I secretly kept my fingers crossed about the horse's chances as I did not really expect the surgical wound to heal in time for the race, especially when it was in full work, doing the daily winding-up gallops that were needed before the big race. But it did; and to everyone's delight the horse, Victor Norman, won the race to become Champion Hurdler of 1936.

What more could I ask?! Such luck is a bonus indeed!

It was soon after this that the same trainer, Morgan Blair, asked me to operate on a 'roarer' - the name given to a horse suffering from an inability to breathe properly during exertion, and typified by the sounds of roaring and whistling it makes during inspiration at a canter or gallop. This case had already been operated upon unsuccessfully by another surgeon, so it was a wonderful opportunity for me to put it right and gain another influential client; which I did, thank goodness.

The operation involves correcting the inability of one or both of the vocal cords inside the larynx to open well enough during inspiration to allow a free flow of air to reach the lungs. Obviously this problem is a serious handicap for a racehorse. It can be corrected by stripping the mucous membrane from a little pocket behind each vocal cord so that the opposing (now raw) surfaces heal together and pull the protruding cords back out of the way of the airflow.

Needless to say, it is difficult to work inside the larynx, and not every operation on it is a success. In this particular case, I found that I could cure the trouble by merely cutting the vocal cords - another bit of luck for me. My special interest in horses had now reached the stage when I wanted to focus in greater depth on special problems. I chose to do so on the origin and treatment of chronic, often incurable, diseases and paid particular attention to navicular disease which was prevalent, and still is in 1957. It is a crippling complaint that causes much suffering and loss, affecting the navicular bone - a small shuttle-shaped bone within the hoof - which decays prematurely for an unknown reason.

My research into this disease was helped by my radiographic set, as well as by the consignment of hooves from a London knackery that I arranged to be sent to me each week. I could dissect these after x-raying them, and compare my dissection notes with the pictures. After reviewing several hundreds of these, I became an expert interpreter of the radiographs of any horse's foot, and had some of my results published in the professional journals. In this way my work became even better known, and my services were in demand from the main racehorse centres at Newmarket, Lambourn, Epsom and the South Downs.

I designed a travelling darkroom and had it mounted on a trailer for hitching onto my super new Bentley, so that now I could offer on-the-spot development and diagnostic services, as well as travel the long distances required in speedy comfort. I could rarely fit into each day all that I wanted to get done. Two of the leading veterinary horse practitioners of their day became my advisers and friends, E. Brayley Reynolds and Sir Frederick Hobday, and sent many cases to me. Thanks to their kindness in showing me their methods, I was able to develop my own surgical techniques for the more specialised equine operations.

In addition, I gained permission from surgeons at the Surrey County Hospital to attend their operations and study their methods whenever I could manage it. I purchased horses that needed surgery in order to perfect my techniques, and then sold them afterwards. By doing things this way, I acquired skill and confidence without risking my reputation on animals owned by someone else. It was not long before all sorts of specialist equine surgical cases were being referred to me, and visits to training establishments alone were taking up two or three days of my time each week.

The influx of work outgrew our facilities, and made bigger premises an essential next step. We needed more stabling, a saddle room, lofts and, above all, an operating theatre for horses, which meant a barn - the only sort of building likely to be large enough for conversion.

Research Work

My interest in the aetiology of the chronic bone diseases causing lameness in horses had not diminished. I found time to keep abreast of current thinking and developments by reading and entering into discussion with other researchers.

One theory held, concerning disease of the navicular bone, was that it wasted away due to a poor blood supply. An improved blood supply could be obtained by dissecting away the outer layer of the supplying artery. This operation removed the nerve responsible for contracting the artery, so it dilated and provided a better supply of blood below the area dissected. I had applied this technique to several hunters that were lamed by navicular disease with good results.

These results made me wonder if the diagnosis of this condition could be improved by radiography, by demonstrating whether or not the artery was patent. So I experimented on a large number of *postmortem* cases by injecting an opaque medium into their leg arteries, and then x-raying them. I was soon satisfied that most of those with diseased navicular bones also had a relevant branch artery that was shrivelled or occluded in some way.

This radiographic work fascinated me, so much so that I wanted to extend it to other parts of the body and, more importantly, to the living animal in case *postmortem* changes masked or distorted reality. One of the many difficulties to overcome involved the equine head, which had not, at that time, been radiographed successfully. I worked late for many a night, sometimes not able to start until midnight, x-raying an old pony I had purchased, and developing and labelling the resultant films.

After several years, I had a complete *Radiographic Atlas of the Normal Anatomy of the Horse* (including the skull) which was labelled and annotated with interpretations. The manuscript and films filled a large suitcase that I sent to the publishers in London, Ballière, Tindall & Cox, on the eve of the outbreak of the Second World War. The publishers stored it in their vaults until they were able to get started on it. It was a sad blow for me when a bomb wrecked these vaults, and destroyed a work that I can never repeat. The profession still lacks (in 1958) such an atlas in spite of the great advances in radiographic apparatus and technique since that war started.

Another aspect of bone disease that interested me was the possible influence of the parathyroids, embedded in the larger thyroid gland of the horse. Among other things, the parathyroids were said to control calcium levels in the body. This held out the hope to me of trying to prove that diseased parathyroids and diseased bones were linked.

Unfortunately, the measure of efficient parathyroids was the level of calcium in the blood, but nobody knew what that level should be in horses. So I collected blood samples from a large number of horses, and also their histories, age, sex, etc., which took a long time in the daily whirl of a busy practice, and got them analysed by a friendly biochemist who was interested too. Finally, we were able to establish an average normal equine blood level to our satisfaction.

The next logical step seemed to be to remove a gland from a horse that had bone disease as well as an abnormal level of calcium in its blood. Some years later, I came across such a case in one of the training stables I attended. He had been a brilliant sprinter, and was still a splendid young animal, but had lost his form. His trainer said he was 'a dog', would not try, and could no longer gallop well. His owner no longer wanted to meet the expense of keeping him. The only clinical fault I could find was enlargement of one thyroid gland.

I persuaded them to let me keep him in my yard for further observation, where I found his blood calcium was lower than normal and x-rays showed he also had incipient bone disease - a perfect case for experimental surgery! The only snag was that there was no record of anyone ever having removed the thyroid gland from a horse. It proved to be a fairly tricky job because the gland lies against the jugular vein, but luck was with me, and I was able to send it off to a pathologist. He reported the thyroid was abnormal, but could find nothing wrong with the parathyroids.

The horse was returned and put back to work. His trainer was delighted to find the lethargy gone, and had high hopes that he would regain his old form. Unfortunately, we were never to find this out, nor was I able to continue my investigations into this line of work. The war had intervened once again.

It was soon after this operation that I had the bad luck to lose my radiographic set. My travelling darkroom did sterling service being towed around behind my car; it contained all my apparatus, which could be trundled down its ramp with ease, and allowed the development of films on the spot which avoided the need for any return visits to retake unsatisfactory results. It was a reliable and convenient asset that I valued highly.

Its coupling to the car broke one evening while returning home, and it ended its life upside down in a ditch with its contents completely wrecked. To make matters worse, it was not insured!

Twelve years had flown by from the day I put up my plate in 1925 and, apart from occasional solo short breaks, Nora and I had not had a holiday together since our belated honeymoon. Our social life had been almost nonexistent too because, although initially we had dined out and given parties ourselves, I was nearly always called away from them to some urgent business or other. Nora got fed up with making excuses on my behalf, so we felt it was unfair to all those involved, and stopped giving or accepting invitations. We decided that we had now reached a stage when we could take some time off. Michael was away at Picket Post Preparatory School in the New Forest; his sister Ann was happy with nanny, her school friends at St Catherine's, Bramley, and her pony; all our domestic, kennel and stable staff were efficient and reliable, and could be left to care for things in our absence - especially at the slacker period of the year - under the guidance of a capable *locum tenens*.

We took three blissful weeks off and went to Switzerland, returning via Brittany. We toured by car in a luxury made possible by our four-and-a-half litre Bentley open coupé that was purchased for its ability to pull our trailers - horsebox and darkroom - as well as its ability to get me to Newmarket and other distant centres without an unreasonably early start, and yet be in time to meet trainers after their first string had come in from work and, more importantly, its reliability.

During the trip, I visited the famous veterinary school at Zurich to discuss my radiographic work with one of the professors, and Nora and I both called in to see the cavalry school at Samur in Brittany. Otherwise, all our time was spent in luxurious idleness, and the sun shone brilliantly every day!

From faith healer to physician to clinician

PETER ROSSDALE
Beaufort Cottage Stables
High Street
Newmarket
Suffolk CB8 8JS
UK

The origins of man's capacity to heal fellow man goes back to antiquity; to the very origins of altruism, where one individual made the life of another easier, more bearable, more whole.

Whether this was accomplished by physical support, such as that given to the lame or assistance to a mother in the act of birth, by the laying on of hands, in such as massage, or by soothing through the sound of music or of speech, providing associations of tranquillity, optimism and encouragement, whatever the means, those who practised this altruism were the early healers of mankind.

Over time, healing became an art form practised by individuals; but there was little or no knowledge; and faith was the medium by which the giver and the receiver of what we now called medicine was practised. As knowledge about human function developed about 1000 BC, the faith healer gave way to the physician who introduced logic to the methods of healing; and concerns began to surface as to cause and effect, both as an end point as well as to an understanding of the pathways between the two.

In the 19th and early 20th centuries, great strides were made in the practice of medicine and the introduction of surgery. Veterinarians joined in this programme and became members of a profession, they too joined the ranks of physicians but practising their art and science on animals and not on man. Nevertheless, there is essentially no difference between the human and the veterinary physician in their approach, apart from that imposed by the different physiology and behaviour between species.

In the latter decades of the 20th century, the term clinician has come to replace that of physician. The distinction may be taken to celebrate the arrival of clinical science; the science of rigorously tested hypotheses leading to further hypotheses on which clinical skills depend, aided across the board by computers that allow handling of vast volumes of data, inaccessible and unanalysable in the first half of the century; and increasing in effectiveness at an extraponential rate of many magnitudes, almost annually.

The veterinary clinician of today differs from his or her human counterpart only in the degree to which financial, ethical and practical considerations lend emphasis to our evaluation of man compared with animals.

The opportunity, nay the duty, to perform euthanasia is the single most compelling difference between the two professions. The shooting of a horse to relieve its suffering was once one of the most significant attributes of the equine practitioner, albeit one also performed by horse slaughterers and some individuals of the laity. At the end of the century, the means may be less brutal, in the form of chemicals, but the principle remains the same: if the individual is deemed to be suffering unduly or in a terminal illness, its despatch is demanded on humane and/or economic grounds. Not so the human patient, whose life must be preserved almost at all costs, both financial and of the suffering of the individual; and of the friends and the relations of that individual. Surely, the 21st century will see the balance adjusted so that human subjects may receive the same compassion as we provide our animals. Control there must be to safeguard the patient, but the privilege of being able to perform such a service towards the patient must at some stage and in specified circumstances be given to human as to veterinary clinicians.

A horse (having Rheumatism) draped after being steamed. *From Edward Mayhew, reprinted with kind permission of the Royal College of Veterinary Surgeons Library.*

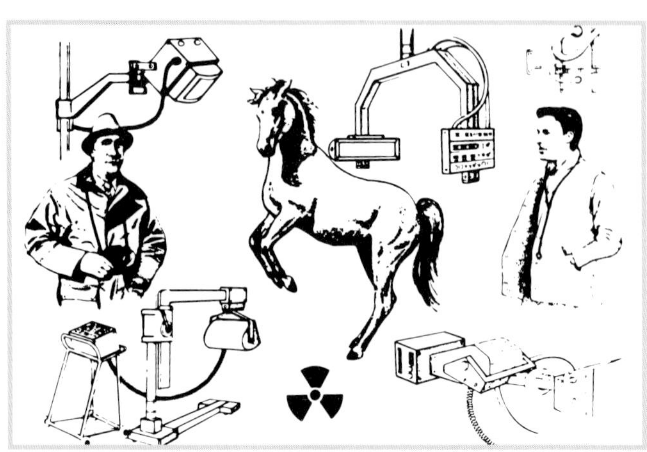

Modern practice is based on technology. Illustration by John Fuller.

As clinicians employ more sophisticated means of diagnosis and therapy, contact between doctors and their patients is becoming increasingly remote. It is as if the patient is merely a cog in the machinery of medicine, turning with the other wheels as they are set in motion. The physician and general practitioner, in this writer's experience, used to be sufficiently close for the need of the patient to become predominant in any decision-making process. In the last quarter of the century, the patient is fortunate to visit the same doctor as before on any given day or to receive a domiciliary visit; the best that can often be achieved is an emergency in which one is transported to the hospital. Once in the hands of the specialist, the GP recedes into the background of their daily routine, in contrast to the past where the patient might expect a visit in hospital from the GP. Small animal veterinary practice has moved more in this direction than equine practice where, on the whole, the clinician retains a close relationship with the patient and, through the patient, to the client. This particularly applies to the larger group equine practices, although the smaller mixed practices may find it difficult to maintain this relationship in view of the manpower required of such a service.

This same limitation has affected the medical profession, the greater the opportunities for service (new technologies, increasing diagnostic and therapeutic aids), the greater the demands upon the individual clinician and the less practical it is for a single individual to meet these demands throughout the year. In the National Health Service and private practice, this system is one of integrated services extending from the general practitioner to the appropriate specialist within the hospital environment; and the system functions to provide a service 24 hours a day for 365 days of the year. In equine veterinary practice, the larger practices fulfil a similar integrated system, but at much greater level of demand upon personnel involved. Practices which refer their cases for specialist diagnosis and for surgery may use a referral practice or one of the university veterinary schools, thereby simulating the human situation of providing primary care but passing their patient to secondary and, possibly, tertiary levels of expertise.

However, the great range and depth of the potential for service is, at the end of the current century, placing impractical demands upon the commitment expected of those who provide the service. Increasing the number of veterinary surgeons and lay personnel involved in the practice (or the university veterinary school clinics) is an obvious solution to provide comfortable rotas for graduates and others who wish to have time for family and other commitments. However, extra personnel entail extra funding; and private practices, at least, have to remain commercially viable, including the need to generate sufficient income to service the high cost of sophisticated apparatus and surgical facilities.

Veterinary schools also find themselves under pressure from the universities to run their clinical facility as a commercially viable operation. The illogicality of today, with all the duplication and competition between the plethora of equine veterinary clinics in practice, in university veterinary schools and the Animal Health Trust in Newmarket, in the context of clinical services and equine research will be resolved in the next century, probably by rationalisation and collaboration between the private, state and charitable sectors. Competition is an excellent spur to increased efficiency, but competition that leads to the stifling of professional development is counterproductive and fails to meet the needs of the public and the profession.

In the evolution from faith healer to physician to clinician, both veterinary and medical professions have adapted to the change by transferring the personal intimate relationship of one to one, of doctor to patient, with the impersonal highly professional and sophisticated approach where documentation, organisation, computerisation and high technological sophistication provides ample opportunity for the previous role of the faith healer and physician to be taken over by carers and ancillary workers. The equine clinician is coming increasingly to rely on nurses, horse handlers and perhaps even horse whisperers to fill the vacuum that modern clinical medicine and surgery, with its absorbing commitment and dedication to diagnostic and therapeutic techniques, creates in areas once occupied by the physician.

It is perhaps relevant to record an item on a BBC programme in August 1998, which reported that there were 7,000 vacancies for training nurses in the UK, but an extra 15,000 nurses were required, pointing to a potential deficit of 22,000 vacant places for training. During the ensuing discussion between a representative of the Royal College of Nursing and a politician, the former remarked that nurses were as much a part of the service as equipment; and that a career structure coupled with salary scales at least relative to other walks of life was an essential ingredient both to recruitment and for qualified nurses to remain in the service.

A parallel may be seen in many walks of medical and professional life, namely that conditions of work, including salaries, are a necessary part of the progress which is perhaps too often regarded as being the advance of technology rather than of the technicians (clinicians) who practise that technology. Care will have to be taken in the next century to ensure that the professional individual is not only well qualified, but given rewards for that qualification. Otherwise, the less qualified will take over increasing roles within the service; cheap labour is the recipe for deterioration of the service and the morale of those who provide it.

But the other side of the coin is and will remain the financial backing to support such services as they expand in breadth and depth. In the case of human medicine and surgery, even the resources of the state are insufficient to meet all the demands of increasing sophistication of procedures; a sophistication marked by time-consuming technological advances involving teams of experts at all levels of professional endeavor in increasing number and dedication. The development of heart surgery is an apt example of progress on the one hand and the demand for resources on the other.

In the veterinary field, the same opportunities for progress exist but the limits are set very much by available resources of manpower and finance; the finance having to come from the private sector and, therefore, from owners who may not or cannot afford to sustain the facilities on which medical and surgical procedures are based. The pathway from faith healer to clinician is littered with failures of application of methods which have become outdated and shown to be false dawns, but the search for new means of diagnosis and therapy continues unabated; professional men and women reach towards the stars but their feet must remain firmly on the ground of practicality and affordability.

From *hippiatroi* to equine surgeon

TIM GREET
Beaufort Cottage Equine Hospital
Cotton End Road
Exning, Newmarket
Suffolk CB8 7NN
UK

From man's first attempts at domestication of the horse, several thousand years ago, lame and sick equine patients have been subjected to a variety of diagnostic and therapeutic procedures. Most of these primitive attempts were based upon superstition, ignorance and fallacy.

Some may argue that very little has changed to the present day. There are records of ancient Egyptians bleeding sick cattle and, in Babylonian times, a doctor of donkeys was paid one-sixth of a shekel in silver if he successfully treated a serious wound but, if the animal died, he had to pay the owner a quarter of its value. Perhaps it is just as well that such a draconian burden is not placed upon veterinary surgeons in the 20th century. In Greek times, vets were *hippiatroi*, literally horse doctors. It was thought in those days that diseases of horses were as numerous as those of man.

In Roman times veterinary surgeons were known as *medicus equarius*, *mulomedici* or *veterinarii*. It seems that the first of these groups were probably military vets and the second may have been rather well-educated slaves. Perhaps not that much difference there, either! In Roman times, treatment of equine disease consisted of bleeding from the jugular vein in order to remove the old polluted blood. It was hoped that, having removed the old blood, it would be replaced with new blood. Bleeding was achieved by using a *sagitta*, a primitive phlebotomy instrument. Another major form of treatment, in Roman times, was the use of purgation of the head (*purgatio capitis*). Initially, the horse was purged and this was followed by cautery of the forehead with the application of a poultice to the area. Cautery was used in other sites and there is description of the use of parallel lines or palm leaf patterns. It should be remembered that even today 'firing' of the chest and abdomen is still performed on cattle and camels in some parts of the world, let alone the equine limb and soft palate!

In Roman times, castration of horses was carried out commonly and horses were usually cast and hobbled before the procedure was performed. There is description of the use of ligatures and some form of early emasculators were also employed. There is even a description of surgery to remove a prolapsed rectum in a horse.

After the decline of the Roman Empire, there are very few historical accounts of equine surgery. In the dark ages the treatment of horses depended entirely upon superstitions and it appears that firing of the forehead was still carried out. After the Roman Empire collapsed, educated Greek and Roman scholars probably emigrated to Persia and translation of Greek and Roman medical texts was carried out by both Arabs and Persians. Until the Renaissance, equine surgery had advanced no further than in Roman times and there is evidence to suggest that veterinary surgery in the Middle Ages was even more primitive than it had been more than a thousand years previously. Following the Renaissance, matters improved significantly. An equerry of Louis XIV, de Solleysel took a great interest in matters equine and criticised the use of firing of the forehead and medicating ears for respiratory disease. Having said that, his surgical treatment for ocular disease involved ligating the facial veins around the eyes.

In 1761, Louis XVI founded the first veterinary school in Lyon under the care of Claude Bourgelat and a veterinary school, in Paris at Maison Alfort, followed in 1766. The Royal Veterinary College in London, was founded with French help in 1791 and it is from the foundation of these first veterinary schools that the birth of modern equine surgery can be dated. During the 15th, 16th, and 17th centuries considerable advances were made in medical knowledge. However, both human and equine surgeons still depended extensively on the hot iron and the fleam for treatment of disease. It should be remembered that much equine surgery in this era was performed by farriers. However the evolution of the veterinary surgeon was by now, well on its way.

The first clinical descriptions of laryngeal hemiplegia appeared in the 16th century, but its initial treatment was by incision of the external nares. The first equine laryngeal surgery was carried out by the Gunthers, in Hanover in the 1830s, and they employed a variety of techniques, including the operation that we know today as Hobdaying. The first laryngoplasty procedure was performed in 1888, by Mr Clarke, a naval surgeon, although his method was to tie back the vocal process rather than the muscular process of the arytenoid cartilage.

Recurrent laryngeal nerve anastomosis was performed in the 1890s by Sir Fredrick Smith, an eminent veterinary surgeon of the day. Many of these early surgical operations were performed on army horses by army veterinary surgeons. Of course, the horse's role as a military accessory and the large collection of horses in army stables meant that there was a great opportunity for the equine surgeon to perform on patients which had to be sound enough to be used for military purposes. Although veterinary surgeons of the late 19th and early 20th centuries were often confronted by equine surgical problems, in many cases they had to perform operations for which they had little experience or training.

The first veterinary surgeons in the modern era were formidable men, and the best of them stand out through the ages like beacons in the darkness. These men were the founding fathers of our profession. They were not only eminent in the veterinary field but, frequently, showed multidisciplinary expertise that would put the modern veterinary surgeon to shame. Names that stand out include those of Smith, Fleming, Mcfadyean and Hobday in the United Kingdom, and Belair, Cadiot, Moller and Williams abroad. They were pioneers all.

The Gunthers of Hanover (father and son), who developed laryngeal surgery in the 1830s and '40s, were classic examples of veterinary surgeons who showed great ingenuity in dealing with a common problem by performing a number of experimental procedures to assess the efficacy of each technique. Many of these noble efforts were doomed to failure because of the contemporary lack of sterility, proper anaesthetic agents, antibiotics and anti-inflammatory drugs; the sequence at the root of medical progress for the past 150 years.

Following in the footsteps of men like Sir Fredrick Hobday, modern equine surgeons owe a great deal to their predecessors. Whereas a number of the most eminent equine surgeons of the Victorian and Edwardian times would perform surgery in a clinic situation, such as at the Royal Veterinary College in London, most had to travel around the countryside performing their surgery on a standing or cast horse at the premises of either local veterinary surgeons or, more commonly, of clients. Remount depots with equine hospitals have been a feature of army units thoughout the history of the British Empire. Indeed, stables of horses associated with the army, police and railways used to have hospital areas associated with them. However, it is really only since the Second World War that the concept of the equine surgical hospital has come to be of importance.

There is little doubt that the modern equine surgeon owes much to the development of better anaesthetic agents. It is here that we encounter Sir Fredrick Hobday who published the first English textbook on anaesthesia in 1915. As a surgeon he had recognised how important a safe and effective anaesthetic was, to allow the surgeon to perform the operation successfully. In his day, chloroform was the agent frequently used. However, since the Second World War and, more particularly, in the last 25 years, anaesthetic regimens used for horses have really improved; of particular importance has been the development of effective and safe injectable anaesthetic agents, e.g. the barbiturates and ketamine, and the use of volatile inhalational agents, e.g. halothane and isoflurane. These new agents were used and combined with the introduction of intraoperative monitoring of intra-arterial pressure, blood gas values and the use of mechanical ventilator systems. These have made the work of the modern equine surgeon much easier, and enabled surgical procedures to become both more intricate and successful.

What of modern equine surgeons? While much minor equine surgery is still carried out at owners' premises, more and more surgery is performed within clinics or hospitals. The provision of a padded anaesthetic recovery box is now regarded as the minimum requirement for carrying out equine surgery. In the great majority of situations, inhalational anaesthetic machines and circuits are in use along with the routine monitoring equipment mentioned above. The British Veterinary Hospitals Association, in combination with BEVA, has formulated a set of guidelines for the minimum standards required for an equine hospital. Many equine practices now provide hospitalisation and surgical facilities.

As for equine surgeons themselves, the days of 'do it yourself' general veterinary surgeons who dabbled in a bit of equine surgery have almost disappeared completely. Following distantly in the footsteps of our illustrious predecessors, the modern equine surgeon has probably undergone a residency at one of the universities or large private practices and obtained postgraduate qualifications in soft tissue or orthopaedic surgery. For many years, the Royal College of Veterinary Surgeons would not accept the concept of a veterinary specialist. Nowadays the Royal College register contains lists of specialists including those in equine surgery. These are colleagues who have undergone postgraduate training and demonstrated their ability in the subject by obtaining postgraduate qualifications, having peer recognition and spending a significant proportion of their working day involved in that speciality.

In fact, the career structure of a modern equine surgeon is now far better set; and follows increasingly the routes travelled by our medical contemporaries. This reflects a massive increase in the equine surgical repertoire over the last quarter of the century.

Techniques such as arthroscopy, fracture repair, and gastrointestinal surgery have become so specialised that some equine surgeons concentrate on only one or other of these individual areas. However, there are still a number of general surgeons in private equine practice and in some of the university veterinary schools, who, it should be emphasised, enjoy the diversity of the life and caseload which has always been the prerogative of the general surgeon in all walks of medical and veterinary life.

Practices in Newmarket

RICHARD GREENWOOD AND DAVID ELLIS
Greenwood, Ellis and Partners
166 High Street
Newmarket
Suffolk CB8 9AQ
UK

PETER ROSSDALE AND SIDNEY RICKETTS
Beaufort Cottage Stables
High Street
Newmarket
Suffolk CB8 8JS
UK

Introduction

Newmarket is the home of the British Jockey Club and has for centuries been the centre of racing and breeding Thoroughbreds. It is not surprising, therefore, that veterinary services have played an important role in the health and welfare of the horse and in the interests of owners, trainers and studfarm management.

Two substantial practices have developed over the course of the century and the account here records their progress and the contribution of a large number of dedicated colleagues whose contributions are justly incorporated in any history of the subject. In addition to the two practices, veterinary surgeons such as the redoubtable Major Charles Townsend, who operated from his own practice in neighbouring Huntingdon, and Frank Chamberlain, of the London Bloodstock Agency, made notable contributions.

Reynolds House

There have been veterinary surgeons at what is now known as Reynolds House, 166 High Street, Newmarket for the entire 20th century.The practice has grown steadily over the years. The senior partner at the end of the century is Richard Greenwood, a much travelled and widely respected veterinarian with expertise in both studfarm and training stable work. David Ellis is similarly a clinician with broad interests who has made a significant contribution to the veterinary literature on the subject of orthopaedics. He is one-time President of BEVA and has held a number of important advisory positions within the racing industry. James Crowhurst is the son of a distinguished father and in an advisory capacity has been closely associated, as was his father, with the Maktoum family. Andrew Edgar has also acted in a similar advisory role and Huw Neal is an eminent stud veterinarian with widely recognised expertise in gynaecological ultrasound and colic surgery. Other partners now include David Dugdale, Benoit Herinckx and Ian Wright, the internationally recognised consultant orthopaedic surgeon.

The partnership and reputation of the practice was largely established in the 1920s by Brayley Reynolds. On his death on 2 March 1967, at the age of 89 years, his obituary in the *Veterinary Record* described Brayley Reynolds as *"one of the greatest veterinary surgeons of this century"*. He was born in Daventry in 1879, one of 11 children of an old established veterinary family in the Midlands. At the outbreak of the South African War in 1899 he enlisted, while still underage, in Lord Chesham's yeomanry and served throughout the campaign as a trooper. On demobilisation he earned his living as an assistant in veterinary practice in Essex and eventually managed to save sufficient money to enter the London Royal Veterinary College as a student. During his studentship he was obliged to perform a number of locums in order to complete his training in which he succeeded eventually in 1912 at the age of 33 years.

In the First World War he was commissioned in the Royal Army Veterinary Corps and served in France and Mesopotamia. He commanded the Military Veterinary Hospital in Baghdad and was awarded an OBE.

After the war he joined the staff at the RVC, where he was appointed Professor of Materia Medica and Head of the Horse Clinic. He was an inspiring teacher, combining scientific logic with great experience. His services as an equine consultant were increasingly sought and he left the college and went into practice with W. Livock in Newmarket in 1926. Here he had great success and was also consultant veterinary surgeon to the Jockey Club, examiner in veterinary surgery at the Royal College of Veterinary Surgeons and a bloodstock authority. He was awarded the Dalrymple-Champneys prize for this outstanding services to the veterinary profession.

Brayley Reynolds lived in a period of tremendous change, passing from the horse-and-buggy stage through the motor car to the jet plane. In his obituary, he is described as working very hard and enjoying life to the full. He was blessed with an extraordinary memory which remained clear to the end. He was extremely adaptable and forward looking, and kept himself abreast of new ideas and techniques. He considered sound advice to be often of more value than drugs.

Geoff Leader, a member of a family of successful trainers, including Ted and Harvey Leader, initially practised on his own in Newmarket but during the 1930s joined Brayley Reynolds to establish the partnership at what was then called March House. He was a racing man of lifelong experience, was well liked and fitted the description of a gentle man.

After the Second World War the practice was joined by Fred Day, who had been one of the pioneers of gynaecological examinations of mares. He worked with Hammond at Cambridge before the war developing reproductive techniques in both cattle and horses. After the war he brought his expertise into general use in stud farm medicine and gained a worldwide reputation. He was a man of strong opinions but great charm, a first class shot, an expert fisherman and a redoubtable opponent at the bridge table. He was the son of a trainer, Reg Day, who came from a long and distinguished racing family. Frederick Thomas Day graduated from the Royal Veterinary College in London in 1935. Bob Crowhurst, writing in his obituary in the *Veterinary Record,* 16 February 1985, described him as an outstanding veterinary surgeon who had gained a high reputation both in veterinary research and practice. In 1937 he gained an award from the Thoroughbred Breeders' Association to join a team under the renowned Sir John Hammond at the Agricultural Research Council Unit at Cambridge to study equine infertility. He studied the control mechanisms of the oestrous cycle and the detection and prediction of how and when ovulation in the mare occurred. He established the period that spermatozoa lived in the mare, and laid the basis for the veterinary gynaecological examinations of mares that is used currently at the end of the century in practice. In 1945, he became a partner in the Newmarket practice of Reynolds and Leader. He established a dominant position in the horse breeding and racing industries.

Robert (Bob) Crowhurst was a good judge of a racehorse and a master of the art of soundness examinations besides being a bold surgeon and skilled clinician in all departments of expertise. He was born in 1915, in Maidstone, into a veterinary family. His father, grandfather, great grandfather, three uncles and elder brother, Arnold, were all veterinary surgeons. He graduated from the Royal Veterinary College at the age of 21 and went straight to Newmarket to work under Professor Brayley Reynolds. At the outbreak of the Second World War he joined the Royal Army Veterinary Corps, taking a yeomanry division of cavalry with 11,000 horses to Palestine in the winter of 1939/40. He subsequently accompanied the ill-fated expedition to Greece in 1941, and with six men narrowly escaped capture by the Germans by sailing a small boat from Crete. For this exploit he was mentioned in dispatches. During the Italian campaign he commanded veterinary hospitals at Persano and Bari, having care for thousands of mules used for transport and mountain warfare.

His war experience trained him to be a bold surgeon but gave him a high regard for conservative treatment, reinforced when he had to run a large hospital in Italy for one week with only salt and water available. He ended the war as a Lieutenant Colonel and was awarded the OBE.

After the war he spent a year in Lexington, Kentucky working under Drs Dimmock and Caslick. He returned to Newmarket in 1946 and rejoined Brayley Reynolds, Geoffrey Leader and Fred Day. He was veterinary surgeon to the British showjumping teams at the Helsinki, Stockholm and Rome Olympic Games.

Donald Simpson became a partner in the practice in 1965. A graduate of the Royal Veterinary College he had worked with John Ingram in Kent before coming to Newmarket. He was the first veterinary surgeon to the new National Stud, which was established in Newmarket in 1963. He was strongly associated with the early success of the stud, and particularly of the renowned stallions Mill Reef, Tudor Melody and Blakeney. Through his work at the National Stud, diagnosis, epidemiology and management of the new disease contagious equine metritis, which had occurred in Europe in 1976 and caused an epidemic in Newmarket in 1977 were established. His educational work, particularly at the National Stud, was renowned. Clear, beautifully illustrated talks which imparted a thorough knowledge and wisdom benefited professional and lay audiences for many years. He was also a founding Examiner for the RCVS Diploma and Certificate in Equine Stud Medicine. Donald Simpson retired from the partnership in 1991.

Robin McEnery became a partner soon after Donald Simpson and, having graduated in Dublin, developed a considerable reputation for both studfarm and flat racehorse medicine and surgery. He came from an Irish family steeped in horse tradition and knowledge (his brother bred Red Rum, the renowned Grand National winner). Robin was a very good judge of a horse and bred some of his own, but decided to retire from practice in 1974 in order to set up his own bloodstock agency. Soon afterwards he developed Alzheimer's disease.

Since the war many very accomplished veterinary surgeons have worked at Reynolds House and gone on to make successful careers elsewhere. They include Derek Grant. Derek was born in Stafforshire in 1923, educated at Tamworth Grammar School and the Royal 'Dick' School of Veterinary Medicine, Edinburgh. He graduated in 1945 and served with the Royal Army Veterinary Corps in India. He then joined the Newmarket practice of Reynolds, Leader, Day and Crowhurst and, in 1957, moved to the National Stud at West Grinstead where he worked with Peter Burrell. His obituary in the *Veterinary Record* on 10 March 1979 contributed by Brian Singleton, described Derek as having a striking personality, being an entertaining conversationalist and capable of stimulating deep thought and being pleasantly provocative.

Others included Peter Murray Hayden (the Curragh), Joe O'Donnell (the Curragh) John Morgan (Scone, New South Wales), Michael Kirby, Bill Eaton Evans and Paul Ferguson (Lambourn), John Chandler (now in stud management in Lexington, Kentucky), Keith Mason (Hong Kong and presently the Jockey Club) and not least Peter Rossdale (Newmarket).

The policy of experienced assistants spending the winter working with Thoroughbreds in the southern hemisphere, which started as exchanges with Murray Bain's practice in Scone, still continues. Many veterinary surgeons who have specialist equine interests have visited the practice from abroad, some spending considerable periods of study. Strong ties with equine veterinary surgeons have been maintained in Australia, South Africa, South America, Hong Kong, Japan, USA, Italy, Greece and France. Both students and graduates have spent time at Reynolds House gaining and contributing knowledge.

Beaufort Cottage Stables

Beaufort Cottage Stables practice was started in Newmarket in 1959. It actually began from the base at Romney House where one of the present authors (PDR) lived with his wife Jill and two young children, one having recently arrived and a third having been conceived. The pioneer of the practice completed a natural science tripos in Cambridge in 1949 and subsequently graduated from the Royal Veterinary College, London, in 1954, gaining a Fellowship in 1967. He achieved a PhD at Cambridge in 1984 on the basis of published work. Among honours bestowed upon him have been Honorary Life Membership of the British Equine

Veterinary Association, a Doctorate of the University of Berne and a fellowship of the Australian College of Veterinary Scientists. In 1998 he received an OBE in the New Year's honours list (for services to equine veterinary science). He has been an inaugural member of the Kentucky Hall of Fame at the Gluck Centre and was President of BEVA in 1976. He has served as Honorary Editor of the *Equine Veterinary Journal* since 1980.

Peter Rossdale was joined by Michael Hunt in 1961 following a period of two years as a single man practice. Michael was the key to survival of the practice. He had been a pupil and assistant of the redoubtable Dr John Burkhart at his practice in Thirsk. The practice had a wide consultative position in Yorkshire and elsewhere, including Newmarket, Lambourn and Malton in the UK, as well as in Chantilly and Normandy in France. Michael hailed from a family of medical men, both his father and brothers practising that profession. He was an experienced horseman both in the hunting field and in point-to-point races. Michael graduated from Cambridge Veterinary School and spent a year at the Animal Health Trust working with the surgeon Jim Roberts. He became an excellent, highly observant and dedicated clinician. He retired to North Wales in 1990.

In 1965, Colin Peace, another Cambridge graduate, joined the practice and remained until 1981 when he moved with his family to take up a post at the University of Guelph in Canada. He developed surgical facilities at the practice based on observations he had made during a journey through American University facilities. He was one of the first equine surgeons in the UK to perform major abdominal surgery, a volvulus of the small intestine in a mare called Denty. The mare survived the surgery and subsequently produced live foals.

Raymond Hopes joined the practice in 1968 following a chance meeting with the present author at a scientific function at the Royal Society of Medicine. Raymond was in the process of leaving the practice in Reading, having served in the Colonial Service in Uganda and been in practice with Alistair Fraser for the best part of 17 years. He had been Veterinary Officer for the Royal Ascot racecourse and his forte and interests were in race training and practice. He collaborated at one time with Sir Charles Strong who introduced the technique of faradic muscular stimulation as a diagnostic and therapeutic tool to equine practice, having applied his physiotherapeutic techniques to the Duke of Edinburgh and his polo ponies. Raymond served for many years on BEVA Council and on a number of Congress Committees. He retired from practice in 1997.

Sidney Ricketts, a Bristol graduate, joined the practice in 1973 after spending a year at New Bolton Center, Pennsylvania as a Thouron scholar. A prodigious worker in clinical science, he has advanced the frontiers of stud medicine with particular emphasis on conditions of the uterus causing subfertility; and has developed the laboratory at Beaufort Cottage Stables into a substantial practice and referral service enterprise. Sidney has been senior veterinary consultant to the Royal Stud Farms at Sandringham and to Juddmonte Farms. He is an Honorary Life Member of BEVA and was made a Lieutenant of the Victorian Order in Her Majesty's birthday honours list in 1998.

Nicholas Wingfield Digby, also a Bristol graduate, brought considerable flair in both areas of racehorse training and studfarm medicine. Hailing from a well known old established Dorset family, he brought additional elements to the practice, including prowess in cricket, game shooting and fishing. His major contribution to the subject of cytology of the mare's endometrium was of particular significance at the time of the CEM outbreak in the 1970s. Nick is an excellent judge of a horse and in great demand for bloodstock advice with respect of foals and yearlings being prepared for sale.

Tim Greet joined the practice in 1982 after the departure of Colin Peace and became chief surgeon to the practice. He developed the new facilities at Exning (Beaufort Cottage Equine Hospital) (see page 244) and brought with him a specialist knowledge of ENT problems while advancing the practice's facility for soft tissue and arthroscopic surgery. Tim is due to become President of BEVA in the year 2000 and has been active in promoting the RCVS Equine Nursing Scheme.

In the '80s, Rob Pilsworth developed the practice scintigraphy service, generously imparting his expertise to colleagues in other practices. Together with Neil Steven, who joined the practice at the same time, they have increased the practice acumen in the area of diagnostic imaging in racehorse practice, establishing a dedicated and meticulous lameness investigation service. Andrew McGladdery was the first HBLB-sponsored resident in 1988, subsequently becoming a partner and developing specialism in reproduction and internal medicine. Fred Barrelet, a graduate of the University of Berne, Switzerland, achieved his RCVS examination in and became a partner in 1997. Fluent in a number of languages, Fred has become internationally respected for his work in artificial insemination and for his veterinary support of the Federation Equestrian Internationale and endurance events. Michael Shepherd, a graduate of Massey University, New Zealand, became a partner in 1997, while Deidre Carson, a graduate of Sydney University, Australia, a dedicated multitalented clinician and Sarah Stoneham, a graduate of Bristol University, with a particular expertise in equine neonatology, became salaried partners in 1995 and 1993, respectively. At the end of the century, the practice consists of 21 veterinary surgeons, including a resident in surgery and several interns. Beaufort Cottage Stables, the original site of the practice, has been retained as an administrative and laboratory centre while the diagnostic unit, at nearby Exning, has been extended by the building of a purpose-built hospital. The development of the practice has been, as with any other organisation of similar character, the consequence of dedicated teamwork provided by many colleagues serving as assistants and it is a pleasure, therefore, to pay tribute to the following who are currently serving or who have moved to greener fields. Each has made a valuable and greatly appreciated contribution: (Present) Nicholas Acworth, Annalisa Barrelet, Nigel Dunn, Philip Dyson, Marcus Head, David Lloyd, Russell Malton, Sam Nugent, Richard Payne, Peter Ramzan, Monte Saulez, W. Neil Steven; (Past) Simon Abbott, Andy Bathe, Philip Burguez, Nicholas Butcher, Harry Frauenfelder, Nicola Holdstock, Nicola Jarvis, Mark Johnston, Desmond Leadon, Jason Lowe, Catherine Mitchell, Haydn Mitchell, Peter Ravenhill, Amanda Scott and Paula Williams.

The Beaufort Cottage practice Visitors' Book

PETER ROSSDALE
Beaufort Cottage Stables
High Street
Newmarket
Suffolk CB8 8JS
UK

Introduction

From the early days of the Beaufort Cottage practice, visitors were asked to sign their names in a book kept specially for the purpose. In the 38 years since the first name appeared, some 1600 names have been recorded. There is space here to make mention only of a few, but the selection has been made with the humility of a judgement that acknowledges the importance of every individual in the aggregate sum of veterinary life. While most of the following are placed in chronological order, may I start with a contribution submitted on request by Dr Woody Asbury who visited first on the 18th November 1977, because his contribution contains in its last paragraph the epitomy of the concept of professional friendships and working relationships for which visitors' books, the world over, are reminders.

Dr Woody Asbury writes:

"Since my early days living on Hampstead Heath, it has always seemed natural to return to England. In fact, later in my career, when involved in the puzzle over the response of the mare's uterus to inflammation, I considered an extended stay among the colleagues at Beaufort Cottage Stables. Reality prevailed, however, as I realised that a long-term involvement in the UK would involve spelling DEFENSE with a C. As a compromise, Peter arranged for a cottage at a local training yard, and my wife Clare and I spent a marvellous November seeing practice. Actually we saw it mostly over the fence (not fense) as we were busy taking in the pleasures of England in the fall.

Woody Asbury when Dean of the Veterinary School at the University of Florida.

"Several other memorable trips to the island stand out in my memory. In 1966, I travelled with George Pope's good horse Hill Rise to Newmarket, where he was to be trained by Noel Murless for a shot at some of your stakes races. During the pleasant few days when I was the guest of the Murless family, I managed to tag along with Mr Fred Day on his broodmare examination rounds. His skills have inspired me to this day. I don't believe I was allowed to associate with that 'other practice' at that time. But in 1978, when the questionable social disease contagious equine metritis was rampant on your side of the ocean, I returned, in the company of John Hughes and Bob Kenney. That tour, designed to exchange information on CEM, included sessions at Cambridge University, Twink Allen's base at Cambridge and a stopover at Beaufort Cottage Stables. Thus began a long and productive association with members of that esteemed group.

Fred Day, Peter Rossdale and Twink Allen (left to right) at the National Stud, Newmarket, in 1974.

"Of course, I had developed a keen appreciation for the Rossdale talent over a long stretch of time. During practice days in California, when he was contributing his wisdom to the Thoroughbred breeders of that state, he occasionally dropped in to check on our progress. Amazingly, those visits always coincided with the worst weather in England!

"My last sortie to Newmarket was in 1992, when Peter and Twink invited me to participate in the John Hughes Workshop on Equine Endometritis. This was a special honour, since the late, great John Hughes was my mentor and associate during my entire professional life, and he continues to be a factor in my thinking after his untimely death in 1998.

"As the 21st century approaches, I realise the temendous impact that colleagues in equine practice and academics have made in my life. International gatherings, working relationships and particularly friendships around the world have special meaning for me."

Marian Silver (Cambridge), pictured with Verena Bracher (Zurich) and Carol Cottrill (Lexington, Kentucky) at a reception during the International Veterinary Perinatology Society in Cambridge, 1995.

The first entry in the visitors book was Dr C. Hansson from Molndal, Sweden, who came in 1961. He was the first of many Swedish veterinarians who visited the practice, often on the occasion of their attending meetings of the British Equine Veterinary Association of which they have been loyal and most welcome supporters. An account of this pleasing relationship is included in the contribution by Harry Petterson on page 90.

Marian Silver (1959) attended Newnham College, Cambridge as an exhibitioner in 1945, attaining a First in Natural Science. She obtained her PhD degree at Reading and, in 1952, joined the Physiology Laboratory at Cambridge where she became Assistant Director of Research, a position she held for 30 years. With Dr Robert Comline, she was the first to achieve techniques for chronic cannulation of the fetal circulation in horses building on techniques pioneered by Donald Baron for fetal sheep research. I first met Marian on a blind date when we were both undergraduates at Cambridge in the late '40s. I subsequently met her again after she had married Ian Silver who was in my year at the Royal Veterinary College in London. For close on 50 years I have therefore had the privilege and pleasure of being not only involved in friendship but also having close collaborative ties in clinical research with each of them; "*a friendship as had mastered Time*".

Apostolos Zafrakas (March 1961) achieved his Diploma in Veterinary Medicine at the Aristotle University, Thessaloniki, Greece in 1957. He subsequently became Director of the Reproductive Laboratory and AI Station in Thessaloniki and, in 1993, he was appointed to a Chair at the University. He has contributed many articles and text on reproductive physiology and pathology of the horse.

Apostolos Zafrakas making a point.

Noud Broojmans (1961) visited the practice on my invitation following my own visit to Utrecht in the previous year in order to discuss with him the advancement of the technique of ECG recordings in the horse. In the late 1950s I had purchased a Cambridge instrument company machine, having read of the work of Professor Jim Steel in Melbourne, Australia. At Jim Steel's request I had recorded an ECG tracing from Hyperion when he was age 27 years by kind permission of the then manager of Lord Derby's Woodlands Stud, Colonel Adrian Scrope. Jim was disappointed at the 'heart score' of the horse, a disappointment which I never understood because, at age 27 years in a horse suffering severe arthritis, the heart size I myself supposed would be considerably reduced from that pertaining to a period of the horse's prowess on the racecourse some 24 years previously. Would it not have been a fascinating subject to pursue employing echocardiography?; are we now taking the opportunity to make such recordings and to preserve them for the sake of those who look back, as we do now, in the future on the past?. My contact with Noud covered a short but rewarding collaboration in which we identified, although never published, a case of a three-year-old horse diagnosed as Wolf-Parkinson-White syndrome; he also introduced me to the facility at Utrecht where I met the redoubtable clinician Dr Kroneman; and my first visit was the forerunner of many more occasions as the school expanded to the excellence of its current status.

Heinz Gerber visited Newmarket on 28th August 1964 with his wife Andree. From an immediate recognition of common interests and shared philosophies of veterinary life and of literature and the arts, not to mention skiing and a knowledge of the beautiful country of Switzerland, a close friendship of 35 years developed. To quote Rudyard Kipling, "*One man in a thousand Solomon says will stick more close than a brother, it is worthwhile seeking him for half your life, if you find him before the other.*" Heinz is, to this author, the epitome of the complete veterinarian, housing in one intellect the elements of practice, research and clinical

Heinz Gerber receiving his Honorary RCVS Associate award from the President Dr Jerry Lucke in 1990.

acumen. He has been kind enough to translate one of my books into German, published by Karger in Basle, and participated in many collaborative ventures of writing and research besides being a charming host and stimulating company. His son Vincent is following in his father's footsteps and will, no doubt, grow increasingly in stature during the next decades. Heinz was made an Honorary Associate of the Royal College of Veterinary Surgeons, London, in 1990. In the official account of this Honour, in the *Veterinary Record* 21 July of that year, the President, Dr Jerry Lucke, observed that:

"Professor Dr Heinz Gerber has spent periods studying abroad in England and the United States and, in 1969, he was appointed full professor and director of the large animal veterinary clinic of the University of Berne. The clinic has thrived under his direction. He has been described as the complete veterinary surgeon with a distinguished record in clinical medicine, teaching and research. He has an international reputation, and contributed significantly to the literature on many aspects of virology, internal and genetic medicine in the horse. He was the founder President of the Swiss Equine Veterinary Association and was appointed to the Sir Frederick Hobday lectureship of the British Equine Veterinary Association in 1988. His presentation was widely hailed as a masterpiece by those who were fortunate enough to hear it. Professor Gerber is well known for his Chairmanship of the Committee of Medication of the International Equestrian Federation."

While compiling this account, his colleague Professor Urs Schatzmann kindly provided me with the following:

"Professor Heinz Gerber, in 1972 freshly appointed director of the large animal department (equine and farm animals), recognised the future needs of specialists not only in the equine department but also in specialised fields like clinical reproduction, radiology and anaesthesiology. Against many difficulties, he forced the creation of new posts for promising young colleagues who, some years later, became first recognised specialists with their own departments on the European continent. This was not possible without enormous personal and financial support, created in a time of more and more limited governmental sources. Professor Gerber retires from the faculty at the end of this century at a time, when both Veterinary Schools (Zurich and Bern) are integrated in Vetsuisse. He leaves the University with the knowledge, that his departments are the basis for veterinary education in the new century."

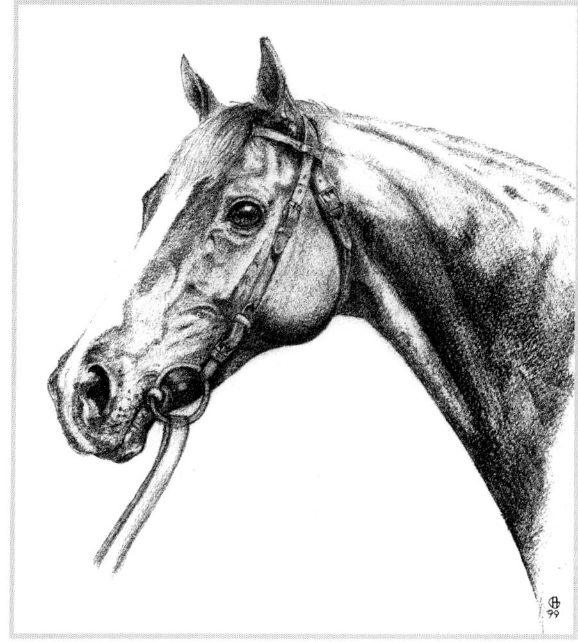

Heinz Gerber's portrait of his horse, Djebel.

Virginia (Ginny) Osborne (26 October 1964) has been the mother figure and mentor for generations of veterinary students at the Faculty of Veterinary Science in Sydney University and is one of those dear souls with a heart of gold and a propensity to think and care about people and horses. She has always been something of a collector of horses and, at her lovely old farm near Windsor in NSW, she keeps a whole range of Thoroughbred and Standardbred horses in training and in retirement. She has played a prominent role in the trotting hierarchy of Sydney and, on one visit to Australia, she took my wife and me to the trotting track when the horse Semmelweiss broke the one mile record. He circuited the course against lights placed at regular intervals which were only extinguished when he passed them. Sure enough he beat the record. In addition to her teaching, Ginny devoted her career to studying the physiology of the ovarian cycle of the mare, as described on page 134–143 by Sidney Ricketts. Among other things, she examined over 8000 mare reproductive tracts at Sydney horse abattoirs from which, in 1966, she published her seminal paper on the annual ovarian cycle of the mare. On one occasion, when she was travelling into the UK from a European country, she replied, when asked by Customs if she had anything to declare, "*Only my ovaries!*" Ginny has come many times to the UK to scientific and veterinary meetings and she has been a loyal attender at the International Equine Reproduction Symposia (see page 123). Whenever and wherever I have met her, she has remained the same dear soul, with her quiet determination and kindly philosophical outlook.

Percy Sykes (17 June 1965) was the first of a number of contacts, including those made during my own visits to Sydney, Australia. His work on haematology of racehorses and his entrepreneurial approach to practice in Sydney, described more fully by Treve Williams (p 250–251), and in other parts including Hong Kong and Iran, gave him a special aura in one's memory, of an energetic and highly motivated clinician.

Terry Boundy (1963) was an enthusiastic supporter of BEVA from the time that the present writer was Honorary Treasurer of the Association. For this chapter he contributed the following on request.

"My first association with horses began when I started to ride at the age of seventeen. This introduction was closely followed by service in the TA.

"Major Arnold Shuttleworth suggested that I joined the Duke of Lancaster's own Yeomanry as a trainee farrier. Two TA camps followed, one during which I worked a groom and batman to Captain John McGee. On the outbreak of war I was called up and we set about shoeing the whole Regiment. In late autumn, the horses were all sent to the Cavalry Brigade in Palestine, much to our sorrow. As I was in a reserved occupation I returned to Liverpool to renew my studies, qualifying in 1942. I volunteered for the RAVC soon after and was called up in early 1943, spent a short time in Doncaster and then on to India.

"At that time in the Corps we were all volunteers; we were young, enthusiastic and with a good measure of discipline. We got

Terry Boundy - always an enthusiastic supporter of BEVA.

on with whatever work we were detailed to do. After all, it was our life's work, and I never heard any complaints. In retrospect, it was an honour to serve in the 14th Army and to be part of the three million volunteers from the continent of India who stopped the Japanese at Kohima, 40 miles from the Indian Border.

"Returning home in 1946, I took over a run-down practice in Montgomery. An agricultural practice dealing with cattle, sheep and a good sprinkling of horses. I started to hunt in 1950 and completed 47 seasons last year. Eleven of those years I was MFH of the Teme Valley Hunt. In 1988, I paraded my hounds at the Royal Welsh Agricultural Show before a tremendous crowd, a day I shall always remember as being one of the best in my life.

"There were so many sheep in my practice area that I had really to specialise from an early date in that species. I visited New Zealand in 1973 and as a result became an enthusiastic advocate for preventive management of disease programmes in all herds and flocks.

"In 1978, I was in Dallas speaking at the AVMA Convention and I lost my wallet. Some days afterward it was returned with a scribbled note to say, "I could not keep the money after finding this belonged to an English vet. I have read *All Creatures Great and Small* and could not steal from an English vet." *Alf Wight was very amused.*

"I joined BEVA in 1962–3 because I wanted to keep up to date. The BEVA specialist and refresher courses gave me exactly what I wanted. I have attended most of the yearly conferences where I meet so many of my old friends and hear all about progress in the equine field. In 1967, I visited Poland for a month to check on facilities for tourist horse riders from the UK. I spent a memorable day with Professor Bialanski in Krakow and returned to the UK full of ideas for AI in mares. Unfortunately, at that time, few people wanted to know. I was too early by far.

"I am still practising and enjoy all my horse work. I especially like to talk to young students and to help them along the hard road to qualification, and follow them with help and advice in their early years. I always acknowledge the great help I myself received from members of the old school e.g. Arnold Shuttleworth, J. G. Wright, Fred Day and Willy Baker to mention just a few. I don't think that, as long as my health remains reasonable, I shall ever want to retire. I only wish I could begin all over again."

Cliff Irvine (6 April 1966), I first met in Christchurch in the early '60s. Cliff has the remarkable distinction of having paid his way through college by driving his own trotters on the track in competitive events. This facility for choosing the right animal and participating at the grass roots of the sport has remained with him ever since. Cliff has performed the role of an endocrinologist of excellence, elucidating many of the mysteries of the hypothalamic, pituitary adrenocortical axis. He has a deep knowledge and understanding of the subject and of molecular pathways often difficult for the average clinician to comprehend, yet Cliff has the capacity to explain the subject clearly. His scientific presentations, despite the complexities of his subjects, carry the simplicity and clarity born of long years of teaching graduates and undergraduates.

W. R. (Twink) Allen and Roger Short (6 December 1966) visited as disciple and mentor respectively. Twink's work has ranged from studies on basic physiological mechanisms to highly practical clinical observations. He subsequently completed a successful doctoral study at Cambridge under the tutelage of Roger Short who, as his supervisor, infused him with a whole new and exciting way of approaching the fundamental questions of reproductive physiology. At the Animal Research Station in Cambridge he was in contact with what might be described as the reproductive giants of the age, namely, E. C. Amoroso, Thaddeus Mann, Chris Polge, Tim Rowson, Bob Moor and Eric Lamming. Roger Short once described Twink as his most successful student and incredibly hard working, dedicated, innovative and stubborn! Perhaps his most significant research has involved the findings he established in a series of painstaking studies on the endometrial cups and their sequence of life from their somewhat paradoxical establishment in the wall of the mare's uterus, producing vast amounts of equine chorionic gonadotrophin and, finally, ending their days at about 120 days gestation in an apparently immunological death. He has won recognition worldwide and has been honoured for many awards, including the Bielanski Gold Medal and being one of the first inductees into the Kentucky Equine Research Hall of Fame.

Roger Short first approached the present author in 1957 with a request that he bring Cambridge veterinary students to see foalings in Newmarket. From this time I developed a lifelong friendship with and a great regard for Roger. He has become the ultimate comparative worker with an interest of great width, becoming involved in such diverse disciplines as behaviour, physiology and the control of human and wildlife populations. That he became a Fellow of the Royal Society (FRS) signifies the regard with which he has been attributed by the scientific community.

Wladyslaw Bielanski (14 September 1966) was Professor of Reproductive Physiology at the Krakow Academy of Agriculture and a full member of the Polish Academy of Sciences. He was a renowned specialist in the field of animal breeding, especially horses. He was born in Krakow in 1911 and graduated from the Veterinary Faculty of Lvov University. After World War II he organised the first horse insemination station in Poland and became head of the Horse Breeding Unit at the Balice Animal Breeding Institute. He conducted original research on the endocrinology of early pregnancy in mares and he greatly improved methods for collecting stallion semen and for preserving it at low temperatures. In particular, he designed the Krakow model open-ended artificial vagina and was responsible for the first birth in Poland of a foal

Rex Butterfield and Peter Rossdale in Professor Butterfield's office at Sydney University.

conceived from semen that had been stored in liquid nitrogen. He also instituted and organised the experiment which resulted in the birth of three Welsh Pony foals in Krakow in 1976, they having been carried to Poland in the oviduct of two rabbits in 1975. The birth of these unique foals coincided with Professor Bielanski's chairmanship of the 9th International Conference on Animal Reproduction and Artificial Insemination (ICAR) which he organised and ran in Krakow despite the rigours and restrictions of the then communist regime in Poland. Bielanski was a true horseman, both in the application of his work to improve the welfare and productivity of horses in Poland and in his capacity as a very capable rider. In a tribute paid to him by Marian Tischner in his obituary, in Supplement 32 of the *Journal of Reproduction and Fertility*, Tischner noted: "*Fittingly his heart failed him on 15th March 1982 while he was out riding his horse, a pastime which he enjoyed almost every day.*"

Jerry Gillespie (16 October 1966) from the cardiopulmonary section of the School of Veterinary Medicine, University of California, Davis, was a friend and close collaborator with Leslie Hall at Cambridge. I subsequently met Jerry on many occasions on visiting California and his visits to Newmarket in what became both a professional and a personal friendship.

Rex Butterfield (6 April, 1967) recalls that on arrival at Beaufort Cottage Stables I greeted him with the question: "*Would you like to wash your hands?*" Thus started a delightful interaction between English reserve and euphemism and Australian forthrightness that has lasted for over 30 years. Although Rex's main interest is in livestock development with respect to meat production, he has strong interests in equids and all that accompanies the species, including performance, breeding and anatomical peculiarities. I heard him give a delightful contribution in Arizona at one of Gene Ensminger's Stockman's Schools in a lecture entitled *How the Horse Sleeps Standing Up*. In his long stint at the University of Sydney as Dean of the Veterinary School and Professor of Anatomy, Rex has contributed substantially to the formation and development of the Equine Research Foundation in Australia. His contribution on page 144 reflects both his insight and his humour, which have been the hallmark of his distinguished career.

On 11 August 1970, Edda Hannington and Sam Hignett visited the practice, both in the capacity of representatives of the Wellcome Trust and Wellcome Foundation in London. This initiated a close working relationship with them both, eventually leading to my becoming a member of the Veterinary Advisory Panel of the Wellcome Trust, a position I held for four years. Edda was an expert on migraine and had written book on the subject, and was a charming, highly organised person with insight into the ways of scientists and scientific research. Sam was someone with great knowledge of the veterinary profession and its services across species. When I first met them at the Wellcome Trust offices in Queen Anne Street, London, when Ian Silver and I successfully applied for a grant to support some work at the Department of Anatomy in Cambridge on lambs delivered with and without clamping of the umbilical cord. We wished to determine by means of radiography whether the procedure affected the initial expansion of the lungs immediately following delivery. This work was performed in conjunction with our interest in the effect of early or late clamping of the cord in horses and, currently at that time, a similar issue with respect to the infant. Jaykka had proposed that early clamping had deprived the infant of placental blood that was destined to assist in the expansion of the pulmonary vascular system to support the inflation of the alveoli, an hypothesis supported by clinicians, including Dr Bonham Carter at the University College Hospital.

Stewart Hastie (22 June 1971), a friend all this author's professional life, reports on page 85 on his experiences with Major Oxspring in the practice at Ashford, Kent, where I first encountered Stewart. Stewart has been Honorary Secretary of BEVA and an active supporter for many many years. 1999 BEVA President Pat Harris writes:

> *"Stewart is deeply interested in all aspects of the horse, its management and care, as well as the industry that surrounds it. He has an immense thirst for knowledge and a real desire to understand how and why things are as they are, he is always keen to dissect and understand problems and, to him, no horse is ordinary and every one has something to tell and to be learnt from."*

Walter Plowright (May 1974) came with Jenny Mumford and Gavin Thompson from the RVC in London, to discuss the subject of respiratory infections in foals (a quarter of a century later, what's new!). Walter is the doyen of veterinary virology and his contributions, succinct, often humorous with a twinkle in the eye, have been enjoyed subsequently in my service on the Veterinary Advisory Committee of the Horserace Betting Levy Board of which we were both members and when serving under his chairmanship of the Scientific Committee of the Equine Viral Foundation, established by Lord Porchester in the '80s. Walter was a fine leader of this effort which resulted in a substantial input of information regarding equine herpes viruses although, unfortunately, not leading as yet to an improved vaccine as was intended and hoped for earlier in the piece. Jenny Mumford, of course, has subsequently risen to the heights of Scientific Director of the Animal Health Trust, a worthy reward for her prestigious efforts on behalf of the infectious diseases department of that organisation.

John Hughes' (27 July 1974) untimely death in 1998 robbed the equine world of one of its most distinguished contributors; and to a large number of people, including the present writer, of a kindly, warm and endearing friend. John was a distinguished Professor of Veterinary Medicine for

John Hughes, at the first meeting of the Brazilian Equine Veterinary Association, on a visit to the Iguacu Falls.

more than four decades, an excellent horseman and a dedicated rancher. He has been described, rightly, as a true gentleman. He was born in Fresno, California, and worked in private practice before, in 1956, joining the faculty of UC Davis School of Veterinary Medicine. He was recognised internationally as an expert on equine reproduction and collaborated in the publication of more than 150 scientific papers and eight book chapters. He was a founding member of the International Symposia in Equine Reproduction (see page 123).

Reinhard Jacobi (1976) was a veterinary student when first visiting the practice for a period of three months. He subsequently wrote that he was grateful to come into close contact with the working life of English veterinarians. After graduating, Reinhard practised in Sottrum (between Bremen and Hamburg), Germany, specialising in orthopaedics and establishing an equine hospital with four assistants and a team of 10 technicians. The practice specialises in orthopaedic surgery with a special contribution of perivascular sympathicectomy for navicular and sesamoid problems.

Lennart Olsson, one time veterinary surgeon to the Swedish National Stud and father of Monica Magnusson Falk.

Monica Magnusson Falk (1977) inherited skills and motivation from her two grandfathers and her father. Her maternal grandfather was Professor Forssell of Forssell operation fame. He was Dean of the Veterinary School at Stockholm. Monica's father Lennart Olsson was veterinary surgeon to the National Stud in Flyinge. She spent two stud seasons at the practice in Newmarket, imprinting herself on our memories for her dedication in the application of intensive care support for convulsive and other sick foals. In one period, a foal out of the mare Villa Tenata suffered severe convulsions and was brought back to life by her efforts over a period of more than three weeks. Unfortunately there was no happy ending and the foal suffered diarrhoea when aged four weeks, collapsed and died instantly. Subsequent to the two seasons she spent in Newmarket, Monica presented a paper on CSF analysis on the foal at the International Equine Reproduction Symposium held at Davis, California in 1978.

Carl Ebbe Gerhard Forssell with his granddaughter Monica (now Monica Magnusson Falk).

William McGee (9 June 1977) is a very highly regarded Kentucky clinician whose practice involves Thoroughbred breeding farms in Lexington. His clinic and surgery, which operated at the time of his visit under title of Hagyard, Davisdon, McGee has incorporated many distinguished clinicians, such as Doug Byars. Bill graduated from Wisconsin State University and served as AAEP President in 1964.

Joe Mayhew (March 1979) visited the practice from Cornell and has subsequently been a good friend in positions at the University of Florida, Gainsville, Animal

Joe Mayhew, eminent veterinary neurologist.

Health Trust, Newmarket and, currently, University of Edinburgh. Neurology is a difficult clinical subject and Joe is an equine neurologist *par excellence,* contributing greatly to individual cases within our own and many other practices, as well as being an outstanding communicator of this subject to graduates and undergraduates alike.

Pinto Moreira (5 June 1979) visited the practice at the same time as Thomas Wolfe (16 July 1979). Two enthusiastic and friendly clinical scientists from Brazil, their contributions have received accolades in many countries in the Northern Hemisphere.

Frank Pipers (21 April 1981) may firstly be described, in the catalogue of colleagues, in terms that Shakespeare described as "*the valued file*". A spirit of deep-thinking eccentricity, he became a staunch friend and supporter of this author's family. During his first visit he left our home for far-off Devon, where he was confronted by a freak snow storm and advised not to drive down a certain road. *"I am an American!"* he declared with enthusiasm; drove down the road and became embedded in a drift!

In July 1984, a remarkable coincidence occurred which, in statistical terms, must have had a P value of very many zeros. On the 2nd of that month, Vanden Bossche Geert visited the practice and signed his name in the Visitors' Book. Nine days later on 11 July a young Italian graduate, Eleondra Guicciardini, was asked to write in the Visitors' Book. As she signed her name and wrote her address on the next line from the colleague from Antwerp I noted the similarity of her surname to the street in which Vanden Bossche Geert lived. On enquiry, she told me that one of her ancestors had lived in Antwerp and had probably had the street named after him because he had been a worthy citizen of the city. If even one visitor had interposed their name and address between these two colleagues, the coincidence probably would never have been noted.

2 July '84	VANDEN BOSSCHE GEERT	Guicciardinistraat, 8 2050 Antwerp
11 July '84	ELEONDRA GUICCIARDINI	v.o. Ghibellina, 73 50122 Florence (ITALY)

To this writer, coincidence serves as an illustration of the fact that all our lives are governed by chance, as Macbeth responded to the three witches, "*If chance will have me king, why chance will crown me without my stir.*"

I first met Robert (Bob) Copelan (1985) in March 1976 in Lexington, Kentucky. He was one of the first, if not *the* first, equine surgeon to construct a purpose-built surgery along the then current standards for human hospital surgical theatres. He has been unfortunately unable to contribute to this book in the chapter on equine hospital facilities (page 244) but he was undoubtedly a pioneer of the subject and an outstanding orthopaedic surgeon.

Marcel Vandeplassche (18 December 1985) was Professor of Obstetrics and Gynaecology in the Faculty of Veterinary Medicine in Gent during an unbroken span of 43 years until his first retirement in 1984. Within only a year, however, his former pupil and close teaching and research colleague, Roger Bouters, died suddenly after taking over the Chair. Marcel was called upon to resume his duties at the age of 71 until a second successor, Professor de Kruif, could be found for this important and prestigious post. In a tribute to him as Honorary Chairman of the Fifth International Symposium on Equine Reproduction, Twink Allen wrote:

"Youth and synonymous terms like vitality, freshness, enthusiasm and fun are all words that should be associated with Marcel Vandeplassche. Despite his 77 years and his long and distinguished academic career, he remains a young man both in body and in spirit. He has a full and highly distinguished career as a clinical research worker whose abiding aim was always to undertake and apply scientific research to reproduction and obstetrics in farm animals. He has produced a total of 240 papers in 35 different scientific and lay journals, 12 book chapters and three text books."

Yoshimasa Nishikawa (1987) completed his degree in veterinary sciences in 1936 and joined the National Institute of Animals Sciences. In 1957, he moved to the Chair of Animal Reproduction at Kyoto University and, in 1976, was elected President of Obihiro University of Agriculture and Veterinary Medicine. He published no fewer than 250 original research papers, 171 review papers and 35 book chapters. Not least of this legacy was a splendid book summarising Nishikawa's studies on reproduction in horses, published by the Japan Racing Association in 1959.

George Stabenfeldt (1987) graduated in veterinary medicine in 1956 and was awarded a PhD by Oklahoma State University in 1968. He then joined the Faculty of Veterinary Medicine at the University of California in Davis where he soon became an excellent teacher and an internationally recognised expert in the field of equine reproductive endocrinology publishing more than 150 scientific papers in a first class academic career that was sadly cut short by cancer. He was a caring and concerned educator and friend to many students and colleagues, including the present writer. He was an accomplished jazz pianist and was a founding member and director of the popular High Wheelers Barber Shop Quartet which still performs throughout Northern California and Nevada.

Doug Antczak (28 April 1988) had been a Cornell National Scholar, captain of the university polo team and a member of the Quill & Dagger Senior Honor Society at Cornell. After completing a degree in veterinary medicine at the University of Pennsylvania of in 1973, Dr Antczak conducted postgraduate research at the University of Cambridge, England, and received a PhD in 1978. Since 1979 he has been on the scientific staff of the Baker Institute. In 1992 he was appointed the Dorothy Havemeyer McConville Professor of Equine Medicine and, in 1994, Director of the James A. Baker Institute for Animal Health.

His scientific research has focused on immunological and genetic aspects of the fetal-maternal relationship, including the Major Histocompatibility Complex genes and molecules, the regulation of their expression in the placenta, the composition and function of uterine lymphocytes and alterations in maternal immune reactivity during pregnancy. Dr Antczak has a worldwide reputation among veterinary scientists for his studies of horse genetics, immunology and reproduction. Currently, he is one of the organisers of the international Horse Genome Project and a member of the Genomics Task force at Cornell.

Bob Kenney (11 April 1997) is a colleague extraordinaire with a deep-rooted scientific approach for problems of reproductive physiology and pathology. His pioneering work on endometrial problems is described by Sidney Ricketts on page 134. Once, when I visited him in his house near Philadelphia, I had the experience of having to travel up the steep hill to the house where he lived. This would normally have been a routine exercise but it so happened there had been an ice storm the previous night and the car drive by Seshu Ganjam slithered sideways halfway up the hill; we had therefore to travel the remainder of the journey to the house on foot. I had flown in from California where the temperature had been in the '80s and I was therefore wearing very light clothing including light shoes. The remaining half of the climb was interesting, to say the least. However, the hospitality and warmth of my receipt was well worth the trip.

"No man is an island" is a truism made famous by John Donne. The story line of this selection from the visitors' book is necessarily incomplete and fails to do justice to those colleagues included or excluded; but it is hoped that it serves as a reminder that all our lives are threads of the fabric of existence.

Tim Greet introduces the Queen to lay members of staff at the official opening of Beaufort Cottage Equine Hospital, 23 April 1998.

Associations and Societies

Associations, societies and publications (BVA, BEVA and IERSC)

PETER ROSSDALE
Beaufort Cottage Stables
High Street
Newmarket
Suffolk CB8 8JS, UK

Introduction

Early Societies and Associations

The term 'associate' is derived from the Latin *associatus* and defined as *"joined in function or status"*; and the term society, as *"living in association, aggregate of persons living together, selection of persons forming a community, the association of persons united by a common aim, interest or principle"*. The Royal Society of London was founded in 1662 *"to promote scientific discussion"*.

Societies and associations, as we understand the definitions of today, may be regarded as the logical endpoint of an evolutionary instinct of mankind, for individuals to band together for the better prospects of survival. Intellectually, the aphorism that 'two heads are better than one' describes the building bricks of civilisation and Society itself. Societies of art and religion would seem to be the earliest motivation of association between individuals. The earlier societies of art consisted solely of practising artists and existed chiefly for their mutual protection and, to a lesser extent, for their social betterment. They had their origins in mediaeval lodges, groups of craftsmen working together on ecclesiastical building projects. In the 14th century, painters and sculptors seceded from the lodges and attached themselves to guilds. In Florence, the appropriate guild for a surgeon was the apothecaries, for which a special branch for artists was formed, in 1360, with compulsory membership!

Learned associations of today are those whose members are united in some common interest and organised with definitive objectives, usually basing their activities on meetings and the publication of periodicals called journals.

Veterinary societies have been known in practically all countries and their purpose has been to advance the standards of the profession and improve its services to society. Publications of these associations include the *Veterinary Record*, a weekly publication of the British Veterinary Association, the *Journal of the American Veterinary Medical Association*, published biweekly, and the *American Journal of Veterinary Research*, published quarterly by the American Veterinary Medical Association. These associations were established in the 19th century, but those devoted to the horse have mostly been formed in the second half of the 20th century. These include the American Association of Equine Practitioners and the British Equine Veterinary Association. There are many other associations and societies that have developed in the last three decades of this century, based upon the developing progress of specialisation. The International Equine Reproduction Symposia Committee was, for example, formed in 1964 in order to bring together those colleagues, clinicians and scientists interested in equine reproductive research. As described later in this chapter, this Association started as a composite approach to reproduction, forming an umbrella over the specialist activities of those with particular interest in the stallion, barren mare, pregnant mare and neonatal foal. These branches are increasingly becoming subjects in their own right and, as with so many societies of generality in the past, are subject to the pressure to fragment into specialism of their members. Societies of ultrasonography, radiography and nuclear medicine are other examples of fragmentation from wider generalities into disciplinary specialisms.

In the late 1950s, fraternal exchanges between practices and practitioners were considerably less evolved than they are today at the end of the century. One of the main objectives of forming an equine association was to bring colleagues together under an umbrella from which an exchange of scientific and clinical knowledge could be exchanged; and contacts developed between the more senior and experienced clinicians and those who were younger and less experienced, for the common benefit of all. From the second half of this century, these objectives have been largely achieved by associations such as the American Association of Equine Practitioners (AAEP) and the British Equine Veterinary Association (BEVA) and those in other countries which have followed the example of these two senior organisations.

There follows an account of a selected number of societies (associations) whose objectives encompass advancement of veterinary science applied for the benefit of the horse and for those who care for and own the animal, to which this present celebratory volume is dedicated.

1. British Veterinary Association

In 1792, the Royal Veterinary College opened in London, followed, in 1823, by the Dick Veterinary College in Edinburgh. Until 1844, both colleges granted certificates of competence to practise the veterinary art but practitioners were not really a profession and it was not until 1844 when the Royal College of Veterinary Surgeons was granted the Royal Charter that the term veterinary surgeon was reserved for the graduates of the two colleges, and veterinary medicine declared to be a profession.

From that time onwards, local associations were formed, some of the oldest being in the West of Scotland, Lancashire, Yorkshire and the Midlands. By 1880 there were 15 associations, and George Banham, a graduate of the Royal Veterinary College, attended the Congress of the British

Medical Association in Cambridge, where he perceived the idea of holding a National Veterinary Congress.

The first of these was held in London with George Banham as secretary and George Flemming, President of the Royal College of Veterinary Surgeons, as President. The new Association was created in 1882 and held its first meeting in 1883. In the early years, it was the annual meeting that was the only function of the association but, in 1887, it was proposed that local associations should become affiliated to the national body. Over the period of some years this idea came to fruition and, by 1912, almost all local societies were affiliated. In 1919, the enlarged association changed its name to the National Veterinary Medical Association of Great Britain and Ireland. In 1920, the *Veterinary Record* was purchased and has been the mouthpiece of the Association ever since. In 1952, the Association changed its name to the British Veterinary Association (BVA) which now has 8,000 members. There are 28 territorial divisions and 19 special interest groups which have become affiliated and have influence on BVA policy through their representation on the Association's Council.

The horse was the major concern of BVA members up to the Second World War; and the replacement by other species, including farm and small animals, has corresponded with the changing emphasis of the times; changes which have led to specialist associations being developed, as in the case of the British Small Animal Association and the British Equine Veterinary Association.

2. The British Equine Veterinary Association

Origins

The origins of BEVA involved independent individual aspirations of colleagues for an umbrella organisation, similar to the American Association of Equine Practitioners (AAEP) established in 1955. For example, Maxie Cosgrove in Ireland, John Gray in Lambourn and Alistair Fraser in Wokingham, were of a like mind regarding the need for such an association, but the initiating force came from Newmarket where Leo Mahaffey, pathologist at the Equine Research Station, proved to be the catalyst of action.

Leo Mahaffey.

Mahaffey had a vision which brought him from Australia to the UK in search of European culture to which he was immensely drawn by its artistic and literary history in which he had become well versed. He was one of the first, perhaps, in our profession who advocated the European ideal of a community stretching from the Urals to the west coast of Ireland. He was born at Bega in New South Wales in 1917, graduated from the Veterinary Faculty of the University of Sydney in 1938, and had already developed a keen awareness of the place of his profession in the mainstream of European culture by the time of his arrival in England in 1953. After a short period in this country he went to Tunis to work with Drs Renoux and Alton at the Pasteur Institute, and then returned to take up the position of Pathologist at the Animal Health Trust's Equine Research Station under William Miller. In 1959, he was given leave of absence to go to Italy as veterinary officer in charge of Ribot at the Razza Dormello and, the following year, went to Peru to advise the Jockey Club of that country on the breeding of racehorses.

The Equine Veterinary Society

The records of a meeting that took place in Newmarket on 16 October 1961 and signed by Leo Mahaffey provides an insight into the original concept of those involved in the formation of BEVA. Minutes of the meeting headed Equine Veterinary Society are reproduced in full as follows:

"The fourth meeting of gentlemen interested in the formation of the Society took place at Romney House, Dullingham Road, Newmarket at 7.45 pm on Monday, October 16th, under the Chairmanship of Mr J. Hickman. Also present were Messrs M. Hunt, L. W. Mahaffey, P. D. Rossdale and I. Silver.

Hickman advised that the inaugural meeting will be held in the Main Hall, Royal Veterinary College, Camden Town, at 2.30 pm on Saturday, November 18th.

He also produced a draft letter to be sent to the Veterinary Record *and a Notice of Meeting, to be inserted in three consecutive issues of the same journal.*

It was agreed to ask Mr A. C. Fraser of Wokingham to attend a further meeting at Cambridge, on Tuesday, October 31st, at 6.00 pm. To this end he was telephoned and he accepted then and there. A main purpose of this meeting is to agree upon the matters and material which several speakers will present on November 18th.

It was agreed:

a) Hickman will produce a proposed agenda for the inaugural meeting.

b) He will, in a Chairman's introduction, give an outline of the steps which have led up to the formation of an E. V. S. and will indicate broadly what kind of services such as Society might render. It was proposed that these be dealt with more specifically by individuals, under the headings as shown:

1) Scientific Services - A. C. Fraser, who might establish that:
a) In a broad sense there is a distinct desirability for equine medicine and surgery to advance in parallel with other specialist

branches of veterinary science. This is not happening at present and probably cannot occur until a Society exists to foster such a development.

b) One of the aims of the Society would be encourage liaison between general equine practitioners, specialised equine consultants and laboratory and academic workers, to the mutual advantage of all.

c) Considerable sums of money are likely to be available in the near future from the Betting Levy Board for veterinary research. It is felt that such a Society, representative of equine practitioners all over the country, could offer guidance to the recipients of grants regarding the type of research work most practitioners urgently required.

2) Political Services - L.W. Mahaffey. The Steering Committee thought he should deal with this as follows:

a) The society should assist in dealing with the many questions concerning all types of horses which are continually arising.

b) It should attempt to establish good relationships with various outside bodies so that the profession might exert the influence for which its special training and knowledge befits it.

c) Such bodies (taken at random) might be the Jockey Club, the various horse societies, the American Equine Practitioners' Association, which is by all accounts flourishing, the Ministry, regarding questions concerning import and export regulations for horses (e.g. whether Mallein testing should continue).

d) In this connection it would be hoped that, as the Society gets into its stride, good public relations with the Press might be established and authoritative comment might be offered upon all matters where veterinary science is or should be involved.

e) Such a Society should be well fitted to assist in having clarified the responsibilities and liabilities of people such as racecourse veterinary surgeons. Private practitioners, too, will probably be faced with numerous problems connected with the use of drugs etc. in their practice as the campaign against doping proceeds and swabbing becomes routine. An Equine Veterinary Society should be able to help here.

f) Establish good relationships with Continental equine societies (or equine practitioners if the former do not yet exist) with the ultimate objective of a European Equine Veterinary Society.

3) Finance - M. Hunt. The necessity to be established upon a sound financial basis and reasons therefore:

e.g.

- *payment of stenographer;*
- *cost of abstracting and distribution of literature;*
- *possibility of inviting distinguished equine veterinary surgeons from any country to address the Society and paying expenses for this.*

4) Editorial Matters - I. Silver. The general dissemination of knowledge.

Hickman will also wind up the discussion at the end of the meeting. He proposes to discuss the possibility of having a 3 day conference in 1962 or 1964 as well as the questions of how many whole and half day meetings per annum are envisaged.

He also asks for any views the Steering Committee may have regarding other matters he should discuss at the beginning and end of the inaugural meeting.

It was suggested that Fraser, Mahaffey, Hunt and Silver bring their prepared statements to the Meeting on October 31st for general comment and, if necessary, amendment.

The following names of men who might be prepared to serve on an Executive Committee were suggested, viz:

Bell, Burkhardt, Brain, Cosgrove, Carey-Foster, Crowhurst, Dawes, Davenport, Dickens, Frank, Gould, Green, Gray, Haselden, Jennings, Littlewort, McDonald, Miller, McCunn, McGeady, Rossdale, Reynolds, Sumner, Silver, Wright, Walter."

Richard Onslow's Narrative

In his book, *The First Twenty Five Years*, published by BEVA, Richard Onslow wrote:

"A man of great energy and enthusiasm for anything he undertook and, above all, vision, Mahaffey was inspired by his strong contacts in France and Italy with the idea of founding a 'European Veterinary Association', which would facilitate the spreading of knowledge, as well as the sharing of experience, and keep its members informed of the latest scientific discoveries in equine research. In long discourses with his friend and colleague, Peter Rossdale, he stated passionately the case for the benefits such an association would bring to all concerned, most especially the horse.

In Rossdale, he found a kindred spirit; he was preaching to one already converted to the urgent need for an element of cohesion in his profession. Readily sharing the enthusiasm of Mahaffey, Rossdale consulted Michael Hunt, another equine veterinary practitioner at Newmarket, who suggested they enlist the support of Colonel John Hickman, whose achievements as a practitioner, academic and serving officer in the Royal Army Veterinary Corps for 11 years had long earned him recognition as one of the most distinguished members of his profession (see also p 34).

At that time, Hickman was Reader in Animal Surgery at the University of Cambridge, a post that he held from 1952 until his retirement in 1980. After graduating from the Royal Veterinary College, London, in 1935, he was commissioned into the RAVC the following year. Serving in the Indian Command from 1937 until 1943, he was attached to the Army Remount Department for much of that time. On returning to Europe he was appointed Deputy Assistant Director of the Veterinary and Remount Services of the 21st Army Group in 1944. The following year he joined the Control Commission for Germany and, having been mentioned in dispatches twice, he was permitted to retire from the Army to resume his profession in civilian life in 1947. He was subsequently Reader in Veterinary Surgery at the Royal Veterinary College, Overseas Visiting Fellow at the Institute of Experimental Medicine at Mayo in the United States, and Senior Scientific Officer at the Animal Health Trust,

Newmarket. He became a Fellow of the Royal College of Veterinary Surgeons in 1963, and Honorary Colonel Commandant of the RAVC from 1970 until 1979. In practice, Hickman was particularly interested in farriery and problems involving the lower part of the horse's leg. He was one of the pioneers of equine orthopaedic surgery in England.

As could have been expected of a man who had proved an innovator in such an important field, as well as an administrator of such considerable ability, Hickman readily agreed to give his help to setting up an association to benefit his profession. At that time, the equine veterinary practitioners were deeply divided into a number of factions, and a further impediment to cooperation lay in the intense rivalry that often existed between local practices. More than anyone else, Hickman stood above these vastly varying interests, and was thus in the ideal position to take the lead in bringing cohesion. In the view of those who worked with him on the Steering Committee, Hickman made the most significant contribution to the establishment of the British Equine Veterinary Association.

The next person to be invited to join the Steering Committee was Ian Silver, who now holds a Chair at Bristol University. A brilliant scientist, he was seen as the ideal representative of the scientific side of the profession. He had made his reputation through the treatment of tumours by radiotherapy, a technique which he introduced into equine practice. He subsequently made important contributions to the study of tendon injuries; and of brain damage in man.

There was, therefore, at the first meeting of the Steering Committee at Romney House, Newmarket, in 1961, Hickman, Rossdale, Hunt, Mahaffey and Silver. Subsequent and equally informal meetings were held at the School of Veterinary Clinical Studies or over dinner at the Arts Theatre Restaurant in Cambridge.

The Steering Committee was strengthened by Alistair Fraser, who had a flourishing equine practice in the Lambourn area of Berkshire and had, quite independently, long been considering the desirability of forming an Association. When he had proposed the idea to a British Veterinary Association (BVA) Congress at Oxford, it had been received enthusiastically. Taking the view that Cambridge, with its long tradition of scientific research, and nearby Newmarket, with its huge horse population, constituted a better area for operation, Fraser generously abandoned the steps he was taking to implement his proposal, and threw in his lot with his colleagues in East Anglia. A very good practitioner of the traditional school, Fraser had always been forward looking, and anxious to see equine work receive formal recognition as an important division of the veterinary profession.

Distinguished members of the profession such as Clifford Formston, Bob Cook and Michael Simons showed themselves in full sympathy with the aims of the Steering Committee. Equally important, Maxie Cosgrove, a leading Irish clinician and member of the AAEP, made it known that he and many of his fellow Irish practitioners would be only too willing to become members.

The late George Sutherland who came from Yorkshire, another extremely experienced practitioner, happily supported the new venture in its earliest stages. He, too, was keenly aware how far equine research had been allowed to lag behind that of other species.

The first perceptible outcome of the meetings and informal discussions between the members of the Steering Committee was the sending out of a questionnaire to 250 veterinarians with known equine connections, all over the country. One hundred and fifty were returned, with the majority in favour of the establishment of an association.

Encouraged by this response, Hickman inserted an advertisement in the Veterinary Record, asking anyone interested to meet him in the main hall of the Royal Veterinary College at Camden Town, London, on Saturday 18th November 1961. This was to be the inaugural meeting of what was to become the British Equine Veterinary Association.

Introduced by Fraser, Hickman explained the purpose of the Association. Fraser then talked about scientific objectives, Mahaffey about other aspects of the work they hoped to do, Silver about editorial matters and Rossdale about finances.

Having deplored the neglect of research into equine medicine and surgery, as well as lack of cooperation between practitioners, Fraser declared that much could be rectified by meetings, lectures and courses of a practical nature. He then went on to emphasise the importance of equine veterinarians engaged in academic work cooperating with those in practice.

By being a representative society, Mahaffey told his audience, they would be able to give a more valuable service to the whole of the equestrian community, and establish good relations with other bodies with obvious equine interests like the Jockey Club, who were currently much concerned about doping. An organised society would be able to give advice on such subjects with authority, and clarify the responsibilities of its members in various spheres of activity, such as those on racecourses, where they had to make decisions about the destruction of valuable Thoroughbreds after serious accidents. Coming to a subject particularly close to his heart, Mahaffey said that he would like to see good relationships with Continental societies, and where such societies did not exist, practitioners could join the one that they were in the process of forming.

Silver spoke of the desirability of printing a quarterly digest of abstracts on world equine veterinary literature. He suggested publication of transcripts of each meeting, so that members unable to attend would be informed of the papers that had been given and ensuing discussions. Mahaffey's suggestion, supported by Rossdale and Hunt, that the name of the society should be the European Equine Veterinary Association, was opposed by Bob Cook who put forward the British Equine Veterinary Association (BEVA). McConnachie, Ingram and Dennis Oliver supported the European prefix but this was opposed by Clifford Formston and Jimmy McCunn, respectively, Professors of Surgery and Anatomy at the RVC. John Ayliffe seconded by Bill Walter proposed an association known as the Equine Veterinary Society. The name BEVA was seconded by Michael Littlewort and on being put to the vote this was carried. Thereby, the British Equine Veterinary Association came into being. Its original crest was designed by Cook's father Colonel Frank Palmer Cook.

The first meeting then proceeded to elect Hickman as President, proposed by Michael Hunt and seconded by Ingram. He was elected unanimously and served for two years. At the meeting, the President proposed Fraser be elected Vice President, Cook was elected Honorary Secretary with Hunt and Rossdale as Joint Honorary Treasurers. Mahaffey and Silver were elected to the Executive Committee in company with Cosgrove, Formston, Simons and Sutherland. Other members included Carey Foster, Fred Day, Charles Frank, Sidney Jennings, George Kelly, William Miller and Arnold Shuttleworth.

After discussion it was agreed that the annual subscription should be three guineas with no entrance fee. Of the 157 founder members, 77 attended the inaugural meeting."

The President and Jill Rossdale receiving guests at the 1976 Congress in the cloisters of Neville's Court, Trinity College, Cambridge.

Board of management at the Waltham Centre for Pet Nutrition, Melton Mowbray (1999). From Left to right: J. Mantell, M. Collins, P. Rossdale, H. Robinson, Pat Harris, J. McEwen and A. Barr.

BEVA 1961–2000

In the four decades of the century during which BEVA has operated, there have been substantial changes at all levels of professional acumen and organisation. Technology has been responsible for increasing specialisation and has made a substantial contribution to the accuracy of diagnosis and the outcome of surgery. These developments have changed the clinical face of the profession, both in practice and in the veterinary schools.

While practices have become increasingly organised into groups and university veterinary schools increasingly concerned with research, career pathways for graduates have become correspondingly altered towards a narrower, yet deeper, commitment across the spectrum of veterinary life; and that life made more exacting by virtue of the progressively increasing number and complexity of statutory legislation on subjects, from the use of medicines to the means of waste disposal; all with direct or indirect effects on equine veterinary practice. These enactments may have logic in terms of human health, the environment or misuse of technology, such as radiology, but they can also have far-reaching and often counterproductive effects within the life of individual veterinarians.

Scenes from the BEVA Congress Birmingham 1998 (top) and Harrogate 1999.

The actions of governing bodies and, even, government to control or alter the way in which horses are used, and the attitude of sales companies to impose conditions with respect to veterinary adjudication of an individual animal's fitness (soundness) at the time of sale, have brought increasing conflicts of interest. Welfare has become much more to the fore and entered into many *quasi* veterinary decision-making processes, in the course of treatment of cases or the approach to experimentation by research workers. International and, more recently, European dimensions of veterinary science and practice have been given increasing weight in the context of equine practice.

However, apart from specialism, the concept of continuing professional development (CPD, not to be confused with Cell Programmed Death, the term used by those interested in apoptosis) has, as in all professions, been a much-advocated process in order to maintain standards in a changing world. It is, perhaps, in this field that BEVA has been most active and has contributed substantially during the last quarter of the century.

In 1962, the first meetings of the Executive Committee (later to be called Council) met at the British Veterinary Association's (BVA) rooms in Mansfield Street, London. There was much discussion as to whether BEVA should establish itself as an independent Association or become one affiliated to BVA. Committee members divided roughly equally between those who supported affiliation, largely on the grounds of the opportunity to have a meeting place available and partly in the hope of carrying more influence under the BVA umbrella. The argument against was based, partly, on the wish for independence by the newly established association and, partly, on a desire for the association to be largely one of science without the need to indulge in the politics of the profession. Affiliation eventually won the day, with the hope that affiliation would remove the need for becoming embroiled in arguments of a very 'political' nature, which could be passed to BVA.

During the next four decades, the landscape of veterinary life has changed and, inevitably, BEVA has been drawn more and more into the 'political' arena of veterinary life. As the activities of the Association have increased, so too has its influence and, in particular, its authority across the spectrum of equine activities and interests. For this reason BVA has increasingly turned to the Association for advice. The Royal College of Veterinary Surgeons has also found BEVA to be an appropriate source of advice on equine matters. At the end of the century, BEVA has been involved in many decision-making processes and members of its Council and Sub-Committees devoting substantial proportions of time in discussion of a multitude of contemporary questions followed by submission of advice to the aforementioned and many other authoritative bodies concerned with the horse from both the lay and professional side of the fence.

Pat Harris and Tim Greet - outgoing and incoming BEVA Presidents 1999/2000, at the annual dinner, Harrogate.

3. Equine Veterinary Journal and Equine Veterinary Education

As the 20th century closes, *Equine Veterinary Journal* (EVJ) has the distinction of being the most widely read peer-reviewed publication devoted to a single species; and its reputation, as a clinical science journal, indicated by ranking second only to *Theriogenology* in the impact factor from the Institute of Scientific Information (ISI) in 1998. The *Journal* is read by subscribers in 50 countries and authorship contributed from 23 countries of which approximately 20% are from the UK and 25% from North America.

EVJ was established in 1968 under its first editor, John Hickman. Before that year, papers presented at BEVA meetings were circulated in an edited form under the direction and control of Ian Silver. Anyone who has participated in attempts to report proceedings at scientific or, indeed, other meetings will appreciate the enormous task of placing the spoken word on record. For example, in 1998, a row developed as to whether the words used by the British Prime Minister, Mr Tony Blair, had been accurately reported in Hansard; a spokesman for Hansard commented that:

> *"If Hansard were a verbatim report of what was spoken in the House, most of it would be quite unintelligible."*

EVJ is, in effect, a journal whose origins came from the demand of members to have a written account of subjects presented at meetings and debated in practice. John Hickman moulded the *Journal* into a peer-reviewed, objective, scientific means of communication. He handed over the editorship to Leo Jeffcott in 1975. Leo was then Head of the Clinical Department at the Animal Health Trust and an active member of the Association. He was assisted by his wife, Tiza, and the *Journal* was printed by Henderson Group One. In 1979, the British Veterinary Association Publications Department, which was responsible for *Veterinary Record*, took on the task of publishing EVJ.

Jeffcott built upon Hickman's work and introduced educational articles of a commissioned nature. The *Journal* still accepted *ad hoc* submissions from any quarter on any subject. These were subjected to peer review and selected on the basis of originality, scientific merit and relevance to clinical practice.

In 1979, this author took over the position as Editor when Leo Jeffcott left to take up a chair in veterinary clinical studies in Melbourne, Australia. My own editorship has lasted (hopefully at the time of writing this!) until the end of the century. During the past 20 years there has been an ever increasing submission rate from authors requesting publication of their work in EVJ. This trend was met, at first, by increasing the size of the *Journal* both in number of pages (from 48 to 88 per issue) and also in number of issues (from four to six) published annually. However, it was realised that it would be impractical to continue to include educational articles and, by 1985, the *Journal* became an entirely peer-reviewed journal based on nonsolicited submissions.

Continuing educational material was then placed in *Equine Veterinary Education* which was started in editorial collaboration with Lawrence Gerring in 1985. At about this time, the affairs of the *Journal* were placed in the hands of Equine Veterinary Journal Limited, a company registered on the 14th December 1984. The objective of forming the company was to remove the day-to-day running and policy of the *Journal* from the confines of the BEVA Executive Committee and Council, where it had been found to occupy too much time in discussion in their meetings throughout the years.

EVJ Limited was constituted on the basis of an Executive Board and the Editor as Chairman and Managing Director. There were, and still are, five members of the Board, the Editor and two members appointed by the Editor and two by BEVA Council. BEVA owns the company and its shareholding is represented at the AGM of the company by two appointees of Council.

The reader may gain some appreciation of the progress made by *Equine Veterinary Journal* over the 30 years of its publication by reference to Table 1.

In 1983 the first supplement to EVJ was published. The concept of supplements was to enable single subjects to be addressed by experts in the field in the form of peer-reviewed papers, some of a review nature. The idea was to follow, somewhat, the format of bulletins published by the

TABLE 1: Quinquennial Analysis of Equine Veterinary Journal Content From Volume 1 to 30.

			No. Original Papers Per Year			
Volume	No. of Issues Per Year	No. of Pages Per Year	Editorial Leaders	General Articles	Short Comms	Case Reports
July 68–Oct 69	4 of 6	184				
1968 (1)	6	296	1	9	5	0
1973 (5)	4	180	0	31	2	0
1978 (10)	4	274	1	47	5	0
1983 (15)	4	384	16	55	10	14
1988 (20)	6	476	17	66	8	24
1993 (25)	6	562	19	65	13	20
1998 (30)	6	552	17	69	7	8

British Medical Journal, publications which the writer and then Editor found most helpful in his own field of perinatology.

The first EVJ Supplement was devoted to work which was being performed under the direction of Ian Silver on tendon injury and repair. The content consisted of work performed at the University of Bristol funded by the Horserace Betting Levy Board. The reason for the funding stemmed from a question asked in the House of Commons regarding the firing (cautery) of horses' tendons and whether this procedure was cruel. As with so many subjects of welfare of animals, though sincerely held, the issues involved were based largely on anthropomorphic and subjective opinion. It is always tempting to throw science into the arena but, as on this occasion, answers fail to satisfy the pros or the antis. In this case, some quarter of a million pounds was expended and failed to conclude that the procedure was cruel, but rather that it was no better nor any more logical than many other therapies of a less aesthetically challenging nature. The funding was not wasted because the work represented a unique basis for a better understanding of equine tendon physiology and pathology; and laid the basis for further work on the subject in the succeeding 20 years.

The issue of firing is considered elsewhere but this author believes that it is not any more cruel to the horse than many other procedures which veterinarians employ, but it gives an aura of the dark ages to those who see it practised. To describe oneself as a veterinary surgeon and resort to the wholesale destruction of tissue is a contradiction of what is nowadays considered to be surgery.

Since the publication of the first supplement there have been 30 others (see Table 2).

Equine Veterinary Journal serves as a vehicle by which authors can communicate their work with a diverse readership extending from clinicians to academics and other research workers. This means of communication is essential in order to justify the extensive funding which is committed to the work leading up to the reporting in print and, importantly, the 'sweat and toil' of many hours, weeks, months and, sometimes, years, which not only the authors but many others have devoted towards the objectives of the endeavours reported. Papers published strengthen the reputation and *curriculum vitae* of the authors and are an essential basis for judgement in the course of their careers, both for promotion and for obtaining further research funding.

The *Journal* has also served as a means of communication for clinicians who have original findings to report and can do so in a manner which is sufficiently objective to pass scrutiny. Clinical communications are as important as basic research, particularly to other clinicians. However, *magnas est veritas* and the *Journal* has to ensure every statement made within the pages of content is objective and a true basis of what is being claimed. Journals of lesser peer-reviewed standard may publish and be damned, but those of high standing must essentially never place themselves in this position.

The style of reporting work in EVJ sometimes provokes comment that many of the papers are regarded as being too esoteric for clinical readership. This is an inevitable critique of quality in all walks of life. From novels to newspapers, from scientific journals to magazines there is a range of quality and a corresponding range of readership. Fortunately, veterinary surgeons are nowadays so highly qualified and enthusiastic for learning that they not only recognise but demand quality in what they read.

As we pass into the next century, we must expect there to be a higher demand from the public for the higher quality of veterinary services. Communication is extending into numerous electronic media, e-mail, CD ROM and internet. While facing a virtual revolution in our capacity to inform and be informed, the printed form still represents an important part of communicating truth, as opposed to fiction and subjective pronouncements. As the poet wrote:

> *"The moving finger writes and having writ moves on, nor all thy piety nor wit can lure it back a single line, nor all thy tears wash out a word of it";*

and the printed word, like the evidence of fossils, always needs to be present as a permanent record that cannot be eliminated from the screen or affected by, for example, a computer virus.

Equine Veterinary Education (EVE) was started in 1989 for the purposes implied by its title. As with all efforts to educate, success depends upon the commitment of those

TABLE 2: Supplements of the Equine Veterinary Journal.

No	Year	Title	Editors
1	1983	A Clinical and Experimental Study of Tendon Injury, Healing and Treatment in the Horse	I. A. Silver and P. D. Rossdale
2	1983	Equine Ophthalmology	K. C. Barnett, P. D. Rossdale and Janette F. Wade
3	1985	Equine Embryo Transfer	W. R. Allen and D. F. Antczak
4	1986	Equine Radiography - A Guide to Interpretation	P. M. Webbon and P. D. Rossdale
5	1988	Perinatology	P. D. Rossdale, M. Silver and R. J. Rose
6	1988	Equine Orthopaedic Injury and Repair	L. R. Bramlage, G. B. Edwards and Janette F. Wade
7	1989	Equine Colic	E. L. Gerring, D. D. Morris, J. N. Moore and N. A. White
8	1989	Equine Embryo Transfer II	W. R. Allen, D. F. Antczak and Janette F. Wade
9	1990	Equine Exercise Physiology	D. H. Leach, R. J. Rose and D H Snow
10	1990	Equine Ophthalmology II	K. C. Barnett, P. D. Rossdale and Janette F. Wade
11	1992	Equine Therapy, Anaesthesiology and Pharmacology	W. W. Muir III, P. D. Rossdale and P. M. Keen
12	1991	Equine Immunology	M. A. Holmes, P. D. Rossdale and Anna F. Arnold
13	1992	Equine Gastroenterology	G. B. Edwards, E. L. Gerring and Anna F. Arnold
14	1993	Foetal Maturation: Comparative Aspects of Normal and Disturbed Development	A. L. Fowden and P. D. Rossdale
15	1993	Equine Embryo Transfer III	W. R. Allen, D. F. Antczak and J. G. Oriol
16	1993	Osteochondrosis in the '90s	L. B. Jeffcott, G. Dalin and Barbara J. Weir
17	1994	Animal Locomotion	H. C. Schamhardt, Hilary M. Clayton and Janette F. Wade
18	1995	Equine Exercise Physiology 4	N. E. Robinson
19	1995	Equine Cardiovascular Medicine	Karen J. Blissitt, Celia M. Marr, P. D. Rossdale and Rachel E. Green
20	1995	Progress Towards Atlanta '96 Vol I	L. B. Jeffcott and A. F. Clarke
22	1996	Progress Towards Atlanta '96 Vol II	L. B. Jeffcott and A. F. Clarke
23	1997	Animal Locomotion	E. Barrey, Helen M. S. Davies, H. C. Schamhardt and P. D. Rossdale
24	1997	Comparative Fetal and Neonatal Physiology: Reviews in memory of Marian Silver	Abigail L. Fowden, P. D. Rossdale and Ann Silver
25	1997	Equine Embryo Transfer IV	W. R. Allen, E. Palmer and Valerie Urwin
26	1998	The Equine Hoof and Laminitis	J. D. Reilly, M. J. Martinelli, C. C. Pollitt and Rachel E. Green
27	1998	Equine Clinical Behaviour	Verena Bracher, Sue McDonnell, Thomas Stohler and Rachel E. Green
28	1999	The Role of the Horse in Europe	Pat Harris, Deborah Goodwin and Rachel E. Green
29	1999	Equine Gastric Ulceration	T. S. Mair, P. D. Rossdale and A. M. Merritt
30	1999	Equine Exercise Physiology 5	L. B. Jeffcott
31	1999	Osteochondrosis and Musculoskeletal Development in the Foal under the Influence of Exercise	P. D. Rossdale, L. B. Jeffcott and E. C. Firth

who teach, in this context to contribute articles, together with the ingredients or material presented and receptivity on the part of those to whom the efforts are directed. An educational journal is attempting to sell information, not only in a commercial sense, but as a transaction between the giver and the receiver. In large measure, EVE has succeeded if success is judged on the enthusiasm of contributors, circulation numbers which have increased exponentionally worldwide, culminating in the arrangement made in 1999 for the American Association of Equine Practitioners to reprint each issue of EVE for distribution to their membership of some 6–7000 colleagues.

It is a pleasure to record here the names of some of those on whose commitment and dedication to continuing education provided the impetus for the genesis and progress of EVE. Lawrence Gerring joined enthusiastically in developing the concept. Lawrence was at the time the consulting equine surgeon at the Royal Veterinary College, Potters Bar. His broad knowledge of subjects and of potential contributors was an essential element in raising the EVE initiative off the ground. Jan Wade was of great help to us both and we gathered around us a team of clinicians in university veterinary schools and in practice who formed an actively participating Editorial Board; these included: Robert G. Allpress, Andrew F. Clarke, Kathy W. Clarke, Murray J. Corke, Goran Dalin, David R. Ellis, Rolf M. Embertson, Leo B. Jeffcott, Desmond P. Leadon, Ietje P. Leendertse, Stephen A. May, I. G. (Joe) Mayhew, Elspeth Milne, Graham A. Munroe, Arthur C. Pickles, Sidney W. Ricketts and John P. Walmsley.

The Editors have been Lawrence Gerring, Joe Mayhew, Sandy Love and Tim Mair, with the present writer moving to the position of Editor-in-Chief on relinquishing the post of Editor. The arrangement with AAEP came about largely through the good auspices of Larry Bramlage, Wayne McIlwraith and Gary Carpenter on their side of the fence and, on BEVA's side, Jeremy Mantell, Howard Robinson and Sue Dyson. A new Board was formed and met for the first time on 26 March 1999 at the AAEP Headquarters in Lexington, Kentucky. The Board consisted of Peter Rossdale, Ed Robinson, Larry Bramlage, Eleanor Green, Pat Harris, Tim Mair and Mark Martinelli.

What of the future? It has been said that *"the educated man is one who keeps learning"*, and there can be little or no doubt that professional men and women in whatever walk of life, will both need and be required to heed this maxim increasingly in the coming century. Audit is an increasing challenge to professional enterprises, including the doctor in practice, the surgeon in the hospital, the teacher in the classroom and, inevitably, the veterinarian in each department of veterinary life. If there is judgement, there must a corresponding commitment to learning and improvement of ones expertise. 'Keeping up with the times' has always been an aim in professional life, but with the explosion of knowledge and technology of the last two decades of the 20th century, we may expect more and more sophistication and precise methods of diagnosis and therapy to challenge those into the 21st century and beyond. Journals of continuing education play an essential role, although they have to be taken into the context of hands-on experience, refresher courses and electronic devices of communication. Each individual may have preference for one or other of these means, but together they stand as the means to the ends of education. EVE and EVJ are, therefore, an integral part of the educational programme for veterinarians who wish to keep up with the times and maintain their professional status under the audit of the horse-owning community and of their peers.

4. BEVA Presidential Reminiscences

J. Robert Bainbridge (1990)

Queen Mother's birthday celebration

In 1990, there was a most important and colourful national occasion, one in which BEVA played a part. On a warm sunny Wednesday afternoon in June, a magnificent parade took place on Horse Guards Parade, as a birthday tribute to Queen Elizabeth, The Queen Mother, on completing her 90th year.

As one of the organisations of which The Queen Mother is a Patron, we had the honour to be invited to join in the fun. Our contribution to the parade lined up in Birdcage Walk, the bowler-hatted President, this author, leading the group, resplendent in the original silver chain of office (now pensioned off), representing the equine practitioner. Captain Anne Ashman, an equine surgeon from the RAVC, in green operating gown, represented our lady members. Research and new product development in the equine field was represented by veterinary surgeon Henry Fielden, in white lab coat, while the equine veterinary nurse was represented by animal nurse of the year, Miss Carole Martin, who completed the quartet.

Next came the two equine stars of our show. The charger Copenhagen, who had been reinstated to health by skilled veterinary attention following his wounding in the IRA bombing outrage in Hyde Park in 1982, was accompanied by the younger charger Iniskillen, who had undergone surgery for colic.

These were followed by a white Range Rover towing a sparkling new Racecourse Horse Ambulance with the BEVA logo prominently displayed on both vehicles. That our display was somewhat obscured by two large bulls from the Royal Herd, in tractor-hauled trailers which veered in front of us just as we passed our Patron at the saluting base, was perhaps unfortunate! However, when Her Majesty later toured in her open car she passed very close to us and hopefully noticed our contribution.

The day was rounded off with a very pleasant dinner attended by past presidents of the Association with their wives at a restaurant in the West End.

The event was the catalyst which brought about the foundation of the BEVA Trust Queen Mother Student Travel Award which has been awarded annually since 1990 to commemorate the birthday of our Patron. It is very gratifying that the standard of the reports by the recipients of the award has been very high and, in recent years, the Trust has been able to assist more than one student per year to travel to a centre of excellence outside the UK. Her Majesty invited past beneficiaries of this award to a small reception at Clarence House in March 1999.

Hawaii Nine-O

How did a party of some three dozen people of assorted nations, but all with an interest in the veterinary problems of the horse, find themselves in Oahu in January 1990? I suppose the germ of an idea must have originated at the equine reproduction course at Newmarket in 1988 when Norman Chandler was talking to Jerry Dilsaver, the equine veterinarian based in Hawaii. I suppose they caught yours truly in a receptive mood and I agreed, with Jerry's help, to organise a BEVA offshore meeting on one of the islands of Hawaii.

An agent was approached and he arranged an exploratory trip to view potential hotels in Waikiki and Maui as well as for the stopover in San Francisco. The event was publicised, especially at Congress in 1989, and a main speaker booked and sponsorship to help with his flight was found. Interest was adequate and widespread and all appeared to be progressing well as Christmas drew nearer. Then, toward the end of November, a fax arrived from Tasmania saying that a potential delegate had tried to book rooms at the Pacific Beach Hotel only to be told that the rooms had been cancelled!

This could not be happening! However a phone call to the hotel proved that it was so. My somewhat irate call to the agent was met with the reassurance that, although the hotel had cancelled, because he had not paid the deposit in time, he had reserved rooms at an even better hotel - in Southern California! Not surprisingly we did not find this a reasonable alternative. Requests for registration were still coming in, especially from AAEP members in the States, but they could not be taken due to the uncertainty about accommodation. Fortunately, contact made on the exploratory trip with a retired travel agent at a Rotary meeting, enabled us to obtain some rooms but at greater cost and although we did not take these, the fact that we could find rooms when our agent thought there were none spurred him into action and adequate rooms were found in a hotel adjacent to the Pacific Beach Hotel. There was even a view of the Waikiki breakers if one leaned over the balcony and peered between the high rise buildings.

So it came about that our party, after an enjoyable, if eventful, stopover in San Francisco - where Paddy Sweeney had the misfortune to be mugged - arrived on Oahu. It was an assorted party of like minds with a thirst for knowledge including representatives from Norway, France, the Netherlands, Ireland, New Zealand, Australia and Hawaii, with a nucleus from Wales, Scotland and England; this included three past presidents of the Association and the President-to-be for 1992.

We were fortunate still to have the conference facilities of the Pacific Beach Hotel available to us, and of these we made full use. Lawrence Gerring set the tone as an excellent main speaker and most of the delegates gave papers. Subjects included a report of the trial use of Cisapride in colic cases, grass sickness and following colic surgery; surgery of the cervix in the mare; surgical removal of fractured splint bones to treatment of strained flexor tendons; and an interesting comparison between sports injuries in the horse and the racing greyhound. Other topics included interesting observations on copper supplementation; the then recently introduced use of arthroscopy in the horse; surgery to correct overriding cervical vertebral dorsal processes; and much, much more. These sessions had excellent scientific content and the discussion which followed invariably overran the time allowed for the use of the room. One might have thought that the call of the beach would be too great for a number of delegates after the first day but this was not so; and there was full attendance on all days and all sessions overran. *"All work and no play..."*? The day excursion to the Polynesian Centre was one which fascinated all of us but you may imagine the reaction of the group when our agent (yes, the same one) could not find the tickets. At the last minute, they appeared from the depths of a travel bag which saved him from being fed to the sharks and we were allowed in to this theme park of Island Pacific culture.

Following our conference the majority of the party moved on to the delightful island of Maui where attendance at a conference on equine fertility was being held at a very luxurious Japanese-owned hotel. Dr Ginther and his team were the main speakers in a programme which concentrated on recent advances in ultrasound techniques. For many of us, this was our first introduction to the possibility of determining the gender of an embryo *in utero*.

The value of BEVA meetings held in venues outside the British Isles is well recognised but the format using one main speaker supported by contributions from the delegates themselves proved to engender great discussion sessions with participation of all delegates. Will someone try it again sometime in the new millennium? It is hoped that they will.

Deborah Baker (1993)

I was completely taken by surprise when Bob Bainbridge, who was President at the time, called me one day to ask whether I would consider being President in 1993.

I had never considered the possibility of this office and moreover was totally in awe of how Presidents were selected. I remember thinking that I was to become the first woman President of the Association by default, as I was very well aware that at least 10 years earlier an eminent veterinarian, Sally Glendining was to have had the honour. Sadly she died before she could become President, but her academic achievements and personal charm were remembered by many. I hope I did not let her down.

I started my Presidential year determined to measure up as far as possible to the other past Presidents but also to pave the way for the future.

Perhaps having my second child two months into office was not one of the greatest examples of strategic planning, and to the first Council meeting I chaired I brought a veritable train consisting of two infants, long-suffering husband, a nanny (of sorts) and piles of child-associated baggage.

Past Presidents were a wonderful resource to draw on (I commend drawing on their wide diversity of skills and experience to all future Presidents of the Association). Andi Ewen was a lifesaver, whose heroic deeds included deciphering illegible scrawls sent by fax, diplomatically offering loads of advice to ensure feathers remained unruffled and putting up with my lamentable habit of speaking at machine gun speed.

My abiding memory of that year in office was of the goodwill from colleagues on Council and from other Associations. Amongst various endeavours, I tried to bring the Association and the world of racing closer together. Six years on I am delighted to see that this relationship is now a close one, and BEVA are asked for their input on many different aspects of equine health and welfare.

On a lighter note, having grappled with the Presidential chain of office, it became clear that this was emphatically not female friendly. Accordingly a flat ribbon chain type was commissioned for all future Presidents, with the original used for high days and holidays.

Ian McNab (1979)

The changing images of BEVA

I attended the inaugural meeting of BEVA in December 1961, having qualified just six months previously. As an undergraduate I had relied heavily on attending lectures with their accompanying visual aids to gain the necessary knowledge. I related much more easily to the spoken rather than the written word. Reading the *Veterinary Record,* as the only avenue left open to me to continue my professional development, did not appeal.

Membership of BEVA reopened the door. The Management Committee speedily installed a programme of day meetings and annual congresses, providing ready access to recent developments in equine veterinary science, in my preferred audiovisual format. Out of these attendances grew a fascination with the technological advantages in investigative techniques and, in particular, the images they created.

Bob Cook, using a rigid endoscope to produce photographs of the larynx, was probably the first to produce images that literally gave an insight into the conscious patient. The mysteries of the guttural pouches were solved. However, with the rapid progress in technology, the fibreoptic endoscope soon became the preferred instrument. Virtuosos such as Geoff Lane gave members a new understanding of laryngeal dysfunction. Although originally a very expensive piece of equipment, a veterinary version was introduced to the market place at the Exeter Congress, and became a 'must-have' for most equine practitioners.

Research at a cellular level also entered a new phase of photomicroscopy. Simple photographs of stained sections were superseded by the wonderful landscapes produced by the scanning electron microscope. Illustrations of alveolar macrophages ingesting virus particles were almost surreal.

I also have clear recollections of being a member of small group at a stud management course that, at the invitation of Twink Allen, went to a nearby studfarm to see a demonstration of a new gadget. The images of the fetal heart, produced by that now rather primitive ultrasound scanner, may have lacked quality but their significance cannot be underestimated. This was the beginning of dynamic investigative techniques in veterinary science.

The boundless uses of ultrasonography were rapidly

explored over the succeeding years. Tendons and other soft tissues were particularly amenable. However, it has its most eloquent expression when used to investigate the cardiovascular system. Viewing for the first time a colour screen showing the contraflow of blood produced by valvular incompetence in an equine heart was particlarly memorable, and due in no small part to the sheer expertise of Celia Marr.

Dynamic images also became available with the advent of the video chip camera. The closed world of arthroscopy became available to a wider audience. Ian Wright, at a meeting at Cirencester, ventured into new ground with a simultaneous projection of a video film and still slides to illustrate his topic. A somewhat schizophrenic experience! This was also the first occasion when I can recall the proceedings being interrupted by a mobile phone.

The respiratory system came under renewed scrutiny with the combined use of the treadmill and the videoendoscope. A short piece of film introduced late in the day at the Warwick Congress in 1991 showing a horse at vigorous exercise and the moment of laryngeal collapse was breathtaking!

Twink Allen, in the meantime, was also exploiting the use of the latest technology. The intrauterine approach he employed, using a videoendoscope, produced some of the most beautiful images we have seen over the years. To complete the picture, at the 1998 AGM, John Walmsley exhibited his technical brilliance in demonstrating the technique of abdominal laparoscopy. His guided tour through the abdomen added a third dimension to understanding the anatomy, even leaving aside the immense possibilities of diagnostic and surgical applications.

One of the hallmarks of BEVA meetings, over the years, has been the standard of presentation. In the early days slides were very much the standard issue white print on a blue background. They did have a rather soporific effect, especially after lunch, even on one occasion on the Chairman! (did no one notice me, or were they too polite to comment?)

Many presenters also proved to be able photographers. Donald Simpson produced excellent slides to augment his practical paper at the time of the CEM outbreak. With the advent of computer-aided design packages, and digital camera, lecture slides have become almost a new art form. Consigning the slides for a whole lecture to a floppy disc will remove the minor embarrassments of upside down and sticking slides, but will it spoil audience participation?

In conclusion, I would like to pay tribute to all those who over the years have informed, instructed and entertained us with the audio visual aids not only for their factual content but also for the artistry.

Richard Jones (1996)

After serving as Sam Hignett's Congress Secretary, Richard recalls filling Congress wallets on the dining room table, a memory common to all those who give voluntary support to organisations such as BEVA. He was active in restarting the equine veterinary nursing training project with Jane Craven, then President of the British Veterinary Nursing Association, an initiative followed subsequently by Tim Greet. The first fast-track equine certificate candidates who will graduate as veterinary nurses are due to take their examination in July 2000.

Peter Rossdale

Brian Singleton (1988)

Brian established the Annual Congress at the conference centre in Harrogate, thereby initiating the upgrading of facilities from those enjoyed at universities and similar centres in the past to more luxurious and spacious surroundings at Harrogate; and leading in 1998 to the even more ambitious step taken under the leadership of the then President Jeremy Mantell when the meeting was held in Birmingham. The Harrogate centre provided exceptional Congress facilities, including an area for the trade exhibition all under the same roof. In May 1998, Brian arranged a visit to Sweden for BEVA Members with the chief objective to view the new equine hospital designed and constructed by Harry Pettersson (see p 248).

Reminiscences of a Congress Secretary

Michael Osborne

I had the unenviable task of acting as BEVA Congress Secretary at the first Dublin Congress in 1966. The Congress Committee functioned under three basic constraints - no experience, no idea and no money. But our instruction from President Maxi Cosgrove was "*don't lose money*"; BEVA could not afford a loss.

Luckily, the enthusiasm of our colleagues from the UK and a plan to entice equine practitioners from the USA and Europe ensured that we had a record attendance augmented by a large number of Irish colleagues who were experiencing a BEVA Congress for the first time.

The party spirit literally and metaphorically pervaded all activities. Two events on the social programme, in particular, are well remembered.

The Ladies' Social Programme was in the very capable hands of Maureeen, wife of a Committee Member, and she arranged a comprehensive itinerary including shopping tours, fashion shows, brewery visits and the usual tourist haunts.

The highlight of this programme was a four hour bus tour of the Wicklow Mountains. This took a slow meandering route on mountain roads encumbered with local sheep and riddled with potholes.

Because of the importance of this tour, Maureen decided that she would act as the tour guide and commentator, using the bus microphone and copious tourist literature. She had a very good knowledge of the area, but passengers from the UK, Europe and USA (in particular two ladies from California) were on their first visit to Ireland.

The bus departed from Dublin at 10 am on a cloudy, rainy day. Maureen with her beautiful speaking voice laced with a hint of brogue commentated as she looked out from the front seat through a clear window as follows:

> *"On your right is Christchurch Cathedral associated with Dean Swift. On your left, Dublin Castle, seat of power during British Rule. On your right is Russborough House, home of Lord and Lady Beit, who own a most valuable collection of Old Masters. We are now approaching Glendalough the house containing St Kevin's bed and a place of great historical and religious interest. St Kevin's bed is hewn from a granite rock."*
>
> *"Oh gee,"* said a Californian. *"I'd sure like to see that and tell Marylou back in Fresno that I lay in an Irish Saint's bed."*

Later, high in the mountains over Dublin the commentary continued. *"On the left is the start of the River Liffey - only a small and narrow stream,"* and so it went on until, arriving back in Dublin, the group applauded and thanked Maureen profusely for her commentary.

On alighting from the bus I asked the California dreamer, *"Did you enjoy the tour?" "Oh yes, it was great,"* she replied, *"but none of us could see out of the bus, all the windows were fogged up. I was wondering if all of the tourist things that the beautiful guide described were really there."*

The other episode from that Congress was a drink-related tale of a heavily tweeded, very obese English practitioner, who decided that while his wife was on the Wicklow Hills Tour, he would take the literary tour of Dublin, based on that described in James Joyce's *Ulysses* when Leopold Bloom does a pub crawl through Dublin. The tourist guides at that time stated that visitors interested in Irish literature should trace Bloom's path from pub to pub. There are signposts *en route* to ensure they could find their way.

Anyway, Mr 'Tweeds' made his way by taxi to the first pub on the route and the taxi driver explained that you must drink a pint of Guinness, a ball of malt and another pint of Guinness in each pub on route. 'Tweeds' said to the taxi driver, *"Come in and get me started."*

The taxi driver, stepping to his chin, made a bee line for the counter ordered the prescribed drinks and proceeded to regale his companion with real and imaginary tales of 'Ould Dublin'.

Eight hours later, in 'Davy Byrne's' famous pub, both Joyceans were paralytically drunk. 'Tweeds' fell asleep with loud snoring. His boozing mate could not wake him, could not stand the noise and left a note with the barman to get 'Tweeds' back to the Shelbourne Hotel; and left money for the fare.

When the Hall Porter at the Shelbourne Hotel saw the prostrate body on the back seat, he brought along some help to load 'Tweeds' onto a hand cart normally used for luggage.

He wheeled the hand cart into the bar where some BEVA delegates were in good spirits. *"Do any of you know this man?"* the hall porter asked.

"Yes, his name is 'Tweeds'," replied a helpful delegate. *"He and his wife are residents."*

"What will I do with him. He is helpless and unconscious - I think."

"Oh, bring him on up to his room in the hand cart."

The knock on the door aroused his wife who enquired, *"Who's there?"*

"Hall porter, mam, I have someone in my hand cart that you may know."

I never saw 'Tweeds' or his wife at the Congress on the following days. Come to think of it, I haven't seen him since.

5. International Equine Reproduction Symposia Committee (IERSC)

In 1973, an initiative developed with the aim of bringing together scientists and veterinarians active in the field of equine reproductive research under the umbrella of an organising committee. As with all such enterprises, someone has to lead and to cajole, push and work towards stated objectives. In the case of the IERSC it was W. R. (Twink) Allen who, at that time, was based at Cambridge.

Twink was an ideal colleague to, as they say, 'get the project off the ground'; his scientific background and motivation, his energy and enthusiasm and his wide knowledge of research workers worldwide, provided the necessary impetus, infecting all with whom he had contact with his own enthusiasm for the idea.

A small group was contacted in the first instance, including John Hughes (California), Doug Mitchell (Alberta, Canada) and Peter Rossdale (Newmarket). The first meeting, in 1974, was financed through the good auspices of Peter Burrell (see Preface) and his wife, through the Richard King Mellon Charitable Trust. In his opening address The Honourable Jakey Astor, Chairman of the Agricultural Research Council and President of the Thoroughbred Breeders' Association, said that:

> *"Against a world background of political conflict, economic confusion and general uncertainty, it is a commendable achievement for distinguished scientists from 22 countries to meet in the pursuit and dissemination of knowledge and to promote its practical application in an area entirely associated with peaceful activities."*

He went on to say:

> *"My experience in the field of agricultural research suggests that it is sometimes just as hard to set up machinery capable of deciding sensible areas for research and so imposing sensible questions, as it is finding scientists capable of supplying answers. It is the responsibility of the biologist and the veterinarian to investigate the mechanisms and problems of reproduction in the laboratory and stables; and to ensure that the results of their findings are made readily available for the benefit of others. It is equally important that breeders and breed societies use any new information wisely to increase the efficiency of horses and the quality of their offspring."*

Participants in this symposium are shown in Figure 1, together with their names. The programme, in this first symposium, was divided under the following headings: *Evolution*, in which Roger Short, Hans Klingel and A. D.

Courtesy of R. M. Butterfield.

Year	Venue	Chairman
1974	Cambridge, UK	W. R. Allen
1978	Davis, California, USA	B. W. Pickett
1982	Sydney, Australia	P. D. Rossdale
1986	Calgary, Canada	J. P. Hughes
1990	Deauville, France	D. Mitchell
1994	Cascombe, Brazil	E. Palmer
1998	Pretoria, South Africa	J. Hyland

TABLE 3: Venues and chairmen of IERSC Committee meetings.

Feist contributed; *Stallion,* in which 28 papers were presented, mostly concerned with the biochemistry, physiology and clinical aspects of semen, its collection, analysis and storage; *Nonpregnant mare,* with 45 contributions under a variety of headings, including clinical and endocrine aspects of the oestrous cycle, fertility, ovary and uterus, and genetics; *Pregnant mare,* with 33 contributions involving the subjects of endocrinology and embryology; and *Fetal and newborn foal,* which comprised 33 contributions covering the fetal environment, endocrinology of late pregnancy and birth, cardiopulmonary adaptation, metabolic adaptation and the immune status of the foal.

Following the meeting, it was concluded that an international committee should be formed, and this became composed of those recorded in Table 3. The system adopted was for the committee to hold a meeting midway between quaternary symposia and for a new chairman to be elected by the committee which, itself, was to be composed of representatives covering the globe. Therefore, from 1974 until 1998 the meeting has been held every four years. The venues and the chairman of the committee are shown in Table 3.

The proceedings of each meeting have been published, in all but two instances (the second and the sixth), as supplements of the *Journal of Reproduction and Fertility*. It seems probable that the organisation will continue into the next century, although modifications of the format and approach may have to adapt to the changing circumstances of the volume of material available and, particularly, its sophistication and specialist nature. Equine reproduction now covers, as in other subjects, a spectrum through molecular biology and the specialism of semenology to intrauterine growth retardating effects, as demonstrated by stereological (three-dimensional) assessment of the density of microstructures. Presenters at these meetings are often those who would prefer to contribute to meetings of their own speciality than to those of generality; and audiences or workers in other fields may not have the time to be concerned with subjects outside their own range of interest and work. The publication of the proceedings becomes increasingly onerous and, to some extent, cumbersome, as the subject matter extends in breadth and depth. Such publications across a broad field, with their unavoidable delay if peer review is applied, gives rise to concern among those who depend, as most research workers, on the need for publication of their results if they are to survive in a competitive environment of funding. It is with these considerations that the IERSC will have to come to terms in the future.

Fig 1: The First International Equine Reproduction Symposium, Kings College, Cambridge, 1974. From left to right: Front row: *K. Kosiniak, I. W. Rowlands, R. V. Short, W. Bielański, Mrs K. Arbeiter, R. M. Moor, Mrs J. K. Barty, Virginia E. Osborne, K. Arbeiter, H. Tillmann, M. Vandeplassche, D. Mitchell, W. R. Allen, P. D. Rossdale, D. W. Holtan, J. S. Cosgrove, J. Hickmann, Ann C. Chandley, J. D. Ansell, R. J. McEnery, M. J. Cooper, Mrs M. Cooper, P. W. Nathanielsz, C. H. G. Irvine, Margaret J. Evans, P. Hernández-Jáuregui, Carole A. Samuel, Isabel A. Forsyth, R. C. Rous, A. W. Patterson;* Second row: *L. Jacob, F. T. Day, S. Kullander, J. M. Owen, J. K. E. Erbsloh, L. F. McManamny, M. C. Morison, G. Manefield, H. Williamson, Beatrice Jousset, E. Palmer, Miss Tillmann, W. Baier, R. Thein, P. S. Jackson, R. R. Pascoe, R. Burrows, A. D. Purvis, D. Codazza, Sally Spence, W. van der Holst, Patricia Ellis, M. Pollitt, J. P. Hughes, K. E. Cudsell, C. J. Roberts, D. P. Neely, G. Malnati, J. Morgan, H. Merkt, V. K. Ganjam, A. M. Nelson;* Third row: *I. Settergren, E. Tolksdorff, D. G. Williams, H. Kitchen, M. Varadin, R. S. Thornbury, R. E. Pattle, P. F. B. Williams, P. C. Belonje, C. H. van Niekerk, J. Spincemaille, H. Onuma, P. Wright, O. Sharma, K. Mason, F. Lagneau, P. Benazet, J. T. Bryans, E. H. Fallon, J. B. Hughes, R. E. S. Greenwood, W. P. Howey, E. Klug, A. M. Larsen, J. L. Hancock, D. R. McCullough;* Fourth row: *E. E. Swierstra, M. A. J. Azzie, W. J. Solomon, J. F. von Lepel, R. Moberg, J. E. Lowe, S. J. Burns, J. W. Evans, A. Zafracas, S. Yamauchi, Y. Nishikawa, Carol C. Alm, J. J. Sullivan, A. Littlejohn, W. G. Parker, A. Hennau, D. D. Hardy, G. H. Stabenfeldt, R. M. Kenney, G. R. Greenhoff, J. L. Voss, J. M. Bowen, J. I. Raeside, G. H. Arthur, J. P. O'Donnell, H. Heinze;* Back row: *B. W. Pickett, C. H. B. Marlow, D. G. L. Faull, H. Leuenberger, R. A. McFeely, R. B. Hillman, W. Jochle, D. M. Witherspoon, J. Thimonier, A. W. Marrable, P. Mauléon, T. M. Nett, W. D. Oxender, Patricia A. Noden, E. L. Squires, R. H. Douglas, D. C. Sharp, J. E. Cox, R. M. Liptrap, D. S. Irvine, K. J. Betteridge, W. E. Allen, S. W. Ricketts, P. F. Flood, R. G. Loy.* (Courtesy of the *Journal of Reproduction and Fertility*)

Beyond the call: the history of the American Association of Equine Practitioners

WAYNE KESTER (1906–1999)
AAEP
4075 Iron Works Parkway
Lexington
Kentucky 40511
USA

NOTE: General Wayne 'Sage' Kester prepared a draft of this manuscript in the fall of 1998 as perhaps his last official action on behalf of the AAEP. His work was then edited and augmented by Julie Kimball of the American Paint Horse Association (former Director of Communications for AAEP) and Gin Preston, Publications Director. Sage's charge, "Do what you are doing, only try to do it a little better"*, continues to be our challenge.*

In the Beginning

In the early history of equine veterinary medicine in the United States, the treatment and care of horses was often determined by the sage wisdom of horsemen and the medical wisdom of those who studied both man and animal. The history of organised equine veterinary medicine, however, was not to come until well into the 20th century when a small group of veterinarians formed the American Association of Equine Practitioners (AAEP) in 1955. Central to the formation of the AAEP was the need to address a challenge, affirm the integrity of, and provide continuing education for the equine practitioner.

From the days of the country's original 13 colonies, horse racing in America, as in many other parts of the world, was a sport that dominated any other. Whether it was a formal affair or a gentleman's bet, horse racing provided entertainment and bragging rights to the owners. But horses were to mean much more in America. America was built on the back of the horse, from a mount during heat of battle to a beast of burden in the movement west. Prior to the first World War, the horse and mule population in the US was nearly 27 million. Veterinary schools abounded and 20,000 veterinarians served the vast population. But with the technological advancements developed during the First and Second World Wars, the need for the horse in these pursuits fell dramatically, and, therefore, so did the equine population. By the early 1950s, interest in equine veterinary medicine had diminished and many veterinary schools had closed. Horse racing, however, was still king of sports and equine veterinary medicine still had this audience. What it didn't have was students and an organisation to protect its integrity.

Two important events occurred in the 1950s. At that time, the regulation of the horse industry was left to those who were not necessarily qualified, but who were appointed to do so through the power of politics. And, in most cases, these were policy-making bodies with no real authority. Therefore, the regulation of medication in racehorses was often left to the National Association of Official Racing Chemists; an organised body that performed chemical testing and drafted rules based on this testing, rather than on what was best for the horse's health. As a result, a number of varying opinions developed among state racing commissions. Some states allowed certain levels of medication while others strictly forbad it. The rather unfortunate label of 'dope' was applied in almost every case where a substance could be detected, be it the dishonest use of narcotics or a truly therapeutic need. And veterinarians were labelled as the source for this 'dope'.

Just prior to the first AAEP convention in 1955, three veterinarians accused of 'doping' horses, were publicly disgraced in a daily Los Angeles newspaper that published the heading, "*Cops Ride With Vets*". While this event itself was not the basis for the development of AAEP, it did serve as a catalyst to drive the momentum to organise the profession.

Organising equine veterinarians had long been the subject of conversation among many practitioners who saw that horse racing was still a robust industry, but was not recognised by recent veterinary school graduates as an opportunity. Exploratory meetings to discuss the formation of AAEP had been held in December 1954 and March 1955, but with the poor publicity generated by the Los Angeles paper, a small, but dedicated group of veterinarians realised the need for action was immediate. Among those attending those first meetings and who would eventually become founding members were Drs H.K Bailey, Wilmington, Ohio; R. F. Butzow, Urbana, Illinois; Edwin A. Churchill, Centreville, Maryland; Robert W. Copelan, New Orleans, Louisiana; Thomas E. Dunkin, Chicago, Illinois; William F. Guard, Columbus, Ohio; L. A. Hartrick, Royal Oak, Michigan; Edward Kennedy, Miamiville, Ohio; Edward Lang, Louisville, Kentucky; W. E. Lickfeldt, Plymouth, Michigan; P. J. Meginnis, Roselle, Illinois; William O. Reed, Elmont, New York; Marian L. Scott, Akron, Ohio; Joseph A. Solomon, Cleveland, Ohio; E. W. Thomas, Lexington, Kentucky and Jordan Woodcock, Port Chester, New York. During one meeting in Louisville, Kentucky, meeting, Dr Scott was named President, Dr Guard, President Elect and Dr Dunkin, Secretary-Treasurer.

General Wayne O. Kester DVM, Brigadier General USAF (VC) Ret. and AAEP past President. In his 70 years of service to the equine industry, he pushed AAEP into active involvement in equine research and disease control and served as its executive director for 25 years.

'Sage' Kester

Key also to the formation of AAEP was retired US Air Force Brigadier General and veterinarian William O. 'Sage' Kester. Unable to attend the Louisville meeting due to his position as Chief of the newly formed US Air Force Veterinary Service, General Kester was nonetheless equally dedicated to the formation of this new body and kept in contact with Dr Scott. And, as President Elect of the American Veterinary Medical Association, General Kester was in a strategic position to promote the mission of these equine practitioners to the nation's largest organised group of veterinarians.

General Kester, while recognising the racetrack problem, was also convinced that the horse industry was on the brink of vast expansion. In 1940, the American Quarter Horse Association had formed, creating the largest market of horse ownership in the world. This movement would spread to include such other breeds as the American Paint Horse; the Appaloosa and several others stock horse breeds which became central to pleasure horse riding in the United States.

The third meeting of AAEP took place in Chicago, in December 1955, to coincide with the American Veterinary Medical Association (AVMA) Executive Board meeting. This tactic proved beneficial, as General Kester presented the racetrack problem to the Board, which determined that the public's poor perception of veterinarians clearly affected the entire profession. However, it was also determined that the AVMA general membership would not support AVMA involvement in racing problems and AAEP was encouraged to continue on its own. While AVMA would not become involved publicly, its board did offer their support and the President, Executive Secretary, Journal editor and four other board members attended the AAEP meeting the next day, becoming members themselves.

Constitution

A constitution was drafted, including a statement that became fundamental to the development of AAEP:

> *"The objectives of the Association shall be to elevate the standards of practice in this branch of veterinary medicine; to further research and knowledge of equine diseases with the purpose of improving the quality of practice; to enlighten various agencies on the need for better methods in horse racing and to assist in formulating them, especially as they pertain to the profession..."*

That statement was refined in 1991 to be more concise, but retained much of the original intent:

> *"The objectives of this Association shall be to improve the health and welfare of the horse, to further the professional development of its members, and to provide resources and leadership for the benefit of the equine industry."*

Developing Events

These statements, along with a number of position statements, were published in many equine and veterinary magazines. AAEP was finally a reality, not only to veterinarians, but also to the horse industry. The first annual meeting included a business session and the presentation of an educational programme. Seventy-four veterinarians attended, including 47 who were already AAEP members. Eight more joined at this meeting for a $15 membership fee.

Clearly, public awareness about both the AAEP and the value of the horse industry to the US economy needed to be cultivated. In addition, the veterinary profession needed to be convinced of equine medicine's bright future.

In 1958, an AAEP study indicated the horse population to be approximately 4.5 million. General Kester reported the results during the 1958 Thoroughbred Racing Association annual meeting, where it was picked up by *Time*, a respected national news magazine, which, in the public perception, added credibility to the figures. Future studies conducted by the American Horse Council over a period of years indicated the steady growth of the horse industry. By 1998, an AHC survey determined the impact on the US economy was $112.1 billion. It also indicated 7.1 million people were involved as either owners (1.9 million), volunteers or service providers, and provided $1.9 billion in taxes and 1.4 million full-time jobs in an industry that included 6.9 million horses.

AAEP's efforts to educate the public and those in its own profession mirrored the growth of the horse industry. The task of informing the media and the deans of the nation's veterinary schools fell on the shoulders, once again, of General Kester and the officers of the association. Due to his previous responsibilities with the Air Force, General Kester had established relationships with all of the veterinary schools. So, he began to work with each of the deans in emphasising the growing horse industry and the need for more undergraduate teaching in equine medicine and surgery, as well as the need for research and graduate students. From throughout the horse industry, the officers of several national organisations were invited to attend AAEP meetings to express their own views.

In turn, AAEP officers attended many organisation meetings. Dr Guard addressed the National Association of State Racing Commissions, while Dr Churchill, as 1958 AAEP President, addressed meetings of the National Association of State Racing Commissioners, the Jockey Club

Round Table and the Thoroughbred Racing Association.

In 1959, General Kester was elected AAEP President and the fact that a Brigadier General was now leading the organisation did not go unnoticed. With his election came a tremendous increase in exposure for AAEP. By the end of his term, General Kester had addressed 24 veterinary and horse organisations, including the American Quarter Horse Association, Arabian Horses Associations, National Association of State Racing Commissioners, the Jockey Club Round Table, Thoroughbred Racing Association and Horsemen's Benevolent and Protective Association, as well as several other breed and regional associations and state racing commissions.

AAEP continued to court the press and sports writers were invited to attend the AAEP meetings. Attending regularly were two of the country's best in Thoroughbred racing, including Joe Estes of *The Blood Horse* and Alex Bauer of *The Thoroughbred Record*, as well as Tom Shehan of the Standardbred racing publication, *The Horsemen's Journal.* All saw the problems in racing as real ones and AAEP as the potential solution, offering off-the-record advice and continued publicity.

Panels were also developed to include members of the horse industry and to address emerging challenges and problems. In addition, AAEP made its first efforts to organise a team of veterinarians to provide service to the international Pan American Games held in Chicago in 1959, a pattern that would repeat itself at numerous major equine sporting events over the next 40 years.

Leadership

AAEP's affinity for electing capable leadership proved to be its strongest asset. Among the Presidents elected were nine distinguished veterinary college professors, three of whom became Deans and one a Provost. Through this illustrious group, relationships with several organisations were solidified to the point where AAEP was viewed as integral to their continued development. Dr Joseph O'Dea, with his many years as the US Olympic team veterinarian, was largely responsible for placing veterinary service in proper perspective for the Olympic Games and related international equestrian events. and also served as a New York State Racing Commissioner. Dr Jordon Woodcock guided the development of veterinary services and practical drug testing policies and programmes with the American Horse Shows Association. Dr Marvin Beeman generated proper veterinary relationships and guidance for the American Horse Council and the American Quarter Horse Association for many years. Dr Stewart Harvey did similar service with the Morgan Horse Association, and Dr Horace Davis did the same for the Thoroughbred Club of America while serving as president. Dr Delano Proctor Jr and General Kester were presidents of the AVMA. Furthermore, General Kester was to be appointed Executive Director in 1962 and remained in that position for 25 years, setting the tone for continued and extensive involvement by its members in the administration of AAEP. Among those volunteers was Dr Frank Milne, a professor at Ontario Veterinary College who was appointed editor of the annual convention Proceedings in 1960. Dr Milne served in that position for 28 years, developing it into a world class, highly sought-after text.

Education and Opportunity

With the establishment of a highly regarded leadership body, AAEP grew rapidly and with little effort put into recruitment. From its original 55 members in 1955, AAEP more than doubled in membership from previous years. It would continue that pattern throughout its history to its 1999 membership of nearly 7,000 in the United States, Canada and 52 other countries. Perhaps the greatest strength of AAEP was the clear vision it had in providing education and opportunity to its members. The leadership of AAEP remained very focused on these goals and established an annual convention and scientific meeting as one of the premier educational meetings in the field. The system first established by the leadership, and one still in effect today, provided that the President Elect of the association organise the meeting. This proved to be a very effective tool in creating a meeting with the highest standards in educational information, as well in ensuring the continued and consistent leadership of the association.

Through the coordinating efforts of the AAEP President Elect, an auspicious body of reviewers was selected thoroughly to review each of the papers submitted. Originally, full papers were submitted for publication in the AAEP Proceedings, but it soon became apparent that in order for more quality papers to be submitted and for further exposure to the entire industry, these papers would need to be in abstracted form. This would allow the authors to submit full papers to other veterinary journals with perhaps an even greater, broader based audience of large, mixed or small animal practitioners who might treat the occasional horse. The result was an immediate increase in the number and quality of papers submitted for review. Another dimension was added in 1996 when 'how to' papers, focusing on the practising veterinarian's discoveries in the field, were added to the programme bringing what many viewed was a practical aspect of the industry to the programme.

The Annual Convention

The AAEP Convention began as strictly business - the presentation of the scientific papers included in the proceedings with no exhibits, no hospitality rooms, and no entertainment. It would remain so for nearly 10 years.

General Kester took over convention management in 1960, the same year the first woman, Dr Pat Lynch, participated. By 1964, with the help of a piano-playing veterinarian's wife, entertainment made its debut. This proved a popular decision for those who wished to mix a little pleasure with their business and for whom the convention meeting was the only time away from a busy practice.

It would not be until 20 years later, in 1984, that AAEP began to accept commercial exhibits, immediately realising the financial benefit of doing so. Under the direction of Dr Gene Carroll, the trade show soon became one of the largest in the profession. Exhibitors also found the AAEP Convention trade show to be financially lucrative. Convention attendance from 1955 to 1970 grew from just under 100 to more than 1000. By the time a trade show was added, in 1984, nearly 2000 AAEP members, students and guests were in attendance and by the end of the century that number swelled to more than 4000.

For veterinarians, it was a perfect opportunity to take an annual inventory of their professional and practice needs and fulfil those needs at the meeting. Veterinarians could satisfy any continuing educational requirements they needed, as well as examine equipment; learn about new pharmaceuticals on the market; and compare pricing prior to purchasing. AAEP also took advantage of this captive audience by holding committee meetings and making decisions about the future of the Association. Committees discussed issues of concern ranging from equine insurance to therapeutic options. As a result, a number of publications were developed with the assistance of many of these committee members. Authored by AAEP members considered experts in their fields, these brochures and booklets were made available free or at very affordable prices to all AAEP members, veterinary colleges and other equine industry groups.

Clearly, the role AAEP played in equine veterinary medicine had become a significant one and the volunteer role of its members was astounding. In addition to the many individuals who ensured the continued success of the annual meeting Dr and Mrs Stanley Teeter, Dr and Mrs Manual Thomas, as well as Dr and Mrs Gene Carroll were the individuals who served as committee chairs and as liaisons to more than a dozen equine industry groups. Where at one time a single veterinarian could work with several of these groups, the input of AAEP member veterinarians had become so valuable, it was common for several to work with a single industry group in assisting them in determining humane treatment and medication policies.

Role of Research

The role of research in equine medicine had always been an important one, but with an impressive line-up of veterinarians providing expert advice and encouragement to several groups, the dollars spent on equine research grew tremendously. Notably, partnerships developed between AAEP and groups who provided research dollars. Among those were the Morris Animal Foundation, the Grayson-Jockey Club Research Foundation (formerly Grayson Foundation until 1989) and the American Quarter Horse Association. Since the formation of these individual foundations, nearly $20 million in funding has been directed toward equine research. Also of note was AAEP's influence in ensuring that a portion of monies earned through pari-mutuel wagering be contributed to equine research.

By the early 1980s, it was apparent that AAEP would need to consider the development of a full-time staff and headquarters building. General Kester, who would serve as AAEP Executive Director for 25 years, was considering retirement. AAEP also faced the challenge of answering emerging needs of its members, as well as those of the equine industry. Housed in General Kester's home in Golden, Colorado, AAEP began to search for a permanent site. While a number of locations were considered, Lexington, Kentucky, got the nod as the new location due to the vast array of equine organisations already in the area. By the time General Kester retired in 1987, boxes and equipment were being packed to move to Kentucky to open the new headquarters. With a new office established

Groundbreaking for the AAEP headquarters building at the Kentucky Horse Park, Lexington, Kentucky, 12 September 1991.

in a downtown Lexington shopping area, AAEP began its role as an employer of four staff members. However, it would only take two years to determine that a change of scenery in both location and staffing would be needed. A capable successor to Dr Kester had not been named and, in 1989, the search was on for that individual as well as a new building location.

In 1990, Gary Carpenter, a young man from west Texas who had been deeply involved in the horse industry throughout the majority of his career, was named Executive Director. With his arrival, came rapid movement toward the purchase of an office site and the development of a professional staff. A key figure in AAEP's recent development, David Foley, took charge of managing the convention in 1989. It was determined that the new building would be located at the National Horse Center of the Kentucky Horse Park, which already housed a number of national equine organisations. But before a shovel would be placed in the dark, rich soil of Kentucky, AAEP would begin building yet another important reputation and a programme that would prove almost indispensable to the American Thoroughbred racing scene.

The 6700 square foot AAEP headquarters were built to accommodate the expansion of facilities and member services. Upon completion, the building was dedicated to General Wayne O. Kester DVM, and named the Kester Building in his honour. The new AAEP headquarters joined 14 other equine organisations and associations in the Kentucky Horse Park's National Horse Center.

Communications with Media

Through the tragic death of the filly Go For Wand in the dramatic closing finish of the 1990 Breeders' Cup, it became apparent to both the veterinary and racing community that a better system of communication and response to the media had to be developed. Perhaps the simplicity of the answer made it more palatable. AAEP proposed to provide, at no charge, qualified veterinarians to be 'on call' to the media in the event a horse was injured during a Thoroughbred race. The proving ground was to be no small event, either. The programme was named after its purpose, *On Call*, and its first assignment was the 1991 Kentucky Derby.

Fortunately, no injuries occurred during that race, but AAEP had planted a seed that would grow to include the entire Triple Crown series, the Breeders' Cup and approximately 60 other Thoroughbred races, as well as a few select arena events, such as the National Reining Horse Association's Futurity and the AQHA World Championship Show. In 1996, the programme won the coveted Public Relations Society of America's Silver Anvil award competition, the 'Oscars' of public relations awards. The programme was honoured by PRSA for its unique approach in providing accurate, veterinary information to the public. *On Call* has been expanded to include the additional racing coverage gained through the development of the National Thoroughbred Racing Association and now services 75 races annually.

On Call provided its longest term of single service during the 1996 Olympic Games, where the servicing veterinarians were called upon to respond to issues ranging from excessive heat to piroplasmosis. *On Call* was a huge success, providing the media with injury reports on both horses and humans within 10 minutes of the close of the cross-country portion of the three-day event, as well as refuting unfounded accusations made by animal rights groups. In addition, the European veterinary community saw the value of the programme and has since modified the programme for other international competition.

AAEP's involvement in advocating responsible animal welfare practices was further bolstered through the development of its annual equine welfare award in 1996. Named the Lavin Cup in honour of AAEP President Gary A. Lavin, VMD, the award sought to recognise those groups that had demonstrated exceptional compassion for or developed and enforced rules and guidelines for the welfare of horses. Recipients of this award have been the California Horse Racing Board, in 1996; the American Quarter Horse Association, in 1997; and the Thoroughbred Retirement Foundation, Inc., in 1998.

Strategic Planning

The decade of the '90s would continue to see rapid growth in both the AAEP and its reputation. To stay ahead of the demands being made on it by both members and the industry, AAEP utilised the tool of strategic planning. Forming a Long-Range Planning Committee in 1992, AAEP set a five year course to develop greater educational opportunities; improve its services to members; and remain effective as a reliable authority to the horse industry in issues affecting the treatment and welfare of the horse. In a speech dedicating the new AAEP headquarters in 1992, The Kester Building, named in honour of General Kester, AAEP President Peter F. Haynes noted this focus.

> *"The AAEP has been recognised since its inception for being pre-eminent in its concern for ethics, standards, continuing education, disease control and prevention, and research to mention a few,"* he said.
>
> *"In short, the health and welfare of the horse, our members and the industry at large is what we are about, and the collective effort and commitment of our members have allowed us to reach the heights of what we enjoy today."*

With the construction of the new headquarters, Carpenter began to expand the scope and number of staff. This expansion allowed for expansion of the AAEP convention; heightened communication with industry groups and government agencies; as well as increased public relations efforts.

AAEP's relationship with a number of companies greatly assisted with its efforts both to educate its members and horse owners. With the assistance of Bayer Corporation, AAEP developed a line of client education brochures distributed by its members to clients. The popular series, written for the lay audience, addressed such issues as equine insurance, newborn foals and euthanasia, as well as educate horse owners on such diseases as equine protozoal myelitis. Purina Mills joined in this effort by adding brochures addressing the nutritional needs of the horse. Nearly four million brochures have been distributed since the programme's inception. Bayer also created a valuable service in the creation of the Equine Connection, providing a toll-free number to horse owners in search of a veterinarian. Through 1-800-GET-A-DVM, horse owners could be provided with a list of veterinarians in their immediate area.

Practice and Management

In 1992, with the assistance of Boehringer Ingelheim, AAEP introduced its first small-group programme with a Practice Management seminar, focusing on the business aspects of veterinary practice. Experts in finances, staff management and client communication provided members with information vital to their success as business owners. 3M has also provided considerable support for AAEP's educational

The Frank Milne State of the Art Lecture bronze.

efforts. With the assistance of Pfizer Animal Health, AAEP added the Frank Milne State of the Art Lecture series to its 1997 convention line-up, focusing on subjects and techniques considered 'state of the art' by the equine veterinary industry.

"The major objective of this series will be to bring equine veterinarians the latest information regarding treatment techniques and research surrounding some of our most common or perplexing problems.

"The idea is to bring a perspective to the subject that can be given only by a researcher with the experience and credibility in the field,"

said Educational Programmes Committee Chair Larry Bramlage, DVM.

Student Programmes

While AAEP continued to focus on the needs of its practicing member, it did not forget the needs of the student. Preparing students to enter the demanding equine veterinary field became a focus in 1975, when AAEP opened a membership category to students. AAEP student chapters were formed in each of the veterinary schools with member advisors. Six student scholarships, funded with the assistance of the American Live Stock Insurance Company, were made available and students could receive many materials at little or no cost.

In 1997, AAEP leadership began to work on perhaps its most ambitious student education programme. In 1998, *Avenues* debuted. AAEP member practices were invited to offer internships to student members while gaining a valuable addition to their practice staff. The programme was made available to fourth-year students who had completed large animal or equine clinical rotations. Graduates were also eligible to apply. Approximately 40 practices implemented programmes by 1998 and were interviewing students for internships to begin in 1999.

The 1990s

The '90s saw new focus placed on the leadership of AAEP itself. The leadership track to the AAEP Board of Directors and, eventually, the AAEP Executive Committee required a commitment of several years from those interested in serving. Many qualified members could not make that commitment. By 1996, a new strategic plan was developed that addressed this issue as one of its goals. As a result, the number of board members was reduced; Directors-at-large were added to bring greater representation to areas with a larger concentration of members; and the number of executive committee members was reduced from five to three. Ascension to the AAEP presidency, then, became a three-year process instead of five. AAEP also took another bold move in 1996, and one that was a definite departure from tradition, when it opened one of its board member positions to a lay person. Labelled the Equine Industry Representative, this position was intended to bring a broader perspective of the horse industry to the leadership body. John Snobelen, a recognised figure in both horse and political community, was the first to take the position in 1997. As Minister of Education in Ontario, Canada, Snobelen brought extensive leadership experience, as well as a wealth of knowledge from the horse industry gained through his experiences in the National Reining Horse Association.

Increased emphasis was placed on AAEP's role in providing the most sought after opportunities in continuing education as the mid-1990s approached. Resort meetings had already become a popular attraction for many veterinarians, as it afforded them an opportunity to gain knowledge about a specific topic in an intimate atmosphere, combined with an opportunity for relaxation. With the market already established, AAEP offered its first Resort Symposium in Maui, Hawaii, in 1999 with three half-days of lectures focusing on lameness, colic and respiratory problems. In addition, realising many of its members could not attend its annual convention due to distance, timing or practice demands, AAEP determined that it would take the best papers from the annual convention and offer a second meeting in a location geographically different from the convention location. *Encore* debuted in August 1999 in Minneapolis, Minnesota, and featured popular in-depth seminars and how-to's from several recent conventions. These additions brought to four the number of meetings hosted by AAEP annually.

The number of AAEP staff had grown to 11 as AAEP prepared to tackle one of its most ambitious projects to date. Negotiations with perhaps one of the most respected publications in equine veterinary medicine had begun in 1998 when a delegation from AAEP began discussions with representatives of the British Equine Veterinary Association journal, *Equine Veterinary Education*. It was decided that an American edition would be developed in 1999, featuring jointly generated articles and to include AAEP material and advertising not included in the BEVA edition. In addition, an editorial board comprised of AAEP and BEVA members was formed to develop close collaboration at all levels of the journal's production. AAEP members would receive a subscription to the bimonthly journal as a part of their membership benefits.

"We in the Journal office and in BEVA welcome this new development with great pleasure and considerable humility,"

said EVE and EVJ editor Peter D. Rossdale.

"Pleasure stems from the fact that the objectives of the two associations are so similar - the aim of both is to assist practitioners in their front-line duties of caring for and improving the welfare of horses. Humility stems from the knowledge of the substantial contribution made to the Journal by American-based authors in recent years."

As AAEP begins looking to the next century, it will remain rooted in those principles on which it was founded and which have so assuredly guided its footsteps - education and service to its members. No doubt greater challenges and opportunities will arise, and will be met with the spirit that has held it steady for more than 40 years - to further, to improve and to provide.

Wayne Kester

The Home of Rest for Horses: a brief history

PAUL JEPSON
Westcroft Stables
Speen Farm, Slad Lane
Lacey Green
Princes Risborough
Bucks HP27 0PP
UK

The foundation of The Home of Rest for Horses was largely due to the efforts of one lady, Miss Ann Lindo, who was appalled at the treatment of many of the working horses on the streets of London.

She canvassed support and on 10 May 1886 it was agreed that a home of rest for horses, mules and donkeys should be started. The first patient was an overworked cab horse that Miss Lindo arranged to be cared for at a farm at Sudbury, near Harrow.

Subscriptions for the new society were canvassed and dinners and balls organised to raise funds. HRH Prince Albert pledged his support and the Duke of Portland, Master of the Royal Household, agreed to become President. By late 1887 more stabling had to be found and an eminent London veterinary surgeon allowed his stables at Neasden Stud Farm to be used. The society was now simply called The Home of Rest for Horses.

By 1889, the Home had outgrown the facilities at Sudbury which was also too far to transport sick and lame horses. A search for larger premises resulted in building 40 loose boxes on a leased site at Acton in North London. It was close to the railway station and horses could easily be transported to and from central London. The society was now sufficiently established to hold a pool of fit, healthy, young horses which were loaned to owners of sick horses and those whose animals needed rest from their daily toils.

By 1908 the society had flourished and was able to buy Westcroft Farm at Cricklewood which despite only being four miles from Marble Arch, enjoyed 20 acres of good pasture and an impressive range of loose boxes.

The 1914-1918 war brought forage rationing which restricted the number of horses which could be cared for. However the society was able to provide a fully equipped

Visiting time, Acton, 1900.

Westcroft Stables, Speen, 1999.

horse ambulance to help the evacuation of wounded horses from the front line in France. At the same time Her Majesty Queen Alexandra agreed to recognise the work of the Home by becoming Patroness and she took an active interest in its work until her death in 1925 when Queen Mary accepted the invitation to continue the royal patronage. The Home continued to be successful and whilst the number of London cab horses declined, there were still thousands of tradesmen's horses requiring help and the Home provided rest and recuperation for approximately 250 horses a year.

Urban spread soon reached Cricklewood and in 1933 Hampstead Council put Westcroft Farm under a compulsory purchase order for development.

The search for new premises took the Home to Boreham Wood in Hertfordshire where a new Westcroft Stables with 75 loose boxes was built on a 25 acre site. It was at this time that a good and enduring liaison was established with the London Royal Veterinary College whose Dean, Sir Frederick Hobday, asserted that the Home of Rest for Horses was the best premises of its kind in the world. The College supported the Home by providing a service for poor owners whose animals were sent to the Home for convalescence.

In 1962 the Home was able to rent an additional 30 acres of land adjacent to Westcroft Stables enabling it to accommodate over eighty horses at any one time.

By the mid-1960s the Home had become sufficiently well known and supported to enjoy an income that exceeded running costs. With a reduction in the number of working horses the Committee decided to seek new ways of extending the Home's activities rather than using its resources to expand what it already did. With the blessing of the Charity Commission it was agreed that grants could be made to other charitable organisations concerned with the welfare of horses. The first recipients of these grants for stabling and equipment were the Royal Veterinary College and the Equine Research Station (now the Animal Health Trust) at Newmarket. Shortly after this the Home's Chairman, Gerald Critchley, instigated the formation of the Riding Schools Act Committee and the Home became the principal financial supporter of the Riding Schools Inspection Team for the next 17 years.

By 1968 the relentless urban sprawl of London had encircled the stables at Boreham Wood and it was necessary to look for new premises again. The search led to a 130 acre freehold property known as Speen Farm in the Chilterns midway between High Wycombe and Aylesbury. The sale of the Boreham Wood site for housing development allowed a new complex, including 85 loose boxes, to be built at Speen Farm which was firmly in the green belt and enjoyed unspoilt views over the rolling Chiltern countryside. The new Westcroft Stables at Speen Farm were officially opened on 15 July 1975. The Home is still based at Speen Farm today and will remain there for the foreseeable future.

A fortunate by-product of the forced sale of the site at Boreham Wood was a modest profit which was to become a cornerstone of the Home's activities over the following 25 years. Wisely invested, this money has produced good capital growth and healthy dividends which has progressively enabled the Home to assume its current position as the leading funder of equine welfare projects. Since those first modest grants in 1965, to the Royal Veterinary College and the Animal Health Trust, the Home has given over £10 million to a wide variety of projects and, at the time of writing, has ongoing commitments of over £4 million. The main beneficiaries have been the university veterinary schools either in the form of grants for improved facilities or the funding of scientific research projects. More recently, the Home has introduced veterinary postgraduate clinical training awards known as residencies or clinical scholarships.

The guiding criteria for successful grant applications has always been that they must be of potential long-term benefit to all types of horse and that any research or investigation must be of a noninvasive nature.

The Home's support of equine welfare projects has not been at the expense of the Home itself which continues to function as a sanctuary for cases of hardship and as a final dignified resting place for a number of old favourites who, after a lifetime of service, provide a living example to the public of exemplary care and responsible ownership. As the millennium comes to a close, the Home can be justifiably proud of its achievements and the way in which it has adapted to the changing demands of welfare of the horse.

Perspectives in...

Stud medicine

SIDNEY RICKETTS AND PETER ROSSDALE
Beaufort Cottage Stables
High Street
Newmarket
Suffolk CB8 8JS
UK

JOHN COX
The University of Liverpool
Faculty of Veterinary Science
Leahurst, Neston
South Wirral L64 7TE
UK

WALTER ZENT
Hagyard-Davidson-McGee
Associates
4250 Iron Works Road
Lexington, Kentucky
USA

In the UK, the veterinary 'turn of the century' was marked by the 1907 publication of Professor J. Wortley Axe's nine volume treatise *The Horse - Its Treatment in Health and Disease* (with a complete guide to breeding, training and management).

Professor Wortley Axe was President of the Royal College of Veterinary Surgeons and a lecturer at the Royal Veterinary College, London. His aim was:

> *"To fill a hiatus in the literature relating to horses, by producing a book of the horse which shall contain information on all the points which are constantly the subject of enquiry among owners of horses."*

His comments on breeding horses, suggest that some aims have not changed:

> *"There is nothing more satisfying to a breeder of horses than to breed a good one...to breed a winner of a classic race or a champion of the first class is unquestionably the end to be aimed at."*

He also comments that:

> *"Many strive to achieve these aims but few succeed."*

This remains very true today, but he offered encouragement:

> *"We could point to many men who, with control of large studs, have spent a lifetime in honest endeavour to realise these high ambitions without attaining success; but they have done the next best thing, they have produced stock of a high standard of excellence which has brought a remunerative average; and, after all, that is what the general breeder desires and what the country requires - a grading up as near to the highest attainable point as can be reached."*

While for many horse breeders the fun and satisfaction of producing good stock remains of most importance, financial return has become the aim or even an essential requirement for many others. It is true to say that, whereas at the turn of the century horse breeding was seldom considered to be more than a sport, it is now an industry and an important livelihood for many. The computer age has given breeders detailed, helpful and fascinating statistics relating to performance and sales prices. All these changes have improved the management and efficiency of horse breeding but there is now more emphasis on planning for short-term financial gain than for 'improving the breed'. Many contemporary commentators recognise the potential problems that this may produce for the industry and, of course, the horse. Rachel Midwood and Darryl Shearer writing in the September 1998 issue of *Pacemaker and Thoroughbred Breeder* stated that:

> *"As we approach the new millennium, one question that continues to vex both breeders and trainers of the thoroughbred is that of soundness. Taken at anecdotal level, the majority in the industry would have you believe that the modern thoroughbred in the UK is less sound than his counterpart of 30 years ago."*

They debate both sides of the argument but conclude that:

> *"A predilection for producing horses for the sale ring does not help".*

Most modern day veterinary surgeons would agree that owners, breeders and veterinarians must never forget that, although unusual individual horses with an exceptional constitution may overcome conformational abnormalities to win a fashionable race, breeding for performance while ignoring conformation has and will continue to threaten the 'soundness' of the horse population.

In 1900, the general requirements of a breeding studfarm in terms of its site, construction and organisation were well established. It was recognised that soil type, ideally a limestone base, was of fundamental importance. The quality and quantity of feed and water supply was known to be important but precise details were unavailable. Following the work of veterinary anatomists, a detailed knowledge of the structure of equine genital organs were well established but knowledge of their function was lacking. It was well recognised that mares were seasonal breeders, evolutionarily timed for foals to be born in the spring time when weather was improving and grass was growing. Wortley Axe states that:

> *"The mare is usually 'in season' (ready to receive the stallion) from April to June, or even later, and the periods when conception is likely to take place during that time recur about once a fortnight or three weeks, and are very brief in some mares - only of two or three days' duration."*

The testes of stallions were known to produce spermatozoa and these are ejaculated into the mare's genital organs at mating, but their significance was clearly misinterpreted. On the subject of 'generation' Wortley Axe states:

> *"A knowledge of the functions of the two distinct sets of organs will leave no room for doubt that the female has the largest share in the perpetuation of the species.* "Omne vivum ex ovo" *is a very familiar quotation but it contains a most important truth. The ovum of the female animal or plant contains all the material necessary for the formation of a new animal or plant. In the ovum or egg there is a germ possessing a dormant vitality, which only*

awaits contact with the sperm-cell of the male to become actively alive and capable of appropriating the material by which it is surrounded, and evolving from inert and shapeless substances all the tissues and organs which constitute the new existence."

He also states that:

"Impregnation is effected by the contact of the sperm-cell of the male with the germ-cell of the female. The precise manner of the contact, and the means employed to ensure it, are of no consequence to the result. In the most highly organised mammals, for instance, the fluids secreted by the testicles of the male (semen), with fluid from the prostate and other glands, is conveyed to the generative organs of the female by means of the intromittent organ, which injects it forcibly into the vagina, and to some extent also through the open mouth of the uterus into that organ. Sperm-cells, or, as they may more correctly be termed, spermatozoa, which have been set free from the germ-cells are abundant in the fluids so injected. These actively moving bodies are the essential agents in impregnation, and whether they reach the germ-cells of the ovum in the natural way, or are conveyed artificially by instrumental means, as in artificial insemination, the effect of their contact is the same. The previously passive germ-cell becomes active under the action of the stimulus imparted by the sperm-cell, which rouses the developmental force, before laying dormant, in the germinal vesicle of the ovum."

He also recognised that:

"Not every contact between the sperm and the germ is fruitful; possibly the power of the sperm-cell may always be active, but it is quite certain that the ova in the ovarium are not at all times ready to react to the mysterious force which the sperm-cell is ready to transmit."

It is therefore clear that the 20th century has seen enormous advances in the knowledge of the microanatomy and the physiology of equine reproduction, facilitated by fundamental technological developments in microscopy, both light and ultrastructural, and in physiology and endocrinology. This has aided enormously our knowledge of equine reproductive health and disease.

The Stallion

It is now recognised that the spermatozoon, rather than imparting a 'mystical force' to the ovum, carries 50% of the genetic material which is required to produce a new individual. Once this was established and the basic technological tools for research became available, the work of Nishikawa in Japan, Bielanski in Poland, Mann in the United Kingdom and Kenney and Pickett in North America defined equine seminal parameters in health and diseases aiding our knowledge of both natural breeding and artificial insemination. Armed with these basic data, we are now better able to evaluate the breeding potential of stallions for natural and artificial mating and are better able to diagnose and manage their difficulties in the face of male infertility or subfertility. That said, our ability to predict fertility in untested stallions remains elusive and there is still a great deal more to learn of this subject.

Requirements for maximising financial return from some stallions has produced new problems. Traditionally up to the 1950s, a fashionable Thoroughbred stallion's 'book' was 30 mares, until syndication became the norm with 40 shares per horse and the number of mares was raised to 40 and even 50. More recently, many are now required to cover 70 to over 100 mares in one hemisphere and then 'shuttle' to the alternate hemisphere where they may cover a similar number of additional mares thereby breeding all year round. It is clear that some stallions 'survive' this better than others. When they mated fewer mares, stallions generally appeared to be either fertile or infertile, but we now appear to see an increasing number of 'subfertile' stallions for whom conceptual 'strike rates' are poor and some who suffer 'bad patches' of conceptual failures. In many cases, semen analysis does not provide a clear answer to individual problems and the often-made diagnosis of 'testicular degeneration' is seldom backed by histopathological proof.

One hypothesis is that although most stallions are endowed with a massive overproduction of capable sperm, allowing adequate compensation for the equally large numbers which are recognised to be structurally and/or functionally 'unsound', the increases in the number of mares put to the stallions and, therefore, ejaculatory frequencies extend the resources of some beyond their natural compensatory abilities. It must be remembered that for stallions, unlike, for instance, bulls, there is no attempt to select for fertility potential and there is little doubt that some high performance blood lines impart subfertile traits in male offspring. If there was a desire to select out subfertile young stallions from the breeding pool, there is little doubt that this would be beneficial, in reproductive terms, but it might deprive the gene pool of some excellent performance characteristics. This conundrum is difficult to solve.

In time, research will progress our knowledge of the prediction of stallion fertility potential in order that at least some of these limitations can be determined, understood and managed by all at an earlier stage. At the present time, there is no reliable therapeutic answer to the subfertile stallion problem and we must rely on careful and sometimes necessarily intensive mare management in order to limit matings per oestrous period to one, as close as possible to the time of ovulation.

The Nonpregnant Mare

While Wortley Axe understood that:

"During the period of life which includes the power of procreation, development of ova is always going on in the substance of the ovary",

the function of the ovarian ovulation fossa was not recognised:

"As the development reaches nearer to the point of perfection, the Graafian follicle in which it is contained and protected advances to the surface of the ovarium, blood circulation in the external membranes increases in volume and rapidity and soon the surface of the graphian follicle is covered with an arboresque arrangement of brightly coloured vessels. In due time the follicle bursts and sets the mature ovum free to pass into the open fimbriated mouth of the fallopian tube, through which it passes to the interior of the uterus."

The precise site and physiology of conception was also unknown at that time:

"At what stage of its process from the ovarium through the

fallopian tubes to the cavity of the uterus the ovum meets the sperm-cell from the seminal fluid is not known. Most probably the point of contact is purely accidental. As spermatozoa are capable of rapid movements, and may meet the advancing ovum at any point of its course, even from the moment of its exit from the Graafian cell. Wherever the contact between the germ-cell and the sperm-cell occurs, the resulting changes are wonderful and also inexplicable."

While the basic principles of ovarian gamete production and of early blastocyst development by cleavage of cells into halves was understood in 1907, it appears that much of this knowledge was extrapolated from the study of hens' eggs. In the 1940s, Andrews and McKenzie from Kentucky published their studies which for the first time accurately described the detailed events of *"oestrus, ovulation and related phenomena in the mare"*. Also in the late 1940s, Burkhardt from the United Kingdom showed that the onset of the equine breeding season was initiated by increasing daylight length and could be advanced by exposing mares to artificial light. Loy and co-workers, during the early 1960s, developed managerial methods to make the use of artificial lighting regimes practical for the commercial horse breeder. Our knowledge in this regard has been refined by Sharp and co-workers in North America and Palmer and co-workers in France, resulting in the now widespread use of artificial lighting programmes at commercial studfarms worldwide. This enables barren and maiden mares to be mated and become pregnant during February and early March, i.e. before the start of the mare's natural breeding season and earlier than is possible without artificial lighting. Not only does this result in foals being born in January and early February, an advantage for owners who produce foals and yearlings for sale and two-year-old racehorses, but also in removing a significant proportion of the stallion's mares 'early', allowing room for more foaling mares to be mated throughout the remainder of the season than would otherwise have been possible. Managing mares to foal earlier in the season gives them more opportunity to recover from foaling injuries, uterine involutionary or other difficulties and still have time to be mated during the same season.

As essential laboratory technology became available, the behavioural dynamics of the oestrous cycle was augmented by knowledge of changes in and interactions of pituitary gonadotrophic and ovarian steroid hormones, especially through the work of Stabenfeldt, Hughes and Loy in North America and Irvine and Evans in New Zealand, among many others internationally. Plasma progesterone is now routinely assayed, under field conditions, as an aid to the diagnosis of ovulation and cyclic activity in mares who are behaving unusually. Human chorionic gonadotrophin (hCG) is used commonly for mares as a form of luteinising hormone to help stimulate ovulation at the time of mating. This treatment has become very much part of modern commercial studfarm practice where the target is to maximise efficiency by achieving successful conception following one mating per oestrous cycle per mare. The widespread use of hCG is probably unnecessary and it has been established that mares produce circulating antibodies to the repeated use of hCG, but there has been no convincing research data nor anecdotal clinical impression to suggest that these antibodies block ovulation. The relatively recent discovery of gonadotrophin-releasing hormones (GnRH), produced in the hypothalamus to stimulate gonadotrophin secretion by the posterior pituitary gland, has led to the commercial development of potent synthetic GnRH analogues which some clinicians believe to be a useful therapeutic alternative, although Michelle and Rossdale were unable to demonstrate its value in a single dose study. Studies using the synthetic GnRH desorelin, suggest that this can produce more reliably timed ovulations than is achievable with hCG. The widespread clinical use of desorelin has not yet stood the test of time and may not be without side effects of its own. Desorelin is not yet licensed for clinical use in Europe.

The discovery, in the early 1970s, of the pivotal role played by prostaglandins in the control of the equine oestrous cycle by causing luteolysis in the absence of early pregnancy, led Allen and colleagues in the United Kingdom to encourage the commercial development of synthetic $PGF2_{\alpha}$ analogues for therapeutic use in practice. This enabled safer veterinary control of the oestrous cycle in the nonpregnant mare without the risk of iatrogenic uterine infection which sometimes occurred following uterine saline irrigation, the recognised therapeutic technique used previously.

As our knowledge of normal equine reproduction developed, our ability to diagnose and accurately define the abnormal presented itself. At the turn of the century, Wortley Axe recognised metritis as:

"A serious infection of the uterus which frequently followed traumatic or abnormal parturition sometimes complicated by lameness."

He erroneously attributed it as arising *"more from pain accompanying movement of the body than from any actual disorder of the limb"* rather than from the subsequently well-recognised postparturient septic metritis/laminitis syndrome. He recognised vaginitis as being *"most frequently associated with traumatic parturition resulting in injury to the vagina"*. He described leucorrhoea ('the whites') as *"a chronic discharge from the vagina"* and although he recommended use of the vaginascope to *"discover the parts most implicated"*, he did not appear to recognise that these conditions were primarily associated with uterine inflammation. In 1928, Dimmock and Edwards from North America published their treatise *Pathology and Bacteriology of the Reproductive Organs of Mares in Relation to Sterility*. This work recognised the role that several species of bacteria played in infecting the uteri of mares and the importance of equine sexually transmitted, i.e. venereal, diseases.

Veterinary surgeons across the world, including Day in the UK, recognised that the mare's ovaries and uterus could be palpated *per rectum* on a regular basis, while taking appropriate care to avoid injury, to follow the development and ovulation of ovarian follicles to aid the management of horse breeding, which, at that time, was frequently associated with poor results. In 1937, Caslick described his vulvoplasty operation designed to overcome the sloping perineal conformation which led to pneumovagina ('windsucking') and ascending endometritis in many Thoroughbred and standardbred mares as they aged. This simple surgical procedure, performed easily and quickly under local anaesthesia, represented a major advance in equine gynaecology and remains today one of the most important aids to improve the fertility of mares with unsatisfactory conformation. At the same time it is probable that more offspring have been produced from mares with unsatisfactory perineal conformation than would otherwise have been, perhaps genetically compounding this anatomical problem in Thoroughbred and Standardbred mares.

In spite of these advances, it was not until the 1960s, following publications by Mahaffey, Hunt and Rossdale in the UK and Collins in Ireland, that routine bacteriological examination of the mare's oestrous cervix became part of routine studfarm practice. In the early 1970s, Peterson, McFeeley and David, and Hughes and Loy in North America published research which defined the importance of the natural defence mechanisms of the mare's genital tract in overcoming bacterial endometritis. It became recognised that all mares were effectively 'infected' by environmental and external genital microorganisms at natural mating because, unlike most other species, the stallion's penis enters the mare's open oestrous cervix, at natural mating, resulting in intrauterine ejaculation. Their work demonstrated the difference between young genitally healthy mares who were able to overcome this infectious challenge within 48-72 hours of natural mating and older genitally compromised mares who succumb to persistent endometritis. Kenney and colleagues in North America devised 'minimal contamination techniques' for use with natural mating and AI to help so-called 'susceptible' mares to avoid the development of persistent postmating endometritis. They also highlighted the need to confirm whether cervical/endometrial bacteriological results were associated with acute endometritis or not. In the 1960s Knudsen in Sweden and in the 1970s Wingfield Digby and colleagues in UK established the endometrial smear test as a simple and practical 'red flag' test for the diagnosis of acute endometritis in mares, prior to mating. This resulted in much greater accuracy of diagnosis and therefore more appropriate routine mare management, under practical studfarm conditions.

In 1977, an outbreak of aggressive sexually transmitted endometritis (contagious equine metritis, CEM) occurred at the British National Stud in Newmarket and spread among other local stud farms. This outbreak confirmed to any lingering doubters the significance of equine venereal diseases not only for the health of the mare but for the economics of the international Thoroughbred and, indeed, other horse breeding industries. The causal organism (CEMO) was a previously unrecognised Gram-negative microaerophilic coccobacillus, subsequently named *Taylorella equigenitalis* after the head of the Public Health Laboratory at Addenbrooke's Hospital (Dr Eddie Taylor) who first isolated the organism using human gonococcal culture techniques. The Horserace Betting Levy Board (HBLB) set up an advisory committee which subsequently developed a Code of Practice for the control of this infection in the United Kingdom. This Code has been reviewed and republished annually ever since and has resulted in the eradication of the disease from the United Kingdom and the successful control and elimination of small reintroduced outbreaks since.

The Code has developed to include diagnostic, treatment and control measures for venereal diseases caused by *Klebsiella pneumoniae* (it was recognised that capsule *types 1, 2* and *5* had an association with venereal pathogenicity whereas other capsule types usually behave as opportunists), *Pseudomonas aeruginosa* and subsequently also included Codes of Practice for *Equine Herpesvirus* (EHV) and *Equine Arteritis virus* (EVA) infections. The Code is now a common one agreed to by authorities in Great Britain, France, Germany, Ireland and Italy. Other countries have formed control policies adapted to their own needs. In the United States there are national regulations for the control of infectious disease and, in addition, some horse-producing states, e.g. Kentucky, have additional, more stringent, regulations. Experience with the epidemiology of *T. equigenitalis* infection lead to the realisation that there was a clear need to improve hygienic procedures on studfarms. Stud grooms and others who handled the genitalia of mares during the teasing and mating process were encouraged to wear disposable gloves and veterinary surgeons maintained proper protective clothing on each premises, using disposable equipment, especially rectal sleeves and vaginal specula to prevent accidental lateral transmission of infection. At the same time, it was established that commonly used disinfectant solutions were ineffective in killing *K. pneumoniae* and *Pseudomonas aeruginosa*. Portable (fire-extinguisher-type) and static (shower-type) washing facilities were soon provided by most commercial studfarms for veterinary use for washing mares to avoid the use of infected buckets of disinfectant water.

During the elimination of CEM infection from the National Stud, Simpson and colleagues established the importance of the clitoris and its fossa and sinuses as the sites of persistence of *T. equigenitalis* in the mare. Similarly, the site of persistence in the stallion was established as the urethral fossa and diverticulum and the preputial smegma. It is now clear that in most cases of equine sexually transmitted disease, involving *T. equigenitalis, K. pneumoniae* or *Ps. aeruginosa*, the infection is fundamentally an external contaminant which becomes mechanically transmitted at mating but has the capacity to infect mares of all ages and of varying uterine competence.

The HBLB Code of Practice, the cornerstone of which remains the screening of all stallions and mares for potential venereal disease organisms prior to the start of the breeding season and the exclusion of positive cases from the breeding pool until successfully treated, also emphasised the need for open communication regarding outbreaks of venereal disease on stud farms and other transmissible infectious diseases. There is no doubt that the Code has been enormously beneficial in the United Kingdom and Ireland in improving general and veterinary studfarm management standards.

Experience with *T. equigenitalis*, coupled with the research of Peterson and colleagues and Hughes and colleagues confirmed that infections caused by bacteria other than the three recognised potential equine venereal pathogens, i.e. most commonly the aerobes *Streptococcus zooepidemicus*, *Escherischia coli* and *Staphylococcus aureus* and the anaerobe *Bacteroides fragilis* develop as a result of a failure in individual mares' natural genital defences. Many failures result from anatomical abnormalities, e.g. vulval, vaginal or cervical injury leading to pneumovagina/uterus, many of which can be corrected by surgical reconstruction. In others, a more fundamental deficit in local immunity was suspected but subsequently, following exhaustive research by teams from various parts of the world, no basic aberration in local uterine immunity has been proven. It was not until the 1990s that the work of Allen and Pycock in the UK and Liu and Le Blanc in North America that the role of failure of uterine fluid clearance was established. The importance of flushing the uterus of infection, inflammatory products and fluids with large volumes of sterile saline solution followed by encouraging the uterus to expel remaining content by administering the ecbolic hormone oxytocin intravenously, was established and incorporated into equine studfarm practice. It remains clear that the whole subject of equine uterine competence for controlling infection is a complex and multifactorial problem that can be addressed satisfactorily only by detailed and careful examinations of individual mares. Uterine incompetence leads to a continuum of endometritis which must be resolved before mating, resolved again after mating and prevented throughout pregnancy to result in the birth of a live healthy foal. The 'primary lesion' for incompetence, if there is one, remains elusive and research must continue progressively to better our knowledge of the many degenerative conditions which inevitably occur during the ageing process of the broodmare which lead to failure of uterine competence earlier in some than others. Experience suggests that, in many previously normal mares, the 'switch' is thrown periparturiently and that this period, perhaps involving progressive myometrial damage, and the complex uteroplacental interactions must be important avenues for further research.

In 1972, Rossdale analysed the fertility performance of 26 mares who had won the English Oaks, comparing them to 52 other Thoroughbred mares who had never won a race, selected at random, and found that whereas the latter's records conformed to the national average, the former's breeding potential deteriorated earlier. In 1994, Pemberton and others studied a series of Thoroughbred mares who had been examined and treated for endometritis. Their results suggested that the progression of endometritis in these mares was modified by the nature of the α1–P1 proteins present in their endometria. Without more extensive research data, one can only speculate upon the full significance of these observations, but there is little doubt that genetic influences are important contributing, or even determining factors for mare fertility.

All these facets have provided important pieces to the diagnostic 'jigsaw puzzle' which must be solved in order for veterinary clinicians to help the subfertile mare. The 1970s work of Greenhof and Kenney in North America provided the foundations for the development of strategies for the examination of barren mares during the autumn period with the aim of diagnosing significant genital abnormalities in such mares, developing rational therapeutic strategies, followed by re-examination after a period of sexual rest to confirm improvement to optimal levels possible for that individual. When performed in good time this allows the mare to enjoy a further period of sexual rest and recuperation prior to the start of the next breeding season which she can then start in optimal gynaecological condition. Examinations of perineal conformation, palpation and ultrasound examination of ovaries and uterus, bacteriological examinations of the clitoris and uterus and videoendoscopic examination of the uterus provide essential diagnostic information.

In addition, Kenney and subsequently others, established the technique of endometrial biopsy as a valuable objective means of evaluating the mare's endometrium, principally for inflammatory and degenerative changes. As these are such important factors in the gynaecological health of the broodmare, biopsy information is a very useful diagnostic tool which aids the formulation of treatment strategies and the evaluation of their success or failure. Paired biopsy investigations prior to and following uterine treatments have lead to more accurate prognostic information for use by veterinary gynaecologists and studfarm managers and owners.

Research and experiences gained over the latter part of this century have resulted in a number of useful prophylactic strategies for managing the genitally compromised mare. Their principles are: the initial accurate diagnosis and successful treatment of genital abnormalities in the individual mare; one natural cover just prior to ovulation or artificial insemination with filtered and antibiotic-treated semen, as appropriate; and irrigation of the uterus coupled with antibiotic treatment and stimulation of uterine clearance with oxytocin during the 'window of opportunity' which occurs for the 24–48 hours following ovulation in the mare prior to the fertilised ovum (blastocyst) entering the uterus at approximately Day 5.

There is no doubt that great progress has been made in the fundamental knowledge and practical management of barren mares and this is measurable in the fact that the barren mare rate for the Thoroughbred population of the United Kingdom and Ireland has halved during the last 21 years.

It is possible that at least some of this apparent improvement may be due to better culling of older mares and to changes in the means of reporting results but the trends are clearly encouraging. This is particularly so as brood mares are not selected for their fertility potential but for their pedigree and athletic performance, this apparent improvement is even more encouraging. Nevertheless, we must consider the possibility that our progressive ability to help more less fertile mares become pregnant may adversely effect the inherent genetic fertility potential of the broodmare population.

Pregnant Mare

Although Wortley Axe presents a lengthy discussion of the embryology of the horse, somewhat inaccurate in areas because of reliance of extrapolation from other species, it is clear that he viewed the subject of early pregnancy with some mystification:

"At the outset, the attempt to describe the formation of the

Weatherbys' Annual Return for UK and Irish Thoroughbred Mares

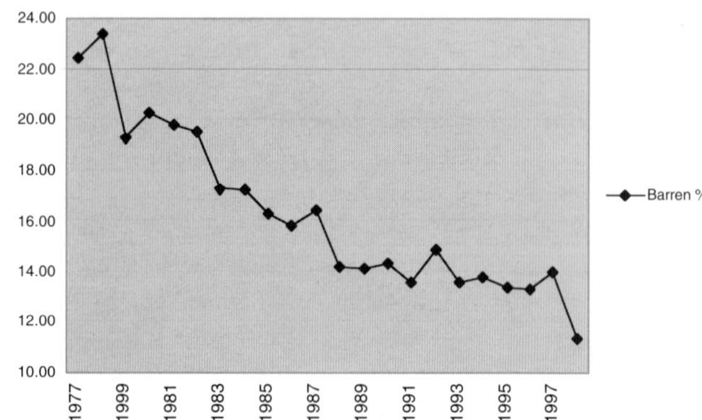

Thoroughbred mares covered by registered Thoroughbred stallions minus those who died, were exported and those who for whom returns were not made - 16,000 mares in 1998.

various parts of the young animal is met by an insuperable difficulty, because by no form of verbal gymnastics is it possible describe a whole set of simultaneous processes by the aid of consecutive phrases."

This is surprising because Cossar Ewart, only 10–20 years previously (*A Critical Period in the Development of the Horse*, 1897), had quite accurately described and drawn equine conceptuses and had described the trophoblastic girdle that Allen was later to show was responsible for invading the endometrium and provoking a cellular reaction that resulted in the formation of endometrial cups. Ewart described:

"In the region of the absorbing area some of the fetal cells blend with the adjacent uterine cells. Around the absorbing area a circular adhesive ring is formed. This ring shrinks as the absorbing area diminishes. A supplementary grappling apparatus appears in the form of a girdle, which becomes, up to the seventh week, more and more complex, and travels towards the ring just mentioned as the allantois increases in size."

It was Allen who demonstrated that it was these chorionic girdle cells which produced the hormone first found in blood by Cole and Cupps and named Pregnant Mare Serum Gonadotrophin and shown by them to originate from the endometrial cups. Allen's later work was to show not only the dynamics of PMSG production, and some of the immunological factors that influenced its production as well as its probable immunological function, but also that a better name for it was equine Chorionic Gonadotrophin by analogy with a similar protein produced by the chorion of pregnant women.

It was also Cole and Cupps who first reported the presence of large quantities of oestrogen in mare blood in late pregnancy, although Zondek had described the presence of vast quantities of oestrogen in pregnant mare urine. Zondek's discovery spawned an industry that still survives today: the harvesting of late pregnant mare urine for therapeutically useful oestrogens. Today, the horse provides the bulk of the Hormone Replacement Therapy that has significantly reduced the prevalence of osteoporosis in older women.

Girard, one of a number of chemists working in France for the burgeoning pharmaceutical industry, isolated from the urine of pregnant mares oestrogens other than the classic oestrone and oestradiol. The enigmatic ring-B unsaturated equilin and equilenin, oestrogens not found elsewhere in nature and whose biosynthetic pathway, nearly 70 years after their first discovery and in spite of brilliant work by Bhavnagni and his colleagues, remain an enigma. What is known is that their precursors are synthesised by the fetal gonads whose prodigious enlargement during pregnancy had also been reported on by Cole and Cupps (though the first to describe the enlargement was Aristotle in 300 BC who observed them in an aborted foal and wondered if they were spare kidneys). The purpose of this enlargement remains as much an enigma as the existence of equilin and equilenin, showing that the horse's biological peculiarities can keep research work going for some time to come.

It is now recognised that equine maternal recognition of pregnancy begins very early in pregnancy. Amoroso and others had observed degenerating oocytes in the Fallopian tubes of mares in early pregnancy and, observing new corpora lutea in the ovaries of these same mares at a stage when they were producing massive amounts of eCG, known to be follicle-stimulating in other species, assumed that all this proved that mares produce follicles under the influence of eCG. They were later to be proved wrong on two counts. Firstly, the later work of Allen on eCG already referred to showed that this hormone merely luteinised follicles growing in the ovary under the influence of pituitary FSH. Secondly, the work of Betteridge and others demonstrated that the mare possesses a unique ability to segregate fertilised and unfertilised eggs and to allow only the former to enter the uterus, whilst the latter remain in the Fallopian tube to degenerate. A cautionary lesson for all who dare to hypothesise! Research on the mechanics of 'maternal recognition of pregnancy' continues. It is believed that at approximately 14 days, the maternal uterus recognises chemical and endocrinological signals from the importantly mobile conceptus, inhibiting endogenous $PGF_{2\alpha}$ release from endometrial glands and therefore blocking normal luteolysis and return to oestrus at the normal three week cycle stage.

It was not until the work of Amoroso in the UK and subsequently Short, Allen, Betteridge and Flood that the anatomy of the early equine blastocyst, with its unique steroid-secreting capsule and the development of the equine placenta was accurately understood. Allen's definition of the development of equine endometrial cups from chorionic girdle cells as the source of production of eCG was fundamental to our understanding of early equine pregnancy. The dynamics of eCG production and the recognition that large quantities of oestrone sulphate are produced by the fetal gonads after day 120 formed the basis for the two laboratory tests for pregnancy in mares, eCG from 45–95 days and oestrone sulphate from 120 days to close to term, both measured in blood samples and both useful at their different stages for the monitoring of normal and abnormal pregnancies. Oestrone sulphate has the added advantage of confirming a viable fetus.

Routine diagnosis of pregnancy developed to a fine art during the 20th century. Wortley Axe observed that:

"In a short time, also, the majority of mares, if they have been irritable and restless previously, become quieter and more docile, if not absolutely torpid, and inclined to become fatter. Seldom is anything more noticed until pregnancy has advanced to the sixth or seventh month; so that though the question is often asked the expert as to whether a mare is in foal before that period, a reply in the affirmative is rather hazardous, and can only be based on the indications just eluded to, unless recourse be had to a manual examination per rectum or through the genital passage, a procedure which is not advisable in all cases".

Dimmock in North America in the 1930s and Day in the UK in the 1940s were clinicians who developed the art of rectal palpation of the ovaries and early pregnancy in mares. It became clear, and is still the case today, that individual clinicians require the experience of large numbers of examinations before they can become safe, confident and accurate in this technique. Nevertheless, serial routine examinations still form the basis for gynaecological management and early pregnancy diagnosis in mares. The 42 day (six week) manual pregnancy examination became the 'gold standard' for confirming pregnancy in mares but, following Van Niekerk's studies in the 1960s, it was recognised that the three week pregnant mare's uterus frequently has a very characteristically palpable tense tone, as if in spasm. Many experienced clinicians used this and the tight, pale and dry appearance of the cervix on vaginascopic examination to predict early pregnancy, which was a help to management at that time. Coupled with a 30 day examination to reconfirm pregnancy and to palpate specifically for twins, before endometrial cups became established and eCG secretion had started, this somewhat helped to reduce the major wastage associated with equine twin pregnancy.

Progress was accelerated with the introduction of *per rectum* linear array ultrasound scanning for routine equine pregnancy diagnosis in the 1980s, firstly by Palmer in France and then Allen in Newmarket and Ginther in USA. Ultrasound scanning has proved to be a watershed for the equine gynaecologist and obstetrician. Experience and great care with the large probes available at that time was required, but clinicians found that they could confirm nonpregnancy with repeated examinations at three weeks after mating and could then use prostaglandin injections to return the mare to oestrus for covering again. This avoided an enormous amount of wasted time for many mares, improving breeding efficiency and reducing the number of mares left barren at the end of the season. It was also found that, with care, experience and attention to detail, twin pregnancy could be diagnosed with much greater accuracy than ever before possible. Clinicians from all over the world developed techniques for manual crushing of twins, leaving one intact. With ever-improving ultrasound technology and ever-increasing clinical experience, the accuracy of early pregnancy diagnosis, early twin and sometimes triplet diagnosis and their reduction to single ongoing pregnancy has never been higher. The incidence of twin abortion in scanned Thoroughbred mares has reduced from approximately 50% of abortions 20 years ago to currently insignificant numbers. There is no doubt that ultrasound scanning, in its many forms and facets, has been one of the major contributions of the veterinary profession to equine studfarm management during the 20th century.

Following the work of Ginther and Holder in USA, clinicians with adequate technology and experience can determine fetal gender by ultrasound scan, with ever-increasing accuracy, between 60 and 70 days. Many North American and some European horse breeders find that this adds valuable information which can be used for long-term planning, e.g. for the level of insurance cover, future purchases, mating lists and auction reserves. Fetal gender determination has become one factor for the selection of mares to be culled and has increased the number of mares carrying filly fetuses for sale at some public auctions. If purchasers of pregnant brood mares are no longer able to assume that they have a 50% chance of buying a colt or filly fetus at many public sales, the international sales companies should seek to find a way to encourage vendors to make honest declarations to protect the long-term interests of everyone concerned.

In the UK Thoroughbred mare population, umbilical cord abnormalities, resulting in vascular embarrassment and fetal cardiovascular collapse, more commonly seen in umbilical cords of greater than 80 cm length, is now the most common cause of abortion. Twenty years ago, twin abortion was the most important cause of Thoroughbred abortion but this problem has been virtually solved by the widespread use of ultrasound scan. The incidence of bacterial and mycotic placentitis has been generally reduced by better management of mares during the breeding season. But an interesting form of placentitis, apparently associated with a focal nocardiform infection, has been recently reported in Kentucky and this will be the subject of further research. Transplacental infection with *Equine Herpesvirus 1* remains the most feared potential cause of epidemic abortion in mares but this has been largely controlled by the widespread use of safe, commercially available vaccines which do not always avoid individual abortions but have reduced the incidence of epidemics to negligible proportions.

Rossdale, Silver, Ousey and colleagues in UK described gross and biochemical changes in the mammary secretions of mares and circulating endocrinological changes which occur during the preparturient period. These studies and others involving 30 years of collaborative perinatal research have led to the concept of fetomaternal 'readiness for birth'. These and transabdominal ultrasound studies have provided the clinician with techniques and reference data with which to evaluate the 'at-risk' or abnormal late pregnancy and to help judge the time of imminent parturition. The latter has helped improve the safety of elective and emergency induction of parturition and caesarean section, in terms of the viability of the foal.

Parturition and the *Postpartum* Period

With perhaps the greater incidence of foaling difficulties seen in the working and heavier breeds of horses, Wortley Axe and similar sources contain long descriptions of foaling difficulties associated with fetal positional and postural abnormalities. With it there are pages of descriptions of mechanical aids from hooks to blades and embryotomes for the correction of such problems. Nevertheless it was not until Jeffcott and colleagues presented radiological studies of parturition in the mare during the 1980s that the dynamic changes that the fetus normally makes just prior to and during parturition were accurately understood. With the remaining importance of the heavier type of mare in mainland Europe, Vandeplassche and colleagues from Belgium continued the traditional expertise in the correction of dystocia and have advanced our knowledge of periparturient abnormalities such as dorsoretroflexion of the uterus, uterine torsion, transverse presentation, uterine prolapse and their treatment and management.

Coupled with Stevens' microscopic anatomical descriptions of equine placental microcotyledons, Vandeplassche emphasised the importance of removing retained equine placentas with caution, using intravenous oxytocin drips, to avoid the traumatic fracture of microcotyledons at their bases, leading to their retention and necrosis in the endometrium. This change of management undoubtedly reduced the incidence of septic periparturient metritis/laminitis in mares, which had been so important to the heavy working mare. Coupled with advances in equine abdominal surgery during the last 30 years, Vandeplassche and equine soft tissue surgeons such as Pearson, Edwards and Greet in UK, taking advantage of clinicians' earlier diagnoses and improved general anaesthetic techniques, have advanced the success and practicality of caesarean section in the mare.

Clinicians experienced in equine stud medicine now readily acknowledge that the 'macho' days of manual dystocia correction should be over and that for the health and welfare of both mare and fetus, an early diagnosis of dystocia which is not immediately simple to correct should be followed by urgent referral to an experienced surgical team, without delay, for caesarean section.

Many clinicians experienced in equine stud medicine recognise the postparturient period i.e. from birth to foal heat as a very important time for maternal genital recovery, the success of which is vital to the fertility of the subsequent breeding season and the rest of the mare's breeding career. Early exercise for both mare and foal, assuming both are healthy and environmental conditions are satisfactory, is undoubtedly beneficial.

Arguments regarding the fertility of the first *postpartum* oestrous period ('foal heat') have persisted throughout the 20th century. Before the benefit of routine gynaecological examinations, it is to be assumed that many mares most reliably 'showed' behavioural oestrous at this time and not when subsequently inhibited by suckling their foals. It was probably for this reason that the foal heat was recommended as the most 'fertile' period for the mare to be covered and this is probably the norm for the feral mare. Particularly in the case of the Thoroughbred mare, factors taken into account were developing knowledge of uterine infectious disease and genital competence for recovery, coupled with practical experience that significant numbers of mares either suffered pregnancy failure followed by intractable infection or conception followed by early pregnancy failure when covered at this time, many owners, managers and clinicians developed the opinion that the foal heat period, coming at 7–12 days after foaling, was 'too early'. Many mares were therefore routinely left for mating until the second *postpartum* oestrous period i.e. at approximately 30 days. Following Loy's survey in Kentucky during the 1980s, many clinicians have formed the opinion that a decision should be made only following detailed gynaecological examinations have been completed at the foal heat period, coupled with consideration of the normality of foaling and placental release. If all indications are that the mare has recovered well then foal heat covering followed by early conception and successful pregnancy will result in the mare foaling at a similar time of year next year, an advantage not only to her owner but to her own long term breeding career.

The idea that the foal heat comes 'too early' has lead some clinicians to develop endocrinological strategies to delay the foal heat period, involving the use of progesterone and oestradiol or progesterone alone. Although some clinicians claim success, most examine mares at their natural foal heat period and form three categories. Those who have a normal foaling and who appear to have recovered normally at foal heat period are recommended for mating at that time, using prophylactic postmating therapeutic techniques as previously discussed.

Those mares who are deemed to have had a normal foaling and do not have an infected uterus but whose uteri have palpably and ultrasonically not involuted fully by their foal heat period are not recommended for mating at that time. In these cases, the subsequent dioestrus period is often shortened with prostaglandin treatment at five or six days following foal heat ovulation, resulting in a gain of approximately one week on the normal 30 day oestrus period.

The third group are mares who suffered an abnormal traumatic parturition and/or postparturient uterine infection and for whom treatment and a full period of recovery and recuperation prior to mating at the 30 day or subsequent oestrous period is recommended. Various endocrinological regimes to delay the foal heat period have been tried, with variable success. Many clinicians remain of the opinion that normal *postpartum* gynaecological recovery is such a critical period for the future genital health and, therefore, breeding potential of all brood mares that mating at the foal heat period is a 'luxury' for which only a few carefully selected mares qualify. When more is known of the complex gynaecological processes involved at this time and therapeutic procedures to aid recovery have been validated, this opinion may be modified.

Neonatal Foal

Wortley Axe dismissed equine neonatal considerations as follows:

> *"The foal itself is not liable to many diseases if properly cared for. At birth the attendant should give it his immediate attention if it does not immediately breathe, as unless he then acts promptly it may die. When it fails to inspire after the navel-string has been divided, he should at once open its mouth, seize the tongue and pull it gently forwards a few times at some seconds interval, blowing hard into the mouth and nostrils while the tongue is forward. Flicking the sides of the chest with a wet towel at intervals may also produce the desired effect."*

Although some neonatal diseases were described in the 1940s and '50s, Rossdale in the 1960s and '70s was the first to describe the complex physiological adaptive processes which are essential for the newborn foal to survive and to discuss the pathology, treatment and management of specific neonatal diseases. His definitions of prematurity and dysmaturity have formed the basis of multicentre basic and applied research that has been conducted since on neonatal critical care. These studies have not only lead to a better understanding of neonatal problems but to the successful saving of progressively more premature and sick foals. He developed the definition 'neonatal maladjustment syndrome' for a number of foal behavioural disturbances which had previously been called by their clinical manifestations 'barkers, wanderers and dummies'. At that time it was the practice for stud grooms to ligate and cut the umbilical cord at foaling and Rossdale, Mahaffey and others pointed out the significant deprivation of placental blood supply to the fetus that this unnecessary procedure caused. Whether this specific change in management resulted in the otherwise unexplained reduction in incidence of neonatal maladjustment syndrome in the UK neonatal foal population is not clear but there is no doubt that equine neonatology has risen to a level of excellence where it is now considered a speciality of its own.

Older Foal and Yearling

While Wortley Axe did not specifically discuss the orthopaedic problems of growing foals and yearlings, veterinarians, stud managers and owners would all benefit from reading his extensive treatise on normal and abnormal conformation of horses. There is little doubt that in the racehorse and other forms of competition and show horse, breeding for performance to the exclusion of all else has resulted in the selection and perpetuation of a number of undesirable conformational traits which are now causing clinical problems. Offset and otherwise unsatisfactory knee conformation and flat-footedness are undoubtedly two examples of conformational difficulties which are well recognised to be perpetuated by certain fashionable Thoroughbred blood lines. These two factors alone are resulting in a high degree of wastage in training. Although unproved, many clinicians believe that some developmental orthopaedic diseases including osteochondrosis have a significant relationship to genetic conformational predisposition and that this has also resulted in significant wastage. It is to be hoped that the now widespread requests from purchasers for comprehensive radiographic examination of yearlings' joints at international Thoroughbred sales will eventually lead to a reduction in the incidence of some of these orthopaedic abnormalities in the breeding population. Substantial improvement has been made in the nutrition of young growing horses, particularly with regard to mineral, vitamin and trace element supplementation, resulting in the prevention and better management of physitis in particular. Better nutritional management and the use of routine regular veterinary assessments of young growing horses has become very popular and aids the optimal development of individuals in preparation for both sales and their performance career.

Artificial Breeding

Wortley Axe discussed artificial insemination in some detail as a means of overcoming "obstructions of one kind or another" in the genital organs of mares. Under this heading he described:

> *"The practice with some stud managers to pass the fingers into the uterus of mares which failed to breed, before putting them to the horse, the object being to open the passage for the entrance of the seminal fluid, and in many instances with the result that pregnancy has followed the service."*

This was presumably used for mares who had suffered vaginal or cervical injury at parturition or at mating and had developed fibrous adhesions. He recommended that:

> *"A more safe and reliable method however is to resort to artificial insemination. This is affected by means of an instrument (inseminator) designed to collect the semen from the male from the vagina of the female after service, and transfer it directly into the uterus. The practice has been largely adopted by breeders and with a considerable amount of success."*

The inseminator is pictured as a metal catheter connected to a rubber aspiration bulb by a rubber tube. He reports that:

> *"In America the operation has been practised on a considerable scale for many years and to a lesser extent, in France, Germany, Russia and India, before its adoption in these islands was at all general."*

The transfer of equine semen from mare to mare was, of course, practised from ancient times, but it was not really until the development and successful use of artificial vaginas by Nishikawa in Japan, Merkt in Germany and subsequently Kenney and Pickett in North America that an ejaculate was divided and used on more than one mare with any success. Following the development of seminal extenders for use specifically in stallions by Kenney, Pickett and their colleagues in North America and the development of chilling techniques in the 1980s and early '90s, cooled and extended semen is transported over quite large distances within a 24–48 hour time frame. Commercially available portable 'refrigeration' devices have become commonly used for shipping cooled semen internationally for use within 24–48 hours of collection.

Following the lead from eastern Europe, particularly Poland, significant progress has been made over the last 10 years in the freezing of equine semen, which has never enjoyed the success that the technique has with some other species. This has resulted in the commercial availability of frozen semen stocks for transportation over long distances and potentially for long-term storage. Reliable quality remains a problem with some commercial sources and there is need for improvement in this regard. Assuming a supply of good quality semen, it is recognised that the key to success for chilled semen and especially frozen semen is good mare management, in particular the accurate prediction of timing of ovulation. Clinicians who are experienced and successful in this field may examine mares 3–4 times a day during late oestrus. The considerable technical and veterinary input required for success frequently makes equine AI much more expensive for the mare owner than natural service unless it avoids international or interstate transport and associated boarding expenses. AI can be helpful (where foal registration authorities allow these techniques to be used) when the presence of infectious disease precludes transporting the mare to the stallion studfarm for natural mating. Fertility rates with shipped or frozen semen still cannot compare with those now achieved for well-managed Thoroughbred studfarms using natural cover and therefore the demand for this service currently remains with performance horse mares and stallions who are required to breed during their continuing performance career, for the international transport of semen rather than mares and to aid management on studfarms in order to allow several mares to be inseminated with one ejaculate (where foal registration authorities allow these techniques to be used).

For the performance mare, another option has become embryo transfer. As results for nonsurgical transfer improve in the hands of experienced clinicians, there is little doubt that this will become more widely used. It must be hard for owners and veterinarians to justify the stress and costs of surgical interference for such a procedure. Results for old and subfertile mares remain less reliable than for younger, genitally healthy mares, but undoubtedly this also will improve in time.

At the 1998 7th International Symposium on Equine Reproduction in Pretoria, a wealth of papers were presented on new artificial breeding techniques, including various techniques for *in vitro* fertilisation. We must wait to see what the future holds in this regard.

Conclusions

At the beginning of the 20th century it was clear that equine reproduction was the 'poor relation' of the art of veterinary surgery. During the 20th century this has been rectified to the extent that well-managed domesticated horses can now achieve excellent levels of fertility.

At the present time one gets the impression that equine reproductive research has to some extent 'run out of steam' because there are fewer obvious major problems inhibiting the natural breeding of horses to solve. There is no doubt that research into artificial breeding will continue apace, but it remains to be seen where such techniques will be usefully applied. It is to be hoped that owners, managers and veterinarians will learn something from the difficulties that financial and economic pressures have produced in the performance horse today. One cannot escape the fact that horse owners can now expect at least 90% conception rates and 80% live foal rates from adequately fertile stallions, with natural mating, when not overused and when their mares are well managed. Some young, well-managed, highly fashionable Thoroughbred stallions, mating 50–75 mares naturally, occasionally achieve 100% conceptions during a breeding season. Artificial breeding techniques, whilst undoubtedly helping to overcome some valid individual difficulties, have fundamentally developed for the benefit of owners rather than horses, for whom unnecessary problems are created.

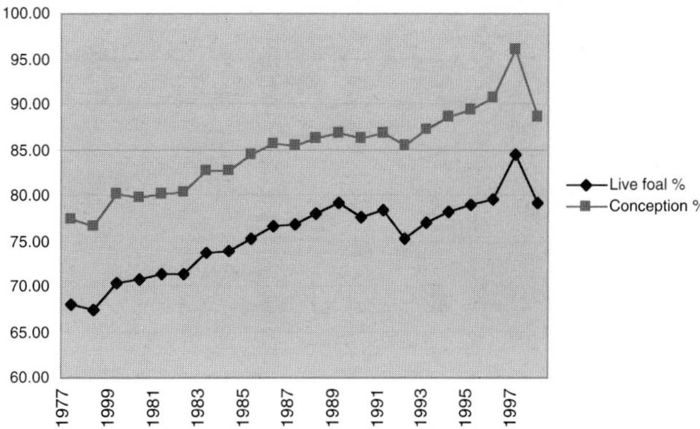

Thoroughbred mares covered by registered Thoroughbred stallions minus those who died, were exported and those who for whom returns were not made - 16,000 mares in 1998.

Nevertheless, there will undoubtedly be new, unexpected and exciting equine reproductive problems which will require solutions from the veterinarians of the 21st century.

Man is the disease of mares

The gaining of knowledge from the *Australian Veterinary Journal* 1940–1980

REX BUTTERFIELD
University of Sydney
56 Queens Road, Lawson
NSW 2783
Australia

It was my helpful nature which got me into this. There on my study floor, a perfect normal distribution no matter from what angle, lay the *Australian Veterinary Journal* (AVJ) from 1940 to 1980. The various eras were easily detectable from the colour of the covers: the austere wartime dark brown of the early 1940s, through the maroon and green in the new-found peace, then a strange shade of pale curry to a final glorious pink.

What do I do with them? I had promised Virginia Osborne I would find them a good home. I browsed their obituaries. Strange how interesting they become as one progresses towards candidacy. How little we really know about people until all is revealed in the obituary.That quietly efficient practitioner had been a hell-raising Spitfire pilot in the second World War! The grumpy Chief Government Veterinary Officer had had a passion for growing violets!

Having scanned the hundreds of 'Tables of Contents', many cunningly concealed among the advertisements to ensure difficult finding, I was struck by how few articles I had seen relating to the horse. Just how much had the AVJ contributed to the knowledge of those of us who had found ourselves involved in equne stud practice? The subject had rated hardly a mention during our undergraduate course; and yet many of us were to find ourselves becoming part of the horse stud scene very soon after graduation.The number of articles dealing with the horse, in any way, in that pile of AVJs, was extremely small. I counted that around 7% of the original articles over the 40 year period were related to the horse. At first this seemed a very low figure, but when assessed against the background of research funding it is really quite high, as less than 1% of the research funds of the animal industries over the period were directed at the horse.

So how did we acquire the knowledge which gave us the confidence to engage in horse stud practice? Although some modern educationalists would have us believe that the old-fashioned idea of veterinary education, whereby we had a basic science training followed by clinical training, must turn out nonthinking morons, it seems that somehow we had an appropriate basis to absorb what the AVJ, virtually our only scientific publication, and daily experience, were to tell us.

The first paper which really kicked along the subject of the involvement of vets in horse stud management was the report (AVJ 1948) of an address given to the NSW Division of the Australian Veterinary Association by Murray Bain, a proud Scot who was then working in New Zealand after a stint in Kentucky. Bain was later to move to Australia and be extremely influential in establishing the role of the veterinary surgeon in stud practice.

At this time, there were few veterinary surgeons working in equine stud practice and the observation that "*...as a profession we do not sufficiently understand the normal mare,*" was certainly an understatement by Murray. Bain's report was heavily influenced by his experience in Kentucky and referred often to the Caslick brothers. It is apparent that, at this stage, Bain had not foreseen the routine use of ovarian palpation which was to be widely adopted later; and he obviously placed heavy store on sexual behaviour and use of the vaginal speculum in detecting oestrus and in predicting ovulation. It is apparent that the oestrous cycle was the basis of his management of mating.

In a narrow sense, the central focus of veterinary function in stud practice is the selection of the optimumal mating time. Bain, at this time, recommended a single mating early in oestrous and presented some Kentucky figures in support of the success of this technique. However, he was uneasy about his inability to reconcile this recommendation with his knowledge of reputed sperm survival time and of the wide variation in the duration of oestrus which he acknowledged as follows:"*The only regularity about the oestrous cycle of the mare is its irregularity.*" He made it clear that: *"Much remains to be determined regarding this subject."*

Although Bain freely quoted the Kentucky fertility figures, he had been around long enough to be cautious of such statistics. Maybe he knew about the old-time travelling Clydesdale stallions who always achieved 100% of their mares in foal at the first jump.

In the audience at Bain's talk, which formed the basis of the AVJ publication, was Norman Larkin, probably the first vet to be involved closely with Thoroughbred horse breeding in Australia. He found some points of both agreement and disagreement with Murray in the discussion that followed.

Bain's talk, and its publication, certainly alerted many of the post-war undergraduates and new graduates who were soon to form the majority of vets providing a service to horse studs in Australia, that there was an important role for them to play. Through his strong personality and highly successful practice, he was a major influence on the development of horse stud practice in Australia, yet he left us uneasy in those early years. Just how could it be possible to get those mares with a three week heat period in foal with a single service? How could simple morons like us interpret the mystical speculum views to allow us to pick the time of mating?

In 1953 Bain again appeared at an AVA Conference with a very large paper on *Diseases in Foals*. This paper (AVJ 1954), supported by a smaller effort by an MRCVS from Victoria, F.H. Wiltshire, was a mini text book on the nonreproductive aspects of the veterinary role in stud practice. Once again, this was a great help to the young practitioner.

Although it was Bain who alerted us to the likely demand for veterinary involvement in horse stud management, and who provided us with much of the vital knowledge, it was Leo Mahaffey who supplied the linchpin for guaranteed success in the prediction of ovulation. He swung the emphasis from the oestrous cycle to the ovarian cycle, from manifestations of oestrous to maturing follicles and from pink vaginal walls to ovulation. For the first time we had an objective basis for veterinary advice on time of mating.

Mahaffey graduated from the University of Sydney in 1938 and then worked with Dr H.W. Bennetts, a world-class pathologist in Western Australia, before setting up in veterinary practice. His papers (AVJ 1950 & 1952) were almost conversational. They would certainly be too long for any modern editor, but the bulk of detail was of great help to those who followed. I suspect that he skilfully manipulated the editor with his text: "*As Topley and Wilson (1946) observe, tables tell much more illuminating tales than curves and graphs, and we set out in Table 6...*" Table 6 turned out to take up four whole pages of the journal.

Essentially, the Mahaffey papers set out to "*...accumulate and publish data which may be of assistance to the Thoroughbred industry generally*". He achieved this superbly. He cleared away much of the confusion that had pervaded the industry and which had resulted in the studs having more 'free returns' each year than they had new bookings to their stallions. His statement that "*it is impossible to devise a schedule of matings for the unassisted breeder which will ensure fertility in all potentially fertile mares*", was backed up by convincing analyses and by fertility levels in WA studs varying "*from 17 to 50% before veterinary assistance was obtained*". He swept away the hopeless feeling which confronted the breeder trying to obtain pregnancies in mares with highly variable heat periods as follows: "*The duration of oestrus, whether short or long, has not in itself presented any obstacle to conception in our work.*" From this statement alone he inspired confidence in the young graduates that they could be sure to improve fertility on almost any stud where they were given the opportunity to control mating by ovarian palpation.

The vaginal speculum allowed the vet, and no doubt the more adventurous of the stud staff, to peer knowingly into the genital depths and maybe gain suggestions of what might be occurring in the so near but so cunningly concealed ovaries. The speculum was becoming the snake-oil instrument of subjective predictions of ovulation and was rightfully downgraded by Mahaffey's statement that: "*The state of the vagina and cervix of the mare is not a sufficiently reliable guide to ovulation even in the hands of the expert observer.*"

I sighed with relief when I read that! So! It was not just me who could not make sense out of the claims of those who saw magical views of the vagina which were denied to me. I was so impressed that I determined that my speculum should be stored under all the other untidy gear in the boot of my car, so that it would be used only as a last resort. It soon gathered a lot of dust. It was necessary for Mahaffey to challenge the practices and writings of some of the big names and he did this with objectivity. How could the practice of a single mating early in oestrous result in high conception rates when ovulation occurred (in his mares) from the seventh to the 21st day? He was critical of Caslick, of labial embroidery fame, for being "*erroneous and confusing*" in his use of the term "*ovulation period*" in the absence of ovarian palpation.

Mahaffey moved on to the UK where he had a profound influence. Sadly, this is recorded in his all too early obituary in the AVJ (1973).

By the end of the 1950s there were many of us in practice doing some stud work and we were only too well aware of the problems of mares not ovulating when we most desired. There were those mares who just would not start until late in the season and worse, those who did not ovulate at all during the season. However, we had little idea of what the overall ovulation pattern of mares was outside the calendar breeding season. All was revealed in a paper published in 1966, setting out the ovulation pattern of mares in eastern Australia. Its relevance to most major horse breeding areas throughout the world was soon clearly apparent. It appeared under the title of *An Analysis of the Pattern of Ovulation as it Occurs in the Annual Reproductive Cycle of the Mare in Australia*, and it was written by Virginia E. Osborne, who, since graduating from the University of Sydney during the second World War, had been teaching her beloved horse anatomy while enjoying breeding and racing Standardbreds and later Thoroughbreds.

A large and cooperative knackery near Sydney provided the opportunity for her to obtain a regular supply of complete sets of mare genitalia. Who else but Virginia could charm a knacker carefully to remove the entire female tract from thousands of mares and to dispatch them regularly to the Department of Veterinary Anatomy?

She examined many hundreds of milk cans full of genitalia (actually 6,763 samples) over the period 1959 to 1965 and these specimens comprised the entire throughput of mares in the knackery.

Unlike Mahaffey's study, where a mass of tabulated data made understanding easy, Virginia produced the simple frequency distribution curve of ovulation, overlaid on the months of the years and, more particularly, the calendar breeding seasons, which left no doubt of the major importance of the study. The true breeding season and the calendar breeding season were barely talking to one another.

The study clearly established that "*The period of optimal activity is only partially encompassed by the stud season, and mares remaining anovular either throughout or until late in the season will have little or no opportunity for a successful mating.*" She confirmed the level of around 8% of mares that did not ovulate during the breeding season, which had been the experience of practitioners in other areas of Australia. There appeared to be no doubt that a higher level of fertility would be achievable if the breeding season was shifted to extend over the summer after a later start in the spring.

Change seemed a great idea; however, nothing could be so simple. The complexity of the racing calendar along with the Mediterranean climate of many of our breeding areas, have been the basis of maintaining the status quo. Thirty plus years later the Thoroughbred industry still finds it impossible to respond.

For later foals to be profitable, there would need to be a thorough overhaul of the racing calendar. The difficulty of this task, along with the problems of young foals being born into the stark dryness of midsummer in the southern regions of Australia, has been sufficient to outweigh the advantages of producing more foals in a later Thoroughbred season. However, the Standardbred industry, where the emphasis on early two-year-olds is much less, did delay the start of their season from 1987.

So, Virginia's massive amount of work remains, to the Thoroughbred world, a very neat piece of work which has had no opportunity to realise its potential to increase Thoroughbred fertility. But certainly it has helped us and, hopefully, our clients to understand that there is a group of around 10% of mares from which we have little, if any, chance of producing a foal in any year, unless we continue mating beyond Christmas (in the southern hemisphere), and that those 10% of mares are quite normal. It is we who are abnormal in our expectations.

The publications of Bain, Mahaffey and Osborne created peaks in the rather barren landscape of Australian equine reproduction writing during the 1940–80 period; but there were others. Way back in the early 1940s, Bazeley presented a series of papers on *Streptococcus equi*, recording work which led to the production of the CSL vaccine which was frequently mentioned by later writers in relation to horse stud practice.

Reg Pascoe, one of those rare practitioners who regularly finds time to write, contributed 1.2 papers per year for over 20 years. His writings touched on a wide range of problems associated with horse production and he has been a most influential practitioner. There are, of course, others who have made significant contributions, but I must return to the trio of Bain, Mahaffey and Osborne.

From Murray Bain we received the initial stimulus that there was a role for the veterinary surgeon in horse stud practice; from Leo Mahaffey came the mechanism to enable the simple graduates to do better; and from Virginia Osborne came the explanation of why we could never be perfect. It was these three who did so much to remind us that the major limitation on the fertility of mares is the restriction imposed upon them by man. Yes Virginia! man still is the disease of mares.

Rex relaxing in the Blue Mountains of New South Wales.

The birth of perinatal medicine

PETER ROSSDALE
Beaufort Cottage Stables
High Street
Newmarket
Suffolk CB8 8AU
UK

JOHN DAVIS
Four Mile House
1 Cambridge Road
Gt Shelford
Cambridge CB2 5JE
UK

The survival of any species depends upon the replacement of ageing individuals with new and younger members. Nature has developed two strategies for this purpose. The multigravid short gestation pregnancy, which relies on balancing high mortality through increased litter size, and the unigravid conception followed by a long period of gestation as adopted by our species and the horse. This latter strategy in turn may be associated with either a comparatively long period after birth during which the young move slowly towards independence, as in our own species, and those which, as in the horse, the altricious; or the precocious form of development where they run with the herd almost from birth.

In the natural state, the relationship between parent and offspring is determined mainly by the intensity of the care the latter require for maximum survival while they remain dependent as regards nourishment, maintenance of body temperature (the smaller an animal, the larger the ratio of heat-losing surface area to heat-generating volume), and protection. In the altricious state, the young usually have to be guided to the mammae for suckling and cuddled to minimise heat loss, whereas precocious offspring to some degree seek out the care that they need.

At birth, the survival of the fetus depends on the establishment of independent respiration: as Joseph Barcroft put it, "*breathing is living and the first respiration is the beginning of life*". By and large, it is only in our species that assistance is provided when a baby is asphyxiated at birth, neonatal resuscitation having been developed almost as an art form backed by the technology of so-called 'intensive care'. Such interference has now been adapted by veterinarians to the care at birth of Thoroughbred foals; illustrating the maxim of the Jesuit philosopher, Teilhard de Chardin that "*animals know, but man knows that he knows*." Thus modern obstetrics and neonatology are based upon scientific understanding of the physiological processes involved and their pathology in order to circumvent natural wastage.

Attitudes to the newborn have, as one might expect, changed markedly over the centuries. In the Middle Ages, as before, the young were often subjected to sacrificial ceremonies and the standard of care given frequently fell below that required for survival. Poverty, ignorance and a degree of indifference were, as they still are in many parts of the world, a threat to the survival of the young in animals and humans alike; infant mortality being of an order that bore out the words of King Lear: "*The oldest hath seen the most and those that are young shall never see so much nor live as long.*" It is, in fact, only through positive action, i.e. intervention, that what was seen as inevitable natural wastage can be reduced or avoided. This is the *raison d'être* of perinatal medicine - including surgery.

Historically, intervention was, even in comparatively recent times, primitive or even counterproductive, giving rise to a fatalistic belief that 'nature knows best'. It was in fact not until about after the establishment of the NHS, and following the publication in the USA of Clement Smith's account of what was then known as 'the physiology of the newborn infant', building on the work of Joseph Barcroft before the war, that clinicians began to apply scientific knowledge to the care of babies at and after birth. It was the formation of the Neonatal Society that brought together a distinguished group of neonatal physiologists (Kenneth Cross of London, Geoffrey Dawes of Oxford and McCance of Cambridge, to name a few), and a number of pioneering paediatricians, obstetricians, pathologists and - if last, certainly not least! - veterinarians, that led to an explosion of research at all levels whereby theory and practice were synthesised in a Hegelian that generated new insights in fields ranging from biochemistry to psychology. A good

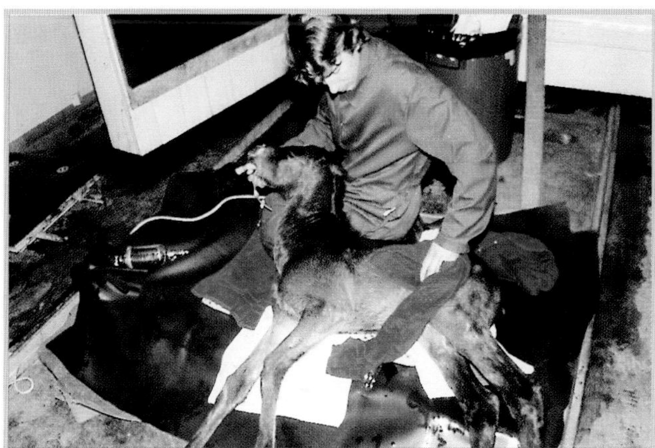

Foal receiving critical care including oxygen-enriched air following delivery by caesarean section.

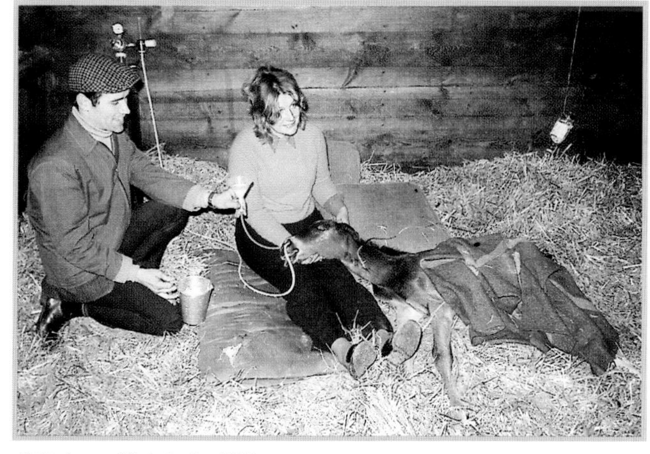

Critical care of foals in the 1970s.

example is the elucidation of the aetiology of the so-called Respiratory Distress Syndrome (hyaline membrane disease) that was the major cause of mortality in premature babies and those born to diabetic mothers.

Following its experimental production in animals, the serendipitous discovery by Pattle when studying the effects of poison gas on the lungs rabbits at Porton Down of pulmonary surfactant confirmed the supposition of Radford's in the USA that wet alveoli would collapse under the influence of surface tension in the absece of a factor tending to reduce it. Mary Ellen Avery in the USA and Pam Davies in Oxford drew attention to the likelihood that RDS was the consequence of a lack or denaturing of the natural surfactant discovered by Pattle in babies born before the switch from growth to maturation at the end of pregnancy mediated by adrenal steroids. The resultant understanding of its pathogenesis revolutionised the management of RDS and was followed by a dramatic and still-continuing increase in the survival rates of immature babies mainly brought about by the development of relatively safe and effective assisted ventilation. This was accompanied by an appreciable morbidity which is still the subject of anxious enquiry and by increasingly successful attempts at prevention either by induction of surfactant secretion in the fetus or the administration of exogenous surfactant after birth.

Only now is it becoming clear what a profound influence early vicissitudes - even in the womb - may have on subsequent well being; a realisation that should balance the present almost exclusive focus on genetics and molecular biology in medical research. Those who help care for inbred Thoroughbred horses may well have a special contribution to make in this area in working out the interaction between genes, environment and capacity.

In the horse, the understanding of neonatology and its application to equine paediatric medicine began in the 1950s. The first breakthrough was from the work of Robin Coombs who led the team that elucidated the reason for haemolytic disease in newborn Thoroughbred foals and, therefore, gave grounds for curing or, importantly, avoiding the condition. In the '60s, the work of Leo Mahaffey and others furthered the understanding of the 'Barker' syndrome and the concept of the Neonatal Maladjustment Syndrome with its underlying cerebral pathology described by Tony Palmer at Cambridge. This led, in turn, to a better understanding for premature and dysmature foals and the importance of adrenalcortical function in maturation of the equine fetus. This work was developed by Peter Rossdale, Marian Silver, Abby Fowden and Jenny Ousey at Cambridge/Newmarket and, in the subsequent decade of the development of intensive (critical) care facilities worldwide, particularly in Newmarket and, in the USA, led by Anne Koterba and Tim Cudd in Florida and Bill Rood in Kentucky.

The value of Thoroughbred and Standardbred foals encouraged owners to support intensive care procedures although, at the end of the century, it is apparent that considerations of cost, consequent upon expensive technology and labour-intensive protocols, are causing problems of decision as to the extent and duration to which measures may be applied economically in referral centres established for the purpose of therapy and support of the newly born foal. Further, in the case of performance horses, the prognosis for athletic survival has to be added to that of survival of the individual *per se*.

In the late '80s and '90s and, undoubtedly, into the next century, the concept of perinatal medicine has developed and will develop as it has in human medicine. It is customary, even for paediatricians, to speak of life of the individual as if it starts at birth. This applies, of course, to independent existence but, for the individual, life starts at fertilisation of the maternal ovum; and it is from this point that the potential for conditions of the newly born and, indeed, older individual, as highlighted by the original observations of David Barker, take their origin in many instances. Many studies in man and animal have now confirmed the influence of intrauterine growth retarding effects (IUGR) and subtle postnatal consequences ranging from cardiopulmonary diseases to metabolic disturbances.

In the horse, this awareness is increasingly being established in the minds of veterinary clinicians and a search made for pre-natal origins of disease. The words of T.S. Eliot are particularly apt applied to the individual at birth: "*For every end there is a beginning, the end is where we start from.*" The end of gestation sees the delivery of an individual with an anamnesis based upon prenatal experiences of environmental and untoward challenges, thus underwriting or destabilising depending upon the gestational circumstances, the start of extrauterine existence for the individual.

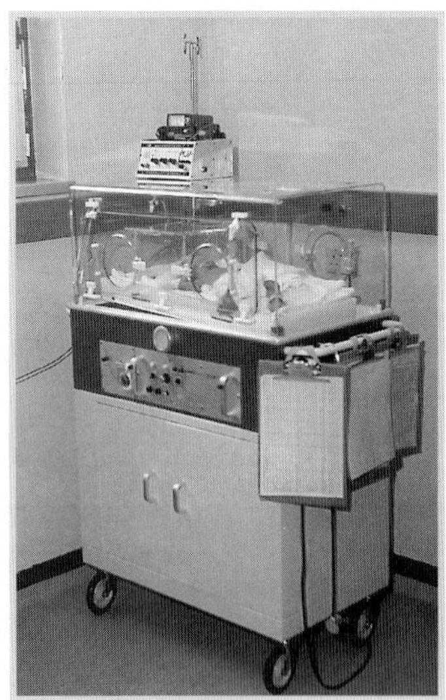

Intensive critical care for the human infant.

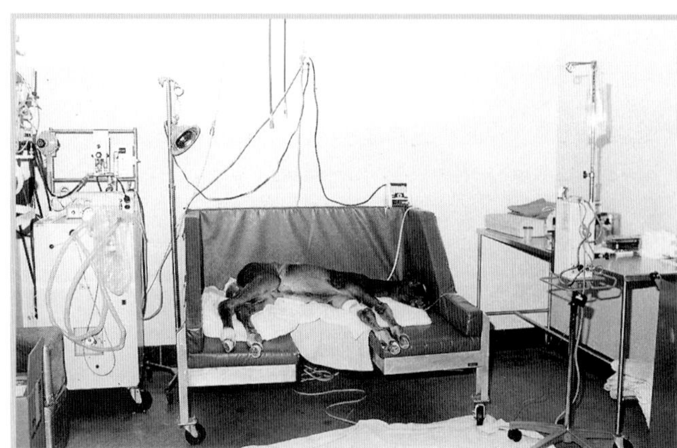

Modern facillities for foal critical care.

Changes in equine feeding practices

PAT HARRIS
Equine Studies Group
WALTHAM Centre for Pet Nutrition
Waltham-on-the-Wolds
Melton Mowbray
Leics LE14 4RT
UK

Since its first domestication around 5000 BC the role of the horse in society, as discussed more fully elsewhere (p 29) in this book, has varied according to man's requirements. Initially the horse was kept for its flesh and milk but soon became used for transport. One of the first examples of a man on horseback is believed to be the bone engraving of the Susa horseman (2800 BC).

Selective breeding meant that, by the 10th century BC horses had become essential to the skilled horseman turned warrior. Horse racing developed in parallel with horse riding, the very popular Roman chariot races evolving into modern day racing.Domestication and selective breeding resulted in changes in conformation leading to the different breeds and types of the modern day horse. The heavy horses, for example, were bred in the 18th century to transport heavy loads and to work on the farms, whereas fast trotting horses, capable of carrying a man over long distances, were bred and used to transport mail. Both of these types have become less common in the last century due to mechanisation, whereas breeds such as the Quarter Horse, Standardbred and Thoroughbred all used for racing, have become more popular. The Thoroughbred was originally used for stamina racing around the reign of Charles II, the first general stud book being published by Weatherbys in 1791.

The Thoroughbred, together with many other breeds or types originally selected for a variety of specific purposes, is mainly used today for pleasure. A large variety of competitions have developed to provide a competitive angle to pleasure riding, including racing, eventing, show-jumping, gymkhana and endurance rides. The challenge recently for the nutritionists has been to determine how and when horses competing in the various disciplines can be optimally fed.

As the role of the horse has changed, so have the conditions under which it is kept. It was common in previous centuries for there to be large stables where horsemanship was passed down from generation to generation. But especially in the later part of this century, there are now increasing numbers of people with no family history of horse ownership keeping one or two horses. Veterinary surgeons, feed companies and the various horse societies are becoming more and more involved in providing advice on horse management and feeding. While good nutrition may not be able to improve the intrinsic ability of a horse, poor or inappropriate nutrition may impose limitations and may lead not only to impaired performance but also to overt clinical problems.Today there is no general feeding or management practice and it is probable that almost any permutation of feeding regimen can be found somewhere in the world.

At the middle of this century it was felt that there had been little real advancement in horse nutritional knowledge over the previous 50 years compared to the growth of knowledge in farm animal nutrition. However, this situation changed in the latter half of the century.There has recently been a great expansion in the number of equine-orientated courses at universities and colleges throughout the world.At the same time, there has been a great increase in the amount of equine nutrition research being carried out and papers being published in various journals. It is not possible to cover all the changes in equine nutrition and feeding that have occurred in the last millennium or indeed even in the last century. Aspects of these developments are therefore covered later in this section and in the chapters from Professors Hintz and Meyer (pp 153 and 158), both currently eminent in equine nutrition.

This research has resulted in some major as well as minor changes in the way that we feed and manage our horses. But what horses are fed has obviously depended, to a certain extent, on where they lived and what feedstuffs were available. For example, at the beginning of this century kulthi, gram, moth, urad and mung (Indian beans/peas) were commonly fed ingredients according to a UK-published animal management book and this probably reflected the geographical destination of the manual. This manual also stated that *"meat was utilised successfully during the siege of Metz by being cut into small pieces and rolled in bran, and Norwegian stock of all kinds is accustomed to consume a soup made from boiled fish when mixed with other food"*. Although the use of meat would be altogether frowned upon today, Icelandic ponies apparently may still be fed herring in the winter. In some countries horses are fed a very different and wider variety of vegetables and fruits compared with the UK. Horses in some less developed countries may, at times, survive on feedstuffs, such as cardboard soaked in a sugar solution, which are unlikely to be on a UK horse's menu. Little written information is available in the mainstream nutritional textbooks as to what feedstuffs are currently fed to horses in such countries.

Which Feedstuffs Are Fed?

In many countries, most of the feedstuffs listed as being suitable for horses at the beginning of this century are still fed today, e.g. lucerne, oats, maize, barley and linseed, although soya has tended to replace linseed as one of the major protein sources for horses. In the late 1920s it was stated that *"custom has decreed that the staple diet of working horses should consist of hay and oats supplemented or substituted by straw, maize, beans or dried grains"*.

One of the biggest changes in the last part of this century has been the increased use of manufactured commercial feeds for horses. The impetus for such feeds came initially in the 19th century from the military and those involved with using horses for transportation. At the start of this century *"compressed food cakes consisting of a mix of oats, beans, corn, bran and sometimes chaff"* were mentioned as possible feeds but it was recommended that they be broken up before being fed damp. The few manufactured feeds available tended to be expensive and contained poor quality ingredients such as ground corn stalks and sawdust. By the late 1920s, for convenience, 'prepared chop' could be purchased which was reported to contain mainly cereal straw, bruised oats (of indeterminate quality), broken maize, kibbled locust beans, and other beans, but it was recommended that *"horse owners should buy and mix the food for the horses themselves, then they know exactly what their animals are getting and that the food is of good quality"*. Pelleted feeds were being fed as early as 1917 but their popularity did not increase dramatically until the 1960s. Increased competition and improved knowledge, as well as more ethical companies and government regulations have resulted in a large industry producing mainly high quality pelleted and coarse mix feeds (sweet feeds) often tailored for the different types or uses of the horse. The next section includes short communications from three horse feed manufacturers in the UK who explain their particular involvement in certain areas of this development into the common and widespread use of commercial horse feeds.

Spillers: The Development of Pelleted Feeds for Horses

"The animal feed industry has its roots in the human feed industry. The major animal feed companies either developed from using by-products of the oilseed crushing industries or from using by-products of flour milling. Spillers developed from the latter and had been producing feeds for farm livestock since the early part of this century.

In the postwar years the focus in agriculture was on maximum human food production and, in an increasingly mechanised environment, the feeding needs of horses were given less importance. Therefore the acreage of oats grown was declining steadily and new forms of harvesting meant that grain was taken directly from the field to the animals instead of the traditional method of maturing harvested oats in stacks. This was thought to have affected its nutritional value and palatability. In addition, to these changes, traditional meadow hay made on permanent pasture was becoming less available.

Nutritionists at Spillers therefore reasoned that it must be possible to make a nutritionally balanced cubed feed for horses using feed technology adapted from farm feeds. The principle was to use the traditional cereal by-products to make a versatile feed that could fuel a certain amount of work in the horse and if necessary replace some of the hay portion of the diet. Throughout the 1950s trials were carried out matching recipe to requirements until in 1958 Spillers Horse and Pony Cubes were launched which quickly became, and have remained, very popular over 40 years later.

Once the principle of the cubed feed was established, other variations quickly followed on and in the early 1960s Spillers produced the first racehorse, stud and complete cubed products."

The amount of energy available for use by the horse varies according to the feedstuff itself. Corn has more net (useable) energy than barley and oats. Barley has around twice that of good hay, which in turn is over twice that of wheat straw. It can be noted that, back in Grecian times, barley was referred to as aiding performance by providing additional energy over and above forage – possibly the first ergogenic aid. Although the basic type of grain fed to horses may be identical from the last few centuries to today (oats, barley, corn), there are differences in how they might be presented to horses. Back at the start of this century it was appreciated that crushing, soaking, boiling or parching certain grains, in particular corn and barley, helped improve the digestibility of these grains. It was also suggested that 'bruising' or 'crushing' improved the digestibility if not the storage of oats. Recent work, mainly carried out in Germany has looked at the effects of processing on precaecal starch digestibility. This showed considerable individual variability in precaecal starch digestion due partially to chewing activity and amylase activity. In general, processing had relatively little effect on the precaecal digestion of oat starch (around 80–90%) but it had a significant effect on barley and in particular corn precaecal starch digestibility, increasing from around 30, 50 to approximately 90% for whole, ground and popped corn respectively. Today many compound feeds fed to horses contain steam-cooked, micronised or extruded cereal grains with the aim of improving starch availability and precaecal digestion.

Baileys: Feeding Bread to Horses?

"Feeding bread to horses is not such a novel idea. In fact, it transpires that bread was fed to racehorses as early as the 17th and throughout the 18th and 19th centuries. Racehorses at that time were termed 'running' horses, as, contrary to today's practice, racing was over long distances and consequently horses required stamina and endurance. Staying power was the most important feature in a horse and this necessitated a nutritious diet with readily available energy. Before 1733, the diet consisted of barley, beans, wheatsheaves, butter, white wine and up to 25 cloves of garlic per feed. By 1733, feeding was fragmented into four fortnightly intervals, termed the First Bread, the Second Bread and so on, at which points the diet was altered subtly by changing the quantity of pecks of beans and wheat. In other words, the fitter the horse became the more wheat it had and the less beans.

The main ingredients of the stages consisted of:

	First bread	Second bread	Fourth bread
Pecks of clean beans	3	2	1
Pecks of fine wheat	1	2	3

The above were kneaded together and mixed with 'barm' (the froth on the top of fermenting malt liquors or yeast leaven) and 'lightning' (a strong alcoholic spirit) with only a little water and then baked. It was recommended that the bread should not be given before it was at least three days old and then mixed with oats. By the Fourth Bread the diet had been expanded to encompass yet more dairy products. The lightning was now replaced by 'new strong ale' and the whites of 20 eggs or more, with no water.

So why not feed bread to 20th century horses? George Knowles of Baileys horse feeds discovered that it had been fed before when his avid interest in all aspects of polo stimulated him to research equine nutrition. Bread is an excellent source of carbohydrate and, therefore, is ideal for promoting weight gain and coat condition and he found that horses looked good and performed well when fed dried breadcrumbs.

With the latest developments in equine nutrition bread is no longer used as a primary ingredient. However the principle of cooking cereals to improve digestibility remains the same. Bread is, in fact, the precursor of today's micronised wheat."

Dodson and Horrell: From Boiling Barley to Micronising Mueslis: The Development of Processing Cereals

"Throughout the 20th century and before, oats and peas were utilised as the main energy sources for horses. Historically, feeders of horses would boil barley and feed bread to put weight on a horse (both wheat and barley are excellent sources of starch). Unwittingly they were processing this starch when trying to put condition on a horse. Boiling barley and processing the wheat gelatinises the starch and makes the starch more available to the enzymes in the small intestine. Even today feeders are more inclined to feed barley rather than any other type of cereal to put weight on a horse, although now with the development of manufacturing technology there is no need so to do.

In the 1970s Dodson and Horrell pioneered the development of a completely new manufacturing technology known as micronising. Micronising builds on the traditional method of boiling to gelatinise starch but is obviously a considerably more controlled, sophisticated and scientific procedure. Cereals are first brought to a closely monitored moisture level and steeped in a manner similar to that used by the brewing industry, to hydrolyse the starch to a predetermined level. Each cereal type is then cooked for different times temperatures under infrared cookers to gelatinise the starch. The cereals are then precision flaked before cooling to maintain the stretch of the starch molecule and prevent it returning to its helical structure. As well as improving the digestibility of the starch, micronising effectively sterilise the cereals to human feed grade."

One of the major differences one would notice between the lists of feedstuffs considered suitable for horses at the beginning of the century and today would be the current inclusion of supplementary oil in the diets of many horses, especially competition horses, and the availability of high oil (~15%) commercially prepared complementary feeds. The major key to optimal sport performance has been said to be the proper production and control of energy. To this end, the appropriate biomechanical, psychological and physiological training, specific to the nature of the athletic event, will improve the control and utilisation of the various energy systems and maximise energy efficiency and production. However nutrition can also play a part.

WINERGY®: Feeding Supplemental Oil to Horses

"The horse evolved as a grazing animal which escaped predators by flight and is adapted to an almost constant supply of forage, which is predominantly digested in the hindgut. Today, the horse might be expected to carry a rider and undertake fairly exhausting, repetitive work. The horse, therefore, often needs more energy than would have been required out in the wild and often can not obtain sufficient energy from forage alone. This can be explained if we look at how the horse obtains its energy from its feed. The Gross (chemical) Energy (GE) of the feed is decreased by the energy lost through ingestion, foraging, chewing and then fermenting the feed. In addition, a fairly large proportion of the energy contained in the diet is not available to the horse and is lost in the faeces. This leaves us with the Digestible Energy (DE) content of a diet. Potential energy is also lost via gas production from the fermentation processes and via urea in the urine. This results in the Metabolic Energy (ME) content of the feed being lower than the Digestible Energy content. The conversion of the chemical energy in the feed to mechanical energy of movement etc. is not 100% efficient (energy being 'lost' as heat). So the actual energy or Net Energy (NE) available for work is even lower.

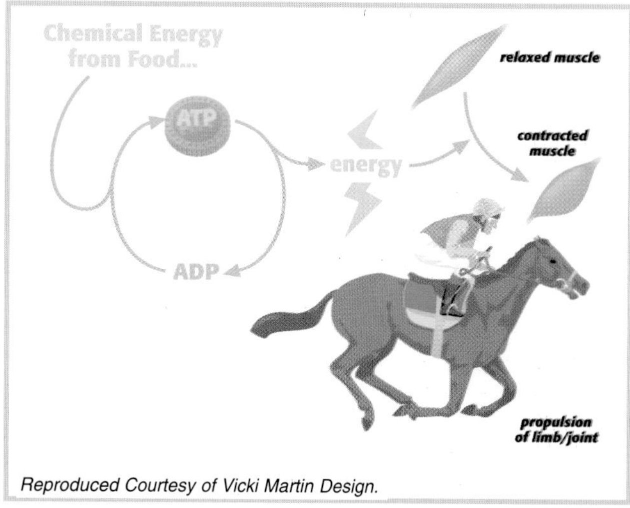

Reproduced Courtesy of Vicki Martin Design.

Oil is a very energy-dense nutrient, which has a high Net Energy value for the horse. Feeding supplemental oil can reduce the amount of concentrates that may need to be fed in order to maintain energy intake and, therefore, help to reduce the risks associated with high starch/sugar feeding in the horse. Supplemental oil feeding may also help to maintain the desired forage (low NE value in general) intake. Because the conversion of the chemical energy in oil to mechanical energy available to the horse is more efficient than for many other feedstuffs it can result in a decreased thermal load which may be very important under hot and humid conditions. Oil has many other potential advantages when horses are fed appropriately and trained on oil supplemented diets. WINERGY® provided the first balanced, fortified, high oil (~15%) coarse mixes for horses in Europe."

What about Minerals and Vitamins?

At the start of this century, as discussed later, very little was known about the importance of even the macrominerals; the role of trace elements had not been established and the work on vitamins was about to start. In an animal management manual published at the start of this century, it was stated that *"the addition of salt to a horse's food is not a necessity, they may be kept in the best condition without it, all the salt they actually require for the body's nourishment being contained in their food"*. No mention of salt could be found in some later nutrition books. Today, perhaps because of the increased demands placed on our horses (especially our competition horses), supplementary salt is considered an important part of the diet for a performance horse. It is now well appreciated that sodium requirements vary in line with the amount of sweat produced and a lot of research has recently been carried out into the electrolyte losses in the sweat of horses, in particular exercising those under conditions of high heat and humidity.

At the beginning of the century, while it was appreciated that mineral elements of lime were needed, especially for young growing animals, the importance of 'vitamins' and the trace elements was not appreciated. By the late 1920s calcium, sodium, potassium, magnesium, iron, phosphorus, chlorine, sulphur and iodine were known to be important. It was appreciated that other trace elements were also important *"but little is as yet known of their function"* and *"vitamins, or accessory food factors as many prefer to call them, are substances which, in view of the results of recent research work, we may assume to be definite chemical entities"... "they have a profound influence on the tissues of the body"... "at least five definite vitamins so far recognised"... "These have been denoted by the letters 'A', 'B', 'C', 'D' and 'E'"*. Selenium was not recognised as an essential nutrient until the 1950s. Vitamin B12 was not identified until the 1940s. This area is emphasised in the two articles by Professors Hintz and Meyer (p 153 and 158).

What of the Future?

Even in this author's time of feeding horses I have seen both the type of feeds fed and the nutritional advice given develop and change dramatically. Feedstuffs such as broad flaked wheat bran were commonly fed in my youth but are perhaps less common now, due both to a change in the nature of the bran itself and an increased appreciation of the nutrient content and the potential impact of feeding quantities of bran either consistently or intermittently. Coarse mixes have gained in popularity and I am sure that new formats and ingredients, which will benefit the horses that we feed, will be discovered. More practical and applicable ways of determining and assessing the nutritional content of feeds are needed, as well as a greater understanding of the potentially differing nutritional needs of horses competing in the various activities. A better appreciation of how and when to feed different categories of horses is also needed. In addition, a better understanding is needed of the effects of different feeds, as well as when, how and with what they are fed, on digestibility in various parts of the GIT and how the end products arising from the digestion of these different feeds are metabolised under different circumstances. The answers to these questions will enable us to be in a better position to modify horse diets in such a way to maximise, health and performance whilst minimising risks.

Developments in equine nutrition in the past century

HAROLD HINTZ
Cornell University
Ithaca
New York
USA

In the summer of 1998, the American Film Institute published a list of what they considered to be the hundred greatest American movies. Shortly after, Random House published a list of what they considered to be the hundred greatest American novels. In both cases there was considerable negative response. As might be expected, many film lovers and bibliophiles were upset because their favourites did not appear on the list. Dr B. M. W. Schrapnel wrote, "*The Random House roster is preposterously ignorant of contemporary literature. Only four of their selections were published after 1975.*"

The fear of lawsuits and, coincidently or perhaps incidently, the number of jokes about lawyers has greatly increased since 1900. It has become fashionable to put disclaimers on products. I hope that there will be no great furore caused by those who fail to find their favourite nutritional developments in the following pages nor do I expect any lawsuits. However, in the spirit of the times and of fair play, I put a disclaimer on this article. One of the admonitions of the editors was that I should enjoy writing it; I did. I have not attempted to rank the importance of the various developments. It is not a top ten list but rather a list of ten. Nor do I have any delusions that I have listed all the important world developments in equine nutrition. I include the developments that I enjoyed discussing and those that are most familiar to me; therefore, most of the developments discussed are those that originated from North America. Readers are encouraged to send me developments that they feel should have been included. Such suggestions should provide more than enough material for another article (perhaps at the end of the next millennium!). However, I hope those willing to send nominations will not label me as preposterously ignorant.

The term 'NAHMS survey' appears in several places in the article. This refers to the National Animal Health Monitoring System, which was an extensive survey of equine operations in the United States published in 1998. Operation in NAHMS does not refer to a surgical procedure but rather to "*an area of land managed as a unit by an individual, partnership or hired manager.*"

1. Calcium and Nutritional Secondary Hyperparathyroidism

It might seem odd that the impact of calcium on the skeletal integrity of the horse was not widely recognised until the 20th century. According to McCay, the importance of calcium was first demonstrated scientifically by Chossat in 1842 in experiments with pigeons. Röll in 1856 demonstrated that lions and cheetahs fed only meat developed skeletal malformations unless given bones or calcium supplements. But apparently this knowledge about the need for calcium for bone development was not effectively communicated to the horse industry. Many reports of 'big head' or osteoporosis can be found in publications for farmers and in veterinary journals published in the United States in the late 1800s and early 1900s. Reports published in the 1890s demonstrated that big head was common throughout the United States. In 1890, Berns reported that hundreds of horses were lost annually in New York City because of big head disease. Another report stated that of 220 horses owned by a railway company in Chicago, 47 had big head disease. When calcium is removed from the skull due to hyperparathyroidism caused by calcium deficiency, fibrous connective tissue increases and the head enlarges. Therefore, although the importance of calcium for bones was illustrated more than 50 years earlier, calcium deficiency was still widespread in horses throughout the United States. The horses suffered not only from the lack of calcium, but from the treatments of the disease as well. It was recommended by some that the swollen area of the head should be penetrated in several spots with a hot iron. Others suggested puncturing the enlarged area with an awl and pouring arsenic into the openings.

Many suggested causes of big head disease can be found in articles published during 1890 to 1910. The suggestions included poor ventilation due to poisonous gases (one author wrote that he never saw big head in horses in stables on the second floor or in stables with a cellar underneath), fungus infection, infectious disease and inherited disease. Many derided those that proposed it was a dietary problem. However, in the late 1890s and early 1900s, increased attention was given to nutrition. Some veterinarians reported that removing the grain from the diet and turning the horses out to pasture greatly improved the condition. Grain has a very low calcium content. Some reported that the feeding of wheat bran could induce big head (which, of course, was true because wheat bran contains a high concentration of phosphorus but little calcium, leading to a Ca:P imbalance). Others recommended the addition of lime to the water or feed of affected horses. But some veterinarians reported that lime was not of value and others even recommended that phosphorus should be added to the diet. The value of calcium was not readily accepted. Even as late as 1901, the famous veterinarian James Law wrote: "*We are still in the dark as to the essential cause of rarefaction of bone.... Faulty food - a lack of lime has been a favorite explanation....but there is a growing tendency to suspect a microbial origin.*" Dadd in 1920 wrote: "*Osteoporosis is a disease about which very little of a reliable character has ever been said or written.*" He wrote that incidence of the disease still seemed to be increasing and he considered it to be of hereditary origin.

However, in the 1920s and 1930s several experiments, such as those conducted by Niimi in 1927, Crawford in 1927 and Groenwald in 1937 provided evidence that could not be ignored. Calcium was the answer. Krook and Lowe in 1964 demonstrated that feeding a diet with an imbalance of calcium and phosphorus could cause lameness in growing horses within 12 weeks. Their elegant descriptions of the histological changes provided basic information about nutritional secondary hyperparathyroidism (NSH) which is a better term than big head disease.

However, in spite of the knowledge of the cause of NSH and the greatly improved methods of communication, NSH is still being reported. In the 1990s, there were reports of NSH in horses from Brazil, Japan, South Africa and Ethiopia. Therefore, the education of horse owners about the importance of calcium cannot be ignored.

Many studies since 1960 have increased our knowledge of calcium metabolism in horses, including information about endogenous losses and requirements. The elucidation of factors such as oxalic acid that inhibit calcium utilisation has significantly benefited the nutritional status of horses.

2. Selenium

Selenium is one of the most interesting of all minerals. It was named after the Greek goddess of the moon (Selene). Although selenium has fewer phases than the moon, it does have two distinct ones - a toxic phase and an essential phase. Selenium toxicity was recognised long before selenium was determined to be an essential nutrient. Trelease and Breath, in 1949, suggested that Marco Polo, in 1295, may have been referring to selenium toxicity when he noted that the eating of certain plants in what is now western China, caused "*the hoof of animals to drop off.*" Many areas of the United States, particularly in Nebraska, Wyoming, Montana, South Dakota and North Dakota, have soils with high concentrations of selenium. In fact it has been claimed that the US Cavalry lost more horses to selenium toxicity in the above areas than they lost in battles with the Indians. Wilcox, in 1944, suggested that Custer's fall at Little Big Horn was due partially to selenium toxicity. Troops that Custer requested to come to his aid did not reach him in time because their pack train travelled at a much slower rate than usual. They could travel only 10 miles/day rather than 30 miles as expected because the pack animals' feet were sore and some animals acted crazily, which may have been signs of selenium toxicity. The animals had been wintering in an area now recognised to have highly seleniferous soils. I relate this story to students to dramatise the effects of selenium toxicity. I conclude that Custer really died of selenium toxicity and point out that the loss of hair is also a sign of selenium toxicity. Of course, I do not think that the reserve troops could have saved Custer, even if they had arrived before his defeat, and Custer was not scalped. But the story helps make a point about selenium toxicity.

The discovery in the 1950s that selenium was essential for the prevention of white muscle disease has saved many foals. Selenium supplementation may also improve reproductive performance and help in the treatment of some cases of exertional myopathies. The addition of selenium to commercial horse feeds has greatly decreased the incidence of selenium deficiency in many parts of the world, but cases of deficiency in foals are still being reported. White muscle disease is rarely seen in mature horses but recently eight mature horses on a farm in Mexico apparently died because of severe muscle degeneration due to selenium deficiency.

Selenium can also be the basis for an excellent example of the interrelationships of minerals. Selenium and arsenic are antagonistic. A rancher in a high selenium soil area in Colorado was having no difficulties with selenium toxicity until he changed the water source for his animals. The initial water source contained arsenic, which negated some of the selenium in the feed. When the water with arsenic was no longer used, the horses developed selenium toxicity. Because of the selenium-arsenic interactions, I have suggested that Napoleon had a shortened life span because of selenium deficiency. Analyses of hair from Napoleon suggested that he had been given arsenic. If Napoleon had taken selenium pills, the effects of arsenic could have been prevented and perhaps he might have returned to France once again.

3. Copper and Zinc

A series of studies at Ohio State University greatly increased the awareness of the importance of trace minerals such as copper and zinc in the diets of young horses for the optimal development of the skeleton and prevention of developmental orthopedic disease. Recent studies from New Zealand demonstrated that the trace mineral content of the diet of a pregnant mare can also significantly influence the skeletal development of the foal.

4. Changes in Growth Rate

Horses grow at a faster rate now, than they did in the late 1890s and early 1900s. Perhaps the increased rate is because of more nutritional diets, increased feeding of grain and selection, intentional or unintentional, for increased rates of gain. The increased growth rate is not due to increased birth weight. The birth weight of foals seems to be about 9 or 10% of the mare's weight. Boussingault, in 1847, reported values of about 10%. Meston in 1894 also reported that the typical birth weight of a foal is 9 or 10% and studies in the 1980s and 1990s reported similar average values.

I reviewed four reports published from 1905 to 1945 that indicated horses of light breeds might be expected to attain 40, 60 and 73% of their mature weight at 6, 12 and 18 months, respectively. A review of eight reports published from 1969 to 1981 indicated that horses of light breeds might be expected to attain 46, 66 and 81% of their mature weight at 6, 12 and 18 months, respectively. Recent reports suggest that Thoroughbreds from Kentucky may be growing even faster. Therefore, it appears that horses are growing at a faster rate than they did during the early 1900s.

An increased rate of gain increases the daily requirements

for protein, vitamins and minerals. A more rapid growth is frequently associated with an increased incidence of developmental orthopaedic disease, which is perhaps related to an increased mineral and vitamin requirement or possibly because of other reasons.

5. Changes in Opportunities to Pasture Horse

What do metabolic bone disease and the movies *Jaws*, *ET*, *Raiders of the Lost Ark*, *Schindler's List* and *Jurassic Park* have in common? The answer is found later is this section.

One of the arguments for the increased need of fortified commercial horse feeds or supplements is that horses, in many parts of the world, do not have as great an opportunity to obtain as many nutrients from pasture as did their ancestors, due to the horse owner's desire to house horses near large population centres where adequate pasture may not be available. Pasture can be an excellent source of many nutrients. It can also help decrease the incidence of stable vices and digestive problems, such as colic. There is an old saying that Dr Green (pasture) can cure many problems. For example, equine motor neuron disease, which may be related to vitamin E deficiency, is found only in horses with no access to pasture. Therefore, there is no doubt that the absence of good quality pasture necessitates that greater attention be paid to the feeding programme to ensure that the supply of nutrients is adequate.

However, concern over the lack of pasture may not be of any greater significance now than it was in the late 1890s. The NAHMS survey indicated that the majority of horse operations in 1997 had pasture available during the summer. The average maximum number of equids/acre at one time was 0.8. But pasture may not be less available to more horses now than in the late 1800s. The large cities, in the late 1800s and early 1900s, required a great number of horses for hauling of goods and transportation. Michael Crichton has written many interesting novels such as *Disclosure*, *Rising Sun*, *The Andromeda Strain* and *Jurassic Park*. But the novel written by Mr Crichton that I enjoyed the most is *The Great Train Robbery*. In addition to an excellent plot, Mr Crichton also provided insights into life in London in the 1800s. He pointed out that there was great concern about traffic jams caused by horse-drawn vehicles. He wrote,

> *"In the midst of this [traffic jam] the street sweepers began their day's labours. In the ammonia-rich air, they collected the first droppings of horse dung, dashing among the carts and omnibuses. And they were busy: an ordinary London horse, according to Henry Mayhew, deposited six tons of dung in the streets each year, and there were at least a million horses in the city."*

It is unlikely these horses had significant exposure to pasture.

Large numbers of horses were housed in other major cities such as New York and Chicago. As mentioned in the section on calcium, many of these horses developed NSH. They were often housed in poorly ventilated, filthy stalls with no access to pasture.

Michael Crichton's novel *Jurassic Park* was made by Steven Spielberg into an enormously popular movie, which was credited as the cause of a great increase of interest in dinosaurs. The movie may have led to an increased interest in iguanas because of their resemblance to dinosaurs. In fact, in the first few years following the release of *Jurassic Park*, as many as one million iguanas were imported to the United States annually to be sold as pets. Many of these iguanas developed metabolic bone disease because of lack of calcium and sunlight. So what do the movies listed earlier in this section and metabolic bone diseases have in common? One might say they were all caused by Steven Spielberg because he directed all of the movies in the list and *Jurassic Park* led to bone disease in iguanas in the United States.

6. Increased Use of Commercial Feeds

The use of commercial feeds for horses has greatly increased, while the use of home-grown grains has decreased in the United States. The NAHMS survey indicated that 87% of the grain/concentrate fed to horses was purchased from a retail source in bags, 5% was purchased as bulk delivery and only 6% was home grown. Unpelleted sweet feed (grain mixed with molasses and usually fortified with protein, vitamins and minerals) was fed on 57% of all equid operations. Complete feed pellets or grain mix with pellets was fed on 40% of the operations. Commercial feeds are particularly useful in the United States because, according to the NAHMS survey, 79% of all equine operations have five or fewer horses. These operations are not likely to have significant feed mixing and storage facilities. It is much more convenient to purchase a feed and not be concerned about the need to add proper amounts of micronutrients. However, about one-third of horse owners purchase vitamin and mineral supplements. Commercial feeds also provide diets specifically designed for various classes of horses, such as weanlings, broodmares and performance horses. Another example of a speciality feed is that designed for geriatric horses which will be discussed later.

The diets for horses in the late 1800s and early 1900s probably provided adequate energy and protein, in most cases, but they may have been lacking in minerals and vitamins. The lack of calcium in the diets fed to horses in the 1800s and early 1900s was mentioned in Section 1. Many of these diets were very simple. Henry, in 1908, referred to studies conducted, in the 1870s and 1880s, with horses owned by the Paris Omnibus Company. The company employed about 10,000 horses, therefore even a small change in the cost of feeding a horse could have a major economic impact which is why they commissioned the studies. The typical diet was 18.7 lb oats and 1.8 lb wheat bran fed with hay and straw. In one study corn was used to replace 6.6 lb oats. Weight increased slightly. The horses were considered to be calmer when fed the corn and the company saved $9.26/horse/year. In another study, with 362 Paris horses, a diet of 9.5 lb oats, 6.7 lb corn, 2.1 lb horse beans, 1.1 lb bran, 10.4 lb hay and 11 lb straw was fed daily with no problems reported. Henry reported that the horses of US Cavalry weighed 950 to 1,150 lb and were fed 12 lb grain (varying mixture of oats, corn or barley) and 14 lb hay. German cavalry horses (average weight 1,050 lb) were fed 10 lb oats, 5.5 lb hay and 7.7 lb straw.

According to Henry, many horse owners preferred to feed a diet of oats and hay but he suggested that:

"When we consider the number and complexity of the components of bone and nerve, we can believe that these are better nourished by several kinds of grain and forage plants than by one or two only."

Some commercial feeds were available in the late 1800s and early 1900s. Most were of questionable nutritional value. Many contained inferior ingredients. Most were advertised to be fed to all species of livestock. Blatchford's Royal Stock Food of Chicago, Illinois was advertised in 1886 as the most complete feeding cake ever made and to be invaluable for cattle, horses, swine and sheep. Raven's Horse, Cattle and Poultry Food was claimed in 1893 to make hens lay, cure cholera and improve breeding animals. H.O. Horse Feed in 1898 contained only oat feed (by-products from the manufacturer of oatmeal for man) and corn. Blomo, in 1903, was a mixture of dried blood, molasses and ground corn stalks.

Some commercial feeds were recommended by the Experiment Stations. In 1893, a report from New Jersey said:

"A farmer who intelligently exchanges farm products for commercial feeds may secure not only an increase in feeding value but also a gain in fertility."

A report from Massachusetts in 1914 indicated that some commercial horse feeds were very satisfactory but usually more expensive than home-mixed foods.

By the 1930s, commercial horse feeds contained added calcium which helped reduce the incidence of NSH. By-products which were effective sources of B-vitamins were also included and most companies provided better quality ingredients than those found in some of the earlier feeds.

7. Use of Body Scores to Evaluate Horses

Body score systems to evaluate body condition and body fat have been developed for most livestock. Systems are available for beef cattle, dairy cattle, sheep and swine. Systems are also available for dogs, cats and some exotic animals.

Some forms of body score systems for horses were used in ancient times. Xenophon (430–355 BC) recommended that horses should have a double back, which I assume means that the areas along both sides of the vertebrate should be developed so that a groove is formed. Columella (65 AD) recommended that horses have a double seat. Oppian (200 AD) recommended that horses have a double chine. Morgan in 1893 wrote:

"Horses are in good condition when the flesh rises on each side of the spine so that the latter does not stick up like a ridge but lies in a slight depression."

In modern times, the interest in body scores of horses was stimulated by Henneke and colleagues in the early 1980s. They published papers that described a detailed body score system and demonstrated the significant relationship of body score and reproductive efficiency. The papers by Henneke and others such as Carroll and Huntington, in 1988, demonstrate clearly that body scoring can be an effective management tool and its use should be encouraged. Energy requirements have been estimated for horses but there is considerable variation among horses. Therefore, the best indicator of energy adequacy of the diet is the horse. A body score system is an organised method by which the horse can be evaluated.

8. Use of Supplemental Fat

Dr Larry Slade and co-workers, at Colorado State University, reported, in 1975, that the addition of fat to the diet of horses performing prolonged exercise could be beneficial. A similar finding was reported from Cornell University. Extensive studies conducted at Texas A&M University, by Dr Gary Potter and colleagues, demonstrated that fat supplementation could be beneficial for many classes of horses. Benefits of fat supplementation include the potential to delay onset of fatigue, increase nutrient density, lessen gut fill, reduce chance of founder when some of the calories supplied by starch are replaced, decrease heat production which could be beneficial when exercise is performed during hot weather, and improve performance in horses with polysaccharide storage disease and geriatric horses.

I do not know how many horses are fed supplemental fat, but many feed companies provide formulations that contain supplemental fat and it appears that many horse owners use products such as rice bran, which contains 20% fat, or corn oil. A survey conducted by Kristin Goodrich in 1997 indicated that 96% of the entrants in the Western States Endurance Ride, one of the premiere endurance rides in the United States, gave supplemental fat to their horses.

There are historical reports on the use of supplemental fat in horses. Sydney, in *The Book of the Horse* in 1856, wrote,

"The Arabians fed their horses balls of barley flour kneaded with sheep tail fat. The horses could go 150 miles per day."

In 1886, Loudon wrote in *Encyclopedia Agricultura:*

"In parts of India, salt, pepper and other spices are made into balls, as big as billiard balls with flour and butter, and thrust down the horse's throat."

Perhaps the horses developed more endurance by working to get away from such treatment. In any case, the use of supplemental fat was not common until the latter part of the 20th century.

9. Nutrition of Geriatric Horses

The number of geriatric horses has increased in the United States. It has been estimated that 10 to 15% of all horses are age 20 years or more. The increase is probably due to better veterinary care, such as improved parasite control, and changes in the function of the horses. The majority of horses in the United States are now used for recreation rather than for work. Recreational use is usually not as hard on the horse as heavy work. Many of the owners of recreational horses have strong bonds with their animals and are willing to spend resources to keep older animals, even when the ability to function has decreased. Some older horses do not need special care or nutrition, but some respond to diets that contain higher concentrations of protein and less fibre, and a more digestible fibre than is usually provided horses. The addition of fat provides a highly digestible energy source. Purina Mills was the first company to manufacture a feed specifically designed for geriatric horses on a national basis. Many other manufacturers now provide diets for senior horses. The NAHMS survey found that about 8% of all equine operations purchase some geriatric rations. Of course, other factors such as dental and veterinary care are needed to prolong the lives of the horses but the geriatric diets can be very useful.

Another indication of the number of older horses is that the NAHMS survey claimed "*the largest percentages of death for equines more than 30 days of age were attributed to old age [29.5%].*" The comedian Steven Wright once asked: *"How old does a person have to be to die of old age?"* The same can be asked for horses. Of course no horse really dies of old age but rather from complications that happen in old horses. Nevertheless it appears evident that equine life expectancy has increased significantly. Previously, life expectancy was thought to be 20 to 25 years for horses but now 30 to 40 years does not seem unreasonable.

10. Sources of Information about Horse Nutrition

The NAHMS survey confirmed earlier reports that, in the United States, the veterinarian is considered by horse owners to be the most important source of information about horse nutrition. Eighty-five percent of equine operations said the veterinarian was a very important or a somewhat important source. Seventy-two percent said the same about feed store personnel and 64% said the same about the farrier. Only 31% of operations considered the extension agent or university instructor and only 30% an equine nutritionist to be important sources of nutrition information.

Conclusion

Many changes have taken place since 1900. And many more will take place in the future. More sophisticated and elegant procedures are available to study the nutrition of the horse but many questions remain to be answered.

Acknowledgements

The author thanks Terry Kinsman and Katie Simmons for their indispensable help in the preparation of this manuscript.

References

Anon (1989) *Nutrient Requirements of Horses*, National Academy Press, Washington DC.

Henneke, D.R., Potter, G.D., Kreider, J.L. and Yeates, B.F. (1983) Relationship between condition score, physical measurement, and body fat percentage in mares. *Equine vet. J.* **15**, 371-372.

Henry, W.A. (1908) *Feeds and Feeding*, 8th edn, W.A. Henry, Madison, Wisconsin.

Hintz, H.F. (1983) *Horse Nutrition: A Practical Guide,* Arco. Publ., New York.

Krook, L. and Lowe, J.E. (1964) Nutritional secondary hyperparathyroidism in the horse. *Path. Vet. 1, Suppl.* **1**, 1-98.

National Animal Health Monitoring System (NAHMS) (1998) *Part I. Baseline Reference of 1998 Equine Health and Management. Part II. Baseline Reference of 1998.* Equine Health and Management, USDA.

Slade, L.M., Lewis, L.D., Quinn, C.R. and Chandler, M.L. (1975) Nutritional adaptations of horses for endurance performance. *Proceedings of the 4th Equine Nutrition Society.* pp 114-128.

Horse nutrition in central Europe: 1000 years of empirical knowledge, 100 years of research

HELMUT MEYER
c/o Institute für Tierernahrung
Bischofsholer Damm 15
D-30173 Hannover
Germany

"*A horse! A horse! My kingdom for a horse!*" was King Richard III's plea at the end of a hopeless battle. However, one horse alone would not have been enough to help him if it was not, or could not be, properly fed. The horse owner, however, seldom talks about the horse's feed; to him its pedigree, physical advantages and character are of much more importance. This is the reason why I would like to venture on a 'ride' into the history of horse nutrition, because it is so closely related to the practice of the veterinary art and science.

When the West Roman Empire collapsed in the 5th century, it took several hundred years before the horse was again able to play a central role in trade, agriculture and war as a power source for the transportation of people and merchandise. How was this power source fed? What was considered to be suitable, how much and in which composition? These questions have been answered over time, starting from the lifetime of Charles the Great and throughout the following 1000 years, by trial and error and learning from positive and negative experiences.

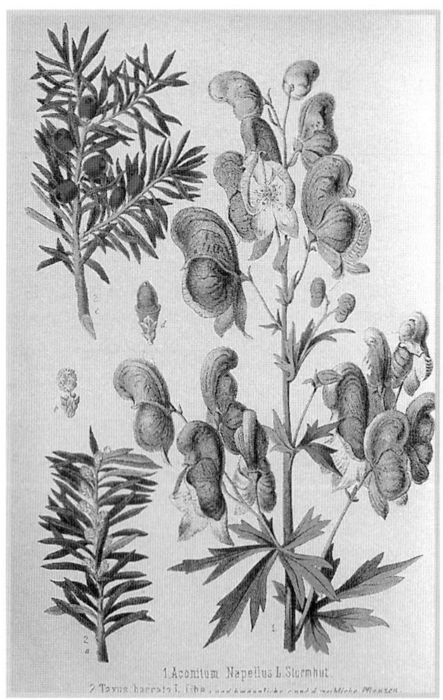

Fig 1: Painting of toxic plants in veterinary textbooks: Aconitum napellus *and* Taxus baccata*; from Dammann, K. (1886):* Gesundheitspeflege. *Parey, Berlin.*

Initial reports were mainly verbal, but with the invention of printing, discoveries could be recorded. M. Fugger's 1578 work *From The Studfarm*, for example, is an in-depth description of how a stud of good, expensive warhorses was looked after and fed.

Veterinarians: Pioneers in the Nutritional Science for Horses

With the founding of veterinary schools at the end of the 18th century, veterinary teachers started to gather information based on experiences over the previous 1000 years in the field of horse nutrition. The first ever book published on this subject was by the Scottish veterinary teacher J. Clark. His *Treatise on the Prevention of Diseases Incidental to Horses* (1788) was a great success, being published in the USA and translated into several European languages. Later the continent was dominated by G.C. Haubner's book *Care of Health* (1845, 4th edn 1881) which carried much more extensive information on food for horses, their likes and dislikes, and feeding technology, with possible connections between feeding and diseases. The first book entirely dedicated to general horse nutrition (not just dietetics), was written by the Dutch veterinarian H. Mars and entitled *De Voeding en de Voedsels van het Paard in Nederlandisch-Indie* (1887) (The Feeding and Feedstuffs of Horses in Dutch India).

At the end of the 19th century, when scientific experiments on horse nutrition began, veterinarians remained leaders in the field of horse nutrition, even though many agricultural researchers, including Wolff of Stuttgart-Hohenheim in 1886, had also started to think about the subject on behalf of the agricultural workhorse. However, with the decline of the farmhorse during the second half of the 20th century, science in this area in Central Europe shifted again, mainly to veterinary medical schools.

Results from Empirical Knowledge and Research - a Comparison

Veterinary reports on nutrition that date from the time of purely empirical knowledge about feeding suitability, appropriate quantities and preparations are relatively near the mark. Much of this material can still be found in modern scientific books on horse nutrition. For example,

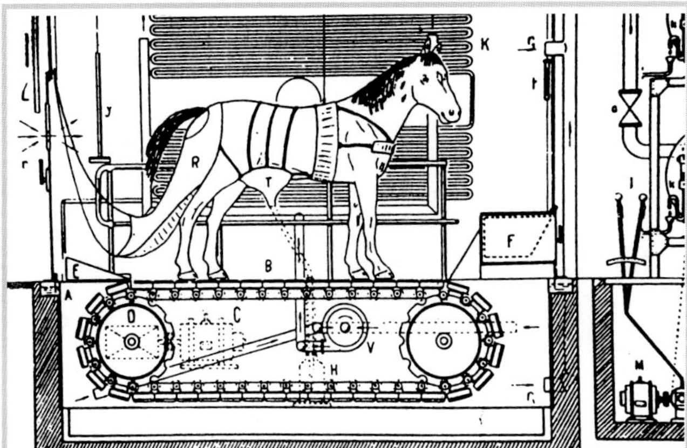

Fig 2: Chamber for respiration and balance experiments with a treadmill. Leipzig-Mockern after Fingerling.

Fig 3: Taking a sample from a horse with a caecal fistula; Hannover 1980.

Fig 4: Big Head; from Leblanc, P, Cadeac, C. Carougeau, C. (1902): Pathologie Chirurgicale Generale. *Balliere, Paris.*

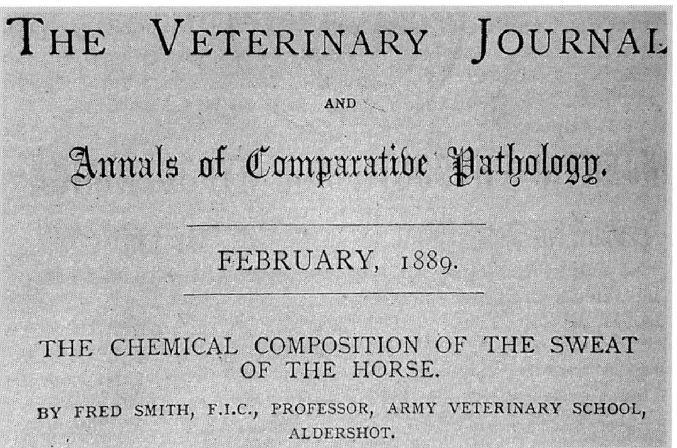

THE VETERINARY JOURNAL

AND

Annals of Comparative Pathology.

FEBRUARY, 1889.

THE CHEMICAL COMPOSITION OF THE SWEAT OF THE HORSE.

BY FRED SMITH, F.I.C., PROFESSOR, ARMY VETERINARY SCHOOL, ALDERSHOT.

Fig 5: Title page of the publication by Professor Smith on the chemical composition of horse sweat.

valid information on poisonous plants and their effects has been explained in depth and carefully sketched in the books of the 19th century (Fig 1). If a comparison is made between recommended feed for certain energy requirements for gravid or lactating mares, foals or military horses, in the 18th or 19th century and today, it can be seen that they are quite close. A thousand years of empirical knowledge, therefore, drew similar conclusions to 100 years of scientific research. However, there are important differences. In earlier times, knowledge of the basic reasons for the recommendations was nonexistent and, in addition, empirical data only becomes valid after a considerable period and are costly to acquire.

When in 1876 the Austrian army asked the question, "Oats or maize?" hundreds of horses in 60 military units received the same quantity of either oats or maize over a period of approximately two months. Independent observers were given the task of carefully evaluating the horses and from 60 main reports discovered that feeding maize to horses led to improved physical condition and the horses were stronger and sweated earlier. According to recent findings, this can be traced to the digestibility and energy content of maize, and the localisation of maize starch digestion within the intestinal tract (mostly within the large intestine). However, back then, such issues could be decided only on a speculative basis and it was assumed that maize was more digestible than oats. Actual values for the digestibility of different grains had eventually to be derived from initial tests with pigs and ruminants.

Early Motives for Nutritional Research - Clarification of Causes of Illnesses

Although nutritional research became popular during the 19th century, with animals (especially dogs) as well as humans being investigated, the diet of horses did not improve immediately with the new understanding of the digestive tract and metabolism (Fig 2). However, G. Colin (1825–1896) in Paris, W. Ellenberger (1848–1929) in Dresden and N. Zuntz (1847–1920) in Berlin started work on the digestive physiology and metabolism of horses, later continued by A. Scheunert (1897–1957) in Leipzig and by F. Alexander (1917-1998) in Edinburgh, after the Second World War. They were able to build a basis for the rational, specific feeding of the horse and also supply information on the pathogenics of the most feared illness in horses, colic.

In the 1970s and 1980s, when this work was continued, there was a significant interaction between the progress in the abdominal surgery of horses on the one side and nutritional physiological examinations on the other. Modern surgical technology, in comparison with earlier techniques going back to the 19th century, meant that it was now possible to carry out permanent fistulatomy lasting months or years (Fig 3). This opened the door to the detailed study of processes within the digestive tract, e.g. the enormous water and electrolytic circulation within the intestine, as well as the passage of food and its digestion within different sections of the intestinal tract. With this knowledge it was possible to improve therapeutic measures and clarify pathogenesis of different illnesses, particularly colic but also laminitis.

It became progressively clearer that mistakes in hygiene, the quality and quantity of rations and faults in the preparation of food were the most important causes of colic, although some veterinary practitioners still remained loyal to explanations based on weather, neurodystonia or parasites.

Other research activities in this century have been based on deficiency illnesses such as calcium or iodine deficiency and others that were already known or assumed (selenium or copper) or ignored (sodium, chloride). Ways and means to gain the required knowledge are not always straightforward and problems do not only appear when and where we have the necessary knowledge and research capabilities to solve them. When veterinarians and research groups in different countries with different parts of the puzzle work together, however, research can be stimulated and the solutions made easier. An example of this can be seen with big head (*Osteodystrophia fibrosa*) (Fig 4). This condition was a problem in the last century, mainly in the USA, South Africa, the Philippines and Australia, countries which at that time unfortunately lacked research establishments. Ideas about the causes of big head remained speculative up to the turn of the century: damp stables, bad ventilation, sour grass and, of course, infection were fashionably mentioned. Therapy was correspondingly exotic and included tooth extraction, burning, and rubbing down with tar or lard. Looking back, it has been said of the veterinary practitioners of the time within the USA "*that they existed in the main as ignorant as the animals they treated*".

European veterinary practitioners had fewer problems with this illness because it did not occur as often and then only after excessive feeding with bran (Miller's disease). The question was posed whether it was possible to influence positively or even prevent this illness by changing diet. Histological examination and bone analyses in the middle of the last century allowed the cause of big head to be traced. However, the comprehensive clarification of the condition and some of its accompanying clinical signs (e.g. nonspecific lameness) did not originate from Europe but in areas with big head problems, e.g. Japan, India, Ceylon and South Africa. In-depth surveys on the calcium and phosphorus intake, together with digestibility and dietary balance studies, were carried out in the first third of the 20th century. We can mainly thank veterinary officers posted to the abovementioned countries for these examinations. But it was not until 1940 that the American H. Schmidt carried out an in-depth scientific evaluation and determination of the calcium and phosphorus requirements of a horse.

In the 1970s, decisive examinations were initiated on calcium, phosphorus and magnesium metabolism, first in the USA, then later in Europe. Intestinal metabolism was further clarified, e.g. the influence of phosphorus and oxalic acid on calcium absorption, regulation of blood content and renal excretion. Basic data for estimating calcium and phosphorus requirements for gravid and lactating mares or growing foals are now available.

Old problems (such as hypocalcaemia in mares) or new questions (hypocalcaemia in high-performance horses) are now being tackled. A significant gap, however, between practical problems and scientific findings has tended to characterise questions of electrolyte metabolism. For instance, even though there was a death rate of approximately 10% during the long distance rides that were the fashion in the military around the turn of the century, e.g. from Berlin to Vienna, Strasbourg to Granada, Saarbrücken to Rome, Metz to Bucharest, Peking to Tientsin, to mention only a few, and these competitions were cynically completed under the heading of "*with or without the death of the horse*", there was little effort made to explain these deaths. However, after 1889, when Professor Smith at the Army Veterinary School in Aldershot published his analysis on the sodium, chloride and potassium content of horse sweat, still valid today (Fig 5), it should have been common knowledge that horses lose a significant amount of water and electrolyte fluids when sweating. This work should have had an important impact in clarifying such deaths. Unfortunately, Smith's results remained in the academic sphere and were hardly ever mentioned. The suggestion that this link was practically important came in the 1960s from a hot country, Egypt, whose scientists gave the subject of cutaneous water and electrolyte losses in horses much more attention. Subsequent projects clarified many details and drew attention to how best to improve the supply of such elements before and during long rides.

Research into trace elements has thrown up many curiosities that would have been totally unforeseeable if they had not been revealed by life itself. One such example is the importance of iodine to the horse. Due to its deficiency, goitre in a horse was once as common as it was in human subjects and other domesticated animals. When, in 1940, reports appeared about goitres in foals whose dams were fed on seaweed, no one knew why. It was not until 30 years later that the cause of this paradoxical phenomenon became apparent, that an excess of iodine was as liable as a deficiency to result in this condition (Fig 6).

This discovery was made firstly by the in-depth study of the human medical literature (where the problem was well known), secondly by the careful observations of two veterinary practitioners, and thirdly by coincidence, when two related stud managers, whose studfarms were 1000 miles apart, realised that they had both fed a seaweed

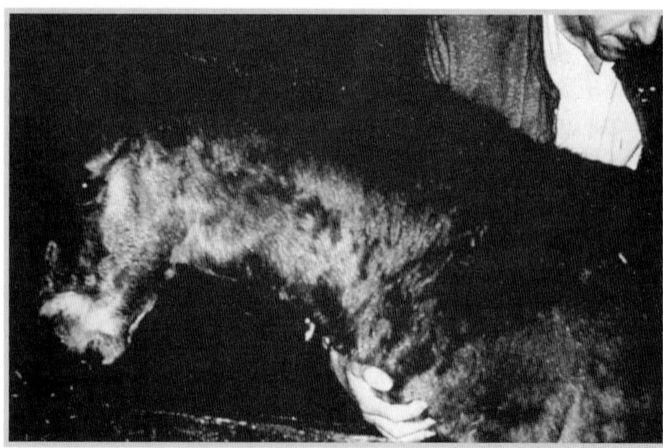

Fig 6: Foal with goitre after excessive iodine intake of its mother; from Silva et al. *(1987)* Pferdeheilkunde *3, 271-276.*

TABLE 1: Original publications concerning minerals and vitamins in horses in Europe and North America.

Period	Macro elements		Trace elements		Vitamins	
	Europe	North America	Europe	North America	Europe	North America
1900–1950	91	31	48	16	41	37
1951–1979	96	84	67	42	83	40
1980–1995/96	98	72	62	95	68	43

From Ohlendorf (1998).

preparation to their gravid mares. This pointed to a new phenomenon in horse nutrition: from deficiency to excess! Moderation is not a human quality, not even when feeding animals. There are sufficient examples to illustrate this statement, e.g. energy, protein, vitamin A and vitamin D. There are, for example, more reports on the causes of vitamin D excess, than vitamin D deficiency, in horses. However, behind the abuse of vitamin D there is a further mistake, namely the uncritical transfer of findings gained from other species. The horse is no rat with hooves, it has its own distinctive characteristics, even in its specific metabolism. Vitamin D metabolism in horses seems to differ from that reported in other species. Selenium and copper are further examples. When, during the last century and the first half of this one, selenium was described as a toxic danger, nobody anticipated that in many parts of the world there was an urgent need to include it in horse food. Reports from Scandinavia, for example, spoke of damaged muscles in foals long before the discovery that selenium is an essential element. Regional environments clearly have a part to play in horse nutrition.

Copper enjoys a different history. Between 1920 and 1930, scientists in Trakehnen, East Prussia, had already tried to get poorly growing foals 'back on their feet' with the so-called 'Trakehnen Copper Solution'. The only empirical knowledge they had was the fact that copper acts as a roborant. However, this had been long forgotten when approximately 50 years later copper was 'rediscovered' in Kentucky after indications that it could play a role in the development of orthopaedic diseases (DOD) in foals. After initial euphoric activity and heavy counter-attacks, it was not until the dust had settled that the truth gradually emerged, as often occurs in science. Copper supply for gravid mares and copper storage in the fetal liver should be observed, but copper was not the only answer to all DOD problems.

Europe and North America in Competition

During the 19th century, Europe seemed to be the only continent that carried out nutritional research on horses. The Americans at that time were dependent on the flow of European science information. Even in the first half of the 20th century, Europe clearly dominated research on quantitative values and trace elements. Apart from work in vitamin research, this changed in the second half of the 20th century, when North America drew level with or even overtook Europe; a case of the pupil starting to teach the master. Of course, the number of publications in itself does not reveal anything about the quality of the work; however, generally this has increased in standard on both sides of the Atlantic.

TABLE 2: Components and nutrients of a feedconserve[1] from the German army (World War I).

Components	(%)[1]	Nutrients/kg[2]
Oats	42	95 g digestible crude protein
Yeast	8	11 MJ digestible energy
Potato flocks	27	130 g crude fibre
Hay, chopped	13	
Straw, chopped	10	

[1]Pressblocks of about 5 kg; [2]Calculated.

Aiming for New Horizons

As long as the horse was used in farming, up to the middle of the 20th century, feeding on farms remained conventional. Hay and oats were the 'daily bread' for horses. It was the urban transport firms and especially the military, who demanded a handy, concentrated, easily transportable and space-saving feed. Those requirements were met by the English horse biscuit or the bread loaf, which were on offer in the 19th century. During the Franco-German war of 1870–71, necklace-like strings of feeding breads were often seen hanging from the saddles of the cavalry, while the Prussian military had already tried products like the so-called 'Russian rusk' at the beginning of the century. However, pea bread, tested by the Prussian Horse Guard, was unsuccessful.

As commercially produced supplements were added to roughage in the civilian arena, 'tonic feeds' also became the fashion for horses at the turn of the century. They contained special herbs in addition to the usual components, and also several undefined substances. This reminds us of today's herbal feeds, which are enjoying a renaissance after 100 years despite the fact that apart from their fragrance there is not much substantial evidence on their effects. Maybe we should take to heart some advice given in 1906 in a Louisiana report: "*If your animals are in good health, they need no tonic and if they are sick it is cheaper to consult a veterinarian.*"

The horsemen of the army tried persistently to come up with a complete feed. Before the First World War, for example, a food preserve was developed in Germany and pressed in blocks, which besides oats, hay and straw also contained malt germs, draff, barley, molasses, sesame and peanut cakes. The raw protein content was relatively high, obviously because they were unable to distance themselves from Justus von Liebig's (1803–1873) erroneous theory, which supposed protein to be broken down by working muscles. Even today, there are so-called 'horse experts' who believe the secret forces of protein influence muscle movement performance.

During the Second World War the German army, which at that time had more than one million horses, introduced feed preservatives. The Russians also conducted successful trials in the 1930s. The products, which had a similar energy density to oats, had the character of a complete feed, mainly because of their high content of chew-stimulating raw fibres.

Current thinking on the numerous trials (mainly carried out by the military), to produce a mixed feed, is that they tend to look like finger exercises for the benefit of the mixed feed industry. Soon after the Second World War, particularly from the 1960s onwards, a new phase of horse nutrition started. In mixed feed, oats are partly or totally replaced with by-products or other grains. However, those feeds were offered as pellets or cobs after the extensive crushing of the components also containing raw fibre. The American army, thinking more economically than the Germans or Russians, already used this product at the end of the Second World War. As the pelleting required the fine chopping of components containing chew-stimulating fibre, these mixed feeds, contrary to some intentions, were unsuitable as a complete feed. In the civilian area after the war it was not practical to pay such a high cost for the preparation, storage and transport of a complete feed, even though it had been standard procedure for the military in Central Europe during the war.

Mixed feeds as a complementary or crib food have now asserted themselves, despite several problems and reservations, because they contain the complete nutritional requirement in one ration, rather than in individual grain varieties. Deficiency illnesses can therefore almost be discounted by their usage. New technologies have made it possible to include many new components in the mixed feed by simultaneously reducing the oat content.

Oats have been favoured over other grains for feeding horses for approximately 1000 years in Central Europe. This is for good reason, as we have finally discovered. Its advantages stem not just from the high husk proportion, which is responsible for the improved tolerance by safeguarding loose storage within the stomach, but more importantly from the high precaecal digestibility of the smaller grain oat starch in comparison to maize or barley starch, despite the low amylase activity in the small intestine of the horse. This helps to ensure good utilisation in the small intestine, so preventing excessive starch reaching the large intestine and causing potential digestive disturbances. Through technical know-how during feed preparation it is currently possible for the mixed feed industry accurately to measure differences between individual grains and to influence their digestion. However, there are questions remaining, especially as regards a truly complete feed. The mixed feed industry still remains an important motor and sponsor in the nutritional science of horses in today's postmilitary phase of the role of the horse.

There is another area which supports the research into horse feeding: the so-called 'horse industry' with its focus on the racehorse. This has driven work in two main directions, namely the influence of feed on fertility and secondly and perhaps more importantly, on racing performance. While today it is clear that certain mistakes in feeding have led to a failure in reproduction, convincing progress is still lacking on the effect of nutrition on racing performance area. Despite

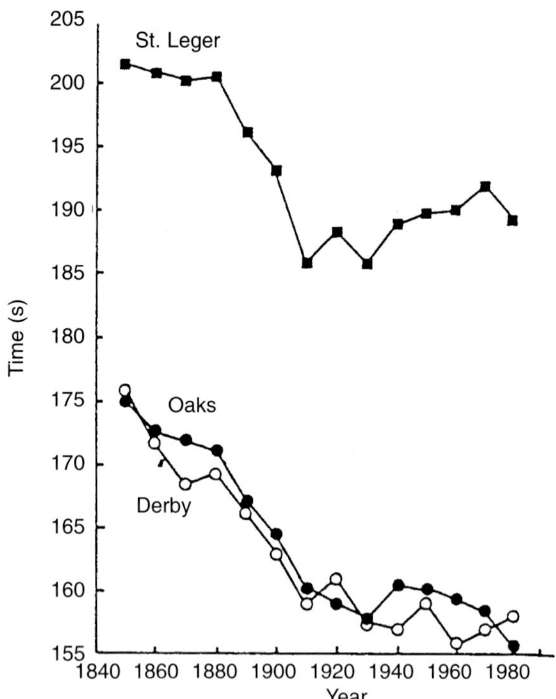

Fig 7: Trends in winning times of the 3 principal classic races in the UK. Ten year average winning times are plotted. From Gaffney, B. and Cunningham, E. P. (1988), Nature *332, 722-723 with permission.*

concerted efforts in breeding, training and feeding, horses have not improved their speed during the last 70 years (Fig 7). Therefore, the search for a feed or feed supplement that works like a catalyst on horses and makes them faster, could still be compared with the efforts of the mediaeval alchemists to produce gold.

'Feeding to win' misrepresents the possibilities of feeding in relation to performance. We cannot expect miracles from feeding in general or from single nutrients. However, if feeding is inadequate, we should not be surprised if a horse's performance is somewhat less than could have been achieved otherwise. In this context 'feeding not to lose' would be a better expression, because research suggests nutrients cannot improve performance beyond the physical capability of an animal.

If one looks back over the last 100 years of scientific research and practice in the feeding of horses, one realises, paradoxically, that the horse, a peaceful creature which tends to flee rather than fight, has profited largely from the activities of military vets. It has not been until the second half of the 20th century that new promoters have appeared in the research of nutrition for horses. However, on a long-term basis, horse owners and friends of the horse have to determine for themselves the direction of nutritional research. The only aim must be the horse's welfare. Our challenge is to develop species-specific, health-promoting nutrition to ensure a long, well-fed life.

Equine medicine as a speciality

DOUG BYARS
Hagyard-Davidson-McGee, PSC
Equine Internal Medicine Hospital
4250 Ironworks Pike
Lexington, Kentucky 40511
USA

During the preparation of this article our profession sadly lost one of the founding specialists in large animal internal medicine, Dr Bill Rebhun. Bill brought clinical knowledge, expertise and a commitment to teaching with a fun-loving camaradarie to his colleagues and students. Bill left us too soon at age 51, and this article is respectfully dedicated to him.

It seems to me that all practising veterinarians practise 'medicine'. Our background education gives us the means by which we identify the problem and arrive at some form of diagnosis. Eventually we reach for a syringe to complete the task of practising the administration of 'medicine'.

This historical perspective began a rapid evolution some 25–30 years ago as key players within institutions began emphasising medicine in their academic careers, and academicians gradually carved niches within their departments and later in the private sector. The latter started in Newmarket, England, with the pioneering work of Peter Rossdale and Sidney Ricketts who gracefully brought academic medicine to the private sector and presented the challenges of equine reproduction and neonatal medicine to the rest of the world.

In the United States, academic specialists cornered other organ system diseases. Humphrey Knight tackled respiratory disease, Bud Tennant focused on liver disease, Al Merritt drifted onto diarrhoea and gastroenterology, Joe Mayhew chose neurological disease and Bob Whitlock and Tom Divers let our profession realise that horses had kidneys that could fail. Medicine created an outlet for personalities best described as problem solvers with patience, somewhat different to our surgeon mentors who liked to 'get on with it'. Medicine was initially a discipline perceived as too slow and too complicated, but a necessary part of practice that a few took to heart.

Medicine is performed routinely by each veterinarian whether their personal speciality is surgery, theriogenology, ophthalmology, or any other practice preference we enjoy. Medicine epitomises the structured principles of the diagnostic, therapeutic and prognostic approach, but then so does veterinary medicine in general.

Test for Inflammation of the bladder. *From Edward Mayhew, reprinted with kind permission of the Royal College of Veterinary Surgeons Library.*

"We learn and teach so much information it is easy to forget the benefits of a proper physical examination." - I. G. Mayhew

So how is it medicine is now considered a speciality? Part of the reason is the information explosion, with too much to know, and the advent of technology. Also, there is the fact that the public's perceptions and expectations of human medicine are now being applied to their animals. Then there were those of us who fit that niche of wanting to know more about specific problems but still liked a bit of everything. Medicine was perfect, as we could be recognised as specialists and still do the eyes, heart, skin, kidneys, nerves, etc., yet recognise that we are not ophthalmologists, cardiologists, dermatologists, urologists or neurologists. We became members of an 'umbrella' speciality that knew a little more about of lot of different things, although less than the true organ specialists. Internal medicine became a referral buffer from our colleagues in general practice as well as a triage group to the elite specialist concerned with a single body organ or system.

During the 20th century human medicine organised into services far beyond the 'country doctor'. Surgery became the discipline that introduced the public to a hospital facility with designs and staff capable of improved care. Groups of physicians and staff communicated on a daily basis and individuals emerged with special interests. Over time, specialities emerged which formalised into colleges with speciality examinations for credentials. The support professions of nursing and laboratory technicians also matured and a gradual exodus of specialists from academic institutions occurred into the private sector.

Eventually, large hospital and research facilities followed, complete with mandatory internships and residency training programmes within the medical profession. Today, both general practitioners, often with advanced family practice training, and specialists exist within communities, at community hospitals and with respective local offices. Veterinary medicine has followed the same course, albeit at a slower pace because of economics and the commitment to the rural community.

But the course is set and we will continue to follow the lead of human medicine as regards what is professionally realistic. Wherever human medicine has gone and stayed, we will also go, although the product of our services will be customised to veterinary medicine. Speciality boards are now commonplace and spreading throughout the world of veterinary medicine as recognition and application of clinical expertise. This response is the result of the precedent established by human medicine, the educational changes within the veterinary curriculums and the public awareness of increasing veterinary medical services along with the recognition of liabilities.

The trek behind human medicine began to show itself with hospitals, diagnostic facilities, support staffing and recognition by referring veterinarians who similarly recognised the information explosion and the benefits of technology. Most knew there was too much now for everyone to know and that attorneys were primed to be sure of it. The wide application by capable group practices created a professional environment capable of absorbing the infiltration of clinical 'experts' into the private sector, the current arena for one of our profession's growth opportunities.

So if the stage was set, who were other players and what happened to establish the momentum? The pioneering of Rossdale and Ricketts provided the credibility of practitioners by the recognition of their scholarly publications. Visiting clinicians and a generation of students, such as John Freestone and Fairfield Bain, travelled to England to study.

> *"The laboratory results can be wrong, but they keep giving the same consistent numbers, you might look closer at the patient who will eventually fit the laboratory description."* - F. T. Bain

The neonatal foal provided a patient that required advanced knowledge of all the body systems and a plethora for advancing knowledge. A generation of neonatologists evolved, with the private sector having set in motion the academic pursuits of the institutions, initially followed, within the United States, by the University of Florida.

Meanwhile, myself being a graduate and familiar with the scenario at the University of California, respected surgeons like John Wheat developed confidence in the medical skills of Humphrey Knight. Medicine as a discipline became established, along with a burgeoning of speciality-orientated clinicians that provided the medical subspecialities of cardiology (Ed Rhode), ophthalmology (Robert Cello), dermatology (Tony Stannard) and oncology (Gordon Theilen). The theme seemed to present faculty with knowing how much they didn't, but being confident in knowing the things they did! These clinicians, and colleagues at other colleges and universities, established speciality interests and the need for clinical recognition.

The formation and chartering in 1972 of the American College of Veterinary Internal Medicine (ACVIM) was pivotal and provided the formal credential process needed for recognition. The medicine purists established their bylaws, residency training requirements and examination criteria. The icon of the pursuit of clinical excellence, as demonstrated by being board-certified, was Jim Coffman, who was then at the University of Missouri and who set the standard which future clinicians strove to emulate. Dr Coffman exemplified the credibility of the boarded internist, and the man and his credentials were perceived as the prototype capable of achieving the highest levels of institutional administration.

Board certification was both fashionable and desirable within clinical institutions and was acknowledged by both faculty and administration. It also offered clinical recognition by the private sector, something the PhD did not provide directly. Other American institutions concurrently took the same path from their respective leaders and this precedence mentored a second generation of internists, such as Gary Carlson and Joe Mayhew, who sought both sequential board certification and advanced degrees. The profile of an equine clinician transformed on being board-certified with primary leaders, such as Jill Beech (the great lady of Medicine, University of Pennsylvania), Brad Smith (California), Steve Reed (Washington State University), Catherine Kohn (Ohio State University), Leon Scrutchfield (Texas A and M University) and Bob Whitlock then at the University of Georgia. Being boarded in internal medicine was now perceived as speeding a clinician's reputation and credibility among peers, referring veterinarians and, even, students.

When the wave of new veterinary schools opened during the 1970s and 1980s, the standard was set at Florida, North Carolina, Tufts, Oregon, Mississippi and Prince Edward Island with the clinical faculty requirements including board certification.

> *"Borrow heavily from human medicine, but apply it cautiously to the horse as a unique species. On humility, I once had a horse with a chronically infected hip...I did every test, treated with antibiotics and local lavage without much change. The surgeon, Dr Frank, walks by and says: 'There's probably a stick in there.' I stuck my fingers in and pulled out a small stick my mind recorded as a log."* - J. R. Coffman

The University of Georgia obtained special status as assembling a team of internists capable of national prominence. Bob Whitlock hired Lisle George, and soon Tom Divers and myself came on board and were tailored to the team. Those days were early enough that Divers and I never completed the residency programmes but, under the tutelage of Whitlock and George, we sat the examinations and got boarded. The University of Georgia now had four boarded clinicians, residency programmes and a dramatic increase in caseload. In the early 1980s the group disseminated and Whitlock (losing his hair by the turmoil we other three had fostered) went to Pennsylvania where he then recruited Divers, George went to California, and myself, being the least balanced in the skills of research, teaching and service, wound up in Kentucky in the private practice of Hagyard-Davidson-McGee (HDM). Divers' pre-eminence in international clinical medicine continues today from Cornell University.

> *"There are three patient categories: the one which will recover without treatment; the one that will die regardless; and, the one that will live with the proper treatment. I prefer the gain of satisfaction from the last category, but my favorite mentor, Dr Dilmus Blackmon, once said: 'Never retreat from taking credit for any recovery.' He also said of the patient about to die regardless: 'We arrived too soon!'"* - T. J. Divers

There were other boarded internists who entered practice, such as, Scott McAllister and David McCarrol, but Lexington offered the opportunity to practise specifically internal medicine. Medicine came to Kentucky because the timing was right for the support of HDM. Fairfield Bain, then from Florida, stated:

"Hagyard-Davidson-McGee provided the reputation for the development and public acceptance of the private referral hospital."

The blessings of the economy along with the coexistence of Norm Rantanen (an ultrasound guru who also came to Kentucky in 1983) allowed for the interpretive abilities of internal medicine to affix to technology's most profound diagnostic blessing, the ultrasound machine. Ultrasound gave us the noninvasive gift to look inside the patient without hurting. As Peter Rossdale has said:

"Imaging has blessed our profession with seeing as believing."

Medicine was quickly accepted by the mainstream veterinary community and began a growth phase that still exists today. The private sector absorbed and developed demands for the service area similar to human medicine. Equine internal medicine developed a needed commercial recognition and the service began dissemination throughout North America as representing, perhaps, the most dynamic area of occupational opportunity for the next generation of internists. I prefer to think that internists continue to advance the standards of general practice. Other countries now also provided for advanced training and speciality credentials with the Royal College of Veterinary Surgeons, in England, and Australia being initiators. The section editor, Tim Mair, represents the current generation with advanced degrees and speciality certification within the private sector, while those, such as John Freestone in Australia, provide our 'umbrella' skills slowly to elevate the standards of veterinary practice.

"I remember most Jim Pinsent who taught me you never forget a good teacher, practice being the teacher that shows the student to learn from your mistakes." - T. S. Mair

It is my belief that medicine is moving toward the millennium with professional and public acceptance that will not reverse or be deleted from institutions or the private sector. A growth phase exists which mirrors human medicine while being tempered by our contact with the realities of veterinary medicine: the patient's environment, economics, and that wonderful 'umbrella' of the versatility that is instilled into our training. Our influence into reproduction, sports medicine, neonatology and postoperative care will continue; and our participation in the newer disciplines such as critical care medicine will maintain that influence into the dynamics of the next century.

"My father would today eat his words about the cautions of all the advanced education I pursued...today he would realise that our level of professional training and achievement is second to none." - F. T. Bain

Millennium bugs: a selective review of developments in equine virology over the past century

RICHARD NEWTON AND KEN SMITH
Animal Health Trust
Lanwades Park, Kentford
Newmarket
Suffolk CB8 7UU
UK

Introduction

In preparing this review, we have been conscious of the enormous advances in understanding of the major equine viruses over the past century. For most viral diseases of importance to the equine industry, this progress has entailed a rapid acceleration from basic clinical definition of individual disease syndromes to painstaking molecular dissection of the pathogens involved and the host immune responses that are evoked.

In some recent cases, such as the Hendra virus outbreaks in Australia, this accumulation of knowledge from first recognition of a new disease to its effective control has occurred within a period of less than one decade. In the case of other viruses, such as equine herpesvirus-1 and -4, the translation of basic scientific data into improved methods of disease control continues to provide a challenge to the scientific community despite over 50 years of sustained research effort.

Our backbone for the review has been the eight International Conferences on Equine Infectious Diseases that have moved around most of the major horse breeding and racing centres of the world from the first conference in Stresa in 1963 to the recent extravaganza in Dubai in 1998. Those conferences provide an admirable example of international collaboration and friendship in the control of viral pathogens that increasingly present global rather than regional threats to equine health and welfare. Considerable credit must be given to Heinz Gerber and Jack Bryans for their foresight and effort in establishing the early conferences and not least their arranging for publication of the proceedings which provide an invaluable record of developments in equine virology.

In order to provide a brief introduction for the general veterinary reader to the ever-expanding field of literature on veterinary virology, we have restricted our list of references to comprehensive review articles that provide rapid primers on the current state of knowledge for each virus.

African Horse Sickness Virus (AHSV)

African horse sickness (AHS), caused by an orbivirus, has nine serotypes, all transmitted by *Culicoides* midges. The disease occurs regularly in most countries of sub-Saharan Africa, being endemic and subclinical in zebras, and is likely to assume increasing importance with changes in global weather patterns and increased international movement of horses. A disease resembling African horse sickness is mentioned as early as 1327 in an Arabian document reporting on an outbreak of disease in the Yemen, and there were sporadic reports of peracute disease in horses imported from Europe into endemic areas in the succeeding centuries. Experiments in 1900 by McFadyean resulted in transmission of disease with bacteria-free filtrate of blood from an infected horse, consistent with a viral pathogenesis. Research into AHS has naturally been concentrated in South Africa, and the siting of the Veterinary Research Institute at Onderstepoort in 1908 was in large part due to the high prevalence of AHS in the immediate area. In 1903, Pitchford and Theiler demonstrated that horses could be protected against infection by housing in mosquito-proof enclosures and, in 1944, Du Toit reported that the midge *Culicoides imicola* is a major vector of both AHS and bluetongue viruses.

Major epidemics of AHS occurred in southern Africa at roughly 20–30 year intervals over the period leading up to the 1950s. Observations on these outbreaks and on experimental infections led to the accumulation of a mass of data on the clinical signs and lesions induced by AHS infection. The epidemiology, clinical signs and macroscopic changes are often sufficiently characteristic to allow a provisional diagnosis to be made. The diagnosis can be confirmed by virus isolation from specimens of blood collected during the febrile phase of the infection, or from necropsy samples of lung, spleen and lymph nodes.

A polyvalent vaccine against AHS is available in southern Africa, and has limited severe losses due to the disease, but epidemics have occurred in recent years in countries outside the endemic regions of Africa. Current research is underway to try and develop a cheap and effective subunit vaccine using recombinant technology. An intriguing recent observation on AHS epidemiology suggests that recent incidents of infection in southern Spain, Portugal and Morocco may be associated with the El Niño weather phenomenon, with spells of drought followed by heavy rainfall resulting in an explosion of the biting midge that acts as a vector of infection. The implications of those data in terms of possible increases in other diseases spread by flying insects will become apparent in the next millennium[1].

Equine Herpesvirus-1 and -4 (EHV-1, EHV-4)

Equine herpesvirus abortion was first recognised in Kentucky in 1932 following examination of an aborted fetus by Dimock and Edwards. Detailed descriptions of the fetal lesions followed from the same group in the 1930s and 1940s. At that time, the virus was termed equine influenza virus because of the influenza-like symptoms that it produced, and it was not until 1954 that it was shown that equine rhinopneumonitis and equine abortion were caused by the same agent. Neurological manifestations associated with abortion were also an early observation in the 1940s, although the virus was not isolated from nervous tissue until 1966, by Finn Saxegaard in Norway. In 1959, major antigenic differences between EHV-1 strains were noted by workers in Japan, and the meticulous observations of Bob Burrows and David Goodridge on the Pirbright pony herd in the 1970s subsequently led to the concept that EHV-1 strains associated with respiratory disease and abortion were different virus subtypes. Restriction endonuclease fingerprinting subsequently demonstrated that the two subtypes were genetically distinct viruses that were renamed EHV-1 (formerly subtype 1) and EHV-4 (formerly subtype 2), and those results were published independently by three different laboratories in 1981.

Detailed studies of the pathogenesis of the neurological syndrome associated with EHV-1 infection were performed by Jackson and colleagues at the University of Davis, California, in the 1970s, and involved experimental infections of horses with the Army 183 isolate. Their work emphasised the importance of vasculitis and local thromboischaemic necrosis of neuropil in the induction of the paralytic syndrome. In the 1980s Neil Edington and his group at the Royal Veterinary College in London used immunostaining methods specifically to demonstrate viral antigen expression in endothelial cells. Endotheliotropism in relation to abortigenic disease was shown to be of importance in parallel studies using the Ab4 isolate of EHV-1 in London and at the Animal Health Trust in Newmarket. Those studies included the novel finding that infection of the fetus could be incidental to the abortion episode, although such virologically negative fetuses have not yet been recognised in spontaneous abortion epizootics.

Equine herpesvirus infections caused some respiratory problems in a few stables in England in the 1970s and major epidemics of paralysis and abortion in the 1980s caused great concern in the equine industry. This situation led Lord Porchester (now Earl of Caernarvon) and a small band of industry supporters to set up a privately funded research body, the Equine Virology Research Foundation, in 1986. The Foundation was under the scientific direction of Professor Walter Plowright, and had the specific aim of developing a more effective vaccine for herpesvirus abortion and paresis. Funding from that group certainly led to better understanding of the detailed structure of EHV-1 and EHV-4, with both viruses being completely sequenced, although the ultimate goal of a better abortion vaccine remained elusive when the Foundation wound up in the late 1990s.

The 1990s have seen the application of novel molecular techniques for the rapid diagnosis of EHV-1 abortion and respiratory disease. In particular, use of the PCR for diagnosis of abortion is now used routinely in laboratories in Newmarket, the Netherlands and New Zealand. The development of sensitive PCR assays for the detection of EHV-1 and -4 nucleic acids also led to better understanding of viral latency. Edington and co-workers had shown in the 1980s that EHV-1 infections could be reactivated by administration of corticosteroids, and that work was reproduced for EHV-4 infections by Browning and co-workers in Australia. The site of latency was first thought to be primarily lymphoreticular, with detection of viral DNA particularly in lymph nodes draining the respiratory tract. Work by Slater and co-workers in Cambridge and Berlin, using specific pathogen-free foals, indicated that the trigeminal ganglion could also be a site of EHV-1 latency and reactivation. It is likely that both sites of latency can coexist in an infected animal.

Studies of the immune response to EHV-1 infection concentrated for many years on the demonstration of complement-fixing and virus-neutralising antibody. Those serological assays are useful in determining EHV-1 exposure during epizootics but no serological measure has been shown specifically to correlate with protection. More recent development of an assay for EHV-1 cytotoxic T-lymphocytes shows greater promise as a measure of EHV-1 immunity likely to be helpful in evaluating new vaccines.

The understanding from pathogenesis studies that high virulence isolates of EHV-1 such as Ab4 and Army 183 have a particular predilection for endothelial cells has led to studies examining the molecular basis of virulence and possible genetic differences between high and low virulence isolates of EHV-1 and EHV-4. That work has not yet led to clear molecular markers of virulence, despite the generation and characterisation of specific EHV-1 deletion mutants, including viruses lacking four nonessential genes which are not found in other alphaherpesviruses. Better understanding of the molecular basis of variation in pathogenicity between and within EHV-1 and EHV-4, and the manipulation of that knowledge in development of more effective vaccines, is a key goal for equine herpesvirus research into the next millennium[2–4].

Equine Infectious Anaemia (EIA)

Equine infectious anaemia was first recognised as a viral disease by Vallee and Carre in 1904, and initial attempts were made by Bankier in 1945 to develop an inactivated vaccine. The pace of research was slow over the first six decades of the century, being hampered both by the failure to transmit the virus to nonequine hosts that could be used as models of the disease, and by a lack of methods for *in vitro* cultivation of the agent. The latter problem was resolved in the 1960s, by Kobayashi and co-workers. An important milestone in EIA research was the development of an effective diagnostic test in 1970.

The ability to identify seropositive horses by the Coggins test enabled the spread of infection to be controlled in endemic areas through limitation on the movement of seropositive horses and prevention of contact with seronegative horses. Effective control by these techniques inhibited active research into improved EIA vaccines in the

1970s. Research blossomed again in the mid-1980s after it was shown that a lentivirus which was serologically cross-reactive with EIA was the cause of AIDS, thereby opening new funding opportunities that used EIA as a model for certain aspects of the human infection. Recent areas of research that have been facilitated by this renewed interest include examinations of the structure and function of the structural and regulatory proteins of the virus; identifying the molecular basis for antigenic drift; defining viral and host determinants in pathogenesis; and dissecting the immune response to whole virus or specific viral components, in order to identify immunological correlates of protection[5].

Equine Influenza Virus (EIV, 'flu')

A disease of horses clinically indistinguishable from influenza and referred to as a 'distemper' was described as long ago as 1732. Many similar references were made subsequently, but there was some confusion with other viral diseases, with some observers attributing 'pink-eye' and abortions to influenza. In the 1930s, German researchers comparing epidemic coughing in young racehorses with the then recently isolated swine influenza virus, showed for the first time that the disease was due to a filterable virus and that it was experimentally reproducible. The disease had many pseudonyms, including 'laryngotracheobronchitis', 'infectious bronchitis', 'infectious catarrh', 'Hoppengarten cough', 'Gulf Stream disease', 'epizootic cough' and 'Newmarket cough'. Influenza became recognised as a highly contagious respiratory disease characterised by acute pyrexia and a harsh dry cough that rapidly spread both within and between groups of young horses, particularly in racing yards. There were few deaths or complications when horses were rested and recovery usually occurred in two to three weeks.

The first demonstration of the correct nature of the causative virus of equine influenza occurred in 1955 when it was shown that horses in a respiratory disease epidemic in Sweden seroconverted to a soluble human influenza virus antigen. Shortly afterwards an influenza virus was isolated for the first time from coughing horses in Czechoslovakia and this prototype virus was named A/equine-1/Prague/56. Retrospective serological surveys demonstrated that the virus had been the cause of disease in many areas of the world. Serological and virological monitoring of epidemic respiratory disease demonstrated that this prototype virus continued to be responsible for disease outbreaks in predominantly young horses in many countries between 1957 and 1963. In January 1963 there was an outbreak of rapidly spreading acute respiratory disease among horses at several racetracks in Miami. A characteristic of this outbreak that differentiated it from earlier outbreaks was that it affected all ages rather than predominantly younger horses. A novel virus, antigenically distinct from A/equine-1/Prague/56, was isolated and named A/equine-2/Miami/63. This new virus was subsequently responsible for an equine influenza pandemic of such significance that it was the stimulus for convening the First Conference on Equine Infectious Diseases. A serological survey of A/equine-2 antibodies following the epidemic of A/equine-1 influenza in the UK in 1963 demonstrated that British horses were completely susceptible to the new virus and an epidemic was predicted. Despite the start of production of a vaccine, insufficient stocks were available before the disease was first seen in February 1965 on two studs in Sussex. The stud had recently received mares from France, where the disease had been present for about one month.

Following the equine influenza pandemic of 1963–65 there was much work done in the areas of serological and virological diagnoses, vaccine development and experimental infections. By the mid-1970s, by extrapolation from experience with human influenza outbreaks the phenomena of antigenic drift and shift of equine influenza isolates began to be explored and the need for continual surveillance of the disease in horse populations around the world was recognised.

In 1979 in the UK there was a significant and widespread epidemic of A/equine-2 influenza initially among unvaccinated horses and later in vaccinated animals. Antigenic examination of isolates from epidemics that year confirmed antigenic drift among A/equine-2 viruses. From March 1981 and following the loss of racing because of the 1979 epidemic, the Jockey Club in the UK made influenza vaccination mandatory for all horses running at British racecourses. In 1983 it was recommended that representatives of both subgroups should be included in future equine influenza vaccines to increase the relevance of vaccinal to circulating strains. In the UK it was recognised that in order to develop and test effective vaccines, there was a need for an accurate experimental model for equine influenza infection. Models were gradually developed in naive ponies using different routes of administration and infectious doses and these have since been repeatedly used in the successful licensing of equine vaccines in the UK.

As with most other viruses, the last two decades have seen an increase in the detailed antigenic and genetic characterisation of sequential influenza viruses which has led to a much improved understanding of strain variation. The predicted need in 1987 for vaccines to be periodically updated was proved correct when in 1989 there were outbreaks of influenza seen among recently vaccinated horses. This subsequently led to an update of strains in UK vaccines. The continued occurrence of outbreaks among vaccinated as well as unvaccinated populations of horses and the emergence of a highly fatal avian reassortant in China in 1989, have reinforced the need for ongoing epidemiological surveillance. Phylogenetic characterisation has recently recognised two antigenically divergent subtypes of A/equine-2, the so-called 'American-like' and European-like' strains, and experimental infections have confirmed field observations that there is a need for inclusion of representatives of both strains if future vaccines are to remain effective.

As the next millennium approaches, observations of natural outbreaks are confirming the validity of experimental challenge models and increasingly these data will used mathematically to model the disease in different situations. Similarly, attention is turning to mucosal and cell-mediated immunity as alternatives to circulating antibody production as mechanisms of protective immunity against influenza. The call to recognise homoeopathic preparations as a safer alternative to conventional vaccines appears to be gaining ground in certain equine disciplines. However, the lack of any efficacy data and the resistance of homoeopathic practitioners to undertake properly conducted clinical trials does little to sway scientific argument in favour of the preventive capabilities of such 'alternative' products[6,7,8,9].

Hendra Virus (HeV, previously referred to as equine morbillivirus)

In September 1994 there was an outbreak of acute severe respiratory disease in racehorses stabled in Brisbane, Queensland, Australia. During the outbreak 18 horses were clinically affected and 14 died or were subjected to euthanasia. Two human contacts became ill, including the trainer, who later died of a pneumonic condition. Following notification to the Department of Primary Industries (DPI), a veterinary team conducted an exhaustive investigation of the outbreak. Quarantine and movement restrictions were immediately implemented, all horseracing in Queensland was halted and all equine deaths were made notifiable. The investigation did not demonstrate infection with any known equine infectious agents, but quickly identified a previously unrecognised virus (now referred to as Hendra virus - HeV) similar to other morbilliviruses (others in the group include measles, rinderpest and distemper) in all autopsied equine cases. Transmission studies satisfied Koch's postulates by reproducing clinical disease and causing death in experimentally infected horses and HeV was recovered from all four animals at autopsy. A serological test for neutralising antibody was rapidly developed and validated by the Australian Animal Health Laboratory (AAHL) and was used to test all contact humans and horses on premises within 1 km of the affected stables. Seven horses, which were all stabled on the affected premises and included recovered cases, were found to be seropositive for HeV. The decision was made by the DPI to destroy these animals and their seronegative contacts, in order to minimise risk of further transmission. There were no further human or equine cases identified in this outbreak.

In October 1995, a farmer in northern Queensland, 1000 km from the original outbreak, died in hospital following a progressive neurological illness. Subsequent autopsy investigation demonstrated that brain tissue from the dead man was positive for HeV and serum was positive for neutralising antibody. In August 1994 the man had assisted his wife, a veterinary surgeon, with autopsies on two horses which had been diagnosed with 'avocado poisoning' and 'brown snake bite' on the basis of autopsy findings. The dead man had suffered mild meningoencephalitis soon after the horse deaths in 1994 but had recovered without apparent complication. Direct fluorescence antibody and PCR tests subsequently conducted by the AAHL on archived tissues from the autopsied horses revealed that they had been infected with HeV.

These findings prompted a statewide serological survey of humans, horses and likely reservoir host species capable of transmission between the two separate outbreaks. This investigation showed that all tested humans and horses had no serological evidence of HeV but a possible natural reservoir was identified. The *Pteropus* species of bat (otherwise known as fruit bats or flying foxes) were found to have an HeV seroprevalence of 9%. However, there have been no reports of disease in fruit bats or cases of infection in humans with exposure to these animals. Further investigations have shown that the infection is associated with the uterine fluid of pregnant fruit bats and transmission between bats may take place during birth. Fruit bats, normally tree-dwelling animals, give birth on the ground, and it may be contact with infectious uterine fluid that explains the transmission of HeV to horses.

A further case of HeV occurred in January 1999, with the death of a mature adult Thoroughbred mare within 24 hours of becoming ill. The diagnosis was based on histological, immunoperoxidase and PCR tests conducted by the AAHL on fixed lung tissue from the affected horse. The mare was one of two horses kept in a paddock in a residential area of Cairns, but the second horse was negative for HeV when tested by ELISA in February 1999. There had been no other contact with other horses for at least two months but the paddock contained trees that were occasionally visited by fruit bats. It was concluded that the infection in this mare was unlikely to have originated from or spread to another horse but probably occurred following contact with a reservoir host.

Investigations are continuing in order to eliminate other possible reservoirs and elucidate the complex biological relationship between fruit bats (or other reservoir host species), horses and HeV that explains the sudden emergence of this new and fatal disease. There are many lessons to be learned from HeV, which provides an excellent example of how a novel and fatal viral zoonosis can be efficiently, effectively and collaboratively investigated, controlled and monitored[10,11,12].

Equine Arteritis Virus (EAV)

The symptoms of the disease 'pink-eye', now known as equine viral arteritis (EVA), were first reported over 100 years ago, but there was clearly some confusion with other equine viral diseases as the condition was also referred to as 'equine influenza'. Early workers described the clinical signs as including "*weakness, watering of the eyes, injected conjunctiva, swelled legs and diffuse swelling on the under-part of the abdomen*". There was also recognition that the disease could be spread from stallions to mares at covering and that this spread continued for a long period after stallions were first affected. Abortion was sometimes observed and it was recognised that strict isolation could successfully control the disease.

The next major advance in the understanding of EVA came when the causative agent, equine arteritis virus (EAV), was first isolated from horses during an outbreak of severe respiratory disease and abortion on a Standardbred studfarm in the town of Bucyrus, Ohio, in 1953. The observation that different disease outbreaks often presented with differing severity of signs then led to speculation that different strains of EAV could exist. A difference in virulence was recognised as a potential source of protection through use of a modified virus strain in a live vaccine. Following its initial isolation, the morphological and physicochemical properties of EAV were described by the early 1970s, by which time it had been appreciated that there were two different viruses capable of causing abortion in mares (i.e. EHV and EAV). Around the same time detailed observations on the respiratory form of the disease were made in Kentucky during experimental infections which contributed to understanding of the pathogenesis. The now standard serological assays of complement fixation (CF) and virus neutralisation (VN) were also developed and described by the mid-1970s. These techniques allowed accurate diagnosis and surveillance of EVA in many areas of the world.

The outbreak in Kentucky in 1984 led to a major breakthrough in the understanding of the epidemiology of EVA that provided an explanation for the postcoital infections that had been described at the turn of the century. Testosterone-dependent persistence of EAV infection localised in the accessory sexual organs was found to occur in around one-third of infected sexually mature stallions and was reproduced experimentally. This pivotal understanding in the epidemiology of EVA offered for the first time the realistic prospect of control and even elimination of this disease from endemically infected horse populations.

The rapid advances in molecular biological techniques in the last decade have inevitably led to an explosion of extremely detailed knowledge regarding the genetic structure of EAV, even leading to its taxonomic reclassification as a member of the *Arteriviridae* genus. These molecular advances have already led to more sensitive and rapid diagnostic techniques such as polymerase chain reaction (PCR) and offer the real prospect of novel vaccines in the future. However, it is worth remembering that with the increased international movement of horses, the last 10 years have also seen the first outbreaks of EVA in the United Kingdom and South Africa, both countries that had relied on stringent controls to prevent importation of the disease. The UK has recognised the importance of EVA as a potentially devastating disease for its equine breeding industry with its inclusion in the HBLB Codes of Practice and the implementation of the Equine Viral Arteritis Order 1995, which made the disease notifiable in stallions.

As we enter the next millennium, these recent EVA outbreaks serve to remind us that there is still a real threat posed from infectious viral diseases by the international movement of horses or even just their semen. The situation for EVA is exacerbated because different nations currently have very different attitudes to this disease[13,14,15].

Other Viruses Causing Neurological Disease

A variety of other viruses, including rabies virus, Borna disease virus and the arthropod-borne alphaviruses, cause encephalitis in horses. Rabies continues to be the most important of these infections in view of its zoonotic implications, and is endemic on all continents with the exception of Australia. The disease has been successfully excluded from the United Kingdom by an isolation and quarantine scheme for incoming animals, although this scheme is now likely to be progressively replaced by a vaccination and microchip-based strategy. Infection in horses is generally acquired by traumatic inoculation of virus in saliva from an infected carnivore, and the horse is the dead-end host for the infection (with the possible exception of the low risk to laboratory staff examining rabid horses at necropsy). Clinical signs in horses are highly variable, but may include apparent lameness, maniacal behaviour or colic. Diagnosis of equine rabies is made at *postmortem* examination by the recognition of Negri bodies in sections or smears of the cerebrum, cerebellum and hippocampus, supplemented by immunofluorescent staining of sections of brain and/or transmission studies using neonatal mice. Current research is concentrated upon improved methods for vaccination of susceptible wildlife species in order to limit the reservoir of infection in endemic areas[16].

Borna disease (BD) is a transmissible subacute polioencephalomyelitis, with most reports of disease occurring in horses and sheep in endemic areas of Germany and Switzerland. The first descriptions of clinical signs likely to be due to Borna disease in horses date back to 1767. An outbreak of disease occurred at a military stud close to Stuttgart in 1823 and resulted in the death of two-thirds of the horses on the premises. Early descriptions of the microscopic lesions of the disease were made by Dexler in 1900 and Joest and Degen in 1909 and 1911. In 1924 the disease was successfully reproduced in rabbits by intracerebral inoculation of brain material from an infected horse. This work was followed by further passages from rabbit to rabbit and transmission back to the horse, and induction of BD with filtered brain material in 1926 suggested a viral aetiology.

Research continued sporadically over subsequent decades, but decisive characterisation of the causal virus proved problematic until the mid-1990s, when the agent was defined as an enveloped virion containing an intranuclearly replicating single-, negative-stranded RNA of 8.9 kB, which has now been sequenced. Serosurveys in horses suggest that exposure to the virus is more widespread than clinical disease, and it is likely that a high proportion of infections in horses run a subclinical course. It is thought that infection of the central nervous system is persistent and that the lesions of encephalitis seen in some infected animals are the consequence of a delayed type hypersensitivity reaction. At the end of the century interest in BD has been rekindled by the suggestion that the virus could be involved in some cases of mood disturbance, chronic fatigue syndrome and other psychiatric disorders in humans[17].

The arthropod-borne encephalitis viruses of principal importance in horses are the alphaviruses causing Eastern (EEE), Venezualan (VEE) and Western equine encephalitis (WEE) and the flavivirus causing Japanese encephalitis. The three alphaviruses cause epizootics of encephalitis in horses and humans in North, Central and South America. EEE has been recognised as an important infection in American horses since the 19th century, when the first clinical descriptions of disease were recorded[18]. The virus was first isolated during an outbreak of disease extending across Delaware, Virginia and New Jersey in 1933. The morbidity during outbreaks is high, with 80–90% of infected horses developing acute fatal disease in some epizootics, and severe chronic neurological deficits are common in those animals that survive the acute phase. Current issues of concern in relation to EEE include outbreaks of disease in previously unaffected areas of North America, including Kentucky; vaccine failures in young horses; and involvement of recently introduced species of mosquitoes and birds in the complex epidemiology of the infection.

Outbreaks of disease due to Venezualan equine encephalitis virus in endemic areas can involve tens to hundreds of thousands of cases in horses and man. In common with EEE, the clinical signs in humans range from inapparent to severe encephalitis, and mortality rates in horses vary from 19–83%. Western equine encephalitis virus was first isolated during an outbreak of disease in California in 1930, and has caused periodic equine epizootics in many parts of North America, with severe losses occurring in the 1930s–1950s. The declining use of horses for agricultural purposes in North America has limited the extent of alphavirus disease outbreaks, but the infections remain of major significance because of their zoonotic potential. The most important of the arthropod-borne encephalitis viruses in terms of the frequency, morbidity and mortality rates of disease, in addition the wide geographical occurrence of infection, is Japanese encephalitis virus (JEV). The virus has been isolated in Japan, China, India, Indonesia, Korea, Malaysia, Nepal, Singapore, Sri Lanka, Taiwan and Thailand. A mass vaccination programme for equines was begun in Japan in 1948, and has resulted in a gradual decline in human and equine deaths since then, but the incidence of disease is increasing in India, Nepal and other parts of Southeast Asia where vector populations are uncontrolled and vaccination is not practised[19].

Other Respiratory and Miscellaneous Viruses

Following the first isolations of viruses from cases of rhinopneumonitis, viral arteritis and influenza during the 1950s, other viruses were isolated during the 1960s and 1970s from cases of equine respiratory disease particularly in young horses and occasionally from only immune-compromised foals. Equine rhinovirus-1 (ERV-1) was first isolated in the UK in 1962 and in North America in 1965, and this was followed by the isolation of the antigenically distinct serotypes ERV-2 reported in 1972 and ERV-3 in 1978. Equine adenovirus was first isolated in 1969 and a relationship with immune incompetence, particularly in Arab foals, was postulated. Acid-stable picornavirus and equine herpesvirus-2 (EHV-2) were also isolated from the respiratory tract of horses in the 1970s. Subsequent serological surveys have demonstrated that infections with these viruses are widespread in horse populations with most horses becoming infected at a young age.

There continues to be debate as to the precise role that these viruses play in causing clinical respiratory disease, with many subclinical infections identified. Despite recent epidemiological evidence that bacterial and mycoplasmal infections are closely associated with respiratory disease in young racehorses, there continues to be speculation that these viral infections play a primary and predisposing role. The role of enteroviruses as a possible cause of chronic fatigue in horses, analogous to persistent Cox-sackie B virus infection in postviral fatigue syndrome (also referred to as ME or myalgic encephalomyelitis) in man, has been preliminarily investigated, but no conclusive results have yet been forthcoming[20,21,22,23].

Coital exanthema, an acute, contagious disease characterised by vesicles, pustules and erosions of the external genitalia, has been historically described in cattle, horses and man. The causative virus was first isolated from horses in 1968 by several workers and was described as a novel herpesvirus that was antigenically distinct from that causing rhinopneumonitis (EHV-1). Identification of the viral cause of coital exanthema confirmed that the disease in horses was analogous to the genital herpes infections of cattle and man. The virus was subsequently referred to as equine herpesvirus-3 (EHV-3) and a virus-neutralising serological test was developed. As the disease was found not to cause abortion or infertility, the infection was generally considered a nuisance rather than a significant venereal pathogen. Consequently since its detailed descriptions in the early 1970s, coital exanthema has not been the focus of such intensive research as other equine herpesviruses. However, it is clear from clinical observations that animals do become latently infected, with recrudescences appearing repeatedly, in some cases causing real problems[24].

Rotavirus had been identified as a potential pathogen since the mid-1970s but even as late as 1985 the aetiology of foal diarrhoea was still poorly understood. A three year epidemiological study in Kentucky helped demonstrate the primary pathogenic role of rotavirus, which was responsible for more than 90% of the major US outbreaks investigated between 1986 and 1988. Work since then has concentrated largely on the development of a vaccine for administration to mares in late pregnancy for boosting colostral antibody and so providing protective immunity for foals in the critical first weeks of life. However, in a situation analogous to that of respiratory disease, further studies have shown that *Clostridium perfringens* is associated with a substantially greater proportion of disease cases[25].

Conclusions

It is clear from this all too brief and extremely selective review of ever-expanding equine virology that the subject has advanced enormously over the past 100 years, from the earliest and sometimes confused disease descriptions to the plethora of current molecular knowledge. In concluding, it is appropriate to note that scientists from around the world considered the subject's future in a meeting at the Eighth Conference of Equine Infectious Diseases held in Dubai in March 1998 where recommendations regarding priorities for future research were drawn up. Whilst the full list of recommendations can be found in the Conference proceedings, the general priorities pertaining to equine virology are summarised as follows. The need for the development of improved, more rapid and internationally validated diagnostic tests was recognised, as was the need to improve the understanding of viral disease epidemiology, pathogenesis, virulence determinants and correlates of immunity. These advances would enable better models of disease to be developed and subsequently lead to the marketing of effective and safer vaccines. Improved and multidisciplinary approaches to surveillance and control of equine diseases were also required, particularly in light of the increasing international movement of horses and not least because of the potential for novel interspecies and zoonotic viral transmission.

Acknowledgements

We would like to thank colleagues at the Animal Health Trust for their constructive comments on the manuscript.

References

[1]Coetzer, J.A.W. and Erasmus, B.J. (1994) African horsesickness. In: *Livestock Diseases of Southern Africa.* pp 460-475.

[2]Allen, G.P. and Bryans, J.T. (1986) Molecular epizootiology, pathogenesis and prophylaxis of equine herpesvirus-1 infections. *Progress in Veterinary Microbiology and Immunology* **2**, 78-144.

[3]Crabb, B.S. and Studdert, M.J. (1994) Equine herpesvirus-4 (equine rhinopneumonitis virus) and -1 (equine abortion virus). *Advances in Virus Research* **45**, 153-190.

[4]Allen, G.P., Kydd, J.H., Slater, J.D. and Smith, K.C. (1999) Advances in understanding of the pathogenesis, epidemiology and immunological control of equine herpesvirus abortion. In: *Equine Infectious Diseases VIII: Proceedings of the Eighth International Conference on Equine Infectious Diseases*, Eds: U. Wernery, J.F. Wade, J.A. Mumford and O.R. Kaaden, R & W Publications Ltd., Newmarket, UK. pp 129-146.

[5]Cook, R.F., Issel, C.J. and Montelaro, R.C. (1996) Equine infectious anaemia. In: *Virus Infections of Equines, Virus Infections of Vertebrates,* Vol 6, Elsevier, Amsterdam. pp 297-323.

[6]Gerber, H. (1970) Equine influenza: clinical features, sequelae and epidemiology of equine influenza. In: *Equine Infectious Diseases II: Proceedings of the Second International Conference on Equine Infectious Diseases*, Ed: J.T. Bryans, Karger Basel, New York. pp 63-80.

[7]Wood, J.L.N. (1991) *Equine Influenza: History and Epidemiology and a Description of a Recent Outbreak,* MSc Dissertation, LSHTM, University of London.

[8]Mumford, J.A. (1992) Progress in the control of equine influenza. In: *Equine Infectious Diseases VI: Proceedings of the Sixth International Conference on Equine Infectious Diseases,* Eds: W. Plowright, P.D. Rossdale and J.F. Wade, R & W Publications Ltd., Newmarket, UK. pp 207-217.

[9]Hannant, D. and Mumford, J.A. (1996) *Equine Influenza. Virus Infections of Equines*, Ed: M.J. Studdert, Elsevier, Oxford. pp 285-293.

[10]Murray, K., Selleck, P., Hooper, P., Hyatt, A., Gould, A., Gleeson, L., Westbury, H., Hiley, L., Selvey, L., Rodwell, B. and Ketterer, P. (1995) A morbillivirus that caused fatal disease in horses and humans. *Science* **268**, 94-97.

[11]Murray, K., Dunn, K. and Murray, G. (1999) Hendra virus (equine morbillivirus): a model for national responses to disease emergencies. In: *Equine Infectious Diseases VIII: Proceedings of the Eighth International Conference on Equine Infectious Diseases,* Eds: U. Wernery, J.F. Wade, J.A. Mumford and O.R. Kaaden, R & W Publications Ltd., Newmarket, UK. pp 3-10.

[12]Young, P.L., Halpin, K., Selleck, P.W., Field, H., Gravel, J.L., Kelly, M.A. and Mackenzie, J.S. (1996) Serologic evidence for the presence in *Pteropus* bats of a paramyxovirus related to equine morbillivirus. *Emerging Infectious Diseases* **2**, 239-240.

[13]Chirnside, E.D. (1992) Equine arteritis virus: an overview. *Br. vet.J.* **148**, 181-197.

[14]Timoney, P.J. and McCollum, W.H. (1993) Equine viral arteritis. *Vet. Clin. N. Am.: Equine Pract.* **9**, 295-309.

[15]Wood, J.L.N. (1994) Equine Viral Arteritis: progress in the last 100 years? *Equine vet. Educ.* **6**, 348.

[16]Turner, G.S. (1994) Equine rabies. *Equine vet. Educ.* **6**, 197-199.

[17]Durrwald, R. and Ludwig, L. (1997) Borna disease virus (BDV), a (zoonotic?) worldwide pathogen. A review of the history of the disease and the virus infection with comprehensive bibliography. *J. vet. Med.* **44**, 147-184.

[18]Scott, T. W. and Weaver, S.C. (1989) Eastern equine encephalomyelitis virus: epidemiology and evolution of mosquito transmission. *Advances in Virus Research* **37**, 277-328.

[19]Weaver, S.C., Powers, A.M., Brault, A.C. and Barrett, A.D.T. (1999) Molecular epidemiological studies of veterinary arboviral encephalitides. *Vet. J.* **157**, 123-138.

[20]Burrows, R. and Goodridge, D. (1978) Observations of picornavirus, adenovirus, and equine herpesvirus infections in the Pirbright pony herd. In: *Equine Infectious Diseases IV: Proceedings of the Fourth International Conference on Equine Infectious Diseases*, 1976. Eds: J.T. Bryans and H. Gerber, Karger Basel, New York. pp 155-164.

[21]Mumford, J.A. and Thomson, G.R. (1978) Studies on picornaviruses isolated from the respiratory tract of horses. In: *Equine Infectious Diseases IV: Proceedings of the Fourth International Conference on Equine Infectious Diseases*, Eds: J.T. Bryans and H. Gerber, Karger Basel, New York. pp 419-429.

[22]Steck, F., Hofer, B., Schaeren, B., Nicolet, J. and Gerber, H. (1978) Equine rhinoviruses: new serotypes. In: *Equine Infectious Diseases IV: Proceedings of the Fourth International Conference on Equine Infectious Diseases*, Eds: J.T. Bryans and H. Gerber, Karger Basel, New York. pp 321-328.

[23]Murray, M.J., Eichorn, E.S., Dubovi, E.J., Ley, W.B. and Cavey, D.M. (1996) Equine herpesvirus type 2: prevalence and seroepidemiology in foals. *Equine vet. J.* **28**, 432-436.

[24]Bryans, J.T. and Allen, G.P. (1972) *In vitro* and *in vivo* studies of equine 'coital' exanthema. In: *Equine Infectious Diseases III: Proceedings of the Third International Conference on Equine Infectious Diseases,* Eds: J.T. Bryans and H. Gerber, Karger Basel, New York. pp 322-336.

[25]Dwyer, R.M. (1993) Rotaviral diarrhoea. *Vet. Clin. N. Am.: Equine Pract.* **9**, 311-319.

Equine respiratory viral vaccines: an ode to immunology

DUNCAN HANNANT
Animal Health Trust
Lanwades Park
Kentford
Newmarket
Suffolk CB8 7UU
UK

In days of old, or so we're told,
the equids found it hard to hold
their own against successful germs,
which triumphed on unequal terms.

Strangles, scours, and EAV[1]
they were the dreaded enemy.
EHV[2] *and influenza*
added more to this cadenza.

An endless list - we were unsure
if vets would ever find a cure.
But cure's a word we should not mention,
to stop disease we need prevention.

The way to start this task, of course,
was asking questions of the horse.
The scene was set for vets in practice
to use immunoprophylaxis.

Towards prevention you can't go,
'til pathogenesis you know.
A sidetrack which seemed very nice
involved the use of furry mice.

But mice (and hamsters) had a plan
to differ from the horse, like man.
So after trawling alleys blind,
we went back to the equine kind.

In Newmarket back 20 years
the flu struck, filling us with fear.
The nation waited, horror facing,
that this could mean the end of racing.

And so they built the EVU[3]
to try to halt the horrid flu.
Located at the AHT[4],
part paid by equine industry.

Proud Jenny Mumford led her team
and saw the future in a dream.
Their purpose: to investigate
then beat the dread H3N8[5].

After research in her lab
all horses had to have a jab
of virus which was subjugated,
the vaccine was inactivated.

However, due to variation
and viral skills at quick mutation,
virus spread was just abated
and vaccines had to be updated.

The virus, with one hideous bound,
amino acids changed around.
H3N8 produced its sequel
to which the vaccine was unequal

Into battle one more time,
the virus changed in '89,
but Mumford rallied, yet again
to try and beat this mutant strain.

The manufacturers were keen
that vets in practice would be seen
to use their products to the max
and halt the virus in its tracks.

The only way this was achieved
(equine vets were much relieved)
was adding vaccine strains updated
to beat each virus which mutated.

But still it didn't go away,
its friends from Europe and USA
would circulate in the same yard
and make controlling very hard.

The truth is, while you can be sure
we won each battle, not the war,
this cloud had got a silver lining,
it stopped the research jobs declining.

Some novel routes of vaccination
are giving cause for celebration.
The needle's reign draws to a close:
"apply the vaccine up the nose".

Yes, intranasal is in fashion,
arousing scientific passion.
The route of treatment is mucosal,
no problems of syringe disposal.

Enough of flu, let's draw a veil
and head off on another trail.

Equine herpesvirus 1
has been the demon which has won
the most attention, research grants,
to try to halt its vile advance.

The vaccines used for EHV
made lots of serum IgG[6]*,*
but antibodies could not zap
and beat this horrid viral chap.

No matter how the vets injected
the horse was simply not protected.
Another way had to be found,
this problem we must get around.

Seemed best to go for CMI[7]*,*
and if you seek the reason why,
to kill the virus in the cell
you need to have good CTL[8]

These killer chaps will only see
infected cells, not virus-free.
The way the antigens are shown
leads to the killing act, full blown.

By processing endogenous
the viral peptides, without fuss,
go straight to MHC class I[9]
where recognition has begun.

Then many activations start
with IL-2[10] *a leading part.*
The target cells go comatose,
in fact they mostly apoptose[11]*.*

Inactivated vaccines fail
to stimulate this complex trail.
Some lateral thought came into force
to make it work and help the horse.

Live virus seemed the only way.
Not native EHV per se,
but mutant virus incompleted,
its glycoprotein genes deleted.

Some of these mutants very soon
proved they could make a horse immune
to challenge with EHV1,
at last some progress had begun.

Adding genes was tried as well,
expressed upon infected cells.
The hope was that they would direct
immune responses, all correct.

But added genes meant 'GMO'[12]*,*
at present, that's a big no-no.
These beastly things must be confined,
not free to roam, like natural kind.

Environmental risks are great
'cos if these mutants procreate,
there is a chance to recombine
to start a new and lethal line.

So safety problems have a hold
on vaccine workers being bold,
at least until there is no chance
that reassortants will advance.

However, vaccine trials can be
so hard to do for EHV,
because for years we've had to wait
to find an immune correlate.

There is a possibility
that measuring CTLp[13]
might estimate immunity
of equine herds to EHV.

Let's hope the research to be done
beyond the new millennium,
will show that EHV can be
controlled for all eternity.

The best way forward seems by far
to use our skills molecular
and find the genes that there should be
to stimulate immunity.

However, years of evolution
gives viruses the best solution.
They simply change their DNA
and live to fight another day.

MORAL[14]
This story has a simple moral
with which the wise will hardly quarrel;
Remember that it scarcely ever
pays to be too bloody clever.

---

[1]*Equine arteritis virus*
[2]*Equid herpes virus (type 1 = EHV1)*
[3]*Equine Virology Unit*
[4]*Animal Health Trust*
[5]*Subtype 2 of influenza/A/equine*
[6]*Immunoglobulin G*
[7]*Cell mediated immunity*
[8]*Cytotoxic T lymphocyte*
[9]*Major histocompatibility complex class I molecule*
[10]*Interleukin-2*
[11]*Cell death triggered by CTL activity*
[12]*Genetically modified organism*
[13]*CTL precursors (more accurately, CTLp frequency)*
[14]*Moral by Prof. J Maynard Smith* (In: *The Pattern of Vertebrate Evolution* (1969) Ed: L.B. Halstead, University Reviews in Biology, Oliver and Boyd, Edinburgh.)

Duncan Hannant

The ear, the nose and the lie in the throat

BOB COOK
Tufts University
School of Veterinary Medicine
Boston
USA

HYPERION was foaled in 1930. Not that I was aware of this when I too was born later the same year. As a child, I had no real awareness of horses in general, let alone one particular horse. As an adolescent, I regarded horses with the same fascination that I might have had for a cobra.

As a student, seeing practice in Newmarket[1], during the spring of 1951, I can remember being with Mr Fred Day as he motored at a snail's pace behind a small chestnut horse that was being led down Snailwell Road. He asked, "*Do you know what horse that is*?" I had no idea. The next time I saw Hyperion, he had changed from chestnut to bronze. During my eight years at the Equine Research Station, I often took a walk down Snailwell Road and paid my respects to John Skeaping's sculpture in the crescent that Lord Derby created for it out of Hyperion's old paddock[2]. By this time, I already had Hyperion's larynx in a museum jar, a gift from William Miller, the previous director. I was also beginning to appreciate what a most unusual larynx it was... a 30-year-old Thoroughbred larynx with no macroscopic evidence of recurrent laryngeal neuropathy.

If admission to the Royal Veterinary College, in 1948, had depended on the standards required today I might never have become a veterinary surgeon. Leaving school at 16, I worked for a year on a dairy farm and at a riding stables but, as a 17-year-old, jumping straight into the second year of a five year course, I was still lamentably unprepared. The student translation of the College motto seemed far too apt: "*Venienti occurite morbo...*" (When we come, death occurs). Most of my classmates were exservicemen and, unlike today, there were only a handful of girls in a class of 60. From a ragbag of memories, I pull a random selection.

In those days of steam locomotives and fossil fuel, the nearby railroad stables were full of Clydesdales. I remember 'Jimmy' McCunn, our Professor of Anatomy, telling us in class that no draught horse should ever be worked on the road at a pace faster than a trot. He had hardly completed the sentence, when a great clattering of iron-shod hooves was heard in the street below, as a Clydesdale with an empty coal cart struck up a cacophony on the granite cobbles as it cantered homewards. As Edward Mayhew remarked in 1860, "*The pace is always more willing when returning to captivity.*"

Thinking of 'nosebag time', Professor 'Fred' Hobday had instituted, some 20 years before, the 'Nosebag Fund' to raise money for rebuilding the old college. Pennies were collected in miniature paper nosebags[3]. They carried a drawing of a retired cavalry horse by the name of Brenda and the legend "*Don't say neigh*". McCunn used to tell the story of a predecessor in his chair, Professor Shave, who was on the faculty during the dying fall of the old building, when its walls were shored up with wooden buttresses. Shave was in the habit of lecturing on the move and would pace up and down in front of the class like a caged tiger. Suddenly, a large chunk of plaster fell from the ceiling, narrowly missing one of the students, who exclaimed, "*Jesus Christ*!" The professor paused in his perambulation and addressed the student gravely, "*It is no good calling on that gentleman, Mr Smith, he was a carpenter not a plasterer.*"

Physiology was under the command of the great (and terrifying) Professor Amoroso. By the time I entered College, this distinguished member of faculty and Fellow of the Royal Society, who spoke the King's English so beautifully, had won his spurs long ago. But when he first joined the faculty, students gave him a much harder time than we would have dared. Young, inexperienced lecturers, as I was reminded years later, were always considered fair game by students and 'Amo' was no exception. Professor Tony King, who was a demonstrator in anatomy in my time, has given me a couple of stories about Amo's early days. I cannot do better than pass them on in his own words:

> *"It was related that, on one occasion, a student took a cannon ball into the lecture room and seated himself on the back row at the top of one of those long flights of wooden steps. Halfway through the lecture he pushed the ball over the top step, and it descended in a series of thunderous crashes. Amo stopped speaking. When the ball finished moving he said, 'Would the gentleman who has just dropped his head kindly come down here and collect it.'*
>
> *"When I was in Amo's class, he used to stamp out minor riots by suddenly pointing in the general direction of the disturbance and shouting, 'You there, come and see me afterwards.' Since his finger pointed in one direction and his eyes in two other totally different directions, half the class*

[1] My student case book for this period contains the following aside: *"The record for the journey from London to Newmarket by road is held by H.H. Aga Khan who, early in the morning, before the war, did it in 59 minutes"*.

[2] Now it has been moved to grace the forecourt of the Jockey Club.

[3] An 1873 entry in *Nature* records the ingenuity of a pigeon that had seemingly learned to fly at the horse's head when the supply of grain had been exhausted from nosebag droppings. The frightened horse would raise its head suddenly and, in so doing, would sprinkle a fresh supply on the ground.

Fig 1: Casting with heavy hobbles. This engraving carried the caption, "The present method of casting a horse for an operation." *It was frowned upon by Mayhew.*

would be standing before him at the end of the lecture."

The highlight of College days, of course, was the final year at Streatley-on-Thames. Lectures were given in an old Nissen hut in the garden of Streatley House, the Georgian townhouse to which the Field Station had moved after the College had been evacuated to Sonning during the war. Food rationing was beginning to end. Professor 'Cliff' Formston, Geoff Arthur, Jim Roberts, Leslie Vaughan and Teddy Yeats, performed *plein-air* surgery on their knees, in a small paddock on the side of the hill. We learned how to cast horses with heavy hobbles. The method we used can be accurately illustrated by an engraving from Edward Mayhew's excellent book[4]. The only thing that had changed in 100 years was the dress code (Fig 1). We also witnessed the art of administering chloral hydrate by stomach tube and chloroform by mask. Students had the privilege of watching surgery but not participating. A large and rather cumbersome x-ray machine was housed in the stables at Streatley House, though I do not recall ever seeing it being used. I do remember that we did have one lecture on x-rays. Systemic penicillin was not in use but, in the course on *Materia Medica*, we learned how to dispense medicines and fold powders into neat little envelopes.

In my final year, I was fortunate to see practice with Colonel 'Mouse' Townsend. Jeffery Brain, who qualified the year before me, was his assistant. Townsend had retired from the Royal Army Veterinary Corps and bought a farm at Southrop, in the Cotswolds. I think he had intended to retire as a veterinary surgeon but his hunting and polo friends would not permit it and, before long, he had a impressive roster of clients and some difficulty in finding the time he needed to hunt three days a week. His 'Hobdaying' instruments were kept neatly in an old army ammunition box, cushioned and protected by the greasy felt lining. As his 'ollybolly' man, it was my job to lay them out for him on a nice clean towel, placed on top of a bale of straw. I don't remember that they were ever sterilised but I may have forgotten.

Qualified as an 'MRCVS' (there was no university degree to be had in those days) and licensed to learn at 21, I was trustingly employed by Messrs Hale and Brown, in Chippenham, Wiltshire, the members of which firm had been kind to me as a student over several summers. This was a predominantly agricultural practice. It did not represent a departure from any grand plan on my part because, at the time, I had no thought of being anything other than a farm animal vet. The salary was ten pounds a week and I thought it princely. Derek Hale, the senior partner and a wise and wonderful mentor, did most of the horse work. He was a keen hunting man and much devoted to Robin, his grey cob. It was thanks to Mr Hale (I never called him Derek) that I was initiated into the pleasures of riding across country. A few years previously, he had done a similar favour for another assistant, Richard Hartley (later to become President of BEVA) by introducing him to the gentle art of fly fishing.

In 1955, I had the temerity to propose myself as a partner to Jeffrey Brain who, by this time, was working single-handed in Townsend's old practice, 'Mouse' having died in the saddle during a game of polo. I thought Brain could do with some help, without stopping to question myself as to whether I was the right person to provide it! My first choice of digs was The Fox Inn at Great Barrington, where my bedroom was lit by oil lamp and the only telephone was downstairs, in the room behind the bar! The custom in this practice, when examining a horse for soundness, was to ride the horse ourselves to test its wind. Not being an experienced horseman, I learned more about riding during the next three years than I ever did about unsoundness of wind! I also learned how to blister and fire a horse; practices which at the time were considered quite acceptable.

In 1958, the nine-year-old School of Veterinary Medicine at Cambridge advertised for a Hospital Surgeon. Although having had no special training in surgery, I nevertheless thought I was an eligible candidate but the Appointments Committee thought otherwise. Professor Leslie Pugh, however, mentioned that a House Surgeon position was vacant and advised me that if I took this for a year, I might be in a better position to compete for a faculty appointment when one cropped up. It was good advice. Under the tutelage of John Hickman, Leslie Hall, Mike Littlewort, Rob Walker and many others, I benefited from a much-needed year of further education. My flatmate, the other House Surgeon at Cambridge, was Mike Rex, who went on to achieve academic distinction in Australia. It was his Labrador/Retriever that ate my first research project.

Being expected to carry out research, but having no idea what to research or how, I eventually recalled that the function of the horse's guttural pouch was unknown. Clutching at this straw, I determined that this is what I would discover. I started by making a plaster cast of the guttural pouch from a fresh cadaver and laboriously pencilled in every landmark on its blood-stained surface. After several weeks, the cast was crowded with information, none of which was backed-up, as it should have been, with photographs and a paper record. I kept the cast on a bookshelf in the flat where, in our absence, it was eaten by Mike's dog. I never have discovered the function of the guttural pouch, though I have toyed with a number of hypotheses over the years. Currently, my favourite is that this diverticulum of the auditory tube in the horse and hyrax amplifies the voice for long distance communication. But

[4]Edward Mayhew, MRCVS (1890) *The Illustrated Horse Doctor*, 17th edn, W.H. Allen, London.

the great tragedy of science is, as Thomas Huxley said, the slaying of a beautiful hypothesis by an ugly fact. How does this hypothesis survive the embarrassing presence of a guttural pouch in that almost silent animal, the tapir? Perhaps the tapir is only silent to our ears but not to those of other tapirs?

After Cambridge, I moved to a newly established lectureship in the Department of Surgery at the recently opened Royal Veterinary College Field Station at Potters Bar. Professor Formston took me into his office and said, "*Well I don't know what you are going to teach, as the syllabus is already being covered by existing members of faculty. But I'll tell you what we'll do. I have been lecturing on the head, neck and chest. As your interest is the guttural pouch and my interest is the eye, I will keep the eye and you can take the rest.*" In this way, Formston set my career compass. I groped around to discover the medical speciality that most nearly corresponded to the current veterinary surgical work in this region and decided it was the ear, nose and throat speciality.

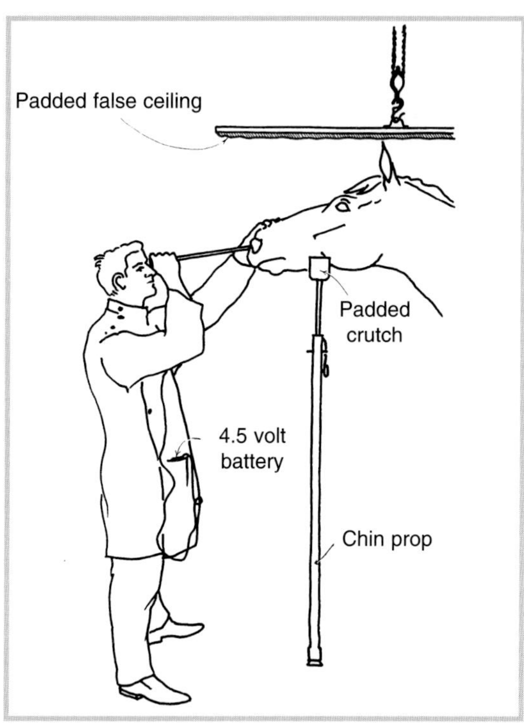

Fig 2: The perils and precautions of endoscopy in the early days. My equine model for this diagram was Persian War, three times winner of the Champion Hurdle.

Accordingly, I browsed through the medical literature in this field and did what I could to model my veterinary studies along ENT lines.

In this I was helped by a fortuitous turn of events. Fred Day phoned to say that he was sending me a Thoroughbred colt of Bernard Van Cutsem's with a septic sinusitus and that a friend of Van Cutsem's, a Harley Street ENT surgeon, wished to be present when I operated. This, I recognised, was a kind way of telling me that they wanted the horse to get the benefit of medical expertise. I spent a feverish weekend in the necropsy room, knowing that the first question an ENT surgeon might ask me would be the exact position of the sinus ostia, a detail on which the veterinary surgery texts (there were very few in those days) maintained a majestic silence. On Monday, a scholarly but sympathetic man arrived, wearing pince-nez glasses. Thus I came to know Alfred Alexander: surgeon, musicologist, farmer, foxhunter, linguist and author. Alfred became both mentor

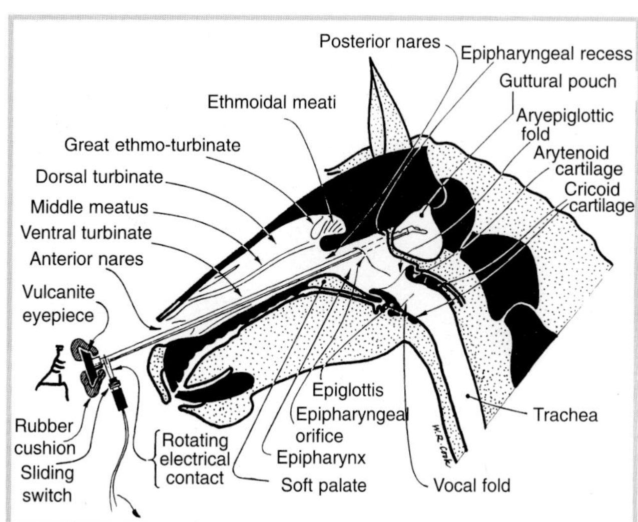

Fig 3: The trick of diverticuloscopy.

and friend. During many a weekend at his farm in Hampshire, I enjoyed a day's hunting, interlarded with frequent discussions (often in the saddle) about comparative aspects of laryngology. Thanks to him, I was at Covent Garden for a performance of *Lucia di Lammermoor* on the night that Joan Sutherland took 14 curtain calls.

The equipment grant for the new Field Station had funded the purchase of a rhinolaryngoscope. When I joined the faculty, there it was in its clean wooden box, untouched by human hand. The trick was first to discover how to get this rigid metal endoscope, with glass optics, safely into a conscious horse's nasal cavity and then to recognise what it was I was looking at by the dim light of a distal bulb (Fig 2). Xylazine sedation would have been a boon and a blessing but, in those days (1960–65), there was no such thing as a tranquilliser. I bent several endoscopes (Formston was amazingly patient and forgiving) and bled a few noses but, finally, endoscopy became a routine part of my examination and opened up a field of research that, at the time, had been only scantily explored. Michael Simons, for example, referred a horse to me with an interesting vascular mass in the roof of its nasal cavity; my first sighting of a disease that Mike Littlewort and I were to later dub 'Progressive Ethmoidal Haematoma'.

The winner of the Epsom Derby in 1934 was Windsor Lad, owned by the Maharajah of Rajpipla, familiarly known as 'Mr Pip'. Later the same year, the Maharajah found himself with a cash flow problem and sold the horse to Martin H. Benson, owner of a well-known bookmaking firm with the motto 'Duggie Never Owes'. At stud in 1938, and heavily insured, Windsor Lad developed a mysterious and possibly malignant disease of the sinuses. Benson filed a claim with the insurance company to have the stallion destroyed on humane grounds, but the underwriters debated the necessity and a High Court action followed. Distinguished medical and veterinary pathologists were called as expert witnesses but a definitive diagnosis was never arrived at, and the debate as to whether this was or was not a cancer was left an open question. Twenty years later, thanks to Benita Horder, the librarian at the RCVS, who allowed Littlewort and I to examine the court transcript, we felt confident that it was possible to make a retrospective diagnosis of Progressive Ethmoidal Haematoma.

With the help of an angled bulb and some sleight-of-

Fig 4: 'What's he up to now?' From left to right, John Hickman, Leslie Vaughan, Clifford Formston and Derek Tavernor at the RVC in 1961, watching 'young Cook'!

Fig 5: BEVA crest designed by Frank Palmer Cook.

hand, one could even get the 'borescope' into the guttural pouch (Fig 3). As a result, I began to recognise the frequency of a problem that had not then been fully described or recognised as a disease entity. Now it seemed to be turning into an epidemic. To Formston's bemused incredulity, there was one week in which the majority of the loose boxes assigned to the surgery department were occupied by horses whose case record sheets carried the unfamiliar diagnosis, 'guttural pouch mycosis' (Fig 4).

Which brings me to another retrospective diagnosis, this time on Humorist, winner of the Epsom Derby in 1921, ridden by Steve Donoghue. A vivid description of this horse's death by exsanguination on a Sunday afternoon, soon after Ascot week in 1921, is provided by Sir Alfred Munnings in his autobiography. At the time, the cause of death was attributed variously to pulmonary tuberculosis or a ruptured aorta but, in hindsight, a diagnosis of guttural pouch mycosis seems much more likely.

When the British Equine Veterinary Association (BEVA) was formed in 1961, I became its first Honorary Secretary and prevailed upon my father to submit a design for the BEVA crest. This is the one that was accepted and is still used today (Fig 5). An alternative logo was offered by a veterinary surgeon/artist by the name, I think, of Murphy. His delightful engraving of a horse was rejected on the grounds that it had something wrong with its left hind leg. But horsemen are notoriously difficult to please on such matters. I am reminded of John Singer Sargent's definition of a portrait as being "*a painting with something wrong about the mouth*".

Prior to forming the association, there was a great throwing about of brains concerning the feasibility of such a project. Looking back, it now seems incredible that one of the very real fears was that horse vets, being such fiercely territorial, suspicious, jealous and secretive individuals, would surely never be prepared to talk to each other, let alone share their knowledge! Needless to say, these fears were dispelled at the first meeting. It is one of the unsung achievements of BEVA that these barriers were removed overnight. Destruction of the Berlin Wall was not more impressive! I cannot resist slipping in an item of trivia at this point. The first paper given at the first Congress was entitled *Observations on the Equine Soft Palate* and the author was the person that John Hickman always referred to as 'young Cook'.

After three years as 'Hon Sec.' for BEVA, I became its Public Relations Officer. The congress that year was in London, with a trip to the Field Station at Potters Bar on the last day. In those days, the strictures against advertising were so rigorous that a veterinary surgeon whose name was mentioned in the press ran the risk of being struck off the register. Because of this, the Executive Committee[5] wanted the name of the association to be mentioned and the topics under discussion but absolutely no human interest. I spent the first two days of the Congress shepherding the press members around and pointing out the significance of all the fascinating material that was being presented by these necessarily anonymous speakers, but all to no avail. Not a paragraph appeared in the newspapers. On the last afternoon, a large group of practitioners, together with members of the press, were gathered around a horse in the paddock outside the Field Station's operating barn (we were still operating on our knees at this period) as Derek Tavernor and I gave a joint demonstration. Derek was introducing the relatively new concept of closed-circuit halothane anaesthesia and I, with my head under a black cloth to keep out the sun, was giving a running commentary on what I could see, endoscopically. In the guttural pouch, of course, I mentioned the fascinating throb of the external and internal carotid arteries. In parrying questions from one curious spectator, Derek overlooked the fact that, in the meantime, oxygen was still bubbling merrily through the halothane in the vaporiser. I shall long remember the moment when he joined me under the shroud and asked, in a whisper, "*Can you still see those arteries pulsing*?" I checked quickly and confirmed his worst suspicions. As soon as the spectators realised that an emergency had occurred they began to take an intense interest. Many were already of the opinion that this newfangled method of anaesthesia was too clever by half and here was the proof - a dead horse.

By this time, Derek was busy squeezing the rebreathing bag and I, for want of something to do, invented on the spot a method for carrying out external cardiac massage: kicking the horse repeatedly on the sternum. Neither Derek nor I had ever known a horse to recover from cardiac arrest. Nevertheless, we felt obliged to show willing and to be seen

[5]Members of the Executive Committee attending meetings at BVA headquarters in London arrived wearing bowler hats and carrying furled umbrellas.

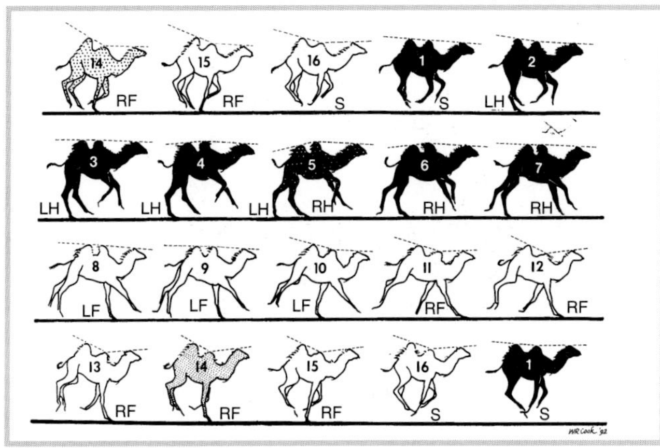

Fig 6: Respiratory/locomotor coupling in the camel. This series of diagrams I based on Eadweard Muybridge's classical work, to show how inspiration (solid camels) takes place when the hind legs are weight bearing and expiration (open camels) when the forelegs are weight bearing. For camel read horse - the respiratory sequence is identical.

to be doing something. So, sweating profusely, we persevered with our pumping and kicking. Remembering, after a while, that the press were watching and guessing that they might misinterpret my good intentions, I stopped the 'massage' for a moment to take off my shoes. After what seemed like an eternity and, much to our surprise, the horse gave a gasp and began to recover. The crowd melted away. The next morning, while shaving in the bathroom and listening to the BBC news I heard, to my dismay, that "*Bob Cook kicked a horse to life yesterday at the Royal Veterinary College*."

This same bathroom was where I later had the 'eureka' experience of knowing that one could cure unilateral guttural pouch tympany by cutting a hole in the median septum. Another happy experience at the Royal Veterinary College occurred one spring morning in 1963. While riding a client's horse to test its wind, I suddenly realised what it was about a canter that made me want to burst into song. The poetry of motion was engendered by the synchronised rhythm of hoof beat and breath; the horse was breathing in time with its legs. Like Chaucer's Cook, I could have clawed myself with pleasure. The joy of this discovery, however, concerning what has since become known as respiratory/ locomotor coupling and found to be a feature of many mammals (Fig 6), was somewhat dissipated when I searched the literature and found that Dr Wittke in Germany had already made the same observation a few years previously.

After London, there followed five years at Glasgow, under the guidance of Sir William Wiepers. Whenever I think about him, I recall Basha's haiku,

Unknowingly, he
guided us
over pathless hills
with wisps of hay.

One of these 'hills' included a memorable year teaching small animal medicine and surgery in Kenya. Margaret and I recall, among many other treasured family memories, the anachronistic charm of racing at Nairobi and Limuru.

I moved, in 1969, to the Animal Health Trust's Equine Research Station in Newmarket. Dr Richard Archer, the 'king of the eosinophil' and director of the ERS, arranged for me to be registered at his own college, Trinity Hall, to study for a PhD at Cambridge. Kenneth Wilsdon, the senior ENT consultant at Addenbrookes Hospital, volunteered to become my supervisor. Once again, I profited by the comparative medicine approach and the enthusiastic interest of a member of the medical profession. One of my examiners, however, was less than fascinated by my eventual thesis on idiopathic laryngeal paralysis. Tiring of his task, during a train journey between London and Edinburgh, he heaved my weighty tome onto the luggage rack and left it there. My deathless prose travelled up and down the country for three months, quite undisturbed.

At Newmarket, I came to the conclusion that, for physiological reasons, laryngeal surgery was never likely to restore normal function to the larynx of a horse with recurrent laryngeal neuropathy (RLN). There being no satisfactory treatment, the next logical step was to focus on prevention. Firmly believing that RLN was largely inherited, I spent many years chasing a genetic will o' the wisp. It was my fond hope that a measure of the coefficient of inbreeding of a Thoroughbred might provide an effective method of selection. The less inbred the better, I argued, as this would reduce the likelihood that a given horse would develop diseases caused by harmful recessives. Unfortunately, having struggled to develop a method for measuring the coefficient based on 20 generations, I came to realise that even this depth of analysis was insufficient and that, even if it had been practical to measure the coefficient right back to the foundation animals in the General Stud Book (which it wasn't!), there would be insufficient variation in the coefficient for this parameter to be useful as a basis for selection.

A population that has a closed stud book and has been inbreeding for 30 or more generations is, inevitably, becoming more inbred with each succeeding generation. It is only to be expected that such a breeding policy, coupled with inadequate culling, will result in the inexorable escalation of recessive diseases, infertility and loss of stamina. Thoroughbreds are destined, therefore, to become increasingly delicate. Like the problem of breakages with precious porcelain, owners may in future find that they are too fragile for everyday purposes and will not withstand being thrown in the racecourse 'dishwasher'. Those who can afford the replacement costs will continue to use 'porcelain' but others may decide that a sturdier equine 'pottery' is more practical for daily use. The heretical solution comes to mind that, in the next millennium, perhaps the racing world will come to recognise the virtue of the hybrid. This, after all, is the basis for success in most commercial animal and plant breeding ventures. Mule racing, as a vehicle for gambling, would be as good as Thoroughbred racing and might even prove better. Mules would have a wider appeal and mule athletes, lasting longer, would become more familiar to the punter. The monitoring of mule racing would be relatively simple as each animal would be earmarked and, being infertile, there could be no cheating. The sturdier mule would require less maintenance and there would be savings for the owner on veterinary fees and replacement costs. Dream on Cook!

While at Newmarket, I tried to find a way to make a horse close its larynx on demand and in such a way that the larynx could be observed endoscopically, without any interference. I thought that such a test would enable adductor function to be better assessed. After a number of false starts, it occurred to me that, during defaecation, we

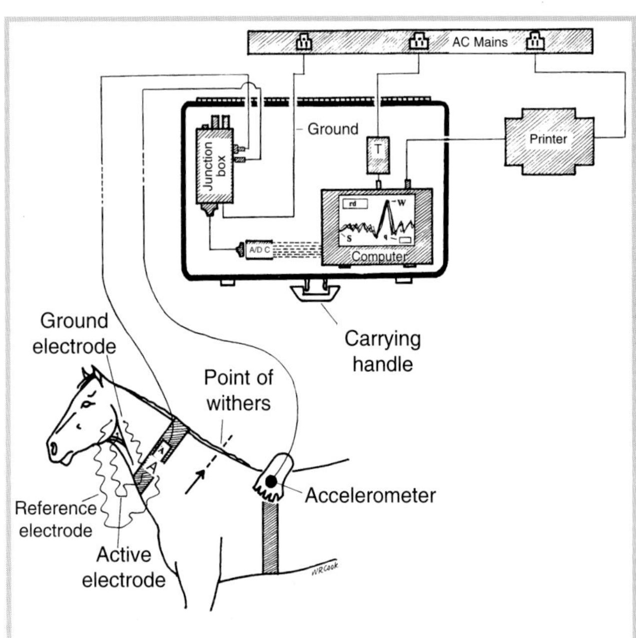

Fig 7: The Mark III ELG circuit.

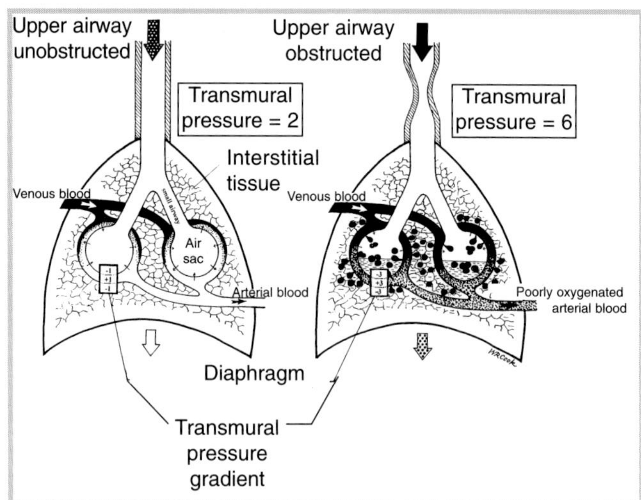

Fig 8: Explaining the mechanism of the upper airway obstruction hypothesis regarding the cause of pulmonary haemorrhage. The transmural pressures shown are fictitious units but serve to demonstrate the principle involved.

close our glottis. What if, I thought, I placed something in the rectum and an endoscope in the nose and waited for the grunt from the glottis? Accordingly, I inserted a cylindrical party balloon in the rectum, then filled the balloon with warm water. But the horse just stood there, with its ears cocked, not a bit concerned about the foreign body under its tail and, certainly, quite 'unmoved'. After a while, I realised that my idea was not going to work. Nevertheless, I went on watching the larynx as Bill Foster, my assistant, withdrew the balloon. I was still watching a moment later when Foster walked up the left side of the horse and consoled the horse with a pat on the back. "*Do that again!*" I cried. And every time he slapped, the right side of the larynx gave a little adductory flicker. Soon I found that this was a crossed reflex and that, if a healthy horse was slapped on the right side of the back, the left side of the larynx would respond. So was established the existence of the thoracolaryngeal reflex, popularly known as the 'slap' reflex. Another decade passed before it dawned on me, as the result of discussions with Hans Thalhammer[6] when we were both on the faculty at Tufts University, that if the latency of the reflex was measured, this would provide an objective method for grading both recurrent laryngeal neuropathy and degeneration of the cervico-thoracic spine[7]. After another decade of development, I have the Mark IV version of a portable instrument I call an electrolaryngeograph, or ELG (Fig 7). With a ten minute examination, it is now possible to measure the recurrent laryngeal status of a horse and assign it a letter grade. Early results hint at the presence of a correlation between ELG grades in yearlings and their racing performance as three-year-olds.

As my interest in guttural pouch mycosis 'bleeders' became known, I was given the chance to examine many racehorses that exhibited what was then referred to as 'epistaxis' or the 'broken blood vessel' problem. I was able to rule out the likelihood that such bleeding originated in the nasal cavity, as we used to think, and concluded, in a 1974 paper, that it was coming from the lungs. This conclusion was subsequently supported by Richard Pascoe and has since become widely accepted. So much for the source of the blood. Unfortunately, another suggestion which I inserted as a tailpiece to the 1974 paper has also been widely accepted, that the cause of the bleeding might be some low grade pulmonary inflammation. Since then, as a result of collecting new and conflicting evidence, I have abandoned this hypothesis but it still has many adherents. I now support the theory first suggested by James Rooney, that this is a problem caused by asphyxia. Any obstruction of the upper airway can, I believe, produce this secondary effect on the lungs (Fig 8). Shakespeare seems to have unconsciously crystallised this domino effect when, in *Hamlet*, he minted the phrase "*the lie i' th' throat as deep as to the lungs*". The causes of obstruction are legion for, sadly, horses are often required to draw their breath in pain. The list includes, but is not limited to: poll flexion and soft palate mobility (both commonly caused by the bit; see below); narrow jaws (therefore, stenotic nasopharynges); recurrent laryngeal neuropathy; and tracheal deformity (Fig 9). I now propose that a suitable name for the problem is asphyxia-induced pulmonary oedema (AIPE).

Anecdotal support for the AIPE hypothesis comes from a diary entry for 7 May 1662, when John Evelyn attended a meeting of an assembly which, three months later, was to receive a charter and be named the Royal Society.

> *"I waited on Prince Rupert to our Assembly where we tried several experiments in Mr Boyle's vacuum. A man thrusting in his arm, upon exhaustion of the air, had his flesh immediately swelled so as the blood was near bursting the veins: he drawing it out we found it all speckled."*

During a sabbatical leave from Tufts University, in 1986, I was able - thanks to Michael Osborne and the support of Sheikh Mohammed - to do some research at Kildangan

[6]Currently Professor and Head of Clinical Sciences at the School of Veterinary Medicine, University of Vienna, Austria.

[7]J.F. Smithcors noted in *Evolution of the Veterinary Art* (1957) that the French phrase "*mort du chain*" (death of the spinal cord) was corrupted in the late Middle Ages by the British into the phrase that Shakespeare used in *Taming of the Shrew* "*mourning in the chine*". The theory was that excess bile in the horse, an animal without a gall bladder, was carried to the spinal cord, then the brain and on into the nasal cavity, from where it was discharged at the nostril and recognised as glanders.

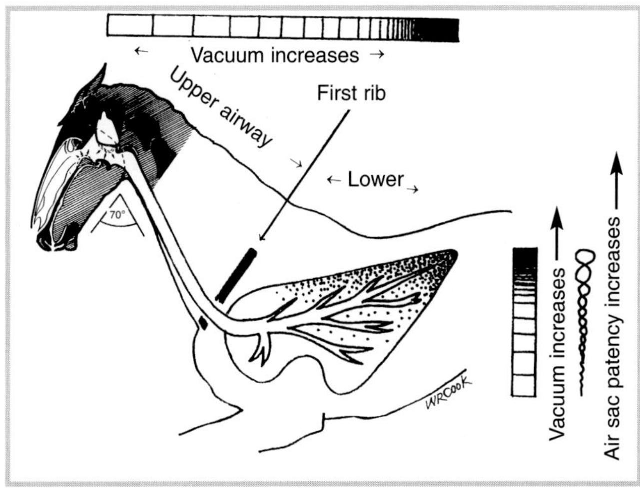

Fig 9: Showing how the upper airway obstruction hypothesis is consistent with the distribution of lesions in pulmonary haemorrhage. In this particular instance, the source of obstruction is poll flexion, elevation of the soft palate and flaccidity of the nasopharynx.

- *Bilateral symmetry of lesions is what the hypothesis would predict.*
- *Dorsal distribution is what would be predicted on the grounds that the dorsal alveoli are more patent than the ventral and, therefore, more exposed to barotrauma on inspiration, when exaggerated negative pressures are developed.*
- *Caudal distribution is what would be predicted on the aerodynamic principle that in gas flow along an obstructed tube, the pressure drop distal to the point of obstruction increases with distance from the point of that obstruction. On inspiration, therefore, pressure would be lowest at the caudal extremity of the lung.*

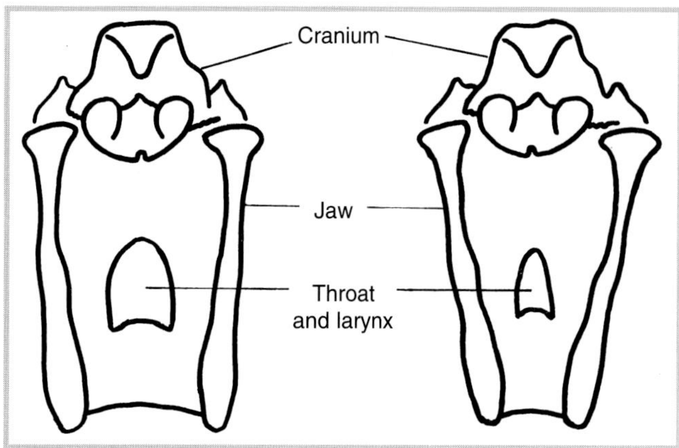

Fig 10: Two diagrams of skulls, viewed from the rear, illustrating good (left) and poor (right) conformation of the lower jaw, together with the effect this has on the cross-sectional area of the nasopharynx. The diagram on the left is drawn from the skull of Brown Jack, one of the most famous stayers in English racing history. He won the 2 mile 6 furlong Alexandra Stakes at Royal Ascot six years running.

Stud in Ireland. It was there that I first became aware of the importance to the horse of a wide jaw. Since then, I have had no reason to change my mind. Width of jaw is, I believe, one point of conformation that really does correlate with performance. Having come to this conclusion, I was delighted to be told by Sheikh Mohammed that the Bedouin horseman has always regarded width of jaw as being a factor that can make the difference between life and death. In tribal warfare, the Bedouin knew that he had a far better chance of outpacing his pursuers following a raid if he was riding a horse with a wide jaw. The citing of individual instances in support of a general theory is rightly frowned on as being unscientific. Nevertheless, as a matter of anecdotal interest, I would encourage anyone to spend an afternoon in the bone room basement of the British Museum and contemplate the lower jaw of Brown Jack (Fig 10). Alternatively, visit the Irish Horse Museum at the National Stud and ogle Arkle.

Two years ago, I received a telephone call from Allan Buck, a dressage instructor in California. He told me that he had developed a new bitless bridle but was having difficulty in persuading the horse-owning public of its merit. Having read my book[8] he thought that I might be interested. To cut a long story short, he sent me a bridle. I put it on an awkward Thoroughbred that, with a snaffle bit, was a headshaker, a stumbler and a pain to ride; and I was an instant convert. Many similarly enlightening experiences since then have led me to ask myself some fundamental questions about what a bit does to a horse. As a result, I have realised that the bit is physiologically contraindicated, counter-productive and, in the wrong hands, cruel. Many physiological facts can be mustered to support this conclusion but I will content myself with explaining only one.

As soon as a bit is placed in a horse's mouth, alimentary reflexes are initiated. Accordingly, the lips and muzzle start to move, salivation commences, a chewing reflex is stimulated, the mouth opens, the tongue constantly explores the bit and, because of the tongue's mobility, the soft palate intermittently rises and obstructs the nasopharynx. So far so good. But now the horse is mounted and set in motion and an entirely opposite set of cardiovascular reflexes are initiated. For exercise, the lips should be 'set', the oral cavity should be dry, the jaw stationary, the mouth closed, the tongue immobile and the soft palate lowered. By using a bit, man is asking a horse to eat and exercise simultaneously, something that nature never intended (Fig 11). Digestion is governed by the parasympathetic nervous system, whereas exercise is governed by the sympathetic nervous system. A horse can graze or it can gallop, but it should not be expected to do both at the same time. Yet this is what man has been expecting of the horse for 6000 years.

I am now convinced that the bit is responsible for a number of serious problems, over and above the long list of bit aversion and associated problems that have been well recognised for generations (Fig 12). The problems as yet unrecognised include many manifestations of laryngeal stridor (especially intermittent laryngeal stridor)[9], dorsal displacement of the soft palate, headshaking and poor action. I now have no hesitation in recommending that the first thing to do by way of investigating all four of these problems, is to remove the bit.

Curiously enough, horses have been controlled reasonably well without bits for quite as long as they have been controlled with bits. The bosal, the hackamore and the sidepull are not perfect but they cause fewer and less serious problems than the bit. Buck's bitless bridle overcomes these problems and offers riders and drivers the advantages of going bitless without any of its disadvantages. The new bridle, known as the

[8] *Specifications for Speed in the Racehorse: the Airflow Factors* (1993) The Russell Meerdink Company Ltd., Menasha, Wisconsin 54952.

[9] Laryngeal stridor can be caused by nasopharyngeal obstruction and is not specific to laryngeal obstruction, caused by the ubiquitous recurrent laryngeal neuropathy or occasional laryngeal chondritis.

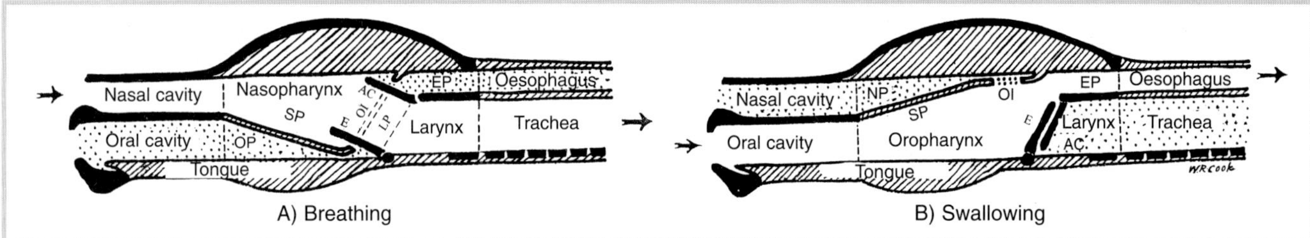

Fig 11: Showing the physiological conflicts caused by placing a bit in a horse's mouth. The bit promotes the swallowing orientation of the pharynx rather than the breathing orientation.

Fig 12: A reminder that the problems of the bit, as illustrated by Mayhew, are still very much with us today, over a hundred years later. This engraving carried the caption "Various modes of forming that which all men speak of with admiration, as "a good mouth.'"

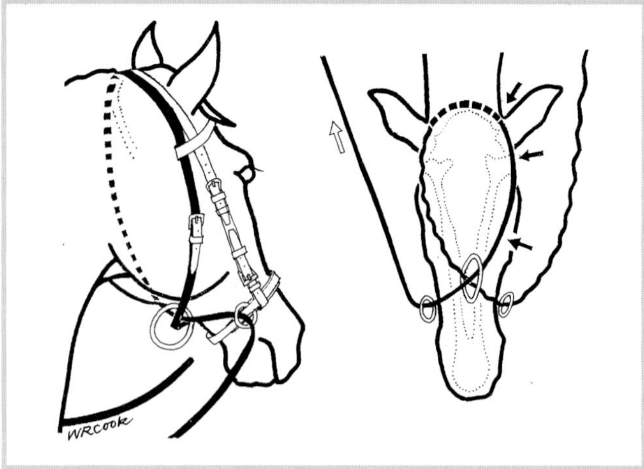

Fig 13: Showing how the Bitless Bridle 2000 controls by pushing, diffusely and painlessly, unlike the bit which pulls, focally and painfully.

Bitless Bridle 2000[10], does not control the horse by pressure on the mouth, which is the principle mode of action of all bits. Instead it controls primarily by applying pressure behind the ears and over the poll (Fig 13). Its overall effect enables the rider to put a benevolent grip on the whole of the head, including nose and chin. The bridle provides effective control, without inflicting pain. It represents a humane and physiologically defensible method for controlling the horse at exercise. As a new millennium commences, it is good to be able to recommend an acceptable alternative to the Bronze Age technology of the bit.

Before I become as tedious as a tired horse, let me close with an item that is for the welfare of the veterinary surgeon and any one else who, like myself, has an aptitude for falling asleep at inopportune moments, such as when driving a car. It might save a life or two. My advice is to overcome any inhibitions you may have about the habit, and chew gum. The rationale for its effectiveness becomes apparent if you watch a horse grazing. At every chew, a pulse of blood can be seen travelling towards the heart in the jugular vein. This results from compression of the large venous sinus that lies within the masseter muscle. In the horse, this muscle pump assists the cardiac circulation to overcome the effects of gravity when the head is lowered. In sedentary man, the same effect maintains a good circulation to the brain and keeps you alert[11].

I would like to thank the horse for teaching me so much; the owners for trusting their horses to my care; and the referring practitioners for giving me the opportunity to learn. I am grateful for the encouragement I have derived from the times when colleagues have agreed with my clinical conclusions. I am especially grateful for the stimulation I have derived from the many occasions when they have disagreed. I wish all future seekers after knowledge good hunting, coupled with the hope that they will enjoy the hunt as much as I have.

> *"For there is good news yet to hear and fine things to be seen,*
> *Before we go to Paradise by way of Kensal Green"*
> \- G. K.Chesterton

[10]ELG Inc., 206 Birch Run Road, Chestertown, Maryland 21620, USA. Tel: (410) 778 9005 and on the web at www.bitlessbridle.com
[11]Robert Louis Stevenson noted that Yoshiba, a Japanese scholar, avoided falling asleep over his books by stuffing mosquitoes up his sleeve.

Lower airway obstruction, heaves or broken wind

ED ROBINSON
Department of Large Animal Clinical Sciences,
Michigan State University,
East Lansing, Michigan 48824-1314
USA

"It was my original intention to publish nothing until I had gone over the field of equine physiology, but I found, after several years of work, that the information I had collected was a mere drop in the ocean, for inquiries of this kind are necessarily slow, and there appeared no reasonable prospect of covering within the space of one life the ground I had mapped out."

\- Sir Frederick Smith, 1892.

When I was a young clinician, I was frustrated by the use of a stethoscope to diagnose horse lung disease. So I was delighted when, in 1967, Jerry Gillespie asked me to be his graduate student.

I was convinced that physiological investigations would allow me to quantify the extent of disease and understand its pathogenesis. I came to Michigan State University in 1972, intent on building a research group to study animal lungs, especially horse lung disease. Fortunately, like Sir Frederick Smith, I had all the ambition and naivete of youth and, being unaware of the pitfalls, I set forth on my quest.

I have been blessed by numerous excellent graduate students and interactions with colleagues both in the US and elsewhere and bruised by reviews of papers and proposals. A quarter century later, I can see what progress we have made but it is 'a mere drop in the ocean' in relation to the knowledge we need totally to understand equine airway disease. This article is a mixture of science, saga and philosophy, and provides my own personal history and opinions about equine lower airway disease. So that we remain humble in this age of biotechnology, I have included quotations from books written in earlier centuries. You will come to realise that, although we can now explain disease pathogenesis in greater detail, some concepts were well in place at the end of the 1800s and some 200 years earlier.

The Term 'COPD'

Severe, inflammatory obstructive airway disease of the older horse is known to the layman as 'heaves' or 'broken wind'. The term chronic obstructive pulmonary disease (COPD) was coined by Sasse to describe this syndrome in horses that are stabled for much of their lives, have virtually unending exposure to hay dusts and, therefore, continuous airway obstruction. In man, COPD is a disease associated with smoking, in which airway obstruction is due primarily to mucus accumulation and structural changes in the airways and surrounding lung parenchyma. Human airway obstruction is not easily reversed by use of bronchodilators and is not very responsive to steroid therapy. This is quite unlike equine COPD in which airway obstruction is intermittent, dependent on environmental factors, and due largely to bronchospasm that can be reversed by use of bronchodilators. Unlike human COPD, equine COPD is alleviated by use of corticosteroids. Equine COPD is, therefore, more akin to human asthma than to human COPD.

Unfortunately, the use of the term COPD has been broadened to include many younger horses with less severe airway inflammation. There has been no conclusive demonstration that airway obstruction accompanies this milder airway inflammation and there is certainly no evidence that it progresses to the severe syndrome called 'heaves' in the older horse.

It is time to rename equine inflammatory airway disease. The severe syndrome of older horses should be renamed 'recurrent airway obstruction' (RAO) or 'equine asthma'. Both of these terms recognise the intermittent nature of airway obstruction and its potential reversibility. 'Inflammatory airway disease' (IAD) has been suggested by Moore as the name for the less severe syndrome that is observed in younger horses, particularly racehorses in training. For the remainder of this article, I will use the term 'heaves' so that both veterinarian and layman know that I am describing the severe syndrome seen in the mature horse.

Whatever Happened to 'Emphysema'?

In the 19th century, veterinarians recognised that the lungs of heaves-affected horses were hyperinflated, that air was trapped in the 'air cells' of the lung and escaped into the interstitium. This emphysema was thought by some to be the primary cause of broken wind and the reason for its irreversibility. Others, who realised that the severity of clinical signs varied from day to day and almost disappeared with suitable management of the horse, concluded that the emphysema was secondary to airway obstruction caused by bronchospasm and mucus. Gresswell and Gresswell (1885) went so far as to state that *"Emphysema is in no means the prime cause"*. In this century, the debate has continued, but it is now accepted that the primary lesion in horses with heaves is chronic bronchiolitis and bronchitis. The associated bronchospasm leads to gas trapping and hyperinflation of the lung. Heaves can be associated with true emphysema, i.e. destruction of alveolar septa, but lesions are not extensive and tend to be restricted to the margins of the lung.

Is Heaves a Form of Asthma?

The idea that heaves or broken wind is a form of asthma was posed as early as 1738 by Bracken who wrote that the *"horse (is) subject to fevers and asthmas, which last is what farriers call a broken wind"*. Asthma is defined by the following criteria: 1) intermittent, naturally occurring, reversible airway obstruction; 2) airway hyper-responsiveness; and 3) airway inflammation. Heaves fulfills all of these criteria.

Reversible Airway Obstruction

Tyler and Gillespie at the University of California were the first to quantify the severity of airway obstruction in heaves-affected horses. Their results have been confirmed repeatedly. Reversibility of airway obstruction by environmental management was recognised long ago. Markham (1636) wrote that *"The best cure in this regard is grass in summer and hay sprinkled with water in winter."* Several authors in the 19th century repeated this observation. In North America in 1860, Jennings recognised that *"The disease has no existence on the prairies - and affected horses taken there are soon well."* Reversibility with bronchodilators is now well accepted but it was recognised as early as 1885 by Gresswell and Gresswell who recommended the use of belladonna (atropine) for treatment of equine asthma and broken wind. These authors described the spasmodic contraction of the circular nonstriped muscle of the bronchial tubes. However, their concept of the function of bronchial smooth muscle was very different from ours. Whereas our present understanding is that bronchospasm is protective and prevents entry of inhaled irritants into the alveoli, Gresswell and Gresswell believed that bronchial smooth muscle pumped air out of the lungs. Bronchospasm prevented this normal function and, hence, the broken-winded horse used its abdominal muscles to aid exhalation.

Airway Hyper-Responsiveness

Our laboratory at Michigan State University began investigating the similarities between asthma and heaves in the 1970s. Fred Derksen, then a graduate student, was investigating the neural reflexes that control airways in horses. One of his experimental ponies had a dramatic response to a relatively innocuous challenge and it dawned on us that horses with heaves may provide a good animal model for the study of airway hyper-responsiveness. Armed with preliminary data from only one animal, I sent my first research proposal to NIH and was funded. An older, wiser investigator would not have had such gall but, at that time, NIH was funding about 25% of applications and the knock-out mouse had not been discovered. We were then faced with finding a population of heaves-affected horses in order to fulfill the objectives of my grant proposal. We should have given that first pony a golden pasture because studies that emanated from that first observation have funded us ever since.

Our laboratory was not the first to describe airway hyper-responsiveness in heaves. Obel and Schmitterlow in Sweden had made the same observation almost 30 years earlier! Professor Deegen's group in Hannover, Germany described hyper-responsiveness in heaves-affected horses at the same time as we did. In equine medicine, there is a tendency to make generalisations based on a small amount of research and that has certainly been the case with airway hyper-responsiveness. The term 'hyper-reactive airways syndrome' is used commonly to describe poorly performing horses with evidence of airway inflammation, but airway hyper-responsiveness has not been documented in this group of animals. It is clear that heaves-affected horses have nonspecific airway hyper-responsiveness, which becomes particularly severe during exacerbations of the disease. In periods of remission, the hyper-responsiveness wanes, but it takes only a few hours of exposure to hay dust to initiate hyper-responsiveness with heaves.

Airway Inflammation

The third criterion for asthma, airway inflammation, is clearly met by the horse with heaves. However, in human asthma, the most important inflammatory cell is the eosinophil, while in the horse, it is the neutrophil. The importance of inflammation in broken wind was recognised by Gresswell and Gresswell (1885), but it was the introduction of bronchoalveolar lavage into equine medicine by Viel that allowed quantification of the severity of airway inflammation. That, coupled with the use of nuclear imaging has led to an understanding of the time course of airway inflammation. When a heaves-susceptible animal is stabled and fed hay, neutrophils begin to enter the lungs at four hours and their number reaches a plateau by six to seven hours. This migration of neutrophils into the lungs is accompanied by the development of airway obstruction. While there are horses that do not fit the typical trend, the severity of neutrophilic inflammation generally parallels the severity of airway obstruction.

A Nervous, Inflammatory Disease

Gresswell and Gresswell in 1885 referred to broken wind as *"A nervous inflammatory disease"*. It is now clear that in many airway inflammatory conditions there is an intimate interaction between the inflammatory response and the nervous system that regulates smooth muscle tone, mucus secretion, and the cough reflex. The mucosa of the horse's airway is richly supplied with neuropeptide-containing sensory nerves that are particularly dense around the plexus of blood vessels that immediately underlies the epithelium. When these nerves are activated by inhaled 'irritants', neuropeptides are released locally where they cause mucus secretion, vasodilation, increased vascular permeability, and neutrophil chemotaxis. The role of this excitatory nonadrenergic-noncholinergic nervous system (eNANC) in heaves is unknown, but its location makes it a likely candidate for initiation of the airway inflammatory response to inhalation of the contaminants in dusts of stables.

More is known of the critical roles played by other parts of the autonomic nervous system in heaves. The observation that antimuscarinic drugs, such as atropine and ipratropium, reverse a large part of the lung dysfunction seen in heaves has led to the conclusion that bronchospasm mediated by activation of muscarinic receptors on airway smooth muscle is the major cause of airway obstruction. Inflammation upregulates the reflex arc causing bronchospasm. A succession of graduate students in our laboratory at Michigan

Ed Robinson

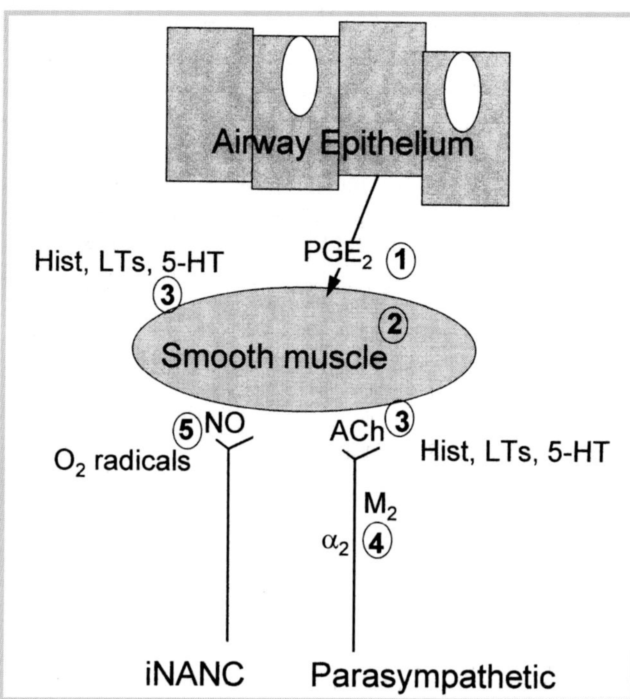

Fig 1: Factors promoting bronchospasm in heaves-affected horses.

1. *Diminished production of prostaglandin E_2 (PGE_2) by airway epithelium. PGE_2 normally inhibits smooth muscle contraction and is antiinflammatory.*
2. *Proliferation of airway smooth muscle.*
3. *Inflammatory mediators such as histamine (Hist), leukotrienes (Lts), and serotonin (5-HT) facilitate smooth muscle contraction by acetylcholine (ACh). Histamine and serotonin also increase release of ACh from parasympathetic nerves.*
4. *Dysfunction of prejunctional muscarinic (M_2) and adrenergic (α_2) receptors that normally inhibit release of ACh from parasympathetic nerves.*
5. *Dysfunction of the inhibitory nonadrenergic noncholinergic (iNANC) nervous system perhaps because the neurotransmitter nitric oxide (NO) is inactivated by oxygen radicals released during inflammation. The iNANC system is the primary nervous system inhibiting smooth muscle contraction.*

State University has investigated the response of smooth muscle to acetylcholine released from parasympathetic nerves and factors regulating release (Fig 1). Inflammatory mediators such as histamine and leukotriene D_4 greatly augment the airway smooth muscle's response to parasympathetic nerve activation. There also appears to be a dysfunction of the alpha$_2$-adrenergic and M_2-muscarinic prejunctional receptors that normally inhibit the release of acetylcholine from parasympathetic nerves. There is also dysfunction of the inhibitory nonadrenergic-noncholinergic nervous system (iNANC), which uses nitric oxide as a neurotransmitter. It is interesting to note that Gresswell and Gresswell (1885) recommended use of a nitric oxide donor, amyl nitrite, as a treatment for broken wind. It is becoming quite clear that heaves is one of a family of airway diseases seen in many mammals in which inflammation and neural regulation are interacting to cause the clinical syndrome.

Mediator Soup and Masses of Protoplasm

When I see a histological section of an inflamed airway, I imagine all the interactions taking place to produce the clinical syndrome of heaves. Inflammatory cells of various types have infiltrated the airway wall and accumulated in the airway lumen and are releasing a veritable soup of mediators. Epithelial cells are producing mucus, smooth muscle is contracting, and blood vessels are leaking under the influence of nerves and inflammatory cells. If one thinks about the melange of cells, mediators, and genes involved in these processes, it is easy to become overwhelmed. However, when I look back, I can see that careful investigation has helped us to make tremendous progress in understanding horse airway disease and that our state of knowledge is not too far from that in human airway disease. How did this occur?

Tennyson wrote: *"Science moves but slowly creeping on from point to point"*, and to me the advance of knowledge is like a large mass of protoplasm moving inexorably forward. Within that mass there is random motion in all directions as hypotheses are propounded and tested, opinionated individuals push for acceptance of their view and are challenged by those who present carefully collected data, meetings occur and investigators return home to try new ideas, and funding priorities change. Gradually, a weight of evidence accumulates, ideas are accepted or discarded, and knowledge moves slowly forward. Within that moving mass of protoplasm, however, each individual investigator must try to produce something solid.

When directing a research group, it is difficult to know when to intervene if a study does not seem to be progressing in the expected direction. In a series of articles entitled *The Retrospectoscope* published in the *American Review of Respiratory Disease,* Julius Comroe pointed out that important discoveries are usually made by chance, and that has certainly been my experience in working with a series of graduate students investigating horse airway disease. Fred Derksen set the future direction of our laboratory by discovering a pony with hyper-reactive airways while studying vagal reflexes. Rick Broadstone discovered lack of iNANC function in heaves while describing autonomic regulation of airways. In his search for a source of the eicosanoid 15-HETE, Peter Gray discovered that airway epithelial cells of horses with heaves have a reduced ability to produce prostaglandin E_2. To test the hypothesis that this deficiency of PGE_2 might be responsible for increased release of acetylcholine (not true) Zhao-Wen Wang established a technique for measurement of acetylcholine release. Xiang-Yang Zhang used the latter technique to determine if exercise-induced levels of catecholamines could inhibit release of acetylcholine. He discovered, for the first time in any species, a beta$_2$-adrenoceptor that augments the release of acetylcholine. Over the years, I have found that when studies do not seem to be producing the expected result, it is unwise to abort the investigation because the horses are trying to tell us something.

"A Very Ignorant Set of Men whose Arguments are Weak and Inconclusive"

Bracken, who applied this description to farriers in 1738, was a physician who wrote a book about horse diseases based largely on his knowledge of human medicine and his realisation that *"The property of the Body is alike in humans and brute creatures"*. As veterinarians, we are not like the farriers of the 18th century. We are aware that discoveries made in the mouse and guinea pig are applicable to both human and animal disease. We realise that research collaborators from biomedical science are essential to progress in understanding horse diseases. Biomedical science advances understanding of the molecular basis of disease and we must be ready to use the knowledge gained to improve the health of horses.

A Focal Source of Dust

Sometimes, a study produces such an obvious result that I am amazed. Such was the case with Pam Woods' study of air quality in our stables. Pam attached personal air samplers to the halters of ponies and compared the dust levels at the nose with those in the stable air a few feet from the manger. When the ponies ate hay, dust levels in the personal samplers were much higher than those in the stall; when they ate pellets, the two levels were the same. These data shouted at us that the horse's exposure to dust depends on where it puts its nose! If there is a focal source of dust such as poorly cured hay on which the horse is feeding for many hours per day, dust exposure is high regardless of overall stable ventilation.

The importance of environmental factors in horse airway disease has been recognised for centuries. Markham (1656) recognised that green grass would help a horse with broken wind, and Peall (1814) devoted a whole chapter of his book to the air in stables. Numerous authors in the 19th century described non-nutritious, bulky feeds as a cause of airway disease. They thought that this type of feed irritated the stomach and, by a reflex involving the 'pneumogastric nerve' (vagus nerve), airway obstruction developed. Now, we believe that these types of feed provide a focal source of dust for inhalation.

We know, from studies in laboratory animals, that numerous inhaled agents can produce airway inflammation. Many of these, such as antigens, dusts, endotoxins, and ammonia are present in the air of stables. So it is not surprising that the incidence of airway inflammation is high among working horses. Reduction of the dust challenge by use of haylage or pelleted feed has very beneficial effects on airway function in heaves-affected horses. Elimination of focal sources of dust must be emphasised again and again to the horse-owning community if we are to reduce the impact of airway disease.

Treatments, or *"How Ventipulmin affected my Life"*

When I lectured on horse airway diseases in the early 1970s, I told practitioners that clenbuterol (Ventipulmin) would soon be available in the USA. However, when we began to test the efficacy of Ventipulmin, we found that only about 25% of heaves-affected horses responded to the dose of Ventipulmin in use in Europe. This was, in part, because FDA required that we prove efficacy without adjunctive treatment such as environmental change. As a consequence of our failure to provide the expected results, company officials from Germany were sent to observe us doing studies, and we were sent to Europe to be shown a horse responding to the drug. The latter trip was associated with the first ever conference on horse airway disease, organised by Professor Deegen from Hannover and Ernst Salomon from Boehringer Ingelheim.

One highlight of the conference was a mediaeval feast at which beer and forcefully administered schnapps had a dramatic effect on the dignity of some of the famous professors! Sober minds later decided that Boehringer scientists would conduct the US clenbuterol efficacy studies. Deb Erichsen laboured long on this project and demonstrated that, in the absence of environmental modifications, about 25% of heaves-affected horses responded to the dose of 0.8 micrograms per kilogram, higher doses being necessary in many horses. Because Ventipulmin was available in Canada, long before it became available in the USA, it frequently 'appeared' in US stables, and was imbued with all sorts of wonderful powers. Regulatory authorities were determined to stamp out illegal use of this wonder drug and developed sensitive detection methods.

In an almost unbelievable confluence of events, an ultrasensitive test for clenbuterol became available almost simultaneously with FDA approval of Ventipulmin syrup in 1998. Now racing authorities are faced with the situation of a legally administered compound that can be detected in the horse's urine for weeks after administration ceases. It is over 20 years since I first told veterinarians about clenbuterol; and I am on the speaking circuit again. This time I am talking to regulators as well as veterinarians about clenbuterol. Over the intervening years, ideas on treatment of airway disease have changed. Bronchodilators are now seen as adjunctive to reduction of inflammation. Now I am telling practitioners that personal inhalers will soon be available to deposit potent anti-inflammatory drugs directly into the airways. I hope that I am not, once again, 20 years too early.

We are now confident of three tenets in the treatment of inflammatory obstructive airway disease: eliminate the cause, reduce the inflammation, and relieve the airway obstruction. The importance of environmental factors in heaves is well accepted but the role of infection in IAD of young horses is still being debated. Most likely we will learn that many factors can interact synergistically to cause airway disease in both man and horse.

The use of inhaled steroids to reduce airway inflammation has become a standard treatment for human asthma. Early use of steroids prevents the airway remodelling that results in more persistent airway obstruction. Systemic corticosteroids are also widely used to treat heaves. Their use, however is generally begun when the horse is showing fairly severe clinical signs and the dose of steroid is decreased as rapidly as possible because of fear of side effects. As convenient inhalers become available for use in horses, we will be able to introduce inhaled steroids into the treatment regime at an early stage of the disease, treat horses for long periods and, hopefully, prevent or slow the long-term deterioration of lung function.

Immunology, Genetics, and Disease Susceptibility

I have left these topics to the end of my article because I see them as the frontier. Why do certain horses develop chronic airway disease while others do not? Why is the inflammatory response so exaggerated in some animals? These same questions are being vigorously investigated in human medicine and the availability of strains of inbred mice with hyper-reactive airways is making the search for answers much easier. The tendency to develop inflammatory obstructive airway disease is most probably dependent on many genes that regulate the inflammatory response and airway physiology. Finding an inbred population of horses susceptible to heaves would greatly simplify the search for genetic factors involved in the disease.

What do we know about the immunology and genetics of heaves? Too little. Although the belief that heaves is a hypersensitivity reaction to inhaled antigens is widely accepted, I have been unable to determine the origin of this idea. Groups working in Glasgow and Edinburgh veterinary schools have focused attention on the importance of allergy to thermophilic fungi that are prevalent in poorly cured hay, but it is likely that chronic exposure to a variety of inhaled allergens can initiate the disease. Human atopic asthmatics respond to antigen challenge with mast cell degranulation that results in bronchospasm within minutes. In many individuals, this immediate obstruction wanes and is followed, four to six hours later, by a more severe airway obstruction in which airway inflammation is accompanied by bronchospasm and mucus secretion. Heaves has the features of a delayed asthmatic response with neutrophil migration into the lung, bronchospasm, and mucus accumulation, four to six hours after environmental challenge. However, an immediate response to antigen has never been reported in horses.

Human asthma is an example of an exaggerated Th2 response. This type of response is directed against prevalent environmental antigens that provide little threat to life. Helper lymphocytes involved in the Th2 response produce a characteristic family of cytokines, including interleukin-4 and -13, that promote maturation, recruitment, and activation of eosinophils in the lung, while stimulating production of IgE. Work by the group at the Royal (Dick) Veterinary School in Edinburgh suggests that CD4+ T-lymphocytes (T-helper cells) and IgE are involved in the development of heaves. It is now time to investigate the pattern of cytokine expression following exposure of susceptible horses to antigens so that we can understand the nature of the immune response and why susceptible horses develop such an overwhelming neutrophilic airway inflammation following inhalation of antigens that are apparently tolerated by other animals.

My Dream for the Future

At present, veterinarians are presented with heaves-affected horses and faced with management of a chronic condition that is already well advanced. It is my dream that increased knowledge of immunology will allow identification of heaves-susceptible horses early in their lives. It might then be possible to advise owners and trainers on management of these animals to prevent the onset of disease. This will be aided by availability of inhaled medications that block the critical parts of the immune response, by improved stable design, and by dust-free feeds and bedding that decrease antigen exposure. Ongoing education of the horse-owning community on the management necessary to reduce the incidence of airway disease is essential if my dreams are to become reality.

Further Reading

Bracken, H. (1737) *Farriery Improved or a Compleat Treatise upon the Art of Farriery.* Printed for J. Clarke, London.

Derksen, F.J., Robinson, N.E., Armstrong, P.J., Stick J.A. and Slocombe, R.F. (1985) Airway reactivity in ponies with recurrent airway obstruction (heaves) *J. appl. Physiol.* **58**, 598-604.

Derksen, F.J., Scott, J.S., Miller, D.C., Slocombe, R.F. and Robinson, N.E. (1985b) Bronchoalveolar lavage in ponies with recurrent airway obstruction (heaves) *Am. Rev. respir. Dis.* **132**, 1066-70.

Fairbairn, S.M., Lees, P. and Page, C.P. (1993) Duration of antigen-induced hyper-responsiveness in horses with allergic respiratory disease and possible links with early airway obstruction. *J. vet. Pharmacol. Ther.* **16**, 469-476.

Fairbairn, S.M., Page, C.P., Lees, P. and Cunningham, F.M. (1993) Early neutrophil but not eosinophil or platelet recruitment to the lungs of allergic horses following antigen exposure. *Clin. expt. Allergy* **23**, 821-828.

Gillespie, J.R. and Tyler, W.S. (1969) Chronic alveolar emphysema in the horse. *Adv. vet. Sci.* **13**, 59-99.

Gresswell, J.B. and Gresswell, A. (1885) *A Manual of the Theory and Practice of Equine Medicine.* Bailliere, Tindall and Cox, London. pp 164-172.

Halliwell, R.E.W., McGorum, B.C., Irving, P. and Dixon, P.M. (1993) Local and systemic antibody production in horses affected with chronic obstructive pulmonary disease. *Vet. Immunol. Immunopath.* **38**, 201-215.

Jennings, R. (1860) *The Horse and his Diseases,* John E. Potter and Company, Philadelphia.

Kaup, F.-J., Drommer, W., Damsch, S. and Deegen, E. (1990) Ultrastructural findings in horses with chronic obstructive pulmonary disease (COPD) II: patho-morphological changes of the terminal airways and the alveolar region. *Equine vet. J.* **22**, 349-55.

Klein, H.-J. and Deegen, E. (1986). Histamine inhalation provocation test: method to identify nonspecific airway reactivity in equids. *Am. J. vet. Res.* **47**, 1796-1800.

Markham, G. (1656) *Markhams Maister-peece: Containing All Knowledge Belonging to the Smith, Farrier, or Horse-leech.* W. Wilson, London.

McGorum, B.C., Dixon, P.M. and Halliwell, R.E.W. (1993). Phenotypic analysis of peripheral blood and bronchoalveolar lavage fluid lymphocytes in control and chronic obstructive pulmonary disease affected horses, before and after 'natural (hay and straw) challenges'. *Vet. Immunol. Immunopath.* **36**, 207-22.

McPherson E.A., Lawson, G.H.K., Murphy, J.R., Nicholson, J.M., Fraser, J.A., Breeze, R.G. and Pirie, H.M. (1978) Chronic obstructive pulmonary disease (COPD): identification of affected horses. *Equine vet. J.* **10**, 47-53.

Moore, B.R. (1996) Lower respiratory tract disease. *Vet. Clin. N. Am.: Equine Pract.* **12**, 457-472.

Obel, N.J. and Schmiterlöw, C.G. (1948) The action of histamine and other drugs on the bronchial tone in horses suffering from alveolar emphysema (heaves). *Pharmacol.* **4**, 71-80.

Peall, T. (1814) *Observations, Chiefly Practical, on Some of the More Common Diseases of the Horse, Together with Remarks upon the General Articles of Diet, and the Ordinary Stable Management of that Animal,* John Bolster, Cork. pp.196-207.

Robinson, N.E., Derksen, F.J., Olszewski, M.A. and Buechner-Maxwell, V.A. (1996) The pathogenesis of chronic obstructive pulmonary disease of horses. *Br. vet. J.* **152**, 283-306.

Sasse, H.H.L. (1971) *Some Pulmonary Function Tests in Horses: An Aid to Early Diagnosis of Chronic Obstructive Pulmonary Disease (Heaves) in Horses,* PhD Thesis, University of Utrecht.

Smith, F. (1892) Preface. In: *A Manual of Veterinary Physiology*, Bailliere, Tindall and Cox, London.

Thurlbeck, W.M. and Lowell, F.C. (1964). Heaves in horses. *Am. Rev. respir. Dis.*

Vandeput, S., Votion, D., Duvivier, D.H., Van Erck, E., Anciaux, N., Art, T. and Lekeux, P. (1998) Effect of a set stabled environmental control on pulmonary function and airway reactivity of COPD affected horses. *Vet. J.* **155**, 189-195.

Viel, L. (1983) *Structural-Functional Correlations of the Lung in Horses with Small Airway Disease.* PhD Thesis, Guelph, Ontario, Canada.

Looking back, looking forward, looking in - a century of development in equine upper respiratory tract endoscopy

GEOFFREY LANE
Department of Clinical Veterinary Science
University of Bristol, Langford House
Langford, Bristol BS40 5DU
UK

Introduction

A retiring senior colleague when asked what he felt had represented the single most significant advance in equine practice in his time in the profession advanced the suggestion "*Heaters in cars*". Those of us with less imagination and shorter memories might have offered developments in chemical restraint, or an item from the plethora of diagnostic aids which have evolved in the latter part of the 20th century. Certainly, when seeing is believing, endoscopy would warrant inclusion on the short list of many equine clinicians.

It has been suggested that "*Any natural orifice should be regarded as an opportunity for endoscopy*" and, in this context, the upper respiratory tract of the horse has proved to be an irresistible target in veterinary diagnosis. Disorders of this region are common and produce effects which range from minor performance limitation to those that are life threatening. The indications for clinical investigation of the respiratory system include nasal discharge, airway obstruction, coughing and perceived limitations of athletic capacity. Also, an assessment of the respiratory tract during quiet breathing, and during exercise, forms an integral part of the veterinary prepurchase examination of horses, particularly those destined for careers in the more arduous equine sports such as racing. It should not be surprising that prospective purchasers frequently request an endoscopic examination as a part of the overall evaluation.

It is fortunate that horses are relatively empty-headed creatures because two effective diagnostic tools, radiology and endoscopy, have evolved which are particularly helpful in the investigation of the cavities of the nose and throat. Radiology is effective here because of the excellent contrast which exists between the bone, cartilage, teeth and air within the head and throat. To complement radiological diagnosis the nostrils provide open and well-tolerated points of entry for effective endoscopy into the air spaces of the front end of the horse. There is every reason to expect advances with both techniques in the early part of the next millennium.

Looking Back: Historical Aspects

1795-1970: Rigid Tubular Endoscopes

In 1795, Bozzini introduced a one candle-powered open tubular instrument for human proctoscopy and hysteroscopy and the major developments which followed in medical endoscopy related to the incorporation of lens systems and improvements in lighting from a single candle to alcohol and turpentine lamps. The discomfort resulting from the heat generated by the light source hardly bears consideration and was the limiting factor for patient acceptance until the incorporation of the miniature electric light bulb at the beginning of the 20th century. In the meantime, a visit to a circus in 1868 inspired Kussmaul to persuade a sword swallower to become a guinea pig for the passage of a prototype rigid gastroscope. However, the experiment was a failure through an inadequate field of view and illumination limited to a small portion of the greater curvature of the stomach. Advances in human gastroscopy were slow until the advent of semiflexible and, later, fully flexible instruments. A driving force for the development of endoscopes came from a military requirement to inspect the lining of gun barrels for faults and in the present age the innards of jet engines are checked using both rigid and flexible instruments.

The first reports of equine endoscopy came from Vienna in 1888 and 1889, when Polansky and Schindelka employed a rigid tubular system to examine the pharynx and larynx. Their endoscope had an external diameter of 30 mm; imagine passing a semiflexible 30 mm endotracheal tube via the nasal meati without causing epistaxis! By 1912 Werth had adopted a human cystoscope for equine laryngoscopy. This instrument had a diameter of 10 mm and length of 62.5 cm and was more suitable to be passed via the nose, but poor illumination limited the diagnostic quality of the image. Thus, line drawings instead of photographs were used to illustrate both normal anatomy and some of the lesions identified, including laryngeal hemiplegia. In the same year, Marek became the first to describe the endoscopic appearance of normal and diseased guttural pouches and he illustrated his technique to pass the

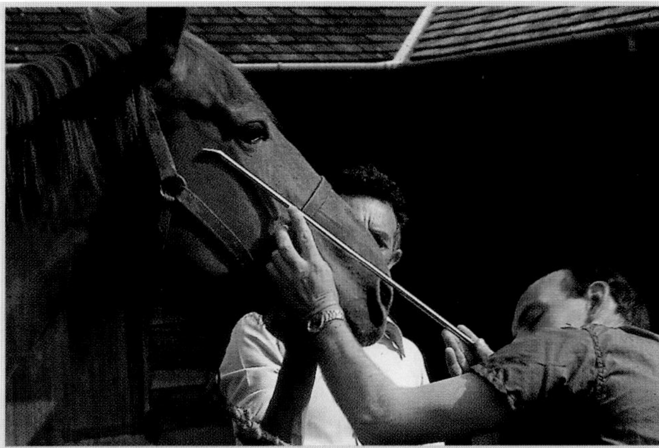

Fig 1: The potential hazards of using rigid instrumentation for URT endoscopy are shown by this 'mock-up' examination. The patient, the clinician and the instrument itself are all at risk of injury.

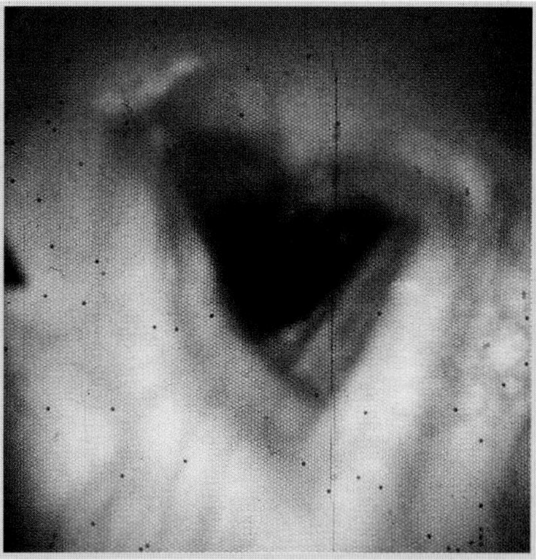

Fig 2: A photograph taken through an early fibreoptic endoscope. Note the granular quality of the picture together with black dots corresponding to broken fibres in the image-carrying bundle. This horse has a grossly deformed trachea.

instrument through the pharyngeal ostium.

Thus, Central Europe was the birthplace of equine endoscopy; and Germany, Austria and Hungary remained pre-eminent in the development of endoscopic instrumentation and a number of endoscopic surveys of the upper respiratory tract of horses were published up until World War II. For example, in 1919 Kral reported endoscopic findings in over 300 horses and evaluated some animals before and after exercise. Throughout this period a major limiting factor with the rigid instruments was that the structures under investigation were viewed at 45°, 60° or 90° to the long axis of the insertion tube. Orientation was, to say the least, challenging even when improved illumination became available.

There appears to have been little interest in equine endoscopy in the English-speaking world until, in the late 1960s, Cook resurrected the use of a rigid rhinolaryngoscope. However, even the enthusiasm stimulated by Cook's work through into the early 1970s was not sustained because of the limited optical quality of the equipment and the potential hazards to patient, clinician and the instrument itself. The difficulties of orientation in a side-viewing system, combined with an inability to clear away discharges, conspired to limit the diagnostic specificity.

1928-1985: Flexible Fibreoptic Endoscopes

Although semiflexible endoscopes incorporating complex lens systems were used for human gastroscopy between 1932-1958 their deathknell had been sounded before they had even been invented. There are no reports that such equipment was ever used in horses. John Logie Baird, better known for the invention of television, took out a British patent on a method to transmit light along flexible glass fibre bundles in 1932. However, it was not until the research of Hopkins in England and Curtiss from the USA that the successful transmission of a sharp image through a coherent fibreoptic bundle that flexible endoscopes became a reality. The first fully flexible human gastroscope was developed by Curtiss and Hirshowitz who reported its use in 1958. Over the following three decades these instruments became highly sophisticated and a wide range of medical, veterinary, forensic and industrial applications have been identified. Medical fibreoptic endoscopes were manufactured in a variety of lengths and widths to suit clinical examinations ranging from the bronchi of infants to the upper reaches of the adult colon. Wherever there was an orifice, an endoscope was made to enter it, and if there was no natural orifice then surgeons felt no inhibition to create a portal. Endoscopes were developed which included a channel for the passage of miniaturised instruments for minor surgical procedures such as biopsy sampling, and the attachment of cameras facilitated case documentation with both still and moving records.

The major explanation for the demise of the rigid rhinolaryngoscope for horses was the report in 1974, again by Cook, of the examination of the equine URT using a flexible

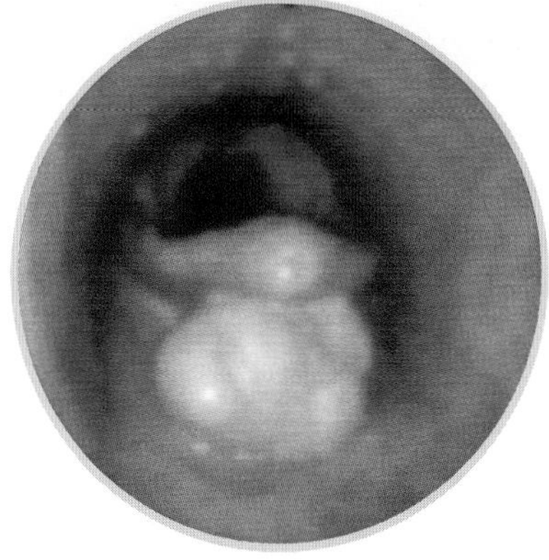

Fig 3: A photograph taken through a fibreoptic endoscope with a 'click-on' chip camera. Compare the quality of image with those obtained through a fibreoptic endoscope (Fig 2) and videoendoscope (Fig 4). A subepiglottal cyst is shown - this condition was first illustrated by Newmann and Kleinpaul in 1944.

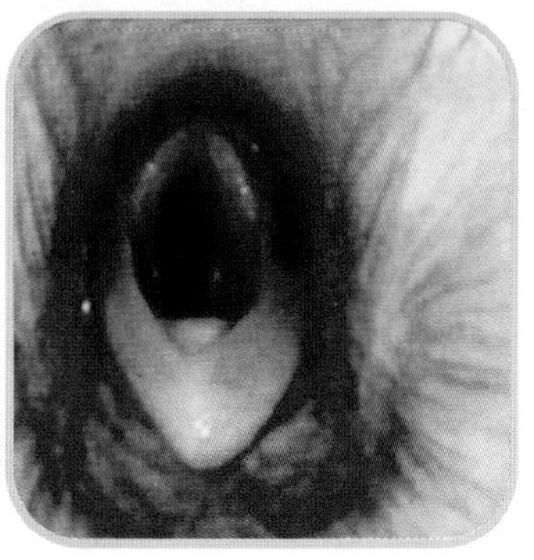

Fig 4: Epiglottal entrapment shown through a second generation videoendoscope. This condition was first recognised by Cook in 1974 and has become a relatively common endoscopic diagnosis.

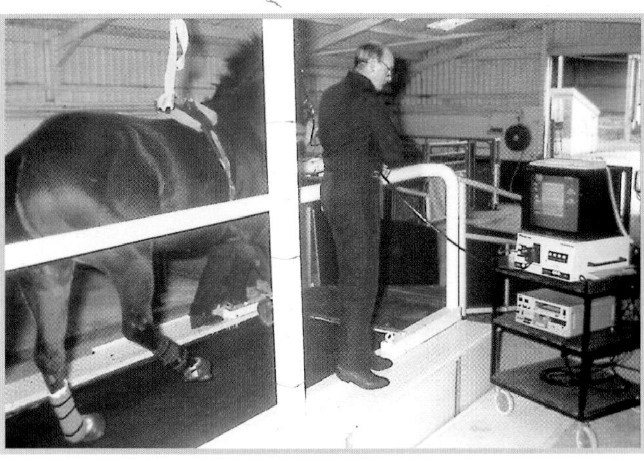

Fig 5: Endoscopy during exercise on a high speed treadmill. This technique now forms an important component in the assessment of horses showing poor performance.

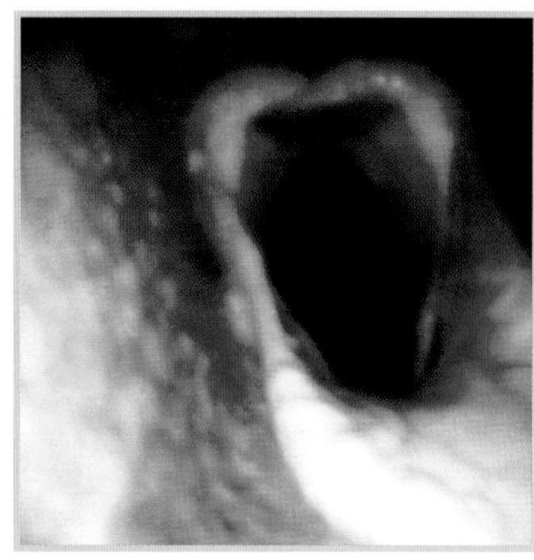

Fig 6: Full symmetrical abduction of the larynx of a horse during exercise.

fibreoptic endoscope. The improved optical quality of image, forward-viewing system and facilities for directional control, objective lens washing and air pump led to increases in the range and specificity of diagnosis. Thus, the history of equine endoscopy, as we know it, goes back little more than 25 years to Cook's pioneering work. Table 1 is intended to give some perspective to the rate at which this method of diagnosis and treatment has evolved. It would be inappropriate to suggest that Cook simply applied equipment to horses which had been developed for medical diagnosis and that it was inevitable that sooner rather than later someone else would have recognised the veterinary potential of flexible endoscopes. Even a quarter of a century later it seems truly extraordinary that so many 'firsts' should have been notched up by him in a single introductory article: mycotic rhinitis; progressive ethmoidal haematoma; pharyngeal lymphoid hyperplasia; pharyngeal paralysis secondary to guttural pouch mycosis; guttural pouch mycosis itself; a pharyngeal stick foreign body; fourth branchial arch defect with rostral displacement of the palatal arch; epiglottal entrapment and arytenoid chondropathy, to name but a few. Some of these conditions had not previously been diagnosed by endoscopy and some of the lesions were totally new to the diagnostic repertoire. Many of the terms used have subsequently become commonplace in the vocabulary of the equine clinician.

With minor exceptions, the pioneers of equine endoscopy, up to and including Cook, left few structural abnormalities to be discovered by the eager beavers of the late 20th century. Although a subepiglottal cyst had first been illustrated by Newmann-Kleinpaul in 1944 it was not until 1978 that Koch and Tate rediscovered the condition and reported a substantial number of cases. Very recently, the author of this commentary thought that he had made a 'new' discovery in the form of acquired strictures of the auditory tube ostia only to find that Cook had already mentioned the disorder in his 1974 masterpiece! Among the few 'new' conditions to have been documented in recent years choanal stenosis, intrapalatal cysts and nasopharyngeal cicatrisation are worthy of mention. Only functional dynamic disorders of the upper respiratory tract escaped detailed interpretation through the inability to conduct endoscopy while the patient was subjected to vigorous exercise.

1985 - Present: Electronic Imaging - Videoendoscopes

In the last 15 years of the millennium the use of videoendoscopes, which convert a digitalised image from a camera at the tip of the insertion tube into a colour picture on a television monitor, has further improved the specificity of diagnosis through the superior imaging systems employed and the facility for storage of recordings on videotape or CD-ROM for subsequent analysis. As part of the growing field of equine sports medicine and performance assessment, critical physiological assessment of respiratory function has enhanced the interpretation of endoscopic findings in terms of the impact which the disorders identified may have on

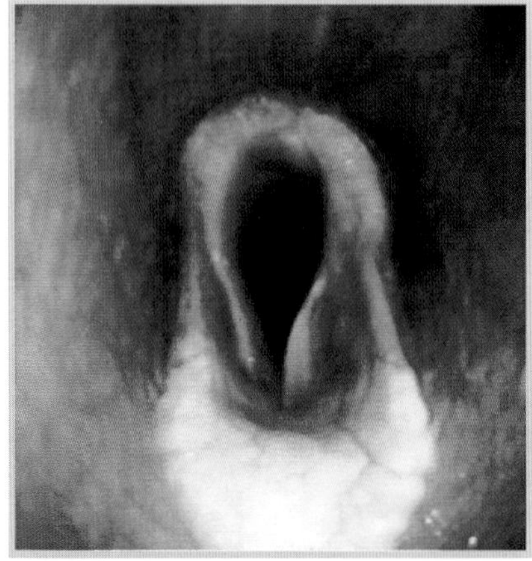

Fig 7: Early collapse of both vocal folds and left arytenoid of a horse with recurrent laryngeal neuropathy. NB in endoscopic images the left side of the patient is shown at the right side of the picture.

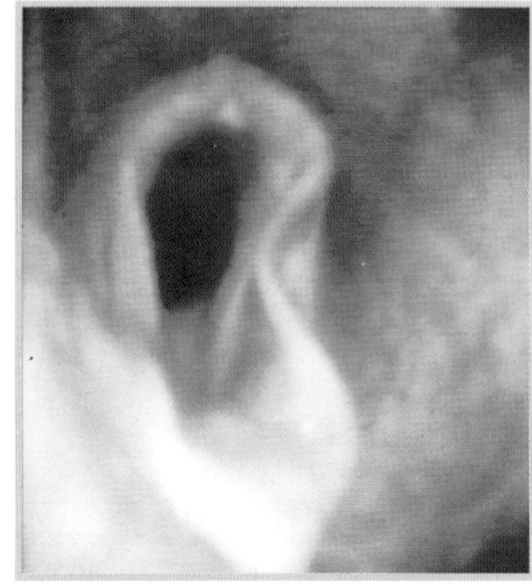

Fig 8: Axial displacement by the left aryepiglottic fold. This is an example of a 'new' diagnosis showing a form dynamic airway obstruction which cannot be appreciated by endoscopy during quiet breathing but which is readily revealed on the treadmill.

the athletic capacity of horses. The combined use of high speed treadmills and videoendoscopes has created the facility to view the dynamic changes which occur in the conducting airways during maximal exercise.

The flexible fibreoptic and videoendoscopes most frequently used by veterinarians are unmodified instruments from human medical practice and few are produced solely for the veterinary profession. The distance between the nostril of the adult horse and its stomach - about 190 cm - has led to the development of exceptionally long gastroscopes, up to 3 m, and this has been rewarded with an insight into the frequency of gastric ulceration in the species. Otherwise, the instrument most favoured by equine practitioners consists of a flexible fibreoptic gastroscope with an insertion tube 1 m long and between 7.0 and 9.5 mm diameter. Such an instrument would be suitable for the examination of the nasal chambers, nasopharynx, auditory tube diverticula (ATDs) and larynx. It would be of little value for oesophagoscopy and yet could be used to view the trachea as far as the thoracic inlet. Colonoscopes usually measure 1.6–1.8 m long and 12–14 mm in diameter and the range of equine procedures for which they can be used is similar to that of the gastroscope, other than that they tend to be difficult to pass into the ATD ostium and their diameter may preclude their use in small foals. On the other hand the additional length is advantageous for tracheoscopy as far as the carina so that colonoscopes are widely used for the collection of aspirate samples from the lower respiratory tract.

Looking In: An Endoscopic Tour of the Equine Upper Respiratory Tract

Endoscopy is usually well accepted by horses and, for most, no more restraint than a twitch is necessary; this helps to stabilise the nostrils as the instrument is passed into the nasal passages but, in excitable animals, may provoke artefactual dorsal displacement of the soft palate. Thus, once the tip of the insertion tube is in place in the pharynx, the twitch can be progressively relaxed, provided that the temperament of the patient permits. Sedatives, such as xylazine, romifidine and detomidine, may be used with very intractable animals where structural abnormalities or the source of nasal discharges are sought, but their role in the evaluation of subtle functional anomalies of the larynx or palatal arch is controversial. General anaesthesia is usually detrimental to effective endoscopy because the postural change produces extensive engorgement of the nasal mucosae and, in recumbency, gravity inhibits the easy passage of the instrument into the guttural pouches. In exceptional circumstances, such as examinations of the mouth, oropharynx and oesophagus, general anaesthesia is indicated to prevent damage to the equipment by biting. Passing the endoscope into the mouth within a mare speculum is a helpful ploy to displace the soft tissues of the oropharynx and thereby to facilitate the view of the structures at the base of the tongue. At the other extreme, for high speed treadmill endoscopy, the videoendoscope is held in the nostril by double velcro tapes or a section of penrose drain which attach to the head collar on either side. The instrument is then held solely at the control housing by the endoscopist. Fibreoptic equipment is not sufficiently robust for use in treadmill endoscopy because the fibres of the image-carrying bundle are vulnerable to fracture.

Nasal Chambers and Paranasal Sinuses

Most horses show apprehension at the initial passage of the endoscope into the nasal meati and, therefore, it should be introduced as far as the nasopharynx via the ventral meatus in a positive manner before inspecting the nasal structures on slow withdrawal. On retraction from the nasopharynx to the choana, dorsal deviation of the instrument reveals the ethmoid labyrinth and the great ethmoturbinate in particular. Novices may confuse this structure for a polyp or tumour and the error is more likely to be made if the horse is heavily sedated or anaesthetised when the tissues become engorged and discoloured. Further withdrawal allows inspection of the nasal septum, dorsal and ventral conchi and the nasal meati.

The term 'turbinate necrosis' appears to have been used quite freely in older texts and yet it is unclear whether it applies to mycotic rhinitis, conchal metaplasia secondary to dental suppuration or to progressive ethmoidal haematoma. Possibly there was no attempt to discriminate between these disorders. Direct inspection of the contents of the frontal, conchofrontal and caudal maxillary sinuses may be performed on the standing horse if a small trephine hole has been created into the CMS under local analgesia. In this manner, haematomas on the frontal aspect of the ethmoid labyrinth or intra-antral mycoses may be identified. It is not exceptional for major abnormalities to be identified by direct endoscopy into the sinuses when conventional examinations *per nasum* have revealed little untoward.

A clinical history and external examination are sometimes insufficient to decide whether or not a nasal discharge is arising from the paranasal sinuses. Endoscopy can be helpful to show pus flowing from the region of the sinus drainage ostia but the demonstration of fluid lines on erect radiographs is more reliable.

All endoscopy of the nasal chambers and paranasal sinuses is best performed on the standing horse because orientation is straightforward and the nasal tissues of the recumbent animal become discoloured and engorged.

Nasopharynx

Congenital choanal atresia is likely to cause extreme dyspnoea in the neonate if the condition is bilateral and it is likely that most afflicted foals die before veterinary attention can be sought. However, when the obstruction is incomplete - stenosis - a horse with nasal stridor may be presented for endoscopy which shows varying degrees of persistence of the buccopharyngeal membrane.

The diagnosis of pharyngeal paralysis as a cause of nasal regurgitation of ingesta is straightforward when the pharyngeal walls lack tone, the palatal arch is persistently dorsally displaced and food debris and saliva are present in the lumen. Further inspection of the ATDs is indicated as mycosis is a likely explanation for this glossopharyngeal neuropathy. In most cases the disorder is, in the strictest sense, pharyngeal hemiplegia because the paralysis is unilateral. This may be confirmed by observing the ostia of the ATDs for their ability to dilate during swallowing.

An early endoscopic revelation was the frequent

existence of extensive lymphoid hyperplasia of the walls of the pharyngeal recess and nasopharynx. The term 'follicular pharyngitis' is inappropriate because lymphoid hyperplasia has a 100% incidence in young horses and the significance which should be attached to the finding is doubtful. Recent evidence suggests that there is little interference with the performance of those adolescent animals which have marked lymphoid hyperplasia, but some clinicians believe that the disturbance of laminar airflow over the protuberances causes adventitious noise and the discomfort of engorged follicles provokes episodic gurgling.

In a single report from the USA, a substantial series of horses was described with endoscopic evidence of nasopharyngeal cicatrices which were thought to be responsible for abnormal respiratory noises and/or exercise intolerance. The condition was commonly found to arise concurrent with arytenoid chondritis or deformities of the epiglottis and ATD ostia. The condition has not yet been reported in Europe or Australasia.

Auditory Tube Diverticula (ATDs) (Guttural Pouches)

The simplest way to pass an endoscope into the pouch is by using a wire leader protruding from the biopsy channel. This channel is invariably eccentric and thus the wire can be used to raise the cartilage flap before advancing into the duct beyond. However, the manoeuvre is invariably unsuccessful unless the ostium is approached via the ventral nasal meatus. In many horses both pouches can be entered by way of one nostril.

ATD diseases are not as common as is popularly supposed. The overdiagnosis of ATD disease arises partly because attention was drawn to the area by reports in the scientific literature and partly because ATD disorders can be lifethreatening. Guttural pouch mycosis is by far the most important disease of the ATD encountered in temperate climates but the worldwide incidence of the condition is highly variable. Although the identification of a mycotic plaque within the ATD confirms the diagnosis, there are practical pitfalls in its investigation by endoscopy. The stress to the horse of being handled may precipitate a fatal epistaxis or the passage of the endoscope into a pouch after a recent haemorrhage may dislodge the haematoma, again provoking a severe loss of blood. Secondly, endoscopy may be unrewarding after a recent haemorrhage. Visibility within the affected pouch may be poor because of the presence of occult blood, and accurate location of the lesion may not be possible. However, it is generally possible to identify whether or not the external carotid artery is healthy as it passes through the lateral compartment. This would be useful as a definitive means to rule out those rare cases when the maxillary branch of the carotid is diseased, although in at least 120 of the 125 cases reported in the literature between 1968 and 1987 the internal carotid was the source of haemorrhage. If the epistaxis has been recent, it may be sufficient to identify the stream of blood flowing from the pharyngeal drainage ostium.

In approximately 60% of grey horses ectopic melanotic deposits can be found in the mucosa of the ATD. The most common site for this to be found is in the lateral compartment adjacent to the maxillary artery. Melanomas may also be identified in this position and it is conjectured that these represent the primary tumour deposits from which secondary melanomas arise in the parotid region.

Endoscopy is less helpful in the diagnosis of other diseases of the eustachian diverticula including tympany, empyema and chondroids. Pharyngeal compression by ATD distension in tympany or empyema may be observed endoscopically and this may help in the planning of the anaesthetic regime for surgery. It has been suggested that fistulation of the medial septum to relieve tympany can be performed by diathermy through the endoscope but no details or results of the technique have been reported. However, this is also an obvious condition which would lend itself to the use of the ND:YAG laser.

Palatal Arch

Midline defects of the arcus palatopharyngeus are the usual explanation for the nasal reflux of milk in newborn foals. The palatal clefts in foals presented in the first few weeks of life are usually narrow midline defects confined to the soft tissues of the caudal portion and less frequently extend forwards to involve the hard palate. Some congenital palatal defects escape attention until maturity is reached and can be difficult to differentiate from iatrogenic defects following overenthusiastic palatal resections. This is because the congenital defects which are more likely to survive without diagnosis until later in life are those not involving the midline but consist of unilateral hypoplasia of the soft palate. In all of the conditions where the palatal seal is defective the horse is likely to be presented with an intractable cough and an intermittent bilateral nasal discharge generally stained by ingesta. Congenital cysts attached to the free border of the palatal arch represent another cause of dysphagia in the neonatal foal and in contrast to the defects described above they may lend themselves to simple and effective surgical removal. Thus, dysphagia in a foal need not necessarily be a grave prognostic sign and endoscopy is a worthwhile measure to clarify the cause. Congenital cysts within the palatal tissues may also cause pharyngeal dysfunction in the forms of dysphagia or respiratory malfunction but they do not carry such an optimistic prognosis.

The primary role of endoscopy during quiet breathing in the examination of horses which sustain dynamic dorsal displacement of the palatal arch (DDSP) is to eliminate other causes of airway obstruction. Owners and trainers often expect the endoscopist to be able to make a positive diagnosis of 'soft palate'. Yet this is rarely possible, least of all at a prepurchase examination. The diagnosis is made primarily on the history provided by the rider, and secondarily, by a process of elimination of other possibilities. Endoscopy during highspeed treadmill exercise is the only means by which to make a definitive diagnosis of DDSP. Treadmill endoscopy is facilitating a better understanding of the normal anatomical relationships between the larynx, epiglottis and palatal arch, during exercise and of the mechanisms by which DDSP arises. It had previously been conjectured that DDSP is invariably a sequel to deglutition through disruption of the link between the respiratory and locomotor cycles. However, recent studies have confirmed that deglutition has no role to play in triggering DDSP. Weakness of the palatal musculature and an inability to maintain an effective oropharyngeal seal appear to be responsible.

TABLE 1: A historical overview of 'firsts' in equine endoscopy.

Date	Technique/Disorder recognised by endoscopy	Author(s)
1888	Upper respiratory tract endoscopy using rigid instrumentation	Polansky and Schindelka
1912	Laryngeal hemiplegia	Werth
1912	Guttural pouch endoscopy	Marek
1914	Bilateral laryngeal paralysis	Frese
1943	Guttural pouch empyema	Gratzl
1944	Dorsal displacement of the soft palate	Newmann and Kleinpaul
1944	Subepiglottic cyst	Newmann and Kleinpaul
1966	Guttural pouch mycosis	Cook
1974	Upper respiratory tract endoscopy using flexible fibreoptic endoscope	Cook
1974	Epiglottal entrapment	Cook
1974	Fourth branchial arch defects (RDPA)	Cook
1974	Pharyngeal lymphoid hyperplasia	Cook
1974	Cleft of the secondary palate	Cook
1974	Tracheobronchial parasitism	Cook
1974	Evidence of previous laryngeal surgery	Cook
1974	Progressive ethmoidal haematoma	Cook and Littlewort
1974	Exercise induced pulmonary haemorrhage	Cook
1978	Pharyngeal cysts	Koch and Tate
1980	Arytenoid chondropathy	Haynes *et al.*
1981	Tracheobronchial foreign body	Lane; Urquhart *et al.*
1981	Nasal aspergillosis	Greet
1984	Transendoscopic tracheal aspirate sampling	Whitwell and Greet
1986	Transendoscopic laser treatment of equine URT disorders	Tate
1987	Pharyngeal cicatrisation	Schumacher and Hanselka
1987	Direct sinus endoscopy	Lane
1988	Transnasal relief of epiglottal entrapment	Honnas and Wheat
1989	Highspeed treadmill endoscopy	Stick and Derksen
1989	Dynamic collapse in laryngeal hemiplegia	Stick and Derksen
1990	Transendoscopic laser treatment of epiglottal entrapment	Tulleners; Tate *et al.*
1990	Transendoscopic ventriculectomy by laser	Shires *et al.*
1990	Dynamic dorsal displacement of soft palate	Morris and Seeherman
1990	Transendoscopic laser treatment of arytenoid chondropathy	Hay and Tulleners
1991	Intermittent epiglottal entrapment at exercise	Morris and Seeherman
1992	Dynamic pharyngeal collapse	Ducharme
1994	Choanal stenosis	Richardson *et al.*
1995	Axial collapse of aryepiglottic folds	Kannegieter and Dore
1998	Transendoscopic intralesional treatment of progressive ethmoidal haematoma	Schumacher *et al.*
1998	Epiglottal retroversion	Parente *et al.*
1998	Correlation between equivocal laryngeal function at rest and dynamic dysfunction at exercise	Hammer *et al.*

Epiglottis

Prior to the advent of the fibrescope, anomalies of the equine epiglottis were practically unrecognised but at the end of the 20th century epiglottal entrapment by the glossoepiglottic and aryepiglottic folds is a frequent diagnosis in horses. Entrapments may be intermittent, and as a part of routine URT endoscopy of horses it is advisable to induce a series of deglutition sequences in an attempt to provoke entrapment. A transnasal technique to relieve epiglottal entrapment in the standing horse has been described using a hooked bistoury passed through one nostril while endoscopic surveillance is maintained through the other. There is the risk during this surgery of serious injury to the soft palate and it is advisable that the patient is heavily sedated and that the pharynx is thoroughly desensitised by the generous application of local anaesthetic spray. The availability of a TV monitor is invaluable. The obvious advantage of a standing method of surgical relief is that the horse can return to training more quickly and, more recently, with the same goal in view, transendoscopic laser ablation of the entrapping mucosa has been reported.

The most common site for congenital or developmental pharyngeal cysts is in the subepiglottic mucosa and these lesions are thought to arise from remnants of the thyroglossal duct or following local trauma. Endoscopic diagnosis is usually straightforward except when the cyst is masked by a dorsally displaced palatal arch. A plain lateral radiograph can provide invaluable complimentary diagnostic evidence.

Oropharyngeal foreign bodies such as twigs and pieces of bramble may become arrested in the lateral food channels lateral to the aryepiglottal folds. Afflicted horses typically show sudden onset dysphagia but the foreign matter itself may not be visible *per os* or by endoscopy *per nasum.*

However, marked swelling of the aryepiglottal mucosa or deviation of the epiglottis itself may be present and this finding should be sufficient to justify an oropharyngeal examination under general anaesthesia. Both peracute and subacute epiglottitis are described in horses. The peracute form, with oedema and cellulitis, is probably a complication of URT viral infections and can be so severe that a potentially fatal airway obstruction occurs.

Larynx

Of all the structures of the equine URT subjected to endoscopic scrutiny, none is more open to controversy and inconsistent interpretation than the larynx. The larynx is a dynamic structure and yet, in clinical veterinary practice, examinations are performed during quiet breathing or, at best, immediately on return from exercise, to be used as the basis for an informed guess at the events that may or may not be occurring during peak exertion. Thus, it should not be surprising that erroneous laryngoscopic diagnoses are commonplace and that surgery of this region is frequently of a speculative nature. Only endoscopy during treadmill exercise can provide an accurate impression of the dynamic changes taking place in the pharynx and larynx under conditions of exertion. In general equine practice, it is unwise to depend upon endoscopy alone for the diagnosis of recurrent laryngeal neuropathy. Suspect horses or those examined prior to sale should be subjected to a routine which includes endoscopy, palpation and an observed exercise test. The significance of untoward respiratory noises during exercise should never be dismissed on the basis of normal endoscopic findings during quiet breathing.

The asymmetry of the *rima glottidis* in cases of true left laryngeal hemiplegia is usually obvious at endoscopy, although the perspective distortion which arises from the eccentric position of the endoscope in the nasopharynx must be taken into account. There is general acceptance that a grading system for lesser degrees of laryngeal dysfunction with reproducible parameters is necessary if the subjectivity of endoscopy of the larynx is to be reduced.

In spite of the considerable body of research and clinical experience which has been brought to bear on the subject, there remains no universally accepted definition of how to differentiate between a normal and a diseased larynx. In the short term, endoscopy of horses during treadmill exercise may seem to be something of a fly in the ointment for practitioners who do not have access to such a facility but it does provide a sound basis for the assessment of airway obstructions. Ultimately, decision-making in equine sports medicine depends upon the correlation of diagnostic parameters and physiological dysfunction. The ability to assess the function of the upper airways during exercise, in terms of airflow mechanics and arterial blood gas measurements, provides the means further to match the impact of endoscopic anomalies with performance limitation and this can be extended to assess the efficacy of corrective surgical procedures. Whatever the limitations of ventriculectomy as a means to treat recurrent neuropathy, it is possible by endoscopic inspection of the ventricular openings to provide a dependable opinion on whether a horse has been 'Hobdayed' previously. Endoscopy is also helpful to establish the degree of abduction which has been achieved by prosthetic laryngoplasty ('tie-back') surgery, to check whether it is maintained in the long term and to identify signs of complications such as dysphagia or chondroma formation.

Rostral displacement of the palatal arch (RDPA) provides the endoscopic evidence of a congenital entity produced by maldevelopment of the derivatives of the fourth branchial arch, namely the wings of the thyroid cartilage, together with the cricothyroid articulations, and cricothyroideus and cricopharyngeus muscles. Affected horses produce a wide range of signs including stridor at exercise and colic resulting from true aerophagia arising from an incompetent proximal oesophageal sphincter. However, the diagnosis by endoscopy alone is not always dependable because not all afflicted horses show the classical RDPA and an open oesophagus. For this reason it is suggested that the term Fourth Branchial Arch Defect (4-BAD) is preferable.

Arytenoid chondritis is an acquired disease and, therefore, mature horses which develop exercise intolerance and stridor, possibly with coughing, warrant a particularly critical endoscopic investigation. Differentiation from hemiplegia can be difficult so that when the left arytenoid is involved and initial endoscopy suggests incomplete abduction, the medial surface of the corniculate process should be scrutinised for focal projections into the *rima glottidis* or contact lesions of the contralateral arytenoid. In the later stages of chondritis, large granulomatous projections may be seen which could be mistaken for neoplasia.

Trachea and Bronchi

The primary objectives of tracheobronchoscopy of horses are more in the identification and aspiration of discharges arising from the lower respiratory tract than in the diagnosis of structural changes of the conducting airways themselves. Rare cases of congenital tracheal collapse, particularly in miniature pony breeds, may be confirmed by endoscopy as well as iatrogenic (post-tracheotomy) distortion or traumatic strictures. Isolated cases of foreign body inhalation to the region of the mainstem bronchi have been reported and this possibility should be considered whenever a horse is presented with an intractable cough together with a fetid breath. Confirmation of the diagnosis requires endoscopy, and retrieval of the foreign body is also performed under direct observation.

It was considered a major advance to know that the overwhelming majority of haemorrhages in horses showing epistaxis after exertion arise in the lungs rather than the nasal airways. However, endoscopic surveys have shown that many, if not all, equine athletes intermittently show frank blood in the trachea after exercise and the likelihood of detection is directly related to two factors, the severity of the exertion and the length of the endoscope used! A sinister change in the very meaning of epistaxis has taken place so that it no longer implies whole blood at the nostrils but rather pulmonary haemorrhage, however slight. Tracheal aspirates can be used to show that haemosiderophages are invariably present in horses in training, suggesting that some degree of exercise-induced pulmonary haemorrhage is an inevitable consequence of exertion in this species. Thus, there is some doubt whether the condition is a disease rather than a normal physiological phenomenon in the equine athlete and there is also a divergence of opinion over its influence on the performance of racehorses. The question may be asked why are so many clinicians seeking a cure for an entity which is not a disease!

Although considerable advances have been made in the understanding of the role of particulate allergens in chronic obstructive pulmonary disease (COPD), the part played by endoscopists has been minor. The retrieval of tracheal aspirates by endoscopy has been advocated in horses with acute or chronic coughing. Examination of the samples obtained for cell concentration and morphology hold some prospect of a specific diagnosis, be it one of allergy, parasitism or microbial infection, and in groups of horses exposed to epidemics of viral respiratory infection, endoscopy can be helpful to advise which animals to rest and which to train.

Looking Forward: What Future Developments Can Be Expected for Equine Upper Respiratory Tract Endoscopy?

Few would argue that the advantages brought to equine practice by the popularisation of the flexible endoscope outweigh the detractions. In the URT, the repertoire and specificity of diagnosis has increased extensively. However, the diagnosis of recurrent laryngeal neuropathy still requires careful interpretation of the endoscopic findings, and their correlation with physiological parameters is essential. At the top of any equine ENT surgeon's 'wish list' would surely be the means by which more accurately to evaluate laryngeal dysfunction. The occasions are few when endoscopy alone provides all of the information necessary for diagnosis, prognosis and treatment and, therefore, this equipment must continue to be used in conjunction with the full range of diagnostic aids as they become available.

No doubt there are some 'new' disorders of the equine respiratory tract out there waiting to be recognised. The most fertile area is likely to be amongst the dynamic disorders observed during high speed treadmill exercise, and it is to be hoped that research will enable those obstructive disorders already described to be more accurately interpreted, particularly in terms of their impact on the horse as an athlete.

To date, the use of endoscopy in the treatment of URT disorders has been limited to laser section or ablation of redundant tissues, and to the surveillance of procedures being performed with instruments passed alongside the endoscope. There is every likelihood that the cost of laser equipment will fall so that it will be widely used in equine practice: 25 years ago few would have believed that fibreoptic endoscopes would become affordable outside teaching institutes and yet today all veterinary practices with the slightest commitment to equine medicine own at least one, often several. Similar trends may apply to laser equipment and to high speed treadmills.

It is a matter for wild speculation what avenues of therapeutic endoscopy will be opened when the new millennium dawns. In other species, including man and dogs, the use of lasers to destroy tissues which have been sensitised with photodynamic preparations is a burgeoning field, but it is conceded that the incidence of neoplastic conditions of the equine URT is relatively uncommon. The development of instrumentation to be manipulated through or alongside flexible endoscopes is likely to extend the range of treatments performed *per nasum* in the standing horse. Recently intralesional treatment of progressive ethmoidal haematomas has been reported and this is relatively easily and accurately achieved with a catheter passed through a flexible endoscope. A routine treatment for chronic sinusitis in man comprises the removal of the uncinate process, a cartilage dam which when swollen inhibits free mucociliary drainage. In order to render a comparable technique applicable to horses with sinusitis it will be necessary to overcome the not inconsiderable difficulty of controlling haemorrhage while resecting tissue under endoscopic control. Will guttural pouch mycosis lend itself to treatment by the implantation of occlusion catheters into the diseased artery while the horse is conscious and will endoscopy have a role to play in monitoring the progress of the operation?

The means by which to transmit coloured and moving images via the internet is already here. In the interests of saving the planet by reduced transport costs and protected rain forests, there should no longer be a need to transport horses over long distances to visit an endoscopic expert or for him/her to travel in the opposite direction. The packaging and postage of endoscopic videotapes will soon be as obsolete as dinosaur orthopaedics when diagnosis-at-a-distance becomes the norm. Radiographs and ECG traces are frequently the subject of electronic transmission and remote diagnosis, even across continents. Thus, the telephoned enquiry and the use of the mind's eye to interpret the primary clinician's verbal description of a lesion inside a horse's head 200 miles away will inevitably become obsolete. If a diagnosis can be made from a distance, why not transendoscopic treatments using robotic arms? Such a brave new world must address the questions raised relating to the medicolegal responsibilities of remote diagnosis and treatment, not to mention how the computer-based clinician will earn his/her crust!

At the turn of the last century no one would have believed that Jules Verne's *Incredible Journey* would have become a reality, but it certainly has through the medium of endoscopy. Only a short time ago clinicians may have dreamt that one day it might be possible for jockeys to carry miniaturised equipment to facilitate examinations of the pharynx and larynx of the horse in motion - endoscopy on the high speed treadmill has fulfilled this wish but with the additional advantage that the exercise test can be rigidly controlled. As the millennium dawns it is inevitable that there will be technological developments in endoscopic and ancillary equipment relentlessly improving the acuity of our diagnostic insight.

Epidemiology in clinical equine practice with reference to colic: uncovering causal factors, predicting outcomes and information overload

MALCOLM ROBERTS
Department of Farm Animal Health
and Resource Management
College of Veterinary Medicine
North Carolina State University
Raleigh, North Carolina
27606
USA

Introduction

The signal development in equine medicine and surgery, experienced since graduation over 30 years ago that has a universal impact, is the exponential growth of information.

The clinician in private practice or academia is overwhelmed with the information blitz and even the most proficient exponent of time management has had to restrict knowledge acquisition to a narrow timeframe. To keep as current as possible, we will be forced to make a paradigm shift in how we access and handle information. We must become more discriminating, not only in selecting those articles pertinent to our discipline or speciality, but also in determining the credibility of the findings that are being reported. This applies to textbooks, journals or references, accessed from library searches through the web, material available on the internet and from commercial CD-ROMs. We must question whether the information is pertinent to the cross-section of horses in our practice region. More particularly, when faced with a clinical problem and seeking additional input from colleagues or from various information sources, can we be sure that the findings and conclusions are valid and can therefore assist our decision making?

In concert with the information explosion, the client base is changing. Horse ownership is increasing; there is a proliferation of equestrian events and activities, as a consequence of greater leisure time, disposable income and the innate appeal or aura of the horse, even without a direct marketing promotion. While the racing industry remains a predominant force in the horse industry overall, this growth in equine interest, ownership and economic base has occurred with sports and pleasure horses. The majority of new owners have limited equine background. They avidly seek information and advice from diverse sources.

Veterinarians have the challenge to ensure that they occupy the centre stage in client education and in promoting and implementing health and 'wellness' programmes. More owners are expecting the veterinarian to provide quantitative rather than qualitative information when they consider the cost benefits of instituting preventive health care programmes or assess treatment options relative to an acute or chronic clinical problem. Direct answers are sought for questions. Responses based on anecdotal experience and best guesstimates are no longer adequate. For example, is the treatment effective in achieving a cure and are there complications? How valid is the diagnostic test that is used to indicate freedom from a disease or that the immune response is protective? What is the evidence that the cause of the problem is represented by the serological or laboratory test results? What are the chances of recovery following surgery for large colon torsion? Why did the torsion occur, and what are the risks of reoccurrence? If surgery is performed for this problem, will the horse return to a level of performance similar to, better than, or below that experienced before surgery?

The clinician has to provide answers and formulate recommendations on prognosis, treatment and cause, using best clinical judgment based on experience, diverse sources of information and any owner-imposed cost restraints. Without realising the significance, equine clinicians are employing epidemiological principles in their descriptive and observational assessment of clinical problems. But wait, epidemiology is the remit of production medicine clinicians who deal with large populations of animals, monitor disease outbreaks and treatment regimens, provide statistical data for monitoring and surveillance studies of preventive health measures, and growth and reproductive outcomes under different management systems.

Epidemiology is the study of health and disease in populations. Each equine practice is responsible for a specific population. For instance, the practice may have developed and promoted health programmes to clients in their district, whether they own backyard horses, performance horses or train racehorses. Even if the owner considers his or her horse an individual animal, it represents part of the larger population, relative to demographics, preventive health care, medical history, nutritional programme, type of activity and management system.

Contributions and Expectations in Equine Gastroenterology

Earlier in my career, the concept of a horse as part of a larger population was not readily appreciated. My initial contributions to the body of knowledge were through publications of case reports or case series describing a unique condition and investigative technique, with a definite outcome, often substantiated at necropsy. Similar cases in the literature were alluded to for comparison or contrast. The conditions were not related to the population at large. The individual horse was not considered a sentinel for a problem if no measures of output were applied, such as growth or production targets, as with food animal species.

Few clinicians recognised that suboptimal growth in weanlings or reduced reproductive performance at a studfarm represented a production problem with an economic cost that should be investigated more thoroughly than treating one or two individuals. It is clear that comprehensive record keeping is essential to identify inputs and outputs. Strategies to resolve the problem can be devised if valid data exist.

My research training contributed to an understanding of the pathophysiology of the equine gastrointestinal tract at a time when there was meager information on normal function. Subsequent research efforts were directed at developing experimentally induced models of impaction colic and acute colitis to study the underlying pathophysiological events. *In vivo* studies were augmented increasingly by utilising *in vitro* techniques, for reasons of cost, the more stringent limitations on approval for animal experimentation, and to control the variables inherent in working with the live animal. Descriptive research has been complemented and superseded by the mechanistic approach to function and dysfunction. Graduate students have investigated fluid and electrolyte transport across the colon in response to different feeding frequencies, adaptive responses to extensive small bowel resection, the role of inflammatory mediators in acute colitis, and mechanisms of intestinal injury and repair. Scientific methods have involved the use of tissues, cells, and subcellular components. As the focus has narrowed down towards the molecular level, the application time and transfer to the live animal problem lengthens. This is a product of maintaining research quality and credibility to remain competitive to attract external sources of funding.

Advances in equine gastroenterological research have been astounding in the past three decades, as exemplified by the increase in knowledge of gastric ulcer disease, endotoxaemia and its ramifications in acute abdominal disease, and the promise that studies on mucosal barrier restitution holds for managing postoperative events in the remaining intestine after surgical resection of ischaemic bowel. However, we as clinical investigators must not lose sight of the big picture, namely, horses in the general population. Combining the rich vein of research progress with an approach to identify those factors that influence the development of the major gastrointestinal diseases through epidemiological studies will amplify the impact that the clinician can exert in dealing with this diverse population.

The overall management of acute abdominal disease, through earlier recognition, aggressive volume replacement and attention to endotoxaemia, excellent anaesthaesia and surgical techniques, has contributed to increased survival rates at recovery and at the time of discharge for many horses with problems that previously would have been considered not only poor risks for surgery but also for survival. As a consequence of these developments, the immediate postoperative phase has become the rate-limiting stage in the outcome, and intensive care management is directed at controlling pain, ameliorating smooth muscle motility disorders and the manifestations of continued endotoxaemia.

The challenge to the equine clinician extends beyond predicting those horses that will survive. The expectation is to give meaningful information on the probability of return to performance if the problem is uncomplicated. The owner questions why this horse developed colic in the first place. Economic prosperity and urban development have imposed pressures on equine operations, particularly in periurban areas, affecting the availability and access to pastures and turnout. The majority of athletic horses, whether used for racing, sport or pleasure, receive processed feed material, high in energy and density, twice daily with limited fibre as dried forage and spend the large proportion of time in a stall environment rather than outside on pasture. Activity levels comprise varying degrees of exercise from intermittent, irregular periods to sustained repetitive training programmes. The development of many equine clinical problems can be linked to nutrition and management practices and the immediate environment. Identifying specific factors in animals with a problem compared with those that are disease free, or comparing a group exposed to factors with a group not exposed with respect to development of a disease forms the basis of observational studies in epidemiology. Knowledge of the risk factors will aid the clinician to formulate recommendations on management and other changes that can reduce the magnitude of the problem, therefore improving the health and wellbeing of the horse. However, the proposed intervention may not be cost effective or practical to implement by the owner or caregiver. Consequently, will the incidence of colic at the farm increase if no remedial action is taken to alleviate the purported risk factors? An affirmative answer would substantiate the clinician's recommendations. Evidence exists from a well-designed study to predict the probable number of colics based on the animal population at risk.

Epidemiological Considerations in Equine Colic

Epidemiological studies in equine colic are not restricted to referral teaching hospitals. They can be conducted in private practices. Unfortunately, medical records data may be difficult to access, are often incomplete, and lack uniformity between and among practices and referral teaching hospitals. However, with the advent of new software programmes to manage medical records information, several practices could generate compatible material for collation by a study leader at a central location. The equine clinician does not have to be a mathematician or well versed in epidemiology or biostatistics to be an active partner in a project in which medical records information on colic cases is analysed to provide valid data. However, the project requires organisation, planning and the input of specialists to avoid any fishing expeditions for potential associations.

Several equine clinicians have stepped forward, acquired formal training in epidemiology and become major contributors in the colic field, including Drs Reeves, Cohen and Tinker in the USA, and a cadre of other investigators in the USA and the United Kingdom and elsewhere who have approached a broad range of equine disorders from an epidemiological perspective. The potential impact of equine epidemiological studies and findings have been highlighted in three recent editorials in the *Equine Veterinary Journal* and one in the *Veterinary Journal*. Two of these addressed equine colic. While uncontrolled retrospective or prospective case series have continued to be published, there has been a profusion of more credible studies with strict selection criteria for case inclusion and controls that have appeared in the literature and on the programmes of national and international meetings. This trend is evident at the Colic Research Symposium held at the University of Georgia every three or four years. Although epidemiologic studies have been included on the programme since the mid-1980s, oral and poster presentations show a continued improvement in study design, methods and validity of results. Many studies have been published in peer-reviewed journals, and several were the subject of the aforementioned editorials.

Nevertheless, these studies on equine colic will have little impact unless clinicians in the field are aware of the findings and understand how the results were derived and can be applied. For example, do the populations and management systems resemble those in their practice region? Clearly, reports of survival of medical colics at referral teaching hospitals may not be representative of the cases seen in a typical private practice. Can results of a study conducted in Texas on a predominantly Quarter Horse population be extrapolated to a highly urbanised sport and pleasure horse practice population in the Home Counties of England? In an attempt to provide answers, information from studies published in the last decade will serve to highlight the progress that has been made and underscore that much remains to be determined.

Epidemiological Concepts and Findings

Epidemiological studies are undertaken to examine factors that influence the development, presentation and outcome of a condition. They focus on the assessment of risk, cause and prognosis. The concept of risk is fundamental to understanding prognosis, treatment and cause. Studies cannot prove with certainty that a cause-effect relationship exists, only that an association exists; and the direction and magnitude (strength) of that association. Initial studies concentrated on survival rates for surgical and medical colics. A plethora of variables or indices were advocated from retrospective and prospective studies from referral centres to aid in more accurately predicting survival probability.

Prediction models were developed and independently validated to provide an indication of prognosis and the need for surgery. Results of this macroanalysis were not unexpected. Significant variables for prognosis reflected the cardiovascular status: peripheral pulse strength, heart rate, capillary refill time and packed cell volume. Variables that described the status of the gastrointestinal tract - rectal findings, frequency of pain, frequency of abdominal sounds - were significant for the need for surgery. However, clinical impression and intuition appear no less accurate in assessing outcome as prediction models, computer programmes or colic severity score systems. House officers in one prospective case study from this college predicted accurately horses that would survive surgery on the basis of clinical findings and judgment. Training enhanced their ability to predict survivors. Furthermore, this predictive ability did not depend on predicting the site or type of lesion.

Risk factors for equine colic have been determined from data drawn from referral centre, practice and horse farm populations in three landmark studies that have addressed the host, management and the environment. Two were case-control studies: the Texas practitioner study of Dr Cohen, and the multicentre hospital-based study from north-east and central USA and Ontario by Dr Reeves. Case-control studies are based on outcomes, and compare a group of diseased animals with a group of healthy animals with respect to exposure to hypothesised causal factors. Prevalence is determined. Usually, they are low cost, and can be conducted with existing data (medical records), with questionnaires or through telephone interviews. Studies are susceptible to bias, depending upon the controls selected and the methods for obtaining the information. The cohort study, considered the gold standard design, conducted at Virginia–Maryland horse farms by Dr Tinker and her colleagues, compared a group exposed to factors with a group not exposed with respect to development of disease. A level of risk of developing the disease is calculated relative to exposure to the hypothesised causal factors. The cohort study is prospective and provides more control over the quality of data. All animals are free of the disease at the outset. The period of study can be protracted, therefore is more expensive to conduct. Owner compliance can falter and animals can be lost to follow-up. However, it provides a measure of incidence (the risk of becoming a case) and incidence density, an assessment of the number of new events or cases per total number of animal days or years at risk.

The Texas case control study provided information through monthly questionnaires of 821 colic cases during a 15 month period. A similar number of controls represented the next noncolic emergency treated each month. The multicentre hospital-based study was conducted over a 10 month period and involved 406 colic and 406 control horses. These were selected randomly from a list of all noncolic admissions in the same week as the colic case. The prospective cohort study of 31 farms in Virginia-Maryland extended over one year, used questionnaires and event calendars and required extensive time commitments, both from the designated farm personnel and the collating group members. Descriptive information from 1427 horses was collected at the initiation of the study and updated at three month intervals. The study provided the first estimate of colic incidence in a general horse population. All animals started the study unaffected. The controls were the randomly selected horse population.

Risk Factors and Colic

Significant risk factors in the Texas study included a history of previous colic or of previous abdominal surgery, recent changes in diet, recent changes in stabling conditions and recent changes in activity level during two weeks prior to the time of examination. Additional risk factors emerged when the data were analysed for a subset of horses with chronic intermittent colic. The incriminating risk factors were age (greater than age eight years), feeding coastal bermuda hay, Arabian breed, being an intact male or a gelding and low density (less than 0.5 horses per acre). The multicentre case control study revealed significant associations for whole grain corn consumption, number of pastures accessed in the past four weeks, horses in outdoor enclosures without a continuous supply of water, Arabian breed, age of horse and dry lot use, type of caregiver and previous colic history.

The cohort study showed that colic risk was intensified with increased concentrate intakes from below 2.5 kg per day to above 5 kg per day, previous colic history, in horses age 2–10 years and frequent changes in concentrate or hay. Activity level was important. Horses in active work or training were at significantly higher risk for colic, whereas horses used for lessons or no defined use had significantly lower risk. Mature horses on forage only and horses with no problems necessitating treatment were at lowest risk for colic.

Despite differences in study design and methodology, biases present in data collection, difficulties in defining and quantifying relevant exposure measures, and differences in the equine populations and management systems in the three regional locations, there were several common risk factors. These highlight the crucial role played by management and nutrition in the development of colic and offer the prospect of intervention that could reduce the incidence of the problem. The risk factors are potentially alterable. Horse factors such as age, sex, breed, and previous colic surgery are unalterable and may be confounding variables. For example, old horses appear more likely to require surgical intervention and tend to have a lower overall survival rate. However, the risk may be attributable to the type of lesion present, such as strangulating lipoma or epiploic foramen entrapment.

Another perspective on the principal findings from these three studies can be gained by reference to the USDA National Animal Health Monitoring System (NAHMS) Equine '98 study. This national epidemiological and statistical project obtained data on horse management and health on farms representing operations with three or more horses, excluding racetracks, and represented greater than 80% of horses from 28 states. Data acquisition included demographics, use of a veterinarian, preventive health, morbidity, mortality, biosecurity, nutrition, facility management and horse management. Except for injury/wounds and leg/hoof problems, colic was the most significant cause of morbidity and was responsible for the greatest number of days of loss of use and the greatest cost to the operation. Furthermore, colic was the most significant cause of death in the age ranges 6 months–5 years and 5–20 years. The horse farm cohort study provided the first estimate of colic incidence in a general horse population. The significant take-home message is that a farm with 200 horses could be predicted yearly to have 20 colic episodes, five deaths from all causes, with one or two of these deaths attributable to colic. If management and nutrition risk factors are alterable, then logic would dictate that the effects of this scourge can be reduced. Presentation of the NAHMS data, according to regional distribution, enables a degree of comparison to be made with the three landmark studies, particularly relative to nutrition (hay and concentrate feeding), water access and confinement by season.

As an aside, the data on the role of the veterinarian in horse health, nutrition and management serve as a salutary reminder that the profession cannot take for granted that horse owners recognise the value of the veterinarian in maximising health and wellness and being the primary consultant on management issues. A vigorous marketing strategy is overdue to connect with those owners who do not interact with a veterinarian.

Lists of factors associated with the development of colic can be found in the literature. These predominantly incriminate the host, environment and management. The epidemiological studies have provided evidence to substantiate several of these associations in a more scientific manner, and indicated several factors that deserve closer scrutiny. Variations in the findings reflect differences in study design, selection of cases and controls, the population at risk and differences in management. Although results should be kept in the context of the study design and population, the implications of the common findings can be transferable to other populations.

Evidence-based Medicine

The application of epidemiological principles to a range of equine clinical disorders has gained momentum in the USA and the UK. The recent Horserace Betting Levy Board-initiated workshop attests to an increasing level of awareness and hopefully of acceptance of this type of study. It is critical that the findings of the initial well-designed studies are relevant to the industry, and that appropriate actions can be taken by the equine clinician in a timely manner to enhance health, performance and productivity. Information should be presented as clearly and unambiguously as possible, and a degree in higher mathematics should not be a prerequisite to interpret the statistical complexity of the findings. The concept of evidence-based medicine is assuming great importance in human medicine as a means to approach clinical problems using the current best evidence from clinical case research in the management of individual patients. The process involves generating an answerable question, and then locating, appraising and integrating the best available clinical evidence into the practice.

Returning full circle to the dilemma of information overload, none of us can hope to keep pace with the growth in information. The task is daunting. Yet we need to provide optimal care for our equine patients. Evidence-based medicine will provide a framework to achieve this objective. Key published material and clinical trials data will be located through computer searches initiated in the practice. Technological advances will enable information to be accessed animal side with a laptop computer. However, the clinician still needs time to assess critically the validity of the material to help in formulating recommendations on treatment options, surgical outcome, probability of return to performance, etc., sought by the client. Unfortunately, the body of knowledge available for most equine topics is relatively small. A single well-designed study may constitute the current best evidence, although this may be appropriate to aid decision making. Critical appraisal of the evidence is the most important step before initiating an action. Additional information has to be accumulated. The challenge is to generate data for the best evidence, the power of which is increased through population studies including clinical trials.

The example cited of the colic studies indicates the level of progress made in understanding the multifactorial complexity of colic. Careful assessment of this type of evidence, together with our clinical experience and pragmatism will help to establish the quality assurance in health care delivery to our patients. Nevertheless, if clients expect the best available evidence, we should not be remiss in charging accordingly for this level of service. Evidence-based medicine will become a powerful tool in progressive practices. In the near future, many graduates will have been exposed to this process during their veterinary curriculum. All of us in clinical practice can participate in expanding the best evidence information. Clinical practice deals with large horse populations. Advances in software programmes should enable appropriate information to be collected. Complex models and large budgets are not prerequisites for epidemiologic studies. Case control studies offer the opportunity for clinicians in practice and at referral teaching hospitals to cooperate in assessing risk factors for colic or other problems affecting horse populations in their region. Prospective cohort studies can be conducted if several practices are willing to collaborate over a designated time period. For such observational studies and for clinical trials, time spent in planning and in study design is critical. Many participants will gain a working knowledge of epidemiology. A uniform protocol for data collection, record keeping and standardisation of clinical signs and diagnosis should be devised with input from a coordinator who may be an equine clinician with epidemiological and biostatistical skills.

Informatics is here, and will continue to assume greater importance in our clinical activities. Advances in computer technology not only will provide access to overwhelming volumes of information but also will distil it to meaningful conclusions for practical application. Practices will have the greatest repository of original clinical information. Analysis of these data will ensure that epidemiology plays an important role in the quality of the service delivered by the progressive equine practice of the 21st century.

Epidemiology: reinventing the wheel or making it go faster?

JAMES WOOD
Animal Health Trust
Newmarket
Suffolk CB8 7DW
UK

Over the course of the last century, general perception of what constitutes epidemiology has shifted from clinical observations of the pattern of disease through to rigorous scientific study, sometimes observational and sometimes actually involving a controlled intervention to assess a preventive or curative measure.

In this respect, the shift seen in equine epidemiology is probably little different to that in other species of veterinary significance. However, the shift in veterinary science has lagged someway behind the same changes in human medicine. Although, in most respects, this lag is a substantial disadvantage, we do have the chance to learn from the medical experience and avoid some of the pitfalls that epidemiology has encountered in its evolution.

Case Report

In the early days of the 20th century, clinical observations, in the form of case reports, and observational epidemiology were virtually indistinguishable. Uncontrolled case reports are still widely published in the veterinary literature, particularly by clinicians and they play an important role in raising awareness of new syndromes or associations and stimulating new ideas[1].

Epidemiological Methods

Above the case report, there is a of epidemiological methods that can be employed in the fight against all important diseases. Many have been used in equine science and include observational or aetiological studies that identify causal or predisposing risk factors for disease and quantify their effects e.g. cyathostomiasis[2], colic (Roberts p 196) and grass sickness or dysautonomia[3] (an excellent example of one of the earliest properly conducted case control studies in veterinary science). Further examples are musculoskeletal injury in racehorses[4,5,6,7,8] and assessment of the relative significance of different diseases through comparison of rates (including incidence, prevalence and possibly mortality rates, e.g. causes of wastage in racehorses[9], equine respiratory disease syndromes in racehorses[10] and causes of anaesthetic death[11]). Randomised controlled intervention or experimental studies are really the only effective way to determine the real benefits of different interventions or treatments for specific diseases. A strength of the epidemiological approach, whatever the chosen method, is that the likelihood of its success is considerably enhanced by close collaboration with appropriate scientific and clinical disciplines. Multicentre collaborative studies[12] fit well in the discipline.

Surveillance

Two other methods used by epidemiologists include surveillance of infectious and new and emerging diseases and computer simulation modelling. Surveillance of infectious diseases, particularly when combined with appropriate control measures, will always be a vital weapon in the armoury of the equine industry. The need for good quality surveillance information will continue to increase as disease patterns change with global warming and the increased international transport of competition horses.

Risk Assessment

Our ability to develop useful mathematical models which can predict disease incidence in different situations has been revolutionised by the developments in computer technology in recent years. These models will be used increasingly to optimise vaccination use and to assess risks or advantages of different programmes. Quantitative risk assessment models are already being used as the basis of international trade regulations and their use is being encouraged by the World Trade Organisation (WTO) and the General Agreement on Trade and Tariffs (GATT). The equine industry will benefit substantially from working closely with regulators to ensure that risk assessment models are realistic and appropriate for the disease in question.

The example of respiratory disease in racehorses illustrates an epidemiological research into an important disease.

Epidemiology of Respiratory Disease in Young Racehorses

It has long been recognised that respiratory disease is common and important in British racehorses and is associated with several infections. Professor Evans reported to the Joint Racing Board[13] that the question of vaccination against equine influenza was confused because several different infections might produce identical clinical signs and he recommended: "*A long-term project for investigating equine respiratory diseases and the effects of vaccination against influenza should be instigated.*"

As a result, the Horserace Betting Levy Board (HBLB) helped to establish a tripartite arrangement of an epidemiologist/extension worker at the Animal Health Trust

(Dr David Powell) supported by laboratory services at the Animal Virus Research Institute, Pirbright (under Dr Bob Burrows), now the Institute for Animal Health, and at the Royal Veterinary College (under Professor Walter Plowright). The two laboratories provided diagnostic services for the equine industry and carried out research projects.

Several research projects were carried out, in particular a study of infectious agents detected in outbreaks of disease in racehorses, between 1971 and 1976[14], and a study more focused on equine herpesviruses[15]. Influenza was identified as an important cause of outbreaks of disease. In one study, equine herpesvirus (EHV) was associated with 10% of outbreaks of acute respiratory disease and a lower proportion of outbreaks of subacute disease[15], but the other study concluded that EHV was associated with around 50% of outbreaks of disease[14].

During this time, substantial efforts were made to assess any role that bacteria and mycoplasma infections played in equine respiratory disease, but no clear association was ever demonstrated. Perhaps because of this, it became increasingly 'established' in dogma that equine respiratory disease, particularly in racehorses, was caused by viruses, although there was little real evidence to support this supposition.

A serious epidemic of equine influenza that severely disrupted racing and a major outbreak of neurological disease caused by equine herpesvirus-1 on a Newmarket studfarm in 1979, led in 1981, to the establishment of a virology unit at the Animal Health Trust (AHT) under Dr Jenny Mumford, to provide dedicated diagnostic services for the equine industry. A more detailed description of the development of equine virology is included elsewhere in this volume (Newton and Smith, see p 166).

The Key Importance of Differentiating the Affected Site in the Respiratory Tract

Through the 1960s and 1970s, all respiratory samples collected from racehorses originated from the nasal passages or nasopharynx. An HBLB scholar, Mike Burrell, initially working at Glasgow Veterinary School and subsequently at the AHT, pioneered the routine use of flexible endoscopes in the UK to examine the airways below the larynx and collect specimens from this site[16,17]. Work carried out by Mike Burrell identified the lower airways as an important site of disease, both in terms of the frequency of disease and its occurrence in outbreaks in young racehorses.

Disease of the upper respiratory tract is principally evidenced by nasal discharge, with or without pyrexia or coughing[18,19], whereas disease of the lung and lower respiratory tract may be evidenced by coughing or pyrexia[19,20,21]. Upper respiratory tract disease is usually diagnosed by simple clinical examination but, in racehorses, disease of the lower respiratory tract, which is often mild, requires endoscopic and cytological evaluation of the airways. Auscultation is rarely sufficiently sensitive in such cases[22]. Although it had been realised for many years that COPD in older horses was a disease of the lower respiratory tract, it has taken longer to reach wide recognition that acute or subacute respiratory disease in younger horses also had a major impact in the lower airways, despite earlier comments by respected clinical observers[23].

A pilot epidemiological study carried out in a Newmarket training yard in the early 1980s, when analysed using appropriate statistical methods[24], demonstrated that inflammatory lower airway disease was the most common form of respiratory disease in the young racehorse[19]. This syndrome was closely associated with bacterial infection (especially *S. zooepidemicus*). A role for *S. pneumoniae* was also established[25,26]. The small-scale study was not large enough to assess the precise role that viruses or less common bacteria played, although the investigations demonstrated clearly that acute inflammatory airway disease was usually not associated with viral infections[20].

Disease of the lower respiratory tract, diagnosed endoscopically and cytologically, often occurred in the absence of disease of the upper respiratory tract (demonstrated by a nasal discharge), although the two syndromes can be present simultaneously. These studies were really the first to make this fundamentally important distinction between lower and upper respiratory tract disease. Also, it was demonstrated clearly that coughing was an insensitive sign of inflammatory airway disease (IAD), with horses only coughing for 38% of the time that they were affected[19]. Thus, it was demonstrated that IAD can be assessed objectively only through the cytology of specimens from the large airways or lungs[27], preferably accompanied by endoscopy of the trachea after exercise[17,19]. Despite the subclinical nature of IAD[19,28], it is associated with poor racing performance[22,29] and reduced respiratory performance parameters[30,31].

In assessing racehorses for the presence of IAD, it is important that endoscopy of the airways is carried out after exercise, as without this, excess mucus may not be visible in the trachea[17]. This is not always done routinely and, in a series of horses referred because of suspected upper respiratory tract disorders, 20% were found to have increased mucus in the trachea, which only became apparent after exercise[32]. Therefore, the protocol used for collecting tracheal wash samples must be considered when comparing studies.

Both upper and lower airway disease can present acutely or more chronically (or at least subacutely). Animals may have a nasal discharge for one day, or it may persist for several weeks. Lower airway disease can also present acutely[20], although it is generally subacute or chronic, its mean duration being around seven weeks[19].

These epidemiological observations stimulated interest in the role of bacteria in respiratory disease and, in particular, work progressed on *S. pneumoniae* through the 1980s, culminating in the demonstration that this bacterium could act as a primary respiratory pathogen in ponies[33].

More Recent Epidemiological Studies of IAD

In 1990, with HBLB funding, the author was appointed to the AHT to work on equine infectious disease epidemiology. Cytology and bacteriology from tracheal wash specimens held on file were used to demonstrate that some species of bacteria (*S. zooepidemicus*, *Actinobacillus/Pasteurella* spp. and *S. pneumoniae*) were associated with lower respiratory tract disease[34]. This provided clear evidence for a pathogenic role for these bacteria, as infections were not the most common upper respiratory tract commensals, as might have been expected if bacterial infection of the lower airways occurred purely as a result of contamination or passive colonisation from the upper airways.

At this stage, a large scale, multidisciplinary epidemiological study of respiratory disease in young racehorses was planned and implemented between 1993 and 1997 in five yards in three different training centres around the UK, requiring close involvement with racehorse trainers and their veterinary surgeons. Epidemiologists and clinicians from the AHT, as well as bacteriologists, virologists, cytologists, pathologists and mycoplasma experts were involved. The study was designed specifically to investigate the role that both bacteria and viral infections play in upper and lower equine respiratory tract disease. Just as the study was due to begin in November 1993, we were asked to investigate an outbreak of respiratory disease in one of the participating yards. Clinical signs included acute respiratory disease with pyrexia, coughing and loss of performance. Conventional tests revealed significant lower airway disease, but laboratory tests did not reveal an obvious cause. Collaborative investigations subsequently demonstrated that the outbreak was attributable to *Mycoplasma felis* infection[35].

This outbreak demonstrated again the critical importance of the site of sampling when investigating respiratory disease as the inconclusive investigations of mycoplasma infections in the 1970s relied only on samples from the nasopharynx. The main study subsequently included mycoplasma investigations.

One hundred and forty-eight horses, mostly age two to four years, were studied prospectively. The results, based on detailed microbiological, cytological and clinical assessments, including endoscopic evaluation of the trachea after exercise, demonstrated that respiratory disease was common[36]. The prevalence of upper respiratory tract disease, defined as an abnormal nasal discharge, was 4.1% whereas the prevalence of lower airway disease, termed inflammatory airway disease (IAD) was 13.8%. The estimate of prevalence of IAD adjusted for the clustering of disease at the horse level was 10.2%. The incidence of IAD was 8.9 cases per 100 horses per month and the incidence of nasal discharge was 2.6 cases per 100 horses per month. The prevalence of both upper and lower respiratory tract disease varied significantly with age, decreasing markedly in the older horses, consistent with the development of immunity[10]. The prevalence of IAD varied markedly between training yards, due mostly to differences in incidence rather than duration.

Different infections were associated with upper and lower respiratory tract diseases. *Streptococcus zooepidemicus, Actinobacillus/Pasteurella* spp., *Streptococcus pneumoniae, Mycoplasma equirhinis, Acinetobacter* spp. and EHV-1/4 seroconversion were associated with IAD, whereas only *influenza A/equi-2* and infection with a group of glucose fermenting mycoplasma distinct from *M. felis* were clearly associated with upper respiratory tract disease.

In general, the incidence rates of bacterial infections (including mycoplasma) were much greater than those of known equine viruses. These studies importantly demonstrated both that bacteria play a much more important role in respiratory disease in racehorses in the UK than hitherto reported and that their association with disease is not dependent on prior viral infection[36].

The Future for Respiratory Disease Research

In common with other epidemiological studies, many avenues for future study were identified, not all involving epidemiology. One of the most important was the stimulus to study further the detailed epidemiology, pathogenesis and prospects for control by vaccination of the most important bacteria, *S. zooepidemicus* and *Actinobacillus* spp.

Molecular tools to distinguish strains of *S. zooepidemicus* have already been identified[37] which complement the previously identified serological and genetic markers[38,39]. We are now applying these tools to estimate the incidence and prevalence of different types within individual horses and circulating within defined populations and to determine the proportion of lower airway disease episodes associated with persistent infection by one type, the proportion associated with several types or with a clonal succession of different types. If episodes of disease are predominantly associated with a clonal succession of different types of *S. zooepidemicus* it may indicate that the prolonged nature of the disease is related to the time it takes to acquire immunity sequentially to the most prevalent types. These investigations will also provide insight into whether immunity to strains is type specific and may guide the selection of types upon which studies of pathogenicity and immunity deserve most attention.

Concurrent detailed bacteriology and epidemiology investigations were performed during our investigations to study the role that different *Actinobacillus* spp. may play[40]. Over 50% of types were found to be *Actinobacillus equuli*, and some types of *Actinobacillus* spp. (e.g. *A. suis*) were selectively associated with disease[40]. There is need to carry similar molecular epidemiological investigations, as described for *S. zooepidemicus*, for this group of bacteria to clarify the role that different strains play.

When effective vaccines against these two bacteria have been developed, there will be realistic prospects for the prevention of inflammatory airway disease, the second most important cause of wastage in TB racehorses[9]. Ideally, efficacy of such vaccines would be proven in randomised controlled trials of products in populations suffering from the natural disease. If this could be done, then the epidemiological approach could justifiably claim to have made real progress in preventing and controlling this important disease. Perversely, if immunised horses spend less time resting due to respiratory problems, then there may be an impact on musculoskeletal problems as well!

Epidemiology in the New Millennium

This review has concentrated on a disease syndrome where some progress has been made by following an epidemiological approach. There are many other examples, such as identification of factors predisposing to sarcoid[41]. In the field of anaesthetic death[11], the researchers have already started performing randomised controlled trials designed to test different agents so that the death rate can be reduced.

Epidemiological methods are able to provide unique and fundamentally important tools in our move towards evidence-based medicine, the significance of which is rightly growing as it becomes increasingly unacceptable to base our clinical practice on unsupported opinion. It is vital that scientific evidence that guides our practice is gathered, wherever possible and appropriate, from real cases rather than from experimental models, particularly if they are conducted in species other than the horse and not carefully validated.

Some might argue that epidemiological studies are

expensive, time-consuming and prone to bias. However, the risks of depending on poorly quantified clinical opinion when considering important equine diseases and their relative significance are unquestionably greater than the risks associated with conducting carefully designed epidemiological studies involving close collaboration with clinical experts.

References

[1]Vandenbrouke, J.P. (1999) Case reports in an evidence-based world. *J. Royal Soc. Med.* **92**, 159-163.

[2]Reid, S.W.J., Mair, T.S., Hillyer, M.H. and Love, S. (1995) Epidemiological risk factors associated with a diagnosis of clinical cyathostomiasis in the horse. *Equine vet. J.* **27**, 127-130.

[3]Gilmour, J.S. and Jolly, G.M. (1974) Some aspects of the epidemiology of equine grass sickness. *Vet. Rec.* **95**, 77-80.

[4]Robinson, R.A., Kobluk, C., Clanton, C., Martin, F., Gordon, B., Ames, T., Trent, M. and Ruth, G. (1988) Epidemiological studies of musculoskeletal racing and training injuries in Thoroughbred horses, Minnesota, USA. *Acta. Vet. Scand., Suppl.* **84**, 340-343.

[5]Mohammed, H. O., Hill, T. and Lowe, J. (1991) Risk factors associated with injuries in Thoroughbred horses. *Equine vet. J.* **23**, 445-448.

[6]Stover, S.M., Johnson, B..J., Daft, B.M., Read, D.H., Andersen, M., Barr, B.C., Kinde, H., Moore, J., Stoltz, J., Ardans, A.A. and Pool, R.R. (1992) An association between complete and incomplete stress fractures of the humerus in racehorses. *Equine vet. J.* **24**, 260-263.

[7]Estberg, L., Stover, S.M., Gardner, I.A., Drake, C.M., Johnson, B.J. and Ardans, A. (1996) High speed exercise history and catastrophic racing fracture in Thoroughbreds. *Am. J. vet. Res.* **57**, 1549-1555.

[8]Bailey, C.J., Reid, S.W.J., Hodgson, D.R., Suann, C.J. and Rose, R.J. (1997) Risk factors associated with musculoskeletal injuries in Australian Thoroughbred racehorses. *Prev. vet. Med.* **32**, 47-55.

[9]Rossdale, P.D., Hopes, R., Wingfield-Digby, N.J. and Offord, K. (1985). Epidemiological study of wastage among racehorses 1982 and 1983. *Vet. Rec.* **116**, 66-69.

[10]Wood J.L.N., Newton J.R., Chanter N., Townsend H.G.G., Lakhani, K.H., Mumford J.A., Sinclair, R., Burrell, M.H., Pilsworth, R.C., Shepherd, M., Dugdale, D., Herinckx, B.M.B., Main, J.P.M., Windsor, H. and Windsor, D. (1999) Respiratory disease in racehorses: an epidemiological study carried out in young horses in training, in particular of the causes of lower respiratory tract disease. *Eighth International Conference on Equine Infectious Diseases.* In press.

[11]Johnston, G.M., Taylor, P.M, Holmes, M.A. and Wood, J.L.N. (1995) Confidential enquiry of perioperative equine fatalities (CEPEF-1): preliminary results. *Equine vet. J.* **27**, 193-200.

[12]Selborne (1997) *Report of the Committee of Enquiry into Veterinary Research.* RCVS Trust Fund.

[13]Evans, D. G. (1971) *Vaccination Against Equine Influenza: A Report to the Joint Racing Board,* Joint Racing Board, London. p 16.

[14]Powell, D.G., Burrows, R., Spooner P., Goodridge, D., Thomson, G.R. and Mumford, J.A. (1978) A study of infectious respiratory disease among horses in Great Britain, 1971 to 1976. In: *Proceedings of the Fourth International Conference on Equine Infectious Diseases,* Eds: J.T. Bryans and H. Gerber. pp 451-459.

[15]Thomson, G.R. (1978) *The Role of Equid Herpesvirus 1 in Acute Respiratory Disease of Horses and the Use of Inactivated Antigens to Immunize Against the Infection.* PhD Thesis, University of London.

[16]Whitwell, K.E. and Greet, T.R.C. (1984). Collection and evaluation of tracheo-bronchial washes in the horse. *Equine vet. J.* **16**, 499-508.

[17]Burrell, M.H. (1985) Endoscopic and virological observations on respiratory disease in a group of young Thoroughbred horses in training. *Equine vet. J.* **17**, 99-103.

[18]Morley, P.S. (1995) *Epidemiology of Infectious Upper Respiratory Tract Disease in Horses.* PhD thesis, University of Saskatchewan.

[19]Burrell, M.H., Whitwell, K.E., Wood, J.L.N., Chanter, N. and Mumford, J.A. (1996) Respiratory disease in Thoroughbred horses in training: the relationship between disease and viruses, bacteria and environment. *Vet. Rec.* **139**, 308-313.

[20]Burrell, M.H., Whitwell, K.E., Wood, J.L.N. and Mumford, J.A. (1994) Investigations of pyrexia in young Thoroughbred Racehorses in training. *Vet. Rec.* **134**, 219-220.

[21]Moore, B.R. (1996) Lower respiratory tract disease. *Vet. Clin. N. Am.: Equine Pract.* **12**, 457-472.

[22]Divers, T.J. (1988) The poor performance horse. *Equine Diagnostics and Therapeutics: Proceedings of the Tenth Bain-Fallon Memorial Lectures,* Adelaide, Australia. pp 81-84.

[23]Gerber, H. (1970) Clinical features, sequelae and epidemiology of equine influenza. In: *Proceedings of the Second International Conference on Equine Infectious Diseases,* Eds: J.S. Gilmour and G.M. Jolly, Karger, New York, pp 63-80.

[24]Wood, J.L.N. and Burrell, M.H. (1993) Epidemiological studies with multiple episodes as outcome: a suggested analytical technique using a cohort study of respiratory disease in horses. *Proceedings of the Society for Veterinary Epidemiology and Preventive Medicine,* pp 213-224.

[25]Burrell, M.H., Mackintosh, M.E. and Taylor, C.E.D. (1986) Isolation of *Streptococcus pneumoniae* from the respiratory tract of horses. *Equine vet. J.* **18**, 183-186.

[26]Mackintosh, M.E., Grant, S.T. and Burrell, M.H. (1988) Evidence for *Streptococcus pneumoniae* as a cause of respiratory disease in young Thoroughbred horses in training. In: *Proceedings of the Fifth International Conference on Equine Infectious Diseases,* Ed: D. G. Powell, pp 41-44.

[27]Moore, B.R., Krakowka, S., McVey, D.S., Cummins, J.M. and Robertson, J.T. (1995) Cytologic evaluation of bronchoalveolar fluid obtained from Standardbred racehorses with inflammatory airway disease. *Am. J. vet. Res.* **56**, 562-567.

[28]Sweeney, C.R., Humber, K.A. and Roby, K.A.W. (1992) Cytologic findings of tracheobronchial aspirates from 66 Thoroughbred racehorses. *Am. J. vet. Res.* **53**, 1172-1175.

[29]MacNamara, B., Bauer, S. and Iafe, J. (1990) Endoscopic evaluation of exercise-induced pulmonary haemorrhage and chronic obstructive pulmonary disease in association with poor performance in racing Standardbreds. *J. Am. vet. med. Ass.* **196**, 443-445.

[30]McKane, S.A., Rose, R.J. and Evans, D.L. (1992) Comparison of bronchoalveolar lavage findings and measurements of gas exchange during exercise in horses with poor racing performance. *New Zealand vet. J.* **43**, 179-182.

[31]Couëtil, L. and Danicola, D. (1997) Correlation between bronchoalveolar lavage fluid cytology and arterial blood gases in racehorses with small airway disease. In: *Proceedings of the Comparative Respiratory Physiology Society,* Liege, Belgium, November 1997.

[32]Lumsden, J.M., Stick, J.A., Caron, J.J., Nickels, F.A., Brown, C.M., Godber, L.M. and Derksen, F.J. (1995) Upper airway function in performance horses: videoendoscopy during high-speed treadmill exercise. *Comp. cont. Educ. pract. Vet.* **17**, 1134-1143.

[33]Blunden, A.S., Hannant, D., Livesay, G. and Mumford, J.A. (1994) Susceptibility of ponies to infection with *Streptococcus pneumoniae* (capsule type 3). *Equine vet. J.* **26**, 22-28.

[34]Wood, J.L.N., Burrell, M.H., Roberts, C., Shaw, Y. and Chanter, N. (1993) Streptococci and Pasteurella associated with disease of the equine lower respiratory tract. *Equine vet. J.* **25**, 314-318.

[35]Wood, J.L.N., Chanter, N., Newton, J.R., Burrell, M.H., Dugdale, D., Windsor, H.M., Windsor, G.D., Rosendal, S. and Townsend, H.G.G. (1997) An outbreak of respiratory disease in racehorses associated with *Mycoplasma felis* infection. *Vet. Rec.* **140**, 138-192.

[36]Wood, J.L.N. (1998) *An Epidemiological Investigation of Respiratory Disease in Racehorses.* PhD Thesis, Open University.

[37]Chanter, N., Collin, N., Holmes, N., Binns, M.M. and Mumford, J.A. (1997) Characterisation of the Lancefield Group C streptococcus 16S-23S RNA gene intergenic spacer and its potential for identification and sub-specific typing. *Epidemiology and Infection* **118**, 125-135.

[38]Moore, B.O. and Bryans, J.T. (1970) Type-specific antigenicity of group *C. streptococci* from diseases of the horse. *Proceedings of the Second International Conference on Equine Infectious Diseases,* Karger, New York. pp 231-238

[39]Walker, J.A. and Timoney, J.F. (1998) The molecular variation in protective *Streptococcus zooepidemicus* proteins. *Am. J. vet. Res.* **59**, 1129-1133.

[40]Ward, C., Wood, J.L.N., Houghton, S.B., Mumford, J.A. and Chanter, N. (1998) *Actinobacillus* and *Pasteurella* isolates from the distal trachea of horses with bacterial lower airway disease. *Vet. Rec.* **143**, 277-279.

[41]Reid, S.W.J. and Mohammed, H.O. (1997) Longitudinal and cross-sectional studies to evaluate the risk of sarcoid associated with castration. *Can. J. vet. Res.* **61**, 89-93.

Equine gastroenterology: yesterday and today

AL MERRITT
Department of Large Animal Clinical Studies
College of Veterinary Medicine
University of Florida
Gainesville
Florida 32610
USA

In trying to organise my thoughts concerning the best way to approach this subject, I have chosen the reference point to be the early 1960s when I was attending that formidable institution on the hill in Ithaca, New York.

What was the 'state of the art' at that time - at least according to the Cornell dogma, where, as far as large animals were concerned, the curriculum leaned more towards food animals than horses? I would say, however, that what we were taught about horses was fairly representative of what other schools were preaching at that time, as my successive moves to University of California and the University of Pennsylvania, within two years of graduation, indicated to me. As far as equine gastroenterology was concerned, it was pretty primitive by today's standards. For instance, a rectal examination for other than a reproductive problem was not discussed because a horse's rectum was considered to be too friable for such a procedure, and a laparotomy was considered a last resort that often ended in the animal's demise due to peritonitis.

That being said, I will focus this discussion on some diagnostic and therapeutic techniques where I think the most important advances have been made over the last 35 years in the field of equine gastroenterology. With regard to diagnostic aids, these would include rectal examination, collection and evaluation of peritoneal fluid, nasogastric intubation to inspect and quantify the volume of gastric contents, tests to evaluate small intestinal absorptive capacity, endoscopy, radiography and ultrasonography. As for therapeutics, nasogastric intubation to keep the stomach decompressed, surgical intervention to correct a problem causing colic and aggressive fluid therapy are, in my opinion, where major advances to increase survival rates in equine gastrointestinal problems have occurred.

In retrospect, I cannot understand why in the early '60s the rectal examination of a horse for evaluation of a GI problem was so shunned. True, a horse's rectum can be more easily perforated than a cow's, but descriptions of the use of the procedure go back to at least the late 19th century. The *Illustrated American Stock Book*[1], published in 1891, mentions the use of a rectal examination as the "*infallible test, under all circumstances*" for the diagnosis of "*enteritis*". A detailed set of directions for performing the technique is followed by the statement that, "*This is the only sure test, and no false delicacy or squeamishness should stand in the way of performing it*" (Fig 1). Furthermore, textbooks held in high regard in the 1930s contained quite detailed discourses on its use to evaluate a colicky patient, including palpation of the anterior (cranial) mesenteric artery[2,3]. However, Greatorex's comprehensive paper[4], published in the first volume of the *Equine Veterinary Journal* (EVJ) in 1968, provided a major impetus for serious application of 'medical' rectal examination of the horse as we know it today. I never had the pleasure of meeting Professor Greatorex, but understand that his physique was particularly amenable to a thorough evaluation of the abdomen of even the largest of horses! Classic contributions to the subject since then include Kopf's excellent (and widely imitated) drawings presented at the First Equine Colic Research Symposium[5] in Athens, Georgia in 1982, and the extensive illustrated discussion by Nat White in his 1990 text, *The Equine Acute Abdomen*[6]. The current judicious use of anticholinergic agents or lidocaine enemas to relax the rectum has aided us in this task and reduced the chances of perforation.

My first introduction to peritoneal fluid analysis as an important component of full evaluation of an equine abdominal problem was through watching Lea Bach and

Fig 1: Woodcut figure from the 1891 Illustrated American Stock Book *demonstrating how to perform a rectal examination on a horse. This was regarded by the authors of this tome as* "the infallable test, under all circumstances" *for the diagnosis of* "enteritis".

Sidney Ricketts at New Bolton Center develop a systematic approach to collection and evaluation of the fluid, which culminated in their very influential paper that appeared in EVJ in 1974[7]. This paper gave appropriate reference to the previous work on this subject, but its particular importance as a benchmark was that it was the first to describe a simple method for obtaining fluid samples and to relate examples of various changes in colour and cell count to specific intra-abdominal problems. We were all pretty happy with the simple needle technique described by Bach and Ricketts until, in that occasional case, pure colonic contents instead of peritoneal fluid began dripping from the hub. Whereas there were more serious subcutaneous rather than peritoneal infections that occurred from this development, it provoked the usage of more involved procedures (e.g. local anaesthesia, stab incision) utilising blunter instruments, such as the venerable teat cannula[8]. I have seen the use, as well, of all sorts of catheters and bits of tubing of various length introduced transcutaneously into the equine abdomen at diverse sites in an attempt to avoid a dry tap; you know there has to be some there, dammit, and you're gonna get it, come hell or high water! This is because further advances in centesis technique and fluid analysis over the last 25 years have brought us to a point where, today, we rely heavily on peritoneal fluid status in our evaluation of many putative intra-abdominal problems of the horse.

An age-old adage is that horses cannot vomit. Numerous theories for why have been advanced, but a definitive answer still evades us. It remains one of those great mysteries of equine gastroenterology. Therefore, back in the early 1970s at New Bolton Center we thought we were pretty smart when we 'discovered' that nasogastric intubation and subsequent drainage of large volumes of gastric contents from some colic patients provided immediate relief (and perhaps prevented gastric rupture?) If we had been really smart, we'd have known that this was not a new discovery but, rather, a rediscovery of the technique that ultimately resulted in increased application and, therefore, increased survival rate. In his 1939 edition of *The Practice of Veterinary Medicine*[3], Udall describes it as part of the treatment of acute gastric dilatation: "*Evacuated fluids are reddish in colour and emit a sour penetrating odour...*" This sounds like what we currently regard as consistent with proximal duodentitis/jejunitis to me. He goes on to state: "*Escape through the tube may be assisted by first introducing a little water.*" When was it that you first realised the importance of creating a siphon? I can remember a few horses that died of gastric rupture in spite of attempts to drain the stomach by nasogastric tube because we did not try to create a siphon. Tubes, preferably of silastic rubber to reduce the chances of oesophageal perforation, are now sometimes left in place for days so that we easily decompress on schedule or demand. The volume of gastric contents collected is measured to provide diagnostic information, and guidance for intravenous fluid maintenance and replacement needs.

Carbohydrate feeding studies to evaluate small intestinal absorptive capacity, using hexose-based sugars, were first applied to the horse in the early 1970s[9,10]. These were shortly followed by reports of the use of the pentose, xylose, in accordance with the rationale that this sugar was found only in very small quantities within the body except for a short time after being fed and, therefore, was a better specific marker for evaluating absorptive capacity[11,12]. Although it has its limitations, the xylose absorption study pointed out that horses do suffer from small intestinal malabsorptive diseases and that, contrary to what is seen in monogastric species that are not hindgut fermenters, horses with severe malabsorption have normal-appearing faeces if the malfunction is confined to the small intestine. As clinicians, this was an important concept for us to learn, as it broadened our appreciation of the complexity of equine gut function and showed us the danger of making too many generalisations in comparative gastroenterology.

The first piece of equipment even resembling an endoscope that I ever saw in use in the horse was the rigid laryngoscope that was passed through the nose; one false move could result in a very unhappy horse with a giant nosebleed and/or one very unhappy clinician with a black eye. Also, one prayed that the connection between the battery pack and the instrument, which depended upon a clip system, would maintain a good contact, and that there was not a giant glob of mucus adhered to the lens. Dr Charlie Raker, at Penn, was very slick at using the rigid laryngoscope; he would be in and out before the horse knew what was happening. Nevertheless, the subsequent ACMI flexible, two-way directional fibreoptic endoscope was a Rolls Royce in comparison. For an equine gastroenterologist, however, the early flexible endoscopes developed for human use were tantalising with regard to potential but frustrating in their lack of sufficient length. The first published description of gastroscopy in the mature horse, using a specially made 2.74 metre long fibrescope, did not appear until 1985[13]. The recent development of the commercially available video endoscopes with small diameters, four-way directional capability and working lengths up to 3 metres has opened up a whole new line of business directed at diagnosis and treatment of peptic ulcer disease in horses.

Other forms of imaging, such as radiography, ultrasonography and scintigraphy are still in their early stages of application to equine gastroenterology. For the first two, the foal was the natural place to start[14] but with increasingly better equipment and advanced expertise on the part of the operators, the adult abdomen is yielding to inspection well beyond the indistinguishable blur - "*Wow, there is an enterolith there!!*"[15] Furthermore, abdominal ultrasonography is now considered an essential component of the evaluation of a colicky foal; imaging of an intussusception early in the course of the illness can, for example, mean the difference between life and death[16]. With regard to scintigraphy, gastric emptying of a radioisotopically labelled meal as an indicator of gut function is already being explored[17]. Who knows where all of this will go; most of it was not even envisaged in 1963 when I received my veterinary degree!

As mentioned above, I believe that the two greatest advances in therapy of equine GI diseases have involved surgery and fluid therapy. It was an exciting time in the mid '60s to see a number of equine surgeons at various institutions begin to challenge the old taboo about the sanctity of the equine abdomen. It is probably safe to say that Dr J. D. Wheat at the University of California, Davis, was at the head of the charge. At least, he was the first to show me that abdominal surgery could be done successfully, the lucky patient being a colicky weanling that I had seen on an ambulatory call and had no idea how to handle that turned out to have an intussusception. That was in 1964.

Consultations with Don Wheat were always informative, but the structure of the conversation is what I remember best

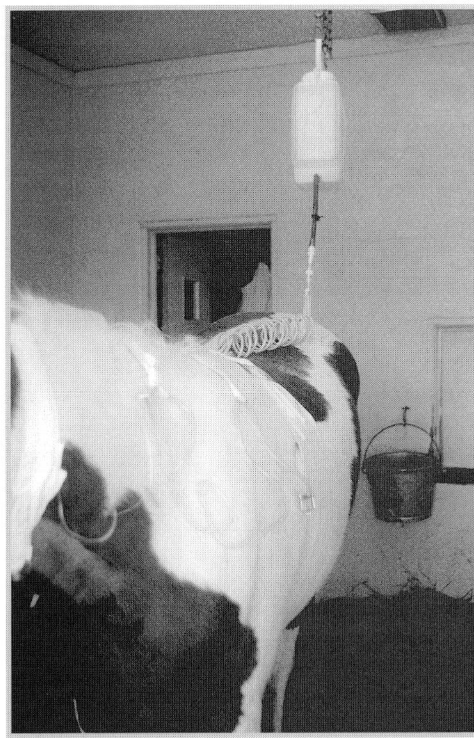

Fig 2: A 1978 version of a home-made constant intravenous fluid delivery system for a horse. The 10 litre container, which has a screw cap and holds a sterilised isotonic poly-electrolyte 'replacement' fluid prepared by the pharmacy personnel, hangs from the ceiling via a swivel snap that allowed the container to turn (hopefully!) as the animal moved around the stall. The coiled tubing on the horse's back was obtained from a supplier to the compressed air industry. The drip chamber between the container and the coil was from a commercially available delivery set, and the system between the coil and the horse was fashioned from bulk plastic tubing. Rate of fluid flow was controlled by the clamp on the tubing.

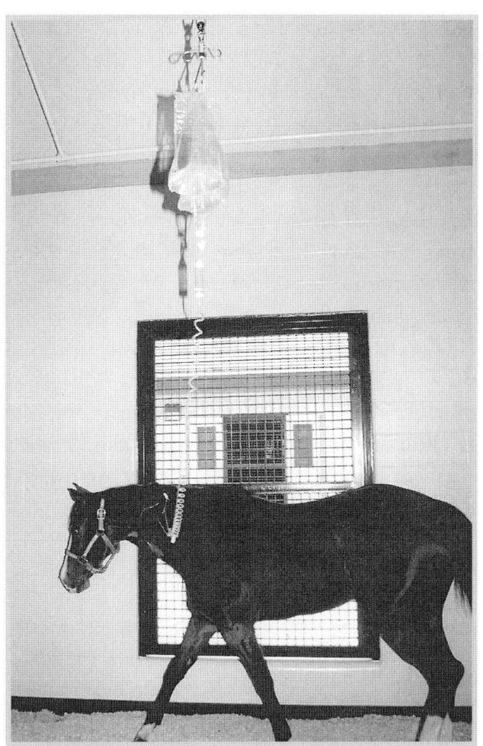

Fig 3: A 1998 version of a constant intravenous fluid delivery system for a horse, all components of which are commercially available. The suspension device for the bags of fluids, which can be easily raised and lowered by the integrated pully, turns on a highly machined ball bearing swivel and will hold up to four 5 litre fluid units at one time. The drip chamber is large and accessible, if needed, through extra ports, and fluid flow rate can be quite precisely controlled by a screw clamp that is part of the system.

- clipped, pointed sound bites delivered almost offhandedly, with no eye contact. Sort of like two cats sitting back-to-back that you know are communicating with each other. It was a pleasure to run into him again in 1974 at the First (and only) International Equine Veterinary Congress, organised by Maurice Azzie and held under a tent in Kruger National Park in South Africa (it's an interesting sensation to have baboons drop in to listen to your lecture). There were a number of papers presented on the state of the art of colic surgery at that time, including one by Wheat[18] and another by my Cornell classmate and then Penn colleague, Bill Donawick[19]. From watching Donawick develop a programme at Penn, in the early '70s, I had really learned what it took to be successful: confidence, good preparation, aggressive metabolic and anaesthetic support, dogged adherence to aseptic technique and, of course, excellent surgical skill (that is why I have remained an internist!). Many points covered in those papers at that meeting in South Africa formed, I think, the benchmark for what is being done today as a fairly routine procedure in academic and private equine practices throughout the world.

Finally, the success we enjoy today in managing all sorts of equine gastrointestinal problems would not be possible without the major advances in fluid therapy that have been made over the last 35 years. Looking back through the old books one finds all forms of vile concoctions and practices recommended for treating colic and diarrhoea that make one wonder whether if the horse survived it did so in spite of the therapy. For treatment of "*inflammation of the bowels*" the *Farmer's Own Book* published by J.D. Koogle in 1858[20] advocates, "*...bleeding profusely, taking at least 7 or 8 quarts [litres] of blood, or as much as the horse can bear, which must be done immediately or a fatal termination may be looked for*". So much for supporting blood volume here! The *Illustrated American Stock Book*[1] of 1891, on the other hand, recommended removing only a quart (~1 litre) of blood and replacing it with 1 pint (~ 500 ml) of "*blood-warm water*" for treatment of enteritis, and it cautioned against the injection of air with the use of a "*quart syringe with a fine-curved point*". This, therefore, was the introduction of a device to deliver intravenous fluids to a horse. Many procedures of that era and on into the first half of the 20th century directed at equine GI disease involved either gastric or rectal instillation of multiple litres of water mixed with various chemicals, including electrolytes which, no doubt, provided some sorely needed fluid replacement.

I think it is safe to say, however, that the major advances in fluid therapy for horses have been made within the realm of my own veterinary experience. The signal of the dawn of a new era could very well be a paper by Drs John Tasker and Ned Olson (1964) presented at the Tenth Annual Convention of the American Association of Equine Practitioners entitled *Fluid Therapy in the Severely Dehydrated Horse*[21]. I had the pleasure of being taught pathology by Jack Tasker when I was a veterinary student, but was unaware at that time of his studies of fluid balance in horses, and the subject never came up in any of our contemporary therapeutics classes. Jack's subsequent series of papers on the subject that appeared in the Conrell Veterinarian in 1967 really set the stage. Encouraged by Tasker's data and the haranguing of David Kronfeld at Penn in the early '70s, I, along with close colleagues such as Bill Donawick and Charlie Ramberg, struggled with these principles and the various ways to apply them in a practical manner to clinical problems. Clinicians at other institutes, such as Jim Coffman at Missouri, Bob Michell at London, Reuben Rose at Sydney and Gary Carlson at UC Davis were going through a similar process. Part of the struggle concerned the best way to deliver a large volume of appropriately designed fluid on a continuous basis that required the least amount of effort on the part of the attendant staff and the horse. Initially this required the preparation and sterile bulk storage of large volumes of fluids by the pharmacy staff and the jury rigging of various delivery devices (Fig 2). Home-made intravenous catheters were part of this process. Leaks, bleeds and air injection were common; it's a miracle the animals survived - again, in spite of us! Today's clinicians are definitely spoiled (Fig 3), but much to the benefit of the patients. This is the way it always will, and should be.

References

[1]Anon (1891) *Illustrated American Stock Book,* American Livestock Publ. Co., Chicago.

[2]Malkmus, B. (1936) *Clinical Diagnostics of the Internal Diseases of Domestic Animals,* Alexander Eger, Chicago.

[3]Udall, D.H. (1939) *The Practice of Veterinary Medicine,* D.H. Udall, Ithaca, New York.

[4]Greatorex, J.C. (1968) Rectal exploration as an aid to the diagnosis of some medical conditions in the horse. *Equine vet. J.* **1**, 26-30.

[5]Kopf, N. (1982) Rectal findings in horses with intestinal obstruction. *Proceedings of the 1st Equine Colic Research Symposium.* pp 236-260.

[6]White, N.A. (1990) *The Equine Acute Abdomen,* Lea and Febiger, Philadelphia.

[7]Bach, L.G. and Ricketts, S.W. (1974) Paracentesis as an aid to the diagnosis of abdominal disease in the horse. *Equine vet. J.* **6**, 116-121.

[8]Nelson, A.W. (1979) Analysis of equine peritoneal fluid. *Vet. Clin. N. Am: Large anim. Pract.* **1**, 267-274.

[9]Loeb, W.F., McKenzie, L.D. and Hoffsis, G.F. (1972) The carbohydrate digestion-absorption test in the horse. *Cornell Vet.* **62**, 524-531.

[10]Breukink, H.J. (1974) Oral mono- and disaccharide tolerance tests in ponies. *Am. J. vet. Res.* **35**, 1523-1527.

[11]Roberts, M.C. (1974) The D(+)xylose absorption test in the horse. *Equine vet. J.* **5**, 171-173.

[12]Bolton, J.R., Merritt, A.M., Cimprich, R.E., Ramberg, C.F. and Streett, W. (1976) Normal and abnormal xylose absorption in the horse. *Cornell Vet.* **66**, 183-197.

[13]Brown, C.M., Slocombe, R.F. and Derksen, F.J. (1985) Fiberoptic gastroduodenoscopy in the horse. *J. Am. vet. med. Ass.* **186**, 965-968.

[14]Cudd, T.A., Toal, R.L. and Embertson, R.M. (1987) The use of clinical findings, abdominocentesis and abdominal radiographs to assess surgical versus non-surgical abdominal disease in the foal. *Proc. Am. Ass. equine Practnrs.* **33**, 41-52.

[15]Yarbrough, T.M., Langer, D.L., Snyder, J.R., Gardner, I.A. and O'Brien, T.R. (1994) Abdominal radiography for diagnosis of enterolithiasis in horses: 141 cases (1990-1992). *J. Am. vet. med. Ass.* **205**, 592-595.

[16]Bernard, W.V., Reef, V.B., Reimer, J.M., Humber, K.A. and Orsini, J.A. (1989) Ultrasonographic diagnosis of small-intestinal intussusception in three foals. *J. Am. vet. med. Ass.* **194**, 395-397.

[17]Ringger, N.C., Lester, G.D., Neuwirth, L., Merritt, A.M., Vetro, T. and Harrison, J. (1996) Effect of bethanechol or erythromycin on gastric emptying in horses. *Am. J. vet. Res.* **57**, 1771-1775.

[18]Wheat, J.D. (1975) Causes of colic and types requiring surgical intervention. *J. S. Afr. vet. Ass.* **46**, 95-100.

[19]Donawick, W.J. (1975) Metabolic management of the horse with an acute abdominal crisis. *J. S. Afr. vet. Ass.* **46**, 107-110.

[20]Koogle, J.D. (1858) *The Farmer's Own Book: A Treatise on the Numerous Diseases of the Horse,* J.D. Koogle, Middletown, Maryland.

Colic: has it always been a pain?

JIM MOORE
College of Veterinary Medicine
University of Georgia
Athens, Georgia
USA

The simple answer to the question put forth in the title of this article is yes, without a doubt. In the words written by another James Moore[1] (no relation) 110 years ago in London, *"Colic ('gripes') is a very common disease, and consists of severe griping pains."*

As is a common occurrence when one delves into the veterinary literature of centuries past, one is immediately struck by the strength and accuracy of the author's observations. In fact, the images created exceed those of most veterinary texts today. We concentrate on pathophysiology, while authors of old described the animal so the reader could actually see it.

When we find ourselves expounding to veterinary students about the purported molecular mechanisms responsible for the synthesis and release of inflammatory mediators during endotoxaemia, we need to consider such early descriptions of enteritis:

> *"Enteritis begins in most cases with dulness; heavy eyes; staring coat; restlessness and moving about from one place to another; the pulse and breathing are both quickened; no appetite. Some are preceded by colic. Other cases begin with shivering. The animal paws, kicks, and rolls about in the most violent manner; he tries often and strains hard to pass water, but either none, or only a few drops, come away; the pain is most intense, and does not cease for a moment; it is increased by pressure and moving about; the belly is hot, tucked up, and hard, unless there be wind in the bowels, when it will be more or less swelled; the bowels are very much bound, although small, hard, dry masses may be passed; the legs and ears are intensely cold; the pulse is small and hard; and sweat breaks out all over."*

That author may have been ignorant of endotoxin, cyclooxygenases, tumour necrosis factor and such, but he saw the same diseases that we see today. Clearly, he and his contemporaries wrestled with making the distinction between colic caused by intestinal obstruction or displacement and enteritis. Yes, colic was a pain for them too.

Some of the more difficult questions we face today deal with the underlying cause for the onset of colic in individual horses. Moore offered that colic is caused by *"bound bowels; hard, dry dung, gathered together in a mass; large quantities of green food, from which gas is given off during fermentation; tumours; worms and stones"*. Although we might not agree with his suggestion that *"sudden application of cold air to the warm skin"* also is a cause, we would have little disagreement with his other conclusions. Unfortunately, in many instances we might have relatively little to add. In fact, many of the questions about colic that existed 100 years ago persist today.

It is readily apparent, from the available literature at the time, that colic was a pain on this side of the Atlantic too. In fact, some of the authors were obviously frustrated by the many faces of colic and that there were so many experts around to offer their opinions on the most appropriate treatments. Michener in 1907[2], in the United States, reported:

> *"The disease of the horse that is most frequently met with is what is termed 'colic,' and many are the remedies that are reputed to be 'sure cures' for this disease.*
>
> *"Let us discover, then, what the word 'colic' means. This term is applied loosely to almost all diseases of the organs of the abdomen that are accompanied by pain. If the horse evinces abdominal pain, he is likely to be put down as suffering with colic, no matter whether the difficulty be a cramp of the bowel, an internal hernia, overloading of the stomach, or a painful disease of the bladder or liver. Since these conditions differ so much in their causation and their nature, it is manifestly absurd to treat them alike and to expect the same drugs or procedures to relieve them all. Therefore, it is important that the various diseased states that are so roughly classed together as colic shall, so far as possible, be separated and individualised in order that appropriate treatments may be prescribed. With this object in view, colic should be considered under the following headings: (1) engorgement colic; (2) obstruction colic; (3) tympanitic colic; (4) spasmodic colic; and (5) worm colic."*

Whilst to some it may be surprising, to others it will be reassuring to see that our thought processes and diagnostic approaches haven't changed that much in the past century. Horses still suffer from abdominal pain, people tend to lump many causes for the pain together, there are many 'sure cures' available, and we must remind ourselves that by classifying an individual horse's problem according to most likely cause, one can best determine the most appropriate treatment.

Common prescriptions at the end of last century included 10 drops of aconitum or colocynthis, nux vomica, or ammonium causticum in a wineglassful of water every 15 or 20 minutes. Veterinarians also relied upon camphor, opium, morphine, cannabis indica, arsenicum and belladonna for the treatment of specific causes of colic. While these drugs differ considerably from what we use today, Campbell in his 1914 treatise *Colics and Their Treatment*[3] reported that he enjoyed considerable success with a new treatment that he termed the *"vest pocket stomach tube"* - salicylic acid. Interestingly, as Campbell warned that the

> *"The wily practitioner... must remember throughout the examination of the patient the possibility of the absence of certain important symptoms that are masked consequent upon*

previous administration of medicine given by the owner or caretaker in a usually misguided effort to effect a cure",

We have the same concern about the masking effects of today's more potent renditions of salicylic acid. Consequently, none of us would have any problems with Campbell's two laws for the treatment of colic: 1) Do not use any treatment that may kill; and 2) Do not use any treatment that will mask the symptoms.

We also need to recognise that one of our mainstays in the evaluation and treatment of colic in horses, the stomach tube, was not introduced into day-to-day practice until after the turn of the century. In fact, much of the credit for popularising its use among equine practitioners rested with D. O. Knisely of Topeka, Kansas, who extolled its virtues repeatedly in the *American Journal of Veterinary Medicine*. Dr Knisely was very persistent in his advocacy for stomach lavage to remove *"the cause of the trouble at its source expeditiously, safely and surely"*. Prior to Dr Knisely's efforts to perfect a rubber stomach tube and injection pump, stomach tubes were stiff, awkward to pass and were discarded as impractical. We and nearly a century's worth of horses owe a great deal to D. O. Knisely's persistence.

Of the many questions about colic that remain unanswered in my mind is the question of incidence. Just how commonly does colic occur in horses and what is its effect on the horse industry? Although there have been some surveys performed in selected practices in individual areas of the world, most of the studies in the literature deal with horses with colic presented to university hospitals. Clearly, these cases represent the tip of the proverbial iceberg and therefore it is impossible to determine the magnitude of the effects caused by colic. With the apparent increase in the number of colic surgeries being performed these days, one is tempted to try, however. For instance, if one assumes that on average each of the 50 states in the United States has a clinic that performs 50 colic surgeries a year and that the average colic surgery lasts 3.5 hours from induction to full recovery from anaesthesia, then one could conclude with a moderately straight face that there is a horse undergoing colic surgery somewhere in the country at any time during the year. If this bit of freewheeling extrapolation is even remotely accurate, then studies designed to document the incidence and effects of colic are sorely needed. Perhaps equally sorely needed will be astute editors and grant reviewers to reject manuscripts and grant proposals that quote the above calculation as fact!

While the majority of this paper has highlighted the cleverness of our predecessors, we cannot ignore the fact that there have been rather astounding advances made in the treatment of sick horses in the past 25 years or so. Colic surgeries have become commonplace and, in many instances, comprise the vast majority of a clinic's after-hours caseload. We have made startling improvements in intensive care, preoperative evaluation and preparation of the horse, anaesthesia, surgical techniques, facilities and more. These improvements came against some rather high odds and the wisdom of some impressive names in veterinary medicine. For instance, L.A. Merillat of the M'Killip Veterinary College in Chicago, Illinois, reported in 1914[4]:

"As Professor Hobday has stated, and as Doctor Blattenburg has reaffirmed, I shall repeat, that we are not today and probably never shall be able to invade the abdominal viscera to any great extent."

How many times at 2 am near the dawn of the new millennium might anesthetist, surgeon or veterinary technician lament, *"Oh, were that only still true."*

References

[1]Moore, J. (1889) *Veterinary Homeopathy*, 10th edn, Ed: T. Moore, Leath and Ross, London. pp 71-82.

[2]Michener, C.B. (1907) Diseases of the digestive organs. In: *Special Report on Diseases of the Horse*, US Department of Agriculture, Government Printing Office, Washington DC. pp 34-74.

[3]Campbell, D.M. (1914) In: *Colics and Their Treatment*, Ed: D.M. Campbell, Kenfield Leash Co., Chicago, Illinois. pp 11-13.

[4]Merillat, L.A. (1914) Surgical treatment of colics in horses. In: *Colics and Their Treatment*, Ed: D.M. Campbell, Kenfield Leash Co., Chicago, Illinois. pp 53-84.

Equine intensive (critical) care

TOM DIVERS
Department of Clinical Sciences
College of Veterinary Medicine
Cornell University, Ithaca
New Jersey 14853
USA

The terms 'critical care' and 'intensive care' are used to describe the treatment of illness of crisis proportion (critical care) and/or those requiring a high level of forceful treatment (intensive care). Although the terms have different meanings, they are often used interchangeably when discussing a serious illness of crisis proportion. In this article, I will use the term critical care.

Equine critical care has been present to some extent as long as trained and educated veterinarians have been treating horses. Even before the advent of newer medications, equine veterinarians have tried to provide some form of critical care. It was basically a situation of 'do what you can with the resources and knowledge available'. In my opinion, the old treatment of standing the acutely founded horse in cold water was a form of critical care. This old practice is not a lot different than the current belief by many physicians that critically ill human patients with cerebral oedema and/or organ failure may benefit from some degree of organ hypothermia. There are many other examples of informal critical care that equine practitioners were clever enough to discover and have provided throughout the 20th century; it's just that it wasn't called critical care at that time.

As best as I can determine, a more formal equine critical care began in the late 1960s or early 1970s. This corresponds temporally to the use of intravenous catheters in horses which enabled the initiation of large volume fluid therapy. It seems appropriate but also somewhat ironic that more formal critical care began with the institution of large volume fluid therapy and yet today intravenous therapy remains the most potent treatment for shock in both man and animals. I frequently tell my students that the most effective 'drug' we have for treating sick horses is intravenous fluids.

Certainly, fluid therapy has been fine-tuned over the years by the addition and use of hypertonic crystalloids and colloids. Plasma probably deserves special mention as a sometimes life-saving fluid of the 1980s and 1990s. I believe we are fortunate too have had easily obtainable and safe commercial supplies of this natural intravascular fluid for equine use. To my knowledge, we have had no transmission of infectious diseases by commercial plasma transfusion. No widespread retrovirus infection has tainted the equine blood pool. Although the efficacy of antiendotoxin, anti-TNF and other anti-'whatever' antibodies have been questioned, there is little argument that the body's own proteins (fibronectin, alpha-macroglobulin, albumin, etc.) are beneficial in treating the critically ill equine patient. Hypertonic saline has permitted the provision of 'on the farm' emergency critical care fluid therapy. Although the physiological improvement is brief, it has allowed horses to make it to critical care facilities such that more long-term care with isotonic crystalloids can be provided. Unfortunately, in horses with systemic inflammatory response, large volume isotonic fluids move quickly from the intravascular bed, decreasing their efficacy. It remains to be seen if synthetic colloids, which should retain the isotonic fluids in the vascular compartment longer, or oxyglobin for improved tissue oxygeneration become important armamentariums in our fluid therapy for the new millennium.

The development of equine critical care has been a multidiscipline contribution. Progress in critical care coincided with the formation of the colleges of veterinary internal medicine, veterinary surgery, and veterinary anaesthesia and the sharing of common expertise in these areas and in the care of the critically ill horse. In large animal medicine, individuals such as Humphrey Knight, Bob Whitlock, Al Merritt, Bud Tennant, and many others began to apply antimicrobial treatment regimens and organ-failure treatments from human medicine to horses and validate pharmacokinetics, treatment protocols, etc, in those horses. At a similar time, Bill Donawick and colleagues made significant progress in the surgical treatments of abdominal pain.

Much of the progress in abdominal surgery can be attributed to improved surgical speed and technique and improved cardiopulmonary function during anaesthesia while other successes can be attributed to the studies on more effective treatments of endotoxaemia in the horse, which were pioneered by Harold Garner, Jack Fessler and their colleagues. This area has been further improved by focused investigation by several centres into endotoxin and cytokine proliferation in horses with inflammatory disease. Special recognition must be given to Jim Moore and his colleagues at the University of Georgia for their lead in the endotoxin/cytokine work and their efforts to organise international colic symposia. Finally, critical care could not be complete without skilful anaesthetists who are required to maintain organ perfusion and oxygeneration during surgery. Newer machinery and more experienced anaesthesiologists, trained in anaesthesia of the horse, have completed the intensive care team of internist, surgeon and anaesthesiologist. Will we, like the small animal profession, now begin to provide specialists in emergency and critical care, a person skilfully trained in all three disciplines?

In addition to abdominal pain and endotoxaemia, other problems surfaced, became very common in the horse and required newer intensive care treatments and diagnostic aids. These are too numerous to list but include developments in critical care treatment of equine pleuropneumonia by Jill Beech and Doug Byars. Prior to the 1980s, I recall our mortality rate of septic pleuropneumonia was very high but now survival rates approach 70 to 90%. Our responsibility should now go beyond the treatment of equine pleuropneumonia but should also include prevention. Information provided by our colleagues in the United Kingdom and New Zealand on proper husbandry of racehorses along with development of more efficacious vaccines might help prevent this costly disease.

Diarrhoeal diseases remain, after abdominal pain, one of the most frequent and serious critical care conditions in the horse. Our medical and small animal colleagues often have difficulty understanding why equine colitis is so often a life-threatening condition. With an understanding of the fluid volume and electrolytes that can be lost, the amount of endotoxin which can be absorbed and cytokines released, it is not surprising that horses with colitis almost routinely require critical care. Traditional therapies used in other species such as PeptoBismol etc. just get lost in the flood. There has been some rather dramatic progress, though, in treating equine colitis. Tetracycline has proved an almost antidote-like treatment for equine monocytic ehrlichiosis (EME, Potomac Horse Fever). Interestingly, our experiences with EME have taught us that tetracycline can be given safely to critically ill horses; this was considered malpractice in the 1980s. Of course, many veterinarians who also practiced in the 1960s and 1970s never believed that it was improper to use tetracycline in any critical care equine case, but it took our experiences with EME to prove it to the doubting Thomases. Clostridiosis has been the critical care enteric infectious disease of the 1990s in horses. The emergence of *Clostridium difficile* as an important enteric disease of the horse seems to be worldwide and is demonstrated by the almost simultaneous research on the disease in Sweden, England, Canada, and the US. Clostridiosis now has replaced salmonellosis as the most common and serious infectious enteric disease of the mature horse housed in critical care facilities. It is a valid concern of critical care providers that *Clostridium difficile* contamination of the critical care unit may be much more serious than a *Salmonella* spp. contamination problem. This by no means suggests that salmonellosis is no longer an important cause of critical illness. In fact, it is still a significant equine and human health concern. Unfortunately, compared to treatments for EME or clostridiosis, little progress in the treatment of salmonellosis other than supportive care has been made.

Certainly one of the greatest advances in equine critical care has been in the area of perinatology. Equine perinatal critical care was initially developed by Tim Cudd, a practitioner from Kentucky, Anne Koterba at the University of Florida, and by Peter Rossdale and associates in the UK. Other schools and practices throughout the world quickly followed their lead by developing neonatal intensive care units. Some of the progress made in perinatology at the University of Florida developed from their important collaboration with perineonatologists and respiratory physiologists at the university medical school. Likewise, Peter Rossdale made important contributions to this area by personal observation, scientific studies, and collaboration with human perinatologists/physiologists in the United Kingdom. Most schools now have perinatal units and some, such as the University of Pennsylvania, have faculties dedicated almost solely to the advancement of perinatal care. Two private practices in Kentucky now each see more than 200 critical neonates yearly. Special areas of progress in neonatal intensive care have been ventilation therapy and parenteral nutrition. Ventilation therapy still has great room for improvement but has progressed beyond the early 1980s when we were pretty ignorant of the pathophysiology of neonatal lung injury and mechanisms of the ventilator and often did as much harm as good. I remember in 1984 being so disappointed with a string of unsuccessful ventilatory cases that the label to the euthanasia solution was taped to the machine. Was it Austin Powers who said, *"We've come a long way, baby"*? The ability to feed the neonate with parenteral nutrition undoubtedly gave a lot of a foals a further chance to be treated with critical care. Parenteral nutrition has been safely and easily used in large animal critical care. Its frequent, if not widespread, use in the early to mid-1980s marked one time we beat our small animal colleagues to the punch (although, to be honest, it was probably first used in calves in 1980 as a lifesaving measure for chronic diarrhoea and cachexia). Some credit for the development of the use of parenteral nutrition in foals should be given to Mike Ward and Baxter Laboratory for showing financial and educational support for its use in calves and foals. Baxter and many other pharmaceutical and medical supply companies, too numerous to mention, deserve a special thanks for helping us promote equine critical care. Likewise, we are also grateful for owners who were willing to spend the money and give us a chance to improve critical care as we applied drugs from human patients and ideas to equine critical care.

Currently, most university hospitals and many private practices have critical care units dedicated solely to the critical care patients. Most, if not all, of the units are staffed by skilled ICU nurses who are every bit as important as the attending veterinarians! The most frequently used equipment in these units are portable electrolyte and acid-base machines and the ultrasound machine. The ultrasound is one of the most vital pieces of equipment for the critical care unit! Familiarity with its use and interpretation of the findings are imperative in monitoring the critical care patient.

We have travelled many important roads but many remain to be travelled. Commonly performed aspects of critical care in human medicine, such as drug monitoring, central venous pressure measurement, and routine arterial pressure measurements are procedures that should and can easily be done in equine critical care in the new millennium.

As the equine practitioners of the early 20th century developed the first critical care, I am sure equine practitioners will continue to develop the more formal critical care well into the new millennium. The amounts of money owners are willing to spend and the finance available for research will be the limiting factors, not the creativity and zeal of the practitioner.

Equine urinary tract disorders: from 'pissing' blood to seeing its source and determining its cause

HAROLD SCHOTT
Department of Large Animal Clinical Sciences
D-202 Veterinary Medical Center
College of Veterinary Medicine
Michigan State University
East Lansing, Michigan 48824-1314
USA

By the start of the 20th century, knowledge about urinary tract disorders in the horse had not advanced considerably from that described in monographs dating back several hundred years. For example, the following passage from *The English Farrier or Approved Remedies to Cure all Diseases in Horses* (Printed for J. Wright, at the Kings Head in Old Bayley, 1649) provides a fairly accurate assessment of myoglobinuria consequent to rhabdomyolysis:

> *"But if it [urine] be red, and of the colour almost of blood, then is the blood more inflamed, which came of over-hard riding, which may prove dangerous to his life. But if it be of a pale greenish colour, thick, and viscous, then certainly his back is growne weak."*

The latter portion of this excerpt appears to describe a case of sabulous urolithiasis, potentially complicated by an ascending urinary tract infection. Although we have spent the past 100 years discounting the horseman's assertion that back soreness is a consequence of kidney pain, this writing may actually prove insightful to the perplexing problem of accumulation of sediment in the bladder of affected horses. Specifically, abnormalities in the lower back or lumbosacral area, supported by recent nuclear scintigraphic findings, suggest that sabulous urolithiasis in some affected geldings may be secondary to incomplete bladder emptying due to pain associated with posturing to urinate. Although kidney pain remains an all too common (and unsubstantiated) presenting complaint for sore-backed horses, back pain leading to urine retention, bladder distension, and accumulation of urine sediment may truly play a role in lower urinary tract disease. As we progress during the next millennium, it is reasonable to expect that technology currently being tried in human patients may lead to development of implantable 'bladder pacemakers' as a novel treatment for this and other causes of bladder paresis in horses.

In addition to early recognition of 'pissing blood' as a consequence of rhabdomyolysis, 17th and 18th century writings also describe uroliths in the bladder, ureters, and kidneys resulting in stranguria and haematuria. These older monographs would lead us to believe that urolithiasis was more common in prior centuries; however, I suspect that the attention devoted to 'the stone' is attributable, at least in part, to uroliths being quite remarkable *postmortem* findings. Since the start of the industrial revolution, there has been a shift from a preponderance of cystoliths to increasing numbers of upper tract uroliths in man, but whether there have been changes in prevalence or location of equine uroliths remains a mystery.

The syndrome of chronic renal failure (referred to as diabetes or profuse staling) was also fairly accurately described a couple of centuries ago by the veterinary surgeon William Gibson in *A New Treatise on the Diseases of Horses* (2nd edn, printed for A. Millar, in the Strand, London, 1754):

> *"A diabetes is a frequent and profuse staling, attended with great weakness, loss of flesh, and often with an atrophy and decay… And when this happens to a horse of a weakly constitution, it becomes very difficult to remove it. He soon loses both his flesh and appetite, grows feeble, his hair stares and his bones stick out; his eyes look weak and watery; and when it is of long standing, he grows unfit for all kinds of business. I have seen several horses with this malady, but they are often incurable, unless in the beginning; for if the pissing in a true diabetes is not soon conquered, it usually ends in rottenness."*

The last sentence in this passage also appears to describe the polyuric, convalescent phase of acute renal failure. Therefore, essentially the entire spectrum of equine urinary tract disorders (acute renal failure, chronic renal failure, urolithiasis, urinary tract infection, pigmenturia and bladder paresis) appears to have been recognised by our predecessors centuries ago.

So what advances have actually been made in the last century? First, and most obvious, was development of laboratory assays of blood to detect accumulation of nitrogenous waste products (azotaemia). Rapid measurement of blood urea nitrogen (BUN) and serum creatinine (Cr) concentrations is so commonplace that today's equine practitioners would be at a loss without this diagnostic aid. Second, urine analysis was expanded from a crude observational skill to a quick and informative field test, requiring only a hand-held refractometer and multiple-test reagent strips. In addition, development of simple

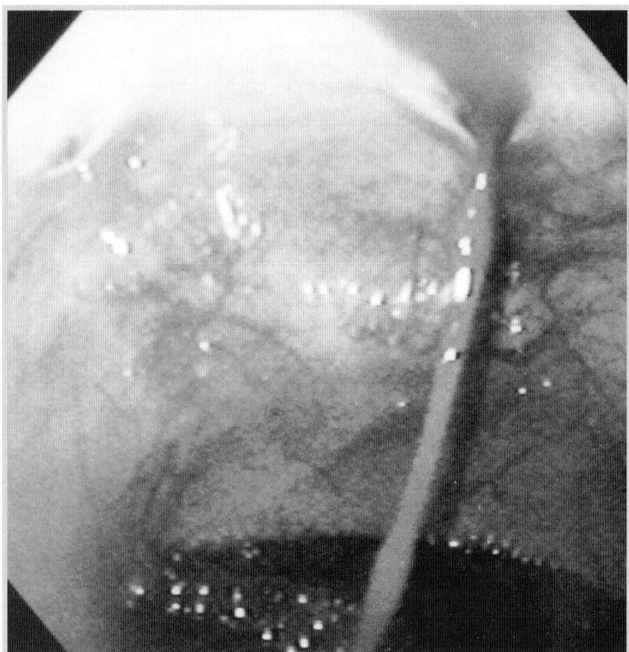

Fig 1: *Endoscopic image of a large blood clot exiting the right ureteral opening of a gelding with idiopathic renal haematuria.*

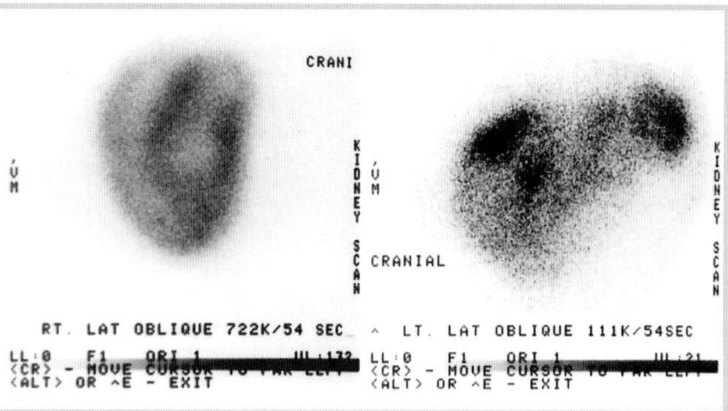

Fig 2: *Renal scintigraphic image using ^{99m}Tc tagged to glucoheptanate in a gelding with unilateral left-sided pyelonephritis revealed inhomogeneous uptake of the radionuclide and lesser count emission over the same time period in comparison to the normal right kidney. The scintigraphic study, which provided both anatomical and functional information, supported pursuit of unilateral nephrectomy, rather than prolonged antibiotic administration, as the treatment of choice in this horse.*

bladder catheterisation techniques has overcome the problem of waiting for the shy horse to void a sample. Microscopic sediment examination and further biochemical testing can also be pursued to evaluate glomerular integrity (proteinuria) and tubular function (fractional electrolyte clearances) or damage (casts and enzymuria).

In select cases, urine produced by each kidney can also be examined by collection of samples via ureteral catheterisation (during endoscopy in either sex or manually in the mare). Third, and perhaps most informative, was development of diagnostic imaging tools for evaluation of disorders of both the upper and lower urinary tract. Over the past two decades ultrasonography has evolved from a tool allowing detection of two kidneys (and perhaps a large nephrolith) to a modality for Doppler measurement of renal blood flow. Similarly, videoendoscopy has become a simple procedure for evaluation of the lower urinary tract and accessory sex glands and is the diagnostic tool of choice for evaluating the source of haematuria (Fig 1).

The combined use of these imaging tools has allowed characterisation of previously unrecognised problems including proximal urethral defects in Quarter Horse stallions and geldings (producing haemospermia and haematuria at the end of urination), unilateral pyelonephritis, and idiopathic renal haematuria. Nuclear scintgraphy, the most recent addition to our diagnostic imaging capabilities, has also been used to evaluate renal anatomy and function with several radiopharmaceuticals and will probably become a more valuable diagnostic tool in the next millennium (Fig 2). Fourth, histopathological examination of tissue collected via percutaneous renal biopsy has allowed *antemortem* diagnosis of renal neoplasia as well as pathophysiologic characterisation of renal disease. For example, renal biopsy may allow acute or chronic renal failure to be attributed to congenital disorders (renal dysplasia, polycystic kidney disease), glomerular disease (glomerulonephritis consequent to immune-complex deposition [streptococcal and equine infectious anaemia virus antigens] or autoimmune disease), or tubulointerstitial disease (tubular nephrosis, interstitial nephritis, or pyelonephritis).

Despite having the potential to be a powerful diagnostic tool, development of renal biopsy techniques has not been without complication (massive and life-threatening haemorrhage/ haematuria in an occasional horse) and its role in assessment of equine renal disease has not yet been as well defined as in human medicine. Although use of ultrasound guidance and triggered biopsy instruments has decreased the risk of complications associated with renal biopsy, detailed examination of the tissue collected (including routine immunohistochemistry and ultrastructural evaluation) has not yet been developed. These techniques are of considerable value in characterisation of human glomerular diseases and greater use of various staining techniques and electron microscopy will probably improve our abilities to detect, understand and, perhaps, intervene in future cases of equine renal disease.

Next, although the impact cannot be assessed quantitatively, improved veterinary care of dehydrated patients, especially fluid therapy, has most certainly decreased the incidence of acute renal failure accompanying rhabdomyolysis, colic, enterocolitis, and other disorders leading to severe fluid and electrolyte depletion. Advances have also been made for treatment of specific equine urinary tract disorders. For example, pharmacological agents are now available to promote dilation of renal arterioles (dopamine) and to induce urine flow (frusemide, mannitol) in horses with oliguric acute renal failure. Unfortunately, development and widespread use of medications has been accompanied by production of adverse effects. Gentamicin nephrotoxicity (tubular nephrosis) and analgesic nephropathy (papillary necrosis and associated nephrolithiasis) are probably the best recognised renal complications of drug administration. However, once recognised, these adverse effects have been largely eliminated by adequate hydration of at-risk patients. Further, research efforts have led to implementation of strategies to limit renal tubular damage (once-daily aminoglycoside dosing and monitoring of trough serum aminoglycoside concentrations) and development of less nephrotoxic analgesic medications (e.g. ketoprofen < flunixin meglumine < phenylbutazone).

During the 20th century, several surgical techniques were developed and antimicrobial agents also became available

Harold Schott

Fig 3: A small nephrolith lodged in the renal pelvis resulted in ureteral obstruction and development of hydronephrosis in a Standardbred gelding which had a history of receiving phenylbutazone for a period of four years.

specifically to address urolithiasis and urinary tract infections. Electrohydraulic lithotripsy was also used for removal of cystic and ureteral calculi in a few horses and with further advances in the technology of endoscopes, other less invasive methods of stone disruption will probably be developed for treatment of equine uroliths. However, as technological advances lead to novel treatment options, it is important not to lose sight of either the expected outcome or more practical and economic approaches to urolithiasis. For example, treatment of upper tract stones has rarely had a favourable outcome to date, because extensive loss of renal function occurred typically before horses were presented for evaluation. This should not be a surprise because, unlike upper urinary tract stones in man, the vast majority of nephroliths and ureteroliths in horses appear to develop secondary to damage to renal parenchyma (e.g. papillary necrosis with analgesic nephropathy [Fig 3], chronic interstitial nephritis, or pyelonephritis).

The exception may be the nonazotaemic horse with unilateral nephrolithiasis or ureterolithiasis for which nephrectomy currently remains the treatment of choice. Thus, the need for improved ability to detect early renal disease is certainly as great as the need for development of more sophisticated treatments. With regard to practical and economic treatment alternatives, cystic calculi can often be removed nonsurgically from mares after manual dilation of the urethra. In fact, although the procedure is not described in any current surgical texts, practitioners with small hands can usually insert their entire hand into a sedated mare's bladder after only a few minutes of manual urethral dilation.

Another problem to be addressed in the coming millennium is recurrence of lower urinary tract stones following surgical removal. Although not well documented, recurrence probably occurs in as many as 25% of operated horses. Nevertheless, predisposing factors for development and recurrence of urinary calculi in horses have received little attention. Similarly, despite the fact that the rather unique composition of equine urine (rich in calcium carbonate crystals and lubricating mucous) has been recognised for centuries, the importance of this species difference in the pathophysiology of urolithiasis remains poorly understood. However, anyone with even limited experience with indwelling bladder catheters can attest to the rapidity with which crystalline material coats the surface of the catheter. Similarly, following instrumentation or trauma, a layer of adherent crystalloid material quickly covers any damaged uroepithelium. In light of this response, it is somewhat remarkable that urolithiasis is not a more significant problem in horses. To improve the outcome of lower urinary tract stone disease (i.e. to decrease recurrence), further studies of the composition and function of the mucous secreted in the renal pelvis and ureter, of dietary and nondietary factors contributing to variation in urinary calcium excretion in horses, and methods of urinary acidification (e.g. changing dietary cation-anion balance) are warranted in the future.

In contrast to the advances in diagnosis and treatment of acute renal failure and urolithiasis, we have made few advances during the past 100 years in our ability to alter the progression of chronic renal disease. Since the mainstays of treatment of human patients with chronic renal failure, haemodialysis and renal transplantation, are not yet available for horses, this lack of progress should come as no great surprise. However, there is no reason that these procedures will not become accepted treatments for horses in renal failure in the next millennium. In fact, dialysis is currently offered for treatment of renal failure in dogs at several institutions and haemodialysis has already been successfully used in a foal with acute renal failure consequent to administration of oxytetracycline.

Similarly, although renal transplantation has been somewhat problematic in dogs, the procedure is now a successful treatment for chronic renal disease in cats. To date, renal transplantation has also been attempted in at least one horse. The latter procedure was performed by Dr Barrie Grant, in 1989, during my residency in internal medicine at Washington State University. The donor kidney was implanted subcutaneously into the throatlatch area of a donated normal horse. Vascular anastomoses were made with branches of the carotid artery and jugular vein and a stoma for the ureteral stump was created along the ventral aspect of the upper neck. No attempt at immunosuppression was made: the goals were to determine the feasibility of the surgical procedure and whether perfusion of and urine production by the transplanted kidney could be established for a period of a few days. Although unsuccessful, to my knowledge it remains the first and only attempt at renal transplantation in the horse. Clearly, renal transplantation will never be in high demand in horses but, as our clients continue to become more knowledgeable about human medicine, more requests for this procedure may be voiced, especially for valuable breeding animals.

So what are the challenges of the coming millennium? First, our clients' goals for their horses are changing and we must be able to provide a greater number of options to address their concerns. Specifically, horses are no longer simply thought of as draught animals. Rather, they have become important companions and their owners are demanding treatment options to maintain them during a comfortable retirement period, often into a fourth decade of life. A clear example of this change is increased recognition and treatment of equine Cushing's disease. Similarly, although humane euthanasia remains a valuable option for equine patients with chronic disease, more and more owners desire to maintain their horses for months to years before selecting this alternative. Therefore, there is a need for investigations of dietary management of horses with acute and chronic renal failure as well as those affected by urolithiasis. Next, the effects of partial loss of renal function on development of chronic renal failure will require long-term follow-up studies of horses that have recovered from acute renal failure or other disorders treated with a prolonged course of aminoglycoside antibiotics or analgesic medications. More detailed clinical evaluation of renal function (e.g. serial measurements of glomerular filtration rate or identification of more sensitive and quantitative indices of renal function) in combination with refinement of examination methods for tissue collected by renal biopsy should allow more accurate characterisation of subclinical renal disease and progression to renal failure. However, it warrants mention that despite advances in diagnostic capabilities in human medicine, progression of chronic renal disease remains rather variable (and unpredictable). Therefore, as greater understanding of the events responsible for initiation and progression of glomerular and tubular cell injury is derived from basic research studies (ranging from inflammatory mediators to gene signalling), it may be realistic to expect that novel interventions to halt or reverse the progression of renal failure may be found. Perhaps by the eve of the 22nd century, genetic strategies to initiate growth of new nephrons may have replaced renal transplantation as the primary treatment for chronic renal failure. Alternatively, technological advances may lead to design of a truly artificial kidney that can be implanted during a routine visit to one of our future physician colleagues.

Selected References

The English Farrier or Approved Remedies to Cure all Diseases in Horses. Printed for J. Wright, at the Kings Head in Old Bayley, 1649.

Gibson, W. *A New Treatise on the Diseases of Horses*, 2nd edn, Printed for A. Millar, in the Strand, London, 1754.

Schott, H.C. and Bayly, W.M. (1997) Urinary tract diseases. In: *Equine Internal Medicine*, Eds: S.M. Reed and W.M. Bayly, W. B. Saunders, Co., Philadelphia, Pennsylvania. pp 807-911.

The evolution of equine cardiology

CHRISTOPHER BROWN
Department of Veterinary Clinical Sciences
College of Veterinary Medicine
Iowa State University
Ames, Iowa 50011
USA

Introduction

"...for it is the heart by whose virtue and pulse the blood is moved, perfected, made apt to nourish and is preserved from corruption and coagulation... It is indeed the fountain of life, the source of all action."

William Harvey
Exercitatio de Mortu Cordis et Sanguinis (1628)

As I was finishing my year as houseman at Bristol University in 1973, I was trying to decide what to do next with my career. Jim Pinsent had been a very strong influence on my development as a clinician, and I wanted to stay involved with clinical medicine.

I also felt that I needed to obtain some advanced training in one area or another. By chance I had helped Dr Jim Holmes with a few cardiac cases, and he was always on the look out for a 'Likely Lad'. Just before my year was to end he proposed that I study with him in equine cardiology for a PhD. At that time, he did not have funding to support a postgraduate student, so that weekend he put together a proposal to the Horserace Betting Levy Board, and sent it off, handwritten, to meet an imminent deadline. Amazingly it was funded, and I began my studies with him.

We chose to study the generation of intracardiac pressure and sound in horses. We decided to use the then very new Millar Micro-Tip catheters, which give high fidelity records. The problem was that they were made in Houston, Texas, and for the length of catheter we needed, a special order was required; thus a nine-month wait for the instrument ensued. As a result I had plenty of time to prepare my review of the literature, and I became well known in the library in Langford.

I recall one day ordering a reprint of the Rev. Stephen Hales' book *Statical Essays: Containing Hemostatics*, originally published in 1733. I had expected a facsimile reprint, but the central library sent me an original copy! Hales was an amazing man, and had done some blood pressure recordings on horses. There was something very moving about holding a book that was over 240 years old and contained the results of some of the first equine cardiovascular experiments. This and other experiences sparked my interest in the history of equine cardiology, and I reviewed material that spread over two centuries. Much of what we now take for granted was not known to our Victorian colleagues.

With the advent of the application of the scientific method in human medicine, similar applications were made in equine medicine. As instrumentation evolved (e.g. the ECG), new insights were gained into the function and malfunction of the equine heart. In fact, findings in horses often preceded those in people, and the horse made significant contributions to the early foundations of basic cardiovascular physiology and cardiac medicine. However, just as medical sciences began to boom and knowledge was increasing at an exponential rate, the horse began to go into a decline as a power source, and the incentives to study equine cardiac function became less compelling. Horses were much less numerous and less likely to be chosen as experimental animals for cardiac investigations; and the dog became the experimental animal from the 1920s to the '90s.

In order to set the stage for the significant developments that have taken place in equine cardiology over the last 100 years it would be beneficial to summarise what had been learnt prior to that time. What was the knowledge base from which the early workers started?

The Early Years - Pre-1900

In 1628, Harvey had published his observations on the circulation of the blood, laying the foundations for scientific cardiac medicine. However, wide acceptance of his concepts did not occur. As mentioned above, Hales in 1733 had performed several experiments on live horses in which he directly measured the pressure in a cannulated artery. His values are well within the published ranges of today. In addition, he created a model of hypovolaemic shock by sequentially removing blood, one quart at a time, from a mare and recording her blood pressure during the exsanguination. If his data are plotted graphically they clearly show an initial drop in pressure after the first few quarts, followed by a long plateau, then a final fall to zero as the mare expired with the loss of 17 quarts of blood. The plateau demonstrated the vasomotor response to a falling intravascular volume and the reflex attempt to maintain blood pressure during blood loss. Hales, however, was not in a position to apply our current knowledge of hypovolaemic shock to his results.

The technique of auscultation was developed in human medicine in France by Laënnec, and first described in 1819 in French, and in English in 1821. As a result many physicians from around Europe went to Laënnec's clinic to learn the technique. One of these people was James Hope, from London. On his return to England he began a series of investigations to determine the origins of the heart sounds.

His first investigation was done at the premises of John Fields, a veterinary surgeon in Oxford Street. They used an ass, which was "*instantly deprived of sensation and motion by a smart blow on the head*", and then ventilated via a tracheostomy using a large pair of bellows. The chest was opened and the heart exposed by removal of the pericardium. They observed the sequence of chamber contraction, and then applied the stethoscope directly to the surface of the heart and noted the timing of the heart sounds. They concluded that the auricles contracted first, and that the first sound was heard when the ventricles contracted. The animal died before they could investigate the timing of the second sound, although they did conclude that the sound was "*occasioned by the diastole of the ventricles*".

They performed three more experiments, again using asses, and concluded that the second sound was due to diastolic relaxation of the ventricles, and subsequent ventricular filling. This concept was challenged by Rouanet, who had experimental evidence to support the valvular origin of the second sound. Hope and his team of observers therefore performed a final series of investigations in 1834, again at the surgery of Mr Fields. This time they demonstrated that the second sound was loudest over the root of the aorta and pulmonary artery. They found that if they occluded the aorta and the pulmonary artery the second sound disappeared. They then passed a long-handled hook down the pulmonary artery to the level of the valve, and pulled the valve aside. They noted that the second sound "*was impaired, and a hissing murmur accompanied it. Another hook was passed into the aorta, so as to act in the same way on the aortic valves: the second sound entirely ceased, and was replaced by a prolonged hissing (heard by several). When the hooks were withdrawn the second sound returned, and the hissing ceased.*" They had clearly demonstrated the role of the intact aortic and pulmonary valves in the origins of the second sound.

The first record of cardiac catheterisation was in 1844, and Claude Bernard performed it in a horse. His objective was not to measure the intracardiac pressure, but the temperature difference between the right and left ventricular blood. This was prompted by a current controversy, as over 40 years earlier Lavoisier had proposed that animal heat was produced as a result of gas exchanges in the lung. If this were the case, then the left ventricular blood should be warmer than the right ventricular blood. Bernard's experiments, however, showed the opposite to be true, and this supported the hypothesis that metabolic heat and carbon dioxide, were predominantly produced elsewhere.

Interestingly, Bernard obtained his horse with help from the legendary physiologist Magendie, who was chairman of a commission on horse hygiene, and the horse had glanders. Bernard later did move on to measure intracardiac pressures in both dogs and horses, but it was Chauveau and Marey who really made significant breakthroughs in this area, and added a great deal to the understanding of cardiac function. Chauveau was a professor at the veterinary school in Lyon, and Marey was a young Parisian physician. Their initial objective was to determine what part of the cardiac cycle was responsible for the apex beat, which can be palpated on the chest wall with each cardiac cycle.

Harvey, 200 years earlier, had proposed that ventricular systole was responsible, but the issue had never been settled. Chaveau and Marey used horses as experimental subjects, and developed intracardiac catheters and a recording system that gave incredibly good records (almost as good as those we obtained with our fancy, expensive, Texan catheters and computer recorders over a hundred years later!). They published their data in 1861 and 1863 and were the first to describe the different intracardiac pressure curves. They also demonstrated that the apex beat was caused by ventricular contraction.

In 1870, Adolph Fick published a note in which he indicated that the volume of blood flowing through the lungs can be calculated from the difference between arterial and mixed venous oxygen or carbon dioxide content, and the amount of oxygen taken up, or carbon dioxide given off, by the lungs in a given time. This is the famous Fick Principle for measuring cardiac output (or stroke volume if heart rate is known). Surprisingly, he never tested his hypothesis experimentally, and it was used initially to a limited extent in dogs in 1886 by Grehart and Quinquard. However, Zuntz and Hagemann extensively applied it in a series of experiments in horses between 1886 and 1894. They performed some scientifically very exacting investigations into gas exchange, respiratory work, cardiac output and systolic ejection velocity in horses at rest and at exercise. This resulted in the publication in 1898 of a 438 page report of their work. This appears to have been the first attempt to assess the effects of exercise on equine cardiac function.

So, as the 19th century came to close, there was a significant amount of knowledge regarding the structure and function of the equine cardiovascular system, much of it based on accurate scientific observation. However, from a clinical point of view there had been few attempts to correlate what was known about normal function with the pathological findings and clinical signs. Mayhew, writing in 1864, commented that although *"all conditions which can affect the heart have been described in the horse, they were discovered by examination instituted after death, when, unfortunately, all opportunity of observing symptoms had ceased"*. He further stated: "*Veterinary science cannot distinguish one (cardiac) state from another while life exists.*" He added: "*Diseases of the heart of horses are incurable*" and "*apparently little attention has been paid to the diagnosis and treatment of them.*"

In Robertson's 1890 edition of a *Text-book on the Practice of Equine Medicine* 37 of the 774 pages are devoted to the heart (4.8% of the total) and in Reed and Bayly's 1998 *Equine Internal Medicine* 81 of the 1092 pages are similarly assigned (7.4% of the total). This apparent increase in proportional importance of cardiac conditions is even more strongly emphasised when one compares the contents of the two chapters. In the 1890 text, most of the material is related to examination and pathology of the system. Clinical signs are often described at length, but are very similar, no matter what the condition! Treatment is given for three conditions: palpitations, pericarditis and endocarditis. The latter two today would be regarded as the most challenging, and, for the most part, untreatable. In the 1998 text the situation is dramatically different. John Bonagura and Virginia Reef have prepared a comprehensive review of our current knowledge of this subject to date, packed with diagnostic information, therapies, outcomes and extensive illustrations. We have obviously come a long way in the last century, and I will now try to cover some of the major achievements along the way.

1900 to 2000 - The Applications of Science and the Emergence of Technology

In the early years of the 20th century, many of the innovations which occurred in veterinary, and human, medicine took place in Germany, Austria and Hungary. As the horse was still the major source of power for transportation, it was the major species to which veterinarians devoted their time, and much clinical and applied research was undertaken. At this time new diagnostic techniques, such as electrocardiology and radiology were being developed and applied in human medicine; and drug use was moving rapidly from alchemy to pharmacology. The new ideas were quickly picked up by veterinary medicine and applied to the horse.

Einthoven pioneered the development of electrocardiology in Germany and, in fact, the first illustration of an equine ECG was recorded by him, and was published in 1910 in a paper by Tschermak. As noted in the first section, abnormalities in rhythm were often lumped together as palpitations, tachycardia or bradycardia. Prior to the development of the ECG, and an understanding of its physiological basis, it was not possible to classify arrythmias based on auscultation and palpation alone. Nörr is credited with being the first to describe the normal equine ECG. He was working in Dresden and his work appeared in 1913. His second paper characterised the now familiar second-degree artrioventricular block, and showed by simultaneous recording of the pulse pressures that there was a stepwise increase in arterial pressure to a threshold which then induced a missed beat and a return of the pressure to a lower level. He also described extrasystoles, some with compensatory pauses, atrial fibrillation (AF), paroxysmal tachycardia and various bradycardias. Over the next few years he added to our knowledge with several other papers. In addition, others such as Wirth, in Vienna, and Krupski, in Zurich, were publishing their observations and electrocardiographic findings. A very familiar Scandinavian name also crops up in this area of research, Nils Obel. Although it was his grading system for the severity of equine laminitis that earned him immortality, he also made significant contributions to equine electrocardiology in the early 1940s.

Interestingly, the horse had played a pivotal role in the understanding of AF in man. Lewis, a physician working in London, had been involved in a debate on the cause of this common arrythmia seen in man. The characteristic nature of the ECG of AF had been described, but the cause of the rapid irregular waveforms seen on the baseline was not determined. In 1915, Lewis published his observations on five horses which had the typical electrocardiographic findings of AF. He was able to anaesthetise two of them and expose their hearts via a thoracotomy. The atria were clearly seen to be quivering or fasiculating in a chaotic and uncoordinated way. He therefore used his observations on horses to explain the ECG finding of an important human disease.

Although it was clear that advances were being made in equine cardiology, the information did not always appear to cross the Channel. On 7 July, 1934, Mr J. McCunn of the Royal Veterinary College, addressed the Central Veterinary Society at the Conway Hall in London. His address was entitled *Remarks on Heart Disease in the Horse* and, although he mentioned tachycardia, bradycardia and other cardiac conditions, he never once alluded to electrocardiography or engaged in a critical commentary on auscultation, as diagnostic aids.

In the late 1930s and '40s, several workers in Germany, Italy and France published their results of phonocardiographic examinations of normal and abnormal equine hearts. These authors included Neumann-Kleinpaul, Steffan, Corticelli, Charton, Bressou and Minot. Many of these workers also pioneered other areas of equine medicine such as equine endoscopy, indicating their broad range of interests and keen inquiring minds. These graphic recordings advanced our understanding of the equine heart sounds, and confirmed that a third sound is normal in many horses, as is the fourth or atrial sound.

Early in the century, the Russian physician, Korotkov, established the now familiar indirect blood pressure measurement widely used in human medicine, reporting his findings in 1905. In this technique an inflatable cuff is applied to the upper arm, and used to arrest arterial blood flow. As the pressure in the cuff is lowered, flow returns. The return of flow can be detected by listening with a stethoscope over an artery distal to the cuff. The sounds produced are called the 'sounds of Korotkov' and the cuff pressure at which they appear and disappear reflect the level of diastolic and systolic pressures, respectively. Schmid was the first to report on this technique in the horse in 1912 and, over the next 60 years, a paper appeared on the application of the technique in the horse from places around the world every two to four years.

Workers in Russia including Sudakov, Laskov, Sharabrin, Filatov and Sobolev, applied the techniques to evaluate blood pressure in a variety of conditions, such as pregnancy, feeding, exercise, infectious illnesses and the differences associated with age. Although an international effort has been made to prove the values of this technique in the horse, from India to Australia, from Russia to France and Germany, as well as in the United States and United Kingdom, it has failed to become part of the mainstream of equine medicine. This is for two reasons. First, the technique is more difficult to use than in man, and the sounds of Korotkov cannot be used to determine the return of pulsatile blood flow. Other techniques such as oscillometric methods and Doppler ultrasound must be used. Second, horses don't suffer from hypertensive disorders, which is one of the major reasons for the widespread use of the technique in human medicine. There is however an established role for the technique in monitoring the anaesthetised horse.

After the Second World War, reports from Germany in the area of equine cardiology declined, although some workers such as Von Deegan were very active. Over the next 40 years, several major centres emerged in different parts of the world, including Detweiler and his group in Pennsylvania, Spörri in Zurich, Muylle and Oyaert in Ghent, Broojmans in Utrecht, Steel in Melbourne, Holmes in Bristol, Hamlin and others in Ohio, and Amada, Senta and others in Tokyo. Each had different areas of emphasis and varied in prominence depending upon the success of their research, the availability of funds and the efforts of their postgraduate students! There was often friendly, and, perhaps, not so friendly, rivalry. I remember Dr Holmes being quite put out after the 1st International Equine Veterinary Conference in South Africa, in 1974, where Dr Steel had advocated his 'Heart Score' concept as a means of predicting equine performance. Dr Holmes was very concerned about the implications of "*hanging numbers on horses*".

This was a period of consolidation and refinement. It consisted of the application to the horse of the expanding understanding of cardiac physiology. For example, it included the efforts by Jim Holmes and his postgraduate students to develop a lead system which would allow the ECG to be used to assess cardiac size or conduction abnormalities, such as bundle branch blocks. This work required the mapping of the equine cardiac electric field, and the application of these findings to derive a semi-orthogonal system for vector analysis. A lot of this detailed and exacting work was done by Peter Darke, who, on completion of his PhD, took up small animal medicine and small animal cardiology, and did not return to equine studies for over 25 years. When one looks at the detail and complexity of some of the studies one can understand why! A lot of effort was expended by many groups around the world to try to show that certain types of cardiac disorders were associated with specific changes in the ECG, recorded by a variety of lead systems, including Hanák in the former Czechoslovakia. For the most part this has failed to pan out, which is not surprising, as Muylle and Oyaert and others had shown that the pattern of depolarisation of the equine ventricles is such that much of their activity is not represented on the body surface ECG. For the most part the equine ECG is most valuable for the characterisation of arrythmias.

One of the biggest challenges which still faces the equine clinician is deciding the significance of a particular clinical finding, such as a soft systolic murmur, or an occasional ventricular ectopic beat. Several attempts have been made to cast more light on these problems, including a large abattoir survey, which was part of Rod Else's PhD study. By chance, there was an equine slaughterhouse about 15 miles from the Bristol veterinary school, and the owner was sometimes cooperative. Jim Holmes and Rod examined hundreds of horses at the abattoir and then performed a detailed *postmortem* examination of their hearts. They recorded ECGs on those with rhythm abnormalities and made tape recordings of murmurs if present. Several years later we would replay those tapes as we selected examples for continuing education programmes. It was quite sobering to be listening to the regular soft sounds of the heart beat with a murmur and suddenly hear a loud crack in the background, which had come from the next building. Another poor unfortunate had begun its final trip to France! Obviously these were trying conditions under which to gather scientific information. But as Jim used to say as the equipment played up or the horses failed to cooperate, "*If it was easy someone else would have done it already.*"

The problem of dealing with the significance of arrythmias was advanced in several centres by the use of radiotelemetry units or tape recorders mounted on the horse. This allowed the frequency and nature of the irregularity to be determined at various heart rates and at different levels of work. Further understanding of the effects of exercise on the equine cardiovascular system has been made by the use of high speed treadmills. Around the world, most major equine referral centres have such a treadmill as part of an equine sports medicine programme. Murli Manohar, in Illinois, is one who has pioneered much of the basic investigations on the haemodynamic changes associated with exercise in the horse.

In the last 20 years, echocardiography has become a widely used diagnostic aid in equine cardiology. Frank Pipers, then at Ohio, was the first to report on this technique in 1977. Since that time there have been improvements in ultrasound machines, and the quality of recordings has improved dramatically. The use of colour-flow Doppler and pulsed Doppler have added to the precision of this diagnostic tool. It is now possible to measure the size of the various chambers in the beating heart, assess valve and wall motion, the competency of the valves, demonstrate abnormal blood flow and estimate pressure gradients across valves, and all of this without invading the animal. It is a particularly useful aid in the assessment of suspect congenital cardiac conditions. Reef in Pennsylvania, Bonagura in Missouri (formerly in Ohio), Stadler in Munich, Marr in London and Blissitt in Edinburgh, have made major contributions.

Not only have we got better at documenting what might be wrong with a horse's heart we can at times, reverse or control the underlying pathophysiological problems. Roos in 1924 was the first to report the successful treatment of AF in horses using quinidine sulphate. Since then, many reports have appeared on the management of this disease and a better understanding of the prognostic factors has emerged, together with modifications to the original protocols. Combining therapy with other drugs, prolonging the therapy in 'refractory' cases, and the use of intravenous quinidine preparations have all been added to the management options for this problem. A lot of useful pharmacokinetic data have been generated on many drugs that affect the equine cardiovascular system, and major contributions have been made by Bill Muir and his co-workers at Ohio. John Bonagura and Virginia Reef, in their chapter in Reed and Bayly's 1998 book, list 16 medications which might be considered to treat heart failure in the horse. In Robertson's text of 1890 there are only three, and only one of which, digitalis, would be considered by today's veterinarians to have potential beneficial cardiac effects. There is even a clinical report of an mature horse being fitted with a pacemaker, and going on to be evented successfully.

In conclusion, we have undoubtedly come a long way from the days of palpitations and evil humours. Our understanding of equine cardiac function and malfunction has increased by a huge amount. We still have many grey areas. Our explanations of some of our clinical findings and their significance are still very empirical, particularly for the subtle abnormalities in flow or occasional changes in rhythm. We are still challenged to decide their potential impact on performance, or often more critically, safety. But we do have more in our support than the option expressed by Mayhew in 1864, which was basically no treatment followed by a thorough *postmortem* examination.

Orthopaedics and rheumatology: past, present and future

STEPHEN MAY
Department of Farm Animal and Equine
Medicine and Surgery
Royal Veterinary College
Hawkshead House
North Mymms, Hatfield
Herts AL9 7TA
UK

Early Diagnoses and Treatments
1000-1500

It is difficult to gauge the standards of horse care in the first century of the current millennium. As in other areas, the Dark Ages were an era of lack of progress and, to a certain extent, after the Greeks and Romans, there was little advance in knowledge for a period of about 1000 years.

Two important compilations of classical authors had taken place during the previous 500 years in an attempt to preserve the collective veterinary knowledge of the Roman Empire. In the second half of the 5th century, Publius Vegetius Renatus produced his *Artis Veterinariae*, which was the first book of the modern era devoted to veterinary medicine. Vegetius was not a veterinary surgeon. He appears to have been an educated man determined to restore veterinary science and its practitioners to a respected position. His work is based on earlier Latin authors and, also, the knowledge and opinions of the veterinarians and physicians of his day in the remains of the Western Roman Empire. About 450 years later, in the early part of the 10th century, Constantine the Seventh recognised that the continued degeneration of culture in the remains of the Eastern Roman Empire was endangering the survival of the remaining classical manuscripts on veterinary matters. He commissioned a compilation entitled the *Hippiatrika*, which included what remained of the works of, among others, the 4th century authors, Apsyrtus, Chiron, Himerius, Hippocrates, Pelagonius and Hierocles.

The lack of printed versions of these works, as well as widespread illiteracy, must have meant that relatively few had access to this sum total of human knowledge. For much of the current millennium, it is clear that the best practice of the day existed alongside ignorance; and compassionate therapies which complemented natural healing processes were applied at the same time as, frankly, barbaric practices. Both knowledge derived from the few literary sources, and knowledge gained from observant empiricism, must have been promulgated in an haphazard fashion. As now, the recognition of progress and the perceived need for dissemination of knowledge led, from time to time, to the production of a manuscript. In the first half of the 13th century, Frederick the Second of Sicily, an educated man interested in animals, like Vegetius, recognised the importance of Arabic sources of knowledge, and determined to combine such sources with the best Western knowledge of his day to regenerate the lost art of equine medicine and surgery. To this end, he commissioned Jordanus Ruffus, his chief court veterinarian, to undertake the task, which was completed after Frederick's death.

In order to assess progress made, it is important to recognise how much of each new work was recycled material and how much new. Ruffus appears to have collated his material and defined terms in an original way, which was later copied by other authors. He draws on Byzantine sources, but in his descriptions of conditions of the distal limb, foot problems and shoeing, his knowledge, probably supported by Arabic literature, is far superior to that of the classical authors. Among other diseases, he deals with ringbone, spavin and splints as causes of lameness, as well as aspects of the recognition of lameness.

The next major author demanding attention is Laurence Rusius who lived 100 years later. He adopted the same structure and plagiarised whole chapters from the work of Ruffus. However, as a practitioner, he clearly added some of his own knowledge, and his style and greater completeness added to the body of knowledge created by Ruffus. Lameness and shoeing are dealt with well. In relation to the feet, Rusius's diagnoses include laminitis, sandcrack, quittor and canker. With regard to limb injuries, he deals with severed tendons and recommends suturing the divided ends.

1500-1800

As in other fields, the introduction of printed text both stimulated the writing of new books and also permitted the broader dissemination of knowledge. Perhaps appropriately, two of the earliest printed veterinary books were a version of Vegetius published by Nuenare, in Basle, in 1528, and a version of the *Hippiatrika*, published by Ruellius, in Paris, in 1530. Both were in Latin! The earliest veterinary literature printed in English would appear to be *Proprytees & Medicynes of Hors* from the late 15th century, followed by the larger *Medicines for Horses* in the early part of the 16th century. The authors of both works are anonymous.

However, the floodgates then opened. A series of original English works and translations, many heavily plagiarised from predecessors, became available. These included important works by Thomas Blundeville (1566)[1], Conrad

Heresbach (English translation 1577)[2], Leonard Mascall (1587)[3], Gervase Markham (1610)[4], Thomas de Gray (1639)[5], Jacques Labessie de Solleysel (English translation 1696)[6], William Gibson (1720, 1751)[7,8], Henry Bracken (1737)[9], Jeremiah Bridges (1751)[10], J. Bartlet (1753)[11], E. G. La Fosse (English translation 1755)[12], William Osmer (1759)[13] and James Clark (1770)[14]. Blundeville appears to have relied on Martin Shelley of Artois, who had gained his veterinary knowledge in Italy, as his contemporary advisor, and drawn on Vegetius, Ruffus and Rusius. Markham relied heavily on Blundeville for chapter titles and paraphrased much of the substance of the latter's work. De Gray plagiarised Markham's works, but his section on lameness is essentially that of Blundeville. Gibson relied on Solleysel, and Bracken plagiarised both Gibson and Solleysel.

The appreciation of this body of knowledge, the recognition of pockets of good practice and the identification of the need for better standards and more widespread dissemination of best practice, led to the foundation of the first veterinary school in England, in 1791. Available for inclusion in its library were works dealing with the recognition of lameness, and a range of diagnoses together with therapies for each of these conditions. Interestingly, as most of these writers demonstrate, their original veterinary sources did not lack powers of observation. Many of the accounts of lame horses and tips on the identification of lameness are recognisably related to the systems which we use today. Similarly, descriptions of topographical changes which take place in diseases of the bones and joints, and *postmortem* changes, can be related to conditions which we regularly recognise. It is the attempt to give meaning to these changes which led to error, and the construction of therapies based on mistaken conclusions regarding physiological and pathological processes which makes many of the described treatments absurd.

By the late 18th century, osteoarthritis of low motion joints (ringbone and bone spavin) was well recognised. Seventeenth century authors had identified the need to distinguish different swellings in the hock region, and de Gray appears to have introduced the term 'bog' spavin as well as referring to blood spavin. Various blisters were regarded as effective treatments for hock swellings, but, interestingly, de Gray records them as disappointing for lameness associated with bone spavin. The only cure, in his view, was one so aggressive that the blister exposed the bone on the medial aspect of the hock. As such heroic treatment might have precipitated an inflammatory reaction, leading to ankylosis of the joint, this might be the earliest record of arthrodesis as a treatment for this condition; alternatively, it might be regarded as a local neurectomy!

Stringhalt. *From Edward Mayhew, reprinted with kind permission of the Royal College of Veterinary Surgeons Library.*

The need to reduce and stabilise fractures in man has been recognised since the earliest times, but Vegetius and subsequent authors recognised, in the case of the horse, the need to protect such treatments by using slings to relieve the damaged part of the weight of this heavy animal. Various conditions were recognised and diagnosed by their typical gait, although their underlying causes remained unknown. J. Fitzherbert (1523)[15] described stringhalt, already using that term, as did Solleysel (who also described upward fixation of the patella, mistakenly attributing it to a hock problem). Bracken related tendon disease to overstretching, suggesting that while minor problems might resolve, severe problems were likely to be incurable.

Regarding the foot, the term 'coffin' appears to have been introduced by Blundeville. The elastic nature of the foot and the 'squeezing' of the navicular bone on heel contraction, was first described by Osmer. A number of authors, including Blundeville and Solleysel, had recognised the importance of strong/long heels in the forefeet, but, despite this, the practice of cutting away the heels and leaving the toe long seems to have been widespread. Indeed, Charles Vial de St Bel, the original Professor of the Royal Veterinary College, is described by John Lawrence as having lamed many horses by lowering the heels. In 1761, Henry Herbert[16], Earl of Pembroke, was emphatic that a training institution should be formed to teach horseshoeing, so great was the ignorance. He was keen that the frog should be left relatively untrimmed and the toe cut short and square, to prevent foot problems. Solleysel recognised pointing of the feet as an unsoundness, but the underlying cause was not understood until the early 19th century. La Fosse described cases of pedal and navicular bone fractures misdiagnosed as shoulder lamenesses due to lack of external evidence of the site of disease. Interestingly, he comments that the hoof should immobilise pedal bone fractures sufficiently for them to heal. However, he did not think this could happen for navicular fractures, or fractures of the second phalanx.

La Fosse also identified nail wounds to the centre of the foot as a particular problem, as they caused sepsis in the region of the navicular bone and this, as far as he was concerned, was incurable. Osmer observed that, when foot lameness is sufficiently severe, there may be wasting of the shoulder muscles, leading to this being identified as the likely region of the problem. This seems to have been one of the first attempts to explain, and apologise for, colleagues making this error. Laminitis is referred to in the *Hippiatrika*, and Blundeville suggested that severe cases should be put in slings to aid treatment. Rusius discussed sandcracks and quittor. Solleysel treated the first condition by wiring and clamping, and the latter by excising the diseased cartilage. After excision, Clark recommended the provision of drainage through the wall if it was required. Bridges advocated a tourniquet at the level of the pastern, as an aid to foot surgery, particularly quittor operations. He thought it very helpful in distinguishing between diseased and normal tissue. Heresbach described nailbind, and emphasised the need for drainage, if required, before the infection broke out above the hoof.

Treatments seem to have followed that well-known rule to the effect that the number of treatments in use is inversely proportional to the amount known about the cause of a problem. Markham casts light on the huge emphasis on therapy rather than diagnosis. He makes it clear that his readers were not interested in diagnoses as they had already undertaken that task themselves! However, the reader needed recipes and 'cures' to put right the problem. Markham's *Maisterpeece*, based on this principle, went through numerous editions, the first in 1610, and what appears to have been the last, the 21st, in 1734, 124 years later! However, not all practitioners were happy with this approach. Bracken warned against the wholesale use of drugs, in particular, those based on family recipes and complex, nauseating mixtures. He emphasised that time and rest are the most important healers, particularly when it comes to injuries and lameness. How often do we forget such wisdom, at our peril?

Lameness Diagnosis
1800–1999

> *"You must be so clever! It is so much harder treating animals than people, because animals cannot tell you where it hurts!"*

This is a widespread public perception of the nature of the veterinary surgeon, which the profession does not take the trouble to deny. However, such logic suggests that the veterinarian should make room on his podium for the paediatrician! There are ways of getting around the problem, including diagnostic analgesia and diagnostic imaging, but these were clearly unavailable to practitioners in the early 19th century.

Despite the excellent work of La Fosse and others over the previous hundred years, there was a marked tendency for all chronic, obscure lamenesses in the forelimbs to be branded shoulder lamenesses, and hindlimb problems to be attributed to the hip and back. However, in the 1820s, James Turner finally confirmed the association between chronic forelimb lameness and degeneration of the navicular bone[17]. Clearly, there was an awareness of this condition before the 1820s, and some have attributed the first description to Jeremiah Bridges in 1751[10]. However, while the typical pointing of the foot was described by Solleysel in 1664, and 'squeezing' of the navicular bone is mentioned in Osmer (1759)[13] as a cause of foot lameness, the full picture does not seem to have emerged until the late 18th or early 19th century. Bridges does not mention navicular disease in his excellent little treatise. William Moorcroft appears to have described it in a letter of 1804 to a client, and in a letter to the *Calcutta Journal* of 1819 he claimed that he had recognised navicular degeneration, as a cause of foot lameness, since just before the turn of the century[18]. Certainly, by 1830, Joseph Goodwin[19] was confidently stating that most cases presumed to be lameness of the shoulder should more correctly be diagnosed as navicular disease, and most cases regarded as hip lamenesses, or back problems, should be diagnosed as cases of bone spavin.

In the days before nerve blocks and x-rays, the prevailing wisdom seems to have conformed to the adage 'common things are common'! A chronic forelimb lameness was likely to be navicular disease and, in the absence of a cure, effective symptomatic therapy was neurectomy. Moorcroft seems to have been practising neurectomies from the 1790s onwards, but the treatment became widespread when publicised around 1820 by William Sewell and other, later authors[18,20].

The success of neurectomy as a treatment pointed to temporary interruption of nerve function as a diagnostic method. Cocaine was used by Kohler, in 1884, for local analgesia of the eye, and Halsted described nerve blocks one year later[21]. Sir Frederick Hobday popularised the use of cocaine in veterinary surgery in England and Liautard, in the USA, seems to have tried ether, chloroform and, finally, cocaine as aids in the diagnosis of lameness[22]. From regional and surface analgesia, it was then only a matter of time before intra-articular analgesia was contemplated, with Forssell starting to use this approach in the early 1920s[23]. In our age of sophisticated noninvasive imaging techniques, local analgesic techniques remain the only conclusive way of bridging the communication gap between the veterinary surgeon and his dumb patient. All other evidence, that derived from physical examination as well as that present on images, can be regarded as circumstantial, although, in the case of a fracture, the circumstantial evidence is compelling! It is only when the pain has been eliminated from a particular area, and the animal no longer shows any signs of lameness, that a site of the body, or even a lesion, can be identified as the source of pain with absolute certainty.

A survey of the historical literature reveals that the *postmortem* examination was not a routine means of advancing knowledge until relatively recently. Greek and Roman authors demonstrated considerable knowledge of internal pathology in disease but, up until the 18th century, this important source of information seems to have been neglected. The recognition by La Fosse of fractures of the bones of the foot as causes of foot lameness, and subsequent observations on navicular disease, indicated clearly the value of close scrutiny of the limbs, *postmortem*, to discover the causes of unidentified lamenesses. In the case of hindlimb lamenesses not associated with enlargements at the seat of spavin, and thus once more attributed to the back or hip, William Percivall (1849)[24] was able, at *postmortem*, to confirm an association with 'ulcerative disease', erosion of the cartilage in the absence of large amounts of new bone formation, the lytic form of bone spavin. Unfortunately, it was clearly not possible to view the bones and joints, in detail, *antemortem*, prior to radiography, so attempts were made to link detailed clinical observations with known *postmortem* findings. However, it was the advent of radiography, in the late 19th century, which marked the most important advance in lameness diagnosis after the use of local analgesic agents.

Within a year of the first description of x-rays by Roentgen in 1895, five papers had appeared on their use for diagnostic imaging in animals. The first lateromedial projection of a foot of a horse was published in the *Veterinary Journal* in March 1896. Despite this, very little progress in equine radiography seems to have been made for at least 30 years. X-ray machines were not very robust, and horses liked neither the equipment nor the noises which emanated from it! In Britain, the Royal Army Veterinary Corps took the lead in the 1930s, with A. A. Pryer (1931)[25] contradicting the then widespread view that because you could not radiograph every part of a horse's body, radiography was neither economical nor useful in that species. He pointed out that, as most lamenesses occurred in the distal limb and this region of the horse could be radiographed, there was plenty of scope for this form of diagnostic imaging. Taking over from Pryer, Oxspring (1935)[26] went on to publish what is, arguably, after Turner (1829)[17], the most important paper in the diagnosis of navicular disease, *The radiology of navicular disease with observations on its pathology*. Still radiography did not take off. Between the two World Wars, medical radiographers helped out at the Royal Veterinary College and Edinburgh on a private basis, and Liverpool and Glasgow did not have any x-ray facilities until the late 1940s[27]. Therefore, it is only in the latter half of the 20th century that radiography has been of widespread practical value.

The great limitation of radiography is its inability to image soft tissues in the same detail as bone. It cannot even distinguish between a fluid-filled structure and a solid soft tissue mass. To a certain extent, the latter problem is solved by the use of liquid contrast agents, but this still does not answer most diagnostic questions relating to diseases of the soft tissues. In the 1970s, Hounsfield of EMI recognised that the information contained in an altered x-ray beam, emerging from a patient, could be artificially manipulated to create an image in which the soft tissue information was enhanced[28]. This became known as computed tomography, where expansion of the grey scale related to the soft tissue part of an image allowed separation of tissues which appeared as one homogeneous mass on photographic film. Therefore, skin, tendons and ligaments could all be distinguished in a way not previously possible. Unfortunately, the machines required to generate the images use linked tube-detector systems mounted in a housing with an aperture designed to take a human body. This means that only the distal limb, and the head and the cranial neck of the horse can be imaged. This limitation, together with the expense of these machines, has meant that they have not achieved widespread use in equine practice, a situation with which A. A. Pryer was all too familiar in relation to radiography!

The limitations of radiography, and even computed tomography, led to the investigation of alternatives to x-rays for diagnostic imaging. Three of these are used in the diagnosis of clinical problems in animals and therefore deserve mention here. Ultrasonography was first introduced into equine veterinary practice in the early 1980s, predominantly for its value in pregnancy diagnosis and investigation of the reproductive tract. Static B-mode scans were soon replaced by real time images and it became clear that these were valuable for all soft tissue investigations, including tendons and ligaments[29]. The only limitation is the ability to get the ultrasound beam to the part being imaged and back to the probe in order to generate the image.

Another imaging system of particular value in soft tissue investigations is magnetic resonance imaging (MRI), previously known as nuclear magnetic resonance (NMR) imaging[30]. Unlike radiography and ultrasonography, MRI is sensitive to cell and tissue composition, giving information on these, associated with pathological change, in the absence of anatomical changes.

The final imaging system which yields physiological/pathological information, far more than anatomical information, is scintigraphy. Introduced in the early 1970s for the detection of primary and metastatic bone tumours in man, it soon became clear that scintigraphy could detect a range of pathological processes in bone, including inflammation, infection, fractures and neoplasia[31]. Ueltschi first used the technique in the horse in 1977, and since then the ^{99m}Technetium-methylene diphosphonate bone scan has become a routine approach in the investigation of acute and severe, but obscure, lamenesses in racehorses. It has revolutionised our understanding of stress fractures in horses and prefracture disease through the work of Pilsworth and Webbon (1988)[32], in Newmarket, and Stover and her colleagues in Davis, California[33].

Management and Treatment of Orthopaedic Problems

The 19th Century

In the 19th, as the 20th century, veterinary surgeons were frequently challenged by trauma to the musculoskeletal system in the form of fractures, open joints and disruptions of the suspensory apparatus, including the flexor tendons. The need for protection of the damaged part, by preventing full weightbearing, was well recognised and slings were applied routinely. Vegetius advocated slings, but one problem with their use was the creation of severe pressure sores leading to inflammation, infection and, ultimately, death. La Fosse seems to have recognised that it was futile to use slings in horses which could not use their limbs at all to support their weight and, therefore, were unable to alternate between resting in slings and partial self-support during recovery. Von Sind (1772) also recognised this important balance between resting and weightbearing, without the need to use the damaged limb, and designed slings in the form of a sheet, providing a large area for support[22]. Wooden splints were important in the stabilisation of fractures, but various stiffened bandages were also used, such as that described by Thomas Turner (1829)[34], James Turner's brother, using wheat flour and table beer!

In 1831, John William Gloag[35] reported the treatment of a complete fracture of the distal radius in a carthorse stallion. He shaped green wood in boiling water and applied these customised splints from 22.5 cm above to 15 cm below the carpus. He covered all the ends with tow to prevent rubbing. After six weeks he was able to take the horse out of slings. It had a relatively large callus but it returned to its original use. His only disappointment appears to have been that his reduction of the fracture had been slightly imperfect, so the horse was left with the limb slightly turned out. Gloag's justification for the report was that,

> *"in many cases of fracture we should be justified in endeavouring to save the animal".*

In 1838, Thomas Mayer[36] reported successful fixation of a tibial fracture by wrapping the limb in an adhesive plaster and providing support with six splints, three placed laterally and three medially. In 1848, John Nelson[37] described the treatment of a tibial fracture in a carthorse mare with splints and slings, giving details of its convalescence. For five weeks the horse bore little weight on the limb, but by 10 weeks the limb was strong enough to carry the horse. At that stage, the horse was walked out during the day and put back in slings at night. At 11 weeks, the horse was turned out for one month, followed by a gradual return to work. In the same year as Mayer's case report, William Charles Spooner (1838)[38] treated a nondisplaced fracture of the ulna with two months' box rest, followed by several months rest at grass. At the end of this, the horse was sound. He also commented on the problems of displaced ulnar fractures. In the days before internal fixation, he recognised that, due to the pull of the triceps muscle, it was impossible to maintain reduction.

In this preantibiotic era, it was clear that removal of small fractures was the best option, particularly if these were associated with wounds to joints. In 1829, William Dick[39] described a horse with a fracture of its medial femoral condyle. He removed a fragment measuring 7.5 cm x 4 cm x 2.5 cm which involved a large part of the articular surface of the condyle. The animal recovered to a point at which Dick regarded it as virtually sound at the trot. The horse's main residual problem was that it slightly adducted the limb as it moved!

The tibial fissure/stress fracture caused some puzzlement to veterinary surgeons in the early part of the 19th century, as evidenced by reports to *The Veterinarian* in the 1830s. In one report, three cases are described in which horses went suddenly, severely lame for no apparent reason[40]. Foot problems were eliminated so the horses were box-rested for several days. The first was then turned out and found, one morning, with a tibial fracture just above the hock. The second developed a complete tibial fracture while in the stable, and the third developed a complete tibial fracture 11 days after the onset of lameness, three days after being turned out. In another article, a horse owner took a person to court for throwing a stone at his horse and causing its death. The horse finished its work and walked home after the incident. However, several days later, it suddenly developed a complete tibial fracture. The judge ruled that the horse owner did not have a case as it would not have been possible for a tibial fracture to have gone unnoticed for several days, so the stone could not have caused it[36]!

Even in La Fosse's day, open joints were already recognised as a major problem. Once infected, he thought a joint was incurable. With large wounds, particular difficulties were covering the area, to prevent further contamination, and reducing motion, to encourage healing. Thomas Turner (1829)[34] advocated his wheat flour and beer bandage, which formed a 'skinlike splint' allowing the wound to heal underneath. He also used his bandaging system for injured and severed tendons. He left the 'cast' in place for several months and, as with open joints, he felt that the quality of healing was better than that gained from other methods.

Up until the mid-19th century, surgery which required a recumbent animal involved casting the horse on the ground and immobilising the animal, for a procedure which was performed without the aid of anaesthesia. In 1779, Sir Humphrey Davy had observed how nitrous oxide could induce general anaesthesia in a cat and had proposed its use for surgery in animals. However, it was not until the 1840s that nitrous oxide, ether and chloroform were all recognised as serious contenders to relieve the suffering of animals and people undergoing surgical procedures[22]. In 1848, one year after Sir James Simpson's demonstration of chloroform's efficacy in man, descriptions started to appear of its use in horses, with Pickering[41] describing its use for castration and Cockburn using it for a neurectomy in a lame horse[42]. By the 1880s, chloroform was being reported regularly as a part of equine surgery, and it had been joined by intravenous anaesthesia, in the form of chloral hydrate, the use of which in the horse was first described by Humbert in 1875[23].

Even today, horses and ponies are still placed under general anaesthesia, in paddocks and yards, for minor procedures such as castration, ventriculectomy and wound repair. However, by the mid-19th century, some were starting to question the suitability of hard ground as a landing place for both the conscious and unconscious horse. In 1862, R. H. Dyer[43] wrote about a less traumatic 'operating bed' for horses, which he created by filling a hole, about one metre deep, with layers of furze, tan and straw. This he described as cushioning the fall and preventing the horse bouncing on hard ground. Thus, injury associated with the casting or anaesthetic induction procedure, was minimised.

Management and Treatment of Orthopaedic Problems

The 20th Century

It is, perhaps, surprising, given the heroic approach of 19th century veterinary surgeons to all types of equine disorder, including long bone fractures, that the early part of the 20th century did not become a period of consolidation and rapid development of orthopaedic techniques, in parallel with the situation in human hospitals. In part, this was probably due to the steady decline in economic importance of the horse following the First World War; but it was also due to the continued challenge of dealing with such a large and heavy animal. The two key problems of fracture stabilisation and the prevention of infection remained to be conquered.

Ignatz Semmelweiss recognised, in 1847, the association between 'dirty' surgeons and puerperal fever in women leading to high maternal mortality in hospital births[22]. He recommended the practice of washing in chlorine, as an antiseptic, to prevent transmission of infection between patients. Twenty years later, Joseph Lister introduced antisepsis into surgical practice, gaining a marked reduction in mortality in a series of patients with open fractures by spraying the wounds with phenol. Pasteur himself had recognised the value of boiling surgical instruments and, in 1886, von Bergmann introduced steam sterilisation to human surgery. This was followed, in 1890, by Halsted's introduction of surgical rubber gloves and in 1900 by Hunter's advocacy of face masks. Despite this, the antiseptic approach remained the usual practice for barehanded veterinary surgeons into the 1940s and beyond, meaning that most wounds healed by second intention and procedures relying on sterility were, on the whole, not attempted[44].

Antibacterial agents were the other big development which unlocked the potential for successful fracture therapy in horses, when appropriate implants could be developed. The introduction of the antibacterial agent, prontosil and, subsequently, other sulphonamides, in the late 1930s, and the antibiotic, penicillin, in the 1940s, revolutionised the treatment of bacterial infections[44]. These agents also offered the possibility of prophylaxis in surgical wounds, at least in theory enhancing the likelihood of first intention healing. Despite the threat of antibiotic resistance, partly as a result of overuse of this group of drugs, there is now a wide range of antibacterial agents available for use in animals. Combinations of penicillin or cephalosporins, and aminoglycosides, such as gentamicin and amikacin, provide broad spectrum efficacy in infected wounds and reassuring prophylactic cover for the treatment of closed fractures.

The introduction of implants into fracture therapy in people did stimulate some interest amongst adventurous veterinary surgeons. As early as 1829, Lavert had implanted gold, silver, lead and platinum in dogs, and concluded that platinum was the most inert of these metals. Subsequently, wire was used to repair a fractured patella in a human subject in 1862, and reports exist of a horse maxillary fracture treated with wire in 1923[44] and a dog calcaneal fracture successfully treated by McCunn in 1933[45]. However, it was not until 1910, when Lane introduced high carbon steel as an appropriate material for bone plates, that any major progress was made in terms of a strong medical implant. For the next 50 years, Lane bone plates, and the wider Sherman plates introduced two years later, became the standard implants of this type for internal fixation of fractures in man. The same year as it was introduced, the bone plate was used successfully to repair a fractured humerus in a dog, and internal fixation gradually became an accepted treatment in small animals. Unfortunately, the application of plates and screws to equine fractures generally led to implant failure, with only the odd case report, such as that of Pallister and Archibald in 1953 concerning double Sherman plating of a metacarpal fracture, illustrating that a few animals could be treated in this way[44]. A report published early in 1966, by the Orthopaedic Research Committee of the American Association of Equine Practitioners[46], offers a snapshot of the state of equine fracture therapy at that time. Humeral fractures were, on the whole, a disaster, but could be treated by an intramedullary nail in some foals. Nondisplaced ulnar/olecranon fractures could be treated conservatively, but attempts to pin displaced fractures usually failed. Some radial and tibial fractures could be immobilised with plaster casts, with the help of transfixation pins, and third metacarpal and metatarsal fractures could also be placed in a cast. Femoral fractures in foals could, in some cases, be sufficiently stabilised to heal with a modified Thomas extension splint.

In fact, it was not until the late 1960s and early 1970s that there was significant progress in the use of bone plates in horses. This arose from the development, by the Association for the Study of Internal Fixation, of superior implants for use in man. These offered the possibility of stronger repair in horses, and heralded the start of the modern era of equine fracture fixation. The group emphasised anatomical reduction and early mobilisation, the former an essential feature of stability and, in the case of intra-articular fractures, an important factor preventing secondary arthritis; the latter an unavoidable sequel to surgery in animals. Jacques Jenny (1968)[47], in particular, was quick to see the relevance of this thinking to equine fractures and to recognise that, combined with aseptic surgical techniques and modern antibiosis, aimed at preventing catastrophic infection, this new approach was a significant advance on previous techniques. In 1969, Gertsen and Brinker[48] reported on the successful use of the new bone plates in compound third metatarsal fractures in two ponies and, in 1972, four papers appeared, in the *Proceedings of the Annual Convention of the American Association of Equine Practitioners*, reporting on larger numbers of fractures which had been treated using the new implants and equipment.

Thirty-three years after the Orthopaedic Research Committee's report, there has been considerable progress[49]. Humeral and femoral fractures remain a problem, particularly in mature individuals, but more successful case reports have appeared involving young animals treated with either intramedullary nails or plates. Compound fractures are a challenge, due to the development of osteomyelitis which either prevents healing or leads to loosening of implants before healing can take place. However, double plating is a successful treatment for about 50% of simple, closed fractures of the radius, and it has also been successfully applied to tibial fractures. Ulnar/olecranon fractures can be repaired using conventional plates or, in cases with only a small proximal fragment, a hooked plate. The prognosis for such fractures is excellent.

In the case of intra-articular fractures, removal of small fragments and replacement and stabilisation of large fragments has become standard practice where economics permit, minimising the likelihood of secondary arthritis and maximising the chances of a horse or pony returning to work. Initially, such fragment removal was via an arthrotomy, in some cases causing significant damage to ligaments and other periarticular tissues, leading to convalescence periods of several months. The relatively large incisions in highly mobile periarticular tissues were also prone to breakdown, with the attendant risk of joint infection, so there was a need to develop techniques which minimised the invasive nature of the surgery.

Arthroscopy had first been used to examine a human knee by Takagi in 1918, with the first equine joint examination, that of a hock, being performed by Watanabe, a pupil of Takagi, in 1949[50]. However, it was not until the 1960s that a practical arthroscopy system for routine clinical use was developed. This was introduced into the USA in the 1970s, and quickly developed by a number of equine surgeons, including, in the late 1970s and early 1980s, Wayne McIlwraith, who produced the first edition of the definitive text on equine arthroscopy in 1984. Gradually, arthroscopic approaches have been developed to all the equine synovial cavities which will permit access and manipulation of the arthroscope and surgical equipment. Smaller arthroscopic incisions are much less likely to break down than arthrotomy wounds and the reduction in damage to periarticular structures means that athletic horses can be returned to training and competition much more rapidly than was previously possible.

The biggest challenge for a large orthopaedic repair is the recovery from anaesthesia. In parallel with better surgical techniques and implants, new combinations of sedatives, induction and maintenance agents have both eased induction and, more importantly, improved the quality of recovery from general anaesthesia. The alpha$_2$-agonist, xylazine, and other similar drugs, have provided a level and quality of sedation undreamed of even 20 years ago and, used as a premedicant, together with ketamine as an induction agent, it is possible to achieve the gentlest of inductions. In the late 1950s and early 1960s, halothane replaced other gaseous agents as the standard drug for maintenance of anaesthesia in horses[23], and maintenance of arterial blood pressure, by careful monitoring and titration of anaesthetic depth, has largely eliminated myopathies associated with prolonged recumbency, if the duration of anaesthesia is kept to less than four hours.

At one time, anaesthesia was all about fast recoveries. Now, following lengthy orthopaedic procedures, it is routine practice to 'top up' horses with alpha$_2$-agonists in the recovery box, to keep them recumbent until the bulk of the anaesthetic agents have been eliminated and redistributed. This leads to a much more coordinated effort to stand when the horse is ready. In some cases, this effort to stand may be assisted. Particularly in ponies and small horses, three people inside the recovery box, one at the head, one at the tail and one at the side of the animal, can help an animal maintain its footing once it is ready to stand, or, alternatively, tail and head ropes may be applied and used to help an animal stand by looping them over pulleys in the box and assisting from outside. Other ingenious methods have been tried to convert a recumbent horse into a standing horse! Slings are still used, particularly with non-Thoroughbred horses, and can be of great value both at recovery and also in the convalescent period. Suspending the unconscious horse in a box full of grain or small balls, so that its legs are immobilised and its trunk supported, and allowing it to wake up, has been tried, with varying degrees of success. Jenny pioneered the use of a swimming pool, with the horse suspended on a raft, and others have used smaller flotation tanks to restrain the limbs and also reduce weightbearing. Unfortunately, none of these methods is straightforward; and keeping water away from a surgical wound, and also keeping the water in small tanks clean, are major problems.

In the belated recognition by veterinary surgeons of the importance of aseptic surgery, in addition to the surgeon and the surgical equipment, the operating theatre, induction area and surgical bed have received considerable attention. Soft areas are important for induction of anaesthesia, but the type of furze/tan/straw surface recommended by Dyer is difficult to keep clean and sterile. Padded floors made of rubber or plastic-covered foam have superseded straw beds, and the induction/recovery area has now been separated from the operating theatre itself. This has led to the development of different systems for moving the recumbent, anaesthetised horse into the adjacent room. Some systems use overhead gantries and hoists, with horses either being lifted in hammocks or via hobbles attached to their pasterns. Alternatively, the floor of the induction box may have a mobile portion which can be wheeled into the operating theatre and, in some cases, attached to a hydraulic ram to provide a variable height table. The surgical table will have a soft surface, provided either by padding or various custom-made air beds. These, the table and the rest of the operating theatre can be cleaned to minimise bacterial contamination and, in the more sophisticated facilities, positive pressure ventilation, with filtered air, excludes contamination by airborne organisms. Many equine hospitals now have two operating theatres: one reserved for clean surgery, in particular for bone and joint problems, the other for 'dirty' cases, such as colics and wounds. This minimises animal-derived contamination of the orthopaedic theatre, again reducing the risk of catastrophic infection of a fracture repair.

It would be wrong to give the impression that sophisticated internal fixation has completely replaced older techniques in fracture repair. Plaster of Paris, used for hundreds of years in man to stabilise fractures, always had disadvantages in the horse due to its prolonged setting time, tendency to disintegrate as soon as it became damp, and sheer weight when applied in sufficient quantity to support a horse's limb. However, the introduction of water-resistant, lighter casting materials, with faster setting times, in the 1960s/1970s, provided much improved external support for fractures[51]. These materials are used by themselves in the distal limb, particularly where economics prohibit internal fixation, and also to give added support to implants during the critical time of anaesthetic recovery. Resin-based casts are also used with transfixation pins to promote extra stability in comminuted fractures.

The Future

The 20th century has seen great strides in our ability to treat horses with bone and joint problems. However, it is perhaps appropriate to separate our superior technological knowledge from our wisdom as a profession, to measure ourselves against our forebears. One hundred and sixty years after Goodwin suggested that, in the case of forelimb lamenesses, navicular disease was a more likely diagnosis than shoulder lameness and, in the case of hindlimb lameness, spavins were more likely to be the cause than a hip or back problem, we seem to have failed in our duty to educate horse owners, as chronic lamenesses are still being blamed on the shoulder and back!

A constant criticism, throughout the 19th century, of the Royal Veterinary College and other professional groups and institutions as they developed was that each of these was run by men with vested interests in their own fame and careers, rather than a concern for the profession and the animals which it treated. Seniority and experience was frequently equated to ability, a mistake which is still made today. A journal, *The Veterinarian*, was established with the specific aim of righting all that was wrong with the Royal Veterinary College. Arguably, we are no different, and the tension of 'egos versus animals' remains. Veterinary education in the United Kingdom is divided between six veterinary schools, leading to fragmentation of the teaching and research resource, and a curious blend of cooperation and rivalry to the detriment of progress in our collective missions. The understanding between general practice and university hospitals, whereby the universities largely avoided first opinion work in exchange for the practices' second opinion work, has largely broken down, meaning that there will be increased competition for cases of all types in the future.

We have seen that the past was a time of plagiarism, in the literal sense, with material transferred verbatim between texts over hundreds of years. However, increased emphasis on results now means that much modern research is of the 'me too' variety, with ideas plagiarised and republished on a daily basis. Computerised databases and an explosion in publications mean that most literature reviews only search backwards for a few years, so ideas and techniques from only 10 or 20 years before go unnoticed and unacknowledged. An even more sinister development is the reliance on abstracts as primary sources. There is a tendency for young scientists to use virtual libraries, relying on summaries of papers - which are essentially interpretations of data - for ideas and support for their own research. This means that original data in papers is less subject to critical scrutiny than in the past and, rather than alternative interpretations being rejected, they are not even considered.

Particularly before the production of printed books, but even after, it is clear, with our current knowledge, that accurate clinical observation and commonsense treatments existed alongside misguided, often barbaric practices. At times, we pride ourselves in more effective dissemination of knowledge and more consistency of practice, but horses all over the world are still receiving treatments, like firing for tendons, which are based more on tradition and folklore than good science. Equine hospitals within a few miles of each other are still recommending completely different and even conflicting, methods of handling equine diseases, based on the whims of their senior staff. No doubt, in 100 years' time, our successors will be identifying and marvelling at the combination of knowledge and ignorance which will be our legacy, in the same way as we can marvel at the contradictions of the last thousand years.

The 20th century has seen great strides in our ability to remove small fractures and also place screws and plates across larger fractures. However, although we can replace the pieces in the right order, we are frequently frustrated by the slowness and, in some cases, the absence of nature's healing powers. As basic research focuses on growth factors and the turnover of connective tissue matrix molecules, it is to be hoped that lessons will be learnt which will allow manipulation of the healing process in the horse. This should allow a better quality of repair and, hopefully, a more functional repair than that which our current knowledge permits. In the case of cartilage and bone, resynthesis of these tissues might allow the return of joints to a near normal anatomical structure and restoration of function. This better quality repair will never be instantaneous, so there is a need to improve our ability to recover horses from general anaesthesia. A practical system for getting horses back on their feet, without implant failure, and reducing weightbearing during the convalescent period, would be a major advance in terms of saving the lives of injured animals.

Difficulties in restoring diseased tissues to their original state should lead us to pay more attention to the prevention of problems. As in the days of Markham, cures are worth far more in a market economy than advice aimed at preventing disease. Therefore, much more money is available for, and has been spent on, the development of therapeutic agents than research into better training methods and work surfaces, show jumps, horse shoes, saddles and all the other factors which might contribute to clinical and subclinical problems in horses. It is to be hoped that welfare groups will combine to redress this balance, so that we can deliver our duty of care to horses and ponies in return for the pleasure which they give us.

There is no doubt that our ability to look inside the horse, both directly with various endoscopes, and indirectly with x-rays and ultrasound, has greatly increased our ability to diagnose problems and also the range of conditions which we recognise compared to our predecessors. However, we remain ignorant of many complex conditions, such as those which genuinely emanate from the upper limb and back. In these regions, we still need techniques which allow us to identify the site of pain and the nature of the disease process affecting the tissues. Above all, as early diagnoses are more and more essential, we need objective criteria for identifying subtle problems which may be evident to a rider only and invisible to all other observers.

To conclude, we should pay tribute to the observational skills of many of the founders of our profession. Wherever one looks in the early literature, one common theme is clear. Among the charlatans there are many very able clinicians. Their descriptions of disease are frequently extremely detailed, and easily recognisable to the modern veterinarian. Many treatments seem ill conceived, but where individuals had the interests of the horse at heart there are records of therapy founded on commonsense and empiricism which have stood the test of time. We should reflect on whether our reliance on technology sometimes means we miss the obvious, and whether our childlike interest in gadgets and medicines, often our predecessors' downfall, means that our own treatments stray from being those best suited to our patients and their owners. This is not to neglect the benefits of empiricism, which accounts for most of our progress to date. That is assuming that empiricism is an avenue left open to us by international and national government bodies in the 21st century!

Acknowledgements

I am grateful to the staff of the Royal Veterinary College Library who have enthusiastically supported many forays into the historical collection over the last 15 years. In particular, I would like to acknowledge the help of the late Linda Warden and Jane Kingsley who is the current librarian with responsibility for this valuable resource.

References

[1]Blundeville, T. (1566) *The Fower Chiefyst Offices belongyng to Horsemanshippe*, Willyam Seres, London.

[2]Heresbach, C. (1577) *The Foure Bookes of Husbandrie*, translated by B. Googe. R. Watkins, London.

[3]Mascall, L. (1587) *The Second Booke of Cattel*, Iohn Wolfe, London.

[4]Markham, G. (1610) *Markham's Maisterpeece*, Nicholas Okes for Arthur Iohnson, London.

[5]de Gray, T. (1639) *The Compleat Horseman and Expert Ferrier*, Thomas Harper for Nicholas Vavafour, London.

[6]de Solleysel, J.L. (1696) *The Parfait Mareschal or Compleat Farrier*, translated by W. Hope, George Mosman, Edinburgh.

[7]Gibson, W. (1720) *The Farrier's New Guide*, London.

[8]Gibson, W. (1751) *A New Treatise on the Diseases of Horses*, A. Millar, London.

[9]Bracken, H. (1737) *Farriery Improved*, J. Shuckburgh, London.

[10]Bridges, J. (1751) *No Foot No Horse*, J. Brindley, London.

[11]Bartlet, J. (1753) *The Gentleman's Farriery*, J. Nourse, London.

[12]La Fosse, E.G. (1755) *Observations and Discoveries made upon Horses with a new Method of Shoeing*, J. Nourse, London.

[13]Osmer, W. (1759) *A Treatise on the Diseases and Lameness of Horses*, London.

[14]Clark, J. (1770) *Observations upon the Shoeing of Horses*, A. Donaldson, Edinburgh.

[15]Fitzherbert, J. (1523) *The Boke of Husbandrie*, Rycharde Pynson, London.

[16]Herbert, H. (1761) *A Method of Breaking Horses and Teaching Soldiers to Ride, Designed for the Use of the Army*, J. Hughs, London.

[17]Turner, J. (1829) The navicular disease or chronic lameness in the feet of horses. *The Veterinarian* **2**, 53-66.

[18]Smith, F. (1976) *The Early History of Veterinary Literature*, Vol. 3. J.A. Allen, London.

[19]Goodwin, J. (1830) On the navicular disease and spavin. *The Veterinarian* **3**, 145-158.

[20]Youatt, W. (1836) Neurotomy, Lecture VII. *The Veterinarian* **9**, 361-368.

[21]Thurmon, J.C., Tranquilli, W.J. and Benson, G.J. (1996) History and Outline of Animal Anesthesia. In: *Lumb and Jones' Veterinary Anesthesia*, 3rd edn, William Wilkins, Baltimore.

[22]Dunlop, R.H. and Williams, D.J. (1996) *Veterinary Medicine: An Illustrated History*, Mosby, St Louis.

[23]Hall, L.W. (1971) *Wright's Veterinary Anaesthesia and Analgesia*, 7th edn, Bailliere Tindall, London.

[24]Percivall, W. (1849) *Hippopathology, Vol. 4, Part 1: Lameness in the Horse*, Longman, London.

[25]Pryer, A.A. (1931) The uses and limitations of the x-rays in horse practice. *Vet. Rec.* **11**, 899-903.

[26]Oxspring, G.E. (1935) The Radiology of Navicular Disease with Observations on its Pathology. *Vet. Rec.* **15**, 1433-1446.

[27]Williamson, H.D. (1978) The new photography - A short history of veterinary diagnostic radiology. *Vet. Rec.* **103**, 84-87.

[28]Lee, R. (1995) Introduction. In: *BSAVA Manual of Small Animal Diagnostic Imaging*, Ed: R. Lee, BSAVA, Cheltenham. pp 13-14.

[29]Reef, V.B. (1991) Advances in diagnostic ultrasonography. *Vet. Clin. N. Am.: Equine Pract.* **7**, 451-466.

[30]O'Callaghan, M.W. (1991) Future diagnostic methods. *Vet. Clin. N. Am.: Equine Pract.* **7**, 467-479.

[31]Steckel, R.R. (1991) The role of scintigraphy in the lameness evaluation. *Vet. Clin. N. Am.: Equine Pract.* **7**, 207-239.

[32]Pilsworth, R.C. and Webbon, P.M. (1988) The use of radionuclide bone scanning in the diagnosis of tibial stress fractures in the horse. *Equine vet. J., Suppl.* **6**, 60-65.

[33]Mackey, V., Trout, D., Meagher, D. and Hornof, W. (1987) Stress fractures of the humerus, radius and tibia in horses. *Veterinary Radiology* **28**, 26-31.

[34]Turner, T. (1829) On opened joints, and particularly the knee. *The Veterinarian* **2**, 272-278.

[35]Gloag, J.W. (1831) A case of fracture of the radius. *The Veterinarian* **4**, 421-422.

[36]Mayer, T.W. (1838) On fractures of the extremities in the horse. *The Veterinarian* **11**, 144-146.

[37]Nelson, J. (1848) Fractured limbs of horses. *The Veterinarian* **21**, 501-506.

[38]Spooner, W.C. (1838) Case of fracture of the ulna. *The Veterinarian* **11**, 208-209.

[39]Dick, W. (1829) Fracture of the inner anterior condyle of the femur in the horse. *The Veterinarian* **2**, 140-142.

[40]Trump (1830) Singular cases of fracture. *The Veterinarian* **3**, 394.

[41]Pickering, J.C. (1848) Castration under the influence of chloroform. *The Veterinarian* **21**, 137-138.

[42]Anon (1848) Application of chloroform to animals. *The Veterinarian* **21**, 3.

[43]Dyer, R.H. (1862) Operating bed for horses. *The Veterinarian* **35**, 572-573.

[44]Pettit, G.D. (1990) A history of veterinary orthopedic surgery. In: *Canine Orthopedics*, 2nd edn, Ed: W. G. Whittick, Lea and Febiger, Philadelphia. pp 3-20.

[45]McCunn, J. (1933) Fractures and dislocations in small animals. *Vet. Rec.* **13**, 1236.

[46]Anon (1966) Repairable fractures in horses. Report of the Orthopedic Research Committee of the American Association of Equine Practitioners *J. Am. vet. med. Ass.* **148**, 435-438.

[47]Jenny, J. (1968) ASIF technique for fixation of fractures in horses. *Proc. Am. Ass. equine Practnrs.* **14**, 99-104.

[48]Gertsen, K.E. and Brinker, W.O. (1969) Fracture repair in ponies using bone plates. *J. Am. vet. med. Ass.* **154**, 900-905.

[49]Nixon, A.J. (1996) *Equine Fracture Repair*, W.B. Saunders Co., Philadelphia.

[50]McIlwraith, C.W. (1990) *Diagnostic and Surgical Arthroscopy in the Horse*, 2nd edn, Lea and Febiger, Philadelphia.

[51]Edwards, G.B. and Clayton Jones, D.G. (1978) Use of hexcelite for the immobilisation of limbs of large animals. *Vet. Rec.* **102**, 397-399.

The horse's gait: moving with the times

HILARY CLAYTON
Large Animal Clinical Sciences
College of Veterinary Medicine
Michigan State University
East Lansing
Michigan 48824-1314
USA

Since prehistoric times, scientists and artists alike have been fascinated by the horse in motion. Scientific interest in equine locomotion dates back at least to Xenophon, who recognised that the hindquarters were the horse's 'motor'; and to Aristotle, who gave an early description of the sequence of limb placements during locomotion.

Leonardo Da Vinci integrated his interests in art and science to produce some fine drawings of horses in motion that are now housed in the British Royal Collection in Windsor Castle. An eloquent account of the history and evolution of equine locomotion in art, science and veterinary medicine has been written by Rene van Weeren for a new text on equine locomotion[1].

Although horses have been a favourite subject of many artists, they have not always been depicted accurately. From the time of the ancient rock paintings that were drawn 30,000 years ago until the 18th and early 19th centuries, artists often represented horses in poses that modern photography has shown are unnatural. Galloping horses were typically shown in an airborne phase with the hindlimbs extended behind and the forelimbs stretched out in front (Fig 1). From cine films and videotapes, we have learned that horses do not actually adopt this position in any of their gaits. Occasionally, a horse galloping at racing speed may show an exceedingly brief airborne phase between lift off of the leading hind limb and contact of the trailing forelimb, but certainly not of the magnitude depicted in the paintings.

Fig 1: Typical representation of a galloping horse.

The presence of an airborne (suspension) phase in certain gaits is now well accepted, but this was not always the case. Indeed, one of the great controversies surrounding equine locomotion in the 19th century revolved around whether there was a phase of the horse's stride in which contact of the hooves with the ground was lost. Joseph Gamgee, from Edinburgh, and Neville Goodman, from Cambridge, conducted a debate on this topic in the pages of the *Journal of Anatomy and Physiology* in the early 1870s[2–5]. Gamgee stated that:

> *"The horse in the fast paces, as in the slowest movement, has never less than two of his feet acting on the ground."*

Goodman disagreed, but did not have the means to prove that he was correct. That task was assigned to the great inventor Eadweard Muybridge. Although British by birth, Muybridge established himself as a landscape photographer in California. He was employed by Leland Stanford, railroad magnate and founder of Stanford University, to prove beyond doubt that the trotting gait had an airborne (suspension) phase. Stanford's horse Occident, who held the world record for trotting a mile in 2 minutes 16 seconds, was the subject of Muybridge's experiments. At the time Stanford assigned this task to Muybridge in 1872, photography was restricted to stationery objects, since shutter speeds were too slow to capture moving subjects without blurring. Muybridge developed a method of reducing the exposure time sufficiently to capture a rather indistinct photograph of Occident in an airborne phase. He continued to improve his technique and devised an ingenious system of still cameras triggered in sequence to record sequential photographs. Several years later, when he worked at the University of Pennsylvania, Muybridge took tens of thousands of photographs of people and animals engaged in various activities. His book *Animal Locomotion* was first published in 1887, and has been reprinted several times[6]. An example of one of the more unusual photographs of a mule on a swing is shown in Figure 2. Muybridge must have had phenomenal powers of persuasion, because almost all his subjects performed naked, including the first Dean of the veterinary faculty at the University of Pennsylvania. Also worthy of note are the exceptionally brave (or foolhardy) farriers, who were photographed working at the anvil and shoeing horses without a stitch of clothing (Fig 3).

As a result of their superior locomotor capabilities, horses have been used as beasts of burden, as vehicles of war and as

Fig 2: Denver, the mule, on a swing. Note how he uses the mass of his head and neck to produce the swinging motion.

partners in sports and recreation. With the recent explosion in the popularity of equestrian sports, equine sports science has become a thriving academic discipline. Gait analysis, which is the study of locomotion, is an area of equine sports science that has made great strides (quite literally) in the last 30 years. The availability of high speed cine cameras and video techniques greatly enhanced our ability to study and understand movement; and their use has been pivotal in the development of equine gait analysis as a scientific discipline. In the second half of the 20th century, frame-by-frame analysis of high speed cine films of moving horses was pioneered by researchers at the Swedish University of Agricultural Sciences in Uppsala. The early Swedish works were published in a series of landmark papers in what was, at that time, quite a new publication, the *Equine Veterinary Journal* (e.g. Fredricson and Drevemo 1971[7]). Today, gait laboratories rely on videography or optoelectronic systems for motion analysis. Different systems vary in the degree of automation, sophistication and flexibility of use. Some are able to locate marker coordinates automatically in real time, others allow manual digitisation without the need for markers, which is useful for studying competitive performances, but is much more time-consuming.

By 1991, animal locomotion was sufficiently established as a scientific discipline to warrant its own conference. The first International Workshop on Animal Locomotion (IWAL) was organised by Henk Schamhardt and Ton van den Bogert at Utrecht University. The workshop was a great success, both for the dissemination of new information and as a catalyst in fostering international collaborations between laboratories. Subsequent IWALs were held in California in 1993 and in Saumur, France in 1996, with IWAL4 being planned for Vienna in 2000. The proceedings have been published[8–10].

Although IWAL encourages papers on all animal species, the vast majority of the presentations have always been related to horses. The early workshops were heavily oriented toward techniques and methodologies, many of which were being adapted from the human field. Methods of reducing errors and improving accuracy were introduced, and many of these are now used routinely. Descriptive reports established the stride characteristics and force profiles of different gaits, providing normal databases for comparison with pathological gait patterns. Studies of the effects of training, shoeing and lameness on the stride variables were reported, together with comparisons of treadmill and overground locomotion.

Input from physicists and engineers has broadened the scope of the discipline and has led to the development of innovative new techniques and the application of a more sophisticated level of computational analysis. With computer power estimated to be doubling every 18 months, our horizons continue to expand.

From a veterinary viewpoint, evaluation of lameness is one of the more interesting applications of gait analysis. Visual analysis by an experienced clinician will always be the primary method of gait analysis in evaluating lameness. Kinematic analysis goes a stage further in quantifying what the clinician's eye is seeing, and detects movements that are beyond the spatial and temporal resolution of the human eye. The kinematic characteristics of supporting limb lameness have been described by Buchner and co-workers[11,12]. Kinematic analysis, however, is only part of the story, since it does not take account of the forces that produce the movements. These are measured by kinetic analysis. The force plate was introduced to equine studies in the 1970s[13] and has proven to be a sensitive tool both for detecting lameness and for identifying the affected limb[14].

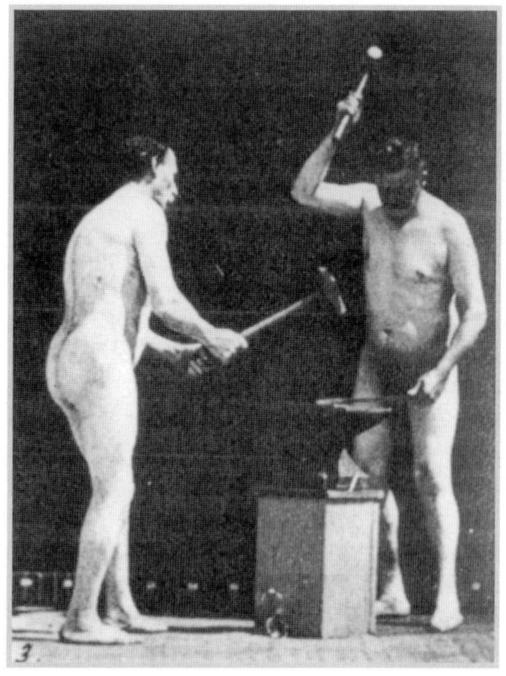

Fig 3: The smith, a mighty man is he...

Neither kinematic nor force variables have proven useful, however, in localising the site of lameness within a limb. Indeed, there is evidence to suggest that horses compensate in a similar manner for a variety of different lamenesses.

Recently, the technique of inverse dynamics has been applied to the equine limbs[15–18]. In this technique the limbs are represented by a series of rigid segments linked by hinge joints, with the muscular action around each joint being represented by a torque generator. The net joint moment (torque) is the result of the combination of muscular forces acting across the joints. The value of this technique lies in the fact that a horse can redistribute its joint torques without visibly changing the gait pattern. For example, extension of the hind limb at the end of the stance phase could be accomplished by an extensor torque at the hip only, by an extensor torque at the stifle only, or by any combination of these[19]. Inverse dynamic analysis reveals the net effect of these differences in muscle coordination patterns.

A further step in the inverse dynamic analysis is to calculate the mechanical power output across the joint to investigate the sites of mechanical power generation for locomotion. In man, inverse dynamics is an established technique for studying normal and pathological gait, and is used to guide decisions regarding treatment, for example in making surgical decisions for children with cerebral palsy[20], and in assessing the response to such treatments. In equine gait analysis, the value of inverse dynamics for lameness analysis and for assessment of the effects of treatment are being explored[21].

We can look back on the 20th century as a time of unprecedented advancement of knowledge of equine locomotion. Computerisation and other technological advances have brought significant progress, but this is not a time for complacency. Our current knowledge represents only the tip of a large iceberg. As we move into the new millennium, gait analysis is poised to become a practical tool for assessing performance and lameness. In future, the greatest advances in our understanding of equine locomotion are likely to come from using an integrated approach to the discipline. Motion studies will be combined with data describing ground reaction forces, tissue loading and muscle activation patterns to provide a more comprehensive picture of the horse in motion. There is reason for considerable optimism regarding the future of gait analysis as we move into the 21st century.

References

[1]Van Weeren, P.R. (2000) History. In: *Equine Locomotion*. Eds: W. Back and H.M. Clayton, W.B. Saunders.

[2]Gamgee, J. (1869) On the action of the horse. *J. Anat. Physiol.* **3**, 370-376.

[3]Gamgee, J. (1870) The action of the horse. *J. Anat. Physiol.* **4**, 235-236.

[4]Goodman, N. (1870) The action of the horse. *J. Anat. Physiol.* **4**, 8-11.

[5]Goodman, N. (1871) The action of the horse. *J. Anat. Physiol.* **5**, 89-91.

[6]Muybridge, E. (1887) *Animal Locomotion.* Republished (1979) as *Human and Animal Locomotion*, Dover Publications, Inc., New York.

[7]Fredricson, I. and Drevemo, S. (1971) A new method of investigating equine locomotion. *Equine vet. J.* **3**, 137-140.

[8]Leach, D.H., and Schamhardt, H.C. (1993) First (ESB) Workshop on Animal Locomotion. *Acta. Anat.* **146**, issues 2-3.

[9]Schamhardt, H.C.C., Clayton, H.M. and Wade, J.F. (Eds) (1994) Proceedings of the Second International Workshop on Animal Locomotion. *Equine vet. J., Suppl.* **17**, 85 pages.

[10]Barrey, E., Davies, H.M.S., Schamhardt, H.C. and Rossdale, P.D. (1997) Proceedings of the Third International Workshop on Animal Locomotion. *Equine vet. J., Suppl.* **23**, (112 pages).

[11]Buchner, H.H.F., Savelberg, H.H.C.M., Schamhardt, H.C. and Barneveld, A. (1996a) Limb movement adaptations in horses with experimentally induced fore or hind limb lameness. *Equine vet. J.* **28**, 63-70.

[12]Buchner, H.H.F., Savelberg, H.H.C.M., Schamhardt, H.C. and Barneveld, A. (1996b) Head and trunk movement adaptations in horses with experimentally induced fore or hind limb lameness. *Equine vet. J.* **28**, 71-76.

[13]Pratt, G.W. Jr. and O'Connor, J.T. Jr. (1976) Force plate studies of equine biomechanics. *Am. J. vet. Res.* **37**, 1251-1255.

[14]Merkens, H.W. and Schamhardt, H.C. (1988) Evaluation of equine locomotion during different degrees of experimentally induced lameness. II: Distribution of ground reaction force patterns of the concurrently loaded limbs. *Equine vet. J., Suppl.* **6**, 107-112.

[15]Colborne, G.R., Lanovaz, J.L., Sprigings, E.J., Schamhardt, H.C., and Clayton, H.M. (1997) Forelimb joint moments and power in the equine walk. *Equine vet. J., Suppl.* **23**, 37-40.

[16]Colborne, G.R., Lanovaz, J.L., Sprigings, E.J., Schamhardt, H.C. and Clayton, H.M. (1998) Forelimb joint moments and power during the walking stance phase of horses. *Am. J. vet. Res.* **59**, 609-614.

[17]Clayton, H.M., Lanovaz, J.L., Schamhardt, H.C., Willemen, M.A. and Colborne, G.L. (1998) Net joint moments and powers in the equine forelimb in the stance phase of the trot. *Equine vet. J.* **30**, 384-389.

[18]Lanovaz, J.L., Clayton, H.M., Colborne, G.R. and Schamhardt, H.C. (1999) Forelimb kinematics and joint moments during the swing phase of the trot. *Equine vet. J.* In Press.

[19]Van den Bogert, A.J. (1998) Computer-assisted gait analysis in equine orthopaedic practice: the case for inverse dynamic analysis. *Equine vet. J.* **30**, 362-363.

[20]Rose, S.A., DeLuca, P.A., Davis, R.B., Ounpuu, S. and Gage, J.R. (1993) Kinematic and kinetic evaluation of the ankle after lengthening of the gastrocnemius fascia in children with cerebral palsy. *J. Pediatr. Orthop.* **13**, 727-732.

[21]Clayton, H.M., Schamhardt, H.C., Lanovaz, J.L., Colborne, G.R., Willemen, M.A. (1999) Superficial digital flexor tendinitis: 2. Net joint moments and joint powers. *Am. J. vet. Res.* In Press.

Equine colic surgery: past, present and future

BARRIE EDWARDS
The University of Liverpool
Veterinary Field Station
Leahurst, Neston
South Wirral L64 7TE
UK

Considerable advances have been made in all aspects of equine surgery but none more so than in surgery of the alimentary tract which has been one of the major success stories in the past 30 years. In a relatively short period we have advanced from a situation where horses with serious intestinal obstructions endured severe pain until they died or, hopefully, were subjected to euthanasia, to one where the great majority can be treated successfully by surgery.

Expectations for survival 30 years ago were not high, but this has changed as publicity accompanying the successful treatment of high profile horses like Desert Orchid and Milton has made horse owners and the public aware of what can be achieved. While this places additional pressure on veterinary surgeons, it also makes owners more prepared to agree to their horses undergoing surgery without delay.

History

Colic surgery is by no means a new innovation. There are references, attributed to Aristotle in approximately 350 BC, to colic due to inguinal hernia for which castration was prescribed. The first account of successful intestinal surgery in the horse, cited by Smithcors, dates to 1695 when a farrier, against his better judgement, decided to operate on a horse that had been staked in the abdomen. The animal was placed on its back and the torn gut withdrawn through the wound. After being emptied and cleaned, the gut was sutured and returned to the abdomen. After an uneventful recovery, the horse returned to the plough six weeks later.

In 1829, King of Stanmore operated on a mare which had shown signs of colic for 13 days, during which time she had been bled, purged and poulticed without benefit. Exploration of the abdomen through the left flank in the standing animal revealed a 12 inch portion of the small intestine impacted with firm material and distension of the proximal small intestine with fluid. The impaction was cleared by massage but the mare died six hours later. It is interesting to speculate that this may have been the first recorded case of ileal impaction in the horse.

Felizet was more successful in 1849. Unaided by anaesthetics or antiseptics he removed an enterolith from the small colon of a nine-year-old horse belonging to the local miller. The horse had been showing abdominal pain for 16 hours, but had shown signs of constipation on two or three occasions during the previous four months. Rectal examination had revealed a concretion the size of a child's head at the beginning of the descending colon. After removing the concretion, Felizet closed the incision in the colon with a furrier's suture. The horse was poulticed on the loins and bled six times at intervals of three hours, 21 pints altogether being withdrawn. Despite this, or because of it, the horse started to eat on the sixth day and was put back to work on the land two weeks later.

Although there were notable exceptions, such as correction of large colon torsions (Marek) and incarceration of small intestine in the epiploic foramen (Forsell) at the turn of the century, most reports over the next 100 years were of unsuccessful attempts; and death was mainly attributable to the operation being delayed too long. This, to a lesser extent, is true today. When I first embarked on colic surgery the horses referred had frequently been walked for several hours, by which time both they and their owners were hardly capable of standing. As a result, horses with strangulating lesions were in an advanced state of endotoxic and hypovolaemic shock and were unlikely to survive.

The surgery was often protracted and a significant proportion of cases died as the final skin suture was inserted or within the first few hours after surgery. At that time, dead horses at the Royal Veterinary College were transported to the *postmortem* room on a sledge and as I drove in to the car park in the morning, I would look with apprehension for the telltale parallel lines leading from the box which would mark another unsuccessful attempt. Naturally, it was very disappointing and disheartening to lose those cases but the experience gained in locating, identifying and correcting a large variety of obstructions was invaluable in the context of saving future cases which were referred much earlier and, therefore, had a much better chance of surviving. It wasn't until the late 1960s and early 1970s that significant progress was made due to the pioneering efforts of veterinary surgeons such as Vaughan and Donawick in the United States, Pearson and Greenwood in the United Kingdom, Kersjes and Bras in the Netherlands but, particularly, Huskamp at Hochmoor in Germany who, without any doubt, has had the biggest influence on colic surgery.

Every colic surgeon worldwide has reason to be grateful to him, not only for his immense contribution to the subject through his innovative approach to a vast array of problems, but also for disseminating his knowledge and experience through his many publications, books and presentations at scientific meetings to the benefit of countless thousands of horses. The overall survival rates reported in 11 surgical colic case studies totalling 2260 horses between 1971 and 1984 were only modest (35–60%), with the notable exception of those from the Hochmoor Clinic which were significantly higher. By achieving a success rate greater than 80% in horses allowed to recover from anaesthesia, Huskamp showed what could be achieved and set a standard for everyone else to attempt to emulate. The last 15 years has seen a steady improvement in the percentage of horses surviving colic surgery and this can be attributed to a number of factors.

Bernard Huskamp (left) with Harry Pettersson (centre) and Goran Dalin at Equitana in Essen.

Diagnosing the Need for Surgery

Early recognition of the need for surgery holds the key to improved survival rates. A similar view was expressed in relation to intestinal obstruction in man by Sir Heneague Ogilvie who wrote:

> *"In acute abdominal emergencies the difference between the best and worst surgery is infinitely less than that between early and late surgery and the greatest sacrifice of all is the sacrifice of time."*

The majority of obstructions are strangulation obstructions which, predictably, carry a less favourable prognosis than simple, nonstrangulating obstructions. Because, largely, the prognosis for survival is directly related to the patient's postoperative cardiovascular and metabolic status, it becomes increasingly important for surgical intervention to be undertaken as early as possible before deterioration in the horse's condition occurs. Delay is sometimes unavoidable, for example when the horse has been in colic for several hours before it is discovered by the owner. In many cases, however, the delay is due to failure to interpret the clinical signs correctly.

Education of veterinary surgeons through publications, lectures and continuing professional development courses and, particularly, of undergraduates who during their clinical rotations are closely involved in the postoperative management of colic cases and have the opportunity to witness for themselves the benefit of early surgery, is having the desired effect. In the early stages, following intestinal obstruction, the presenting signs are less pronounced and are open to different interpretations. As the condition progresses the diagnosis becomes easier but treatment is more difficult.

The veterinarian in practice must therefore investigate even minor pathophysiological abnormalities with great care, evaluating the clinical findings in the context of his/her knowledge of the pathophysiology of obstruction, and arrive at a diagnosis. He or she is a vital member of the 'team' and can make a considerable contribution to successful surgery by early referral. A specific diagnosis is not necessary; it is sufficient to have a reason to suspect an intestinal obstruction and then to organise referral to a surgical facility. Some cases will turn out not to require surgery but the owners will appreciate the reasons for referring the horses and will doubtless be pleased not to have to pay a large fee for surgery!

The diagnosis is still based on a thorough systematic clinical examination of the gastrointestinal and cardiovascular systems, but advances in the use of ancillary diagnostic modalities can contribute to increased survival rates and more economic case management. Abdominal ultrasonography was used primarily in foals where it compensated for our inability to carry out rectal examination. Recently, more refined equipment and greater experience of its use in mature horses with colic has enabled a variety of both small and large intestinal obstructions to be detected.

Similarly, as experience in its use has increased, so has the application of laparoscopy to horses with colic. It may be used to evaluate abnormal findings on abdominal palpation, radiography or abdominocentesis. Its use in horses with acute colic may be restricted by severe intestinal distension, but it can be of considerable value when signs are not conclusive enough to indicate surgical exploration. Small intestinal incarcerations, strangulation obstructions, large colon volvulus or oedema and proximal enteritis have been diagnosed by laparoscopy. Exploratory laparoscopy should be considered in horses with chronic colic or weight loss, particularly if there are abnormal rectal examination or ultrasound findings. Guided visceral biopsies may be accomplished in the standing or recumbent patient.

The availability of videoendoscopes 2 or 3 m in length has allowed the detection of gastric ulceration and neoplasia, conditions which can result in clinical signs that are indistinguishable from those of recurrent or chronic colic.

Abdominal radiography is of greatest value in evaluation of foals with colic but, despite the large size of the mature horse's abdomen, it has been shown to be useful in the diagnosis of sand obstructions, enterolithiasis, gastric impaction and diaphragmatic hernia.

Therapeutic Strategies

A greatly improved understanding of the systemic pathophysiological response to intestinal disease is enabling therapeutic strategies to be developed to counter the complex and far-reaching effects of endotoxaemia. These include cardiovascular collapse, pulmonary and systemic hypertension and abnormalities in the intravascular coagulation pathways that lead to the formation of microvascular thrombi and subsequent tissue hypoxia. The principal therapy to combat the effects of endotoxaemia involves aggressive fluid therapy to restore plasma volume, improve tissue perfusion and correct fluid shifts that occur with increases in capillary permeability. Nonsteroidal anti-inflammatory drugs have been shown to have a beneficial effect by arresting or attenuating mediator effects of endotoxin through inhibition of the cyclo-oxygenase and, possibly, lipoxygenase pathways.

Other treatment modalities are designed to target

specific conserved sites of the endotoxin molecule itself, namely the lipid-A portion or specific mediators in the inflammatory cascade. Ideally, hyperimmune serum and monoclonal antibodies directed against the lipid-A core of lipopolysaccharide should be given to neutralise the endotoxin before the inflammatory pathway is initiated. Polymyxin B may be used to bind the lipid-A portion directly. Future methods to minimise endotoxaemia that remain experimental at this time include the use of immunotherapy directed specifically at the inflammatory mediators TNF, IL-1 and the lipid-A portion of lipopolysaccharide.

By the time the horse is presented to a surgical referral facility, various metabolic derangements may exist that make the horse a poor anaesthetic candidate. Consequently, the presurgical stabilisation and management of the patient can be a medical challenge and can potentially influence surgical outcome. Although these derangements should, if possible, be corrected before surgery, in many cases the severity of the colic precludes prolonged delay in commencing surgery. Additionally the degree of hypovolaemia may be so great that the deficit cannot be replaced in a reasonable period. In such cases, 7.5% sodium chloride solution administered at a rate of 4 ml/kg bwt over 15–20 minutes is effective in expanding plasma volume rapidly, stimulating cardiac contractility and improving tissue perfusion through peripheral dilation.

Anaesthesia

The first colic surgery I saw was performed by Professor John George Wright in 1962 shortly before he retired. The operation on a Standardbred gelding was performed in a paddock with the patient anaesthetised with intravenous chloral hydrate supplemented with local infiltration of the flank which was the surgical approach employed. Fortunately, colic surgery has literally come in from the cold since that time and the cornerstone of the considerable progress in equine emergency abdominal surgery has been the development of modern volatile anaesthetic agents and the means of administering them to the large animal patient. The contribution made by an experienced anaesthetist cannot be overemphasised and I am deeply indebted to my anaesthetist colleagues over the years for their great contribution to any success achieved. In addition to achieving a quiet induction and smooth recovery and providing abdominal relaxation, the anaesthetist is able, by constant intraoperative monitoring, to respond promptly to changes in pulse rate and character, ECG and mean arterial and venous pressure and blood gases, and institute remedial measures.

The duration of anaesthesia and surgery is critical. Surgery needs to be performed as quickly and expeditiously as possible but without sacrificing surgical standards. The problem must be identified and corrected with a minimum of delay. Although experience gained from necropsies is a great help in achieving this goal, recognition of lesions in the intestine spread out on the *postmortem* room floor is no substitute for a knowledge of pathological anatomy *in situ*. Many of the technical problems related to equine intestinal surgery have been overcome and the horse has shown that it tolerates extensive interferences, often involving resection of considerable lengths of bowel, extremely well. Experience has shown that horses which have undergone major intestinal surgery are able to return to their previous level of performance at the highest level. In addition to an ever-increasing wealth of clinical experience, there has been scientific evaluation of surgical techniques including anastomosis, abdominal closure, suture patterns and materials, and of the effects of intestinal resection.

Intestinal Viability

Accurate intraoperative assessment of intestinal viability remains a dilemma confronting the surgeon. Visual assessment, which is still the method most commonly employed, is generally subjective and unreliable. Several methods to evaluate blood flow and tissue oxygenation including fluorescein dye, laser Doppler, Doppler ultrasonography, and pulse and surface oximetry have been used but each has its limitations and the often expensive equipment may not be available. When doubt exists regarding the viability of small intestine, the decision may be taken to resect the suspect bowel. Such an approach is less applicable when evaluating the large colon which has been involved in a 360° volvulus.

The most accurate method requires an evaluation of blood flow to the tissue and the morphological insult following an ischaemic injury. The best methods are surface oximetry or laser Doppler combined with the morphological evaluation of frozen tissue sections. Factors correlating with nonsurvival are lack of haemorrhage at the enterotomy site; packed cell volume (PCV) values >50% and body temperature >102°F at the time of admission; and divergence of PCV and total solids values during surgery. A recent prospective study in which colonic lumen pressure was measured using a simple manometer may offer a more practical solution.

Another aspect of assessing viability is the determination of how much intestine can be resected without creating malabsorption problems. Clinical experience and experimental studies suggests that horses can be managed successfully even without dietary changes, after loss of 70% of the small intestine. Accurate intraoperative measurement of long lengths of jejunum is difficult and is complicated by the fact that strangulated small intestine can undergo an increase in length by up to 25% which can lead to overestimation of the true proportion of intestine involved.

Anastomosis

Most methods of anastomosis work well in the hands of their proponents and all suffer from some limitations that influence a surgeon's preference. Stapling instruments which are now widely used in gastrointestinal surgery have the advantages of speed, reduced tissue handling, improved tissue blood flow and minimal contamination. The most important disadvantages of staples are expense and a greater risk of intestinal leakage and adhesions. Major large colon resection which, ten years ago, was largely an experimental procedure, is now employed in the clinical situation as an alternative to euthanasia for horses with colon of questionable viability after volvulus. Although this results in removal of more than 80% of the large colon, the gastrointestinal tract adapts to this loss without the need for special dietary requirements.

Postoperative Management

The postoperative management of equine colic patients is just as important as the most heroic corrective surgery. Its success depends on adequate intensive care based on close monitoring of physiological parameters. The two factors which affect cases adversely, in the immediate postoperative period, are cardiovascular insufficiency (shock) and loss of gut propulsive activity (ileus). Although the incidence of ileus appears to be on the decline in many clinics, it remains a significant problem and is often fatal. It may be due to specific causes, such as mechanical obstruction or peritonitis, or may fall into the category of idiopathic ileus, the causes of which are not fully understood.

Predisposing factors which have been implicated in its development include ischaemia, chronic distension, abnormal electrolyte levels, endotoxaemia and anaesthesia. Ileus may arise within the first 24 hours following surgery or less frequently between the second and seventh day, and occurs particularly in horses with small intestinal obstructions in which there has been delay in referral for surgery.

The usual measures for prophylaxis and conservative therapy comprise removal of gastric fluid every three or four hours and adequate intravenous fluid therapy. In addition, drugs which stimulate small and large intestinal motility are to be recommended. Although a variety of prokinetic drugs has been investigated, there is as yet no universally accepted pharmacological treatment for idiopathic ileus. Pharmacological therapy is directed towards agents which block adrenoceptors (acepromazine, yohimbine), prostaglandins and dopamine (metacloramide) and the release of acetylcholine (neostigmine, bethanecol, cisapride and erythromycin). Lignocaine, which has several mechanisms of action, is also used. If conservative treatment fails, horses that continue to require gastric decompression for 24–36 hours are candidates for relaparotomy. Experience has shown that decompression of the distended small intestine is the most effective procedure in these cases.

It may be difficult to distinguish between postoperative ileus and mechanical obstructions due to stomal obstruction, obstruction by a haematoma, peristomal volvulus, adhesions or ischaemic intestine. Although a second laparotomy is expensive, it has the advantages of saving on the expense of protracted, unsuccessful medical therapy, a definitive diagnosis of the problem, an opportunity to relieve a mechanical obstruction before irreparable changes have taken place in the intestinal wall, prevention of suffering and expense by subjecting a case to euthanasia with an untreatable complication and an opportunity to treat postoperative ileus by decompressing distended small intestine.

There may be a tendency to underestimate the contributory role of mechanical obstruction in postoperative gastrointestinal stasis. Consequently, this can lead to an overemphasis on pharmacological management of horses after small intestinal resection and a delay in carrying out relaparotomy.

The number of centres at which colic surgery is performed has increased dramatically in recent years. Colic surgery is a team effort and requires expertise, dedication and commitment if it is to be successful. It is, of necessity, expensive, particularly in complicated cases where intensive care extends over several days. Without the benefit of insurance cover, such surgery would not be feasible in many cases and it has allowed much-loved horses and ponies of limited monetary value to be saved.

Adhesions

As the number of abdominal surgeries performed in horses and the postoperative survival rates have increased in recent years, long-term complications such as abdominal adhesion formation are becoming more frequent. The true incidence of adhesions is difficult to determine but after small intestinal surgery varies from 14–22%. However, when all abdominal surgeries were considered, the incidence was approximately 5%. Adhesion formation is associated more commonly with small intestinal disease, intestinal resection and anastomosis, enterotomy and gastrointestinal tract surgery in foals. Adhesions are not unique to the horse. In human patients, they are reported to be the most common cause of intestinal obstruction and female infertility with the majority originating from a previous abdominal surgery. Based on necropsy findings, at least 67% of people having abdominal surgery develop adhesions and this rises to 93% in those having more than one surgery. Although many horses with adhesions have subclinical signs, the most constant manifestation is recurrent colic which, if severe, may require repeat laparotomy or euthanasia. Whereas in human subjects, surgery to treat adhesions is routine, repeat laparotomies are often not financially or humanely feasible in horses. Therefore, the primary focus should be on adhesion prevention rather than on treatment. The principal questions to be answered are:

- What are the significant contributory factors and mediators involved?
- Are there effective pharmacological or physical treatments that can be used to prevent adhesions?
- What are the optimal surgical techniques that can be used to prevent and treat adhesions?

The pathogenesis of adhesions is complex but the two broad categories of peritoneal injury that are thought to predispose to adhesions are ischaemia and inflammation. These increase fibrin deposition and decrease fibrinolysis resulting in excessive or prolonged fibrin deposition leading to the formation of fibrous adhesions.

Most experimental studies using a variety of adhesion models have been carried out in laboratory animals, but variation in adhesion formation between species makes extrapolation from rats or rabbits to the horse questionable. Other variations, such as method and time of adhesion assessment, make comparison between studies evaluating prevention therapies difficult. Experimental studies in the horse are limited by expense but methods of adhesion prevention under investigation include various mediator inhibitors, intraperitoneal infusion of various agents and solutions and physical barriers. Preventative therapies that have been used in equine abdominal surgery mirror those used in human patients and include antibiotics, nonsteroidal anti-inflammatory drugs, dimethyl sulphoxide, intraperitoneal and systemic heparin, sodium carboxymethyl cellulose and surgical barriers. No single treatment has been shown to reduce adhesion formation consistently.

While the preoperative pathological condition may predispose to adhesion formation, the part played by the surgeon in their development must not be overlooked. The surgeon's greatest contribution to prevention is by applying meticulous surgical technique, paying particular attention to atraumatic handling of tissues, removing any ischaemic or potentially ischaemic tissue, precise haemostasis, minimising contamination and the use of nonreactive suture material. Early surgery (before significant endotoxaemia and intestinal distension have occurred) minimising surgical time and avoiding postoperative ileus are other factors which are important in reducing the incidence of adhesions.

Recurrence

Most accidents leading to intestinal obstruction are isolated incidents which are very unlikely to recur. However, recurrence of the same problem does occur, the prime example being volvulus of the large colon particularly in recently foaled mares. Studies have shown that mares which have had one episode of volvulus have 15% chance of recurrence and this rises to approximately 80% if the mare has two or more episodes. Colopexy and, less commonly, partial resection of the colon are employed to prevent recurrence. Colopexy involving suturing the lateral free band of the left ventral colon to the abdominal wall, is carried out at the first surgery for large colon volvulus in young to middle-aged mares on studs with a high incidence of the condition. The technique is not without potential complications, the most devastating of which is rupture of the ventral colon immediately proximal to the colopexy 4–12 weeks after surgery. Use of the technique is usually limited to brood mares because of concern about its effects in performance horses and stallions.

Several nonsurgical methods of managing left dorsal displacement of the colon have been developed, including rolling the horse under general anaesthesia, exercise on a long rein after administration of phenylephrine and simple medical management involving withholding food, administering intravenous fluids and analgesics if required. These are not applicable in every horse and an accurate diagnosis is essential if they are to be successful. Recurrence does occur but, because LDD is rarely life-threatening and can often be managed without recourse to surgery, colopexy is rarely used.

Future Advances

Minimally invasive surgery in man has made great progress over the last decades and similar advances may be anticipated in the horse, limited only by our imagination and the development of proper instrumentation. However, Fischer has warned that we must ensure that procedures developed to replace conventional surgery have a positive benefit to both horse and surgeon, and are not merely the overenthusiastic embrace of new technology. Laparoscopic surgery has been used for selective lysis of adhesions in the abdominal cavity which are accessible only by laparoscopy. Strangulated inguinal hernias are managed with laparoscopic assistance for sectioning the strangulating ring, and assessment of bowel viability and repair of diaphragmatic tears has been attempted laparoscopically. Management of rectal tears will be an area in which laparoscopy can be utilised. Access to rectal tears is very poor by routine flank or ventral celiotomy, but they can be visualised very well by laparoscopy. Intracorporeal suturing may be employed to repair these tears.

Inability to follow intestine systematically from proximal to distal makes laparoscopic-assisted intestinal resection and anastomosis currently impracticable. More specific instrumentation, including large stapling devices, will need to be developed for use in the horse. Ileal biopsy in the standing horse for the diagnosis of grass sickness would be a significant advance.

Our most important advances in the future in the management of colic will require an improved understanding of the disease itself and its varied causes. Epidemiological studies are beginning to provide us with insight into factors involved which could be used to prevent colic in horses. Colic is no respecter of breeding or value and is just as likely to occur in a top class racing Thoroughbred as a child's pony. Many high profile horses have been the victims of severe intestinal obstructions. In the United States the death from colic of a promising Thoroughbred colt called Bolshoi prompted its owner to donate a large sum of money to initiate the Bolshoi gastrointestinal programme of research at the University of Georgia. This money, in addition to financing research and educational programmes for horse owners, sponsored the first Colic Research Symposium in 1982 which established an open international forum to discuss both clinical and research aspects of colic. Such has been the success of this venture, the sixth of these symposia was held in November last year. Eighty-four contributors from 10 countries presented a total of 113 papers or posters at this meeting indicating the breadth of the international research effort into colic which is helping to establish a very comprehensive literature base. However, despite the volume of new information which is published each year, many problems remain to be solved and inevitably new problems will occur in the future which will continue to challenge the skill and ingenuity of clinicians and research workers.

Being involved in colic surgery over the past 30 years has been constantly challenging, sometimes depressing, but mostly very rewarding. I have likened it to being on an emotional roller-coaster but these days the 'highs' considerably outnumber the 'lows'. Despite the disruptions to family life, the lack of sleep and the inevitable frustrations, it is an experience I would not wish to have missed. Colic surgery engenders team spirit and it has been a pleasure to work with professional and lay colleagues, residents and undergraduates, and to have been a member of a large international group of people whose common goal is to help horses with colic.

Famous for 15 minutes - operating on Desert Orchid

TIM GREET
Beaufort Cottage Equine Hospital
Cotton End Road
Exning, Newmarket
Suffolk
UK

I would like to relate the series of events that took place in November, 1992, when a private veterinary practice in Newmarket became a focus of media attention following colic surgery on Desert Orchid, one of the nation's sporting heroes.

For a private veterinary practice used to dealing with a variety of equine patients, a few of which are valuable but without holding any particular interest for the general public, the sudden media attention provided a bizarre almost surreal diversion from the routine of daily practice.

The story started on 24 November, when Desert Orchid was found to be suffering from colic in his stable at Ab Kettleby at approximately 11 am. He showed signs initially of severe abdominal pain and the referring veterinary surgeon Robin Kernohan had treated him medically before deciding that referral to a more specialised clinic was indicated. Even on the journey to Newmarket, the horse had required sedation because of severe pain. However, by the time of his arrival in Newmarket he was quiet, with a slow heart rate of 32 beats per minute, and had passed faeces on the journey.

There was no apparent sign of the drama that was to unfold over the following 24 hours and the horse was admitted for observation. He was given continuous intravenous fluids and his progress was monitored thoughout the night. At no time did he show anything more than low grade discomfort. With the benefit of hindsight it should have been remembered that this was a proven racing champion, a winner of the Cheltenham Gold Cup and a veteran of over 70 racing starts (34 wins, 11 seconds, eight thirds and £654,066 in prize money). So perhaps the low level of pain he displayed was due to the stoicism and courage which had shown itself in no uncertain terms on the racecourse.

The following morning Andy Bathe, my surgical resident at the time, came to see me with a rather anxious look on his face having just carried out another rectal examination. The previous day there had been no signs of any intestinal abnormality, but Andy's worried face was quite understandable when I put an arm into the horse's rectum and could clearly feel tightly distended loops of small intestine. Although the horse's pain level was not significantly worse than noted since admission to the clinic, his packed cell volume had risen from 37 to 46% and his circulating white blood cell count from 10,000 to 15,000. The mucous membranes of the horse also began to look a little congested and I had no doubt that surgical exploration under general anaesthesia was indicated without any further delay.

The owners were consulted and readily agreed to surgery. The referring veterinary surgeon was kept informed. The horse was anaesthetised and an exploratory laparotomy revealed 10 feet of black necrotic small intestine which had become strangulated because of a volvulus. We were amazed by this sight because the horse had shown so little discomfort since his admission to the clinic. It is perhaps surprising in these circumstances that the significance of a patient is completely forgotten as the surgical team works almost on automatic pilot. A routine intestinal resection and end-to-end anastomosis was carried out. Afterwards the horse was moved to a padded anaesthetic recovery box in the usual way, although we did take a number of photographs during these procedures just for posterity. The horse recovered uneventfully from the anaesthetic. Mike Shepherd, the anaesthetist, watched him closely until he stood up. The horse was then moved to one of the heated intensive care boxes where he was attached to an intravenous fluid line and managed like all intestinal resection cases, being deprived food and water and given continuous intravenous fluid support, electrolytes, antibiotics, nonsteroidal anti-inflammatory medication and an intestinal stimulant.

The owner of Desert Orchid, Richard Burridge, and his father Jimmy were obviously concerned about the horse's condition and had tipped off the media that Desert Orchid had been rushed to Newmarket for emergency surgery. So, on the evening of the day of surgery, telephone calls started to filter into the practice from members of the media enquiring about Desert Orchid's condition and seeking confirmation that he had actually undergone surgery. Initially the partners discussed the matter and we decided that we would try to fend off all inquiries with fairly noncommittal descriptions of his progress. However, it soon became apparent that this rather naive approach would be totally inadequate in dealing with a situation obviously outside our experience. So after another hasty discussion it was agreed to hire a security firm to maintain a watch around the clock to try to prevent unwanted intrusion by the media. However, we agreed to give a television interview initially to Sky TV. I remember this as a rather daunting experience, being unused to the ways of the media.

Over the next few days, what had become a trickle of phone calls became an avalanche of enquiries, from the racing press, the broadsheets and, especially, from the tabloid press who undoubtedly felt that the life and death struggle of a racing superstar such as Desert Orchid would provide very good copy. The coverage was not only in the sporting pages but in the general news as well. The wonderful grey horse had been equally popular with knowledgeable racegoers and members of the general public alike. I can remember giving several short radio and television interviews at the time.

Within a day or so a number (it seemed like hundreds to me but was probably only a dozen or so) of photographers were encamped at the end of the driveway of Beaufort Cottage Stables equipped with long lenses or video cameras looking for shots of Desert Orchid with a drip in his neck or being stomach tubed. We were very grateful for the presence of the security guards who kept the media at arms length. Hard-bitten journalists show great ingenuity when trying to obtain stories or photographs and on numerous occasions photographers were seen over the other side of the wall in the Memorial Gardens trying to get a telephoto shot of the stable in which Desert Orchid was kept. We tried to have a press release available on a daily basis which could be read out to interested parties. We did not want to be obstructive as we felt that the situation was of genuine public interest and particularly in this rather critical phase we realised how concerned his many fans were about his progress. However we felt that it was essential that none of this should interfere with his hoped-for recovery.

Despite all our worst fears, Dessie appeared to progress very satisfactorily but we were extremely cautious in giving an overoptimistic forecast because of the great disappointment that would result should his condition suddenly deteriorate. All those who deal with surgical colic patients know only too well how frequently horses appear to make good progress initially only to succumb ultimately to endotoxic shock or other postoperative complications. I have always felt that it is better to be lucky than good. On this occasion our luck held and the horse continued to make excellent postoperative progress.

Although he was deprived of food, Dessie showed every sign of hunger and eagerly awaited the occasional handful of grass that was given to him. Forty-eight hours postoperatively Desert Orchid was walked out and allowed to graze for a few minutes, which he did with considerable relish. On the following day the continuous intravenous fluids were stopped and by the next day, that is four days postoperatively, all his injectable drugs were stopped and his catheter removed. From then on, until his departure from the clinic on 8 December, the hungry horse was given gradually increasing access to food and seemed to grow brighter and stronger every day. Ironically, I felt rather sadly, it seemed as if the general media interest in the horse began to dwindle as soon as it looked as if he might survive. We were still phoned regularly by racing journalists, but he was no longer as newsworthy a story as when the problem first developed.

By now Desert Orchid had appeared for a photo call for the press and a TV interview was filmed with Julian Wilson and shown on *Grandstand*. However all of this media attention was put completely in the shade by the absolutely overwhelming response from the general public and thousands of Desert Orchid fans all over the country. The practice was absolutely inundated with sacks of mail and get well cards, some commercially made, others hand-drawn by young schoolchildren. There were also messages of goodwill from many veterinary colleagues thoughout the country whose support at this time was much appreciated. In fact a small letter of thanks was sent to the *Veterinary Record* as a response to these welcome gestures of support.

Dessie left the premises on 8 December, and all the staff came out to see him off. He was wearing his King George VI Chase Rug which looked very smart. The old horse had hardly lost much condition and his incision was healing well. The Burridges came down later to say thank you and there was a last press call before the practice slipped gradually back to its normal routine. It was very much a case of being famous for 15 minutes, something that many people experience in their lives but that none of us who were involved will ever forget. I think everyone at the practice was very relieved that despite a rather inauspicious beginning it looked as if it was going to end happily. The security guards went home, and passers-by in the street and my newsagent

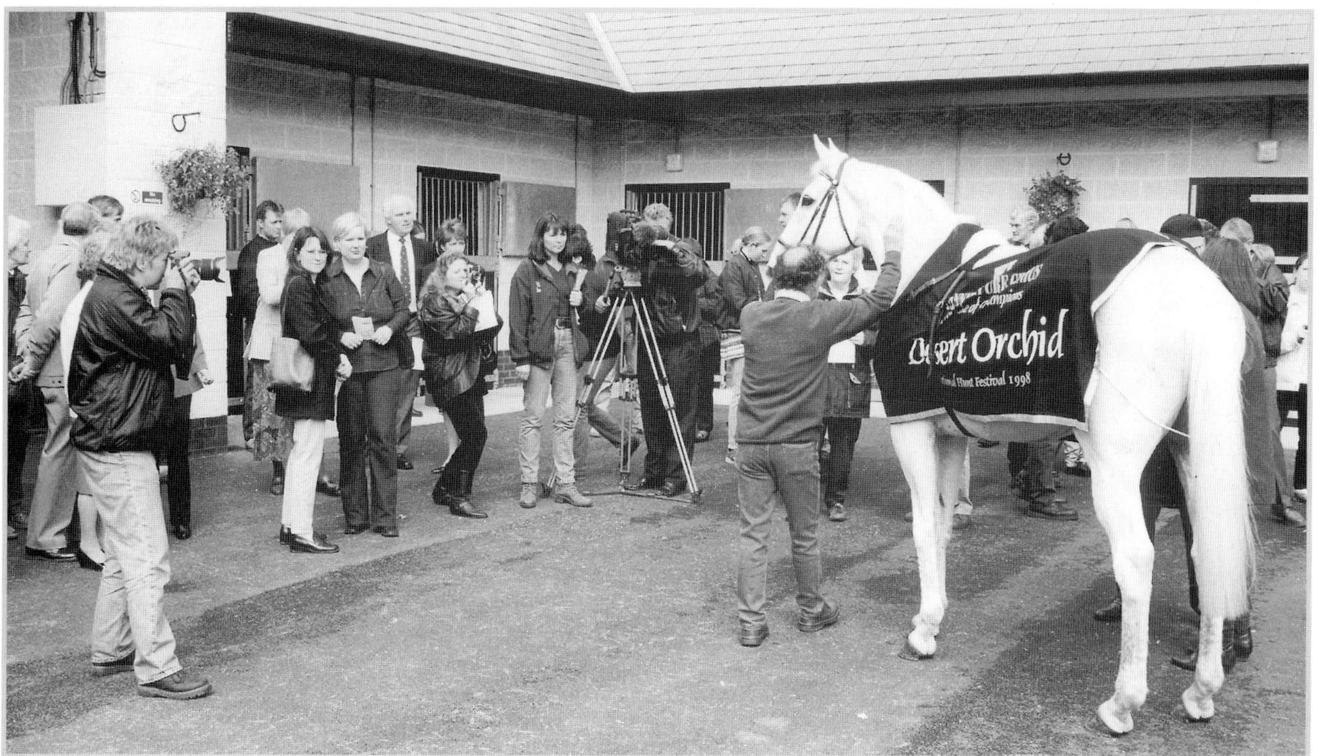

'Dessie' with admirers: Beaufort Cottage Hospital, April 1998.

stopped asking about how the horse was doing.

We totted up his bill which was charged at the normal rate as if he had been any old horse and we sent it out along with the account rendered to us by the security firm. It was rather amusing to note that there was almost no difference between these two figures, one for performing surgical treatment of his life-threatening condition and providing postoperative care, the other for providing a man round the clock to keep guard at one end of the drive while smoking a cigarette. This is rather a sad reflection of our inability to charge realistically as a profession. In the *Racing Post,* when Desert Orchid made his first public appearance following surgery, racegoers were asked to contribute an extra 50p at the gate towards the cost of his veterinary treatment.

Richard Burridge quickly produced an additional chapter to his biography of Desert Orchid, *The Grey Horse.* This chapter described the events surrounding the colic operation and had Andy and myself, along with Bonny Millar, our head nurse, who had been involved with much of his postoperative care, acting in a suitably heroic manner! After that we heard very little about Desert Orchid other than his regular appearances at racecourses and charity events. All members of the practice were delighted that we had been involved in helping such a brave and noble racehorse back to good health.

In 1997 the surgical branch of the practice was moved to a purpose-built hospital in Exning and in 1998 Her Majesty the Queen graciously agreed to open the building. Some years previously Richard Burridge had kindly offered Dessie's support for any practice function. So it was decided that we would hold a public opening for our clients, guests and referring veterinary surgeons and that Dessie would be the star attraction. I had secretly harboured the hope that the Queen might decide to ride on Desert Orchid but in fact she made a private visit two days before his appearance. He arrived, by now a 19-year-old, looking as spritely as ever and on a wonderful sunny afternoon he was absolutely in his element, posing for the photographers and for his mass of admiring fans. We, the members of the practice who had tended him some six years previously, were very proud that he should return to the practice on such a wonderful occasion.

Whither equine laryngeal surgery?

TIM GREET
Beaufort Cottage Equine Hospital
Cotton End Road
Exning, Newmarket,
Suffolk CB8 7NN
UK

Laryngeal hemiplegia (recurrent laryngeal neuropathy) has almost certainly been a significant clinical problem of horses for many centuries. Galen was the first to identify the effect of the recurrent nerve on laryngeal motor function in the second century AD While carrying out experimental chest surgery on a pig he accidentally cut the nerve and noted that the squealing suddenly stopped!

Despite this remarkable observation the correlation between a respiratory noise at exercise and equine recurrent laryngeal neuropathy was not made for another 17 centuries! Until then, obstructive diseases of the upper and lower airway in horses were considered without differentiation. Although in 17th century de Solleysel, an equerry of Louis XIV, described the signs of roaring (*"cornage"*), it was Boulez in 1825 who first identified laryngeal hemiplegia as the cause of an abnormal inspiratory noise in galloping horses.

As early as the 15th century, the earliest form of surgical treatment of respiratory tract obstruction in the horse was performed and involved slitting the false nostril. In the early years of the 19th century, the first tracheostomy was performed, and the technique is still in use to this day.

The Gunthers (father and son) of Hanover were the first to experiment with laryngeal surgery in horses in the 1830s and '40s. They performed cordectomy, ventriculectomy, cordoventriculectomy and arytenoidectomy. However, each technique was abandoned in turn with disappointment.

George Fleming, that pioneer of veterinary medicine, claimed to have solved the problem of laryngeal hemiplegia in the 1880s using arytenoidectomy. Following these claims there was a heated debate in the veterinary literature of the day until Dollar published the 'genuine' results of Fleming's surgery on 71 army horses, stating that none of the operations had been successful!

Professor Williams of Cornell University 'rediscovered' unilateral cordoventriculectomy in the early 1900s and published a number of papers, considering the operation eminently satisfactory. He felt that the arytenoid was held in complete abduction by the formation of an adhesion. However, by 1911 he had abandoned the procedure in favour of simple ventriculectomy. He showed the technique to Professor Hobday in London who adopted and popularised it in this country to such an extent that, to this day, the operation still bears his name. By 1935, Hobday claimed to have operated on more than 4000 roarers and concluded that he could make:

> *"a useless animal into a useful one in about 85% of hunters and 95% of carriage or cart horses. Some will be more or less noisy when galloping, but about 20% become sufficiently sound in wind to pass the average hunting man without comment and, even, to obtain a certificate of soundness from a veterinary surgeon."*

Reynolds (1943) recommended the technique for racehorses and Schebitz (1964) suggested that suturing the margins of the ablated ventricle improved the success of the operation.

Professor Bob Cook (see p 175), a former officer of BEVA, was one of the first veterinary surgeons to look in detail at the effects of laryngeal surgery and to use endoscopy routinely. He expressed doubts about the efficacy of the 'Hobday' operation. Two Americans, Marks and Mackay-Smith were also disappointed by the results of this procedure and were the first to perform radically different surgery for laryngeal hemiplegia. They combined a traditional ventriculectomy with the insertion of an extralaryngeal suture, in the so-called laryngoplasty or tie-back operation. They claimed the procedure to be completely successful in 88% of 121 horses on which they operated.

Interestingly, Clarke (1888), a British naval surgeon, had considered the problem of laryngeal hemiplegia in horses, and commented that "*the most obvious and natural object is to fix the palsied side in the normal position of complete abduction*". To achieve this he used sutures, cautery, and even an ivory pin. Thus the first tie-back operation in a horse was carried out some 80 years before Marks and Mackay-Smith.

Although Clarke's comments on fixed abduction of the left arytenoid cartilage might seem to show remarkable foresight, there is no reason to suppose that he or any of his contemporaries knew what the fully abducted equine larynx looked like. Despite the introduction of the rhinolaryngoscope in the latter part of the 19th century, it was not until the 1960s that regular endoscopic assessment of the equine larynx was practised. In fact, with the advent of flexible fibreoptic endoscopy, major strides were made in the diagnosis of upper airway disease.

Until that time, the majority of horses making an abnormal respiratory noise at exercise were presumed to have laryngeal hemiplegia. The arrival of endoscopy however resulted in a range of new conditions being described, such as epiglottal entrapment, branchial arch anomalies, subepiglottal cysts and arytenoid chondritis. It was also the endoscope that clearly gave the lie to the concept of the ventriculectomy operation producing abduction of the arytenoid cartilage as suggested previously. Whatever the benefits of this operation it certainly produced no significant increase in the size of the *rima glottidis*.

Although endoscopy has revolutionised the diagnosis of

equine laryngeal disease it has precipitated a major debate amongst equine clinicians about the significance of endoscopic findings in laryngeal hemiplegia. In its most advanced and severe form there is usually no doubt about the diagnosis; however, most horses show some discrepancy in movement between left and right sides of the larynx. This is further complicated because the correlation between the abnormal respiratory noise produced at exercise, and the endoscopic appearance of the larynx is often surprisingly poor. Therefore, differentiating between subclinical and clinical laryngeal hemiparesis is extremely subjective. Added to this is the effect of the disease on athletic performance. Some horses perform adequately or even to the top level despite advanced laryngeal hemiplegia e.g sprinting racehorses and show-jumpers. Other horses or those in disciplines with a greater aerobic respiratory requirement may suffer major disability from the disease. There is no method of assessing a horse's laryngeal function accurately under the circumstances of competition, although treadmill endoscopy and measurement of airway resistance approximates this to a considerable degree.

In future small telemetric devices may be inserted atraumatically into the airway to provide this sort of information under top level athletic conditions helping clinicians to evaluate the significance of laryngeal hemiparesis in an individual patient.

Laryngoplasty is currently the preferred choice for treating horses with upper airway obstruction from laryngeal hemiplegia. There are, however, well-recognised complications of this operation including chronic coughing and dysphagia, suture pull-out and infection of the implants. By definition, the position of the arytenoid cartilage ideal for galloping is the opposite of that required to protect the lower airway from food inhalation during swallowing. In practice the arytenoid cartilage is therefore fixed in a compromise position to improve the airway without unacceptable complications such as dysphagia.

The Holy Grail of modern equine laryngeal surgeons has been to find a more physiological method of opening the larynx i.e. only when the horse needs maximal airflow during fast exercise. Nerve anastomosis and neuromuscular pedicle grafts have been well established as a treatment for laryngeal paralysis in human patients. Interestingly, these techniques are used to allow the patient improved vocalisation rather than increased laryngeal airflow. In fact, another British pioneer of veterinary medicine, Sir Fredrick Smith, attempted to reinnervate the laryngeal muscles of a horse by suturing a branch of the spinal accessory nerve to the recurrent laryngeal nerve, as long ago as 1893. However, after initial optimism he abandoned the technique as ineffective. At the turn of the century Tagg also claimed success for nerve anastomosis in three out of six cases when the recurrent laryngeal nerve was grafted locally to the vagus!

In North America, during the late 1980s and early 1990s, Ducharme and Fulton carried out a variety of experimental procedures including direct nerve anastomosis and neuromuscular pedicle grafts. While these techniques have not yet achieved widespread use by equine surgeons, the early results from neuromuscular pedicle grafting have been encouraging. However, evaluating the effects of this operation is quite difficult and endoscopy during fast exercise on a high speed treadmill is necessary to identify left-sided laryngeal movement during fast exercise. Another problem is that compared to traditional surgery, neuromuscular grafts take many months to become established and owners have to be very patient. For this reason the technique is most suitable in very young horses where prolonged convalescence does not matter.

Throughout the history of laryngeal surgery there has been a tendency to reinvent the wheel. For example a number of surgeons have claimed to have 'rediscovered' cordoventriculectomy as a cure for laryngeal hemiplegia. Sometimes such discoveries have been aided by improvements in anaesthetic techniques or by the development of new technology. In recent years the use of Nd:YAG lasers has achieved popularity with some equine laryngeal surgeons. It is now possible to carry out a cordoventriculectomy operation using a laser with the horse under local analgesia. Standing laryngeal surgery is not a novel concept, as in the early days of surgery some surgeons performed this operation in the standing horse. The modern operation allows greater visibility during surgery as the laser beam is transmitted via a glass fibre through an endoscope. Despite this it has always rather amused me to consider that the Nd:YAG laser (usually thought to represent the cutting edge of technology), is nothing more than space age application of firing!

During the last hundred years a number of investigators have attempted to prove that laryngeal hemiplegia is an inherited disease. Obviously, if so, one effective method of resolving the problem would be to breed it out of the equine population. The Thoroughbred, for example, is a highly inbred animal and it is not difficult to imagine in this breed that the incidence of the disease might therefore be quite high. However the necessity for 'seven generation pedigrees' to prove heritability makes investigating diseases in horses a lengthy business because of the slow turnover of generations. Furthermore, there is an understandable reticence by horse owners to publicise the presence of disease in their bloodstock. There are obviously significant economic implications in adopting such a breeding policy. Despite this most expert veterinary opinion supports the hypothesis that equine laryngeal hemiplegia has some sort of heritable basis although the relationship is probably complex.

The title of this essay was "*Whither equine laryngeal surgery?*". It is interesting to speculate about possible developments in equine laryngeal surgery in the next millennium. My belief is that some form of electronic implant will be developed which can be inserted into the abductor muscle of the larynx. The device will be switched on when the horse is required to gallop, providing complete abduction of the left side of the larynx during fast exercise and turned off at all other times preventing the unfortunate complications of food inhalation. However, it remains to be seen whether The Jockey Club or any other regulating authority would allow such a mechanism. Alternatively, by improving the techniques of microsurgery a more effective means of nerve grafting or neuromuscular pedicle grafting will be evolved to better effect than the current techniques.

You may well ask why laryngeal surgery is of importance. Although laryngeal hemiplegia is relatively common and potentially disabling to an equine athlete, you might think more time should be devoted to lameness and to foot problems in particular. After all, "*no foot...no horse*". However I would like to remind you of Bob Cook's adaptation of this maxim: "*No foot...no horse, but, no larynx...no life*"!

The evolution of equine hospitals

PETER ROSSDALE
Beaufort Cottage Equine Hospital
Cotton End Road
Exning, Newmarket
Suffolk CB8 7NN
UK

Introduction

The concept of hospitals is to provide secondary and tertiary care within the confines of one establishment. During the first six or seven decades of the present century the concept of an equine hospital was confined largely to the veterinary schools in Europe, America, South Africa and Australasia and smaller institutes such as Newmarket's Animal Health Trust. These centres attempted to provide medical and surgical referral facilities for clinicians in equine and general practice.

In the latter decades, however, the recognition and success of specialist qualifications, resulting from graduates of high intellectual capacity being selected by veterinary schools worldwide, has eventually produced a cadre of highly skilled equine specialists in the private sector capable of matching that of the veterinary schools. Centres of equine excellence have sprung up in every horse centre worldwide, thereby supplementing facilities at university veterinary schools or elsewhere in the state sector. Private enterprise has increasingly come to occupy a substantial part of clinical referral service and, in the future, will perhaps be of great assistance to the educational needs at undergraduate and graduate levels.

In this chapter a number of entrepreneurial veterinarians who have been responsible for developing equine veterinary hospitals contribute their experiences in order to provide a marker in the evolution of private hospital services to the profession and its clientele, at the beginning of the new millennium.

From Field to Hospital

Equine surgical procedures have been carried out since Grecian times with the patient restrained in a standing position or cast using hobbles, and, in the last 100 years under basal narcosis or general anaesthesia. In the early days of surgery, horses were operated on in the stable or in an adjacent field. Up until recent times a significant number of major surgical procedures were performed in the open air, and in certain parts of the world this is still true today. The first reported case of which I am aware of caesarean section in a mare was from South Africa and was performed on the veldt. I can remember Michael Hunt talking about performing an ovariectomy in the 1950s under an apple tree in a field in Yorkshire. In more recent times Tim Greet has performed surgical procedures such as ovariectomy or internal carotid artery ligation in the open air when there was no alternative; and this author performed neurectomies and castrations in an open yard and an abdominal procedure on a foal on a kitchen table on a studfarm.

In the Victorian era, and certainly in the 20th century, hospitalisation facilities were available at the veterinary schools, and associated with large stables of horses, such as used by the railway companies and the Army. Facilities available at such places were probably rather primitive, but there may have been a set of stocks, and more recently a padded room where horses could be anaesthetised safely.

Since the Second World War, particularly in the last 25 years, there has been a dramatic increase in the number of equine surgical facilities available worldwide. Not only the veterinary schools, but also a number of private facilities have developed sophisticated buildings for equine hospitalisation. These include state-of-the-art operating theatres, padded anaesthetic boxes, intensive care stabling, paediatric units, areas for trotting lame horses, and specialised rooms where diagnostic nerve blocks can be carried out and where radiographic, ultrasonographic, videoendoscopic and scintigraphic examinations can be performed. In a few hospitals there are highly specialised rooms for CAT or MRI scanning.

The development of such facilities has mirrored the development of clinical expertise in various aspects of equine clinical practice. For example as orthopaedic surgery has become more specialised, many surgical facilities provide a specific aseptic orthopaedic operating suite, sometimes accompanied by specialised facilities for recovering horses with fractures from a general anaesthesia. This may be a swimming pool with an inflatable raft such as in the University of Pennsylvania, or a pool where the floor is able to rise up out of the water as the horse wakes up as in one of the private clinics in Southern California.

In the last 30 years or so, a number of famous equine hospitals have been developed, notably Tierklinik Hochmoor in Germany, the Veterinary Hospital at Helsingborg Sweden, and, more recently, in the private equine practice of Rood and Riddle in Kentucky. There are many other equally good hospitals scattered all over the world.

The following section is intended only to record the presence, at the turn of the century,of a burgeoning trend towards the establishment of centres of excellence, serving the horse and its owners worldwide. It is not a comprehensive list but provides examples to bring the reader's attention to this development.

Hospitals around the world

Beaufort Cottage Equine Hospital, Newmarket

TIM GREET
Beaufort Cottage Equine Hospital
Cotton End Road
Exning, Newmarket
Suffolk CB8 7NN
UK

For almost 40 years, our practice in Newmarket had a surgical facility which was adapted within several 18th century stables. Whilst it was possible to perform all sorts of surgical procedures on the premises with great success it was decided in the late 1980s that we required a more modern facility. Several false starts in a variety of locations resulted in the formulation of a basic plan. We also employed a firm of architects to help with the achievement of our aim. Eventually a site was located in a green field adjacent to our Diagnostic Centre in Exning, and detailed plans were submitted to the local planning office for approval.

Although in a conservation area, we were able to progress the project with the help of a vital local ally in the landlord, who was strongly behind the enterprise. The architects designed a very sympathetic exterior to the building, which, although it combined many modern features, was constructed of block in keeping with the surrounding listed local clunch-built barns. We duly obtained permission to go ahead with the project.

Building of a new equine hospital is an expensive project. However, we were extremely fortunate in that our landlord was prepared to underwrite the enterprise and then allowed us a fair lease agreement. Budgeting for such an enterprise is very difficult, and our original budget of £800,000 turned out to be a massive underestimate. Our architects confidently stated that the quantity surveyors would be accurate within 5–10% of the likely quote. However, the minimum quote was £1.8 million and the largest quote nearly £2.5 million pounds. We reconsidered the whole project on receiving the tenders from the building firms we had approached. At the architect's suggestion we asked the two cheapest quotes to rejig the building to keep within the original budget of £800,000. After a number of weeks of recalculation they achieved this; however, it was extremely difficult to believe that we could be having the same building for £800,000 as that which they had quoted £1.8 million for!

The shell of the new building remained more or less similar, but we had lost much of the internal structure that would have been necessary to run a hospital. Changes included a lack of water provision to the stable yard and reducing many features that we had considered essential in a project of this nature. We then chose one of the builders, which as you might imagine caused considerable resentment from the other; not unreasonably, as he had spent a considerable amount of time and effort in restructuring his quote to fit our budget. This builder was somehow placated, and we then went ahead with the painful process of adding back those features that we required as essential to produce a hospital.

It is a golden rule that one should never interfere with the design or construction of a building once the project has started as this usually results in potentially massive increases in costs. However, throughout the entire project additions and alterations were made because we felt that these were essential to the best possible final result.

One of the great difficulties of a building of this size is the fact that not only is one dealing with architects and builders, but also a variety of other specialist advisers. These include mechanical and electrical engineers, subcontracted by the architect. Having designed their various circuitry and plans, they were unhappy to alter these. Thus even when we had the hospital more or less complete, and were seeking hospital status, which required the facility to function in the event of a mains power failure, our generator supply was strong enough to run a coffee percolator in the nurses' office and not much else. It therefore became essential that we found an alternative source of power, and to this effect we subsequently installed an ex-hospital Perkins engine diesel generator which could run the whole building and automatically cut in if the mains electricity failed. This required the tarmac drive, which had just been laid, to be dug up again; indeed, this happened on several other occasions before we had finished the building.

If this sounds a rather chaotic way to design and construct a hospital, it certainly was. The project consumed much of the time of several other partners during the course of the year it took to construct the building. Having said that, we were very fortunate that our builders were very practical and the site foreman had worked on a stud and knew roughly the sort of work we were involved in. Several major pitfalls were avoided by his perceptive observations. One had the feeling that the architectural team were more concerned that the external features of the building should be pleasing to the eye, than that the internal function of the building was adequate. You could imagine them leaning against the wall posing for a photograph for the cover of *Architects' Weekly*. First and foremost a veterinary hospital has

An aerial view of Beaufort Cottage Equine Hospital.

to be practical, and we were adamant that our building should work to our original design.

It would be too long a story to go into the details of the problems we encountered putting in the hoist and runway. Suffice to say that our very first use of an expensive new crane was when we attempted to unload our operating table from the back of a lorry and it became jammed on the hoist, suspended in midair. It was extremely fortunate that it hadn't been a horse as the table could only be released sometime later after we called in the crane manufacturer. Unfortunately this nightmare scenario was repeated on a number of occasions over the first few months with horses. We soon became adept at unloading a suspended animal onto a mobile trolley or an inflatable operating table which we had standing by.

Every new building has teething troubles and ours was no different, but within a very few weeks of opening we realised that the basic system was going to work very effectively, and once we had sorted out the glitches in the hoisting system and had reinstalled our original hoist, the problems resolved almost overnight.

On 23 April 1998 the hospital was officially opened by Her Majesty the Queen in the presence of all our staff. It was a wonderful occasion and two days later we had ex-patient Desert Orchid back with large number of clients and friends of the practice for a big party. Approximately two years after opening the hospital I feel confident to say that it has been as good as we hoped it would be. The pain and anguish of the building project were definitely worthwhile.

Oakey Veterinary Hospital, Australia

REG PASCOE
Oakey Veterinary Hospital Pty Ltd
Box 2 Oakey
Queensland 4401
Australia

In January 1952, the first veterinary practice was established in the small country town of Oakey (population 2000) situated on the north-eastern portion of the Darling Downs, the home of Thoroughbred breeding in Queensland, Australia. My initial practice covered approximately 40,000 dairy cattle, small animals, a very small broodmare farm and two small racing stables.

Initially, tuberculosis eradication and dairy cattle practice formed the core of the practice income. In 1954 a new Thoroughbred farm was established and the first routine three days per week ovarian palpation service offered to horse breeders in this area.

My first veterinary facility was a 4 x 3 metre concrete extension to our garage which had been constructed in my 'spare' time. Both general and equine practice increased, with the closest horse farm being five miles away and the most distant 90 miles from the practice. Much time was wasted travelling and the concept of animals coming to a treatment area was becoming very attractive.

Twelve acres of a hilly farm paddock on the outskirts of the then town limits was acquired in 1957; it was completely bare, had to be boundary fenced, a very deep bore hole drilled for water, and preliminary accommodation built. Thus the beginnings of the current complex began.

My horse farms increased to a total of three with about 300 mares and seven stallions. At this time I was also engaged in a modest way in racetrack practice in Toowoomba, a city 20 miles east of Oakey with about 250 to 300 Thoroughbred horses in training.

Our home and large workshop were built on the new land in 1960. The workshop served as a temporary surgery and consulting area until the completion in 1964 of a 6 x 12 m veterinary facility constructed of cavity concrete block, which became the basis for future expansion needs.

This contained an office, small animal surgery, consulting room, pharmacy, small laboratory and kennels, by the end of which, a third veterinarian joined us, eventually forming our initial partnership of three which remained until 1988 when a fourth partner joined. Progress was slow due to limited finance and the main income producers were still very much dairy cattle medicine, pig practice and small animals.

By 1967, horse farms increased to 10 with approximately 600 mares. Our equipment was still very modest – a second-hand mobile x-ray machine with faulty timer, manual developing, a rigid AO endoscope for scoping horses, an ECG machine and a larger than usual collection of second-hand human surgical instruments purchased cheaply, some of which were excellent and are still in use.

In 1968, I visited practices in Lambourn, Newmarket, Kildare, Lexington, Kentucky and Davis, California. This proved to be highly informative and allowed me to formulate plans for an equine hospital which, through 35 years of careful planning, was able to expand over seven building extensions to its present capacity, with minimal major reconstruction at any time to the then existing main buildings.

Late in 1968, the equine hospital became a reality, following the addition of a cavity concrete block construction comprising a new professional office, small animal and equine operating theatres with a common scrub and instrument storage room, a totally padded recovery room and four stables with five outside yards. A new toilet block and pharmacy were added, thus forming an L-shaped building. All block walls where horse contact occurred were steel rod and concrete-filled for additional strength.

Our first use of the equine operating theatre was 22 March 1969. The operating theatre table was designed around a combination of all the good points I had observed in my overseas visit and constructed by a local engineer. It was a tilt table with manual folding sides on a hydraulic base, capable of tilting both sideways and either end. The table, designed to form part of the recovery room floor, was mounted on industrial nylon wheels allowing the operated horse to be wheeled into the fully padded recovery room. The manually raised sides were fitted with hydraulics in 1990 to meet increasing demands for colic and joint surgery positioning. The original table was constructed out of mild steel to contain costs, and was revamped in 1990 to be galvanised with all exposed surfaces replaced or sheeted in heavy gauge stainless steel.

I have not regretted this second stage; it is extremely functional in many directions. Only two or three persons are required to place most horses on the table and eventually in the recovery room. The table is placed in a vertical position, the horse led alongside, tranquillised, then restrained by head collar, belly band and tail rope; anaesthetic is given and the

The Oakey Veterinary Hospital, Queensland.

horse tipped into a horizontal position, intubated, anaesthetic stabilised and, if necessary, the horse further positioned for surgery.

Fractious horses can, if necessary, be anaesthetised in the recovery room, wheeled to the theatre, operated on and returned to recovery. Any horses subjected to euthanasia on the table are easily tilted onto the tray of a small truck and removed. An emergency power plant provides for lighting and small power usage. In the event of sudden power failure, all hydraulics are capable of returning to normal transport mode with a horse on the table.

Equipment expansion included an in-circle anaesthetic machine, designed with an outer circle 10% fluothane vaporiser, excellent value over many thousand anaesthetics, as well as a Stephens machine for small animals and foals; both are still in use. We started to purchase new surgical instruments and have never regretted always buying the best quality instruments available; longevity, reliability and good service is the reward. A new heavy duty human electrocautery unit and large vacuum suction unit were added.

We entered one of the periodic depressions which the horse industry is prone to experience and, coupled with rising interest rates, our extension programme slowed for 10 years. My only serious expenditure was the purchase of a new fibreoptics scope in 1974. During this period there was a severe economic downturn in the beef industry, affecting the annual sales of yearlings, as well as a portion of our large animal practice.

Our third stage commenced in 1979 with the addition of a large examination area containing two examination crushes, one of which was designed without posts to the floor on one end expressly for limb radiography, the other to be used for standing surgeries and reproductive examinations. An automatic x-ray processor, more toilets, changing room and shower were added to this area. A large professional office for our seven full-time veterinarians, nurses office, an interview/consulting room, laboratory for bacteriology, blood chemistry and microscopy, a larger storage room for consumables, and at a lower level, an autopsy room and general storage area were all added. Four additional reinforced cavity block stables were added to original stables, together with a further eight holding yards and two loading bays. Our x-ray equipment was expanded from one to two portables to cope with extra stable and track practice, and a large condenser discharge mobile unit for the hospital.

All stables had concrete floors, covered with wood shavings, 2 litre automatic waterers, hay racks and floor level chaff feeders made from inside-out large car tyres. These contain feed well, are almost indestructible and don't injure horses. All stable doors are sliding with double drop catches and end holders to prevent horses getting legs caught. Mesh panels in the upper door prevent wind-sucking, weaving and wood-chewing; all exposed door wood and door openings were steel-sheeted to further prevent wood-chewing and three large holding paddocks were constructed.

By means of a research grant in 1982, I was able to introduce the early clumsy Fisher prototype 3.5 MHz ultrasound for everyday mare examinations. This was one of the greatest advances in public relations between veterinarians and stud masters in the breeding industry in this century, as it focused attention on the scan screen and removed so many of the doubts about the pregnancy test that embryonic abortion engendered. In our practice, it also meant the introduction of improved covered examination areas on the farms and, more importantly, the use of crushes (stocks) greatly improved the safety of veterinarians. Portable Aloka 120 ultrasound machines were purchased in 1986 for three full-time veterinarians.

A serious world financial depression for the horse industry occurred in 1988/9, greatly affecting many of our clients and leading to an increase in unpaid fees. This, coupled with a period of high bank interest rates and almost 10 years continuous drought, caused a marked slowdown in yearly case intake. Other equipment that had been added was leased to preserve financial liquidity, including a Frigtronics cryosurgical unit, full arthroscopic surgical suite, completed in 1992 with the welcome addition of a video camera and monitor plus an abdominal telescope.

Fourth stage expansion in 1992 was modest – a totally enclosed shed with 1500 hay bale plus 500 bags lucerne chaff capacity was added. Our small animal practice increased, necessitating expansion and revamping of two small animal consulting rooms, new small animal surgery and new laundry/sterilising room with a 150 litre steam autoclave and 60 litre ethylene oxide gas steriliser added, allowing our capacity to handle increasing surgery more efficiently.

Stage five was the completion of 14 top rail and hilighter plastic coated wire holding paddocks for problem mares, chilled and frozen AI mares. New equipment included Luxar 20 MHz CO_2 laser, video endoscope and monitor, thermography camera, mobile Sonace 6000 ultrasound, upgrade to 5/7.5 MHz reproductive ultrasound machines.

Stage six, in 1997, saw a major reorganisation of the hospital yards. The original outside stables and yards were showing signs of wear, so they were demolished and replaced with a new set of 14 steel box stables, also containing feed and treatment rooms. The eight demountable stables installed during this process have been retained for outside use. A covered farrier's shed/forge has been added.

A self-contained intern flat was added close to the main hospital. A reproduction barn (9 x 14 m) containing a laboratory, storage area for frozen semen, an examination crush (stocks) built adjacent to the outside paddocks, with subdivision of some of the existing paddocks as holding yards for these mares, allowed expansion of AI and ET in the practice, increased convenience, comfort, better more efficient handling of reproductive cases.

In 1999, stage seven saw the addition of the Equine Teaching Unit. This is a joint venture with the University of Queensland School of Veterinary Science for our practice to conduct a major portion of final year clinical training in equine surgery, medicine and reproduction. Further building expansion for the teaching unit included a seminar room, teaching and study computers, slide and data projectors, office, changing room, kitchen and ablutions area. A further (9 x 9 m) covered teaching area and crush (stocks) was added to the reproduction barn for surgery and reproduction practical classes.

Current staff consists of 11 veterinarians, four office secretaries, four qualified veterinary nurses, three stable hands and a hospital cleaner, one part-time veterinarian, two part-time secretaries, two part-time nurse-helpers, and one part-time farrier.

We have on average of over 1500 admissions to the equine hospital yearly, with 350–450 major surgeries, 200 minor surgeries, up to 80 reproduction cases, AI and ET. The majority of the remainder are lameness and medical cases.

Does the facility pay for itself? Yes, with additional benefits of ease of operation for patients, veterinarians, staff and clients, and while not perhaps all 'state of the art', it nevertheless functions well with frequent approval from clients.

What of the future? There is always a need to be able to respond to the problems of horse owners quickly, for the provisions of readily available specialist services, to be able to embrace new technologies where these are perceived to enhance our service at an acceptable financial cost, and to continue to be investigative either directly or collaboratively into equine research.

Endell Veterinary Group Equine Clinic, Wiltshire

MIKE GARLICK
Endell Veterinary Group Equine Clinic
Southampton Road
Clarendon, Salisbury
Wilts SP5 3DG
UK

It is said that getting married and moving house are the most stressful experiences most of us will encounter. Having done the former once and the latter twice I can earnestly confirm that doing both every day would roughly approximate to the demands of developing an equine clinic!

In that case, why do it? Of course, there are all the logical reasons: increasing demand for more comprehensive services; increasing abilities and qualification of staff, both young and old; the need to keep up in a competitive market.

But there are many counterarguments: justification of the high capital input; duplication of services in a limited market; long-term commitment; and many many more that one will not have even considered. To overcome this there is one essential ingredient without which the project is doomed - some would call it dogged determination, others total obsession. It translates into an unshakeable belief that the only way is to move forward, sink or swim.

If you have it, read on! In most equine practices there will have been increasing need for outpatient and inpatient facilities, but to develop a full-blown hospital is still a big step. We did not intend to do it this way at all. We had been using rented farm buildings for over 20 years and had redeveloped the operating facilities 10 years ago. This was intended as Stage 1 of the clinic plan, but unfortunately Stage 2 and onward never happened. Increasing frustration at the stalemate was the trigger, but finding the answer seemed impossible. Many, many potential sites were considered, some with buildings for conversion, others on green field sites for development, but none could satisfy the requirements of position, price, access, planning and suitability. At the lowest ebb we were under six months notice to quit with nowhere to go!

Meanwhile visits to other developments were firming up ideas. It could be done. Universities measure their buildings in acres and their budgets accordingly; others were only mildly out of touch with our (then) idea of reality. Thank you, Alex, Richard, Tim, Alistair, Charlie.

Rough ideas of the necessary budget were floated at partners' meetings and the partnership remained intact, if in disagreement. It was obvious that this level of investment required a freehold site for security and the longevity of the project, and then due to a change of circumstances an offer arose on land alongside our existing site! This seemed ideal; all we needed was planning permission and finance...that was all.

We found a Trusting Savings Bank, which appeared to believe us, but the planners were more difficult. Apparently, views of a dual carriageway are still "*outstandingly beautiful*", and of course the gospel of planning has no chapter devoted to equine clinics. Neither residential, agricultural, industrial nor infill, they fall into the dustbin category where it is safer to recommend refusal. This meant more work in rallying clients to lobby, holding site meetings and negotiations. Common sense and determination have no place here; as it is a rules game and has to be played within them. Stay cool! Oh yes, it took only a year for outline permission to be granted, including signing a legal exclusion on certain aspects of the site and moving the building from one side to the other! In any case, design *should* be given a year.

Design. An architect can build you a great building but how many horses does he treat? You need to do much of the work yourselves. Consider every possible way you want the building to work, then follow your pathway through it. Visit as many other clinics as possible to see their solutions and, more importantly, their errors. When you think you have the perfect result, show it to your wife to find the mistakes!

Finally, the moment we had waited for arrived - the partners meeting to sign the loan agreement (only double the original estimate) to allow construction to begin. Two bank managers from the newly merged consortium were evasive and serious. Yes, they were trying to ditch the whole project on orders from the new head office. It took three months to salvage the deal and the only satisfying moment was seeing the partnership unite as a pack to savage the unfortunate manager more viciously than starving wolves! This was when I knew we would win!

To control construction, we used an architectural

Endell Veterinary Group Equine Clinic

draughtsman who was excellent in building detail and who liased daily with the local workmen; however, this also requires you to be on site virtually every day. The end result should be closer to your ideal and considerably cheaper than a design and build contract, but requires great commitment and will give you many headaches. There were only three disasters in construction: firstly the roof nearly blew off, secondly the entire site, yard and stables flooded and thirdly we were totally let down by a major stable manufacturer.

Equipment and fitting out could not have been completed without considerable recourse to medical sales and auctions where many wonderful bargains were had. I would particularly note the excellent operating lights for £100. Others might be unkind enough to mention the washing machine, which leapt off its stand and tried to destroy itself (successfully) and the building (unsuccessfully). There are still a thousand details to finish but the building is fully in use and is beginning to feel like home.

Was it worth it? There is undoubtedly a great improvement in the service to clients and patients and in working conditions; the partnership is still solvent and talking to the bank manager normally. Can we now relax? There is no chance of that, as new challenges arise requiring solutions. Building the clinic *"Is not the end. It is not even the beginning of the end. But it is, perhaps, the end of the beginning."* I could continue on this theme, but I see the nurse is coming so it must be time for my Valium! Good luck.

Equine Veterinary Hospital, Sweden

HARRY PETTERSSON
The Regional Animal Hospital
Box 22097
Helsingborg S-250 23
Sweden

The Animal Hospital in Helsingborg was founded 1954 by Fritz Sevelius. From the start the hospital has been owned by the Rural Economy Association of Malmöhus county and serves the five southern counties of Sweden. However, horses are also referred from other parts of Sweden as well as from Denmark, Norway and even Finland and Germany. From the beginning, the hospital was of mixed type, with clinics for small and large animals; as the hospital is owned by a farmers' association, it was logical that apart from horses many farm animals were referred to the large animal clinic for treatment during the first two decades.

Later on, the cost for treatment of farm animals in the clinic became too high in relation to the value of these animals. Over the last 20 years the large animal clinic has become more of an equine veterinary hospital, managed separately from the small animal hospital. Certain aspects, such as administration, clinical-chemical and bacteriological laboratory, scintigraphy, the medical engineer and the care of buildings and grounds are shared.

Fritz Sevelius did the pioneer work and, in a few years, the hospital was well known for its knowledge and service and was appreciated in the local area as well as in the whole country. He gave hospitalisation of animals a 'face' in Sweden and the hospital gained confidence from animal owners. This contributed greatly to the future development of the animal hospital in Helsingborg and for the coming hospitalisation in Sweden. Therefore, it was a great privilege for this author and two other young veterinary surgeons to become employed at the hospital in 1961. Very soon Fritz Sevelius taught us that if the hospital was going to develop and survive we should have the best knowledge, give fast service and show a friendly and open attitude to the clients; and handle the animals in a careful and respectful way. After only one year we all three were sent out to different veterinary schools and veterinary practices in Europe and USA for continuing education to bring home new knowledge and ideas. This went on for all the years to come. Fritz himself was an excellent and stimulating teacher and a demanding chief. I was chosen by him to develop the large animal clinic to an equine hospital. I worked closely with Fritz for 15 years until his retirement 1976. An increasing number of horses were admitted for treatment during this time.

In 1965, we introduced inhalation anaesthesia with Fluothane, when we bought the Fisher-Jenning anaesthesia machine. This completely revolutionised our anaesthesic approach and increased the survival rate of horses after prolonged surgeries. New methods of fracture surgery, upper respiratory, colic surgery and so on could be introduced. In spite of expanding in the old buildings by rebuilding three times, the hospital had soon "*grown out of its clothes*".

The equine hospital has acquired a good name. Other reasons for expansion of the clinical work were: 1) The increasing number of horses in our country; 2) The horses became more valuable both economical and emotionally; 3) The horse-owning people had more money to spend; 4) Insurance was introduced to cover most of the cost of the treatment in the hospital. Today, 80% of the horses have such insurance. This insurance has had great importance for the development of the equine veterinary hospital in Helsingborg and for other equine hospitals in Sweden.

We became more and more convinced that the equine hospital had a place in our community and was appreciated by the horse-owning public, as we could offer specialised care 24 hours a day. The horse became more and more exploited in intensive racing and riding sports. People felt that the sick or injured horse had a right to good, fast medical or surgical care.

Mike Garlick

The Helsingborg Animal Hospital's ambulance is manned round the clock.

Plans for a New Equine Veterinary Hospital

For two years, 1978-79 we planned to build a new equine hospital together with a small animal hospital for a cost of 40 million Swedish crowns (£2.8 million). We had travelled a lot to see different new university clinics and some big private clinics to pick the best ideas from each place. Our planning resulted in two very functional clinics with common units in the middle. A colleague joked about our great plans which he said resembled the drawings for the Pentagon. We were very optimistic about the future and relied on the government to finance the new building. But two state investigations came to the conclusion that the financing of animal hospitals was not a concern for the government. We were very disappointed when two years work were thrown away, but we did not give up. With increasing clinical work we earned more money, which could be saved for later investments. People with interest and love for animals donated money to us and we were also fortunate to receive several inheritances. Up to 1998, the hospital has got 35 million Swedish Crowns (£2.5 million) in donations and inheritances. We also started a fund-raising programme and approached the town of Helsingborg, the County of Malmöhus, insurance companies, medical firms, the National Trotting and Racing Association and the Government again. Eventually we were successful and the owner, the Rural Economy Association of Malmöhus County, started a building programme in 1981, which lasted for eleven years.

In 1982 a new building was established with localities for the staff, offices, storage and a modernised laboratory. In 1985 the equine hospital and in 1987 the small animal veterinary hospital were built. In 1991 a building for intensive care of mares and foals, pathology and an isolation clinic for horses was completed.

The Regional Animal Hospital in Helsingborg covers, today, an area of around 7000 m^2. The total cost for the new hospital was 60 million Swedish crowns (£4.25 million).

The Equine Hospital

I should say here a few words about planning design and construction. The planning of all building activities was done by an architect and a group of our own employees including veterinary surgeons and animal technicians representing different units, such as outpatients, stables, medicine, surgery, exercise physiology and imaging. In this way, we obtained the best ideas and knowhow and, above all, everyone was happy when the new hospital was finished. We are proud of the fact that we can offer good a environment for the employees, good service to the clients and, above all, improved welfare for our equine patients.

The Helsingborg Veterinary Ambulance Service

A new concept in emergency animal care and also welfare of the horse was started in 1994. By coordinating the efforts of the Regional Animal Hospital, the technological know-how and official status of the Fire Department of Helsingborg and the commercial Veterinary Ambulance of Helsingborg, a unique model for animal rescue was developed.

With the veterinary experience of the animal hospital, the technological high standard and official status of the fire department in conjunction with the enthusiasm and driving force of the veterinary ambulance staff, the best of three worlds was brought together to create an effective rescue unit. Two ambulances are manned around the clock by specially trained firemen (animedics) and veterinary technicians on duty and therefore the time from alarm to initiation of rescue can be as low as 90 seconds. Drivers are fully trained emergency vehicle drivers, hence full emergency status has been granted to the veterinary ambulance which minimises driving time. Veterinary back-up is supplied on a 24 hour basis by the veterinary surgeon on duty at the Regional Animal Hospital. Other than bringing in diseased or injured horses or other animals to the animal hospital, the ambulances also act at stable fires, traffic accidents and as a mobile clinic at show grounds, on duty around the clock during competitions. The ambulances also support the police when needed.

Economy

As mentioned above, the hospital is fully financed and paid. The yearly turnover for the equine veterinary hospital is around 25 million Swedish crowns (£1.8 million). The profit over the last five years has been around 10%. There are similar figures for the small animal veterinary hospital. With the very professional staff we have today, I think that the facilities will pay for themselves in future and the profit will be used for new investments and continuing education of the employees.

Helsingborg Regional Animal Hospital.

Pferdeklinik Kerken, Germany

MICHAEL BECKER
Pferdeklinik Kerken
Slümer Straβe 5-6
47669 Watchtendonk
Germany

In the late December 1991 the two friends and vets Gerd Bockenhoff and Michael Becker met for a Christmas Dinner. After a good meal and an excellent Bordeaux the idea to found together a private horse clinic was born. We both ran small clinics then, one in Bavaria, the other in the Rhein region. Our goal was a clinic that could be compared with other big private facilities in Germany such as Hochmoor or Telgte or those of the universities, dealing not only with veterinary work but some scientific work as well.

Close to a highway and near the Dutch border we found an old farm and rebuilt it into the Pferdeklinik Kerken within one year. We tried to keep alive the character of the typical old farm of this region from the outside (Fig 1), while from the inside we had to change a pigsty into modern offices.

When, in summer 1993 we officially opened our hospital, we had 50 boxes, two surgery rooms, x-ray, sonography - and nuclear scintigraphy facilities and the first CAT-scan for horses in Germany at our disposal.

In the following years Eberhard Mettenleiter became a partner and five other assistant vets enlarged our team. Besides a remarkable number of publications coming out of our clinic, several young colleagues graduated with doctorates based on their work in the clinic and in cooperation with German and Swiss universities.

One of the pillars of our success has been the treatment of colic patients. Often more than 500 a year are examined of which about 200 are operated on. On the other hand our investment in diagnostic equipment has led to a steadily increasing number of patients with orthopaedic and 'head and neck' problems.

The opening of the European borders was very helpful. We are proud of a good cooperation with German and foreign colleagues and clients from all over Europe, even Great Britain.

The organisation of three successful equine congresses in Maastricht called MICEM, together with the Dutch Dierenkliniek Boxmeer and the big response to it, is another positive sign that the future of our hospital depends on and will be enhanced by the increase of international collaboration in the next millennium.

Fig 1: The Pferdeklinik Kerken, Germany.

Randwick Equine Centre, Australia

TREVE WILLIAMS
Randwick Equine Centre
PO Box 195
Randwick
New South Wales 2031
Australia

Randwick Equine Centre was established as a single-man practice in Sydney in 1951 by Dr Percy Sykes. He was, at that time, one among many small equine ambulatory practices serving the Sydney racing scene and utilising the basic surgical and hospital facilities available at the University of Sydney. It was only in the early 1960s that the portable x-ray machine became available and practitioners were limited to performing surgical procedures under field conditions using short-acting barbituates or Equithesin.

Percy Sykes introduced not only his great clinical acumen into Sydney equine practice, but also made commonplace the use of the stomach tube, standing castration and the use of laboratory aids. The latter, in particular, served to establish his name and the one-man practice was forced to expand to service a rapidly increasing clientele.

The main office was maintained initially at Percy Sykes' home and the laboratory and work were carried out from a block of rented stables. In the early 1960s two semi-detached houses were purchased and converted into offices, laboratory and living accommodation for an associate. Limited surgery was performed at a spelling (resting) farm, which had some facilities, situated about forty miles from Randwick.

The introduction of keen young partners such as this author stimulated the desire to have a central, well-equipped base. The ambulatory mode of the practice, which covered a radius of some 45 miles, also changed at this time and the first purpose-built facility was constructed at Church Lane, Randwick. Ideas were obtained from visiting overseas facilities and a hospital containing a surgical suite, eight hospital boxes, offices and a large, well-equipped laboratory, functioning in its own right and as a referral laboratory for both equine and small animals, was built.

The practice had grown to 12 veterinarians who covered the entire city and some provincial tracks, four studfarms on the perimeter of the metropolitan area and a large number of spelling farms.

The installation of xero-radiography proved to be an instant success, not only with owners and trainers, but because it involved bringing the horse to the clinic for x-ray rather than the portable machine going to the stable. This major change in the attitude of the clientele proved invaluable and although xero-radiography has been replaced because of cost and safety, nevertheless, the standard of other imaging and diagnostic procedures has benefited.

The replacement of the rigid laryngoscope by fibreoptic endoscopes, the introduction and standardisation of ultrasound techniques, hand-held scintigraphy probes, fluid therapy and arthroscopy as opposed to arthrotomy, all occurred during this period of development.

The increasing number of horses arriving at the clinic resulted in an acute lack of space for the vehicles and a shortage of hospital loose boxes and, by 1988, another purpose-built equine clinic and surgery was erected in conjunction with William Inglis and Sons at the periphery of their yearling sales complex, some two miles away. This facility offered two surgical suites, treatment and imaging facilities and an accredited nuclear medicine facility, together with yards and 40 boxes. In conjunction with this, a further building was purchased to house a well-equipped laboratory, office area, accommodation and a modern small animal clinic so as to maximise the use of the many facilities available at the equine hospital.

P. E. Sykes and Partners had now become the Randwick Equine Centre and it was accepted that the age of specialisation had arrived. The clinic now encompasses not only the latest in equipment, but also expertise at the highest level with specialists in surgery, medicine and anaesthesia. Continuing education is actively supported and encouraged and sought-after internship is established and flourishing. This specialist equine clinic now competes more than favourably with the facilities and specialist staff at the universities.

The great benefit of having a large equine centre lies in its ability to produce sufficient income to permit the purchase of sophisticated and expensive equipment whose use, though it may not cover its initial cost, does help to improve diagnostic accuracy and/or a surgical procedure. It also helps in the engagement of keen and bright associates who have professional ambitions and who now form a practice that includes 11 veterinarians and three resident consultants. This has resulted in a very comprehensive group of communicative practitioners who work as a team. The end result is that the clients get an excellent 24-hour-a-day, seven-day-a-week service.

The downside of building such a practice is that it does not happen overnight and involves a lot of personal financial sacrifices over many years to attain the working end result. Unfortunately, few veterinarians, especially within an inner city practice, start out their careers with sufficient capital to build and equip a hospital. Upgrading can only be made in line with an ever-increasing clientele and available finance, this making the ultimate goal a far more expensive exercise.

Randwick Equine Centre, New South Wales.

Having now attained what is considered to be the ultimate at this time, it is important that good staff are rewarded and additional staff selected not only on scholarship, but also equally importantly on their ability to work within a team. Key personnel should be brought into the partnership or encouraged to develop career paths that don't impact directly on the parent body. The core partnership, however, must not be allowed to become too large and unwieldy and there must remain a common purpose.

Finally, if it is to remain and grow, it must be extremely ethical. There is always a very fine line between keeping a neighbouring practice happy and gaining their referrals and encroaching on their territory.

At the end of a long haul, one can say truthfully that big is beautiful since it allows veterinary science to be practised at the highest level, which is not only fulfilling but is also financially viable.

Willesley Equine Clinic, Gloucestershire

SVEND KOLD
Willesley Equine Clinic
Byams Farm
Willesley, Tetbury
Glos GL8 8GU
UK

With a background of 10 years in academia behind me, including a sabbatical year at a North American university, the decision to return to the private sector was not made easily. However, increasing frustration with the politics and management problems in larger institutions was weighing heavily, as was the desire to obtain better and stronger client contacts/interactions, to choose one's own colleagues, and not the least, the likelihood of better financial rewards within the private sector.

The choice of colleagues with whom you enter into a partnership can occur in many ways. In my case contact had been made some while back and a quick succession of meetings soon became a reality. Few, if any, clinical facilities existed within the Lansdown Veterinary Surgeon banner at the time but a number of factors were decisive, such as 1) good geographic location (Tetbury, Gloucestershire) with easy access from major motorways; 2) a well-established clientele of very skilled horse people within an affluent area; and 3) potential partners who had the same visions and interest in developing clinic facilities.

Shiny tiles and brass signs do not make a clinic; more important is a tidy clinical mind obtained from years of clinical training and accumulated experience. Fewer facilities will initially do if the clinician knows his techniques and is skilful in his procedures. On my arrival at the practice, the facilities available were a recovery box and an examination room used for clinical examinations, including radiography. Three stables were available and a young girl was free to hold horses for three hours two mornings a week! Telephone contact to the clinic was via car phone and the first secretary had yet to arrive, let alone develop herself a place to call her office. The main practice office at our small animal hospital 10 miles away doubled up for initial office facilities. Seven years later, we now have new facilities, including an equine theatre, radiology suite with a full-time equine radiographer, new examination rooms, a forge manned two days a week, new offices with three secretaries, a veterinary nurse, a head girl and three resident grooms. An AI department caters for 75 mares a season while most of my own time is now spent doing exactly what I was doing when leaving academia, i.e. receiving referral, orthopaedic and some nonorthopaedic cases from colleagues in practice.

The development of our clinic has been dictated by stage-by-stage conversions of existing buildings as planning permissions were received and extra facilities were required. Some constructions needed more persuasion than others; a £10,000 all-weather arena with state-of-the-art surface was initially thought a luxury, but after the fifth lameness examinations on a wet day in February, it has been generally accepted that life without a series of decent surfaces for an orthopaedic specialist clinic is just not worth living!

I strongly believe that a two-tiered system of equine clinics and equine hospitals is developing. A very small number of 'complete' equine hospitals with the capacity, manpower and expertise to tackle all equine emergencies, will be required in parallel with the services offered by the university clinics; while a larger number of smaller clinics and hospitals will be able to offer a more limited service, includes referrals at a specialist level. This may represent diagnostic imaging, lameness diagnosis and surgery, reproduction and others. The smaller referral clinics will be able to provide better service levels to referring veterinary surgeons and their clients than many university clinics and will be more readily available on a day-to-day basis. Although I feel that it is important for smaller clinics to acknowledge their areas of expertise and equally their limitations, equine medicine and surgery must not become restricted to a small number of hospitals, but should thrive through interaction and communication between a large number of clinics, because only in this way will our colleagues in general and mixed practice reap the advantages and improve their skills to the overall benefit of the welfare of the horse.

Tierklinik Telgte, Germany

FIDI von SALDERN
Tierklinik Telgte
48291 Telgte
Germany

This is the story of Tierklinik Telgte, 17 years old and still going strong. When we faced the farmyard on a beautiful evening in July 1983, the tons of rubbish we saw could not diminish our optimistic view of the future. In front of us stood 18 scrap cars, 15 lorry loads of rubbish and a dilapidated building which used to be a very suitable pigsty - as the overweight farmer told us proudly. When we asked him why he had given up farming, he replied that there is more money in repairing cars.

At this point we changed the subject because we did not allow anything to cast a shadow over our plans for the future: two well-trained young vets as equal partners in a nice small clinic for horses, few but very efficient staff, selective surgery, selected clients, everything small, neat, tidy and private. Finance was not that important as long as it was enough to keep going; leisure time could come later, but first we had to get some clients; as for holidays, a week or two would do - after all, the kids were still small and thus it would be better to stay at home.

The contract with the big-bellied, permanently smoking and steadily drinking landlord was signed a week later. He is still alive, has kept many internists in the medical world busy, and reminds us every day how important it was that we sought legal advice from a solicitor who had experience with farmers right at the beginning of our story.

Two weeks later, the clearing up operations and the building work started. The opening ceremony was on 1 October 1983. The two families of the partners (including six children) and all the helping hands celebrated with self-made sandwiches and sparkling wine. There was also an elderly journalist from the local paper present who produced a well-meaning article praising our abilities in the treatment of animals - in general. As a result we had to treat a 20 foot long python that was brought to our clinic five days later. The snake was cured after we pulled a whole blanket out of its mouth.

Since we had decided not to do calls but to stay in the clinic all the time, at the beginning we had enough time for painting the stables and helping the workmen. However, we did not finish the building in time: thanks to beginners' luck our first patient arrived quite soon. It was a big, grey, promising show-jumper, owned by a well-known rider who was successful in various championships and Olympics already. This horse was the first patient on our operating table and it needed colic surgery twice within two days. After the second surgery, the door of the recovery room burst and the horse stumbled and fell into the storeroom where tools and building machinery were left. There was of course a moment of shock as we briefly thought things like "*Well, that's the end of our clinic's short history*", but the story had a happy ending when the horse won a bronze medal at the Olympic Games in Atlanta the following year. There is still a dusty photo of him in a dark corner of our x-ray room.

This initial success went the around. Horsemen started to talk about the new place: two young partners, no assistants, few but friendly staff, and an emergency service until late at night. Three months after the opening, just before Christmas, a new client came with six horses. He said that he had heard about us and he trusted us. All six horses needed surgery: one castration, one tie back, one spavin, one splint bone, etc. A week later, after he had received the bill, he returned in a BMW and with his beautiful niece. The horses belonged to the niece, who had a cup of coffee, handed the bill back and proclaimed charmingly that they had no money - even the car was leased. In the end we accepted what we could get: a new colour TV for each of us (worth half a surgery) and 20 vouchers for his wife's sunbed studio.

After a while, we needed more stables for the rapidly

Svend Kold

increasing number of clients. The next dozen stables were twice as expensive to build as the first dozen, even though it was only one year later. Due to lack of time no one could control the builders and workmen - and then the bill came! In addition to this it was a harsh winter that year: a lot of snow led to little traffic and even fewer horse trailers on the roads. No phone calls, no horses, empty stables! The clinic was so clean that we could have eaten from the floor. All veterinary journals available were read, the kids got so much attention they were amazed, even the Bach concert in the nearby town was attended with the beloved mother of the children. This was in the times before mobile phones so the phone number of the concert hall had to be left at the clinic and the clerk told the seat number just in case - but no call! We worried whether we would ever have clients and earn money again. Then the weather changed and horses with colic came in. There were so many clients that we could hardly manage. At last we were able to pay the bill for the new stables and we decided that we would never stop doing colic surgery in order to get some free nights and weekends. The weeks with empty stables produced another attitude which influenced the following years: all investments in instruments or in the employment of new staff came too late. We put off building a new stable or examination room, or to employ a new nurse until the pressure became really tough.

Our first Christmas Eve in the clinic we celebrated in our office with two nurses, a secretary, a referring vet and a bottle of wine. Then the red-faced farmer came in with a two litre bottle of cognac. Afterwards we went home on our bikes. Our last Christmas party was celebrated with 48 people: eight vets (two senior partners, two junior partners, four assistants), nurses, accountants, secretaries and stable lads. We had a four course dinner with presents for everybody, free drinks and a taxi shuttle to get everyone home.

The steady change over the years meant a permanent discussion about new investments, new employees, new buildings, tax, future developments, new diagnostic facilities. In short, it took a lot of energy. Back in student times we used to spend endless hours at the microscope in the meat department or in the institute of virology. But what did we learn about investment, tax problems, personnel management or internal controlling? Should we sit back and have a brain-storming session? No time to spare!

After four years, we were doing elective surgery on 10 to 12 horse per day, twice a week. On Tuesdays and Thursdays we worked in two shifts: the first surgeon operated from 6 am until 2 pm; the second from 2 pm until 10 pm. Nevertheless, there was an increasing heap of work left for the next days, week and months.

Instead of making one big step forward we made a hundred little steps; another vet, part-time at first, another nurse, another room, two more stables, etc., never over-ambitiously but always only after the need became dramatic. Additional work was taken on outside the clinic, offering a change from the daily work: acting as vets for the Nations' Cup team, performing selective surgery in other clinics with four or more horses to operate per day, taking arthroscopy workshops twice a year within our own facilities and with our own staff. The well-known workshop lecturers became so familiar in our place that they did not need to be entertained any longer. The course participants came from right across Europe and we supplied them with arthroscopic instruments through our small subsidiary sales company founded for this purpose. At the beginning there was good money in it; a bit later we reported quite a drop in fetlock arthroscopies. After a while, we realised the reason for this - our course participants did it cheaper!

Inspired by our little sales company and encouraged by the great queue of daily clients, our landlord, the farmer, had the idea to found his own company: a fish and chip shop on our parking area. But thanks to our decision to employ a clever, farmer-experienced solicitor back in 1983, we stopped this by showing him the contract!

We did not stop, nor did we sit back until signs of burn-out syndrome began to show. (These manifested themselves as symptoms of midlife crisis, either in the form of young girls appearing on the back of smashing new motorbikes, or as disc hernia surgery followed by two months in a rehabilitation clinic doing gymnastics on a rubber mattress with elderly people.) So we had a brainstorming, which resulted in the admission of younger partners in order to spread the pressure over more shoulders. This way turned out to be quite successful: the daily was organised and managed better and it was no problem that more people were in charge. The only difference was that our business meetings seemed to be never-ending since we had to find democratic solutions even for the most trivial decisions. The learning process took us two years, but by now fewer and shorter meetings seem to be more and more efficient!

Did we learn anything from the past? Or what the future might bring? The red-faced farmer has already announced that the solicitor forgot to put into the contract some square metres that are now urgently needed for a new building. The money he asks for is supposed to enable him to buy a second-hand BMW for his nephew. Well, we will ask our legal advisor first, but we definitely need more stables and six separate offices for the six partners-to-be. For the last seventeen years there have been no separate offices for any of us.

Are we going to buy more expensive equipment in order to diagnose things we are not able to treat? Do we need to have the equipment just to satisfy the the horse owners or even the ambitious young assistant, just out of university? Or are we going to be able to found a diagnostic centre in collaboration with perhaps twenty other horse practices and clinics? Could this centre be a place where great specialists have the best instruments and are ready to use them on horses that really need special diagnosis? Will we have enough time to go to renowned places all over the world, on a regular basis, in order to get new ideas and find out about new ways? Time will tell.

Liphook Equine Hospital, Hampshire

JEREMY MANTELL
The Liphook Equine Hospital
Forest Mere
Liphook
Hants GU30 7JG
UK

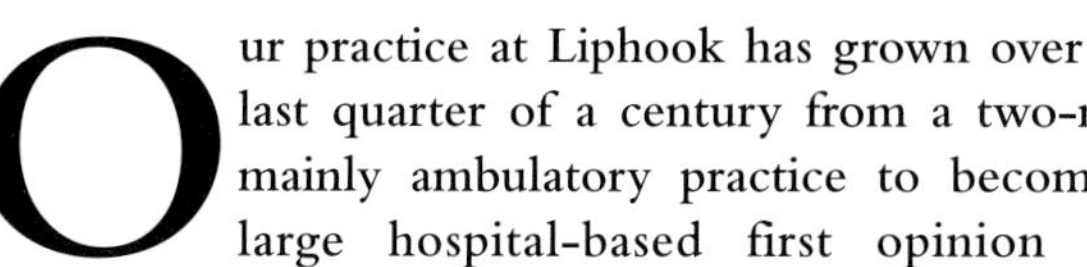

Our practice at Liphook has grown over the last quarter of a century from a two-man mainly ambulatory practice to become a large hospital-based first opinion and

referral centre. The original practice was started by Richard Hartley, a past President of BEVA and, following his sudden death in 1976, the practice was purchased by John Walmsley.

The original ethos of the practice was to provide dedicated equine care at a time when most of the practices in the country were multispecies. The future success of any practice or hospital depends on the leadership and vision of its founders and the particular strength of the Liphook practice has been the development of the team approach, led from the front. John Walmsley, the founder, has demonstrated the classic virtues of all pioneering surgeons, be they human or equine, namely both the determination to persevere and the courage to fail. In the early 1980s, colic and orthopaedic surgery was in its infancy and our records show that less than a quarter of all cases of surgical colic survived until discharge, some of which succumbed later to postoperative complications. Referred cases fared considerably worse than our own, due mainly to delay in referral. In a recent survey of our results published in the *Equine Veterinary Journal*, the majority of surgical colic patients returned to work.

Over the years the team has grown in number, experience and expertise and there are now 13 veterinary surgeons and nearly 60 support staff providing a full first opinion and referral, both ambulatory and surgical, service. The development of 24-hour working nursing cover to complement our 24-hour vets has considerably improved both the care and the recovery rate of our 40 inpatients. Newer members of the veterinary team have brought with them many specialities and strengths (and some weaknesses!) but all follow the common theme of trying to provide first class care both to the horse and to the owner.

The Liphook practice is perhaps unusual in that we have become a large referral practice in an area that is not known as a major centre of racing or equestrianism. There are but a handful of training yards and professional riders in our geographical catchment area and, in the early days at least, the majority of our patients were leisure horses. These horses, often owned by dedicated individuals who were prepared to spend a high proportion of their disposable income on their companion animals, have been greatly assisted by the development of the equine insurance industry. There is no doubt that the rapid development of the surgical facility is due in no small measure to the effect that insurance cover has had. The burgeoning of scientific knowledge and expertise throughout Europe and North America in the '70s and '80s needed a high caseload and the commitment of owners to invest in advanced treatments, if theory was to be put into practice. We were, and still are, fortunate at Liphook that we have been encouraged and supported in developing the practice and especially the referral surgical service by these two groups, owners and insurers, as well as by our colleagues in practice elsewhere. All of our partners have experienced the other side of the fence in agricultural practice. There is little doubt too that perhaps the single greatest threat to the future development and viability of our practice is the availability of good, yet affordable, insurance cover for the competition and leisure market. Just over 50% of our income now comes from referred cases and this trend is steadily increasing. Similarly, approximately 55% of our income comes from hospital-based activities as opposed to our ambulatory practice, a trend that seems set to continue also.

Unlike many institutionalised facilities, we have had to adapt and develop piecemeal over the years. This has been far from ideal and has inevitably led to many compromises in the architecture and design of the hospital complex. Where once we had small but acceptable facilities which were unusual in the region, many smaller practices have now built themselves good but small surgical units for their more routine cases. Although unable to relocate or to rebuild as we might have wished, we have continued to increase the area of our buildings and still have many unfulfilled dreams for the future.

It has been said elsewhere by wiser minds than ours that equine practice demands a peculiarly high price from its practitioners both in terms of time and of commitment. Whilst there is no doubt that the hospital has enabled the professional staff to enjoy a high degree of job satisfaction it is interesting to analyse the economics of this commitment. There is no doubt that the financial cost and return of the surgical cases allows at best only a narrow profit margin, which in the early days meant that we sailed fairly close to the wind. During the development of the practice the surgical side was usually supported by the ambulatory and clinic work and we occasionally discuss whether this continues! Of our annual inpatient intake of some 1600, at least 900 of which are surgical admissions, we find that we have to maintain a high occupancy rate to keep abreast of our overheads, especially staff costs. It has always been the belief and the decision of the partners to continue to develop the practice whenever possible, measured by professional rather than financial criteria. We are, indeed, fortunate that in so doing we have attracted a sufficient caseload to pay for our professional hobbies!

What of the future? The next 25 years may well see further changes in the equine profession within the UK and it is perhaps to be expected that primary, secondary and tertiary levels of care will become more clearly demarcated. The primary care is more likely to be provided by increasing numbers of equine-only practitioners, probably in single-species practices with the secondary cover often being provided by that same practice for diagnostic and routine surgical cover. The further development of tertiary, regional centres for equine surgery is our vision for the practice at Liphook and we aim to continue developing to fulfil the requirements of this niche. Time will tell how successful we will be but, to paraphrase the famous World War I cartoon, "*If we had known of a better 'ole we'd have moved to it by now!*"

Alamo Pintado Equine Medical Center, USA

DOUG HERTHEL
Alamo Pintado Equine Medical Center
2501 Santa Barbara Ave
PO Box 249
Los Olvos
California 93441
USA

The concept of a specialised central equine hospital developed in my mind long before veterinary school. It developed as a result of experiencing hours of valuable time in a veterinary vehicle visiting farms and stables in a very

large section of rural and urban Southern California in the early 1960s. These experiences of observing and assisting my veterinary mentor during junior high and high school were fascinating, satisfying, and extremely important in moulding my future goals as an equine practitioner. The client skills, horse-handling skills, and field medicine and surgery practices were invaluable, but the inefficiency of dealing with critical cases, and the time involved in getting to routine and emergency calls was frustrating at times.

As a result of these wonderful six years of part-time experience with ambulatory practice, I felt that when I got into veterinary school I would also like to develop the skills needed to start a full service veterinary hospital. I did not want to work indoors all the time, as I had observed at a small animal summer job, but I wanted to be able to operate when necessary and give intensive care to cases requiring it. This would require creating an equine medical facility. There were no private equine hospitals in California at that time. During my second year in veterinary school, two private equine hospitals were built in Southern California. Naively, I was crushed that someone else had beaten me to it. However, I felt there was room for at least one more hospital in California, besides the University of California Veterinary Hospital at Davis. In 1967, Davis serviced the entire state of California for referral surgical and medical cases.

I graduated in 1971 from UC Davis and then completed an intensive internship with Dr J.D. Wheat. In 1972, my wife, Sue, and I moved to the Santa Ynez Valley in Central California. We had previously purchased 6 acres of bare land in the very rural Santa Ynez Valley in 1969, and had to come up with $160 per month to meet the mortgage. Sue was an elementary school teacher making $408 per month, while I was in my senior year at veterinary school.

I can remember being told in veterinary school that veterinarians have no problem in acquiring bank loans to build a practice. The part missing was that banks had never heard of an equine veterinary hospital - especially one that would be a home, with a surgery room, office and stalls. In 1972, after seeing over 15 different bankers and being quickly turned down by everyone of them, we were approached by a modern day loan shark. He was willing to give us a building loan at a hefty 18% interest. The most important thing was that we were able to find enough funds to start the construction of the shell of the clinic and home. We put the main emphasis on finishing the surgery room first.

Fortunately, Sue had not only received a teaching degree at Davis, but also had a degree in Home Economics and Design from Davis. I had grown up doing construction of all kinds and landscaping and between the two of us we were able to design and contract the first phase of Alamo Pintado Equine Medical Center at a huge financial savings. We also attained what we needed and wanted, in a full service facility.

At the time we purchased the original six acres in 1969, we did not realise how difficult it would be to get proper zoning for such a facility, especially in Santa Barbara County. Thankfully, after a harrowing two years of meetings and jumping through many hoops, we did get the proper zoning for an equine hospital.

In 1969, there was only one full-time equine veterinarian practising in the Santa Ynez Valley. But, during my internship at Davis, I was also very nervous, because during that time four new equine veterinarians moved in and set up practice, all within five miles of our future 'dream facility'.

Every one of the four separate veterinary practitioners were extremely skilled, very professional and very competitive. They were also well known in the horse community. By the time we arrived in the valley they were established. It took us three months before getting our first call (a sick sheep).

This made us all the more determined to develop a first-class facility and, more importantly, one with excellent patient care and good results. We always felt that anyone could subject a sick horse to euthanasia, but armed with the right equipment, knowledge and willingness to work hard we could save many horses that normally would be put down for colic or fractures. We always knew, *"If we were good, they would come."*

No horse had ever been successfully operated on for colic in the Santa Ynez Valley up until 1972. Fortunately, that changed when Sue and I started operating on them routinely. No longer was the standard of care to merely watch a horse die of strangulated bowel, or obstructed intestines. Dr Robert Miller (of imprinting of foals fame) referred to this phenomenon in his Thousand Oaks practice as *"the dreaded death watch of equine practice"*. He started sending his colics 100 miles north to APEMC. After the first year of keeping track of how many horses came back to him healthy, he deemed colic referral, unheard of in those days, as an important part of his practice. Luckily, nine of 10 horses that first year returned to him after surgery at Alamo Pintado. Dr Miller used the fact that he diagnosed early, and referred early, and had excellent success with our colic surgeries as an important positive alternative to the agonising *"colic death watch"*.

The colic referral surgery caseload grew rapidly, and was an important reputation and income builder for AP. The ability to do ranch calls of all kinds during the day and surgery at night was made possible by having a veterinary hospital. The economics of working days and nights translated into an expanding good reputation and financial rewards that were completely used for more clinic improvements. These improvements increased our services, their quality and, conversely, our overall caseload. Continually reinvesting heavily back into the practice improved caseload, by improving the quality of diagnosis and care.

As the reproduction, lameness, and surgery caseload increased, new staff were added. An important part of the successful growth of the clinic has come from our

Doug Herthel in action.

externship, internship, and residency programmes. Ninety percent of our permanent veterinary associates have come out of this programme. The programme helps to keep us in touch with the most motivated and talented veterinary students and new veterinarians to the profession from universities and private clinics all over the world.

APEMC has a strong commitment to continuing education and in-house research and development of new techniques and surgical procedures. We have sponsored an annual APEMC veterinary symposium for our referral veterinarians for the last 19 years. We feel that this is a great way to show gratitude to our colleagues and to forge lasting friendship between both of us. The symposium's speakers are selected each year with several goals in mind. They must be able to give important useful information to practising veterinarians and share the latest advances in veterinary medicine and surgery.

The Alamo Pintado Equine Medical Center, California, USA.

Alamo Pintado currently employs a staff of 30, 10 of which are veterinarians. The practice continues to grow, but we have put a cap on the number of horses boarded at the clinic. We also are quite happy just to improve our medical and surgical capabilities, but not increase our volume.

The diagnostic tools available at Alamo Pintado include full laboratory services including haematology, blood gases, microbiology, videoendoscopy arthroscopy, laparoscopy, ultrasonography, nuclear scintigraphy, CT and fluoroscopy. Therapy and diagnostic tools include a high speed treadmill, aquatred, and a specially designed water recovery pool for fracture repair. Also for emergency transportation of cases, an equine ambulance was developed and is used in special circumstances.

The future continues to hold more technological sophistication, mixed with motivated veterinarians eager to advance their profession and themselves. Ultrasound will probably continue to be an ever-increasing aspect of our diagnostics, going hand in hand with the use of our CT capabilities. With the use of CT we are learning more about injuries and diseases and we are seeing amazing advancements in our stem cell programme for ligament injuries. We are networking with other universities and clinics, using the new communication and diagnostic modalities. We at Alamo Pintado are looking forward to more exciting advances in veterinary services in the new millennium.

A commentary on the history of equine anaesthesia

BILL MUIR
Department of Veterinary Clinical Sciences
The Ohio State University Veterinary Hospital
601 Vernon L Tharp Street
Columbus, Ohio 43210
USA

Equine anaesthesia, far too long an art, blossomed into a truly recognisable science in the 1970s. This commentary on its history provides a definition and a somewhat philosophical review of where we have been (prior to 1800), how far we have come (1800–1950), includes recent developments (1950–present) and addresses where we appear to be headed (Table 1).

Defining Anaesthesia

The word anaesthesia was first defined in Bailey's English dictionary in 1751 as "*a defect in sensation*". Historically, the word holds special significance because it is often associated with the public demonstration of surgical anaesthesia in man, by William Morton in America, in October, 1846, and subsequently by physicians in London within two days of the docking of the steamboat *Acadia.* This single dramatic and widely publicised event in the wake of earlier unpublicised successes (Crawford Long removed a tumur from the neck of a patient on March 30, 1842) and considerable scepticism, established the idea that drugs could and should be administered to render patients free of pain during surgery.

H.J. Bigelow *(A History of the Discovery of Modern Anaesthesia, A Century of American Medicine 1776-1787,* pp 175-112; 1876) is quoted as stating that: "*No single announcement ever created so great and general excitement in so short a time. Surgeons, sufferers, scientific men, everybody, united in simultaneous demonstration of heartfelt mutual congratulation.*"

Most importantly of all, Morton's demonstration heralded a true paradigm shift, in the sense used by T.S. Kuhn, that it represented a crystallisation of thought capable of producing an achievement sufficiently unprecedented as to attract an enduring group of adherents; and sufficiently open-ended to serve as a new direction and model for future research. Lest it be forgotten, this crystallisation of thought was made possible by the efforts of a mature scientific community including Sir Humphrey Davy, Michael Faraday, Henry Hill Hickman, Crawford Long, Horace Wells, J.Y. Simpson, J. Priestley, John Snow (1813-1856; heralded as the first anaesthesiologist) and others. Like a typical character in George Orwell's *1984*, Morton was "*the victim of history rewritten by the powers that be*". This paradigm shift fostered the secularisation of pain; and a moral transformation, within the Western world, that neither man nor animals should be subjected to or allowed to suffer pain. Based upon Morton's demonstration, the word anaesthesia became synonymous with unconsciousness that provided insensibility to pain, a viewpoint that persisted for almost 50 years. As the clinical use of neuromuscular blocking drugs, opioids and barbiturates became commonplace, however, the beneficial effects of diethyl ether (amnesia, muscle relaxation, attenuation of autonomic responses) became more obvious.

In 1957, P.D. Woodbridge redefined anaesthesia to include four specific components: sensory blockade, motor blockade, sleep or mental blockade (unconsciousness) and blockade of undesirable reflexes of the respiratory, cardiovascular and gastrointestinal systems, a state that could be produced by a single drug or a combination of drugs. Woodbridge believed that different drugs could be used to achieve the different components of anaesthesia, a concept that led to the development of a variety of drug combinations in order to produce a state of so-called "balanced anaesthesia".

Various prominent anaesthesiologists have proposed alternative definitions for the word anaesthesia, as for example C. Prys-Roberts (1987): "*drug-induced unconsciousness... the patient neither perceives nor recalls noxious stimulation*"; M.C. Pinsker (1986): "*paralysis, unconsciousness, and the attenuation of the stress response*"; and E.I. Eger (1993): "*reversible oblivion and immobility*". Few definitions, however, are as descriptive and practically useful as that of Woodbridge. Interestingly, a current edition (26th) of *Stedman's Medical Dictionary* (1995) provides a definition - "*1. Loss of a sensation resulting from pharmacological depression of nerve function or from neurological dysfunction. 2. Broad term for anaesthesiology as a clinical specialty*" - that is not as descriptive as Woodbridge's, although many qualifiers have been added (e.g. local, regional, general, surgical, dissociative).

Given recent advances in our current understanding of the pharmacodynamics (pharmacology, pharmacokinetics) of anaesthetic drugs in horses and the differing requirements of surgery (orthopedic versus abdominal) and patients (age, weight, physical status) a definition of anaesthesia, according to I. Kissin (1997), should include all effects that protect the patient from the trauma of surgery or produce desirable supplements to anaesthesia. This opinion is pointedly demonstrated by recent publications in *Equine Veterinary Journal* describing the use of alpha-2 agonists/dissociative anaesthetic/centrally acting muscle relaxants (detomidine/ketamine/guaifenesin) for total intravenous anaesthesia (TIVA) and the use of established (halothane, isoflurane) or new (sevoflurane) inhalant anaesthetic drugs in combination with various intraoperative anaesthetic adjuncts (ketamine,

TABLE 1: History of anaesthesia websites.

http://umdas.med.miami.edu/aha/aha
http://umdas.med.miami.edu/aha/vma
http://www.acva.org/history.htm
http://www.mandm.ncc.ac.vk/mandmweb/AVA/ECVAhome.html
http://www.oyston.com/history
http://larry.med.yale.edu/info/history.html
http://www.cas.ca/history.htm
http://www.hmcnet.harvard.edu/anaesthesia/history/whoswho.html
http://www.xs4all.nl/~dac/HAS/fhas.htm
http://www.dentaldigest.com/nitrous/nittext.html#history
gopher://gopher.anes.uab.edu
http://www.anes.uab.edu/timeline.htm
http://www.hmcnet.harvard.edu/anaesthesia/history/vandam.html
http://www.asahq.org/wlm/homepage.html

lidocaine, atracurium, dobutamine, calcium-dextrose, atropine) or the simultaneous administration of TIVA with inhalant anaesthetics to produce an "ideal" anaesthetic state. Today, practitioners of veterinary anaesthesia consider hypnosis, analgesia and muscle relaxation to be the core components of anaesthesia. Predictable and easily controlled drugs or drug combinations that produce these qualities, without inducing cardiorespiratory or immune system depression, while simultaneously inhibiting or suppressing the stress response are considered the most desirable.

Where We Have Been and How Far We Have Come (1800-1950)

Rational thought, experimentation, shared information, and the secularisation of pain and its management added to the divergence of herbalism and witchcraft from medicine in the 17th century. By 1800, Sir Humphrey Davy was extolling the inhalation of nitrous oxide as a remedy for the relief of operative pain in "*researches chemical and philosophical chiefly concerning nitrous oxide and its respiration*" and, by 1824, H.H. Hickman had administered carbon dioxide to animals in order to render them unconscious. It was not, however, until 1846 when Morton demonstrated the surgical benefits of diethyl ether that the practice of anaesthesia achieved worldwide recognition. Historical accounts of the human anaesthesia experience are available elsewhere (Table 1). Most of the available equine literature, prior to 1850 (and for a long time thereafter), suggested that the practice of equine anaesthesia was truly an art overly dependent upon herbalism (atropa mandragora, opium, henbane, hemlock) and physical restraint ("a heavy hand") and, at best, a poorly developed science. The practical advantages of anaesthesia and its benefits to equine surgery were advocated by G.H. Dadd one year after Morton's demonstration (1847) and subsequently in his book *Modern Horse Doctor* (1854). The first experimental use of diethyl ether in animals is attributed to Edward Mayhew. Mayhew may at some point have been the first individual to use diethyl ether in horses although similar experiments in animals including horses, were reported in France, Germany, Russia and the United States. Mayhew's experiences (1847) caused him to comment with scepticism:

"The results of these trials are not calculated to inspire any very sanguine hopes. We cannot tell whether the cries emitted are evidence of pain or not but they are suggestive of agony to the listener, and, without testimony to the contrary, must be regarded as indicative of suffering... There has yet been no experiment that I know of made to ascertain the action of the vapor on the horse; but I cannot anticipate that it will be found of service to that animal... We should be cautious lest we become cruel under the mistaken endeavour to be kind."

Others of this era, however, were more optimistic than Mayhew and as Percivall, a graduate physician and veterinarian, stated in that same year, "*We must confess we augur more favurably of the inferences deducible from them [Mayhews experiments] than he would seem to. To us it appears questionable whether the cries emitted by the animals during experiments are to be regarded as evidence of pain.*"

Within one year of Morton's demonstration, 'ether mania' had reached its peak and had begun to subside primarily due to J. Simpson's (1847) demonstration of the advantages of chloroform over ether:

"1st A much less quantity will produce the same effect. 2nd. A more rapid, complete and generally more persistent action, with less preliminary excitement and tendency to exhilaration and talking. 3rd. The inhalation is far more agreeable and pleasant than that of ether. 4th. As a smaller quantity is used, the application is less expensive, which becomes an important consideration if brought into general use. 5th. The perfume is not unpleasant, but the reverse, and more evanescent. 6th. No particular instrumental inhaler is necessary."

Pragmatism, however, was the order of the day with comments from equine surgeons warning: *"It is, in my opinion, very doubtful whether chloroform will ever become an efficient agent in veterinary practice on the horse, as I believe these two bad-conditioned animals [neurotomy surgeries in two horses] suffered more in being reduced to a state of insensibility, and in recovering from the state, than they did from the operation performed"; and "We very often delude ourselves in regard to the operation of medicines, which seldom effect what we suppose them to do. For this reason it is proper that we should be sceptical with regard to new remedies, which hardly ever maintain the character bestowed upon them by their first employers."* An editorial in the Veterinarian in 1848, suggested, *"abandoning the use of this potent chemical [chloroform] agent as an anaesthetic, at least for practical purposes, [instead] let us turn our attention to it as an internal remedy" while other writings suggested that ether and chloroform be reserved for internal use (as vermicides) and that during the 1850s, "Horses continued to be bled and purged with vehemence, and operated on without benefit of anaesthesia."*

These viewpoints gradually changed, however, and as R. Jennings in his book *The Horse and His Diseases* (1860) states: "*In severe operations, humanity dictates the use of some anaesthetic agent to render the animal insensible to pain. Chloroform is the most powerful of this class, and may be administered with perfect safety, provided a moderate quantity of atmospheric air is inhaled during its administration. Sulphuric ether acts very feebly upon the horse, and cannot therefore be successfully used.*" J.N. Naven commented in his text *Veterinary Practice, or Explanatory Horse Doctor* (1873): "*Chloroform may be administered to the horse for the same purpose as it is given to man... I would not recommend its use in any but the more important operations*" and A. Liautard in his *Manual of Operative Veterinary Surgery* (1892), states that for large animals: "*Chloroform used singly has proved itself to be the most effective and safest of all.*"

L.A. Merillat was one of the first veterinary surgeons in the United States to emphasise anaesthesia, albeit cautiously, in his *Principles of Veterinary Surgery* (1906) stating, "*Anaesthesia in veterinary surgery today is a means of restraint and not an expedient to relieve pain. So long as an operation can be performed by forcible restraint… the thought of anaesthesia does not enter into the proposition.*" Merillat, however, goes on to devote over 30 pages of his text to anaesthesia and anaesthetics and suggests "*that the practitioner of the near future will take advantage of the expedient that made the rapid advancement of human surgery possible*". Interestingly, Merillat listed fatalities from chloroform in horses to be 1/800 (0.125%), albeit the surgical procedures performed were of relatively short duration and heavily dependent upon the use physical restraint (hobbles). Shortly thereafter, Sir Frederick Hobday published the first English textbook (*Anaesthesia and Narcosis of Animals and Birds*, 1915) totally devoted to veterinary anaesthesia. Commenting on chloroform Hobday states, "*For the horse and dog, chloroform is by far the best general anaesthetic both in regard to its utility and cheapness and, also, its safety.*" Years later, L.W. Hall commented on Hobday's zeal for using chloroform during the Sir Frederick Hobday memorial address (1982) by stating, "*There is no reason to disbelieve his statement that he personally administered chloroform to thousands of horses without mishap.*" Hall goes on to point out that Hobday "*blamed the method of administration rather than the agent itself for any fatality*", an opinion that has always been and remains a critical issue in the practice of equine anaesthesia. Hobday also pointed out that it was "*safer to chloroform a horse than a dog or cat, one indisputable reason being that the larger animal was perforce hobbled and secured in such a position that its lungs could expand and the chest was not pressed upon by human hands*". An additional factor was the use of lower amounts of anaesthetic due to the use of physical restraint.

One of the many significant contributions of Hobday's text was the introduction of the concept of preanaesthetic medication to: 1) suppress excitement; 2) reduce the anaesthetic requirement (providing safer anaesthesia); 3) decrease the total anaesthesia time; 4) shorten and improve recovery from anaesthesia. Beginning in the early 1940s J.G. Wright who credited Hobday as "*the great pioneer of anaesthesia for animal surgery in this country [England],*" and with being the first to use cocaine as a local anaesthetic in horses, actively taught both the utility and safety of diethyl ether and particularly chloroform in horses as detailed in the first four editions of his book *Veterinary Anaesthesia* first published in 1942.

Subsequent to 1850, the slow development and universal application of veterinary anaesthesia techniques compared to human anaesthesia had many causes, the most important being attributable to a lack of general knowledge, experience, differing opinions and expectations, not to mention inadequate emphasis at many if not most veterinary teaching institutions prior to 1950. Despite slow development (1850–1950), equine anaesthesia emerged with human anaesthesia from herbalism and physical restraint to a science capable of rendering patients insensible to pain. J. F. Smithcors (1957) commented on the tardy pace in *The Early Use Of Anaesthesia In Veterinary Practice* by stating: "*The reasons for veterinarians later (1850–1950) being reluctant to make any considerable use of general anaesthetics are not immediately apparent… Although much progress in anaesthesiology had been made in human medicine, veterinary clinical teachers took few steps to include this adjunct to surgery in school practice… It is likely that more than a few simply thought of anaesthesia as an unnecessary refinement to a practice where a heavy hand was accounted a major asset.*"

These statements remind us of the aphorism, "*The easiest pain to bear is someone else's*" and of the Roman writer Celsius who encouraged "*pitilessness*" as an essential character of surgeons, an attitude that appears to have prevailed in human medicine until 1846 when William Morton demonstrated the surgical benefit of diethyl ether anaesthesia in man and until similar techniques could be developed (approximately 1940), distributed to the rank and file (1960s) and safely applied in equine surgical practice. Smithcors ends his essay by stating: "*Whether it be accounted in the name of humanity to the animal, or for the safety and ease of the surgeon, the relatively recent development (1940s and 1950s) of high calibre techniques of anaesthesiology must be considered a major advance in veterinary medicine.*"

Recent Developments (1950–Present)

Throughout the 1940s and 1950s, J.G. Wright's teachings, at the Beaumont Hospital of the Royal Veterinary College in the United Kingdom, and his texts served as a resource for anaesthetic drugs, principles and techniques for anyone interested in animal and particularly equine anaesthesia. He stated (*Veterinary Anaesthesia and Analgesia*, 4th edn 1957), that: "*Of the inhalation anaesthetics, chloroform is the most potent used in the horse, although… whether or not prenarcosis with chloral hydrate or cannabis indica is induced will depend chiefly on the size of the animal and the magnitude and duration of the operation to be performed.*" By the 1950s, *Cannibus indica* was no longer used in the United States due to human abuse and, shortly thereafter, in the United Kingdom for similar reasons and because it produced "*hyperesthetic activity and the animal (horse) behaved in a maniacal fashion, kicking wildly*".

In 1961, Wright and Hall (*Veterinary Anaesthesia and Analgesia*, 5th edn 1961) summarised earlier experiences with chloroform in horses by stating: "*Over the years chloroform has acquired the reputation of being the most dangerous of all the anaesthetic agents. However, it seems more than likely that many workers have overestimated the danger associated with the use of chloroform in horses.*" Commenting on the inhalation of chloroform they state: "*This can be applied only to the recumbent animal and the horse must be cast either with ropes or by inducing anaesthesia in the standing animal with thiopentone sodium. The dose of thiopentone used for this purpose should not exceed 1 g for 200 lb body weight… After a period of two to three minutes a second dose of half the initial dose of chloroform is given.*" Regarding diethyl ether they comment: "*There is general agreement that, using the ordinary methods of administration described for chloroform, it is an impossibility to obtain concentrations of ether sufficient to provoke anaesthesia in the horse.*"

Wright and Hall also note that "*because of its potency, halothane (used in horses by Hall in 1957) is a most useful inhalation anaesthetic for the horse. It is about twice as potent as chloroform and may be regarded as a much less dangerous anaesthetic agent. Halothane and chloroform both reduce cardiac output and blood pressure but an overdose of halothane causes respiratory failure long before it produces circulatory failure whereas an overdose of chloroform results in almost simultaneous respiratory and circulatory arrest.*" They go on to point out that "*it is usual to restrain the animal with hobbles for about 30 minutes after the administration of the anaesthetic is discontinued.*" From this time (late 1960s) to the present, advances (drugs, techniques, equipment) in the art and science of anaesthesia have had

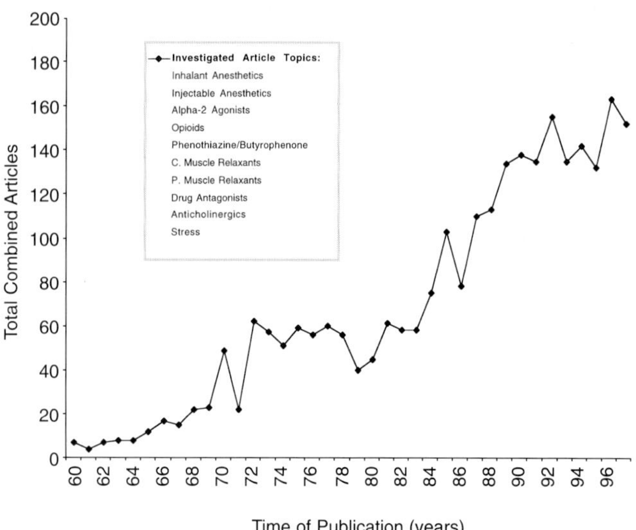

Fig 1: Graphical representation of annual number of equine anaesthesia-related refereed manuscripts (data obtained from Medline: National Library of Medicine).

astounding impact on the practice of anaesthesia in horses as evidenced by the myriad of drugs and anaesthetic adjuncts used to produce anaesthesia.

Occasionally the veterinary experience has coincided with (ketamine) or preceded (alpha-2 agonists) that in man. It is fair to state that what had remained an art prior to 1960 had become a powerfully effective science in the years that followed. L.W. Hall devoted over 20 pages (318-343) to anaesthesia in the horse in the, *Textbook of Veterinary Anaesthesia* edited by L.R. Soma published in the United States in 1971. In this text Hall comments that both chloroform and ether "*still have a place in equine practice*" although he emphasises the use of halothane as "*the principle inhalant anaesthetic to be used in horses*". Methoxyflurane, although very popular in dogs and cats at this time, "*would seem to be only of academic interest (in horses) to the practical anaesthetist. Induction of anaesthesia is very slow, changes in the depth of anaesthesia can only be achieved very gradually and recovery is slow.*" He goes on to state: "*Choral hydrate, the best basal narcotic for horses has been used in veterinary practice for many years.*" Guaifenesin, a centrally acting muscle relaxant introduced in Germany in the 1950s and administered to horses by M. Whethues, R. Fritsch, K.A. Funk and U. Schatzman since the 1960s, was given only cursory mention, but has become the basic ingredient in most intravenous anaesthetic techniques used today. Hall finishes the chapter by stating: "*It is probable that in veterinary anaesthesia generally, too little attention is paid to the relief of pain in the postanaesthetic and postoperative periods, and the use of analgesics in this period warrants further study.*"

The 1970s, '80s and '90s have witnessed exciting and extraordinarily rapid advances in drug development, molecular pharmacology, drug assay techniques, physiology and molecular biology, anaesthetic drug delivery systems and techniques, anaesthetic monitoring equipment and 'point of care' blood and blood chemistry analysers. The evolution of preanaesthetic protocols that render the horse analgesic, uninterested in its surroundings and reluctant to move have eliminated the need for 'a heavy hand' and markedly facilitated 'standing anaesthesia'. The development of new inhalant and total intravenous anaesthetic techniques (TIVA) have revolutionised and facilitated both field and operating suite surgical procedures. Today, computerisation, global networking and new and faster methods for information transfer continue to influence how equine anaesthesia is performed.

Numerous scientific contributions, by E. P. Steffey, describing the effects of inhalant anaesthetics in horses and many others describing the pharmacodynamics and toxicity of intravenous anaesthetic drugs (see Additional Reading) provide ample reading on subjects directly pertaining to both the basic and applied sciences of equine anaesthesia. Annual publications on subjects directly related to equine anaesthesia have increased dramatically since 1960 and continue to increase (Fig 1). In 1991, the first text, *Equine Anaesthesia: Monitoring and Emergency Therapy* (eds: W.W. Muir and J.A.E. Hubbell) was published devoting more than 500 pages to issues associated with the administration and consequences of anaesthetic drug administration to horses.

One highly significant, but less recognised, advance has been the development of a critical mass of highly educated and trained individuals, anaesthesiologists, skilled in the art and science of equine anaesthesia. Thorough review of several sources of information, including the proceedings of the American Association of Equine Practitioners (AAEP; established in 1954), the British Equine Veterinary Association (BEVA; established in 1961), veterinary surgery and anaesthesia texts and numerous manuscripts revealed that the essential ingredient missing from the practice of equine anaesthesia, prior to 1950, was not a lack of appreciation by earlier practitioners of its potential importance or utility (both morally and ethically), but a relative absence of adequately and specifically educated and knowledgeable practitioners of the trade. Academia in particular has fostered and supported this development, both directly and indirectly, in order better to serve their constituents (private practitioners, the public), develop areas of focused research interest and provide a resource (internal and external) for continuing education.

Many private practices have followed suit by employing specialists in medicine and surgery in order to provide better service to the public, a resource to peers and to enhance income from patients that require advanced surgical or diagnostic procedures and special care. Today, one need only look at the index of textbooks of veterinary anaesthesia and many surgery texts to determine the scope of knowledge the speciality expects in terms of prerequisite knowledge. Practitioners of equine anaesthesia must become educated and develop an applied understanding of equine physiology (neurology, respiratory, cardiovascular, endocrine, acid-base and fluid and electrolyte balance), pharmacology (pharmacokinetics, pharmacodynamics, toxicology, drug interactions), chemistry/physics (vapour pressures, solubility coefficients, dissociation constants, pressure, flow, resistance, anaesthetic circuits), electronics (computers, monitors [ECG, EEG]) and principles of emergency medicine and therapy (cardiopulmonary resuscitation and shock). Indeed, most (and if honest all) equine veterinary surgeons would readily admit that they are 'not current in' the science and limited in the art of performing equine anaesthesia, particularly in high risk patients.

It was during the 1960s that many equine surgeons began to realise that a dedicated surgeon could not devote full attention and concentration to surgery and, at the same time, provide the best anaesthesia possible. Stated another way, a poor anaesthetist is the ruin of a good surgeon and

TABLE 2: Historical events important in equine anaesthesia.

Period	Events
Prior to 1500s (Herbalism)	■ Plant extracts produced: atropine, opium, cannabis
1500–1700 (Emerging)	■ Anaesthesia defined as "a defect in sensation"
	■ Ether (1540)
	■ Needles (Intravenous access)
1800s (Developing)	■ Anaesthesia Comes of Age: William Morton (1846) demonstrates ether anaesthesia in America: "*Gentlemen, this is no humbug.*"
	■ Key Drug Developments:
	• Peripheral muscle relaxants: curare (1814)
	• Inhalant anaesthetics: carbon dioxide (1824), ether (Mayhew 1847), chloroform (1845), nitrous oxide (N20, 1844)
	• Intravenous: chloral hydrate (Humbert 1875)
	• Local anaesthetic: cocaine (1885)
	• Equipment: face masks, orotracheal tubes, inhalant anaesthetic apparatus
	• Anaesthetic record keeping
1900–1950 (Achieving)	■ Key Drug Developments:
	• Chloral hydrate (combinations with magnesium sulfate, pentobarbital)
	• Barbiturates (Pentobarbital, thiopental)
	• Local anaesthetic drugs and techniques developed (Procaine)
	• Peripheral muscle relaxants (Succinyl choline)
	■ Compulsory Anaesthetic Use Act in the UK (1919)
	■ Key Texts:
	• E. Stanton Muir, *Materia Medica and Pharmacy* (1904)
	• Atropine, cannabis, humulus, herbane, chloral, cocaine, codeine, morphine, narcotina, heroin, ethyl alcohol, chloroform, ether
	• L.A. Merillat, *Principles of Veterinary Surgery* (1906)
	• First American surgeon to devote dedicated attention to anaesthesia
	• Sir Frederick Hobday, First English Text on Veterinary Anaesthesia: Anaesthesia and Narcosis of Animals and Birds (1915)
	• Introduces concepts of: pre-anaesthetic medication, pain relief and local, regional and spinal anaesthesia
	• J.G. Wright, *Veterinary Anaesthesia*, (1st ed. 1942; 2nd ed. 1947)
	• Cannabis, chloral hydrate, pentobarbital, thiopental, chloroform, ether, morphine, bulbocapnine
	• E.R. Frank, *Veterinary Surgery Notes* (1947)
	• Chloral hydrate and magnesium sulfate, pentobarbital, procaine
1950–2000 (Extending)	■ Art becomes a Science
	■ Controlled studies conducted on horses
	■ Key Drug Developments
	• Central muscle relaxants (ex. Guaifenesin, diazepam)
	• Peripheral muscle relaxants (ex. Atracurium)
	• Phenothiazines (ex. Promazine, acepromazine)
	• Alpha-2 agonists (ex. Xylazine, detomidine, medetomidine, romifidine)
	• Dissociative anaesthetics (ex. Ketamine, tiletamine)
	• Hypnotics (ex. Propofol)
	• Inhalants (ex. Cyclopropane, methoxyflurane, halothane, isoflurane, enflurane, sevoflurane, desflurane)
	• Species specific anaesthetic equipment and ventilators
	• Monitoring techniques and equipment
	■ Key Texts:
	• J.G. Wright, *Veterinary Anaesthesia*, (3rd edn 1952; 4th edn 1957)
	• J.G. Wright , L.W. Hall, *Veterinary Anaesthesia and Analgesia*, 5th edition (1961)
	• Subsequent editions by L.W. Hall and K.W. Clarke
	• L.R. Soma, *Textbook of Veterinary Anaesthesia* (1971)
	• Chapter 23, written by L.W. Hall, described anaesthesia in horses
	• W.V. Lumb, E. Wynn Jones, *Veterinary Anaesthesia* (1973)
	• C.E. Short, *Principles & Practice of Veterinary Anaesthesia* (1987)
	• Chapter 13, Part 1: "Special considerations for equine anaesthesia"
	• Chapter 13, Part 8: "Anaesthetic Considerations in the Conditioned Animal"
	• W.W. Muir, J.A.E. Hubbell, First text on anaesthesia completely devoted to the horse: *Equine Anaesthesia Monitoring and Emergency Therapy* (1991)
	■ Detailed anaesthetic records
	■ Species-specific designed anaesthetic equipment and ventilators
	• Monitoring techniques and equipment
	■ "point of care" blood chemistry (pH, PO_2 , PCO_2 , etc.) equipment
	■ Anaesthesia universally taught as part of veterinary school curriculum
	■ Colleges of American (1975) and European Anaesthesia (1993) established
	■ Information transfer (computer networks and assisted learning)

because both tasks are frequently performed by the same person in most equine practices it behoves veterinary surgeons to become expert in anaesthesia or employ a dedicated anaesthetist, for to become expert in one and not the other produces the same result.

The take-home message is that the body of information and skills required, not to mention the required level of experience and concentration necessary to become a surgeon or an anaesthetist are different, and that to attempt to practise both simultaneously, without these skills, does not provide the best outcome for the patient. Furthermore, the self-imposed scrutiny and vigilance provided by veterinary anaesthetists has significantly impacted the consequences (morbidity) and safety (mortality) of anaesthesia in horses while significantly improving patient wellbeing and lengthening the time (>8 hours) that equine surgery can be safely performed.

It is axiomatic that equine orthopedic and abdominal surgery, as we know it today, would not be possible without these advances. Indeed, early anaesthetic drugs (e.g. diethyl ether, chloroform, cyclopropane, methoxyflurane, chloral hydrate, trimeprazine, perphenazine, pecazine, propionylpromazine) and anaesthetic techniques (e.g. succinyl choline, singular use of thiopental, casting harnesses) have been abandoned for drugs and techniques that provide safer and more predictable effects, greater control of anaesthesia and less opportunity for adverse responses. These ongoing changes, combined with an ever-increasing emphasis upon prevention and treatment of pain, continue to receive special attention in shaping anaesthetic protocols.

The science of veterinary anaesthesia achieved universal recognition as an independent field of study during the 1970s, ultimately culminating in North America by the formation of the American College of Veterinary Anesthesia (ACVA; established on 13 July 1975) and, although heavily represented in the equine anaesthesia literature prior to this time, in Europe by the establishment of the European College of Veterinary Anaesthesia (ECVA; established on 26 April 1993). Both organisations were founded upon the principles of the dissemination of knowledge, the advancement of science and the development and maintenance of minimum standards of care. The development of veterinary anaesthesia teaching (continuing education) and training programmes for both professional and technical practitioners of anaesthesia has been a major focus of these groups. The relatively small number of equine anaesthesia specialists that are competent to provide the education and training needed to perform safe and effective equine anaesthesia is highlighted by the fact that, of the frequently anaesthetised domesticated species, the horse stands alone as being one of the most challenging. The significance of this challenge is dramatised by the 10-fold greater death rate reported for horses (approximately 1%) compared to that for dogs and cats (approximately 0.1%) and 100-fold greater death rate compared to that reported for man (approximately 0.01%)! Interestingly, this percentage (1%) has not changed from values originally reported by W.V. Lumb and E. Wynn Jones in the first (1973) and second (1984) editions of their text *Veterinary Anaesthesia* in which they report values of 2% and 1%, respectively. Death rates associated with equine surgery/anaesthesia become even more dramatic, reaching values of almost 10% when obstetric/colic patients are considered. One is led to ponder the cause for such high death rates in horses, particularly since recent (1998) figures from a veterinary teaching college suggest a much lower number in noncolic/obstetric patients (1/1279; 0.08%) directly attributable to anaesthesia, a number much closer to that in human medicine and my own personal experiences (23/17254; 0.13%) at a veterinary teaching hospital.

Contemplation of these numbers reminds us of the often-quoted phrase, expounded by Robert Smith, "*There are no safe anaesthetic drugs, there are no safe anaesthetic techniques, there are only safe anaesthetists*" and emphasises the absence of any information whatsoever which catalogues or defines the incidence of error in the performance of equine anaesthesia. This issue, error, is relevant to a discussion of the 'current and future state of the art' because of the previously quoted and unacceptable elevated equine anaesthetic death rates and the fact that error is intrinsic to all human endeavurs. Errors occurring immediately before an event (active errors) are knowledge, skill, rule or technically based. Latent errors include inadequacies or failures due to training, policies or protocols. It is important to emphasise that error does not equate with negligence; and that experience does not reduce critical incidents ("*a human error or equipment failure that if not corrected leads to an undesirable outcome*"). Human error will probably always remain a primary cause of accidents but its occurrence can be reduced by knowledge, an understanding of causality and a constructively critical team approach.

The Future (2000 and Beyond)

Many practical issues (e.g. long-term analgesia, hypoxaemia, hypotension, recovery quality, drug-related 'hangover') and new horizons (e.g. immune system modulation, cytokine pathophysiology) require continued investigation. New ideas, drugs, techniques and equipment continue to evolve. It will be interesting to see what direction the current plateau in equine anaesthesia-related scientific publications follows (Fig 1). Although insurrections will occur, another paradigm shift in anaesthesia will be dependent on as yet unrecognised advances in technology and molecular pharmacology. The most immediate issue impacting the practice of equine anaesthesia is the globalisation of information transfer and computer network-based education. The role of equine anaesthetists in equine surgery will be, for many, unquestioned and mandatory. This role being defined by a working understanding of current definitions of the term anaesthesia, the applied and scientific areas in which individuals who perform equine anaesthesia must be adequately educated; and a visceral appreciation for the job at hand, combined with the continuous desire to improve upon the operative and perioperative wellbeing and survival of the horse. If practical and predictable field and hospital anaesthetic techniques are to be performed on sicker patients then more individuals will need to be educated to provide safe and effective anaesthesia. Continued research will be required to provide the qualitative and quantitative data necessary to remove dogma and evaluate new approaches.

Conclusion

In this overview, I have provided a brief and biased overview of equine anaesthesia. I have included a rough chronological review of the various texts, drugs and key developments as they pertain to the development of anaesthesia in the horse (Table 2). Most colleges of veterinary medicine began deliberately and systematically to apply an ever increasing body of knowledge from various scientific specialties (anatomy, physiology, pharmacology) to the clinical practice of anaesthesia in horses during the 1970s and it is since this time that the practice of equine anaesthesia has blossomed from an art dependent on physical restraint to a science based upon focused species specific research.

Horses are a vital part of a grand industry and play an essential role in many peoples lives.

In closing, it is appropriate to remember an excerpt from a poem entitled, *The Horse*, written by Ella Wheeler Wilcox and published in *Poetry's Plea For Animals* in 1927:

The world as we see it now
Is only half man-made;
As the horse recedes with a parting bow
We know the part he has played.
For the wonderful brain of man,
However mighty its force,
Had never achieved its lordly plan
Without the aid of the horse.

Additional Reading

History of Equine Anaesthesia References

Arnstein, F. (1997) Catalogue of human error (review). *Br. J. Anaesth.* **79**, 645-656.

Bigelow, H.J. (1876) A history of the discovery of modern anaesthesia. In: *A Century of American Medicine 1776-1876.* Eds: E.H. Clarke, H.J. Bigelow, S.D. Gross, T.G. Thomas and J.S. Billings, Brinklow, Old Hickory Bookshop. pp 175-212.

Calverley, R.K. and Scheller, M. (1992) Anaesthesia as a specialty: Past, present and future. In: *Clinical Anaesthesia*, 2nd edn, Ed P.G. Barash, B.F. Cullen and R.K. Stoelting, J.B. Lippincott Co., Philadelphia. pp 3-33.

Caton, D. (1985) The secularization of pain. *Anaesthesiology.* **62**, 493-501.

Eger, E.I., II (1993) What is general anaesthetic action? (editorial). *Anesth. Analg.* **77**, 408.

Frank, E.R. (1947) *Veterinary Surgery Notes.* Burgess Publishing Company, Minneapolis, Minnesota. pp 8-10, 25-33.

Glass, P.S.A. (1988) Anaesthetic drug interactions: An insight into general anaesthesia – its mechanism and dosing strategies (editorial). *Anaesthesiology.* **88**, 5-6.

Holzman, R.S. (1998) The legacy of Atropos, the fate who cut the thread of life. *Anaesthesiology.* **89**, 241-249.

James, W. (1982) The varieties of religious experience. In: *A Study in Human Nature*, Penguin Books, New York. pp 297-298.

Johnston, G.M. and Steffey, E. (1995) Letter to the editor (letter). *Vet. Surg.* **24**, 518-519.

Jones, E.W. (1961) Recent advances in equine anaesthesia. *Proc. Am. Ass. Equine Practnrs.* **7**, 153-164.

Jones, R.S. (1993) From hemlock to romifidine. *Equine vet. Educ.* **5**, 197-199.

Keys, T.E. (1945) The beginnings. In: *The History of Surgical Anaesthesia*, Schuman's, New York. pp 5-11.

Kissin, I. (1997) A concept for assessing interactions of general anaesthetics. *Anesth. Analg.* **85**, 204-210.

Kuhn, T.S. (1996) *The Structure of Scientific Revolutions*, 3rd edn, The University of Chicago Press, Chicago and London. pp 43-51.

Lumb, W.V. and Jones, E.W. (1973) *Veterinary Anaesthesia*, 1st edn, Lea & Febiger, Philadelphia. pp 629-631.

Lumb, W.V. and Jones, E.W. (1984) *Veterinary Anaesthesia*, 2nd edn, Lea & Febiger, Philadelphia. pp 623-629.

Mee, A.M., Cripps, P.J. and Jones, R.S. (1998) A retrospective study of mortality associated with general anaesthesia in horses: elective procedures. *Vet. Rec.* **142**, 275-276.

Muir, W.W. and Hubbell J.A.E. (1991) *Equine Anesthesia: Monitoring and Emergency Therapy*, 1st edn, C.V. Mosby Co., St. Louis, Missouri.

Pinsker, M.C. (1986) Anaesthesia: a pragmatic construct. *Anesth. Analg.* **65**, 819-820.

Prys-Roberts, C. (1987) Anaesthesia: a practical or impractical construct? (editorial). *Br. J. Anaesth.* **59**, 1341-1345.

Schwieger, I.M., Hall, R.I. and Hug, C.C., Jr. (1991) Less than additive antinociceptive interaction between midazolam and fentanyl in enflurane-anesthetized dogs. *Anaesthesiology.* **74**, 1060-1066.

Smithcors, J.F. (1957) The early use of anaesthesia in veterinary practice. *Br. vet. J.* **113**, 284-291.

Smithcors, J.F. (1971) History of veterinary anaesthesia. In: *Textbook of Veterinary Anaesthesia*, Ed: L.R. Soma, The Williams & Wilkins Company, Baltimore. pp 1-23.

Stevenson, D.E. (1963) The evolution of veterinary anaesthesia. *Br. J. Anaesth.* **119**, 477-483.

Vandam, L.D. (1994) History of anaesthetic practice, In: *Anaesthesia*, 4th edn, Ed: R.D. Miller, Churchill Livingstone, New York. pp 9-19.

Wilcox, E.W. (1927) The horse. In: *Poetry's Plea for Animals: An Anthology of Justice and Mercy for our Kindred in Fur and Feathers*, Lothrop, Lee & Shepard Co., Boston. pp 238-240.

Woodbridge, P.D. (1957) Changing concepts concerning depth of anaesthesia. *Anaesthesiology.* **18**, 536-550.

Wright, J.G. (1942) *Veterinary Anaesthesia*, 1st edn, Baillière, Tindall & Cox, Great Britain. pp 1-6, 85-106, 120-129.

Wright, J.G. (1948) *Veterinary Anaesthesia*, 2nd edn, Baillière, Tindall & Cox, Great Britain. pp 85-107, 119-128.

Wright, J.G. (1952) *Veterinary Anaesthesia*, 3rd edn, Baillière, Tindall & Cox, Great Britain. pp. 160-188.

Wright, J.G. and Hall, L.W. (1961) Inhalation anaesthesia in horses. In: *Veterinary Anaesthesia and Analgesia*, 5th edn, The Williams & Wilkins Company, Great Britain. pp 262-281.

Fruits of Love: an anaesthetic challenge

SARAH FREEMAN, DYLAN GORVY AND EDDIE CAUVIN
Royal Veterinary College
Hawkshead Lane
North Mymms
Herts AL9 7TA
UK

Approximately one quarter of the Royal Veterinary College Equine Hospital caseload is emergencies. The Sefton Equine Hospital currently has two operating theatres with full anaesthetic facilities and padded induction and recovery boxes. One emergency this year, however, was notable by its unconventional use of the emergency facilities.

Fruits of Love, a four-year-old colt, owned by Mick Doyle and trained by Mark Johnston, was involved in a horsebox incident whilst in transit from Heathrow to Yorkshire. The Royal Veterinary College was notified that a horse had become trapped in the groom's compartment of the horsebox whilst in transit on the M25 motorway. The driver of the box and the grooms had informed the emergency services, who had directed them to the Royal Veterinary College. The fire brigade were first to arrive at the Sefton Equine Hospital, followed shortly by the horsebox.

On arrival, the horse was trapped in left lateral recumbency with its head towards the right side of the box; and wedged in a groom's compartment which was approximately one metre wide. The groom's compartment was separated from the transit area by a wooden partition approximately 1.2 metres high, with a solid wooden bar at the top. The entrance to the groom's compartment was a small door from the driver's cab against which the horse was lying. The horse occupied most of the space, lying transversely, with its head and rump against each side of the box, and its legs partly folded against the partition. It was immediately apparent that the only way to extricate the horse was by cutting and removing the partition.

The accident had occurred shortly before arrival at the Hospital, but the horse was relatively quiet on presentation, only struggling occasionally. There were signs of early shock: the pulse rate was 60 beats per minute and the mucous membranes were slightly congested, but there was a normal capillary refill time. There were superficial abrasions to the head, but otherwise no obvious external injuries. The only access to the horse was over the partition. However due to its position in lateral recumbency with the limbs towards the partition, the safest but difficult access to the head was within the compartment from above the horse (standing on the base of its neck and scapula). The horse was sedated with 0.015 mg/kg bwt detomidine and 0.01 mg/kg butorphanol intravenously to enable the fire brigade to assess the situation. An intravenous catheter was placed into the right jugular vein and hypertonic 7.2% saline was infused at 4 ml/kg bwt to maintain plasma volume and cardiovascular function. Intravenous flunixin meglumine was administered at 1.1 mg/kg for analgesia and its anti-inflammatory action. The horse continued to struggle despite the sedation. The width of the partition meant that the fire brigade were unable to use manual equipment. A power saw was required and therefore general anaesthesia was needed.

Anaesthesia was induced by the intravenous administration of 2.2 mg/kg bwt ketamine and 0.01 mg/kg bwt diazepam. It was maintained using an infusion of guaifenesin, ketamine and xylazine (15% guaifenesin with 1.5 g ketamine and 750 mg xylazine added) administered to effect. The heart rate was between 30 and 40 beats per minute during anaesthesia, and a strong facial arterial pulse was palpable. Active palpebral reflexes were maintained, and intermittent nystagmus occurred. The horse showed spontaneous movement immediately after the partition was removed and 0.1 mg/kg bwt thiopentone was administered to increase the depth of anaesthesia. Once general anaesthesia was stable, the horse was moved onto a drag mat and moved to a short distance to the theatre hoist. It was then hoisted into a padded recovery box. Intravenous xylazine 0.25 mg/kg bwt was administered to reduce the risk of excitement during recovery and the horse was given intranasal oxygen during this time.

The horse made a rapid and smooth recovery from anaesthesia, regaining its feet at the first attempt. Injuries were limited to superficial abrasions over both eyes, withers, back, *tuber coxae* and stifles, and a full thickness laceration over the skin on the medial aspect of the left eye. All the wounds were lavaged and topical treatment was applied. The horse had a normal pulse, respiratory rate and rectal temperature and mildly elevated haematocrit. He was maintained on intravenous Hartmann's solution at a rate of 2 ml/kg/hour overnight and given intravenous 20,000 iu/kg penicillin and 6.6 mg/kg gentamicin. The wound over the left eye was sutured the following day.

There was no haematuria but the horse had frequent micturition, although this resolved within 24 hours following the accident. Fruits of Love was discharged three days after admission, at which time he was loaded without complication into the horsebox and had an uneventful journey home.

A key factor in the successful outcome of this case was the efficiency and cooperation of a team of people working together. The entire procedure from admission to recovery from anaesthesia was effected in less than 45 minutes. Initially, the fire brigade were working to determine the optimal way of removing the partition, whilst the veterinary surgeons were assessing and stabilising the horse prior to anaesthesia.

Preliminary examination of the horse was limited to assessment of the cardiovascular status and any gross external injuries. It was apparent that the horse would require general anaesthesia and the main concerns were therefore hypovolaemia and myopathy as a result of trauma and anaesthesia. Whilst the horse was trapped in the box, it could not be determined whether there were any internal injuries/haemorrhage, although there were signs of early shock. In addition, the horse had recently been raced and shipped from Dubai, and therefore dehydration due to the stress of transport was also possible. Each of these factors could lead to hypovolaemia.

Muscle damage could arise either from direct trauma during struggling, or due to recumbency combined with hypotension (as a result of hypovolaemia or anaesthesia). Hypertonic saline produces rapid expansion of the plasma volume, producing an increase in cardiac output, cardiac contractility and systemic and pulmonary arterial blood pressures. It has been shown to be effective for the treatment of haemorrhagic shock and anaesthetic-induced hypotension[1]. Other advantages include it ease of availability and administration, compared for example with plasma or colloid solutions. Hypertonic saline is highly suitable for use in situations such as this where rapid treatment is essential.

The use of a total intravenous anaesthetic regime was the only feasible option in this case, as there was very limited access to the horse's head and airway, and no access for equipment. Infusion of a combination of xylazine, ketamine and guaifenesin (triple drip) was chosen because this anaesthetic regimen produces minimal cardiovascular depression, and cardiac index, heart rate and arterial blood pressure are usually maintained within normal limits[3,4]. In addition, recovery from this anaesthetic infusion is usually rapid and smooth when used for relatively short duration anaesthesia (less than 60–90 minutes)[4,5]. The greatest concern of the triple drip technique is that ketamine may have some excitatory effects, particularly in a stressful situation such as related to this case. These stimulatory effects of ketamine are due to an increase in noradrenaline release in the central nervous system[6], but as the alpha-2 agonists decrease the activity of central noradrenaline cells[7], they may directly counteract the ketamine excitement reaction. In this case there was some excitement upon the induction of general anaesthesia despite premedication with detomidine. The use of high doses of ketamine can result in a poor recovery, characterised by a prolonged recovery time, incoordination and excitement[8]. Excitement in the recovery period for this case was minimised by using a dark, quiet environment and by the administration of xylazine to decrease noradrenaline release.

Overall, the preanaesthetic hypertonic saline was useful for optimising cardiovascular function. Total intravenous anaesthesia using xylazine, ketamine and guaifenesin allowed the animal to be released with minimal trauma and with a low risk of hypotension and cardiovascular depression.

Fruits of Love went on to win the Hardwicke Stakes at Ascot on 19 June, and to be placed third in the King George at Ascot on 24 July. He was recently described as being "*in the form of his life*".

References

[1]Schmall, L.M., Muir, W.W. and Robertson, J.T. (1990) Haemodynamic effects of small volume hypertonic saline in experimentally induced haemorrhagic shock. *Equine vet. J.* **22**, 272-277.

[2]Dyson, D.H. and Pascoe, P.J. (1990) Influence of preinduction methoxamine, lactated Ringer solution, or hypertonic saline solution infusion or postinduction dobutamine infusion on anesthetic-induced hypotension in horses. *Am. J. vet. Res.* **51**, 17-21.

[3]Muir, W.W., Skarda, R.T. and Sheehan, W. (1978) Evaluation of xylazine, guaifenesin, and ketamine hydrochloride for restraint in horses. *Am. J. vet. Res.* **39**, 1274-1278.

[4]Green, S.A., Thurmon, J.C., Tranquilli, W.J. and Benson, G.J. (1986) Cardiopulmonary effects of continuous intravenous infusion of guaifenesin, ketamine, and xylazine in ponies. *Am. J. vet. Res.* **47**, 2364-2367.

[5]Young, L.E., Bartram, D.H., Diamond, M.J., Gregg, A.S. and Jones, R.S. (1993) Clinical evaluation of an infusion of xylazine, guaifenesin and ketamine for maintenance of anaesthesia in horses. *Equine vet. J.* **25**, 115-119.

[6]Wright, M. (1982) Pharmacologic effects of ketamine and its use in veterinary medicine. *J. Am. vet. med. Ass.* **189**, 1462-1471.

[7]Bylund, D.B. and U'Prichard, D.C. (1983) Characterisation of alpha-1 and alpha-2 adrenergic receptors. *Int. Rev. Neurobiol.* **24**, 343-422.

[8]Muir, W.M., Skarda, R.T. and Milne, D.W. (1977) Evaluation of xylazine and ketamine hydrochloride for anaesthesia in horses. *Am. J. vet. Res.* **38**, 195-201.

The clinical relevance of equine exercise physiology: can we do better?

REUBEN ROSE, DAVID EVANS AND DAVID HODGSON
Equine Performance Laboratory
Faculty of Veterinary Science
University of Sydney
New South Wales 2006
Australia

In equine exercise physiology, the basic issues addressed by studies undertaken during the 1950s and early 1960s relate to key concerns of the horse trainer, which are still relevant today:

- How do I know if this horse is going to be a good or bad performer? What are the chances of a return on investment?
- How do I know if there is some condition that may limit the performance of this horse over the next few days, when it is due to undertake a race start or competition?
- What is the reason that the horse did not race or perform up to expectations?
- How do I know if the horse is fit?

Despite 30 years of intense research, we do not have many answers and there is still a belief in many circles of 'black box' solutions. We hope that we can place some of the issues into context in our look at the past and present and also perhaps a future where the veterinarian with knowledge of exercise physiology will be a valuable asset to the trainer and owner of all performance horses.

Past Studies

Studies relating to the physiology of exercise in horses commenced about 100 years ago[1]. However, there were limited scientific studies and most of the interest over the next 30 years related to energy metabolism and efficiency of work[2]. During this time, the prominence of the car as a form of transport came to the fore and the horse was regarded as old-fashioned, with resulting limited interest in its scientific study.

Scientific studies relating to the horse and its capacity for long distance and intense, short distance exercise, resurfaced in the 1950s, with initial studies recognising the mobility of the erythrocyte pool[3] and the probable importance of this to performance. Because of the simplicity of sample acquisition and the perception that, from a trainer's point of view, this was 'real science', the blood count became an important part of the routine of equine practice in the 1960s[4,5]; and veterinarians began to take blood samples as a routine measure, every few weeks during training. Interestingly, despite the knowledge that the erythrocyte pool was dynamic, veterinarians often adopted a simplistic view of the results obtained. In some cases, horses were withdrawn from races purely on the basis that the veterinarian had indicated that their erythrocyte sedimentation rate was too high. Inappropriate practices persist and many trainers maintain a naive belief in the importance of the blood count, too often supported by veterinary surgeons who appear unaware of the scientific studies that have shown its limitations. Undoubtedly, routine haematology and plasma/serum biochemistry is of value in detecting some subclinical problems, but it is clear that there is no relationship between erythrocyte indices and performance[6,7] or changes in haematology indicating improvements in fitness.

In examining plasma/serum biochemistry, the limitations of use of plasma activities of creatinine kinase (CK) as an aid to diagnosis of rhabdomyolysis are also now better understood. However, in some practices, subclinical rhabdomyolysis is being diagnosed when there are minor fluctuations in CK activities, which are a normal response to exercise and training. While the measurement of electrolyte concentrations has become used routinely, interpretation of changes is often highly flawed. Electrolyte supplementation and i.v. fluid administration are prescribed to treat nonexistent problems; and the diagnosis of potassium deficiency is common in some practices, on the basis of minor changes in plasma or serum concentrations. This approach is inappropriate[8].

The era of science and performance, commencing with the blood count, moved into the 'black box' era with Jim Steel's development of the heart score[9]. The heart score was an attempt by Steel to relate a simple measurement, that is the assessment of heart size, with racing performance. The simplicity of the heart score concept and ready understanding by racehorse trainers, meant that it became extensively used, although always the subject of controversy. Moreover, the technique had the tremendous appeal of theatre in the racing stable, with wires being connected from the horse to an electrocardiograph machine, followed by paper rolling out with amazing squiggles, seemingly uninterpretable to anyone except the veterinarian. While never popularised in the USA, measurement of the heart

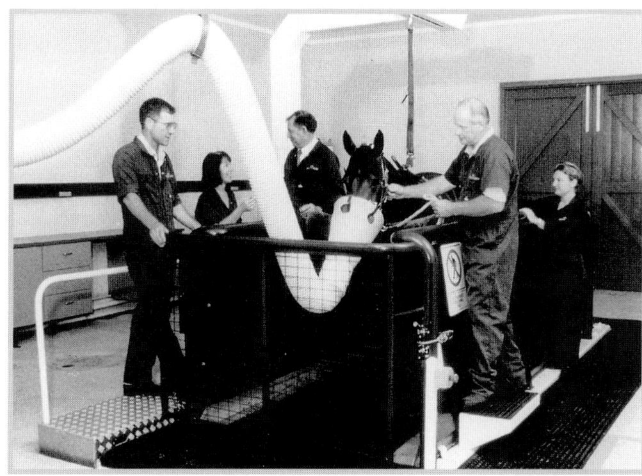

Fig 1: Treadmill at the University of Sydney in 1985, showing respiratory gas collection mask with valves. These types of machines, which allowed horses to be trotted and cantered on a fixed incline, were used on a number of horse studfarms and training establishments.

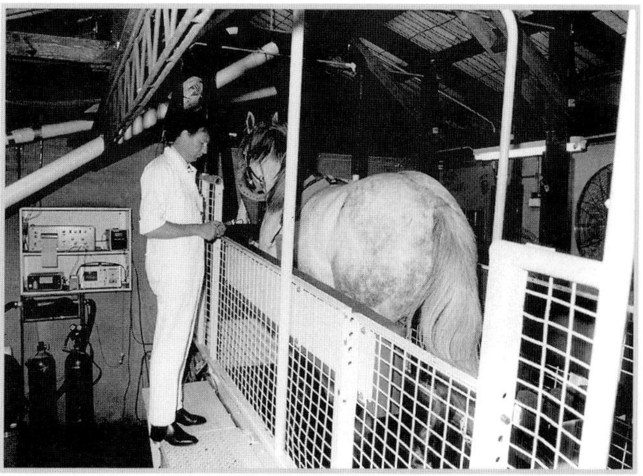

Fig 2: The Beltalong equine treadmill shown in 1989 at the University of Sydney. This machine was developed specifically to allow Thoroughbred horses to be galloped at intensities approaching maximal.

score became widely practised in Australia, New Zealand, South Africa and, to a lesser extent, the UK.

Unfortunately there is still a tendency to adopt new practices for performance prediction that are not predicated on a sound interpretation of research results. Cardiac ultrasonography of yearling horses for determination of future performance potential is an example. There are no published data to support prediction of performance on the basis of cardiac ultrasound in an untrained horse age 12–15 months. In the large prospective study[10] of Thoroughbred yearlings in Ireland, performance as two- and three-year-olds was not correlated with cardiac ultrasound measurements. It is our responsibility to promote new knowledge to horse owners and trainers, using available evidence. It is also important that practitioners and researchers maintain a 'high index of suspicion' until new research findings have been confirmed.

A major conference in 1974 convened by Maurice Azzie and held at the Kruger National Park in South Africa, first brought together the major players in equine exercise physiology. It was here that there were some heated debates involving a number of the delegates and the international nature of the discussions could be seen from the involvement of Richard Archer from the Animal Health Trust in England, Jerry Gillespie of the University of California, Davis, Jim Steel of the University of Melbourne and Sune Persson of the Royal Veterinary College in Stockholm. Steel's work on heart score was regarded as witchcraft by some scientists at the conference, although many practitioners supported the value of the technique. The conference clearly provided a boost to the study of equine exercise physiology and the proceedings of this conference, published in the Journal of the South African Veterinary Association, in 1975, are still cited frequently.

There is no doubt that the blood count and heart score have become widely discredited as some of their proponents have sought to extend interpretation far beyond the boundaries of scientific data. Nonetheless, it is instructive to investigate the reasons behind why these were used, as we attempt in this article to look forward and ask the question: does equine exercise physiology have any useful role in the practice environment, now or in the future, or is it an area of study only for equine exercise physiologists?

The Treadmill Era

Sophisticated human exercise physiology studies accelerated in Scandinavia during the 1950s and it is interesting that many of the early advances in the horse came about from adapting techniques developed in Sweden for human exercise studies, such as muscle biopsy. Interestingly, some of the most important investigators had personal involvement in competitive exercise and the eminent Swedish exercise physiologist, Bengt Saltin, became involved in equine studies because of his orienteering friend Arne Lindholm. Saltin had sought to examine a range of factors associated with elite performance and adaptations to training in human athletes. Arne Lindholm also had identified the importance of muscle and muscle disorders and published the first information on equine muscle fibre types. Working in Saltin's laboratory, Arne undertook what were then extremely sophisticated studies of muscle physiology and physiological responses to exercise in the Swedish Trotter [11–14] on the racetrack and also the treadmill.

The first scientific studies in the horse using a treadmill were those of Sune Persson. Persson's seminal work *On Blood Volume and Working Capacity in Horses* was published in 1963. These studies aroused considerable interest, particularly as he showed a correlation between performance in Swedish trotters and the total haemoglobin concentration. He used Evans blue dye to measure the plasma volume, following mobilisation of the splenic erythrocyte pool by exercise or adminstration of adrenaline. This study was the first to utilise a specially designed equine treadmill to permit samples to be collected during exercise. This treadmill was later used by Bergsten[15] to study cardiovascular function. While this early treadmill was a great breakthrough, the exercise intensity achieved was, however, submaximal and the most important studies undertaken by Persson and Lindholm were performed on the training track or racetrack.

Undoubtedly, the treadmill has been responsible for the upsurge in knowledge about the horse's response to exercise and training. The commercial availability of equine treadmills in the 1980s (Figs 1–3) led to an upsurge in the scientific investigations into cardiorespiratory and muscular responses to exercise. Much of this interest followed the First

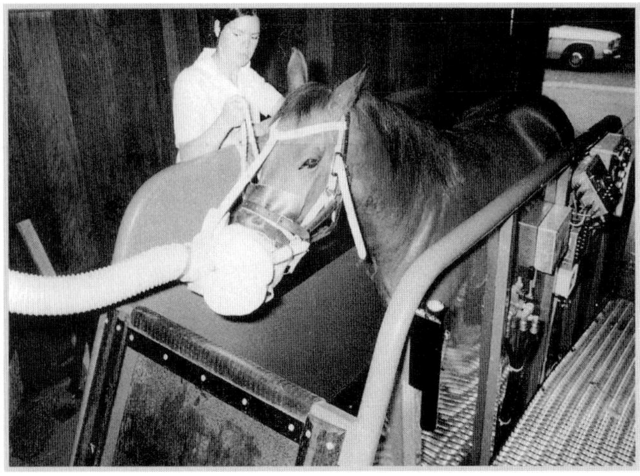

Fig 3: A Mustang treadmill at the University of Sydney Equine Performance Laboratory, Camden, in 1998. This machine is manufactured in Switzerland and our experience is that horses adjust readily to exercise on this treadmill, which is more open in its design.

Fig 4: A French Standardbred trotter having a blood sample collected for determination of blood lactate concentration in a field-based exercise test. A heart rate meter and tachometer with a digital display on the sulky permits the driver to complete a standardised exercise test.

International Conference on Equine Exercise Physiology, held in Oxford, UK, in 1982 and organised by David Snow. A number of key papers were presented by the Swedish research group based at the veterinary school by now relocated from Stockholm to the Swedish University of Agricultural Sciences at Uppsala. Most of the studies were undertaken using an inclined treadmill, with Swedish trotters that exercised at intensities approaching maximal. The sophistication of these studies, compared to other more descriptive studies where blood samples were collected before and after exercise, provided great impetus for research workers to acquire equine treadmills and perform more complex physiological studies in horses exercising at maximal intensities.

This increase in sophistication was apparent in the papers presented at the next major international scientific gathering, in 1986 at the Second International Conference on Equine Exercise Physiology, in San Diego, USA, where a number of research groups reported treadmill-based studies. Importantly, the first descriptions of the measurement of maximal oxygen uptake ($\dot{V}O_{2max}$) and changes with training were described[16,17] and this measurement, widely used in human exercise physiology, subsequently became accepted as a key index of exercise capacity and response to training.

Treadmill-based studies proliferated with research groups around the world embracing treadmill technology and a special supplement (Supplement 9) of *Equine Veterinary Journal*, in 1990, focused on a number of important conceptual physiological advances that were the result of the use of the high speed treadmill. The Third International Conference on Equine Exercise Physiology, held in Uppsala, Sweden, indicated how reliant we had become on treadmills to study exercise in the horse. However, despite the increased sophistication of the studies, most of the papers were descriptive and it was becoming clear that there was a large gulf between what the scientists were studying and what the equine practitioners were expecting. One of the difficulties was the effect *per se* of exposure to the treadmill. This was an important concept that became evident at the Fourth International Conference on Equine Exercise Physiology held in Australia in 1994, and the proceedings of which were published as a special Supplement (Supplement 18) to the *Equine Veterinary Journal*, in 1995.

It was recognised that a range of submaximal indices were altered when horses first became exposed to treadmill exercise[18]. In addition, submaximal measurements of changes in fitness and exercise capacity could be altered by the state of excitement in the horse and also were likely to be altered by horses' repeated exposure to treadmill exercise, which we believe explains some of the unusual findings reported by Harkins and Kamerling[19]. We have observed that some horses have a tendency to increase the energy output during treadmill tests by pushing on the front bar or strap of the treadmill. This behaviour can affect the V_{200} (speed at a heart rate of 200 beats per min) and V_{LA4} (speed at a blood or plasma lactate concentration of 4 mmol/l), both of which are commonly used submaximal indices to measure fitness.

The recognition of the limits of the treadmill, which nonetheless remains an important tool for future studies, is important for progress to be made in equine exercise physiology. There are a very limited number of well-equipped treadmill laboratories around the world, with almost all being located in academic institutions. Treadmills will, in the main, remain the province of academic institutes, where there is the desire to study more basic physiological mechanisms relating to limitations to exercise and performance. Such studies are important, but from a practical viewpoint, it is unlikely that treadmills will become widely used in the practical horse-training environment. The question could be asked, therefore: *have we learnt anything at all that is relevant to the veterinary practitioner from all the exercise physiology studies performed to date?*

What Have We Learnt to Date from the Studies of Equine Exercise Physiology?

We believe that there have been major advances in our knowledge and understanding of how the horse responds to exercise and training, although there is considerable further work needed to move the discipline into the routine field of clinical practice. The most important finding from the hundreds of papers that have been published to date is that there is no 'magic bullet' measurement that can forecast athletic ability or provide an insight into poor performance. Some understanding of the complexity and interrelationship of the major body systems has been gained in studies conducted in a number of horse breeds and athletic uses. Such basic studies are important in providing the groundwork for addressing specific problems and we will highlight some major areas of achievement in exercise physiology studies conducted over the last 25 years.

Endurance Exercise

In the 1960s and 1970s, there was an upsurge in interest in endurance riding, which commenced with riders being interested in trail rides in the USA in various national parks. This became increasingly structured and the Tevis Cup rides of 160 km held in California, became a model for the Tom Quilty endurance ride which commenced in the 1960s in Australia and later endurance events which became popular in Europe and the United Arab Emirates. In the early days of endurance riding, there were substantial numbers of horse deaths associated with prolonged exercise. Investigations into the physiology and biochemistry of endurance exercise provided insight and understanding of the metabolic changes that could lead to serious physiological disturbances[20–22]. The substantial fluid and electrolyte losses that could be incurred during endurance riding were recognised and veterinary clinicians were alerted to the importance of fluid and electrolyte therapy in treating exhausted endurance horses.

The establishment of a relationship between heart rate 30 minutes after exercise and the metabolic derangements that occurred during exercise[21], also provided an important practical tool for evaluation of the 'stressed' endurance horse. The assessment of the heart rate recovery following exercise has become widely used by riders in the training of endurance horses as well as by veterinarians in the assessment of a horse's 'fitness' to continue in an endurance ride.

Metabolic studies, using the technique of muscle biopsy, enabled determination of glycogen utilisation rates and it was demonstrated that slow twitch muscle fibres and the more aerobic fast twitch fibres were recruited preferentially during endurance exercise[23,24]. Muscle glycogen supply is a limiting factor to endurance performance but it is likely that fluid and electrolyte disturbances are more important in restricting exercise capacity.

The recognition of the importance of nonesterified fatty acids as a major energy source during endurance exercise lead to interest in dietary fat supplementation to improve endurance capacity and limit fatigue by sparing glycogen. Some early studies indicated that a fat-supplemented diet resulted in high skeletal muscle glycogen concentrations but there is now some doubt about these results[25–27]. It does seem, however, that a fat-supplemented diet may spare glucose and glycogen use during exercise at low intensity, and promote glycolysis when power is needed for high intensity exercise[26]. A fat-supplemented diet also is useful in horses with equine polysaccharide storage myopathy[28]. There has been recent popularity of strategies that increase muscle glycogen concentration prior to short distance horse racing. It is important to note, however, that this approach may have little value as skeletal muscle glycogen concentration appears unlikely to be a limiting factor for performance in short distance intense exercise[29].

A number of studies have shown the importance of prolonged training in enhancing the metabolic capacity of skeletal muscle[30] and long-term training also increases the resting muscle glycogen concentration[31]. More recent studies have demonstrated that training has the potential to minimise fluid loss[32], improves exercise tolerance and changes the threshold for sweating.

Better understanding of the impact of fluid and electrolyte losses on the tolerance for endurance exercise has led to effective methods for the treatment of exhausted endurance horses and also has resulted in implementation of preventative strategies. The use of oral electrolyte pastes to prevent and treat dehydration has been used by riders before, during and after endurance rides[33] and experimental studies in dehydrated horses have shown the effectiveness of this strategy, when water is available[34]. It also has been noted that successful endurance horses do not lose as much fluid as their less successful competitors[35].

Investigations of Poor Performance

The finding by Bayly and co-workers[36] that many normal horses had profound arterial hypoxaemia during intense exercise stimulated a large number of subsequent studies and a recognition that the lung may well be a major limitation to performance. Wagner and colleagues[37] using the multiple inert gas technique, demonstrated that the most likely cause for the arterial hypoxaemia during exercise is the rapid pulmonary capillary transit time. However, not all horses become hypoxaemic during intense exercise[38] and there is greater degree of hypoxaemia after training[39], suggesting that increases in $\dot{V}O_{2max}$ result in a greater mismatch between alveolar ventilation and pulmonary capillary blood flow. Because there may be a direct relationship between the extent of arterial hyoxaemia and $\dot{V}O_{2max}$, it may be that the fittest horses are at greatest risk of limitation to performance via respiratory disease – whether from the upper or lower respiratory tracts.

A range of investigations into the 'poor performance syndrome' have been undertaken[40–43], utilising resting and treadmill-based exercise studies. These studies have shown that poor performance is often multifactorial and that horses frequently have more than one problem. The detailed studies performed at rest and on the treadmill, have shown that poor racing performance is a complex phenomenon but that the musculoskeletal and respiratory systems frequently are involved as the major causes of performance limitations[43].

One of the major areas of interest for equine exercise physiologists and clinicians is exercise-induced pulmonary haemorrhage (EIPH). Much has been learnt over the last two decades but the question that still needs addressing, given the 100% incidence in racehorses, is: is it really a disease? Some trainers note that it is 'always the good ones' that show postexercise epistaxis. If this is true, we wonder whether running faster or higher cardiac outputs and associated high pulmonary vascular pressure, is the mechanism for the problem. We now know that stress failure of the pulmonary capillaries occurs at pulmonary capillary pressures of 75–100 mmHg. These high pressures are to be expected in the pulmonary vasculature in strenuously exercising horses[44]. Interestingly, swimming also results in high pulmonary artery pressures and many trainers have noted that horses that do not 'bleed' on the track may 'bleed' when swum. Further studies of vascular responses to swimming exercise are warranted, given the popularity of this form of exercise training. Such studies also would assist in testing the novel hypothesis of Schroter and colleagues[45] suggesting an important role of transmitted limb impact forces to the thoracic cavity as a cause of EIPH.

The Atlanta Olympic Games

Following the awarding of the 1996 Summer Olympic Games to Atlanta, there was considerable public concern related to the expected weather conditions and the effects these might have on equine athletes at the games. Based on this, a major international research programme was initiated, the primary aim of which was to determine appropriate strategies for the welfare of horses competing in hot, humid conditions. This research effort was coordinated by Leo Jeffcott, a distinguished equine researcher, FEI delegate and Olympic veterinarian.

Horses competing in the speed and endurance phase of the three-day event were considered to be at greatest risk of heat-related illness, as not only is this test physically demanding; there are four phases – submaximal endurance exercise, steeplechase and jumping over a challenging cross-country course. The expected weather at the Games was for high ambient temperatures (31–36°C) with the relative humidity approaching 100%. In addition, horses would be exposed to high levels of ultraviolet radiation. Thus, the aim of the scientific studies was to determine, using scientific methods, the most appropriate modifications of the speed and endurance event, thereby ensuring the welfare of the horses, yet maintaining a world-class competition.

As discussed earlier, investigations into the thermoregulatory responses of the horse had focused primarily on fluid and electrolyte losses during endurance exercise and the sweating mechanism[46]. In addition, the horse was shown to have a large body mass to skin surface ratio[47], thereby potentially limiting the efficacy of thermoregulation during hot, humid conditions. Hyperthermia during exercise, when extreme, has been shown to have injurious effects on a number of body systems, particularly the central nervous system. To help counteract this, horses have been shown to possess the capacity for selective brain cooling, whereby vital parts of the central nervous system (for example the hypothalamus) are bathed by cool venous blood draining from the face and upper airways[48]. This results in parts of the central nervous system being more than 1°C cooler than the body core during intense exercise in the heat.

Initial studies into the effects of the speed and endurance test of the three-day event provided insights into the metabolic cost of this type of exercise. Elite event horses cover more than 20 km during the test and undergo periods exercise eliciting near maximum heart rates (>220 beats per min) and therefore near $\dot{V}O_{2max}$[49], with horses often having plasma lactate concentrations greater than 20 mmol/l and the conclusion of the test. Carlson and Jones[50] developed a model whereby the energy cost and heat production during this form of exercise could be estimated and indicated that the risk of heat stress in horses would be high if the thermoregulatory mechanisms were inadequate to cope with this large metabolic heat load. Further to this, Kohn and Hinchliff[51] demonstrated that horses competing in the speed and endurance phase of a three-day event achieved higher body temperatures than those competing in cool conditions. In addition, these workers showed that horses undertaking a standardised exercise test on a treadmill in the laboratory under hot, humid conditions had a more rapid rise in core temperature and fatigued more quickly than when performing the same intensity of exercise in cool conditions.

Given that many of the horses coming to Atlanta would be flown in from areas of temperate climate, several groups undertook studies investigating the effects of acclimation to heat and humidity. Geor and co-workers[53] found that as little as five days exposure to heat and humidity (4 hours per day) resulted in a lower core temperature and reduced fluid losses in response to a standardised exercise test. These findings were supported by the studies conducted at the Animal Health Trust[49] where it was shown that horses underwent considerable physiological adaptation in terms of heat tolerance in response to daily exposure for 21 days to conditions of high ambient temperature and humidity.

Based on these studies, scientists, riders, officials and organisers of the equestrian events for the Games were consulted regarding the need to modify the speed and endurance phase of the event to reduce the risk of heat stress. Several groups investigated the different modifications of the test[53–58]. The net result of these studies was a recommendation that the overall metabolic demand of the event should be reduced by ~25% and that the number of mandatory rest periods be increased and extended. In addition, methods designed to cool horses actively were investigated. This involved aggressive bathing with cold water during these rest periods[58–60] and use of misting fans at the rest sites[61]. Furthermore, Schoter and colleagues[62] undertook studies at the Olympic site in the summer of 1995. Using the Wet Bulb Globe Temperature index these investigators showed that environmental heat gain would be minimised if horses exercised early in the morning.

In summary, the well-coordinated and executed studies undertaken prior to the Atlanta Olympic Games resulted in the three-day event competition being substantially modified, yet remaining a true test of horse and rider as is the Olympic tradition. These modifications proved highly successful with no horses suffering heat-related illness in association with the three-day event competition.

What is the Future for Equine Exercise Physiology?

Articles published in EVJ must demonstrate clinical relevance. However, it is likely that many practitioners have difficulty applying or even imagining application of the result of many studies in equine exercise science. These studies generally embrace areas such as physiological and metabolic responses to exercise and training, nutrition, exercise, and biomechanics. These topics reflect the range of investigations presented at the past International Conferences of Equine Exercise Physiology. We suspect that these conferences have been of little interest and relevance to many equine practitioners, and that practitioners might have difficulty identifying aspects of their day-to-day activities that have been influenced by results of research in equine exercise physiology. However, some specialist veterinarians have embraced the opportunities offered to develop new services for horse owners and trainers, and these services are now also offered by nonveterinarians. It is possible that veterinarians may be left behind by alternative service providers?

We believe that owners and trainers will continue to seek information concerning performance prediction and, unfortunately there is very little evidence that any single measurement can accurately predict future performance. As well, more information concerning design of training programmes that reduce the incidence of lameness and fatigue are needed. Improved methods of identifying the stressed horse also are desirable, as are markers of the onset of distress, as found in overtraining. Improved techniques for evaluating horses with poor performance are also a priority. Valuable advances have been made in our understanding of respiratory limits to performance in horses, and new methods for simple, accurate and reliable measurement of pulmonary ventilation during field exercise are needed. Such new techniques would facilitate studies of the effects of airway inflammatory disease on performance, and assist with investigations of treatment and management of the disease. Methods for recognition of subtle lameness are also desirable, and field studies using accelerometers on limbs of exercising horses have potential in this area[63].

Unfortunately, the reliance on treadmills for most equine exercise research has probably contributed to poor rates of technology transfer to equine veterinarians and horse owners. There are few established equine performance laboratories in the world, and many are located remote from racing populations. Establishment of more treadmill laboratories near large populations of racing horses could assist with greater adoption and application of research findings. Cooperation between equine veterinarians and academic researchers would greatly assist development of facilities that provided a service to owners of normal horses in commercial training environments.

Development of new techniques for exercise studies of horses that did not depend on treadmills would also be a major advance. There has been little study of field-based exercise tests, largely because the research protocol is difficult to control, and is subject to influences such as track conditions, skill of jockeys or drivers, and attitudes of horse owners and trainers. However, more field studies should be conducted to develop 'user friendly' exercise tests[64,65]. Field tests (Fig 4) are more likely to be adopted by the industries, and the results may have more relevance than results of studies in abnormal horses, often with a history of poor performance, that have been studied on treadmills. New partnerships between equine exercise scientists and biomedical engineers could also generate new technologies for field studies. For example, field studies of breath-by-breath respiratory gas flows and field ergometry should be possible, building on the innovative studies performed in Germany by Hörnick and colleagues[66]. The techniques for field ergometry have been developed for human athletes, and should be refined for use in horses. The challenge of reliably and accurately measuring respiratory flow rates of over 100 litres per second in a horse galloping or pacing in the field at racing speeds has yet to be conquered.

Field ergometry, coupled with measurements of respiratory function and metabolic responses to exercise, would enable new fundamental studies in many areas of equine exercise physiology. Descriptions of the metabolic and energetic demands of different athletic events would be possible, and design of appropriate training programmes would be facilitated. As well, clinical exercise testing would be more likely to be adopted by trainers and owners. Such 'high tech' clinical exercise tests would contribute to greater knowledge concerning limits to performance in different events (such as anaerobic or aerobic capacity, and maximal rates of oxygen uptake), so building on findings by Harkins and colleagues[67]. Such studies could also help with identification of respiratory limits to performance, with measurements of peak respiratory gas flow rates, and generation of flow volume loops during maximal exercise.

A major difficulty with field studies has been control of the exercise performed by the horse. Ideal standardised tests necessitate control of exercise speeds, duration of exercise, and rates of acceleration. Use of stepwise exercise tests has been usual in treadmill studies, with an increment in speeds used. Such tests enable descriptions of the relationships between speed and variables such as heart rate, blood lactate concentration, and oxygen consumption, to name just a few. Field exercise tests of this sort are not practical, and alternative designs may be needed. Alternatives might include measurement of the responses to a single or pair of exercise bouts. Such field tests need to be designed so that the normal training routines are minimally disrupted. Trainer compliance is unlikely to be high if protocols involve time-consuming and inconvenient disruptions to busy schedules in commercial training establishments.

Many questions in applied equine exercise may be amenable to epidemiological studies. Diseases such as shin soreness ('bucked shins'), tying up, joint disease and tendon strain are common in horses, but there have been few studies of the risk factors for these or other common industry problems. New partnerships between exercise scientists and epidemiologists may contribute to knowledge by studying the horse, management and environmental factors in a disease. Further studies of risk factors for disease could also assist the racing industries by identifying the environmental factors that are associated with lower rates of disease. For example, a study of risk factors for tendon injuries could identify horse training or track management factors that predispose to the disease. Technology transfer could then focus on aspects of horse training or environment that could be better managed to reduce the risk of disease. Such studies would build on recent contributions in this area[68–71].

Prediction of performance is an issue in equine exercise that is of abiding interest to horse owners and trainers, and the topic is always certain to generate an animated conversation. Large scale cross-sectional and prospective studies are required to investigate satisfactorily the use of measurements in young horses as predictors of performance. Cross-sectional studies in large numbers of horses also are required to correlate racing performance with relevant variables. This begs two issues; which dependent variables should be measured, and how is performance measured? The answers will depend on the nature of the event, but our understanding of the metabolic demands of a 1200 m and 2400 m gallop, trot or pace at racing speeds is rudimentary. Is it appropriate to measure $\dot{V}O_{2max}$ as a predictor of performance in a 1200 m race for two-year-old Thoroughbreds? Is there likely to be anything superior to the information derived from skilful use of a stopwatch for prediction of performance of a Quarter Horse?

It is unlikely that any one correlate of future performance will be of much interest or use to industry participants unless it has at least a moderate association with performance, with a coefficient of determination (r^2) of 0.5 or more. Blood lactate responses to standardised treadmill exercise tests have demonstrated coefficients of determination with Thoroughbred racing performance in the United Kingdom of approximately 0.45–0.5[72]. These results suggest that approximately 50% of the variability of racing performance can be accounted for by the variability in the blood lactate response to a submaximal exercise test. Assessment of the current fitness of a horse for racing performance should include measurement of the lactate response to exercise, and comparison of the results to the appropriate reference population. Maximum oxygen consumption is also higher in superior Standardbred racehorses[73]. However, accurate performance prediction is unlikely ever to be based on any one single variable, and a multifactorial approach to the issue should be used.

How will applied equine science be used in the future? Consider a hypothetical scenario that ignores the fashions of breeding and the selection of yearlings on 'blood lines'. An owner/breeder adopts a set of performance criteria applicable for selection of mares and youngsters for racing. The owner is confident that this performance-based approach will work because results of several studies have shown high correlations between racing performance and a set of dependent variables. A close association has also been demonstrated between profiles in results in six-month-old horses and in trained two-year-olds. The studfarm breeds 200 yearlings with the best sires and mares available. The mares have been selected on the basis of racing performance only. There are no mares on the stud that have not won three races. At age six months, all yearlings have been acclimated to treadmill exercise for 4–6 weeks, and can canter happily at 6–8 m/s on a treadmill inclined at 10%. Heart rate, blood lactate and oxygen consumption are measured during standardised exercise tests. Maximal oxygen consumption is measured for each horse, and a performance profile based on a set of measured variables is calculated. The profile might also include measurements of biomechanics, body shape, and results of observations of behaviour of the youngsters in the paddock. Weanlings with a performance profile in the bottom 75% are then discarded. The owner concedes that no set of measurements will be perfect, but is happy to have a small group of horses with elite physiological characteristics. The alternative is to retain a much larger number of horses at high maintenance costs.

Is this hypothetical scenario too fanciful? Educated horse owners and breeders are already considering a future that has performance criteria as the basis for the breeding and racing facets of their commercial operations. In such an industry, fashion would have no place on the equine studfarm or in the racing stable, just as it now has no place in chicken, dairy or pig farms. Criteria for selection of mares and tests for profiling of young horses would be developed and continually modified over time. Geneticists might also contribute by describing the genetic basis of performance. Such studies are already under way in human athletes.

The drive for advances in applied equine exercise physiology must not, however, be at the expense of 'pure' research into the mechanisms of responses and adaptations. Results of such research may not have immediate practical implications, but the science of equine exercise physiology will be the poorer if advances are not made in many fundamental areas. Important recent findings by Pelletier and colleagues[74], Macleay and colleagues[75] and Alexander and colleagues[76,77] have helped answer several fundamental questions. These studies have addressed questions related to regulation of regional blood flow in the lung during exercise, mechanisms of rhabdomyolysis, including the genetic basis of different forms of 'tying up', and mechanisms of equine neuroendocrine responses to the stress and overstress of exercise and overtraining.

Research in equine exercise has created new knowledge; and myths have been exposed. The future will present an exciting array of advances in basic and applied equine exercise physiology. Technological advances should also provide researchers with opportunities for on-board logging of large amounts of data in field studies of equine exercise. We hope that there will be more studies of large populations of normal horses in commercial environments, and that epidemiologists and biomedical engineers will be increasingly invited to collaborate in the efforts to solve industry problems and improve the health and welfare of equine athletes. Greater rates of technology transfer to industry participants are likely, if researchers increase their use of normal horses in commercial training; and if technical developments free researchers from the constraints and limitations of treadmill studies.

References

[1]Zuntz, N. and Hagemann, O. (1898) Untersuchungen uber den Stoffwechsel des Pferdes bei Ruhe und Arbeit. *Landwirtschaftl Jb.* **27** (Suppl. III) p 1-438 (Cited by Thornton *et al* 1987).

[2]Procter, R.C., Brody, S., Jones, M.M. and Crittenden, D.W. (1934) Growth and development. XXXIII. Efficiency of work in horses of different ages and weights. *Univ. Missouri Agr. Exp. Stat. Res. Bull.* **209**, 1-32.

[3]Irvine, C.H.G. (1958) The blood picture in the racehorse. 1. The normal erythrocyte and hemoglobin status: a dynamic concept. *J. Am. vet. med. Ass.* **133**, 97-101.

[4]Steel, J.D. and Whitlock, L.E. (1960) Observations on the haematology of thoroughbred and standardbred horses in training and racing. *Aust. vet. J.* **36**,136-142.

[5]Sykes, P.E. (1966) Hematology as an aid in equine practice. *Proc. Am. Ass. equine Practnrs.* **12**,159-167

[6]Archer, R.K. (1975) Hematology in relation to performance and potential: a general review. *J. S. Afr. vet. Ass.* **45**, 273-277.

[7]Revington, M. (1983) Haematology of the racing Thoroughbred in Australia. I. Reference values and the effect of excitement. II. Haematological values compared to performance. *Equine vet. J.* **152**,141-144

[8]Johnson, P.J., Goetz, T.E. and Foreman, J.H. (1991) Effect of whole-body potassium depletion on plasma, erythrocyte, and middle gluteal muscle potassium concentration of healthy, adult horses. *Am. J vet. Res.* **52**,1676-1683.

[9]Steel, J.D. (1963) *Studies on the Electrocardiogram of the Racehorse*, Australasian Medical Publishing Company, Sydney.

[10]Leadon, D., McAllister, H., Mullins, E. and Osborne, M. (1991) Electrocardiographic and echocardiographic measurements and their relationships in Thoroughbred yearlings to subsequent performance. In: *Equine Exercise Physiology 3*. Eds: S.G.B. Persson, A. Lindholm and L.B. Jeffcott, ICEEP Publications, Davis, California. pp 22-29

[11]Lindholm, A. (1973) *Muscle Morphology and Metabolism in Standardbred horses at Rest and during Exercise.* PhD thesis, Royal Veterinary College, Stockholm.

[12]Lindholm, A. and Saltin, B. (1974) The physiological and biochemical response of standardbred horses to exercise of varying speed and

duration. *Acta vet. Scand.* **15**, 310-324.

[13]Lindholm, A., Bjerneld, H. and Saltin, B. (1974) Glycogen depletion patterns in muscle fibres of trotting horses. *Acta Physiol. Scand.* **90**, 475-484.

[14]Lindholm, A. and Piehl, K. (1974) Fibre composition, enzyme activity and concentrations of metabolites and electrolytes in muscles of standardbred horses. *Acta vet. Scand.* **15**, 287-309

[15]Bergsten, G. (1974) Blood pressure, cardiac output and blood gas tensions in the horse at rest and during exercise. *Acta vet. Scand. Suppl.* **48**.

[16]Rose, R.J. and Evans, D.L. (1987) Cardiovascular and respiratory function in the athletic horse. In: *Equine Exercise Physiology 2*, Eds: J.R. Gillespie and N.E. Robinson, ICEEP Publications, Davis, California. pp 1-24.

[17]Evans, D.L. and Rose, R.J. (1987) Maximum oxygen uptake in racehorses: changes with training state and prediction from submaximal cardiorespiratory measurements. In: *Equine Exercise Physiology 2*, Eds: J.R. Gillespie and N.E. Robinson, ICEEP Publications, Davis, California. pp 52-67.

[18]King, C.M., Evans, D.L. and Rose, R.J. (1995) Acclimation to treadmill exercise. Indices of exercise capacity in horses presented for poor racing performance. *Equine vet. J., Suppl* **18**, 453-456.

[19]Harkins, J.D. and Kamerling, S.G. (1991) Assessment of treadmill interval training on fitness. *J. equine vet. Sci.* **11**, 237-242.

[20]Carlson, G.O., Ocen, P.O and Harrold, D. (1976) Clinicopathologic alterations in normal and exhausted endurance horses. *Theriogenology* **6**, 93-104.

[21]Rose, R.J., Purdue, R.A. and Hensley, W. (1977) Plasma biochemical alterations in horses during an endurance ride. *Equine vet. J.* **9**, 122-126.

[22]Lucke, J.N and Hall, G.N. (1978) Biochemical changes in horses during a 50 mile endurance ride. *Vet. Rec.* **102**, 356-358.

[23]Snow, D.H., Baxter, P. and Rose, R.J. (1981) Muscle fibre composition and glycogen depletion in horses competing in an endurance ride. *Vet. Rec.* **108**, 374-378.

[24]Hodgson, D.R., Rose, R.J. and Allen, J.R. (1983) Muscle glycogen depletion and repletion patterns in horses performing various distances of endurance exercise, In: *Equine Exercise Physiology*, Eds: D.H. Snow, S.G.B. Persson and R.J. Rose, Granta Editions, Cambridge. pp 237-244.

[25]Orme, C.E., Harris, R.C., Marlin, D.J. and Hurley, J. (1997) Metabolic adaptation to a fat-supplemented diet by the thoroughbred horse. *Br. J. Nutrition* **78**, 443-458.

[26]Kronfeld, D.S., Custalow, S.E., Ferrante, P.L., Taylor, L.E., Wilson, J.A. and Tiegs, W. (1998) Acid-base responses of fat-adapted horses - relevance to hard work in the heat. *Appl. anim. behav. Sci.* **59**, 61-72.

[27]Eaton, M.D., Hodgson, D.R., Evans, D.L., Bryden, W.L. and Rose, R.J. (1995) Effect of diet containing supplementary fat on the capacity for high intensity exercise. *Equine vet. J., Suppl.* **18**, 353-356.

[28]Valentine, B.A., Reynolds, A.J., Ducharme, N.G., Hackett, R.P., Hintz, H.F., Petrone, K.S., Carlson, M.D., Barnes, B. and Mountain, P.C. (1997) Dietary therapy of equine polysaccharide storage myopathy *Equine Pract.* **19**, 30-37.

[29]Davie, A.J., Evans, D.L., Hodgson, D.R. and Rose, R.J. (1996) Effects of glycogen depletion on high intensity exercise performance and glycogen utilisation rates. *Pferdeheilkunde* **12**, 482-484.

[30]Hodgson, D.R., Rose, R.J., Allen, J.R. and Di Mauro, J. (1986) Changes in skeletal muscle composition in response to training. *Am. J. vet. Res.* **47**, 12-15.

[31]Tyler, C.M., Golland, L.C., Evans, D.L., Hodgson, D.R. and Rose, R.J. (1998) Skeletal muscle adaptations to prolonged training overtraining and detraining in horses. *Eur. J. Physiol.* **436**, 391-397.

[32]Marlin, D.J., Scott, C.M., Schroter, R.C., Harris, R.C., Harris, P.A., Roberts, C.A. and Mills, P.C. (1999) Physiological responses of horses to a treadmill simulated speed and endurance test in high heat and humidity before and after humid heat acclimation *Equine vet. J.* **31**, 31-42.

[33]Schott, H.C. and Hinchcliff, K.W. (1998) Treatments affecting fluid and electrolyte status during exercise. *Vet. Clin. N. Am.: Equine Pract.* **14**, 175-185.

[34]Sosa Leon, L.A., Hodgson, D.R., Carlson, G.P. and Rose, R.J. (1998) Effects of concentrated electrolytes administered via a paste on fluid, electrolyte and acid base balance in horses. *Am. J. vet. Res.* **59**, 898-902.

[35]Schott, H.C., McGlade, K.S., Molander, H.A. , Leroux, A.J. and Hindes, M.T. (1997) Body weight, fluid, electrolyte and hormonal changes in horses competing in 50 and 100 mile endurance rides. *Am. J. vet. Res.* **58**, 303-309.

[36]Bayly, W.M., Grant, B.D., Breeze, R.G. and Kramer, J.W. (1983) The effects of maximal exercise on acid-base balance and blood-gas tension in Thoroughbred horses. In: *Equine Exercise Physiology*, Eds: D.H. Snow, S.G.B. Persson and R.J. Rose, Granta, Cambridge. pp 400-407.

[37]Wagner, P.D., Gillespie, J.R., Landgren, G.L., Fedde, M.R., Jones, B.W., DeBowes, R.M., Piesche, R.L. and Erickson, H.H. (1989) Mechanism of exercise-induced hypoxemia in horses. *J. appl. Physiol.* **66**, 1227-1233.

[38]Evans, D.L., Silverman, E., Rose, R.J. and Hodgson, D.R. (1994) Gait and respiration in Standardbred horses when pacing and galloping. *Res. vet. Sci*, **57**, 233-239.

[39]Christley, R.M., Hodgson, D.R., Evans, D.L., and Rose, R.J. (1997) Effects of training on the development of exercise-induced arterial hypoxaemia in horses. *Am. J. vet. Res.* **58**, 653-657.

[40]Persson, S.G.B. and Ullberg, L.E. (1974) Blood volume in relation to exercise tolerance in trotters. *J. S. Afr. vet. Ass.* **45,** 293-299.

[41]Rose, R.J., Hendrickson, D.K. and Knight, P.K. (1990) Clinical exercise testing in the normal Thoroughbred racehorse. *Aust. vet. J.* **67**, 345-348.

[42]Morris, E.A. and Seeherman, H.J. (1991) Clinical evaluation of poor performance in the racehorse: the results of 275 evaluations. *Equine vet. J.* **23**, 169-174.

[43]Rose, R.J., King, C.M., Evans, D.L., Tyler, C.M. and Hodgson, D.R. (1995) Indices of exercise capacity in horses presented for poor racing performance. *Equine vet. J., Suppl.* **18**, 418-421.

[44]West, J.B. and Mathieucostello, O.(1994) Stress failure of pulmonary capillaries as a mechanism for exercise induced pulmonary haemorrhage in the horse. *Equine vet. J.* **26,** 441-447.

[45]Schroter, R.C., Marlin, D.J. and Denny, E. (1998) Exercise-induced pulmonary haemorrhage (EIPH) in horses results from locomotory impact induced trauma - a novel, unifying concept. *Equine vet. J.* **30**, 186-189.

[46]Snow, D.H., Kerr, M.G., Nimmo, M.A. and Abbott, E.M. (1982) Alterations in blood, sweat, urine and muscle composition during prolonged exercise in the horse. *Vet. Rec.* **110**, 377-384.

[47]Hodgson, D.R., McCutcheon, L.J., Byrd, S.K., Brown, W.S., Bayly, W.M., Brengelmann, G.L. and Gollnick, P.D. (1993) Dissipation of metabolic heat in the horse during exercise. *J. appl. Physiol.* **74**, 1161-1170.

[48]McConaghy, F.F., Hales, J.R.S., Rose, R.J. and Hodgson, D.R. (1995) Selective brain cooling in the horse during exercise and environmental heat stress. *J. appl. Physiol.* **79**, 1849-1854.

[49]Marlin, D.J., Scott, C.M., Schroter, R.C., Mills, P.C., Harris, R.C., Harris, P.A., Orme, C.E., Roberts, C.A., Marr, C.M., Dyson, S.J. and Barrelet, F. (1996) Physiological responses in nonheat acclimated horses performing treadmill exercise in cool (20°C/40%RH), hot dry (30°C/40%RH) and hot humid (30°C/80%RH). *Equine vet. J., Suppl.* **22**, 70-84.

[50]Carlson G.P. and Jones, J.H. (1995) A mathematical model of energy costs for correlation with field studies. In: *On to Atlanta '96*, Eds: A.F. Clarke and L.B. Jeffcott, The Equine Research Centre, University of Guelph, Guelph. pp 58-61.

[51]Kohn, C.W. and Hinchcliff, K.W. (1995) Physiological responses to the endurance test of a three-day-event during hot and cool weather. *Equine vet. J., Suppl.* **20**, 31-36.

[52]Geor, R.J., McCutcheon, L.J. and Lindinger, M.I. (1996) Adaptations to daily exercise in hot and humid ambient conditions in trained Thoroughbred horses. *Equine vet. J., Suppl.* **22**, 63-68.

[53]Foreman, J.H., Grubb, T.L., Benson, G.J., Frey, L.P., Foglia, R.A. and Griffin, R.L. (1995) Physiological effects of shortening steeplechase in a three-day-event. *Equine vet. J., Suppl.* **20**, 73-77.

[54]Foreman, J.H., Grubb, T.L., Benson, G.J., Frey, L.P., Foglia, R.A. and Griffin, R.L. (1996) Acid-base and electrolyte effects of shortening steeplechase in a three-day-event. *Equine vet. J., Suppl.* **22**, 85-90.

[55]Foreman, J.H. (1998) Equine thermoregulation, three-day-eventing and the Olympic Games. *Atti Accademia Perlortina dei Pericolanti.* **84**, 15-32

[56]Andrews, F.M., White, S.L., Williamson, L.H., Matkuth, P.L., Geiser, D.R., Green, E.M., Ralston, S.L. and Mannsmann, R.A. (1995) Effect of shortening the steeplechase phase (Phase B) of a 3-day-event. *Equine vet. J., Suppl.* **20**, 64-72.

[57]Williamson, L.H., Andrews, F.M., Maykuth, P.L., White, S.L. and Green, E.M. (1996) Biochemical changes in three-day-event horses at the beginning, middle and end of Phase C and after Phase D. *Equine vet. J., Suppl.* **22**, 92-98.

[58]Kohn, C.W., Hinchcliff, K.W., McCutcheon, L.J., Geor, R.J., Foreman,

J.H., Allen, A.K., White, S.L., Matkuth, P.L. and Williamson, L.H. (1995) Physiological responses of horses competing at a modified 1 star 3-day-event. *Equine vet. J., Suppl.* **20**, 97-104.

[59]Kohn, C.W., Hinchcliff, K.W. and McKeever, K.H. (1999) Evaluation of washing with cold water to facilitate heat dissipation in horses exercised in hot, humid conditions. *Am. J. vet. Res.* **60**, 299-305.

[60]Williamson, L.H., White, S.L. L.H., Maykuth, P.L., Andrews, F.M., Sommerdahl, S. and Green, E.M. (1995) Comparison between two postexercise cooling methods. *Equine vet. J., Suppl.* **18**, 337-340.

[61]Bradbury, E. and Allen, A.K. (1994) Equi-mist fan/mist system evaluation. In: *On To Atlanta '96,* Eds: A.F. Clarke and L.B. Jeffcott, Equine Research Centre, University of Guelph, Guelph. pp 75-78.

[62]Schroter, R.C., Marlin, D.J. and Jeffcott, L. (1996) Use of the Wet Bulb Globe Temperature (WBGT) index to quantify environmental heat loads during three-day-event competitions. *Equine vet. J., Suppl.* **22,** 3-6.

[63]Barrey, E. (1999) Methods, applications and limitations of gait analysis in horses. *Vet. J.* **157,** 7-22.

[64]Couroucé, A. (1999) Field exercise testing for assessing fitness in French standardbred trotters. *Vet. J.* **157**, 112-122.

[65]Vonwittke, P., Lindner, A., Deegen, E. and Sommer H.(1994) Effects of training on blood lactate running speed relationship in Thoroughbred racehorses. *J. appl. Physiol.* **77**, 8-302.

[66]Hornicke, H., Meixner, R. and Pollman, U. (1983) Respiration in exercising horses. In: *Equine Exercise Physiology,* Eds: D.H. Snow, S.G.B. Persson and R.J. Rose, Granta Editions, Cambridge. pp 7-16.

[67]Harkins, J.D., Beadle, R.E. and Kamerling S.G. (1993) The correlation of running ability and physiological vasriables in Thoroughbred horses. *Equine vet. J.* **25**, 53-60.

[68]Estberg, L., Gardner, I.A., Stover, S.M., Johnson, B.J., Case, J.T. and Ardans, A. (1995) Cumulative racing-speed exercise distance cluster as a risk factor for fatal musculoskeletal injury in thoroughbred racehorses in California. *Prev. vet. Med.* **24**,253-263.

[69]Estberg, L., Stover, S.M., Gardner, I.A., Drake, C.M., Johnson, B. and Ardans, A. (1996) High-speed exercise history and catastrophic racing fracture in thoroughbreds. *Am. J. vet. Res.* **57**,1549-1555.

[70]Estberg L., Gardner I.A., Stover S.M. and Johnson B.J. (1998) A case-crossover study of intensive racing and training schedules and risk of catastrophic musculoskeletal injury and lay-up in California thoroughbred racehorses. *Prev. vet. Med.* **33**,159-170.

[71]Bailey, C.J., Reid, S.W.J., Hodgson, D.R. and Rose, R.J. (1997) Risk factors associated with musculoskeletal injury in Australian thoroughbred racehorses. *Vet. Epidemiol.* **32**, 47-55.

[72]Evans, D.L., Harris, R.C. and Snow, D.H. (1993) Correlation of racing performance with blood lactate and heart rate after exercise in Thoroughbred horses. *Equine vet. J.,* **25**, 331-445.

[73]Gauvreau, G.M., Staempfli, H., Mccutcheon, L.J., Young, S.S. and Mcdonell, W.N. (1995) Comparison of aerobic capacity between racing standardbred horses. *J. appl. Physiol.,* **78**, 1447-1451.

[74]Pelletier, N., Robinson, N.E., Kaiser, L. and Derksen, F.J. (1998) Regional differences in endothelial function in horse lungs - possible role in blood flow distribution. *J. appl. Physiol.* **85**, 537-542.

[75]MacLeay, J.M., Valberg, S.J., Sorum, S.A., Sorum, M.D., Kassube, T., Santschi, E.M., Mickelson, J,R. and Geyer, C.J. (1999) Heritability of recurrent exertional rhabdomyolysis in Thoroughbred racehorses. *Am. J. vet. Res.* **60**, 250-256.

[76]Alexander S. and Irvine, C.H.G. (1998) Stress in the racing horse: coping versus not coping. *J. equine Sci.* **9**, 77-81.

[77]Alexander, S.L., Irvine, C.H.G. and Donald, R.A. (1996) Dynamics of the regulations of the hypoathalamo-pituitary-adrenal (HPA) axis determined using a nonsurgical method for collecting pituitary venous blood from horses. *Frontiers in Neuroendocrinology* **17**, 1-50.

A brave new world? Thoroughbred genetics in the 21st century

STEPHEN HARRISON
The Royal Agricultural College
Cirencester
Gloucestershire
UK

Introduction

The multifarious Bentleys, Bugattis and Mercedes Benz which once graced the Grand Prix circuit of Brooklands have long ago been superseded by the more specialised Ferraris, McClarens and Williams's. The older cars underwent tests of true stamina, whereas the younger ones have evolved to compete in the shorter distanced, relatively speed-based tests. To the inexperienced, these modern day Formula 1 cars may appear to be structurally indistinguishable. But how can they be? Some win, some lose. Therefore, there must be intrinsic differences, possibly for a limited number of components. The philosophy of 'bigger, better, faster, more' has provided a product which has been designed to a very uniform pattern, using the same universally accepted scientific principles resulting in little obvious superficial variation. A test of stamina was considered to be the ultimate proof of a champion, now it fails to hold the attention.

A parallel can be drawn between Formula 1 and horse racing. The Ascot Gold Cup and the St Leger were once popular races and horses could be unashamedly bred with the possibility of winning these races as an objective. For a variety of reasons, this has changed. It is the middle and shorter distance races that now hold the kudos. They are more valuable and it is understandable that breeders will try to breed horses which are more specialised and not compel trainers to waste time on producing an 'all-rounder'. It is possible that the influx and influences of American bloodstock and racing objectives have played a major role. Horses that can compete over a wide range of distances are very rare and a winner of an English 'triple crown', encompassing the 2000 Guineas over 8 furlongs, the Derby over 12 furlongs and the St Leger over 14 furlongs, is an unlikely prospect. It is true that some winners of the Derby may perform well in the St Leger, and others may not be disgraced in the 2000 Guineas, but the potential to succeed in all is diminished. Regardless of whether this is due to increased competition, lack of interest or greater specialisation within given distances, it would now appear that more horses tend to fall into specific distance categories and their breeding has become representative of this. The true longer distance horse was conformationally different from the speed horse. It could be argued that this is now less true, as horses bred to run over longer distances on the flat no longer exist and those that do are discarded failures from races over the shorter distances. To be bred for extended stamina is now an accident and colts with the ability to perform over longer distances hold no attraction in the breeding world.

A corollary of this is that many of the horses running over the variety of middle distance races and sprints look similar and differ probably in their physiology rather than conformation. This is alluded to by a trainer's need to 'try' horses over different distances, often resulting in failure accompanied by the quote, *"I don't think he got the distance"* or *"He could maybe do with a couple of furlongs further"*. Even National Hunt horses are becoming more classically flat-bred on the sire side. Trends in breeding patterns change and the fashions that prevail at present represent different male lines to those that were used in the earlier part of the century. Some may suggest that the lines being used are limited and that there is a fear on the part of breeders to experiment with the sire lines. Marketing and hype are prevalent. Inevitably, fashions will also determine the quality of mares taken to in-vogue stallions concomitantly resulting in an increase in their popularity. It is obvious that much genetic variation is conserved and provided by the dam lines.

It is not the objective of this article to describe the impact of genetics on every feature of the Thoroughbred industry as that would be a mammoth task. However, it is pertinent to illustrate that it is breeding policies and ideas which have moulded the genetics of the horse to the present. Shifts in fashion, popularity of events, tactics and breeding strategies determine the genetic combinations required in horses and, therefore, affect the way in which the genetic structure of the total population develops. That is, we have determined the variation and types of gene present through selection. This is applicable regardless of whether we are considering Thoroughbreds or any other breed. Our policies have formed everything that is good about the breed and as we are dealing with pedigree animals, we also have to take responsibility for the disadvantages. We may now be entering a period when the reverse may be the case and direct selection of genes will determine breeding policies.

The history of the Thoroughbred has been documented in numerous other articles. Unlike the Formula 1 car, it has been lovingly crafted and developed for, officially, over 200 years and unofficially for as long as 2,000 years if one considers the role of the Romans in bringing Eastern-blooded horses to England to be influential. Mixing, concentration and separation of genetic entities have been achieved by numerous generations of breeders relying on their judgement as horsemen, pedigree knowledge, empirical experience and luck to achieve their end point. Breeders of old, even before the advent of modern, 'Mendel-driven' genetics, recognised the effects of inbreeding, beneficial and detrimental. They knew the value of balanced pedigrees and the avoidance of excessive closebreeding. Bruce Lowe, whose tables clearly and originally demonstrated the value of the dam, made a notable contribution to the development of the Thoroughbred and his work has been shown to have a very firm scientific basis. However, even until recently, many have based their assumptions on the 'mythical' quantity known as a gene which is thought to vary in proportions, duplications and dosage.

The introduction of the General Stud Book has ensured that the population is genetically finite, although not necessarily too invariable. The genepool can be recognised literally as a pool that has delineation. The book ensures that this population has a relatively precise documentation, making studies of breeding straightforward. It presents a more satisfactory working arrangement than a study, for instance, of *Drosophila* flies or field mice and makes problems more solvable.

The degree of genetic knowledge exhibited in different sectors of the racing industry greatly varies. The average race attendee may be able to recognise the names of some sires and dam sires. The same may be true for many owners. However, breeders, owner/breeders, trainers and bloodstock agents generally have a useful knowledge of pedigrees, inbreeding, nicks, stamina indices and performance characteristics. Most scientists will have knowledge of their science, possibly genetics, and may have seen a few horses at best. As genetic science is set to play a greater role, all interested parties would benefit from a knowledge of how important genetic phenomena affect horse-breeding policies and *vice versa*.

Genes, Chromosomes and DNA

In each cell of a horse's body there are around 1.5 metres of DNA molecule which, in the domesticated horse, *Equus caballus*, is packaged into 32 pairs of chromosomes, copies of which reside in the nucleus of every cell. They represent the main type of heritable genetic material. The structure of DNA is outlined in Figure 1. It is essentially a 'ladder-like' molecule with phosphates and sugars forming the 'rails' and organic compounds called bases forming the 'rungs'. There are four bases, adenine (A), thymine (T), guanine (G) and cytosine (C). They interact at the centre of the molecule so that adenine always pairs with thymine on the opposite side and guanine always pairs with cytosine. The frequency and order of occurrence of these bases along the length of the molecule constitute the 'genetic code'. A gene is a specific length of DNA with a particular base order, normally around 1,000 bases in length, which codes for the production of a specific protein within the horse's body. The protein may be an enzyme that affects metabolism, it may directly affect structure, such as collagen, or it might be a hormone, to name a few. Regardless of mode of action, the gene will code for a protein that will have an effect on a bodily trait. A chromosome is, therefore, a long length of DNA, twisted, coiled and compressed, which constitutes a great number of genes.

Genome

The compatible complement of genetic material within any species is referred to as its genome. It is rather like an

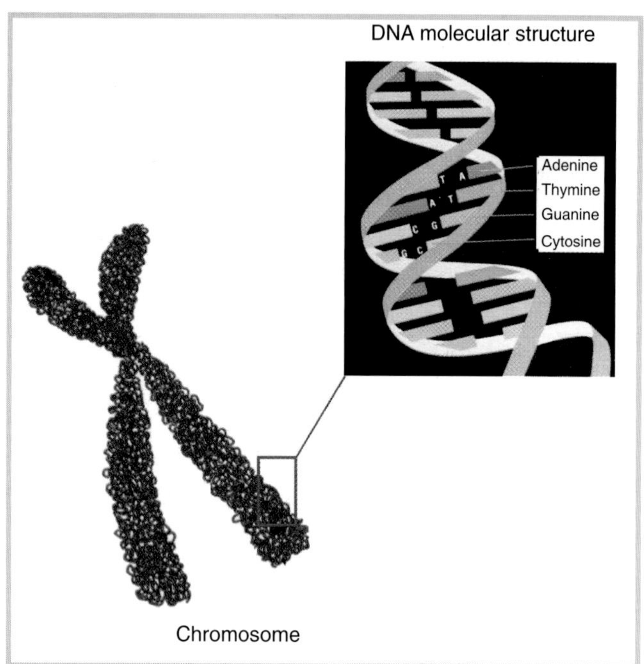

Fig 1: The molecular structure of DNA and its organisation into the chromosome.

encyclopedia of genetic information, where each chromosome represents a different volume. One chromosome of each pair is inherited from the sire and the other from the dam. Each chromosome pair carries different pieces of genetic information from the other pairs. Hypothetically, for instance, the gene for grey coat colour may be carried on a different pair to the one that has genes controlling exhibition of parrot mouth. Importantly, although each parent contributes genes controlling the same functions for each chromosome of a pair, the version of the gene may be slightly different in sequence giving rise to a slightly different protein and therefore affecting the phenotype differently. Versions of a gene are referred to as alleles and fundamentally, it is the presence of different alleles in a population that makes breeding unpredictable in many instances. Sometimes, particularly in very inbred lines or species, a gene governing certain characteristics will have a limited number of alleles. In other, out-bred populations there maybe numerous alleles present for any single gene. The number of different alleles in a population governs the degree of genetic variation within the population.

Mechanisms of Inheritance

Therefore, when considering the inheritance of any single gene we need to take into account the allele of that gene provided to the foal by each of its parents. Sometimes, the allele passed on from each parent will be the same and the foal will inherit two copies of the same allele on the same relative position of each chromosome. This is known a homozygous locus (a locus, plural loci, is the position on a chromosome where a particular gene, or region of DNA occurs). This is a likely condition for many genes in inbred animals, as there is less genetic variation present.

When parents pass on different alleles, the condition of

any such locus is referred to as being heterozygous. In this situation there is a metabolic 'dilemma' as two versions of the same gene are present. Generally, for a variety of reasons, the stronger allele tends to override the weaker and they are referred to as dominant and recessive alleles, respectively. Sometimes the alleles are codominant and an intermediate phenotype may result. This is oversimplified, but is generally the case.

Colour

A good example of the interaction of dominant and recessive alleles is to consider the colour grey. The grey allele is a very dominant allele and it exerts its effect over the nongrey allele by nullifying other genes for other coat colours situated on different chromosomal positions. That is, it will override the effects of the bay genes (known as agouti genes) and chestnut genes (extension genes), causing the loss of original colour seen at birth and the development of grey at a later stage. This happens at different stages depending on breed. A Camargue horse may be four years old, a Thoroughbred normally less than six months. The grey allele is known as epistatic, as it not only overrides its corresponding nongrey allele on the other chromosome in the pair, but overrides other genes in different positions. Other alleles of other genes work in different ways. The ways in which alleles interact in dominance and recession formed the basis of Mendel's laws of inheritance.

Homozygotes and Heterozygotes

During the formation of sperm and ova a process called meiosis takes place which gives rise to a halving of the number of chromosomes in these sex cells. Then, upon fertilisation, the normal chromosome number is restored and the embryo develops from a single fused cell. Therefore, as a horse can pass only one chromosome of a pair to its progeny in each sex cell, it can only pass on one allele for each characteristic. If a particular horse is homozygous for a dominant allele it will always pass that dominant allele to its progeny and the foal will manifest the phenotype determined by that allele. If the horse is homozygous for a recessive allele for a particular characteristic it will pass on only that allele and the foal will exhibit the phenotype directed by the other, more dominant allele if it has been inherited from the other parent. In a heterozygous situation, a horse is capable of passing one of two alleles to its foal. Therefore, it can not be expected to breed true for that character and may sometimes pass on a dominant allele and other times a recessive one. A foal may exhibit the same dominant character as that horse or may show that of the other parent. The allele present and its 'zygosity' for a particular gene is known as a genotype (which controls a specific trait or 'phenotype').

Because of these interactions of dominance, it is not possible to tell from viewing an animal whether a dominant homozygous locus or a heterozygous one controls a particular trait. This can be determined by the laborious and costly task of observing the way the trait is inherited in the progeny of the animal and the progeny of other animals to which it is crossed. A grey horse that is homozygous for that gene will always produce grey progeny whereas one that is heterozygous will only produce greys 50% of the time when crossed to nongreys. After a stallion has been standing for a number of years it is a relatively simple task to assess his progeny for consistently inherited, obvious traits and to obtain an indication of his own genotype for those traits. Assessment of stamina indices of a stallion's progeny roughly works on this basis.

It is less straightforward in the case of new stallions or mares that have produced less progeny. There are a minimum number of matings required to assess the genotype of a specific gene in a horse. In order to demonstrate that two horses are heterozygous at a single locus it is necessary to examine the trait in the progeny from four matings. However, one gene does not make a horse and many genes exist which means that we are not just studying the inheritance of a single variable characteristic, but many. If we were to consider the inheritance of two genes, in order to identify heterozgosity in both horses for both genes then progeny of 16 matings would need to be viewed. As the number of genes that we are simultaneously considering increases, so does the number of progeny that we are required to examine. In fact a formula of 4n, where n is the number of gene pairs involved, demonstrates this. Being able to identify the genetic constitution of horses for particular traits is obviously useful but it is clearly impossible to study huge numbers of progeny from the same repeated mating.

The reason that so many matings are required in order to assess genotype is due to a genetic randomisation of chromosomal material during the formation of the sperm and ova. During meiosis, leading to the formation of these cells, there is an exchange of parts of each chromosome with the other of the pair. This means that alleles of genes that were on one parental chromosome can be 'swapped' with the corresponding alleles of the same genes on the other. This brings together different allelic combinations within these 'recombined' chromosomes so that when they are passed on to a foal via sperm or ova it is a unique genetic identity that results. Another of Mendel's laws recognises that alleles of one gene can be independently inherited of alleles of other genes. That is, unless genes are linked. There are instances where some genes are in such close proximity to one another that they cannot be separated during recombination. In this case certain alleles of one gene may always be coinherited with specific alleles of others. Genes within the same linkage groups can be problematic in that it may be difficult through breeding to separate favourable traits from the less desirable.

Another complicating point to note is that many genes, for instance some of those controlling certain blood proteins, have more than just two alleles, sometimes more than ten. This increases the number of genetic combinations possible within any single horse. Distinction also needs to be made between two types of gene action. Many genes, such as those for coat colour, have an obvious effect and are due to the action of a single or major gene. The trait is either manifested or it is not depending on the inherited allele, that is, it is qualitatively inherited. Other genes, known as polygenes, work as groups and give an affect that is gradual or quantitatively inherited, Genes of this type can be more easily influenced by the environment. For instance, these types of genes control height but an undernourished horse would not realise its full potential.

Performance and Other Traits

It is not only coat colour and obvious traits that are inherited in this way. This type of situation will be applicable to nearly all genes and when one considers that genes also control medical and performance conditions then the interaction between alleles takes on a stronger significance. The basis of breeding programmes is to accumulate the best possible allelic combinations for genes controlling positive characteristics (e.g. performance, temperament, soundness, maturation, etc.) while avoiding accumulation of genes controlling negative effects (e.g. predisposition to ailment, infertility, poor stature). To this end we are aiming to produce an animal with a large number of homozygous dominant loci affecting advantageous traits and fewer homozygous recessive loci which might cause problems. Of course this is not black and white and many positive traits may be governed by recessive alleles and other negative traits, such as parrot mouth, may be passed on by dominant alleles. However, when positive traits are present in a homozygous dominant form they are easily passed on to the next generation and manifested there. This is the basis of prepotency or the ability of a horse to 'stamp its progeny'. This is normally referred to in application to stallions, but mares may also be genetically 'strong' depending on their breeding. Sadler's Wells is thought of as being prepotent and this is demonstrated when one views many of his progeny, for instance, Saddler's Hall and Istabraq. However, when Montjeu, his 1999 French and Irish Derby-winning son, is examined one might consider that his dam (Floripedes by Top Ville) may also be genetically strong.

Prepotency and Inbreeding

Prepotency and the ability to stamp progeny is not only apparent. It might also be hidden in that genes controlling unseen metabolic functions are also subject to the same allelic interactions as those controlling obvious factors such as coat colour. Statistically one might suggest that if a horse strongly resembles a prepotent sire or dam then he is likely also to have inherited many other nonobvious physiological characteristics. The genetic, though not widely realised, basis of inbreeding to a particular animal is to heighten the chances of securing homozygous allelic combinations, or at the least accumulate alleles, for beneficial traits carried by that predecessor. If the former is achieved then the progeny's chances of itself being prepotent increase. Inbreeding increases homozygosity, the drawback of this being that homozygosity of unwanted, detrimental alleles is an unwelcome accompanying feature. If carried out to extreme, this results in the scientific condition referred to as inbreeding depression and the production of substandard progeny. So a balance needs to be achieved. Homozygosity and prepotency does not necessarily guarantee success or the accumulation of the correct alleles. Sometimes it might be a good idea to outcross or outbreed lines in order to introduce and bring together new genetic combinations of alleles for certain characteristics. This would not necessarily ensure the presence of homozygous loci but may result in useful progeny with the correct combination.

However, given the finite nature of the Thoroughbred genepool many crosses will include some duplication in both halves of the pedigree and it is not easy to find completely unrelated animals. The term 'nick' is often applied to a cross of lines which, when repeated consistently, gives rise to acceptable progeny. It is a relatively imprecise term and often relies on the crossing of lines that have obvious common ancestors whose presence is deemed necessary on an empirical basis. Realistically, we do not know whether nicks work because of outbreeding effects or inbreeding effects, i.e. whether is is bringing in new combinations of alleles or is increasing the dosage of certain alleles. Perpetuation of a nick may also be due to trends. Once a nick becomes fashionable, the good mares of the lines are reserved for that cross and it is further enhanced. The importance of the dam line cannot be overstated.

Influence of the Mare

While both parents of a foal contribute one chromosome to each pair, the dam also unilaterally contributes DNA via structures outside of the nucleus called the mitochondria. This can mean that the dam can contribute up to 52% of total DNA and the sire only 48%. As it is passed on only down the female line, the mtDNA, as it is known, could be present in different allelic formats in different female families. When one considers that mtDNA plays a role in respiration, a molecular basis for Bruce Lowe's family classification is provided. Consider all of these types of genetic interaction and add the fact that some alleles are 'switched on' or 'turned off' depending on which parent the foal receives it from and a relatively complicated picture is presented.

Molecular Techniques

Fundamentally, we have relied on pedigrees, performance records and stamina indices to select and genetically judge animals. Recently developed molecular techniques may allow the genetic bases of many traits to be directly assessed and to make better use of the genepool through a greater understanding of inbreeding and outbreeding effects. For a business so obviously reliant on genetic phenomena it is curious that horse breeders are one of the last groups to assimilate genetic studies. This has its advantages in that much of the groundwork has been completed on other species and it is now a matter of transferring the methods and theories. Most equine genetics studies have had a purely veterinary role and have an obvious relevance and financial end point to horse breeders. This is particularly true in the UK where there is less inclination to absorb new scientific reasoning or innovative ideas than in the USA. This also holds for other scientific areas, such as nutrition.

Horse production has been viewed as a largely traditional pastime and some traditional theories have great relevance. Other traditional theories may not be quite as useful and there is a resistance to scientific input into breeding schemes, which have been carried out, unhindered, for hundreds of years. This is quaint and appealing but not necessarily a contribution to true production potential. The majority of scientists are, however, not horsemen or women; and they contribute to the problem by viewing a horse as an organism rather than a product with a specific sporting role and accompanying industry based on it. What is scientifically desirable is not necessarily useful. From a scientific point of view, a genetically healthy population would be an outbred population, genetically heterogeneous and nonspecialised. Breeding for specialisation causes a genetic shift in a particular direction and inevitably requires inbreeding. This same is true of dogs. One would not expect a crossbred mongrel to carry out the work of a spaniel.

The Thoroughbred industry is a well coordinated one. In other spheres of the horse world this might not hold true. Factional infighting and a certain lack of organisation within breed governing bodies can lead to an uncoordinated response to scientific development. Horse production of non-Thoroughbreds is broadly based and has many participants. Not all of them agree on what is best for their breed. Some may be more ambitious or outward looking that others.

Current Studies

Acquisition of funds to carry out general equine genetical studies has not been straightforward. In the past, funding from controlling bodies, such as the Horse Race Betting Levy Board has been directed mainly towards veterinary investigations. Also, in the UK, government funding has not extended to horses, which are not considered to be of agricultural relevance and are seen as leisure items. Naturally, funding will always and primarily be provided for animals that are or produce an edible agricultural product. In the main, this is likely to continue and it will be nongovernment money that will contribute to the major advances in the racing and sports horse sector.

It is not only political reasoning that has held back the studies of equine genetics; there are also logistical scientific problems. Traditional crossing and progeny analyses have not been a feasible approach for the study of equine genetics because of the expense of buying and maintaining horses and, primarily, because of their limitation to mono-ovulation and the restriction of artificial insemination and embryo transfer. Also, it is not a simple matter to define a production objective for a horse. In the case of racehorses, it is a minimum of two or three years before a performance variable can be assessed, making a study of the heritabilty of current stallions and, especially, dams traits an extended process. In summary, as an organism, horses are not amenable to genetic study. No doubt this is why Mendel chose to work on peas and not equids.

Studies based on a molecular understanding of DNA are now commonly applied to horses. On entering the next millennium, the role of DNA will become more publicised and obvious. A number of molecular DNA studies have already been carried out on horses, dating back to 1988. Although these studies have been sporadic they have, together with techniques used on other species laid the foundations for further, major applications to horse production. The current situation is that we are in a grey area where acceptability of new techniques is still reserved but starting to accelerate: *"The fire is lit and will now spread with ferocity."*

Methods of Study

There are many methods for molecular analysis of horse genetics and most of them make use of subtle differences in the DNA constitution of genes and chromosomes. The particular DNA typing test used varies between laboratories and depends mainly upon the type of genetic information required.

Microsatellites: The most common method of DNA analysis utilises the existence of a DNA structure known as a 'microsatellite'. Genes often contain, within their genetic structure, base sequences that have no obvious effect on a trait but are repeated numerous times and are termed 'microsatellites'. The repeated sequence may be very simple, for instance thymline and guanine (TG) repeated 10 or so times. However, the numbers of repeats vary depending on the allele of the gene in question. For instance, again hypothetically, the dominant allele for grey colour may contain a different number of repeats than the recessive allele found in nongreys and, therefore, two versions of a gene controlling the same feature would vary in length. This provides a molecular basis for distinguishing between alleles and is useful in examining inheritance of genes controlling less identifiable features than coat colour that may also have alleles of differing length.

Polymerase chain reaction: The distribution and length of genes containing repeated sequences forms the basis of DNA analyses. DNA can be extracted from small samples of bodily tissue, even hair follicles, but it is usual to extract it from white blood cells taken from each animal. DNA is then utilised in a chemical reaction with other components to visualise and determine the presence of particular alleles in a horse. This is made possible using a process called the polymerase chain reaction (PCR) based on the application of a series of thermal changes. When even a small amount of DNA is placed in this reaction other components, called primers, can be varied to cause amplication of specific pieces of DNA found in the alleles of particular genes. By varying the primers used we can examine alleles of different genes. Actually to visualise the presence of these amplified segments of DNA, a process called electrophoresis is employed. A reaction mixture for each animal is transferred into holes in a jelly-like matrix. Following the application of an electric current, the fragments move along the gel at a rate inversely proportional to their size. The DNA pieces on the electrophoresis gel are then 'stained' with either a chemical or radioactive compound and show up as either one or two bands for each horse.

Bands in a pattern therefore represent fragments of DNA from various chromosomes carrying a gene or genes containing a number of repeat sequences complementary to the primers used. The number of bands appearing in a

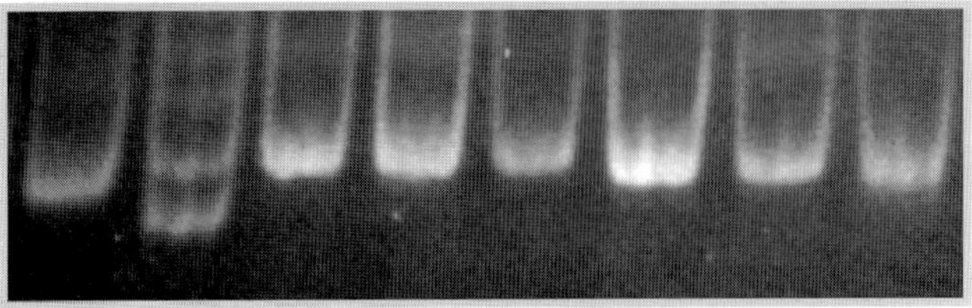

Fig 2: Microsatellite amplifications using a single primer, HMS2 from different Thoroughbred horses. Each lane represents a pattern for a different horse. Most of the animals are homozygous for certain alleles except the one second from the left which is shown to be heterozygous for this locus by the presence of two, more diffuse, bands.

fingerprint can be regulated through choice of primers. Microsatellite repeated sequences are spread widely throughout an animal's genes but can be specifically identified and give rise to one pronounced band (if the animal is homozygous for the locus) or two, more diffuse, bands (if the horse in heterozygous) (Fig 2). Other nonspecific amplified segments (called randomly amplified polymorphic DNAs, RAPDs) can be produced which give rise to a multiple-banded more complicated pattern (see Fig 6). These are less specific but can be used to give a quick indication of the relationship of horses to one another based on band commonality.

Usages of Techniques

It is a relatively simple, yet laborious and time-consuming task, to identify the presence of amplifiable microsatellites. Those scientists that help to generate these tools of analysis must be congratulated for their patience as they provide a favour to those who gain benefit from the tools. The availability of microsatellites opens a series of doorways for further scientific study of immense practical value. They can be used in their own right to study various aspects of population structure and can also be used as instrumental items in the mapping of the horses' genome and the identification of genes responsible for particular traits. The development of these microsatellites in other species is considerably more progressed than for the horse. For obvious reasons, the development of a genomic map has progressed most extensively in the human species. However, agricultural species have also received advanced attention. Examples of the use of molecular techniques are diverse and include such studies as prediction of growth rate and muscular bulk in beef cattle, embryo sexing in dairy cattle and assessment of genetic diversity in chicken populations. In practical terms, the benefits to the production of agricultural animals have been numerous allowing for the selection of quantitative and qualitatively inherited traits.

It is a normal, preliminary step to identify microsatellites without knowing with which gene they are associated. In fact, most of the equine microsatellites in existence have yet to be assigned to a functional gene, although many of their positions on the chromosome have been found. The basis of genome mapping is the ability to assign a microsatellite to a position on a specific chromosome and then to assess whether the occurence in a horse of that microsatellite can be linked to a particular trait. This provides a means of identifying the gene and its chromosomal position and its proximity to other genes. With this knowledge it is then possible to determine the sequence of the DNA which constitutes a certain gene. Indeed mitochondrial DNA has already been sequenced and studies within groups of horses carried out.

First International Equine Gene Mapping Workshop

An international collaboration of laboratories which aims to map the equine genome using a variety of techniques, including microsatellite analysis, had its origins at the First International Equine Gene Mapping Workshop held in Kentucky in 1995. Plans were made for the coordinated acquisition of general genetic information relating to the horse and for the subsequent collation of the data leading to the development of an horse genome map. It was agreed to identify 15 different groups of horses of varying breed each containing a sire and 30–40 of his progeny. DNA from these groups have been used to assess the distribution of microsatellites on the chromosomes and to determine if these pieces of DNA are inherited in a 'Mendelian' fashion, i.e. whether they are passed on in a similar way to genes. By observing the correlation of the microsatellite patterns in groups of horses possessing a similar trait it is possible to assign microsatellites as 'markers' for that gene.

Also, by observing the ways in which markers might be co-inherited, it is possible to determine whether individual genes fall into linkage groups and whether particular alleles for closely situated genes will always be inherited together. Undoubtedly, some traits will be shown to be associated with the sex chromosomes and thus be sexlinked. Obviously, there are many genes controlling numerous characteristics spread over the 32 pairs of chromosomes and it is estimated that, in order to have good chances of finding markers for the entire genome, around 1000–2000 microsatellites must be screened. This is time-consuming and the 'needle-in-the-haystack' analogy is almost applicable. Microsatellite markers can be assigned to chromosomes and linkage groups based on their rates of co-inheritance with other microsatellites. It is also possible physically to visualise their position by labelling them with fluorescent dye and adding this mixture to an isolated horse chromosome preparation that can be viewed under the microscope. The microsatellites will adhere to the common (or homologous) DNA on the whole chromosomes and their position will be shown through fluorescence at that point.

Mapping

This is mapping from 'scratch'. The benefit of being the last group of people to map a species is that many other genes will have been mapped for other species. Many characteristics, predispositions and conditions in these groups will have a similar genetic basis for similar conditions in the horse and often the sequence of the genes will be close. In this instance, it is relatively easy and less time consuming to find the equivalent equine gene because the markers used on the other species can be transferred almost directly without the need repetitively to screen a breed or group of individuals for markers for that characteristic. This type of mapping is probably the most informative.

It would be misleading to suggest that genetic studies of horses have been completely nonexistent. Studies of coat colour inheritance and blood groupings have been commonplace but have essentially been only of scientific interest. A notable exception is the work on blood groups and enzymes, which has allowed identification and parentage registration in recent decades. However, most studies have generally been sporadic and diverse. Molecular methods have been used to study genetic polymorphism and disputed parentage, and extended to analyse the population structure and breed relationship between groups of horses.

Numerous microsatellite markers have been identified for use in equine genetic analysis and many more will be generated during the international effort to map the horse genome. The number of scientific reports detailing microsatellite discoveries has increased noticeably, although not dramatically, in the last three years. Progress in this area is slower compared to the mapping of human genes as the funding is not as great and it is likely that the greatest breakthroughs will be privately funded. Data on the genome mapping of the horse are registered on the internet at the websites of the Roslin Institute, UK, and INRA, France. Indeed, there are now numerous internet sites dedicated to general equine genetics. It is difficult to assess the true status of progress but, as a rough guide, the number of reported potential markers registered on the public Roslin internet site has increased from 100 in February, 1998 to 388 in May, 1999, providing tools for further analysis.

The Future

It is not, however, a prerequisite for mapping of the genome to be complete to achieve benefits from molecular science or to identify horses carrying particular alleles of genes. It is not necessary to know the position of a gene in order for the science to be of use. It is sufficient to know merely if a horse is carrying it. The human genome has not yet been completely sequenced and completion is not expected until around 2005, but benefits to humanity have already accrued and within the first year of the millennium we should expect to witness the emergence of more studies of immediate, practical importance to horses.

The most obvious application is in identification of animals. At present individual horses are identified and parentage tested on the basis of their blood groups and on the presence of different versions of enzymes present in the blood. All Thoroughbred racehorses are blood sampled by a veterinary surgeon as foals; and blood tests are carried out by the certified laboratory appointed by the relevant authoritative body. In the UK and Ireland, the Animal Health Trust and Irish Equine Centre, under the direction of Weatherbys, carry this out. Other major racing nations have similar arrangements. Assessments have already been made on the suitability of a range of microsatellite tests to provide assessable genetic profiles for individual horses. Although a change-over period will be necessary between the systems, these analyses will shortly replace the previous tests. Many organisations or breed societies which have not had the same registration history as Weatherbys can utilise the microsatellite tests immediately and these are at present being used for the identification and registration of competition horses in the UK.

Genetic markers can be sought for a variety of characteristics. Although the heritable nature of many ailments is poorly understood, the obvious area to benefit is that of veterinary genetics. A useful application is in the identification of animals with heterozygous recessive alleles, which will be carriers of that recessively controlled trait. If they are crossed with another animal carrying this allele, they might produce some progeny which are also heterozygous carriers or which may actually manifest the detrimental, homozygous condition controlled by homozygous recessive combination. Progress in the ability to identify carriers of inherited disorders, such as SCID (severe combined immunodeficiency disease) in Arabs, has been achieved. Similarly, the genetic mechanism for the dominant allele of a gene that causes hyperkalaemic periodic paralysis (HYPP) primarily in Quarter Horses has been studied. Prime candidates for research are common, troublesome ailments such as laminitis and navicular disorder, although it is likely that metabolically based disorders such as azoturia will be easier to define. Simply inherited conditions controlled by a single gene will be more amenable for study. There have been indications that a predisposition to roaring (laryngeal hemiplegia) is controlled by a recessive allele and its elucidation is a possibility. However, if a trait or predisposition to an ailment is under the control of numerous genes (polygenic) this will be more difficult to find markers for. Examples of such conditions would be

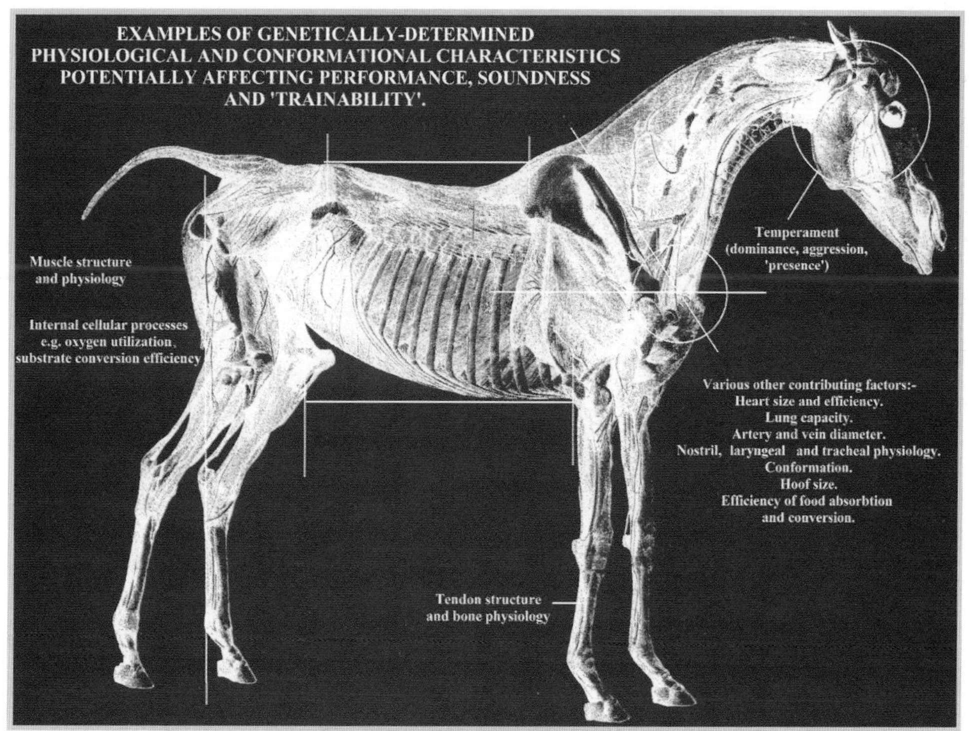

Fig 3: There are many potential genetically controlled factors that contribute to a 'blueprint' for Thoroughbred performance.

chronic obstructive pulmonary disorder (COPD) and, possibly, equine spinal ataxia (wobbles).

Performance

An area of potential study that is consistently of high interest is that of the genetics of performance. Various studies have estimated flat racing performance to be very heritable and suggest that genetics may contribute up to 45% of performance ability. Use of markers may also have the potential to identify beneficial characteristics, which might extend to traits contributing to performance in sport horses. In performing a role as an aid to selection, useful animals could be identified at an earlier age with a subsequent saving of time and money for breeders and trainers or potential optimum distances might be assessed. However, performance is unlikely to be simply inherited and is likely to be controlled by a number of major genes and groups of polygenes. Many varying characteristics under genetic control will affect performance. Some will be physiological, conformational or even psychological and a genetic 'blueprint' might be complex (Fig 3). The ability to find markers for performance would also be dependent on the use of the horse. It may be easier to predict and measure performance in flat racehorses where outright speed is a major criterion than for eventers where many variables are important.

A question that might be posed is that which speculates whether it is possible to produce 'faster' horses using this technology. The procedure of linking genetics to performance is extremely complicated. Performance ability is an interaction between the correct genetic constitution and environment. If performance is determined by genetics by up to 45%, then obviously environmental factors will contribute at least 55%. Not only do environmental influences affect a horse's potential to beat other horses, but they also affect their ability to break records. Racing times over all distances are generally getting progressively better. It is inevitable that horses will occur now and then which, given the right mentality, course conditions and competition will break records. However, tactics, track conditions, course topography and training potential will always play a role in hindering record times. The primary objective of racing is normally to beat the other horses in a race, not to set a new record. This is particularly true of Group One races and specifically the longer distance races.

Genetics of Speed

The concept of the genetics of speed has been addressed in relation to this and it has been suggested that race times for the longer Group races have not significantly improved over recent years for physiological reasons as a result of limited genetic variability in the breed. It is more likely that there are a number of explanations. These include, lack of interest, race tactics and physical and conformational constraints on training.

There are marked differences between the approaches employed by trainers and jockeys in sprint and longer distance races. Longer races are more tactically run and the times are unlikely to improve because of this, particularly in Europe. All races are run differently but, generally, in a longer race the horses may be more strung out at the finish and a horse that is well ahead will not be pressurised to break a record. Alternatively, the race will be determined in a fast finish after an initial slower pace has been set. Generally, better quality races will be run at a faster pace, but it is unlikely that a horse will be pressurised to an extent where injury is risked. It is also general practice to water the courses to prevent injury to horses, particularly over longer distances and records are more frequently set on hard and fast ground.

Role of Training

It can be argued that, if a horse is to be raced to set records over extended, longer distances, it needs to be trained for this. To set continually better record paces means that training levels must be increased or new approaches taken. Unfortunately, improved levels of metabolism required to set records cannot be achieved without sustaining other physical problems, that is, horses cannot withstand the degree of training necessary without suffering physical or psychological penalties. Rather than citing metabolic reasoning as a rate-limiting step to record breaking, it might be more appropriate to consider tendon and bone physiology. A horse which is continually overexerted may win some races but will not be around for very long.

Training methods and racing objectives play a significant role in the ability to utilise genetic potential. There are numerous components of fitness, which require attention and they often require different training approaches to exploit their value. Bone development and remodelling will require a different regime to muscular conditioning and so on. As performance is dictated by the genetic/environmental interaction, the ability to exploit the genetic potential of one variable must be balanced with attention to the others. Good training is the ability to balance an animal's soundness with its performance potential. Horses cannot reach the same levels of metabolic fitness as man, as their physical structure will not allow it. It is inappropriate to assign anthropomorphic physical qualities to horses as their physique and mentalities are quite different from man.

In National Hunt racing, it is currently common to see more Selle Francais or Autre Que Pur Sang (AQPS) horses in training in the UK. Some of these French-bred horses have also been imported for breeding purposes indicating the potential arrival of horses based on these in the Non Thoroughbred Register (NTR). New Zealand-bred horses are also transiently popular, with notable wins for Seagram (1991) and Lord Gyllene (1997) in the Grand National. It is possible that these more robust animals are able to withstand greater levels of training. They have been relatively successful in winning races, although it is clear from the evidence so far presented that many of them also have a short racing life which can be terminated by psychological or physiological injury.

It might appear that the frequency of broken records over shorter distances is higher. A combination of horse psychology, tactical approach and objective priorities would account for this. In a short race a horse may be ridden more vigorously and near the finish, there may be little to separate the better horses. Therefore, the competitive horse will still be striving to beat its rivals and will continue to be racing at full speed at the line. Generally, horses will not be 'strung out' in a sprint. It is also feasible to expect horses to set a faster and more consistent pace for the length of the entire race. Also, importantly, horses can be more muscularly trained for speed under anaerobic conditions without the needs for excessive exercise that might cause greater injury.

Obviously, horses will be bred to perform over particular distances and it is likely that the different genes that are involved will depend on this. And so we return, full circle, to the concepts of fashion in breeding and racing objectives.

The area of the interface between tactics, distance, psychology and genetics is an interesting one and warrants a book in its own right. Some animals may have more 'active' genes or alleles for stamina and not for speed and *vice versa*. However, as we are not entirely sure which characteristics govern speed and stamina, it is not possible to state whether possession of traits for one will be completely mutually exclusive of the other.

For longer distances, we might be selecting horses with the right combination of alleles governing a number of characteristics which will give them the correct balance of alleles for stamina to stay the distance and for the speed to finish and markers would need to be identified for such.

For sprint races, selection should be less complicated and selection of markers for alleles which will play a role in metabolism over shorter distances may be more straightforward. To an extent, the question of whether we can produce faster horses is spurious. Buying or breeding a horse is rather like being dealt a hand of cards. Each card contributes to the overall effect and if one can identify a hand with even a single ace in it then a head start is guaranteed. The average performance level of horses seems to be improving across the breed in general and a certain ideotype horse is desirable. Many horses appear similar, although it is not known to what extent different combinations of alleles carry horses to higher performance levels or how much uniformity exists between them in genes of importance. In a Thoroughbred world now preoccupied, rightly or wrongly, with the effects of inbreeding, it might be appropriate to suggest an Orwellian analogy, *"All animals are equal, but some animals are more equal than others"* (*Animal Farm*). That is, there must be some major, specific genetic components, an ace, present in all top class horses that separate the best from the 'also rans' and that finding genetic markers for these is a possibility. It is not quite as simple as the anatomically obvious *"Four legs good, two legs bad"*, but certain physiological traits and their controlling alleles will be more desirable than others.

It could be argued that intensive selection to fix characteristics based on the use of markers would lead to high degrees of inbreeding. However, contrary to this, DNA technology can be used in a complementary manner to monitor and preserve population structure. Finding a marker for a particular allele represents only a small part of DNA analysis. In addition to finding specific genes, this technology can be used in a less specific, more indicative manner. Looking at the variation in the alleles identified in different animals and assessing the degrees of commonality is a useful way of estimating relatedness. A good example of this is in the application to rarc breeds. Animals of the same breed selected for specific characteristics will inevitably be subjected to a degree of inbreeding, especially if their numbers are low. Their genetic status has often been recorded only by pedigree observations and true status has been unmonitored for numerous generations. Accumulation of deleterious, homozygous-recessive loci due to inbreeding will lead to exhibition of inherited diseases and inbreeding depression.

Pedigree, Inbreeding and Microsatellites

Because of the influences of numerous genetic phenomena it is not entirely sound to rely on pedigree records to predict inheritance; rather they should be used in conjunction with genetic markers. Due to unpredictability in the way genetic material is transmitted from one generation to another, animals may be more or less related to one another than statistically assumed from pedigrees. Poor genetic management through inbreeding of limited family lines will also lead to genetic loss within breeds and a narrowing of their valuable gene pools. Analyses of frequencies of occurrence of DNA markers in populations are good indications of genetic structure and breeding programmes can profitably utilise information taken from these tests to help manage inbreeding levels by selection of suitable parents.

It is assumed that the Thoroughbred has relatively high inbreeding levels and that there is not as much genetic variation within the breed as might be desired. Some of the rare breeds of horse within the UK are, however, presented with a potentially more problematic scenario. Breeding females within breeds recognised by the Rare Breeds Survival Trust (RBST) number less than 1,000 per breed. Some of these breeds have gone through severe genetic bottlenecks. For instance, Suffolk horses can be traced in descent from the line of one stallion. A demonstration of application of these techniques in relation to genetic conservation can be provided by work carried out in our own laboratory (V. Karamatic, J.J. Dooley and S.P. Harrison, unpublished data). Projects sponsored by the RBST had as their aim an investigation of the genetic diversity and relationship within and between various breeds of British horse with a view to providing data, which might aid their preservation.

Figure 4 shows microsatellite bands produced using a single primer for Cleveland Bay and Irish Draught horses. Using comparisons of the occurrence of alleles it has been possible to estimate genetic distances between breeds and to identify distinct breeding lines. Heterozygosity, which roughly indicates the level of outbreeding was examined over 10 different microsatellite loci. The Thoroughbred

a) Irish Draught Horse

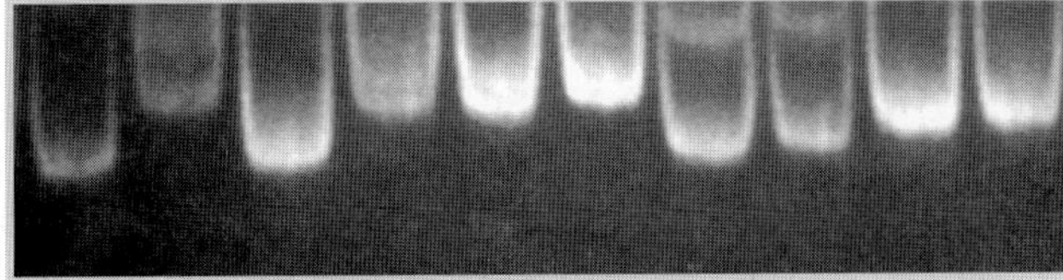

b) Cleveland Bay

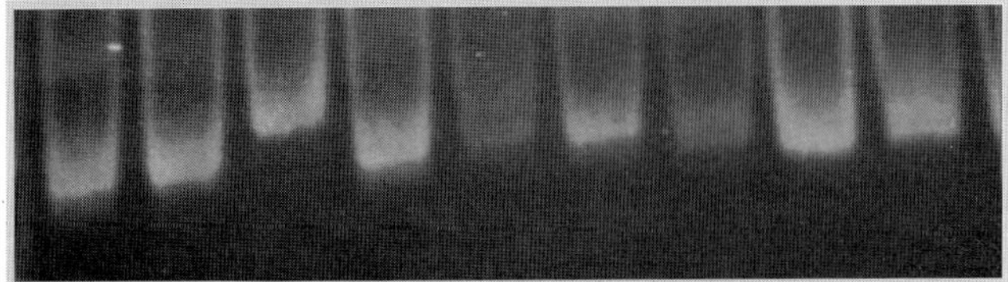

Fig 4: Genetic variation at one microsatellite locus, HMS2, in Irish Draught and Cleveland Bay horses. Note the greater degree of variation here compared to this microsatellite in the Thoroughbred (Fig 2).

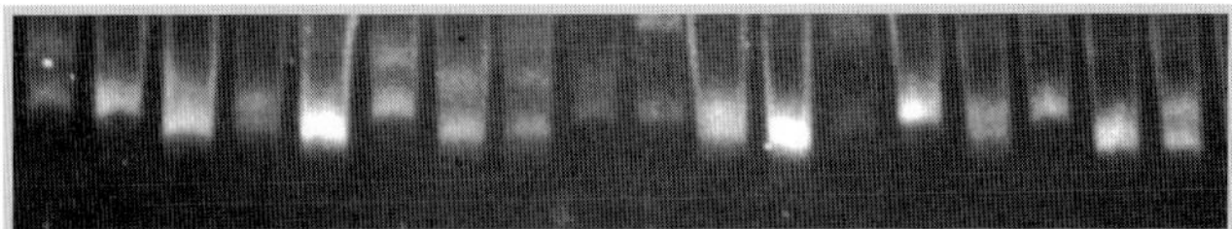

Fig 5: Demonstration that Suffolk horses have good allelic variation and heterozygosity at the HMS2 microsatellite locus.

exhibited greater levels of heterozygosity than most ponies and heavy horses, though not as much as the Irish Draught Horse or, curiously, the hyperinbred Suffolk (Fig 5). There were also indications that the Thoroughbred shared many alleles with other breeds, indicating a common close ancestry. Indeed, the Thoroughbred seems to possess many alleles in common with the Irish Draught and Cleveland Bay. Indications from this study suggest that limited genetic variation in the Thoroughbred may not necessarily be as problematic compared to some other breeds. Veterinary aspects of genetics are a result of an interaction between inbreeding and population management and the occurrence of specific deleterious alleles in a homozygous form. They are inseparable and it is incorrect, from a veterinary viewpoint, to concentrate solely on specific alleles.

Genetic Purity of Breeds

Similarly, in relation to breed preservation, there is concern within some rare breed societies for the integrity of the breeds. At the extreme to inbreeding, there is a question regarding the purity levels of breeding stock. In this instance DNA analyses have the potential to monitor the purity of individual horses by screening the distribution of alleles present in different breeds.

There are indications that certain alleles are characteristic of particular breeds. An allele present only in an Arab horse, for instance, would stand out as being irregular if found in a supposedly purebred Exmoor pony. This may help breed societies concerned about genetic impurity to monitor their animals and provides a basis for exclusion of crossbred animals. In its extreme, this technology could help to eliminate animals carrying nonbreed recessive traits. Figure 6 shows DNA profiles produced in our laboratory from two breeds of horse using the RAPD method (V. Karamatic, J.J. Dooley and S.P. Harrison, unpublished data). Some bands are clearly seen in the profile of the Eriskay ponies but not the

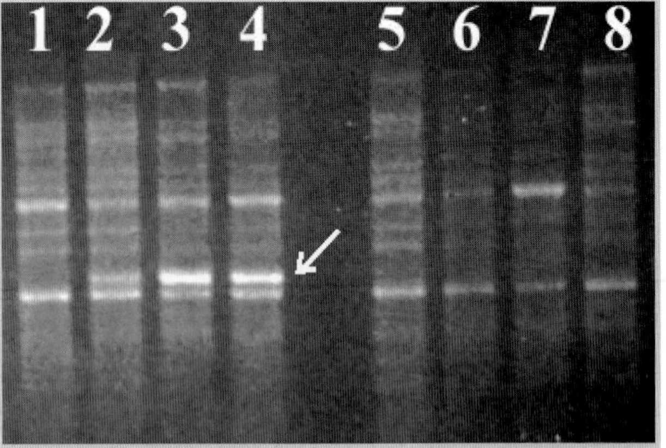

Fig 6: DNA amplification patterns using RAPDs. A band, marked with the arrow, in the profiles of three of the Eriskay horses (lanes 1–4) is not found in the profiles of the Exmoors (lanes 5–8).

Exmoors. Preservation of the purity of native breeds, especially the rare ones, is not only of importance to the breed societies but should also be of interest from a historical and heritage viewpoint.

Even though there are multibreed applications, Thoroughbred breeding can be a lucrative business and will be able to withstand the cost of application of molecular analyses to benefit other breeds. These are expensive to carry out and without subsidies it is unlikely that their application will be easily affordable by the breeders of less expensive animals.

Theories come and go. Galton's law, Vuillier dosage system, Bobinski tables, Bruce Lowe tables and Varola's dosage have all played a role in the development of the Thoroughbred. The validity of these theories have sometimes been viewed with scepticism. Molecular studies present a more solid means of assessing the general population as they actually provide a useful interface between pedigree information and the very entities that affect the horse, the genes.

Pace of Progress

The pace of progress in the area of equine genetic development is building momentum and this is illustrated, not only by the development of the international gene-mapping collaboration, but by the existence and productivity of nonaffiliated laboratories in the field of equine DNA studies. The primary observation regarding the provision of genetic analyses to a cash-buoyant equine world is that there are obviously opportunities for commercialisation, particularly where Thoroughbreds are concerned. As a result of international collaboration much equine genetic information is available for public and general perusal. However, it would be unrealistic and naive to assume that this will continue. Investment requires commercial productivity and some findings will be extremely valuable and patentable. Important markers for prevalent diseases, predispositions and ailments have obvious commercial value in terms of their health-screening potential. If or when performance characteristic markers are found, one should not expect to see their DNA sequence information bandied around far and wide for all to observe. Individuals who are prepared to pay or who have invested will benefit. The goose will not be laying that particular golden egg for everybody, or for free. In this respect, the new technological developments take on a Jekyll and Hyde quality.

Although there are obvious veterinary benefits, traditionalists will argue that this will represent the ruination of the Thoroughbred industry, as only a few major owners will benefit, selection will be based on the presence of markers carried in a limited number of lines and inbreeding levels will increase. Scientists 'invading' their world can add to their fears by insensitively making spurious and ambitious claims as to the potential and capabilities of these studies. There is a place for both viewpoints but they must interact favourably. This is truly a case of 'Copernicus meets Buck Rogers in the 21st century'. *Tempora mutantur, nos et mutamur in illis.* Times change, innovations occur and we need to harness these technologies for their beneficial aspects. The Thoroughbred is now a marketable product and a different perspective will be given to its development. Genetic markers will be used to aid selection but they will also be used to help avoid inbreeding. Other policies, such as extended use of dual-hemisphere-covering 'shuttle' stallions are more likely to reduce genetic variation in the breed *per se* and concerns about inbreeding have not necessarily prevented breeders from utilising related stallions from a narrow genetic background already.

It is feasible that use of these tools to monitor population structure will allow us to scrutinise the genetic constitution of more obscure breeding lines and thus contribute to constructive outbreeding. Useful alleles will be spread amongst many lines and the combinations with which they can be brought together will be great and varied. The Thoroughbred is a biological entity and unlike the Formula 1 car, cannot be designed to a ubiquitous scientific blueprint. Continuation of progress of the development of the breed requires a certain degree of genetic variation. In order to have the potential to produce better horses, genetic variation must be present. Different opinions will exist as to which are the desirable genetic combinations, just as they do regarding the most appropriate conformation. Additionally, the number of coverings and crosses required to 'fix' all advantageous genetic characteristics would be phenomenal.

Cloning?

The only way of consistently producing a horse with all desired traits would be through genetic manipulation and cloning. This is not a viable or desirable option for horses. Its occurrence is so unlikely as not to warrant consideration. Suffice to say that it would be a near biological and legislative impossibility at present. Molecular analyses are a complementary tool for breeders, not a replacement for breeding systems. However, they are important tools and the innovative breeders who embrace them will benefit beyond those that do not. All parties involved in the production of Thoroughbreds are caretakers for the successful, thoughtful and responsible development of the breed and this science must incorporate that philosophy. In summary, specific alleles can be selected for and genetic variation can also be simultaneously maintained.

Many Thoroughbreds have already been analysed in genetically based population studies in order to monitor and help preserve and develop healthy breed structure. At the risk of appearing to be a genetic 'Nostradamus', I would realistically predict that, within the next five years, many Group and Listed race winners and their parents will have undergone some constructive genetic analysis, other than for their compulsory blood test.

Bronze statue by Penny Wheatley.

Imaging Technology: Seeing is Believing

Developments in radiography and radiology

ALISTAIR BARR
Department of Clinical
Veterinary Science
University of Bristol
Langford House, Langford
Bristol BS40 5DU
UK

X-rays were 'discovered' formally on 8 November 1895 by a German physics professor, Wilhelm Conrad Roentgen (1845-1923) (Fig 1), working at the Physical Institute of the University of Wursburg (Fig 2).

Roentgen was investigating light emissions generated by discharging electrical currents through highly evacuated glass tubes (known as 'Crookes Tubes' after their British inventor William Crookes). He noticed that when his cardboard-shrouded tube was charged, a barium platinocyanide screen some distance away began to glow and, subsequently, that if he held his hand between the tube and the screen an image of the bones within the flesh appeared on it. This demonstrated the two critical properties of x-rays in relation to diagnostic imaging, namely their ability to penetrate tissue and be differentially absorbed by it thereby producing a shadowgraph of the tissue based on thickness, density and composition. For his discovery, Wilhelm Roentgen was awarded the first Nobel Prize in Physics in 1901.

The speed with which this discovery was reported and taken up is astonishing by today's standards, despite all the advances in communication technology which we now enjoy. Roentgen gave his first report on his discovery *Uber eine neue Art von Strahlen* to the Wursburg Physical-Medical Society on 28 December 1895 (Fig 3) and, by 1 January, had written to physicists across Europe. His paper was reprinted in *Nature* on 23 January 1896 by which time his discovery was headline news around the world. The discovery was immediately exploited by both medical scientists (Fig 4) and those who recognised the potential for exploitation of the new rays for popular amusement. On the medical front the first angiograms were undertaken on cadaver specimens before the end of January 1896 and March saw the first use of intensifying screens. By May 1896, x-rays were being used clinically in the Italian-Ethiopian Campaign to locate bullets in wounded soldiers. During the first year after Roentgen's discovery, several books and almost 1000 scientific papers were published on x-rays. The first x-ray periodical also appeared in 1896 published in England and called *The Archives of Clinical Skiaography* (Fig 5).

The apparatus necessary to create x-rays was widely available and relatively cheap (Fig 6) with the result that commercial studios opened to take 'bone portraits' and lead underwear was manufactured to foil attempts at peeking with 'x-ray glasses'. The potential deleterious effects of x-rays took some time to recognise. In February of 1896 a physics professor at Vanderbilt University radiographed the skull of the Dean of Medicine. Three weeks later the unfortunate Dean's hair started to fall out - an event that caused much amusement at the time. It was not until some years later that the direct link between radiation and burns to the

Fig 1: Wilhelm Conrad Roentgen (1845-1923). Reprinted with permission of the American College of Radiology.

Fig 2: The Physical Institute of the University of Wursburg. The Roentgens lived in an apartment on the upper story, with laboratories and classrooms in the basement and first floor. Reprinted with permission of the American College of Radiology.

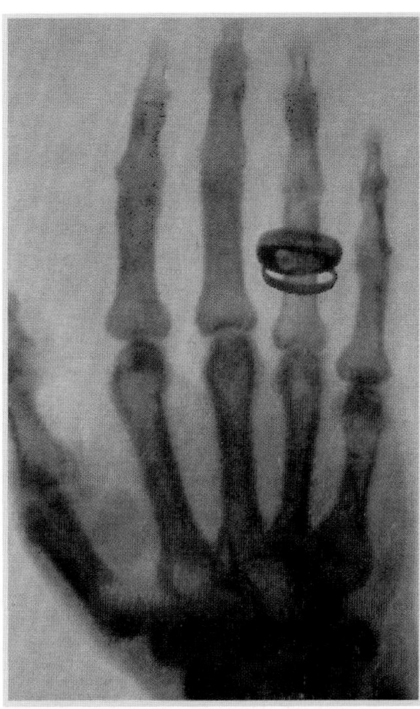

Fig 3: Radiograph of the hand of Albert von Kolliker made at the conclusion of Roentgens lecture and demonstration at The University of Wursburg Physical-Medical Society. Reprinted with permission of the American College of Radiology.

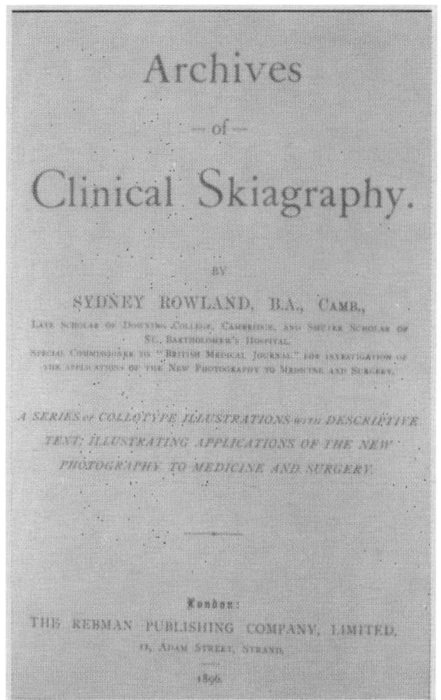

Archives

— of —

Clinical Skiagraphy.

BY

SYDNEY ROWLAND, B.A., CAMB.,

LATE SCHOLAR OF DOWNING COLLEGE, CAMBRIDGE, AND SHUTER SCHOLAR OF ST. BARTHOLOMEW'S HOSPITAL.

SPECIAL COMMISSIONER TO "BRITISH MEDICAL JOURNAL" FOR INVESTIGATION OF THE APPLICATIONS OF THE NEW PHOTOGRAPHY TO MEDICINE AND SURGERY.

A SERIES OF COLLOTYPE ILLUSTRATIONS WITH DESCRIPTIVE TEXT; ILLUSTRATING APPLICATIONS OF THE NEW PHOTOGRAPHY TO MEDICINE AND SURGERY.

London:

THE REBMAN PUBLISHING COMPANY, LIMITED,

11, ADAM STREET, STRAND.

1896.

Fig 5: The first radiology Journal - published in London. Reprinted with permission of the American College of Radiology.

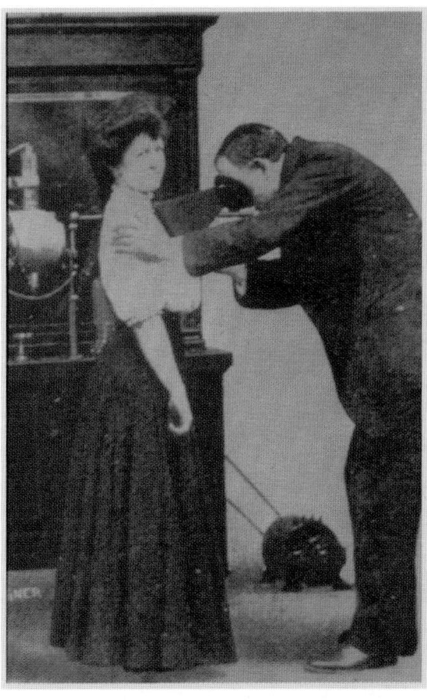

Fig 4: Early demonstration of the 'medical' use of radiography. Reprinted with permission of the American College of Radiology.

Fig 6: Equipment for radiography was easily obtained. It included an anode and cathode in an evacuated glass tube and a generator coil. Reprinted with permission of the American College of Radiology.

extremities and neoplasia became recognised (Fig 7). Even as late as 1953, when a lecturer at the International Veterinary Congress in Stockholm was questioned about slides showing his assistants' hands in the primary beam, he replied to the effect that assistants were replaceable! In the 1950s, x-ray burns on the fingers of veterinarians were so widespread that the American Animal Hospital Association collected a series of 20 or more slides of damage to the skin or even amputation of fingers and sent them around to veterinary meetings for graphic illustration of radiation dangers. At the first International Veterinary Radiology Conference in Dublin, in 1968, a speaker likened veterinary radiography to that in paediatrics in that "*some person must help to control the patient*". He went on to say that: "*If anaesthesia or deep tranquillisation were to be used on all animal patients for radiography it would certainly have a limiting effect upon the usefulness of the x-ray.*" Some 30 years later it is illegal in the United Kingdom to hold a small animal patient for radiography unless there is a good clinical reason for not restraining it by chemical or physical means. Horses are still held for radiography in 1998; what rules will apply in 2038?

To return to the beginning, veterinary interest in 'the new light' was quickly aroused and the first article on the subject was published by J. A. W Dollar in *The Veterinarian* in February 1896. Even before that the topic was addressed by Mr J. Clarkson, the then President of the Yorkshire Veterinary Medical Association at its annual meeting and dinner on 21 January 1896. Mr Clarkson foresaw that the rays could be used for the evaluation of suspected cases of spavin or splints. In the August 1896 issue of *The Veterinarian*, Professor Hobday at the Royal Veterinary College reported

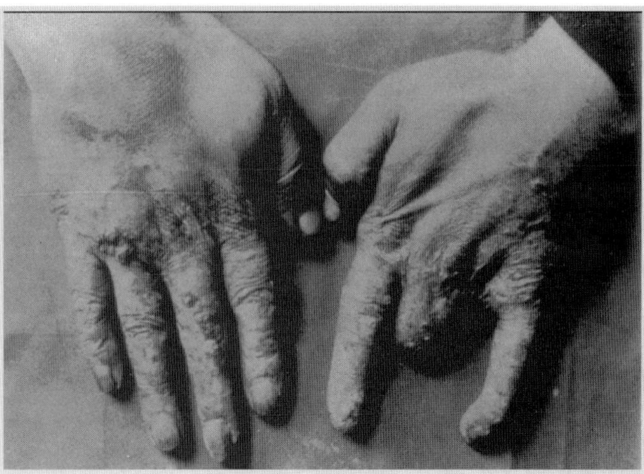

Fig 7: The hands of Mihran Kassabian (1870-1910) an early pioneer of the new rays who suffered progressive necrosis and had serial amputations. Reprinted with permission of the American College of Radiology.

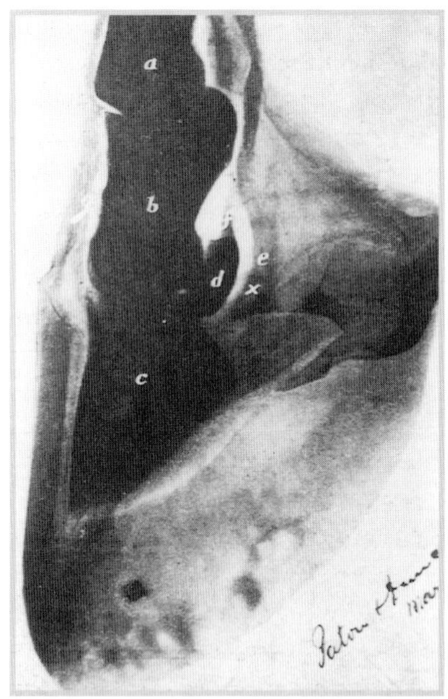

*Fig 8: The first published veterinary radiograph by Paton and Duncan (*The Veterinary Journal *1896).*

that with Mr V. E. Johnson he had obtained radiographs of the knee joints of living horses without anaesthesia. He concluded that the Roentgen rays could be successfully applied to the smaller animals without much difficulty, but that to penetrate through the thicker portions of the horse required greater power than was currently available, or else a prolonged exposure. The technique was adjudged to be useful for abnormalities of the bones of the equine limb such as suspected fractures of the pastern, ringbone, sidebone and foreign bodies in the hoof (Figs 8 and 9).

Despite the enthusiasm of its protagonists, the limitations on the equipment available in the initial stages of radiography were nonetheless severe. Writing in 1925, Ed C. Jerman, an American pioneer of radiography, described some of the difficulties facing the early radiographers:

> *"...If the vacuum of the tube did climb too high or drop too low, if the tube did not puncture, if the patient could be strapped in a stationary position for a long enough period of time, if the motor man could be kept at his job, and provided extreme care was used in the development process a fairly decent radiograph of an extremity might be obtained. It is necessary to use the words 'might be' because of the fact that there were several unknown factors creeping in here and there which upset all our plans from time to time...During this first stage in the progress in the x-ray art the technician required the maximum of ingenuity, initiative, and patience in order to accomplish anything at all worthwhile."*

Fig 9: X-raying a horse October 1898 - location and circumstances unknown.

Subsequent developments, such as the Coolidge hot cathode tube in 1913 and the autotransformer, made standardisation of exposures much easier and lead to more uniform results. Hand in hand with these technical developments came the introduction of training for the technicians involved in radiography. In October 1920, Ed Jerman organised a meeting of a small group of technicians at the Morrison Hotel in Chicago and formed the *American Association of Radiological Technicians*. By 1922, in conjunction with the *Radiological Society of North America*, there was an established register of x-ray technicians.

Progress on the veterinary front was as ever slower and much early work seemed to concentrate on the therapeutic as opposed to the diagnostic capabilities of x-rays in veterinary medicine. One of the early pioneers of veterinary radiology was Professor Alois Pommer at the veterinary School in Vienna and he has subsequently been referred to as the father of veterinary radiology. The first veterinary radiology textbook appears to have been written in Germany by Paul Henkels in 1926: *Lehrbuch der veterinarmedizinischen Rontgenkunde*. The book covered physics, normal anatomy and both diagnosis and therapy. In 1930, Dr Mack Emmerson was the first American veterinary surgeon to receive speciality training in radiology from Professor Pommer in Austria and, in 1938, an x-ray machine for animals was installed at the University of Pennsylvania, however this was again used for therapy rather than diagnostic imaging.

In 1937 Dr Gerry Schnelle, working at the Angel Memorial Hospital in Boston, started publishing a series of articles in *The North American Veterinarian* on diagnostic radiology and, in 1945, he published the first English language textbook on veterinary radiology, *Radiology in Canine Practice*. The American Veterinary Radiological Society (AVRS) was formed in 1954 and published a journal. One of the reasons for its success was the quality of its illustrations which were superior to the reproduction of radiographs in other veterinary journals at that time, although writing in 1968, Dr Schnelle records that the honourable exception was the *Veterinary Record* which "*frequently used insert sheets of high gloss paper on which radiographs were reproduced*". The AVRS eventually led to the formation of the American College ofVeterinary Radiology and its journal *Veterinary Radiology and Ultrasound* which remains a focal point for the publication of veterinary imaging studies to this day.

One of the classic early papers on veterinary radiology was that of Major G. E. Oxspring (see also p 85) of the Royal Army Veterinary Corp published in the *Veterinary Record* in 1935 and entitled *The Radiology of Navicular Disease, with Observations on its Pathology*. This paper combined two emerging elements in veterinary radiological studies, namely the need to publish accounts of case series as opposed to individual case descriptions and the need to correlate images with the underlying gross and histological pathological change. Oxspring's work is described in detail elsewhere in this manual, but his paper interestingly included the observation that:

> *"The definite clinical diagnosis of navicular disease in the incipient stage is usually impossible and in the moderately advanced stage it amounts to a conjecture based on collective symptoms which are very irregular in degree. Even in advanced cases, where the symptoms strongly suggest navicular disease, radiological evidence of its existence is always welcome to the clinician...".*

It is a situation that arguably still exists today.

By the 1950s, radiography was coming into more routine use in veterinary diagnostic procedure with further papers on navicular disease by Sten-Eric Olsson, in 1954, and in the same year a presentation at BVA Congress on radiographic technique by Colonel John Hickman. As the 1960s arrived, technical advances in film screen combinations reduced exposure times and expanded the range of areas of the body, particularly in large animals, that were amenable to routine radiographic examination in practice. Frustrations such as disturbance of subjects by the noise made by clockwork timers were still however present.

In 1962 Derek Tavernor and Leslie Vaughan published an extensive monograph in the *British Veterinary Journal* on radiography of horses and cattle. They emphasised the importance of meticulous care in patient positioning to avoid structures being foreshortened or superimposed on the final image. They also began to discuss the subject of the potential significance of the increasingly more subtle variations in anatomy that could now be detected and the importance of correlating images to the results of physical examination and nerve blocks. Interestingly they also emphasised the potential value of longitudinal studies to assess the change of lesions with time and this remains an area which has not been comprehensively studied in relation to many diseases and injuries.

By 1965, the scope of equine radiology had extended beyond the limb and a technique for radiography of the equine heart (along with a picture of the heart in a 600 kg horse) was presented at the AAEP meeting in Miami Beach. The 1960s also saw the beginnings of the recognition of veterinary radiology as a speciality within the UK with the formation of the British Veterinary Radiology Association (later to become the European Association of Veterinary Diagnostic Imaging) and the development by the RCVS of a postgraduate Diploma in Veterinary Radiology - the DVR. It is interesting that the DVR and Diploma in Veterinary Anaesthesia preceded the plethora of postgraduate clinical qualifications now available at a UK and European level by some 20 years; and the expertise developed by those who developed and examined these qualifications during that time enabled them to act as models for subsequent development of specialisation in other fields many years later.

The 1970s and 1980s might arguably be described as the golden years of conventional veterinary radiology with a stream of clinical publications that described case series and related the radiological information to clinical and in some cases pathological information. O'Brien and colleagues at the University of Davis, California, produced important work in equine radiology some of which drew on novel radiographic projections such as 'skyline' views of the navicular bone and third carpal bone. In the UK, Colles reawakened interest in the radiology of navicular disease, Jeffcott outlined changes seen on radiographic examination of the thoracolumbar spine, Jeffcott and Kold published important studies on the radiology of the stifle, Dyson described radiological changes associated with the shoulder joint, and Gibbs and Lane published on the radiology of the equine head.

What of the future? Conventional radiology is now but one of several imaging techniques available to equine clinicians with diagnostic ultrasound having joined it in the realms of the 'routine' and scintigraphy rapidly following suit. Cross-sectional imaging techniques including CT and MRI will undoubtedly follow and are now readily available in a small number of centres internationally. Progress at the cutting edge is not, however, always followed by consistent progress in the wake. The same attention to detail in patient preparation and positioning, film processing, radiation safety and correlation of images to clinical findings, as was required by the early pioneers, is still necessary today and it cannot be long before more quality assurance and clinical audit procedures to monitor such factors are imposed on the veterinary clinician if we do not do it for ourselves in relation to our day to day radiography. Wilhelm Roentgen's chance observation has made a major contribution to animal welfare and there is no doubt that we have yet to exploit its benefits to the full.

Sources

Davies, J.V. (1995) One hundred years of X-rays: the discovery. *Veterinary International* **7** (2) 3-9.

Carter, H.E. (1995) The early days of veterinary radiography. *Veterinary International* **7** (2) 10-14.

Radiology Centennial Inc., 1891 Preston White Drive, Reston, Virginia 22091, USA. (http://www.xray.hmc.psu.edu/rci/centennial.html)

Developments in nuclear scintigraphy

ROB PILSWORTH
Rossdale and Partners
Beaufort Cottage Stables
High Street
Newmarket
Suffolk CB8 8JS
UK

Introduction

Nuclear medicine developed because technology became available which allowed the tracking of radioactive nuclides, after their injection into the bloodstream. This was made possible by the emission of detectable radiation as these nuclides decayed.

At first, only certain chemicals were available as radioactive elements, and these were mostly unsuitable for medical applications. With the advent of the cyclotron, it became possible deliberately to manufacture very small quantities of the isotope of almost any element. When, in 1942, the nuclear chain reaction was discovered and controlled, it opened the way for the production of these isotopes in commercially viable quantities. In 1946, the journal *Science* announced availability of these agents for research and diagnostic purposes.The science of radiopharmacy, which led eventually to equine scintigraphy, had begun.

The principle of all nuclear medicine is the injection of a radioactive isotope and its tracking within the body subsequent to injection.The first studies used a single probe, moved by hand, giving only numerical data as a read-out, related to the amount of radioactivity detected by the probe at any site.This was superseded by a probe, laboriously moved automatically over the patient in a grid pattern of prefixed points, the rectilinear scanner. The data plotted from each of the grid points formed a very low resolution image of the study site.This rectilinear scanner was similar, in some ways, to the methods later described in examination of the equine pelvis using a probe. In 1957, Anger unveiled the photomultiplier array, coupled to a large scintillation crystal, which forms the basis of all gamma cameras, even today. In this technology, the gamma rays coming from the patient strike a large, fluorescent crystal, causing a small flash of light. This is amplified by a photomultiplier, and the output of all the photomultipliers is pooled and smoothed, to form an image of the origin of the radiation, mostly, in our case, a horse's bone.

Using this technology, the regional function, blood flow, metabolism and morphology of tissues and organs, such as liver, kidney, lung and thyroid can be studied. In the horse, although some early studies on the iodine thyroid axis were carried out, scintigraphy only really came to be a major force with the introduction of the bone-seeking isotopes such as the diphosphonates.

These molecules can be attached to a radioactive chemical, which they will then drag into the bone, mimicking phosphorus in the normal exchange mechanism. Once these 'marker' molecules became available, it rapidly became clear that when attached to a short half-life, unstable isotope, such as technetium (Tc99m), abnormalities and perturbations in bone turnover could be easily monitored by the relative uptake of the MDP-Technicium complex within the bone.

There are many other organ-seeking molecules which will carry technetium into whatever target they are aimed at. There are specific liver, blood pool and vascular flow markers, all of which can be used with the same technicium molecule to look at different organ systems. In the horse, the primary indication of nuclear medicine is still the musculoskeletal bone scan. The other methodologies are gradually creeping into use in small animal medicine, but they are of limited usefulness in the horse because of our peculiar requirements in this species to have a fully functional athlete. This limits the desirability or need for the investigation and monitoring of chronic disease.

Nuclear medicine is a young science, with the first gamma cameras only being introduced into medical practice in the 1960s. The advantage of this to a chronicler is that many of the leading lights, the 'movers and shakers', of this science are still around to talk to. Imagine somebody researching developments in microbiology being able to speak to Lister and Pasteur in the preparation of their paper! Writing this chapter has therefore been a delight, in that it has meant tracing the founding fathers of the science of equine nuclear medicine, most of whom are still active. I have tried to tell the story in the words of the people involved, where possible, using excerpts from interviews conducted in 1998, with the clinicians themselves.There will undoubtedly be some omissions. Some important people, of whom I have not been made aware, will go unmentioned. To them I extend a sincere apology in advance.

Many of the people responsible for the introduction of scintigraphy into veterinary medicine in general and, more particularly, in the horse, did not set out on their career paths with that intention. There was a general interest in nuclear medicine in the early days from the perspective of the threat of atomic bombs, and contamination of livestock by bomb testing programmes. Most of the universities who scaled up to deal with this problem were the ones in which scintigraphic facilities were eventually funded for equine work. Bob Twardock (Figs 1a and b) one of the founding fathers of equine scintigraphy, who by nature would probably be embarrassed to be described as such, takes up the story.

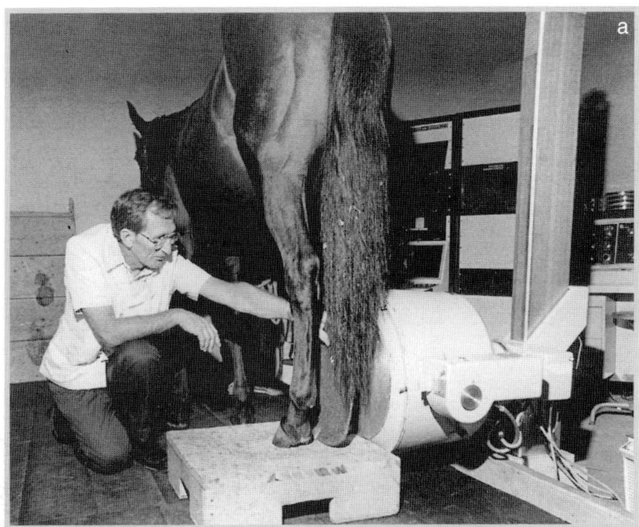

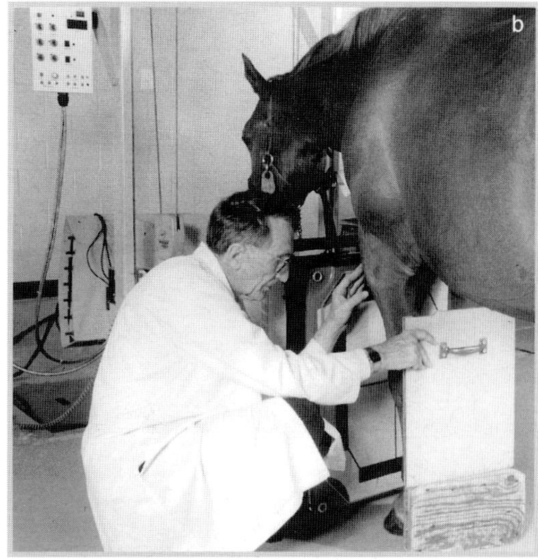

Fig 1: Bob Twardock, pictured in 1979 (a) with his first Siemens 19 tube camera, and in 1998 (b) with his new Omega 500. The moral? Nuclear medicine is good for you!

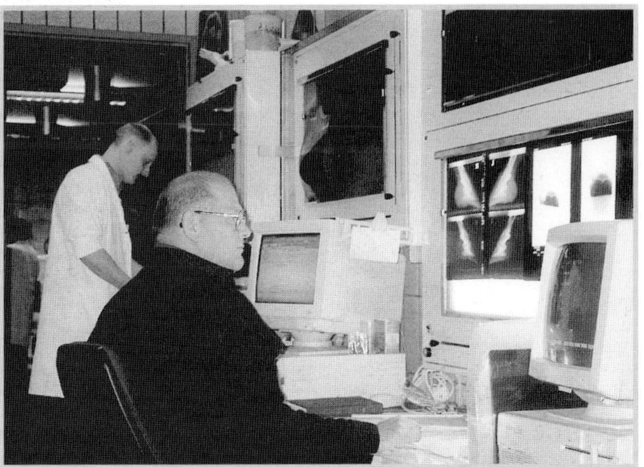

Fig 2: Professor Ueltschi, working at the University of Bern in 1998.

"Open-air testing of nuclear weapons was in full swing in the 1950s. Fission products in radioactive fallout were circulating in the atmosphere and were readily measurable in crops, forage and food. Money was available from the Atomic Energy Commission (AEC) for research on the passage of strontium-89 and -90, cesium-137, iodine-131 and other fission products through the food chain into the human diet. Many of the veterinarians who gained early experience with radionuclides came from backgrounds in the military, and their scientific interests centred on the physiology and metabolism of calcium and bone, and iodine and the thyroid. Dan Hightower and Leo Bustad, in particular, had interests in the latter. Another pioneer was Charlie Reid, who summarised the diagnostic applications of radioisotopes in 1963. His paper included illustrations of thyroid uptake and hand-held probes for detecting thoracic metastases, as well as Kr-85 inhalation for lung studies - very impressive!

During that time at Cornell, a two hour radiobiology course was established for veterinary students. I am sure we taught twice as much as the students needed and ten times more than they wanted! They even had laboratories with hands-on experience with Geiger counters and 'Easter egg' hunts for hidden Co-60 sources! Then, atmospheric testing of nuclear weapons was banned, leading to decreased concerns about nuclear fallout and civil defence. That, and increasing antinuclear sentiment, led to major reductions in our civil defence and radiobiology instruction at Illinois. The laboratory was dropped and we now gave eight lectures on radiobiology, including nuclear medicine, as part of the third year radiology course.

Dan Hightower was Deputy Director of the Division of Nuclear Medicine at Walter Reed Hospital when J. D. McCrady recruited him to join the veterinary physiologists at Texas A & M. Anger cameras, Tc pharmaceuticals and human nuclear medicine evolved in the 1960s, but the technology was too expensive and the early veterinary 'images' were made using rectilinear probes. Articles on bone and brain imaging with rectilinear scanners were also published in the late 1970s.

Gamma cameras were used as early as 1972 at Texas A & M and 1975 at Cornell, but the earliest veterinary image I have seen was in the Journal of the American Radiology Society *in 1974. Tofe and colleagues published a case report on ^{99m}Tc EHDP bone scanning of a chondrosarcoma in a Saint Bernard. The article that especially caught my attention and imagination was Ueltschi's on equine bone scanning in the same journal in 1977. His images demonstrated most vividly the potential usefulness of bone scintigraphy for evaluating equine lameness. Shortly after that, I started questioning our clinicians on their interest and potential use of nuclear imaging. Their estimate of two or three cases a week was encouraging enough to lead us to obtain a 19-tube Siemens camera, which was donated, in 1979 (Fig 1). Mike Devous joined me from Texas A & M as I was about to leave for a sabbatical at Davis, working with Gerry and Sally DeNardo at the human hospital in Sacramento. Tim O'Brien, the Department Head at Davis, was very helpful in arranging this visit, because I think he was hoping that if we obtained a gamma camera up and running, he could then persuade his Dean to get a better one! I suggested to Mike that, while I was away, we should start slowly and feel our way with the clinicians and radiologists, since we were really only physiologists. However, when I came back six months later, he had installed the camera and an image-processing computer and was doing two or three cases a day!"*

In Europe the epicentre of scintigraphic development seems to have been Switzerland, mainly due to the early pioneering work of Professor Ueltschi (Fig 2). Ueltschi occupies a unique position in having progressed the science of scintigraphy in the horse to the very highest levels, in relative clinical isolation. Most of his published work was in German; and this probably slowed down the assimilation of his results in the rest of Europe. He is a quiet, serious man

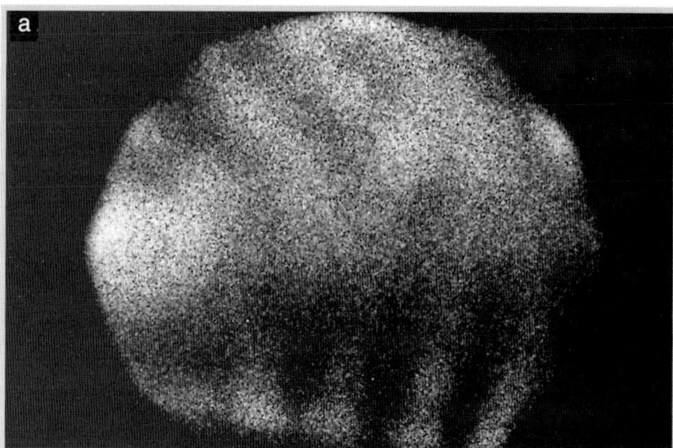

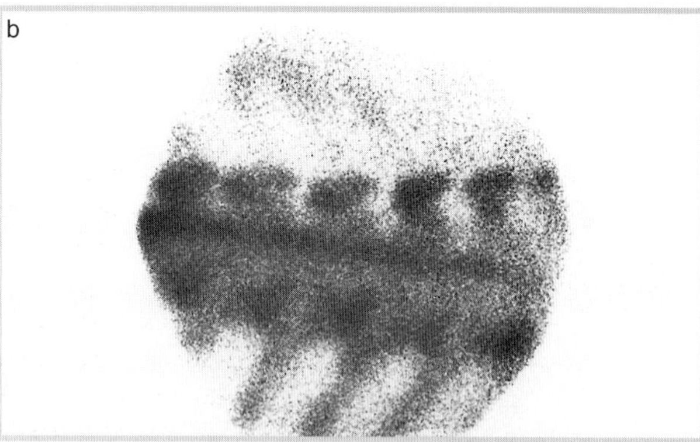

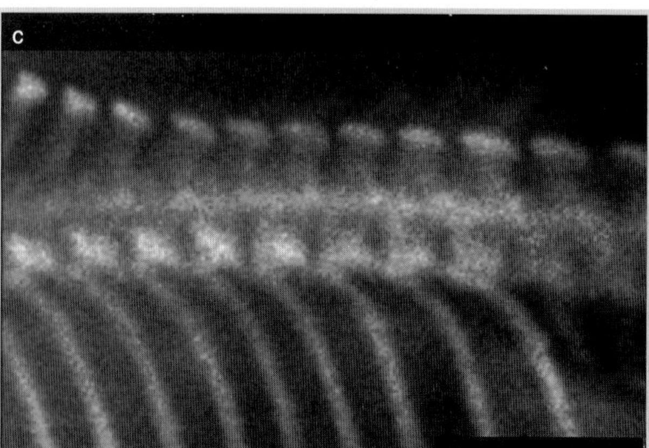

Figs 3a–c: Images of the thoracic spine of a horse, taken by Professor Ueltschi in 1976(a), 1985(b) and 1998(c), illustrating the advances in image quality which have been made during the intervening years.

who has beavered away at developing the methodology for producing bone scans, which are now of startling quality (Figs 3a–c). Professor Ueltschi comments:

"Actually, it was in the early '60s, that was time when we had our first scans, and in those days it was human thyroids we were scanning. With regard to equine work, we observed developments for a few years, and when I came back to the university, we began to look at the possibility of using strontium 90. I was given the possibility of starting in the radiology department in '73, and I started a little project which had a hand-held probe. The methylene diphosphonate and polyphosphonates had just been described and were becoming commercially available in '73. Nobody was using a probe, to my knowledge, at that time and the probe we used was one taken from human thyroid scanning which we modified.

First of all we just looked at the probe in individual horses but were unable to tell much from the results within the individual animal. What we did find was that there were differences between groups of horses and, for instance, in podotrochliosis or in bone spavin of the hock, we found significant differences that were appreciable using the probe. The problem with the probe always seemed to us to be the immense variability in counts and uptake between individual horses. This made the results difficult to interpret. In 1974, we obtained a grant to buy a gamma camera and first of all bought a Selectronics proto-camera. This camera was only suitable for technetium and therefore concentrated our minds on equine bone scanning as this used technetium with the polyphosphonate. I think we were the first gamma camera to be used in Europe. In 1976, I gave a talk at the Veterinary Radiology Meeting in Cambridge and then, in 1977, in the USA, and met up with David Hood and Dan Hightower from Texas. We had tremendous help from the nuclear medicine specialists, particularly Professor Roesler in the Human University Hospital, and he helped both with expertise and to obtain funding for the development of our unit. What I did was to look at the large number of horses, both normal and abnormal. At that time we still had the cavalry, and it was possible to look at several hundred horses. Even in the first year, we had good cases when we could demonstrate a lesion which we could see in no other way, using the gamma camera.

In the future, we may want to use the technique to look at the cervical spine and thoracic spine and back problems in horses. We are now able to see the articular facets, with the modern technology combined with general anaesthesia, and this is very detailed imaging (Fig 3c) I think general anaesthesia is not mandatory for a survey scan of a horse, but for detailed imaging of the spine and for imaging of all deep lying structures for which you might want to use a high resolution collimator, I think it is probably essential."

One of the names which seemed to crop up with everyone I spoke to was Dan Hightower. Dan is now retired, but is still around and was able to speak to me about the very early days of development of nuclear medicine facility at Texas A & M.

"I got into nuclear medicine through the Army radiation biology programme. I did a Masters in Nuclear Engineering and then worked in research in nuclear medicine. In 1966, I retired from the Army and joined Texas A & M University as Associate Professor of Physiology but with the prime purpose of building up a nuclear medicine facility. The Dean at that time, Al Price, wanted to get nuclear medicine going and that was the point of setting up the programme. Texas A & M had quite an active ongoing nuclear interest, but the veterinary side of things had not been developed.

The first scanner we had was a rectilinear scanner with a two inch crystal which we obtained from a Dr M. D. Anderson at the hospital and Tumour Research Institute in Texas. They were getting rid of it, and we said we would like to have it. This was mainly for thyroid work. Things moved on when Don Holmequest, who was Associate Dean of the College of Medicine, managed to get hold of a gamma camera and had nowhere to put it, so we gave him a place! We were working then just on animals, and mostly still thyroids.

Things began to pick up then. We did a lot more cases, but still mostly small animals. Gradually, interest in the technique began to build, and we saw more and more horses, as we began to realise the potential of the bone scan in some of their lameness problems."

Nuclear medicine would undoubtedly have reached equine practice in the United Kingdom without Don Attenburrow. However, Don pioneered so much of the work in this field that he probably brought things forward at least 10 years. Don was, in 1982, the first person in the world to install a gamma camera in private equine practice, and is still actively involved in equine scintigraphy today. The relative geographical isolation of Exeter probably delayed the 'spreading of the gospel' to some extent within the large equine clinics in the UK. Although Don presented his findings at various meetings, and in articles in *Equine Veterinary Journal* and the *Veterinary Annual*, his techniques were not picked up willingly by colleagues in equine practice in the early days. Possibly there was an element of the NIH ('not invented here') syndrome. Also, Don can come across to some as a rather forbidding individual, and certainly not one to suffer fools, gladly or otherwise; and this may have played its part.

Here, in the Rossdale clinic in Newmarket, Don brought his equipment over from Exeter in the early '70s and carried out a small pilot programme on Thoroughbred racehorses, now accepted by most people as being the perfect target for bone scanning. The trial, for one reason or another, was not a success, and the general feeling among the clinicians in this practice was that the technique had nothing to offer. One of my present partners (who, in the light of later events, would probably prefer to remain nameless!) stood up at the first nuclear medicine symposium, held in Exeter in 1984, and declared that, in his opinion, scintigraphy would not become a useful technique in Thoroughbred equine practice in the future!

I was intrigued to know what would make a general equine practitioner, working in the heart of Devon, want to introduce nuclear medicine into his practice, and put this to Don Attenburrow.

"We came to look at the possibility of using scintigraphy, primarily in relation to the horse's back at first. Without wishing to pour scorn on the subject, all my professional life I had difficulty in believing the whole area of slipped vertebrae, of bones being put back in by manipulators. At the time, Dr Vennart was working in the Medical Physics Group at the University of Exeter and it was really in an attempt to address scientifically the problems of the horse's spine that we first used the probe. Our first attempts followed a conference that we attended, probably 20 years ago now, in Oswestry. Our first hand-held probe we made ourselves, in my own engineering workshop. We found the probe interesting for lower limbs, but decided early on that the collimation of 0.75 inch wide allowed far too much extraneous signal to be picked up by the probe and the margin of error, coupled with the angle of presentation, in our opinion was just too great to be clinically useful.

It helped to establish in my mind that scintigraphy could be of use in the horse, and it also brought home to us the ever-present problem of x-radiography understating the pathological evidence in bone. At the time, we could take little from the medical profession as they were not looking at the same kind of problems. When they were developing scintigraphy, in man, most skeleton bone scans were done searching for tumour metastases, in other words, looking for black spots where they should not be. What we were interested in was the normal and eventually abnormal distribution of isotope in the cancellous bone surrounding joints. We related early on that there was a difference in uptake of MDP in the subchondral bone of arthritic joints.

Our first camera, I remember going to fetch from Cardiff, along with Dr Vennart, in a self-hire van! This was a 19 photo multiplier camera, with relatively poor resolution, but it was the first gamma camera to be used in a private practice in the world.

I had an understanding and basic grounding in engineering, because of my involvement with the subject in the Navy. As a flier, one has a vested interest in the safety of the aeroplane in which one is about to take off! The engineering side of development of the gamma camera unit was therefore the least problematic;the physics, I'm afraid, I learnt as I went along, simply because I had to! The great advantage that I have had in my career is close links to the expertise available from colleagues in the Medical Physics Group, Department of Physics, University of Exeter, and I cannot understate the contribution that my colleagues there made.

The one essential piece of equipment to a gamma camera unit, almost more important than the camera or computer, is the possession of an equine skeleton, so that you can learn what it is you are looking at when interpreting the scan images.

I think, in the future, one of the most important goals to strive for is unification in our standards of interpretation and application of scintigraphy. At the moment people seem to be learning from scratch over and over again, as they set up scintigraphic units, rather than combining and standardising knowledge. We should be seeking some kind of unification in the interpretation of our results, using region of interest figures to compare sites, within and between skeletons. The standard nomenclature of mild, moderate and intense uptake is basically meaningless unless it is given a more precise role. Mild uptake in one horse may be normal, whereas in the same situation in another horse could be grossly abnormal. What do we mean by mild and moderate uptake? Mild or moderate in relation to what?"

While Don Attenburrow moved rapidly on from the probe to a gamma camera, his work introduced the possibility of probe-based scintigraphy to other clinicians in the UK. Many of these clinicians were not in a position to install or equip a gamma camera facility at that time, and were therefore led to investigate the use of the hand-held probe more fully. One of those who became interested in the use of hand-held detectors early on was John Walmsley, working in Liphook.

"We actually got interested in the early 1980s because of a client who had been to Don Attenburrow for a bone scan. We hadn't heard much about bone scanning and were intrigued to know more about it, and so gave Don a ring. He had started scanning in the early '70s, I think, and we went down and had a look at the technique. We were quite impressed with the possible usefulness of the technique in some of our lameness problems. I had a friend who was a radiologist in Chichester, who helped us out with expertise and provided us with a probe. We had to build this ourselves and supply lead shielding, and then established a format for scanning the limbs and spine which we used in the clinic for quite a long time. With regard to future possible developments, I think infection is one of the avenues that scintigraphy could help us with. We have been using the gamma camera to look at dental problems and possible tooth root abscessation, when increased bone turnover is involved, but an early infection-seeking agent would definitely

Fig 4: Don Attenburrow, in a 'still' taken from the 1980 BBC documentary Science in the Saddle, *which featured his work, using his early home-made hand-held probe.*

be very helpful. Having now used the gamma camera and the probe, there is obviously much more information available from the camera. Although we did get some exciting cases using the probe, they were relatively few and far between."

Another clinic which was using a hand-held probe at the time was based at the Royal Veterinary College in London, headed up by Peter Webbon. Peter's group arrived at the use of the probe from a slightly different angle, in that it was a technique that they were using in research before, eventually, they decided to try and use the same equipment in the clinical situation. Peter Webbon says:

"We were basically interested in measuring blood flow to horses' feet, purely as a research tool. We looked at many different ways of doing this, including plethysmography, but we eventually met a guy working with xenon 122 clearance in the calf muscle of man in a human hospital situation. This seemed to offer potential to us. We got in touch with a medical research worker, Richard Whiton, who was working at the Whipps Cross Hospital and was married to a veterinary surgeon. He was therefore interested in the veterinary aspects of some of the things we were trying to achieve, and got us organised with a probe and suggested a protocol for technetium labelling of red cells to look at blood flow. Having used the probe, with some degree of success, we realised quite quickly that what we really needed was a gamma camera. We came by our first camera by advertising in the medical physicists' magazine. So, although we ended up using the probe in the clinical situation, our track through to that point was a convergent evolution with Don Attenburrow and his group rather than a direct clinical application of his technology."

Peter Webbon presented some lameness cases which had been investigated using the probe at a BEVA meeting in Jersey in 1985. I was at that meeting, having been sent to represent the Rossdale practice in Newmarket. Although I had only been in the practice two months, it had already become clear that the majority of our lameness cases in young equine athletes were bone related; and that this technique should, therefore, obviously have a major contribution to offer in tracking down the source of these

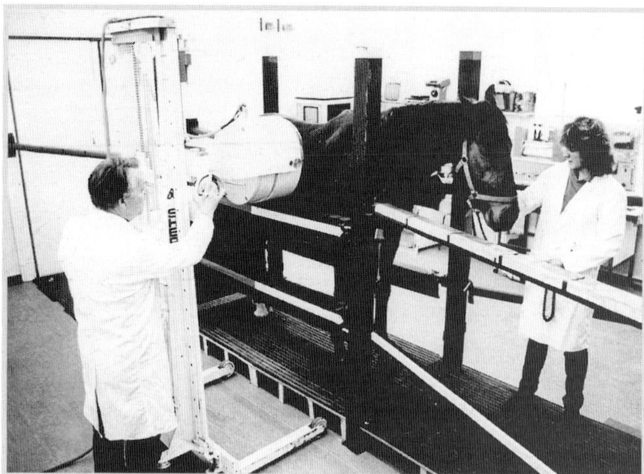

Fig 5: Don Attenburrow pictured performing his first ever equine bone scan with a gamma camera in 1982.

injuries. I came back from the meeting, brimming with enthusiasm to introduce hand-held point counting to our practice, only to discover that the practice had already 'been there and done that', many years before in the trial with Don Attenburrow.

I discussed Peter Webbon's findings with one or two of the partners, and I remember eventually having a meeting with Peter Rossdale, to ask if we could try again. As has always been my experience in this practice, I received nothing but enthusiasm and support for the possibility of introducing an innovation. I contacted Peter Webbon at the Royal Veterinary College and asked him if he would be interested in bringing up his equipment to Newmarket for a half-day trial on a weekly basis to give the technique another chance. Peter was immediately enthusiastic about the idea, and extremely helpful in every respect. He dutifully hammered up and down the M11 every week with the bone scanner in the back of his car, to examine some horses which we had injected with technetium earlier in the morning.

In the first three weeks, we had diagnosed five cases of stress fracture to the tibia, which were subsequently confirmed radiographically, in horses with previously undiagnosed hindlimb lameness. These cases were later published as a joint case series in an *Equine Veterinary Journal* supplement.

The immediate positive response from the second trial of probe point counting, which was purely the result of some luck in the right cases turning up, stimulated my 'bosses' at the time to buy a scaler-rate meter and probe, so that we could have a fully equipped probe point counting unit. We adopted the technique that was orthodox at the time, of listing a series of points on the horses limbs and jotting down the readings at each point. One limb was then compared with the other to see if there were any glaring differences.

We quite quickly realised that one of the problems encountered in this type of situation is that absolute numbers are completely meaningless. The count recorded at any site using the probe would vary with the size and age of the horse, the time from injection and the degree of blood flow to that limb when compared to the other. We felt it would probably be better to calculate the counts as a ratio, compared always to a standard bone. For this we chose the wing of the atlas, easy to find and not often involved in lameness! The 'hot limb-cold limb' phenomenon, which has now been well documented using gamma camera techniques, is a regular occurrence, and caused great difficulties in comparing purely numerical data. More perplexing still, the 'cold limb', in which there is reduced uptake throughout a lame leg, can mask an apparent increase at one site within that leg. What we seemed to need was a visual image which could help us to deal with these artefacts caused by differences in perfusion. We also realised, early on, that detection of pelvic fractures was perhaps the single most important function of scintigraphy in the investigation of orthopaedic problems in the racehorse.

Up to that time, the only investigative technique available was radiography, with all the attendant risks involved of anaesthetising a horse with a suspected fracture to the pelvis. Our early experiments with the probe convinced us that it was possible to detect pelvic fractures in the standing horse using this simple equipment, but we sought a more elegant system than simple paired sampling points. Having discussed our requirements with a couple of computer 'buffs', it seemed obvious that a computer programme was the way to go. We had one initial false start with a fly-by-night computer firm who promised us the earth, and came up with nothing. We ended up owning £5,000 worth of computer equipment and were completely unable to generate the visual plots that we had been promised. Fortunately, we decided to pursue our grievance through litigation, and won. The money which we clawed back from this initial disaster was paid to Mark Holmes, a veterinary surgeon working at the University of Cambridge School of Veterinary Medicine. Mark is one of the rare beings who combine a complete knowledge and familiarity of computers with a clinical grounding in veterinary medicine and was perfectly placed to address our problems. He very rapidly designed the software system to allow visual displays of the data derived from both the limbs and the pelvis which was subsequently marketed as the *Equiscint* programme by Oakfield Instruments. The development of this system was generously aided by a grant from the Home of Rest for Horses and, for a time, gained it fairly widespread acceptance in the smaller equine clinics. Most of these have now gone on to install gamma cameras.

Oakfield Instruments had begun life as John Caunt Scientific, a company making dedicated scaler timer rate meters for use in nuclear radiation detection and measurement. These were used to monitor radiation in the environment and the sheep contaminated during the Chernobyl disaster and its aftermath. Alan Caunt, one of the brothers involved in the initial company and now Managing Director of Oakfield Instruments, describes their early involvement.

"We were basically involved in producing a range of scientific equipment, for use in nuclear radiation detection and measurement. We initially developed a prototype system for Dr Vennart who was working with Don Attenburrow in Exeter. We then supplied a second system to John Walmsley, in Liphook. Peter Webbon of the Royal Veterinary College then purchased a standard SD1 rate meter and collimated sodium iodide probe, which I believe he first used in his research work and, later, for examining horses. This generated early interest and, at the same time, we were developing a small mini probe system for use as a heart monitor in man. This was the size of a hen's egg, and was a lot less cumbersome to use around horses' legs, and the mini probe in conjunction with the scaler rate meter eventually led to the development of the Apple Macintosh software system, by Mark Holmes. This development again generated a spurt of interest both within the UK, Europe and in America. We enjoyed working with the vets enormously during this period; they were much more fun to talk to and deal with than the medics! Although it was never a very commercial part of our organisation, we were keen to see things move forward and help in any way we could. One of the key events to the wider application of the probe was definitely the development of the software."

The use of the hand-held probe, in almost every instance, has led to the clinic concerned eventually acquiring a gamma camera. This was true in our case and, in 1996, we managed to obtain a Technicare Omega 500 camera, from a local hospital, which is in clinical use at the moment. Anyone who has used a camera after the probe needs no convincing over the enormity of the improvements in clinically useful information brought by the camera. The probe does have a place in lameness investigation. It is an excellent fracture detector, even if less useful in other roles. It also gets both clinicians and clients 'hooked' on the benefits of nuclear medicine at low cost. In the United States, although introduced to the Rood and Riddle practice by Larry Bramlage, the probe never really took off, and camera-based scintigraphy became the norm. Initially, this was confined to schools of veterinary medicine although, in the last 10 years, over 30 private practices have installed gamma cameras; and the momentum seems to be picking up continuously.

One of the seminal figures in the development of scintigraphy in America was Bill Hornof who was responsible for the organisation of a nuclear medicine facility at the University of California in Davis. This eventually led to the introduction of the first racetrack facility to have a gamma camera available for track veterinarians in the Dolly Green Centre at Santa Anita Racetrack. Bill Hornof picks up the tale:

"I finished my Masters Degree... and took on a Faculty position which had become available at the University of Davis to develop the veterinary nuclear medicine programme. At the time, the department had an old rectilinear scanner. This wasn't used a lot, and they just used to look at a couple of thyroids a year, something like that. When I started in 1979, the funding was already in place, and we bought a Siemens gamma camera

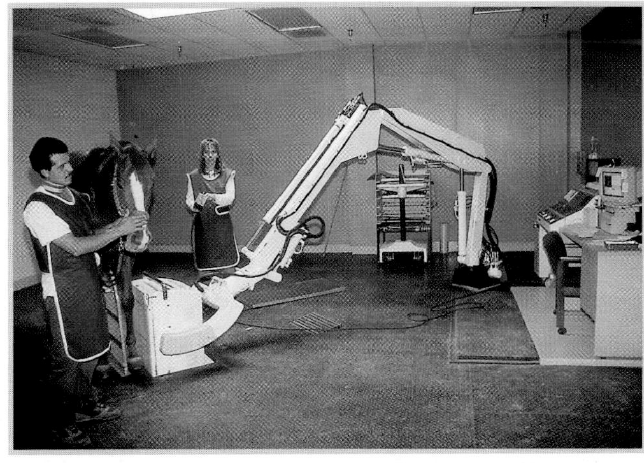

Fig 6: The Dolly Green Foundation gamma camera suite, situated trackside at Santa Anita racetrack in the USA., available to all the racetrack veterinarians and, more importantly, their patients.

which was adapted to a hand-operated fork lift truck. All the appointments at Davis are a 50:50 split between clinical and research and so ours was around the same. Initially, although we had a large racehorse practice with Don Wheat and Dennis Meaher, we didn't see a massive number of straight referrals for bone scan. Don and Dennis saw a lot of horses which showed occult lameness and a lot of these were stress fractures. These were often picked up early, and were radiographically invisible at that time, and these were quite exciting cases in those days. Things really took off in terms of primary interest in bone scan cases, with the work that Sue Stover and her group were doing on the necropsy programme. Sue showed a lot of catastrophic failures that were linked to chronic stress fractures in the same site, and this made us sit up and take notice of these horses who were moving badly on the racetracks. One of the problems we have had in our individual caseload is that this has moved nuclear medicine much further up the line, in terms of the sequence of events in lameness investigation, and so our actual strike rate for stress fractures has declined as more of these injuries are picked up through screening on the tracks."

The unit at Davis, in conjunction with the necropsy programme which Dr Sue Stover was running, generated an enormous amount of interest in the identification of skeletal injuries prior to catastrophic failure. Stover and her group meticulously subjected to *postmortem* examination every single fatality from the racehorse population at the Southern Californian tracks. It soon became apparent that many of these horses were carrying low grade 'occult' stress fractures, at sites which were common predilection sites for catastrophic failure. If it were only possible to detect these lesions in the living horse, some of these failures could probably be avoided. The close association of Sue Stover with the radiology people at Davis turned the focus of attention, in many cases, in novel directions. For instance, the oblique view of the wing of the ilium, described by Bill Hornof and his colleagues, was a retrospective development once the site of the lesion in the ilial wing had been seen repeatedly at *postmortem*. In other words, knowing where to look and thinking of how to look led to the development of novel imaging positions and techniques. At the same time, Rick Arthur, a track veterinarian at the Southern Californian group of racetracks comprising Santa Anita, Hollywood Park and Delmar, was becoming more and more intrigued with the possibilities of scintigraphy and was pondering over the possibility of having a trackside facility developed for the use of all the horses in that racehorse population. Rick Arthur says:

"I have always been interested in diagnostic imaging. My interest in the possibilities of nuclear scintigraphy in equine orthopaedic disease goes back to the late '70s and early '80s, but everything seemed so impractical then... I had been trying to drum up interest from my colleagues to develop a nuclear scintigraphy facility, at Santa Anita or Hollywood Park, for several years, without success. Jay Rose developed the first unit in Southern California at his San Luis Rey Equine Clinic about 1990; Doug Herthel, a few years later, installed a unit at Alamo Pintado, Clinic in the Santa Ynez Valley. Even though one was a few hours north and the other a few hours south of Los Angeles, there were soon horses travelling every few days to one facility or another.

The UC Davis/California Horse Racing Board Necropsy Programme provided the irrefutable information that current diagnostic imaging methods on the track were inadequate for racing horses. The obvious conclusion when analysing Dr Stover's work on the humerus was that nuclear scintigraphy was the diagnostic imaging technique of choice to identify stress fractures. The horrific racing breakdown of Go For Wand in the 1990 Breeders' Cup at Belmont was a wake-up call for racetrack management. They could no longer pretend it was not a problem. Where, before, the Santa Anita management showed no interest in having a nuclear imaging facility on site, they now wanted to be the first track to have one. Mr Robert Strub, the late President of Santa Anita, made sure we had full cooperation from his people.

Gaining funding for this work was easier for us than anyone else I know. I was President of the Southern California Equine Hospital when we received a large bequest from Miss Dolly Green, a racehorse owner (her Brave Raj won the Breeders' Cup Juvenile Fillies race in the mid-'80s) and animal welfare supporter. I was able to convince my board and hospital administrator that this was the ideal first project for these funds, and they agreed. Santa Anita gave us the building to use, and we were off and running. Dr Bill Hornof was our adviser from UCD. Our goal was to have as good a facility as we could afford, and we went first class! The SCEF is a nonprofit organisation and profit was never a consideration, though we try to meet expenses.

We have made diagnoses which simply are not or cannot be made by other means. Humeral, tibial, scapular and pelvic stress fractures are the best example. We find pathology today we never knew existed and others at frequencies we never expected.

Our philosophy when we installed our facility at Santa Anita was that the primary care veterinarian is in a better position to evaluate nuclear scintigraphic findings than anyone else. Obviously there is a learning curve and we are still on it, but I see the future in better management of orthopaedic disease in athletic horses. Most of what we deal with is really overstress of bone. I believe nuclear scintigraphy will become a management factor in 'bone' conditioning. Most trainers of any competence are very adept at cardiovascular conditioning, but they know very little of conditioning bones."

In the United Kingdom, most of the schools of veterinary medicine had by now begged, borrowed or stolen a gamma camera of some description, but no one in these institutions had really set the world alight scintigraphically. The first private racehorse practice to put in a gamma camera was the Valley Equine Hospital in Lambourn. This ambitious young hospital, set up by Barry Park, was really 'buzzing' in the early 1990s. It had attracted a bright young ultrasound specialist, Celia Marr, to leave academia and go back into private practice. Barry Allen, the blood 'guru' from the Animal Health Trust, had joined the team and was running the lab, and other highly motivated clinicians had been recruited to make the hospital a success. I caught up with Barry Park, probably one of the most cheerful vets one could meet, having just sold his hospital and on the verge of becoming a man of leisure, at the December sales in Newmarket.

"We first really thought about scintigraphy after a BEVA lecture given by Ueltschi from Geneva, who described the technique. As we were building a new place, it was the obvious embryonic diagnostic technique to get involved in.

We started with the probe, but quite quickly swopped over

to a gamma camera, for two reasons. Firstly, in that lecture, Ueltschi said that anyone who's serious about nuclear medicine should really use a gamma camera, and I just rate the man very highly Also, we were lucky, in a funny sort of way, in that the very first point counter we had, had a fault on the probe, and it naturally made us suspicious about the technique.

The final straw came when we did one horse five times on the same day, and missed a stress fracture on two of the five occasions. At that point we took everything to pieces and put it on the shelf, and I said I wouldn't use the technique again until we had a gamma camera. It was just luck that, later that night, I heard there was one coming out of a hospital and within six weeks we had one up and running.

Chronologically, it couldn't have happened at a better time. It was just towards the end of building this hospital, I'd already got on board some really good structural engineers and metalwork guys, who didn't even blink when I rang them about the weight of the thing. I just happened to have such good people around me, the logistics of fitting a gamma camera was just another small problem on top of 10,000 others!

I had a chap who was running the unit at that time, Alistair Nelson, who was extremely enthusiastic, and that must have helped to a certain degree in 'selling' the technique to our practice, but I was absolutely astounded how quickly they took to it. Clients loved it, they got into it really quickly, so much so that it almost overpowered us. The only frustration now is getting better pictures, and I don't think you can ever justify Prof. Ueltschi's idea of using general anaesthesia in a lameness diagnosis. I'm told that picture quality will improve with the computer end, and the camera now is as good as it gets. We are already on to our fourth different computer set-up and, again, that's improved the whole thing.

The success of the unit was really thanks to two individuals. One was Alistair Nelson, who was the veterinary surgeon running the show within the practice, and a chap called Nigel Soper, who is the head of the Nuclear Medicine Department with the John Radcliffe hospital in Oxford. It was his constant enthusiasm to appear late at night and at weekends when we were having problems with the computer and things; he kept us driving forward and still does today."

One of the most recent installations in the UK was the introduction of a gamma camera and sophisticated software at the Animal Health Trust in Newmarket. As a major referral institute, the Trust was quite late in going for scintigraphy. This was mainly due to the politics of the place, when during the 1980s it couldn't seem to decide whether to concentrate on research, or clinical work, or, as now, a mixture of both. It was also dogged by the spectre of the possible move to its now excellent site and facilities at Kennet. So although a gamma camera had been at the top of senior clinician Sue Dyson's 'wish-list' for a long time, it wasn't until very recently that she had a camera up and running. Sue had the frustration, for many years, of trying to run a top class referral service, but having to cross-refer her scintigraphic cases to us! Although we tried to offer a reasonable service, it was obviously an unsatisfactory state of affairs, for the horse, its owner and for the Trust. Things had to change and, in 1998, they did.

Sue takes a catchment of cases from a variety of equine sports, and is ideally placed to evaluate the usefulness of scintigraphy in this wider, non-Thoroughbred context, a role which she recently spoke to me about.

"I decided that I wanted a scintigraphic facility after attending Don Attenburrow's first Nuclear Medicine Conference, 13 years ago. However, the main problem through most of that time was funding it We felt that a probe counter just wouldn't be sensitive enough for the type of cases we dealt with. Once we got the eventual go-ahead for our facility, we looked at all the different companies, and had long talks with them in terms of flexibility and what they could offer us, and it was around the middle of last year that we finalised the deal with Nuclear Diagnostics for the Hermes system.

I think that, with the non-Thoroughbred sports horses which we see a lot of here, we are often dealing with more subtle type of problems. We see a different form of multilimb lameness than you get in the racehorse, and often lameness or poor performance which is just a difficulty in doing a specific manoeuvre, rather than an overt lameness. They don't move short, like the Thoroughbreds hurting all over, the clinical signs are very much more subtle. Once we have our scintigraphic images, we have definitely found it immensely useful in our sports horse cases to utilise the software, to manipulate images to analyse them quantitively and to superimpose the scan on top of the x-ray image, to accurately localise these often focal, subtle, lesions.

I think teasing apart the normal and abnormal in these cases is done with some difficulty, but we have been very lucky, and we have had the opportunity to scan quite a lot of normal horses, so we have some degree of database on what to expect in the normal range. We are never happy to assume a diagnosis on a scintigraphic finding alone; I am really opposed to doing anything without good clinical back-up.

I think that standardisation between workers is important. This is something we have been discussing with the group at Uppsala, because they do have the same system and we do have the potential to collaborate. The problem is that they have got a very different horse population and, therefore, you can't put like with like. I think that with sufficient quality images and case numbers, it would be useful to compile an atlas of normal and abnormal scintigraphic images. One of the things that I get a little bit worried about is that, like with all these imaging modalities, more and more people jump on the bandwagon, some with rather inferior imaging capabilities, then they start to make the diagnoses based on dubiously diagnostic quality pictures. I think we really have to try and guard against this.

"For the future here at the Trust, I think because we have got a lot of high detailed scans, we now need to sit down with an enormous number of these scans and go through them in a very rigorous way, because I am sure there is data there that we have missed. I am sure there are diagnoses there that we might have been missing because we have not had time to do a proper study of the data we have accumulated. There is a tendency to get overwhelmed with the clinical cases, without the back-up time this imaging technique deserves and requires. We all just seem to need more time, more days in the week!"

The new, purpose-built facility uses a dual camera-head tomography system, in conjunction with the Nuclear Diagnostics Hermes data processing software. This software allows for correction of patient movement during the acquisition of a scan, which is extremely useful in horses. The respiratory cycle alone introduces several millimetres of cranial and caudal movement in a horse, even when it is apparently perfectly still. Similarly, this software allows the coregistration of radiographic and scintigraphic images, allowing more accurate identification of hot spots in relation

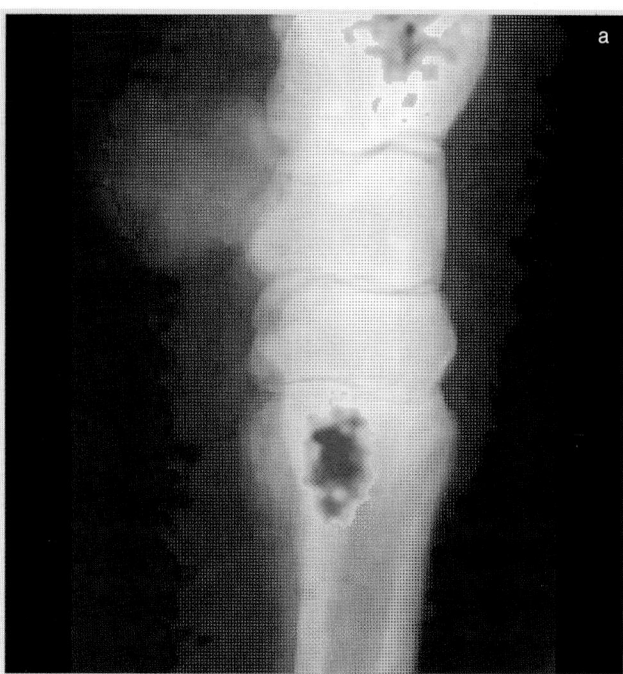

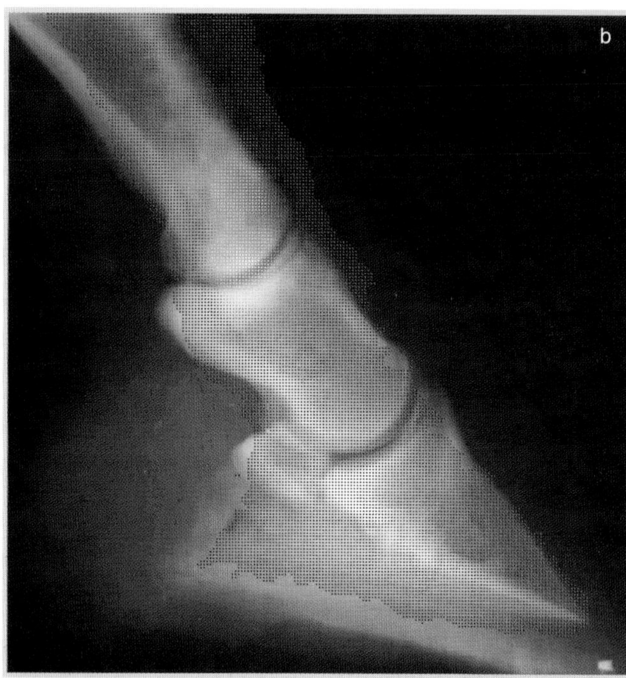

Figs 7a and b: Examples of image coregistration, from the Animal Health Trust, Newmarket. Using the computer software, a radiograph and a nuclear medicine study of the same site are superimposed on top of each other, to highlight the exact location of a 'hot spot'. In these cases, it is identified at the site of a stress fracture in the palmar metacarpus (a) and subchondral bone injury in the proximal interphalangeal joint (b). Both of these lesions initially showed no abnormality on radiography, but were later associated with radiological change.

to bony structures (see Figs 7a,b). Most data-handling software packages have a variety of programmes and protocols which we are only just beginning to play with in equine practice. However, it is unlikely that many of these will achieve the widespread application enjoyed by musculoskeletal scanning. As Peter Webbon commented:

> *"I think bone scanning is, and is probably going to remain, the number one technique in the horse. The use of scintigraphy in man in situations like kidney monitoring and heart monitoring is not really applicable to the horse. The main reason human clinicians want to look at kidney viability and clearance is because of the transplantation programme and, similarly, the only reason we are interested in heart blood flow in man is because of the high incidence of myocardial infarction. Neither of these situations present much of a problem in the horse and, therefore, really the limitations of use of scintigraphy are limitations of indication rather than limitations of ability to carry out that protocol on the horse."*

There are probably a dozen gamma cameras in private equine practice in the UK alone. There is no doubt that, from the introduction of the single hand-held probe into the clinical situation in the late '60s and early '70s, to the now increasing availability of gamma cameras, we have made massive strides forward in our understanding of a variety of orthopaedic conditions which we could only previously guess at. With this understanding, we can sometimes achieve the ultimate goal of the veterinary surgeon, prevention of injury, rather than its treatment.

Catastrophic humeral fractures in the United States have declined to negligible levels in some practices because of screening for the incomplete stress fracture in the same site using the gamma camera. Full blown, displaced, tibial fractures in Newmarket are almost unheard of nowadays, whereas 15 years ago they were not uncommon. Similarly, the occurrence of displaced pelvic fractures has declined, following our ability to pick up these lesions in the early stages, from an integration of scintigraphy and ultrasound. None of these advances would have been possible without the pioneering work carried out by the people described in this article, to whom we, and our equine patients, owe an enormous debt of gratitude.

Acknowledgements

I would like to thank all of the people who were interviewed in the preparation of this chapter for giving up their time so freely. I would also like to thank Dr Sten Carlson, for background on the history of nuclear medicine, and Don Attenburrow, Professor Ueltschi, Bob Twardock, Rick Arthur and Tim Donovan, for provision of illustrations.

Further Reading

Attenburrow, D.P., Bowring, C.S. and Vennart, W. (1984) Radioisotope bone scanning in horses. *Equine vet. J.* **16**, 121-124.

The first description of the use of a probe in equine bone scanning.

Carlsson, S. (1995) A glance at the history of nuclear medicine. *Acta Oncologica* **34**, 1095-1102.

A good synopsis of the development of both radiopharmaceuticals and the electronic technology' involved.

Devous, M.D. and Twardock, A.R. (1984) Techniques and applications of nuclear medicine in the diagnosis of equine lameness. *J. Am. vet. med. Ass.* **184**, 318-325.

One of the milestone papers, describing the technique and some typical case studies.

Mackey V.S., Trout D.R., Meagher D.M. and Hornof, W.J. (1987) Stress fractures of the humerus radius and tibia in horses. *Vet. Radiology* **28**, 26-31.

The first description of many of the stress fractures we now realise are so common in the athletic horse.

O'Callaghan, M.W. (1991) The integration of alternative imaging methods in the diagnosis of equine orthopaedic disease. *Vet Clin. N. Am.: Equine Pract.* **7**, 342.

A good example of the 'extra mile' scintigraphy can give in difficult cases, by one of those responsible for a major input into the development of the science, particularly lung scanning.

Developments in equine diagnostic ultrasonography

NORMAN RANTANEN
PO Box 1351
Fallbrook
California 92088
USA

In 1976, I joined the faculty at Washington State University, College of Veterinary Medicine, Pullman, Washington. One of the topics of discussion with Dr Ron Sande, the Radiology Department Chairman, and Dr Jack Alexander (radiologist), Head of Clinics, was alternative imaging. We discussed the merits of nuclear scintigraphy, computerised tomography (CT) and diagnostic ultrasound over the next couple of years and rapidly realised that the university couldn't afford CT or nuclear medicine. We were negotiating to buy used radiology equipment from human hospitals because the university was not purchasing new equipment for any department.

Ron and I decided that diagnostic ultrasound was to be our venture into alternative imaging. We launched an investigation into the practicality for use both in large and small animals, since it was easier to justify equipment purchase if all species could be examined. Ron Sande allowed me to pursue the technology and gave me encouragement along the way. I attended several workshops given by Sacred Heart Medical Center in Spokane, Washington, to learn the science and to pick the brains of the sonographers regarding equine applications. Several physics types were keen on giving us advice and wished us luck.

After much soul searching, reading, talking to physicists and using the equipment at workshops, WSU was able to purchase our first ultrasound machine for $62,500 from Unirad Ultrasound, Denver, Colorado. The money came from the Autzen foundation, a private source of money. The Dean of the Veterinary School, Dr Leo Bustad, went in to bat for us and helped procure the funds.

The system we purchased was a static B-Mode scanner that was the state of the art at the time. Real time instruments were in their infancy and most medical scanning was performed with the static imagers. The image quality was exquisite, depth of penetration was up to 50 cm and transducer frequencies were available from 2.0 to 12 MHz. The only drawback was that successful use of the B-Mode scanner required some patient cooperation. Since the image was formed by passing the scanhead across the body surface and viewing the image on the monitor, patient movement required the process to be repeated. I spent over one hour unsuccessfully trying to obtain diagnostic images of a horse's liver that had hepatoencephalopathy which caused it to sway to and fro. These systems are referred to as the 'salami slicers' of days gone by because of the necessity to form the image 'slice' manually. Colorado State University purchased similar equipment about the same time. The first paper published on equine imaging with the B-Mode scanner appeared in 1980 in the American Institute of Ultrasound in Medicine proceedings. Articles published after that time in the *Journal of Veterinary Radiology* required an 18 month review before they were accepted because the editorial staff didn't understand the new modality.

Unirad offered a training course that was part of the equipment purchase price. Courses were held in Denver, Colorado, and models were hired to lie on tables for the scanning sessions. Dr Ray Powis was the medical education director for Unirad. He, his wife Wendy, an accomplished sonographer from Australia, Courtney Stanley, renowned sonographer, famous for bizarre real-time scans later on, and others, formed the team that taught the course. WSU had

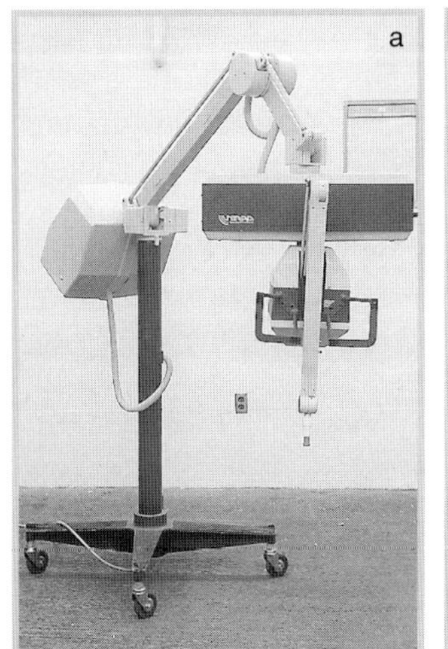

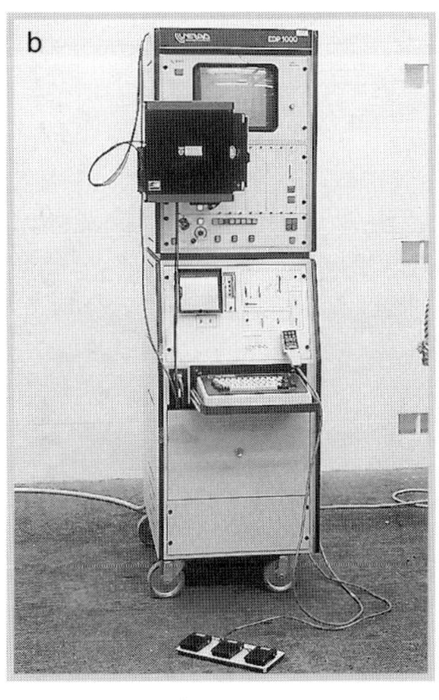

Unirad 'salami slicer' B-Mode scanner in use in 1979 at Washington State University.

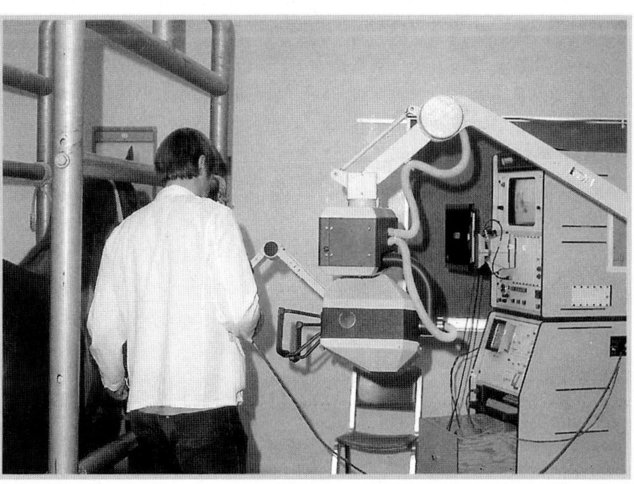

State of the Art!

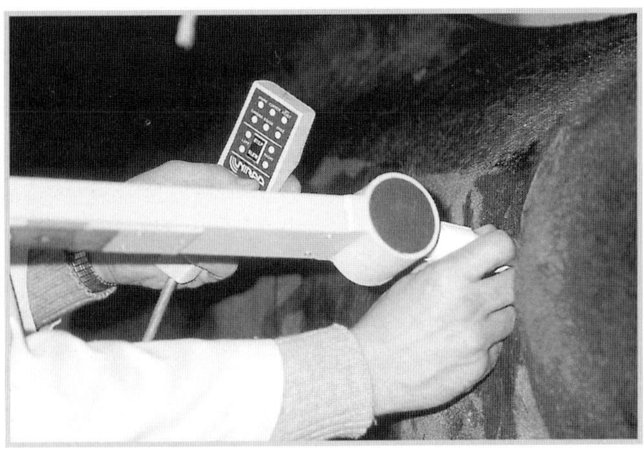

Forming the image by passing the transducer over the skin surface.

hired an on-the-job training person, Robert Ewing, who was to be the ultrasound technician. He attended the course with me, which created some difficulty. The course was given at a motel in Denver on two different floors. The lecture was downstairs and the coffee breaks and scanning lab were upstairs. Since Bob Ewing was confined to a wheelchair, my critique of the course included the 26 stairs that separated the two floors, and the hotel did not have an elevator. Go to lecture, carry Bob to coffee break, back to lecture, carry Bob to lunch... This was truly an aerobic ultrasound course for me. We had good laughs about it, making our friendship even closer and more enjoyable.

Ray Powis, renowned author of *Ultrasound Physics For The Fun Of It*, 34,000 copies of which were distributed by Unirad, did a brilliant job of instructing the class in the intricacies of ultrasonographic imaging in Denver. During one intense session, after he had discussed sound beam penetration, hampered by attenuation of the sound beam by the tissues, I asked, "*What do you do when your patient weighs 1200 lbs?*" This caused some delay in his normally rapid response to enquiries during the lecture and started his relationship with veterinary imaging that has lasted for nearly 20 years. Ray was renowned for his Whisky and Pizza parties that were a part of the short course. He and Wendy have published modern versions of his text entitled *Son of Ultrasound Physics for the Fun of It* in a medical as well as veterinary format. They hope to sell 34,000 copies of the rewrite since the first copies were given away! Ray and Wendy spent many hours at Washington State and allowed us to adapt the equipment to all species. They taught a large portion of the first two veterinary ultrasound short courses given at Washington State University.

When we ventured into real-time imaging, after borrowing a linear array scanner from a Portland hospital, Ray and Wendy were again there for us. Dr Timothy Lee, whose fame included scanning an elephant as well as a successful medical practice, helped us teach the science during the short courses. Dr Marvin Gottschall, Chairman of the Radiology Department at Sacred Heart Medical Center, also helped us teach the short courses and opened his department to us to learn the science. Drs Ernie Carlson, Paul Carson and countless others ensured that we started off on the right track and correctly learned the science from the bottom up.

Steve DuMond helped train Bob Ewing while DuMond was working at a private hospital in Western Washington. Steve later became an application specialist and a veterinary marketing person for Advanced Technology Laboratories (ATL), Bellevue, Washington and went on to become one of the leaders in the veterinary ultrasound market. He currently owns Classic Medical Supply, Tequesta, Florida and has been instrumental in supporting continuing education in veterinary diagnostic ultrasound over the years. During the time when the American Association of Equine Practitioners did not allow exhibitors to display their equipment, Steve would rent a suite and show the instruments. Largely through his effort, the veterinary profession was made aware of what was available to them.

Bob Ewing eventually left Washington State University and pursued formal training in medical ultrasound technology, with some encouragement from Ron Sande and me. He coauthored the first ultrasound articles on ultrasound imaging in horses while at WSU, but went on to bigger and better things in medical imaging.

Mike Hauser, when he was a veterinary student, came to me one day and asked: "*I am interested in the application of ultrasound to horses; is some anatomical area that you think would be important, but don't have time for?*" I told him I thought tendon scanning was going to be important and suggested that he work out the anatomy and that he could be first author on any publications. Thus, tendon scanning was born. Dr Hauser was instrumental in helping two residents complete master's theses in ultrasound application to animals and in producing a videotape on ultrasound guided biopsy in horses, all while he was a veterinary student.

Drs Polly Modransky, Laurie Gage, Mary Rose Paradis, Rick DeBowes, John Foreman, Steve Reed, Warwick Bayly, Pam Wagner and Josie Traub were some of the first equine clinicians to use ultrasound in the early days. In the early 1980s, horses were being scanned for pleuropneumonia, renal calculi, abdominal neoplasia, etc., by the fine team of equine clinicians and residents. Paramount to the success of equine diagnostic ultrasound was Dr Barrie Grant, head of Equine Surgery at WSU. He was the one that dragged me out of the radiology suite after asking me if ultrasound would work for this or that in the horse. Before that time, I didn't know which end of the horse to throw feed to. Because of his diligence and threats to the equine residents (and me) that no cases would escape ultrasound diagnosis if at all possible, equine ultrasound was accelerated at a fast pace.

Word of ultrasound's success in diagnosis was broadcast by Dr William Jones, Editor of the *Journal of Equine Veterinary Science* and *Equine Veterinary Data*. The first use of ultrasound in pregnancy diagnosis in the mare was introduced by Dr Eric Palmer in Europe and reported in the *Theriogenology Journal* (Palmer and Draincourt, 1980). Interest in ultrasound was also generated in Lexington, Kentucky, for application to brood mares and several practitioners (David Parrish, Walter Zent and Bill Baker) came to Pullman for the second short course on equine ultrasound. Prior to that time, Drs David Parrish and Walter Zent, of the Hagyard-Davidson and McGee Equine Practice, travelled to WSU to investigate the new diagnostic modality. Dave Parrish thought he was travelling to the end of the earth landing at Pullman Airport in the middle of winter. He describes this lonely person (me) standing in the snow along the runway waiting for the plane to land. The Dean of the Veterinary School, Dr Leo Bustad, always said that Pullman wasn't the end of the earth, but, if you stood on your tiptoes, you could see it from there.

A visit to Lexington, Kentucky, was arranged by Steve DuMond, then at ATL in Bellevue, Washington. Dr Richard

Torbeck (theriogenologist), Steve and I travelled to Lexington and raced around the countryside scanning pregnant brood mares and I gave a seminar at the Hilton Hotel in Lexington. We absolutely froze to death in the cold Lexington spring. There were no large cars to rent and the ultrasound system was large enough that the small wagon we had was just big enough if the back seat was down. It meant that Torbeck and I had to take turns lying in the back of the station wagon along side the equipment between destinations. That, plus the cold and the stale popcorn and beer, which were our survival rations, nearly killed all three of us. The trip was a success, however, and several sets of twins were found that were unexpected.

Shortly after that time, Dr W. R. Allen came to Lexington from England with linear array ultrasound equipment from Scotland and did a similar programme. We were supposed to be there at the same time, but his travel was delayed. Because the equipment he demonstrated was cheaper than the ATL sector scanner, sales were brisk. There was a down side to the linear array technology available at that time, however. The linear array ultrasound beams had marginal lateral resolution in the near field portion of the beam where the gestational sac(s) were imaged. With the ATL sector scanner, however, the resolution allowed detection of the embryonic cardiac pulse at 20 or 21 days and twins were relatively easy to differentiate. Price of the equipment did win, however, and most people bought the cheaper equipment with the marginal focusing. Needless to say the practice of ultrasound had a shaky start. Some practitioners, by their own admission, allowed seven or eight sets of twins go to term because of missed diagnoses. So the introduction of equine pregnancy scanning in Lexington, Kentucky (and other places) was a disaster because of a simple thing like poor focusing: the equipment wasn't made for high resolution pregnancy scanning in the near field and was 'sold' from the medical market to naive veterinarians.

In 1983, I decided to move my practice to Lexington, Kentucky, at the urging of Rob and Kim Gaines, who were accomplished medical sonographers in Lexington. They wanted to develop the animal scanning to complement their effort in medical imaging. Through their financial backing and patience, animal scanning on a consultation level gained a foothold in Lexington. Just before that time, Dr Douglas Byars joined Hagyard-Davidson and McGee veterinary practice to develop the specialty of equine internal medicine. He and I worked as a team and were able to define a number of equine disease conditions. When I arrived in Lexington, many practitioners told me that an ultrasound consultation practice wouldn't be successful, because horses in Lexington didn't suffer from liver or kidney disease. Ironically, the first horse that I scanned for Dr Byars was a yearling with a primary liver disease and the second was a yearling colt with renal fibrosis, calculi and renal failure. After that, my confidence level increased. Dr James Becht joined their practice shortly after and contributed greatly to the initial investigation of equine ultrasound diagnosis.

About that time, I gave short talks at an AAEP meeting in an upstairs suite (AAEP did not allow exhibitors at that time) and Ron Genovese was in one of the groups that visited throughout the night. The next morning we met and he said that he had to have the technology and we formed a plan. I went to Cleveland and spent a cold, miserable, rainy day scanning with him at his invitation (it's still raining there). He is currently considered the guru of tendon and ligament scanning and is recognised worldwide as the tendon scanning authority.

Mike Hauser came to Lexington in 1984 and worked with me and was able further to develop his expertise in tendon and ligament scanning and racetrack practice. Rob and Kim Gaines had had all the fun they could stand with the effort in starting the practice and offered their assets for sale. Mike Hauser and I came close to working together, but racetrack practice and being able to work with the late Dr Tom Montgomery, who pioneered laser surgery in horses, lured him away.

Ron Genovese, Mike Hauser and I gave a halfday presentation at the 1984 AAEP meeting on diagnostic ultrasound, which more or less launched the technology for all facets of diagnosis. Mike was a new graduate and Ron was a longstanding member of the AAEP and neither one had given any presentations in front of the group. The presentation was given the last afternoon of the meeting and I practically had to hold them both at gun point to keep them from running off. The talks were a success and, I believe, helped convince practitioners that diagnostic ultrasound was a technology that had a bright future in veterinary medicine.

Currently, several textbooks have been written specifically addressing ultrasound diagnosis in horses for virtually all disease conditions. The technology has proven to be efficacious and today, it is unlikely that tendon and ligament injuries are diagnosed or treated without imaging. Pregnancy diagnosis, twin detection, obstetrical problems, etc., are best evaluated with sonography. Strides in diagnosing, treating and managing cardiac, respiratory and abdominal diseases in horses almost always include diagnostic ultrasound imaging. Numerous articles covering virtually all facets of equine medical and surgical diseases have ultrasound at the forefront of the diagnostic procedures. It is truly a technology that is ideal for horses, one of the most difficult species to diagnose musculoskeletal, thoracic and abdominal diseases. It was the only alternate imaging modality that WSU could afford in 1978.

The theoretical limit of resolution in ultrasound has probably been achieved for practical application in horses. Tendon and ligament ultrasound is now being done at 10 MHz. It is interesting that the important parameters in diagnosis and rehabilitation, at this time, seem to be the tendon cross-sectional area, relative lesion size and fibre alignment during healing which don't require the highest frequency and can be evaluated with 7.5 MHz. The application of colourflow Doppler to healing tendons and ligaments, to me, will provide valuable prognostic information. Three-dimensional ultrasound, which is in its early investigation, should provide more information to refine the excellent work done on the two-dimensional tendon images by Dr Ron Genovese. This may have an application in reproductive scanning as well. Instruments have low frequency sector and annular array transducers that display 30 cm fields of view which include most of the tissue accessible through the various 'windows' in horses, including hearts in the largest of the breeds. In my opinion, the future application of ultrasound in horses will once again follow the lead of human imaging and will include the determination of blood flow parameters in injured and diseased tissues and shoud provide us with even more diagnostic parameters to consider.

Equine computed tomography and magnetic resonance imaging: now or (n)ever

KEES DIK
Department of Radiology
Faculty of Veterinary Medicine
University of Utrecht
Yalelaan 10
3584 CM Utrecht
The Netherlands

CHRIS WHITTON
Centre for Equine Studies
Animal Health Trust
Lanwades Park
Kentford, Newmarket
Suffolk CB8 7UU
UK

The most established imaging modality, in the diagnosis and management of equine diseases, is radiography. This technique provides superior detail of bone and bony lesions. However, radiography is of limited value in soft tissue evaluation and superimposition of adjacent structures is unavoidable.

Computed Tomography

Computed tomography (CT) is based on the attenuation of x-rays in a thin cross-sectional slice of the patient. These attenunation measurements are obtained by an x-ray tube-detector device, called the gantry, which rotates around the examined body part.

From the collected series of measurements the computer calculates the specific x-ray attenuation and the associated density of all small volumes (voxels) of the examined slice. Image reconstruction, i.e. translation of voxels in pixels, is then performed by correlation of specific density values to grey values. These gray scale pictures are displayed on a monitor and can be copied to film and/or archived on a disk or tape.

Tissue characterisation: Hounsfield scale

+	3500	
		Bone
+	250	
		Cartilage
+	125	Tendon
+	100	Muscle
+	70	
		Soft tissues, congealed blood
+	50	
		Brain tissue
+	30	
+	0	Water
-	100	Fat
-	500	Lung tissue
-	1000	Air

Fig 1: The Hounsfield scale.

Therefore, CT provides digitised cross-sectional images without overlap of adjacent structures, permits more sensitive soft tissue imaging and enables semiquantitive tissue characterisation by measurement of the Hounsfield level and profile (Fig 1) in the region of interest (ROI). Computed tomography also enables 3-dimensional image reconstruction based on a series of thin contiguous slices.

In human medicine, CT has been used since the early 1970s. CT examination of horses started in the mid-1980s. The large weight and size of horses requires a custom-built examination table, placed over and rigidly coupled to the original human patient table (Fig 2). The diameter of the gantry aperture usually is 60–70 cm and that of the measurement field is approximately 50 cm. This limits the use in horses to the head, the cranial region of the neck and the distal extremities.

Lateral recumbency of the horse facilitates stable positioning of these body parts within the gantry. Therefore, accurate design of the supplementary table requires detailed knowledge of various dimensions of the equine body, such as the length of the head and neck, trunk, limbs, etc. Collection of these data, in many Dutch Warmbloods, provided maximum table dimensions also suitable for other breeds (Fig 3).

For each examination the large animal table is placed over and coupled to the original scan table. The horse is anaesthetised elsewhere, transported to the examination room, lifted on the scan table, placed in lateral recumbency and the body part of interest is accurately positioned within

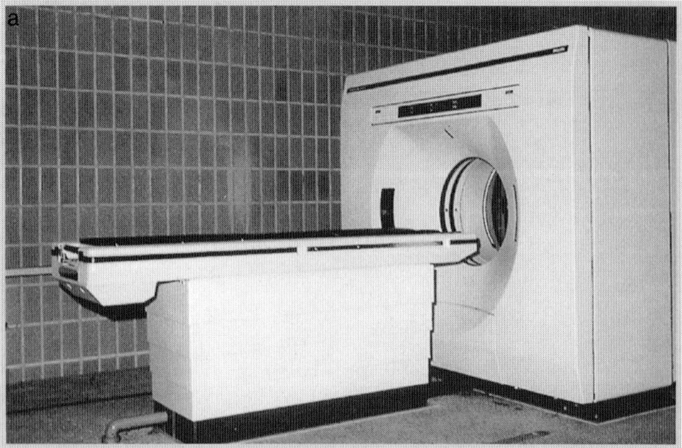

Figs 2: The CT unit with the original human patient table.

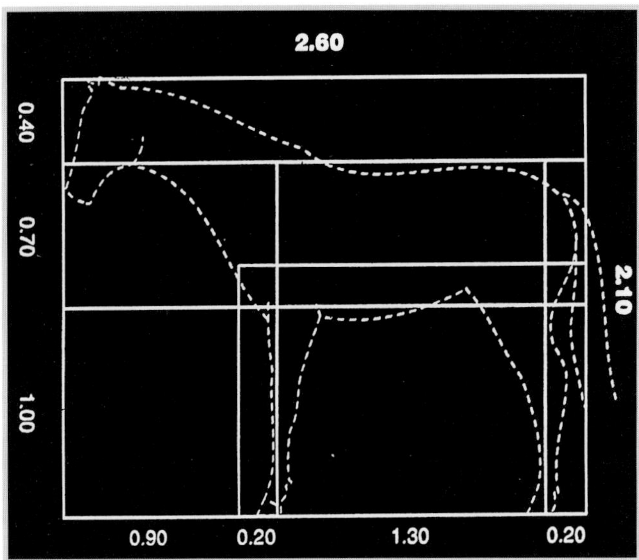

Fig 3: Maximum dimensions of the Dutch Warmblood.

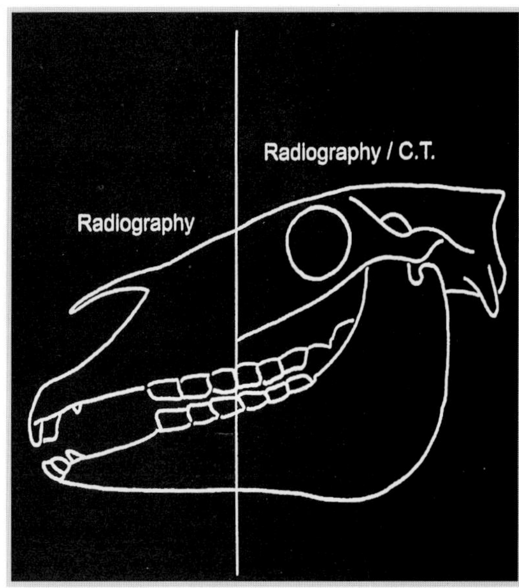

Fig 5: The regions of interest for radiographic versus CT examination of the equine skull.

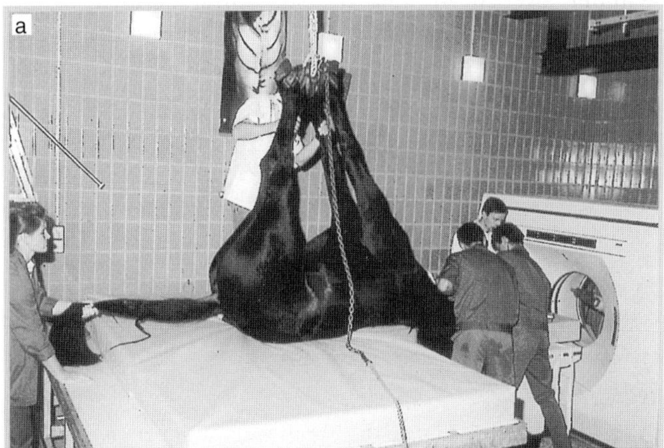

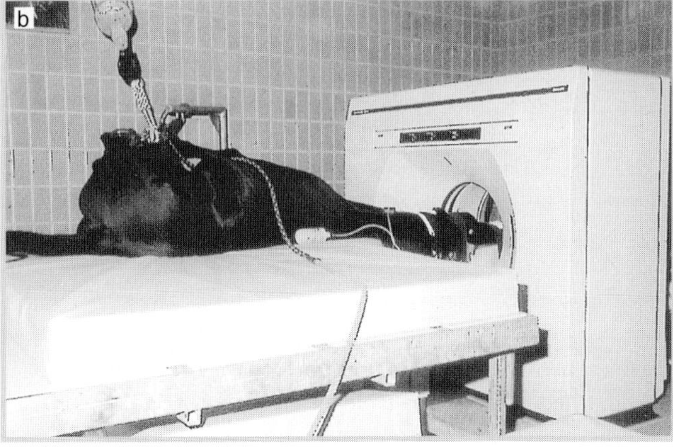

Figs 4a,b: Positioning of the horse for CT evaluation of the head.

the gantry (Figs 4a, b).

Examining the equine head, conventional radiography remains the basic imaging tool. Additional CT has great potential, particularly caudal to the premolar cheek teeth (Fig 5). In this region CT reveals clearly the location, extent, origin and character (Hounsfield level) of dental, conchal, paranasal sinus and ethmoidal abnormalities, thus clarifying the differential diagnosis of associated equivocal radiographic opacities (Figs 6a,b,c, 7, 8 and 9).

CT also enables accurate assessment of skull trauma, e.g. skull base fracture (Fig 10) or orbital trauma, which are frequently not obvious on survey radiographs. In such cases additional three-dimensional image reconstruction facilitates presurgical planning of fracture repair (Figs 11a,b,c).

Temporomandibular joint lesions are usually completely invisible on conventional radiographs, but clearly outlined on CT scans (Fig 12). The superior tool for imaging of the brain is Magnetic Resonance Imaging (MRI). If this modality is not available, CT is the second best option, pre- and/or postcontrast scans revealing a broad range of brain diseases (Figs 13 and 14). However, like radiography CT findings are seldomly specific for particular diseases and normal findings do not exclude brain abnormalities.

CT of the equine neck is rarely performed. In horses with cervical stenotic myelopathy it permits accurate measurement of the minimum sagittal diameter of the vertebral canal and CT evaluation following myelography enables differentiation between circumferential compression of the spinal cord and peripheral compression due to malformed articular facets. However, in horses the results of surgical decompression of the spinal cord are not very promising. Therefore such CT studies are of limited value. Other potential applications are the assessment of parotid gland or guttural pouch disease and abnormalities of the stylohyoid bone, if such lesions are not obvious on conventional radiographs.

Examining the equine limb, CT scans may demonstrate fracture fragments (Fig 15), stress-induced bone remodelling, or focal bone defects which are not apparent on conventional radiographs. Therefore, CT studies of the distal extremities are particularly indicated if radiographic lesions are absent or obscure, despite obvious clinical and/or scintigraphic abnormalities and negative ultrasonographic findings. CT also facilitates presurgical planning of repair of complex (phalangeal) fractures (Figs 16a).

In comparison with conventional radiographs, CT scans of the navicular bone more clearly show irregularity or defects of the flexor and articular surface, small fragments or enthesiophytes at the proximal or distal border and facilitates differentiation between inverted flask-shaped channels and cystic cortical or intramedullary defects. This may contribute to the understanding of the complex pathogenesis of navicular disease, but seldom will be essential for accurate diagnosis. Navicular disease may be limited to the soft tissues,

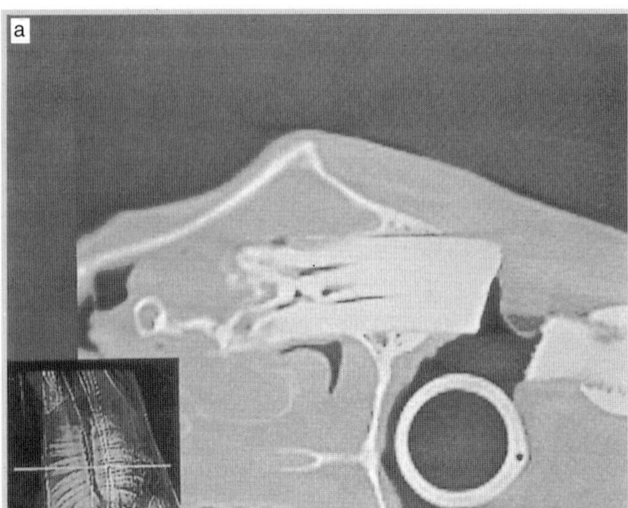

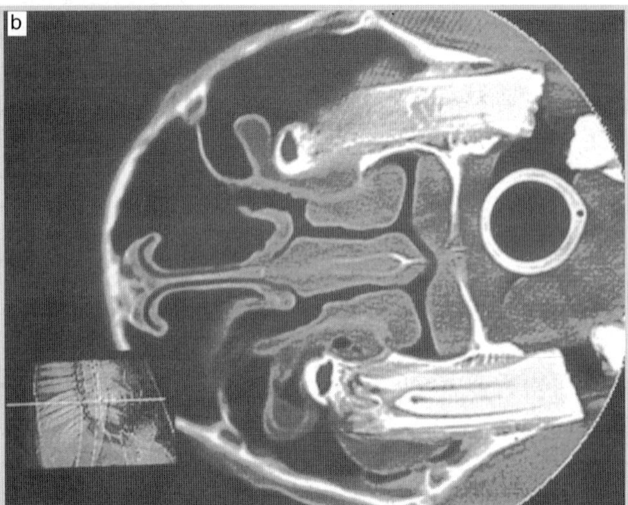

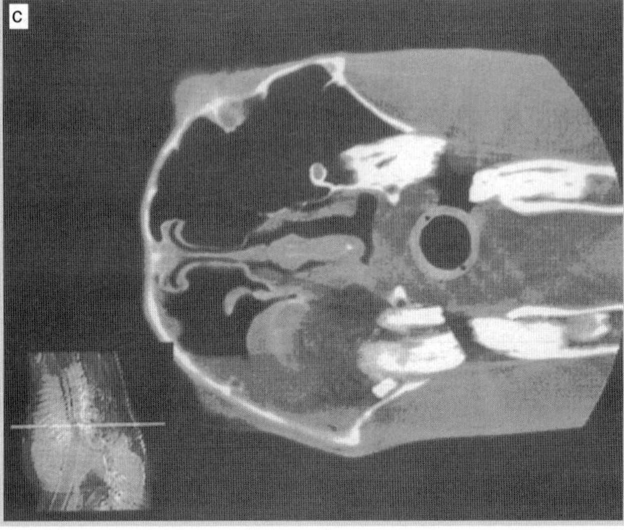

Figs 6a,b,c: Ventral conchal and maxillary sinus opacification combined with intra-alveolar gas (M1) indicating secondary sinusitis (a), versus intraconchal gas superimposing the normal M2 indicating primary sinusitis (b), or consisting of gas and a horizontal fluid level resulting from food impaction through a sagittal M3 fracture (c).

e.g. the deep digital flexor tendon, the navicular bursa and the flexor surface fibrocartilage. Therefore, clinical navicular disease may be present in the absence of radiological changes. The soft tissue resolution of CT is inferior to MRI. Therefore, MRI apparently is the most promising modality for *in vivo* imaging of these structures and for early detection of navicular disease. It may also enable differentiation between navicular disease and other causes of palmar heel pain.

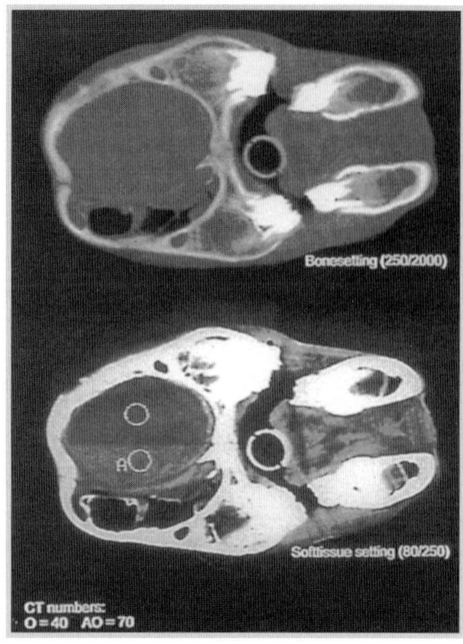

Fig 7: Extensive unilateral conchal opacification (P_3 region) with a horizontal fluid-fluid level separating serum (Hounsfield number 40) from cellular components (Hounsfield number 70), thus indicating a haemorrhagic cyst.

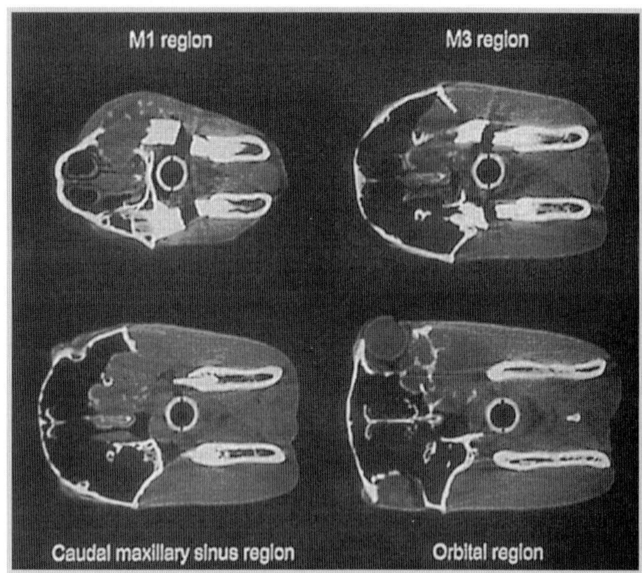

Fig 8: Ventral conchal and maxillary sinus opacification associated with extensive bone destruction, indicating a malignant tumour. Necropsy revealed a squamous cell carcinoma.

The soft tissue resolution of CT is also inferior to ultrasonography, but satisfactory for visualisation of major soft tissue structures. Therefore, CT studies of the equine limb also provide a working knowledge of the cross-sectional anatomy, which is a prerequisite for the appropiate use of cross-sectional imaging modalities, like CT, MRI and ultrasonography.

Presently, conventional radiography and ultrasonography are the main diagnostic imaging tools in equine medicine and surgery.

CT is relatively expensive and requires a custom-built examination table, as well as general anaesthesia. Nevertheless, since its introduction in the mid-1980s it has proven to be a valuable additional tool, particularly for imaging of the head, but also for the distal extremities.

MRI, enabling detailed imaging of bone, soft tissues and cartilage, has even greater potential. Therefore, in the long term, the role of CT in the diagnosis and management of equine diseases may be surpassed by MRI. Time will tell!

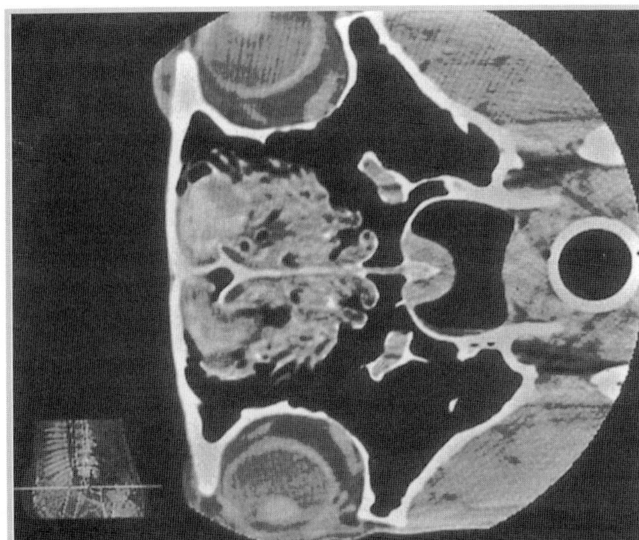

Fig 9: A bilateral mass in the dorsal ethmoturbinate region representing ethmoid haematomas.

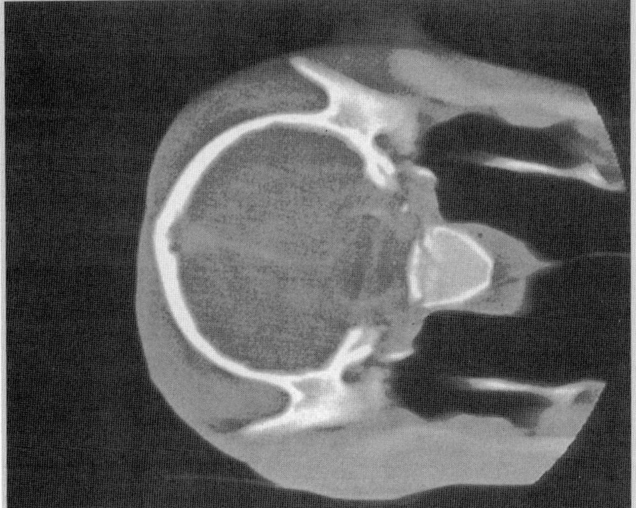

Fig 10: A skull base fracture.

Equine Magnetic Resonance Imaging

Introduction

MRI has been used extensively in human orthopaedics in the diagnosis of a variety of conditions. These include the detection of meniscal injuries[1], synovial thickening[2], pannus formation[3], bone contusions[4,5], articular cartilage erosions[6,7] and tendon pathology[8]. The quality of the information provided by MRI has stimulated some to state that MRI is superior to arthroscopy for examination of the knee joint[9], although this has been questioned by others[10]. However, there is evidence that MRI is extremely sensitive to early collagen degeneration in tendons[11], and it has been demonstrated that it is more sensitive than CT and radiography in detecting subchondral bone lesions in osteoarthritis[12].

The first report of the use of MRI in a cadaver equine limb was published in 1987 by Park and colleagues[13] using a 0.15 tesla device and a T1 weighted spin echo sequence. Crass and colleagues[14] reported the use of MRI to image tendons with acute and chronic injuries using a 1.5 tesla device and demonstrated similar sensitivity to that of ultrasound. The MRI appearance of the normal equine carpus has been reported[15]. The usefulness of midfield MRI for assessing the pathology within the foot has also been demonstrated[16,17]. Recently the imaging of limbs in live horses using a high field device was reported[18].

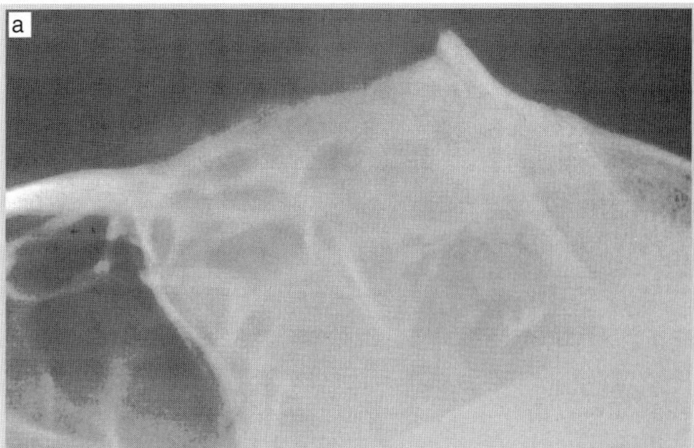

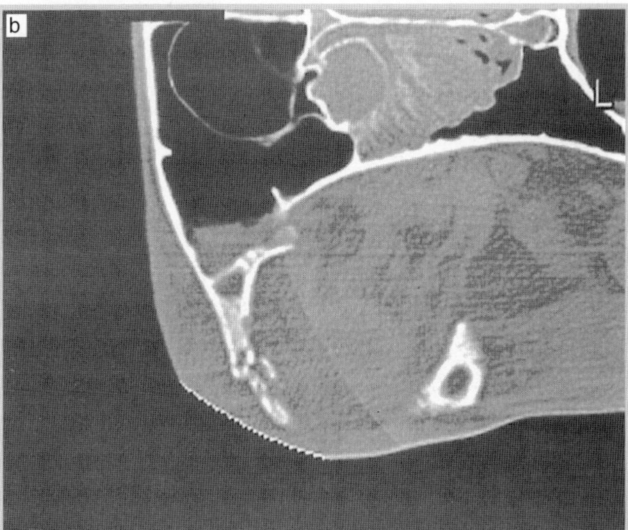

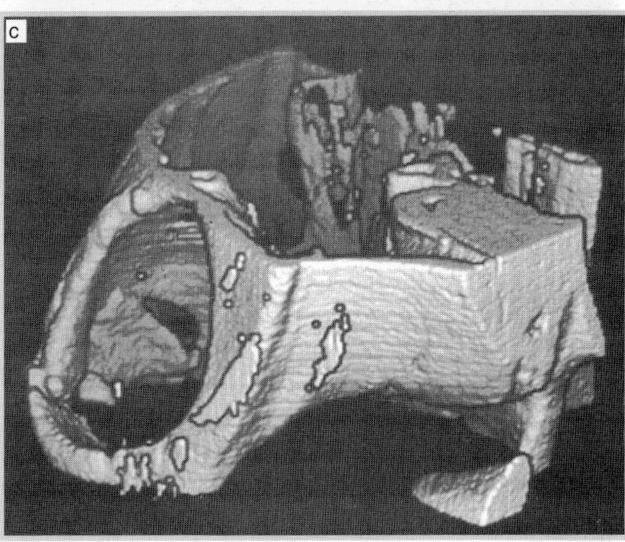

Figs 11a,b,c: Orbital trauma characterised by fragmentation of the supraorbital process, a defect in the inner orbital wall and a corresponding fluid level in the frontal sinus. These abnormalities are not obvious on a conventional dorsoventral oblique radiograph (a), but are clearly visible on CT scans (b) and the corresponding three dimensional image reconstruction (c).

Advantages of MRI Over Other Imaging Modalities

The major advantage of MRI over other diagnostic techniques is its ability to image soft tissues and bone with

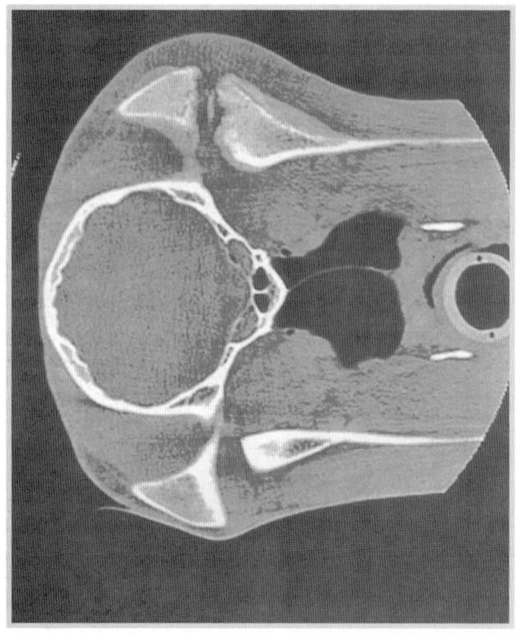

Fig 12: Temporomandibular joint infection resulting from a puncture wound.

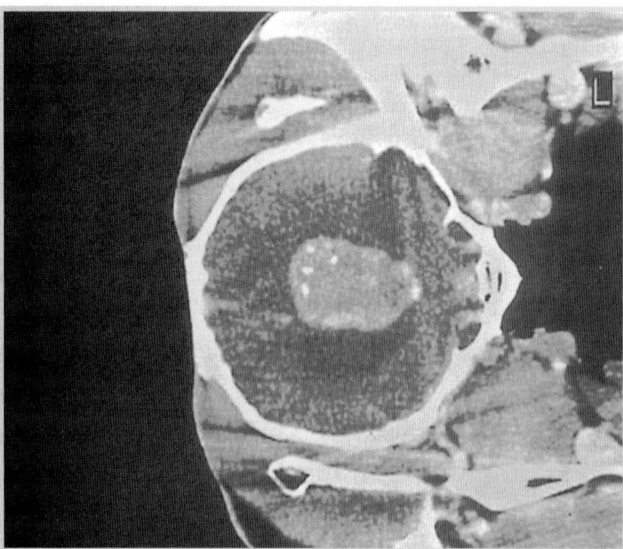

Fig 13: A choleristic granuloma.

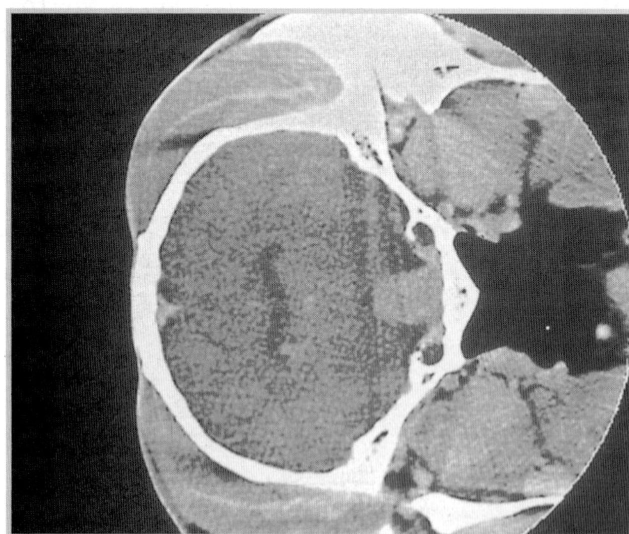

Fig 14: Postcontrast study showing a pituitary gland tumour.

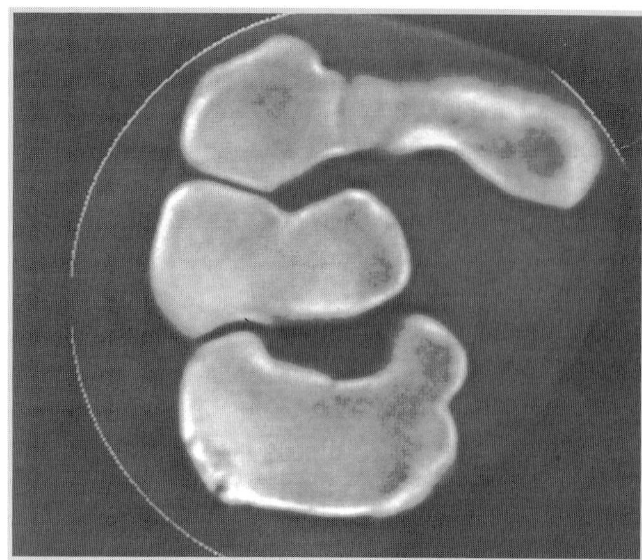

Fig 15: A chip fragment and the corresponding fracture bed in the radiocarpal bone.

high contrast. A single imaging technique can therefore be used to assess bone, ligaments, tendons, joint capsules and articular cartilage. This becomes extremely important when imaging the structures within the equine foot where ultrasound windows are limited due to the presence of the hoof wall, and radiography has been demonstrated to be both insensitive and nonspecific. Using different sequences, various properties of tissues can be assessed. The ability to image in any plane, and to provide three-dimensional information also offers advantages when information on the position of a lesion is important. MRI is the only imaging technique that can image articular cartilage in all parts of a joint[6].

Disadvantages of MRI

The use of MRI in horses is restricted by the huge cost of the equipment. The large size of magnets and the relative inaccessibility of the imaging area of MRI devices also limits the use of MRI in horses. General anaesthesia is required to allow safe positioning of the limbs or head within the magnet and to prevent movement during image acquisition. Handling tables need to be constructed of nonferrous material. The area that can be imaged (field of view) is generally small. Increasing the field of view results in a concomitant loss of resolution, restricting the areas that can be imaged in an imaging session.

Like all imaging techniques, artefacts can interfere with accurate diagnosis. Metal in particular interferes with the image, so that shoes must be removed along with any nail fragments that may be left behind; and areas containing metal implants cannot be imaged. As with other advanced imaging techniques, MRI provides extremely large volumes of information. A single study may provide up to 100 images which need to be reviewed and interpreted.

Live Horse MRI

Due to problems encountered in human medicine with patients with claustrophobia, and the inability to image people who are overweight, there has been a trend towards developing devices which have greater flexibility. Low field open magnets allow much greater accessibility to the

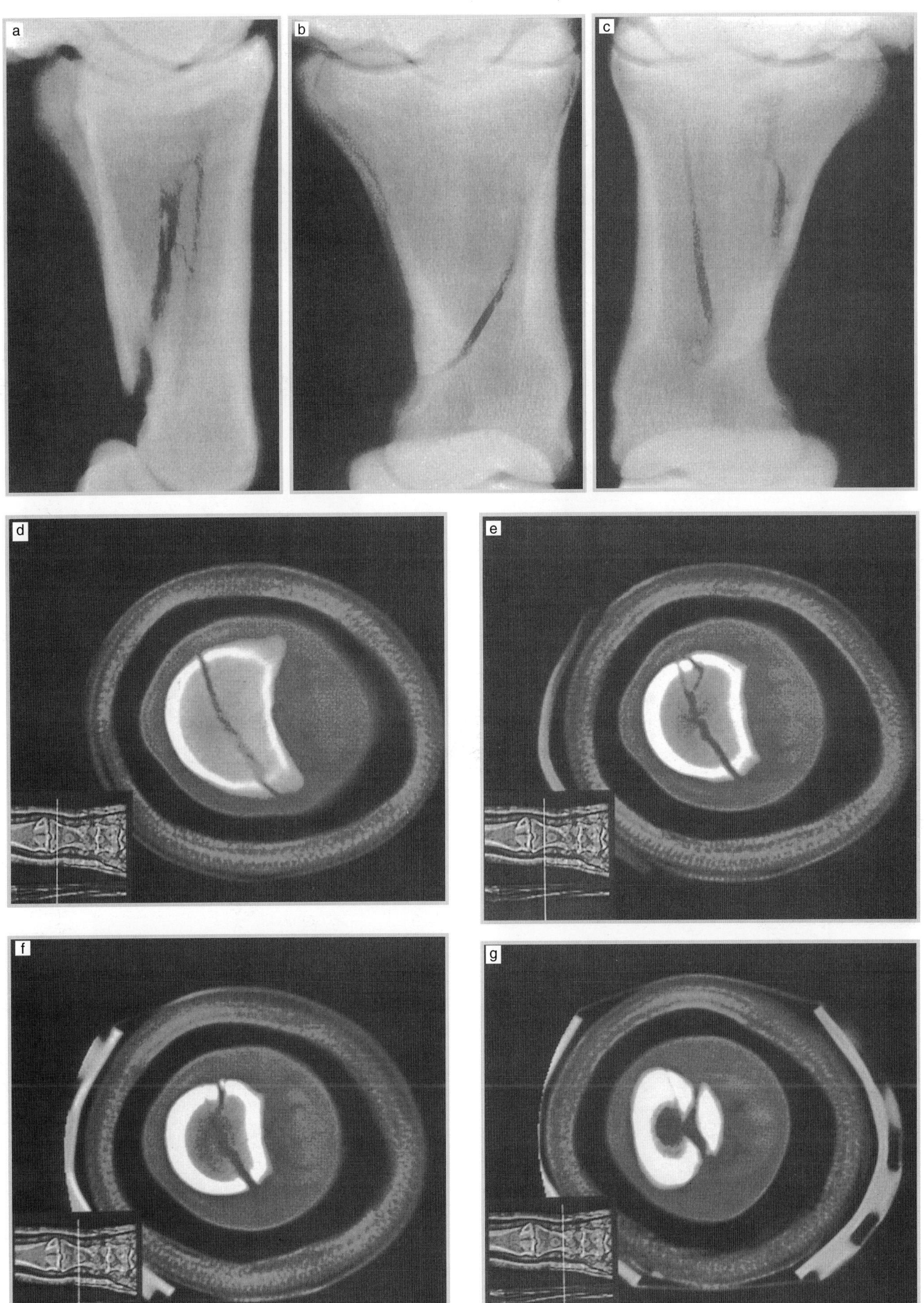

Figs 16a–g: Presurgical CT planning of repair of a fracture of the first phalanx (P_1), beginning with the usual radiographic fracture evaluation, the fracture lines in this horse clearly visible on lateromedial (a), dorsolateral-palmaromedial (b) and dorsomedial-palmarolateral oblique (c) projections. This is followed by CT assessment based on transverse slices of the proximal (d), midproximal (e), mid (f) and middistal (g) P_1 region (continued on following page).

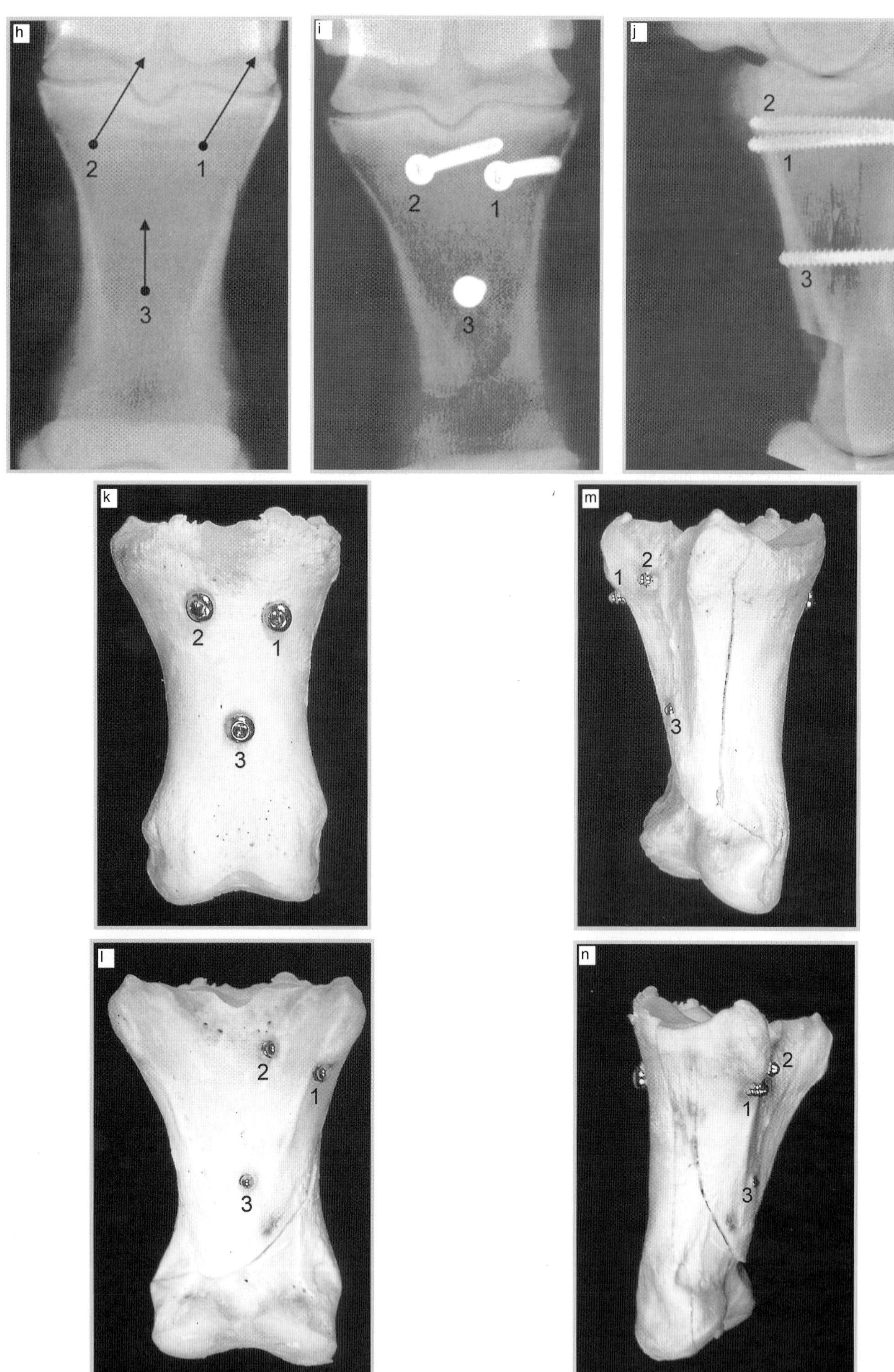

Figs 16h–n: The resulting actual screw plan (based on radiographic evaluation and CT assessment - see Figs 16a–g) is indicated on the presurgical dorsopalmar radiograph (h). The in vivo *result is demonstrated on dorsopalmar (i) and lateromedial (j) postsurgical radiographs. The* in vitro *result is visible on a dorsal (k), palmar (l), dorsolateral (m) and dorsomedial (n) view of the P_1 specimen.*

imaging area as well as being slightly cheaper to purchase and to operate. The accessibility of high field systems has improved with the introduction of short bore magnets with flared ends. The high cost of high field systems has resulted in the development of dedicated orthopaedic systems which are much cheaper to install and run but have a limited field of view and are restricted to human limbs only[19,20]. It is possible to image equine limbs in these devices but resolution is lower than that of high field systems[21].

Imaging horses also requires a nonferrous table to allow positioning of the anaesthetised horse and anaesthetic equipment that is not affected by the magnetic field. The facilities to perform MRI in anaesthetised horses are now available in a limited number of institutions. The technique for obtaining images using a high field short bore magnet is described by Mehl and colleagues[18].

Future Directions

The availability of devices for imaging live horses marks a major leap forward in equine MRI. The potential uses of this imaging modality remain to be fully explored. Due to its expense and the need for general anaesthesia, MRI will be limited to high value horses where other imaging methods have failed to provide an adequate diagnosis. The need to provide a magnetic field of high strength while allowing adequate access to the imaging area is a major problem in MRI device design. It is technically possible to provide a device that would be suitable for imaging standing horses, but this is unlikely to be a reality in the near future. Devices are being designed for use in standing human subjects; however, these are still in the development stages. Sequences that can acquire images with very short imaging times are available, but they result in a compromise in resolution. These devices, by necessity, would be low field, which further reduces resolution. RF coils which are placed around or over the area to be imaged are expensive pieces of hardware and the potential for damage by a conscious horse is high.

Research is perhaps one of the most exciting areas where MRI will be used in the future. The ability to provide both structural and functional information on all orthopaedic tissues noninvasively is unique to MRI and would allow serial examination of tissues in response to various conditions.

References

[1]Cheung, L., Li, K., Hollett, M., Bergman, A. and Herfkens, R. (1997) Meniscal tears of the knee: Accuracy of detection with fast spin-echo MR imaging and arthroscopic correlation in 293 patients. *Radiology* **203**, 508-12.

[2]Fernandez-Madrid, F., Karvonen, R., Teitge, R., Miller, P., An, T., and Negendank, W. (1995) Synovial thickening detected by MR imaging in osteoarthritis of the knee confirmed by biopsy as synovitis. *Magn. Reson. Imaging* **13**,177-83.

[3]Østergaard, M., Gideon, P., Wieslander, S., Henriksen, O. and Lorenzen, I. (1994) Pannus-induced destruction of joint cartilage and subchondral bone. Visualisation and staging by MRI. *Magnetic Resonance Materials in Physics, Biology, and Medicine* **2**, 91-100.

[4]Zeiss, J., Paley, K., Murray, K. and Saddemi, S. (1995) Comparison of bone contusion by MRI in partial and complete tears of the anterior cruciate ligament. *J. Comput. Assist. Tomogr.* **19**, 773-6.

[5]Rangger, C., Kathrein, A., Freund, M., Klestil, T. and Kreczy, A. (1998) Bone bruise of the knee. Histology and cryosections in 5 cases. *Acta. Orthop. Scand.* **69**, 291-4.

[6]Gahunia, H., Babyn, P., Lemaire, C., Kessler, M. and Pritzker, K. (1995) Osteoarthritis staging: comparison between magnetic resonance imaging, gross pathology and histopathology in the rhesus macaque. *Osteoarthritis and Cartilage* **3**, 169-80.

[7]Tervonen, O., Dietz, M., Carmichael, S. and Ehman R. (1993) MR imaging of knee hyaline cartilage: evaluation of two- and three-dimensional sequences. *J. Magn. Reson. Imaging* **3**, 663-8.

[8]Åström, M., Gentz, C., Nilsson, P., Rausing, A., Sjöberg, S. and Westlin, N. (1996) Imaging in chronic achilles tendinopathy: a comparison of ultrasonography, magnetic resonance imaging and surgical findings in 27 histologically verified cases. *Skeletal Radiol* **25**, 615-20.

[9]Rappeport, E., Wieslander, S., Stephensen, S., Lausten, G. and Thomsen, H. (1997) MRI preferable to diagnostic arthroscopy in knee joint injuries. A double-blind comparison of 47 patients. *Acta. Orthop. Scand.* **68**, 277-81.

[10]Blackburn, W., Bernreuter., Rominger, M. and Loose, L. (1994) Arthroscopic evaluation of knee articular cartilage: A comparison with plain radiographs and magnetic resonance imaging. *J. Rheumatol.* **21**, 675-9.

[11]Crues, J. (1994) MRI and the pathogenesis of musculoskeletal disease. *Magnetic Resonance Materials in Physics, Biology, and Medicine* **2**, 233-6.

[12]Nolte-Ernsting, C., Adam, G., Bühne, M., Prescher, A. and Günther, R. (1996) MRI of degenerative bone marrow lesions in experimental osteoarthritis of canine knee joints. *Skeletal Radiol.* **25**, 413-20.

[13]Park, R., Nelson, T. and Hoopes, P. (1987) Magnetic resonance imaging of the normal equine digit and metacarpophalangeal joint. *Vet. Radiol. Ultrasound* **28**, 105-16.

[14]Crass, J., Genovese, R., Render, J. and Bellon, E. (1992) Magnetic resonance, ultrasound and histopathologic correlaton of acute and healing equine tendon injuries. *Vet. Radiol. Ultrasound* **33**, 206-16.

[15]Kaser-Hotz, B., Sartoretti-Schefer, S. and Weiss, R. (1994) Computed tomography and magnetic resonance imaging of the normal equine carpus. *Vet. Radiol. Ultrasound* **35**, 457-61.

[16]Denoix, J., Chevier, N., Roger, B. and Lebas, J. (1993) Magnetic resonance imaging of the equine foot. *Vet. Radiol. Ultrasound* **34**, 405-11.

[17]Whitton, R., Buckley, C., Donovan, T., Wales, A. and Dennis, R. (1998) The diagnosis of lameness associated with distal limb pathology in a horse: a comparison of radiography, computed tomography and magnetic resonance imaging. *Vet. J.* **155**, 223-9.

[18]Mehl, M., Tucker, R., Ragle, C. and Schneider, R. (1998) The use of MRI in the diagnosis of equine limb disorders. *Equine Pract.* **20**, 14-7.

[19]Masciocchi, C., Barile, A. and Navarra, F. (1994) Clinical experience of osteoarticular MRI using a dedicated system. *Magnetic Resonance Materials in Physics, Biology, and Medicine* **2**, 545-50.

[20]Kersting-Sommerhoff, B., Hof, N., Lenz, M. and Gerhardt, P. (1996) MRI of peripheral joints with a low field dedicated system: A reliable and cost-effective alternative to high-field units? *European Radiol.* **6**, 561-5.

[21]Kladny, B., Glückert, K., Swoboda, B., Beyer, W. and Weseloh, G. (1995) Comparison of low-field (0.2 tesla) and high-field (1.5 tesla) magnetic resonance imaging of the knee joint. *Arch. Orthop. Trauma Surg.* **114**, 281-6.

Imaging of the musculoskeletal system: the last 20 years and the future – a personal perspective

SUE DYSON
Centre for Equine Studies,
Animal Health Trust
Lanwades Park, Kentford
Newmarket, Suffolk CB8 7UU
UK

The contributors to this section on diagnostic imaging have already highlighted most of the key developments in this century, but there is little doubt in my mind that it is in the last 20 years that the biggest forward leaps have been made.

There has been vast improvement in radiographic techniques, particularly due to the use of rare earth screens and the development of more powerful portable and semimobile x-ray machines. Diagnostic ultrasonography has blossomed from infancy to maturity. Nuclear scintigraphy has developed from rather crude images, to high detail, motion-corrected images and has greatly increased our diagnostic capabilities.

However, it is important to put all these techniques into perspective. Any imaging technique is only as good as the quality of images obtained, the interpretation of those images and their correlation with clinical findings. It is sadly true to say that many images obtained routinely in equine veterinary practice are of dubious diagnostic quality. Too many practitioners are satisfied with obtaining an image without being critical of the quality of that image. In the quest to seek a diagnosis there is always a tendency to 'lesion spot', without properly evaluating the entire image, and to overinterpret the significance of an abnormality. Sadly, there are few longitudinal prospective studies that give us objective information about the likely behaviour and clinical significance of abnormalities. At the other end of the spectrum, as technology advances, there is a tendency for a diagnostic imager to obtain and interpret images, without correlation with the clinical situation.

Dr Charlie Reid: - an inspiring contributor to equine radiography.

However, the principal aims of this short essay are to pay tribute to some of the key players in the last 20 years, with whom I have had the privilege to have made personal contact; and to look to the future. Many of the advances in recent years have been made by small teams of enthusiasts led by one fanatic. Where are they leading us now?

My first formal and quite terrifying engagement as an intern at New Bolton Center, University of Pennsylvania, in July 1980, was to attend radiology rounds, mandatory for the final year students, interns and residents, and some senior clinicians, and 'hosted' by the indomitable Dr Charlie Reid. Charlie displayed one or more radiographs, sketched a clinical scenario and then randomly (?) picked a member of the audience to describe the radiographs and to face a barrage of questions about the clinical management of the case. The basics of radiography and radiology had been well taught at Cambridge, and while seeing practice I had seen a fair number of radiographs of front feet, fetlocks and hocks.

The first case was a radiograph of the pelvis of a yearling. I sat in fear that I would be 'picked on' since I had no idea what a normal pelvis looked like, let alone the type of abnormality that one might expect to see. Of course, on that occasion I escaped interrogation and, in the future, those sessions became an extremely valuable learning experience. Charlie tried to instill into everyone the principles of reading the radiograph in its entirety – first examining the periphery "*normal, normal, normal...*" and then assessing the internal architecture of the bone. Charlie's enormous experience of equine radiography and radiology, his practical horse sense, his interaction with the senior clinicians and his sense of humour made these incredible learning sessions.

Charlie was a truly gifted teacher and loved to challenge those that shared an interest in radiographic interpretation. He dictated reports about every radiograph that was obtained in the hospital and it was a privilege to be present and have the opportunity to discuss these. His contribution to equine radiography and radiology has been an inspiration to many of us.

Tim O'Brien, University of Davis, California, has also

Dr Tim O'Brien's work at the University of Davis, California, has produced great advances in imaging techniques and interpretation.

made an enormous impact on equine radiography. The correlative work done between the radiology and pathology departments of Davis has provided unique information, particularly related to Thoroughbreds. The enthusiasm of Roy Pool and Sue Stover as pathologists with a keen clinical interest, combined with the innovative approach of Tim O'Brien, have produced great advances in imaging techniques and interpretation. I first visited Tim O'Brien in 1984, and was awestruck by the amount of interpretative information that was supported by previous *postmortem* examinations, and the number of studies that were ongoing.

One of my purposes in visiting Davis was to learn more about nuclear scintigraphy and this was when I first met Bill Hornof, and also Mike O'Callaghan, working there on sabbatical leave. Mike was probably more interested in lung function than the musculoskeletal system, and was the pioneer in ventilation perfusion imaging of the equine lung. However, he was a real enthusiast and innovator and had a lateral-thinking mind, and was an inspiration with whom to discuss imaging techniques. Mike later set up the nuclear medicine facility at Tufts University and the Tufts team, with Howard Seeherman (a final year student at Pennsylvania when I was an intern) have since provided us with an enormous amount of scintigraphic data related to performance horses.

Dr Virginia (Ginny) Reef was a resident at New Bolton Center when I was an intern and it was Ginny who first introduced the technique of diagnostic ultrasonography to me. Ginny, like so many of the pioneering equine ultrasonographers, had the attitude that we could try to scan literally anything and potentially we might learn something. Ginny's prime interest was internal medicine and it was she who recommended that if I really wanted to develop skill in the musculoskeletal system then Ron Genovese was the man to consult. Ron would be the first to pay tribute to Norman Rantanen and Mike Hauser, as the pioneers of imaging tendons and ligaments, but it was Ron who was able really to put the technique to the test, since at Thistledown Racecourse, Cleveland, Ohio, lame horses were the norm. Sound horses were a comparative rarity! Ron's ability as a lameness diagnostician, combined with his enthusiasm for developing diagnostic ultrasonography as far as possible, has resulted in enormous progress. It is a salutary lesson to any practitioner about what can be achieved in a practice situation. I can also confirm Norm Rantanen's observation that it rains a lot in Cleveland and Thistledown is a far from salubrious set-up!

Meanwhile in Europe, Professor Ueltschi from Berne, Switzerland, had been at the forefront of both equine radiography and nuclear scintigraphy. I first heard him give a paper in 1983 in rather slow, stilted English, and I anguished that I spoke no German, since it was clear that he had set quite remarkably high standards in both radiography and nuclear scintigraphy. He had done a large number of studies of normal horses and had vast experience of the Warmblood horses, which were clearly different in some respects from the British and American Thoroughbreds. Professor Ueltschi is a rather quiet, reserved gentleman but a real fund of information if you can win his trust and respect. He has what one might call a typically Swiss, thorough, methodical approach, but his attention to small detail has yielded valuable new information.

Kees Dik, from the University of Utrecht, Holland, has also contributed significant information about the range of radiographic variations and abnormalities which may be encountered in Warmblood horses. Kees has a rather dry sense of humour, and sees things purely through the eye of a diagnostic imager, rather than a clinician, but he does so objectively and methodically. He has also contributed significantly to our knowledge of ultrasonography in the horse.

Jean-Marie Denoix, from Maisons Alfort, France, is another unique individual. A human dynamo, with seemingly endless drive and enthusiasm, Jean-Marie has approached diagnostic imaging from the perspective of both an anatomist and a clinician. His detailed limb dissections and correlation with radiographic and ultrasonographic images and, more recently, with magnetic resonance images, are continually providing us with new information.

Although it is the so-called academics that present the majority of papers relating to diagnostic imaging, the contribution of practitioners must not go unrecognised. Nor must those of us with no knowledge of German ignore what happens in German-speaking countries. At Dr Huskamp's clinic in Germany, nuclear scintigraphy has long been one of the routine clinical tools for lameness diagnosis, and more recently they have been using CAT scanning, led by Michael Nowak.

It is interesting to see how different diagnostic modalities can simultaneously evolve, independently to improve specificity of diagnosis. At a recent meeting, Michael Nowak described deep digital flexor tendon lesions in the foot, diagnosed using CAT scans. Chris Whitton (Animal Health Trust, Newmarket) described similar lesions diagnosed using magnetic resonance imaging and I described their identification using nuclear scintigraphy and arthroscopy of the navicular bursa.

With all imaging modalities it is important to recognise that there are differences between different populations of horses. There have been parallel advances in knowledge related to different populations of horses. Mike Ross, from the University of Pennsylvania, has described a number of new lesions in Standardbred horses, some of which have been described almost simultaneously in England by Rob Pilsworth in Thoroughbreds or myself in both Thoroughbreds and Warmbloods.

So where are we going in the future? The increasing use

of radiography in prepurchase examinations, most particularly in the Thoroughbred sales ring, has stimulated Larry Bramlage and Wayne McIlwraith to set up a longitudinal study to define better what is 'normal' in young Thoroughbreds and what significance lesions might have. Similar studies urgently need to be done in other groups of horses. Digital radiography has found some favour in Europe but its huge cost has prohibited its more widespread uptake. It does have the potential to provide additional more detailed information.

The developments in technology of ultrasound machines now enable much more high detail resolution than formerly: we will have to adjust our standards of what is normal and refine our anatomical knowledge if we are to use these machines to their best advantage. Doppler ultrasonography and power Doppler are still in their infancy in musculoskeletal imaging and their clinical value has yet to be properly explored. Nuclear scintigraphy is moving into a new era with improved computer software, the ability to manipulate and quantify images, and the capability of superimposition of radiographic and scintigraphic images, resulting in much more detailed anatomical information. However, we do desperately need some normal data banks for horses involved in different disciplines and of varying age. Imaging of soft tissue structures in particular within the hoof capsule is moving into a new era with the availability of both CAT scanning and MRI. Which technique is likely to be most useful in the long term remains to be seen.

Whether or not these imaging modalities will ever be possible in the standing, sedated horse remains to be proven. We must always remember that we cannot afford to lose image quality without also losing valuable clinical information. Therefore, it would be inappropriate to use either of these techniques in a standing horse unless it could be done with image quality at least comparable with what can be currently obtained under general anaesthesia.

Finally, with all of these imaging modalities, it is always important that we critically evaluate the sensitivity and specificity of the results, and correlate the results with other techniques such as arthroscopy and tenoscopy and also *postmortem* studies. We must never lose sight of the importance of correlation between clinical findings and the results of technology.

Editors' conclusions

PETER ROSSDALE AND RACHEL GREEN
351 Exning Road
Newmarket
Suffolk CB8 0AU
UK

TIM GREET
Beaufort Cottage
Equine Hospital
Cotton End Road
Exning, Newmarket
Suffolk CB8 7NN
UK

PAT HARRIS
The Equine Studies Group
The WALTHAM Centre for
Pet Nutrition
Waltham on the Wolds
Melton Mowbray
Leicester LE14 4RP, UK

SHERWIN HALL
14 Huntingdon Road
Cambridge
Cambs CB3 0HH
UK

This book is unusual, in that it covers such a wide spectrum of subjects and personal views and reminiscences, with the horse forming the thread that runs through every piece of text; and the focus is provided by an arbitrarily selected moment of time.

The reader may, according to individual preference, have used the text as a reference or have read some parts in depth and others at a glance; some may have bravely read from cover to cover. For all readers we, as Editors, have attempted to perform the objective of presenting a record of the past, with emphasis upon the contribution of veterinary science to the welfare of the horse, giving recognition to those who have been and are the guardians of an animal species which has rendered the human race great service throughout our history.

Rachel Green on Uncle Alf at Rose Hall Stables, Exning - October 1999.

Pat Harris goes clear on Denbow Jeremy - summer 1976.

Sherwin Hall aboard Professor Twink Allen's hunter, Frank - October 1999.

Tim Greet hitches a ride in Sri Lanka, 1983.

Double somersault - Peter Rossdale and Mariner's Locker (owner John Hacking) at Charing racecourse - April 1954. First published in the London Evening News.

Index

A

B

C

I

J

K

L

Mc

M

N

O

P

R

S

T

U

V

W

X

Y

Z

Authors' biographical details

LINDSEY ABEYASEKERE

Lindsey Abeyasekere graduated from Reading University in 1994 with a degree in Zoology. After spells working as an equine veterinary nurse for Rossdale and Partners in Newmarket and as Clinic Manager for Grant and Partners in Somerset she joined Equine Veterinary Journal Ltd. as Production Assistant in 1999.

ALISTAIR BARR

Alistair Barr qualified from Cambridge University in 1982 and, after a year in general practice, moved to the Department of Clinical Veterinary Science at Bristol University. He obtained his PhD in 1990 for studies on carpal injuries in horses. He is currently a senior lecturer in equine orthopaedics and Head of the Division of Companion Animal Studies at Bristol University.

MICHAEL BECKER

Michael Becker completed his PhD in Veterinary Medecine at Munich in 1979 and his career since has been spent in equine practice in Germany. In 1993 he became partowner of the Pferdeklinik Kerken at Watchendonk, near the Dutch border.

VICTOR BERWYN JONES

Victor Berwyn Jones qualified from the Royal Veterinary College in 1925, after which he ran his own mixed practice until 1946, specialising in surgery and radiography. After the war took charge of the Horse Department, Northern Territory, of British Railways. He died in 1968. His son Mike Berwyn-Jones graduated from the RVC in 1953. After a career working as both a veterinary surgeon and freelance writer, he retired in 1985, and now lives in Wiltshire.

JOHN BROOK

John Brook graduated from the Royal (Dick) School of Veterinary Science, Edinburgh University, in 1969. An amateur jockey, who rode 'under rules' from 1961-1971, he runs an equine practice from his home in Warwickshire.

CHRISTOPHER BROWN

Christopher Brown graduated in 1972 from Liverpool University. After 15 years at Michigan State University, in 1994 he became Department Executive Officer (Chair) of Veterinary Clinical Sciences and Director of the Veterinary Teaching Hospital at Iowa State University.

PETER BURRELL

Educated at Eton and the Royal Agricultural College, Cirencester, Peter Burrell CBE began his career in 1926 as assistant manager at Eyrefield Stud in Co. Kildare, Ireland. Within 10 years, he had succeeded Johnson as Director of the National Stud at Tully, in which position he remained for the next 34 years. He engineered the politically difficult move of the stud from the Curragh to temporary premises in Gillingham, Dorset, and single-handedly planned and supervised the building of the present National Stud in Newmarket. Peter Burrell died in 1999.

REX BUTTERFIELD

Rex Butterfield graduated from the University of Sydney in 1950 and after 10 years in rural practice left to undertake PhD studies at the University of Queensland. Six years later he became Foundation Professor of Veterinary Anatomy at the University of Sydney and remained so until retirement in 1986. Since 1987, he has been the Australasian representative of the Keeneland Association of Kentucky.

DOUG BYARS

Doug Byars is a 1974 graduate of the University of California, Davis, School of Veterinary Medicine. Formerly an Associate Professor of Large Animal Medicine at the University of Georgia, he is now the Director of the Internal Medicine Hospital of Hagyard-Davidson-McGee Equine Medicine and Surgery in Lexington, Kentucky.

HILARY CLAYTON

Hilary Clayton graduated from Glasgow University Veterinary College in 1973. After two years in a mixed practice she returned to Glasgow to complete a PhD. Since 1978 she has held academic appointments in the UK, Canada and the USA. In 1997, she became the first incumbent of the Mary Anne McPhail Dressage Chair in Equine Sports Medicine at Michigan State University.

BOB COOK

Bob Cook graduated from the Royal Veterinary College in 1952, and after a spell in practice, became House Surgeon at Cambridge Veterinary School. In 1961, he became the first Honorary Secretary of BEVA. In 1979 he joined Tufts University School of Veterinary Medicine, where he was made Professor Emeritus in 1984.

BRODDY CORCORAN

Broddy Corcoran was one of the youngest vets ever to qualify when he graduated from Dublin in July 1945, and had to practice illegally until he reached 21! He was apprenticed to the mainly equine practitioner Martin Purcell, and eventually purchased Purcell's practice to run himself, continuing in large animal practice for over 50 years.

JOHN DAVIS

Previously Professor of Paediatrics and Child Health, Victoria University of Manchester, and Foundation Professor of Paediatrics at the University of Cambridge Clinical School, John Davis is a James Spence Medallist of the British Paediatric Association. He is one-time Vice-President of the Royal College of Physicians, an Hon. Member of the Neonatal Society and a past Chairman of the Scientific Committee of the Cot Death Foundation.

KEES DIK

Kees Dik graduated from the University of Utrecht in 1967. A Diplomate of Veterinary Radiology from the Royal Netherlands Veterinary Association, he served from 1977–1998 as Chairman of the Department of Radiology, Veterinary Faculty, at the University of Utrecht. He is the Associate Editor of both *Veterinary Radiology & Ultrasound* and *Pferdeheilkunde.*

TOM DIVERS

After graduating from the University of Georgia, Tom Divers undertook post-DVM training at the University of California at Davis and the University of Georgia. He has been a faculty member at the University of Georgia and the University of Pennsylvania, and is currently at Cornell University.

SUE DYSON

Sue Dyson graduated from the University of Cambridge in 1980 and was then awarded a Thouron Scholarship to the University of Pennsylvania. She returned to England to take a position in the Centre for Equine Studies of the Animal Health Trust. She has published widely on lameness diagnosis, radiography and ultrasonography, and is a past President of BEVA.

BARRIE EDWARDS

Barrie Edwards graduated from Liverpool University Veterinary School in 1961, and went on to occupy posts in Large Animal Surgery at Liverpool and the Royal Veterinary College. He was appointed to a newly created Chair in Equine Studies at the University of Liverpool in 1987. His main clinical and research interest over the last 20 years has been equine gastroenterology.

SARAH FREEMAN

Sarah Freeman qualified from London in 1994 and spent a year in mixed general practice before returning to the Royal Veterinary College as a Junior Clinical Training Scholar. She was appointed the Home of Rest for Horses Senior Clinical Training Scholar at the RVC in 1998 and is currently a Lecturer in Equine Surgery.

MIKE GARLICK

Educated in London, Mike Garlick left school after A-levels and joined the Royal Navy for eight years. Following this, he qualified from Bristol University as a veterinary surgeon. and has since worked mainly in equine practice in Salisbury, where he has developed interests in orthopaedics and surgery.

RACHEL GREEN

Educated in Suffolk and Cambridge, Rachel Green started her career at Addenbrooke's Hospital working for two consultants in Oncology. She has worked for Peter Rossdale since 1986, initially as an editorial assistant and for the last four years as Deputy Editor of *Equine Veterinary Journal* and *Equine Veterinary Education*.

RICHARD GREENWOOD

Richard Greenwood graduated from Cambridge University in 1964 and initially worked in Thoroughbred stud practice in Australia before returning to the UK in 1970 to join the Newmarket practice, Day and Partners. He became a partner in 1973.

TIM GREET

Tim qualified from the University of Glasgow in 1976 and worked at the Equine Research Station in Newmarket before joining Rossdale & Partners in 1982. He became a partner in 1984 and is responsible for the surgical department, which is now situated in Beaufort Cottage Equine Hospital. He is due to become President of BEVA in December 1999.

SHERWIN HALL

Sherwin Hall qualified from the Royal Veterinary College, London, in 1953. After five years in large animal practice he joined the Veterinary Investigation Service. He finished his career as the veterinary member of the Chief Scientist's Group of the Ministry of Agriculture. In 1962 he founded the Veterinary History Society.

DUNCAN HANNANT

Duncan Hannant joined the Equine Virology Unit of the Animal Health Trust in 1985 after ten years research in immunology of cancer and respiratory diseases of humans. He was appointed Head of Immunology in 1988.

PAT HARRIS

Pat Harris graduated from Cambridge Veterinary School in 1983 and completed her PhD in 1988 at the Animal Health Trust Newmarket. In 1995 she joined the WALTHAM Centre for Pet Nutrition as their Horse Nutritionist, becoming a Senior Nutritionist a year later. President of BEVA in 1999, Pat also serves on the executive board of Equine Veterinary Journal Ltd.

STEPHEN HARRISON

Stephen Harrison is involved professionally and recreationally with Thoroughbred breeding for National Hunt and flat racing, working as a bloodstock consultant and as an equine geneticist at the Royal Agricultural College. He has had a strong interest in applied DNA analysis of horses since 1991, particularly in the beneficial application to Thoroughbred breeding.

STEWART HASTIE

Stewart Hastie graduated from Glasgow Veterinary School in July 1944 and went into mixed practice in Kent with Major Oxspring OBE MRCVS. In 1956, he became a Partner with Ken Scott, building up a practice in Buckingham. He served as both Honorary PRO and Honorary Secretary for BEVA for several years.

BRIGITTE HEARD

Educated in Suffolk and Lincolnshire, Brigitte Heard worked first in the banking industry, riding out racehorses as a hobby. She subsequently decided to work with horses full time, and spent a winter working for a trainer in Italy, followed by two years in racing yards in England. Since 1988, she has been an assistant at Rossdale & Partners in Newmarket, where she continues to ride out for a local trainer.

DOUG HERTHEL

Doug Herthel graduated from the University of California at Davis, in 1971, and stayed on for another year to complete an internship in equine surgery. In 1972, he and his wife established the internationally recognised Alamo Pintado Equine Medical Center in California to provide advanced diagnostics and therapy for medical and surgical referral cases and to carry out his extensive research.

JOHN HICKMAN

Colonel John Hickman graduated from the Royal Veterinary College in 1935. Following a year as a House Surgeon at the RVC, he joined the Royal Army Veterinary Corps and was posted to India. In 1944, Colonel Hickman took over the Veterinary and Remount Conducting Section, with which he served in France, Belgium and, after VE Day, Germany. After retiring from the RAVC in 1947 he became a Lecturer at the RVC, and from 1952 to his retirement in 1980 he was Reader in Animal Surgery at the Cambridge Veterinary School. In 1961 he became the first President of BEVA.

HAROLD HINTZ

Harold Hintz received his BS from Ohio State University and PhD from Cornell University. He was Assistant Professor at the University of California, Davis, from 1964–1967, when he joined Cornell University, where he is currently Professor of Animal Nutrition in the Department of Animal Sciences.

PAUL JEPSON

Brigadier Paul Jepson graduated from Liverpool Veterinary School in 1972. Between 1994 and 1997, he was the Director of the Royal Army Veterinary Corps, Director of the Ministry of Defence Veterinary Remount Services and the Queen's Honorary Veterinary Surgeon. Since 1997, Brigadier Jepson has been the Chief Executive and Veterinary Director of The Home of Rest for Horses.

WAYNE KESTER

General Wayne Kester served as Executive Director of the American Association of Equine Practitioners for 25 years. In his 70 years of service to the equine industry, he pushed AAEP into active involvement in equine research and disease control. In 1992, the new AAEP headquarters was named The Kester Building in his honour. He died in 1999.

SVEND KOLD

After graduating from the Royal Veterinary and Agricultural University in Copenhagen, Svend Kold went on to work in equine practice in Denmark until 1981, when he moved to the Animal Health Trust in Newmarket as a research scientist. Since 1991, Dr Kold has worked at the Willesley Equine Clinic in Gloucestershire, and was made a partner in 1993.

GEOFFREY LANE

Geoffrey Lane graduated from the Royal Veterinary College in 1969 and for the past 25 years has been a member of the teaching staff in the Department of Clinical Veterinary Science at the University of Bristol. His particular interest is comparative aspects of oto-rhino-laryngology. Geoffrey was President of BEVA in 1989.

DES LEADON

Des Leadon graduated from Trinity College Dublin with a degree in Veterinary Medecine and subsequently worked in Newmarket on the Wellcome Trust-funded Equine Prematurity Project. He joined the Irish Equine Centre in 1984, where he is currently Head of Clinical Pathology. A past President of BEVA, his special interests include the problems of transporting horses by air.

SANDY LITTLEJOHN

After war service in a South African artillery regiment, Sandy Littlejohn graduated from the Onderstepoort Veterinary Faculty (South Africa) in 1949. The subsequent 50 years were spent more or less equally between practice, research, teaching and finally, after retiring as Emeritus Professor of Equine Physiology at the University of Pretoria, as ID assistant at Tattersalls Bloodstock Sales.

JEREMY MANTELL

Jeremy Mantell qualified from the Royal Veterinary College, London, in 1976. After five years in practice in Kent and on Exmoor, in 1981 he moved to Liphook Equine Hospital. A member of the Council of BEVA, he served as President in 1998 and now chairs the working party set up to review the prepurchase examination protocol.

STEPHEN MAY

Stephen May graduated in veterinary science from Cambridge University in 1980. After spending time as Large Animal House Surgeon at Liverpool University and in general practice, he moved to the Royal Veterinary College. His research interests are centred on the inflammatory mediators associated with various equine diseases, particularly cartilage degeneration in equine osteoarthritis.

AL MERRITT

Al Merritt received his undergraduate degree from Bowdoin College in 1959 and his veterinary degree from Cornell University in 1963. He is currently Appleton Professor in Equine Studies and Director of the Island Whirl Equine Colic Research Laboratory in the Department of Large Animal Clinical Sciences at the College of Veterinary Medicine, University of Florida.

HELMUT MEYER

Helmut Meyer studied veterinary medicine at Hannover and Agriculture at Giessen. In 1956 he became Assistant at the Tierärztliche Hochschule, Hannover, where he was later Director of the Institute of Animal Nutrition (from 1967 to 1993). His main research concerns the digestive physiology in horses and dogs.

BONNY MILLAR

Bonny graduated in Animal Health Technology from Harcum College in Pennsylvania, USA, in 1984. She was employed as a medicine charge nurse at the New Bolton Center, Pennsylvania, from 1984 to 1991, when she moved to England, beginning work as Head Nurse at Rossdale & Partners the following summer.

JIM MOORE

Jim Moore has been Professor and Department Head of the Department of Large Animal Medicine at the University of Georgia since 1995. In 1971, he gained his undergraduate degree in Physiology from the University of California, where he went on to gain his veterinary degree in 1974. He obtained a PhD in Physiology from the University of Missouri in 1980.

BILL MUIR

Currently Professor and Head of the Section of Anaesthesia in the Department of Veterinary Clinical Sciences, College of Veterinary Medicine, Ohio State University, Bill Muir obtained his undergraduate degree in veterinary medicine from Michigan State University in 1970 and subsequently gaining a PhD in Cardiovascular Physiology from Ohio State University.

RICHARD NEWTON

After graduating from Liverpool University in July 1991, Richard Newton worked in practice in Herefordshire for two and a half years. In 1994, he joined the Epidemiology Unit of the Animal Health Trust, where his current work includes studies on the epidemiology and control of grass sickness, strangles and influenza.

REG PASCOE

Reg Pascoe graduated from the University of Queensland in 1951. He went into practice in Oakey and in 1969 established a large animal hospital, predominantly for horses. For his contributions to veterinary science, he was made a Member of the Order of Australia in 1987, and was the inaugural inductee to the Queensland Equine Hall of Fame in 1999.

HARRY PETTERSSON

After graduation in 1959 from the Royal Veterinary College, Stockholm, Harry Pettersson worked in general practice until in 1961 when he became an Assistant Veterinary Surgeon at the Large Animal Clinic of the Regional Animal Hospital, Helsingborg. Chief of the hospital from 1976 to his retirement in 1998, he also served as Adjunct Professor of Surgery at the Swedish University of Agricultural Sciences in Uppsala from 1982 to 1988.

ROB PILSWORTH

Rob Pilsworth graduated from the University of Cambridge in 1981. He is a partner at Rossdale and Partners, Newmarket, with particular interest and expertise in orthopaedic problems and imaging techniques.

EDOUARD POURET

Edouard Pouret combines work as a clinician, author, politician and racehorse trainer from his practice in Argentan, France.

JIM POWER

Jim Power has worked in horse racing since 1960, when, aged 14, he joined Bryan Marshall in Lambourn. Now a senior member of stud personnel at Banstead Manor Studfarm, Newmarket, he is also a well-known equestrian artist. His paintings have been exhibited in major London galleries and have won numerous awards. He is an active member of the Society of Equestrian Artists.

NORMAN RANTANEN

Norman Rantanen graduated from Washington State University, Pullman, in 1967. He then joined the US Air Force, completing tours of duty in Vietnam and Germany, as well a Masters Degree at Washington State University in 1971. In 1976, he joined the radiology department at Washington State, before moving to Lexington, where he started an imaging consultation practice in 1983. In 1992, the practice moved to southern California.

JOHN REILLY

Major John Reilly RAVC was educated at Seale-Hayne Agricultural College in Devon and Bristol and Edinburgh Universities. Prior to joining the Royal Army Veterinary Corps, he worked in mixed veterinary practices in the West Country and in research as a Horserace Betting Levy Board Scholar. He is codirecting research at De Montfort University, Leicester, where he is an Honorary Research Fellow.

SIDNEY RICKETTS

Sidney Ricketts, a BEVA Honorary life member, graduated in Biochemistry and Veterinary Science at Bristol University and was Thouron Fellow at the New Bolton Center, Pennsylvania, before joining Rossdale & Partners, Newmarket, where he is now a partner, specialising in stud medecine. In 1998 he was made Lieutenant of the Royal Victorian Order as Senior Veterinary Consultant to the Royal Studs, Sandringham, Norfolk.

MALCOLM ROBERTS

Malcolm Roberts graduated from the University of Liverpool in 1967. After spells at the University of Bristol and in general practice he spent six years as Senior Lecturer in Equine Medicine at the University of Queensland Veterinary School in Australia. He has been Professor of Equine Medicine at the College of Veterinary Medicine, North Carolina State University, since 1981.

ED ROBINSON

Ed Robinson graduated from the Royal Veterinary College, London in 1965. He gained his PhD in 1972 from the University of California, Davis, and has, from 1988, been the Matilda R. Wilson Professor at Michigan State University, directing the Pulmonary Laboratory, studying equine airway disease.

IAN ROBINSON

Ian Robinson graduated from the University of Durham in 1983 with a degree in Zoology specialising in Animal Behaviour, and obtained his PhD from the University of Aberdeen in 1987. The following year, Ian joined the WALTHAM Centre for Pet Nutrition as an Animal Behaviourist.

JIM ROONEY

A graduate of New York State Veterinary College, Cornell University, Jim Rooney is the author of numerous papers on equine pathology and lameness and of seven books on anatomy, pathology and lameness of horses. He has spent sojourns at the Royal Veterinary College, Sweden, and the Animal Health Trust, Newmarket, UK, and has been Professor of Pathology at the School of Veterinary Medecine, University of Pennsylvania, and the Department of Veterinary Science, University of Kentucky.

REUBEN ROSE

Reuben Rose graduated from the University of Sydney Veterinary School in 1972. After completing a postgraduate Diploma in Veterinary Anaesthesia, he worked in equine and mixed practice in New Zealand. He returned to the University of Sydney, completing his PhD in 1980. He is currently Dean of the Faculty of Veterinary Science at the University of Sydney.

PETER ROSSDALE

Peter Rossdale completed a natural science tripos at Cambridge University in 1949, before graduating from the Royal Veterinary College, London, in 1952 and starting Rossdale and Partners, a private equine practice, in Newmarket in 1959. An Honorary Life Member and past President (1976) of BEVA, he has been Editor of the *Equine Veterinary Journal* since 1980. He was awarded an OBE in 1998 for services to equine veterinary science.

FIDI VON SALDERN

Fidi von Saldern graduated from Tierärztliche Hochschule (Veterinary School), Hanover, after which he spent three years as a veterinary assistant in Tierklinik Hochmoor, Germany. Together with Dr K.J. Boening, he founded Tierklinik Munster-Telgte in October 1983, specialising in equine work. He is the official veterinary surgeon for the German national three-day event team.

HAROLD SCHOTT II

Harold Schott gained an undergraduate degree from Cornell University in 1980, followed by a veterinary degree in 1984 from Ohio State University. After spells in private equine practice and at Washington State University, he has, since 1995, been Assistant/Associate Professor at Michigan State University.

ROGER SHORT

Roger Short was foundation Director of the Medical Research Council's Unit of Reproductive Biology in Edinburgh from 1972 to 1982. He held a Personal Chair in Reproductive Biology at Monash University from 1982 to 1995 and in 1996 was appointed Wexler Professorial Fellow in the Department of Perinatal Medicine at the Royal Women's Hospital. He also holds US and EC patents for the use of melatonin to control jetlag.

BRIAN SINGLETON

After graduating from the Royal (Dick) School of Veterinary Studies in 1945, Brian Singleton spent 27 years working in canine and equine practice. He is a past President of the British Small Animal Veterinary Association (1960), the RCVS (1969), the World Small Animal Veterinary Association (1975 –1977) and BEVA (1987). From 1977 to 1988, he served as both the Hon. Veterinary Advisor to The Jockey Club and Director of the Animal Health Trust. In 1974, he was made a CBE.

KEN SMITH

Ken Smith graduated from Edinburgh Veterinary School in 1988 and commenced a pathology residence at the Animal Health Trust. His PhD research concerned the pathogenesis of equid herpesvirus-1 abortion.

ROGER SMITH

After graduating from Cambridge University in 1987 and gaining his Masters degree in 1988, Roger worked in private equine practices before becoming a Clinical Resident at the Royal Veterinary College. He was awarded his PhD in 1997 and went on to work as a Lecturer at the College until 1998, becoming a Senior Lecturer at the beginning of 1999.

LAWSON SOULSBY

Lord Soulsby graduated from Edinburgh in 1948. He spent 15 years as Professor of Parasitology at the University of Pennsylvania, before returning to the UK in 1978 as Professor of Animal Pathology and Head of the Department of Clinical Veterinary Medecine at Cambridge University. He was the first veterinary peer (appointed not inherited!) to sit in the House of Lords.

PETER WEBBON

Peter Webbon graduated from the Royal Veterinary College in 1971. After three years as a Horseracing Betting Levy Board Research Training Scholar, he spent 22 years at the Royal Veterinary College in the Departments of both Surgery and Medicine before moving to The Jockey Club in 1996 as its Chief Veterinary Adviser.

TREVE WILLIAMS

Born in Burma, Treve Williams was educated in Devon and then at Sydney University. Following National Service, he worked as a jackeroo and later as a stockman in Australia. Treve joined Sykes, Bain and Partners in 1964 and became a partner in 1967. Since then, he has become a Director of RANVET and the Australian Feed Company.

JAMES WOOD

James Wood graduated from the Royal Veterinary College in 1988, after which he worked in mixed and small animal practice, ran a lamb production trial and studied scrapie in sheep and goats at Weybridge. Since 1990, he has worked at the Animal Health Trust, where he is now Head of Epidemiology.